OPERATIONS MANAGEMENT

Second Edition

Comments on the first edition:

'Written in a clear style, this book is down to earth in its approach. The examples and case studies are current and engage students' learning. It is clear that Andrew Greasley has reflected on improving students' learning.'

Spencer Onuh, University of Portsmouth

'The attention given to the service industry is a strong selling point.'

Lars Sørensen, Copenhagen Business School

'A comprehensive text that covers all the topics normally covered in the operations management curriculum through a practical, student-friendly approach.'

Professor David Bennett, Aston Business School

OPERATIONS MANAGEMENT

Second Edition

Andrew Greasley

WILEY

A John Wiley and Sons, Ltd, Publication

Copyright © 2009   John Wiley & Sons Ltd, The Atrium, Southern Gate, Chichester,
West Sussex PO19 8SQ, England

Telephone   (+44) 1243 779777

Email (for orders and customer service enquiries): cs-books@wiley.com
Visit our Home Page on www.wiley.com

First edition published in 2006 © John Wiley & Sons Ltd
Images supplied in part by permission of Shutterstock.com

Reprinted, October 2009, February 2010.

Other Wiley Editorial Offices

John Wiley & Sons Inc., 111 River Street, Hoboken, NJ 07030, USA

Jossey-Bass, 989 Market Street, San Francisco, CA 94103-1741, USA

Wiley-VCH Verlag GmbH, Boschstr. 12, D-69469 Weinheim, Germany

John Wiley & Sons Australia Ltd, 42 McDougall Street, Milton, Queensland 4064, Australia

John Wiley & Sons (Asia) Pte Ltd, 2 Clementi Loop #02-01, Jin Xing Distripark, Singapore 129809

John Wiley & Sons Canada Ltd, 6045 Freemont Blvd, Mississauga, ONT, L5R 4J3, Canada

Wiley also publishes its books in a variety of electronic formats. Some content that appears in print may not
be available in electronic books.

Library of Congress Cataloging in Publication Data

Greasley, Andrew.
    Operations management/Andrew Greasley. — 2nd ed.
        p. cm.
    Includes bibliographical references and index.
    ISBN 978-0-470-99761-1 (pbk.)
    1. Production management. 2. Project management. 3. Business logistics. 4. Production
    management—Examinations—Study guides. 5. Project management—Examinations—
    Study guides. 6. Business logistics—Examinations—Study guides. I. Title.
    TS155.G8172 2009
    658.5—dc22

                                                                    2008042469

British Library Cataloguing in Publication Data

A catalogue record for this book is available from the British Library

ISBN 978-0-470-99761-1 (P/B)

Typeset in 10/15pt Georgia by Integra Software Services Pvt. Ltd, Pondicherry, India
Printed and bound by Printer Trento, Italy

Why *WileyPLUS* for Operations Management?

WileyPLUS combines robust course management tools with the complete online text and all of the interactive teaching and learning resources you and your students need in one easy to use system.

"WileyPLUS definitely increased my interest for my course, contributed a lot to my performance on the exams, and improved my grades."

- Student Pardha Saradhi Vishnumolakala

Up-to-date and relevant video clips, tutorials, simulations, interactive demonstration problems, and cases involve students as interested participants. With various ways to learn, retain, and apply the material they have read about or learned in lectures, students build the skills and confidence it takes to perform better.

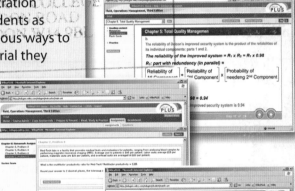

Instructors can easily and immediately assess their students' progress - individually, or by class - using the online gradebook and assessment tools contained in *WileyPLUS*.

"I enjoyed using WileyPLUS because I learned a lot, and performed very well!"

- Student David Villarreal

See and try *WileyPLUS* **at www.wileyplus.com**

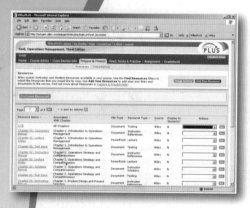
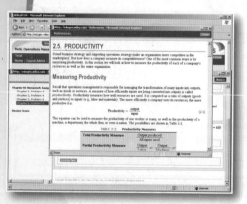

BRIEF CONTENTS

CONTENTS

ABOUT THE AUTHOR

Andrew Greasley MBA PhD FHEA is a lecturer at Aston Business School, Aston University, Birmingham, UK. He lectures in operations management and is a member of the technology and operations management research group at Aston. He is author of the book *Simulation Modelling for Business* published by Ashgate Ltd and is co-author of the book *Business Information Systems* (4th edn) published by Pearson Education Ltd. His research interest is simulation modelling. He has over 50 publications, including papers in journals such as the *International Journal of Operations and Production Management, Journal of the Operational Research Society, Simulation, Technovation* and *Business Process Management Journal*. He has undertaken a number of teaching and consultancy projects in the area of simulation in the UK, Europe and Africa.

PREFACE

Operations management deals with the management of the creation of goods and the delivery of services to the customer. It thus plays an essential role in the success of any organization. The aim of this book is to provide a clear and concise treatment of operations management. The text covers the main areas of operations strategy, the design of the operations system and the management of operations over time. The book is intended as an introduction to operations management and as such attempts to cover all relevant areas in the field but in a clear and concise manner so that the students are not overwhelmed by the amount of material presented. The target audience is undergraduates on business studies and joint degrees where no prior knowledge of the subject area is required. The book will also interest postgraduate students on MBA and specialist masters programmes.

Content

After an introductory chapter, the book is structured into three main parts: introduction, design and management. Within this structure the book consists of 18 chapters. This design has been used in order to maximize the clarity of the presentation of material.

Chapter 1 provides an introduction to the field of operations management. It defines the role of operations in the organization and discusses the increasing role and importance of service operations. Chapter 2 covers the area of operations strategy. The vital role of operations in providing the capability to implement an organization's strategy is covered as well as guidance on how to formulate a successful operations strategy.

The role of design in operations is covered in Chapters 3 to 9. Areas covered include:

- the configuration of processes in manufacturing and services firms
- the design and location of operations facilities
- technology used in the operations process
- product and service design
- the design of the processes that deliver services
- the design of jobs.

An emphasis on service design is provided in this section by covering topics such as business process management and service blueprinting.

The management of operations is covered in Chapters 10 to 18. Areas covered include operations planning and control, capacity management, inventory management, lean operations and JIT, enterprise resource planning, supply chain management and project management. The impact of e-Commerce on operations is covered using topics such as e-procurement. Topics such as total quality management, continuous and breakthrough improvement approaches, statistical process control and acceptance sampling are also covered. The growing influence of Six Sigma programmes is also covered.

New for the Second Edition

The structure of the book has been maintained from the first edition but a number of improvements have been made for the second edition.

- The book has been visually redesigned in full colour to provide a clearer and more interesting layout.
- The number of case studies has been greatly increased. More international case studies are included in this edition.
- New content has been included in such areas such as the quality-gap model, enterprise systems and business process management.
- Chapter material has been organized for greater clarity, in particular Chapter 2 and Chapter 17.
- A greater amount of support material is available for students and lecturers on the companion web site and through the WileyPLUS course.

Learning Aids

The text provides a number of features to help student learning. These include:

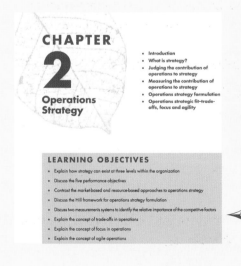

Each chapter begins with a list of the main **learning objectives** for the material covered.

department and an "us versus them" attitude toward other departments within the firm. Each process can be treated using the input/process/output transformation model as with the functional perspective, but there is a clear emphasis on breaking down the barriers between departments and ensuring that output meets customer requirements. Processes can be carried out by separate individuals (individual processes), contained within a department (functional processes) or occur in several functional areas (cross-functional processes).

CASE STUDY 2.1

Findus Foods

Ashburton Products manufactures wooden fireplace mantels. They have a retail showroom in which various models are displayed. A small workshop close to the showroom was taken on a short term lease, and various items of second hand woodworking machinery were acquired. Two joiners were taken on to build the mantels which, for the most part, were custom built to customer requirements.

A mantel consists of three sub-assemblies comprising two legs and a shelf. Sub-assemblies are made from wood which has been cut, sawn, planed and routed. At the sub assembly stage, the various items are brought together, glued and then clamped. The glue takes time to dry, so clamped sub-assemblies are left overnight. The assembly stage is similar. As with sub-assembly, assembly takes place on a specifically designed workbench. One person operates the cutting and planing machines, together with the saw. Another operates the router. Two people are employed

in sub-assembly and final assembly work. Two main categories of mantel are produced from hardwood and medium density fibreboard (MDF). The ratio of MDF mantels to hardwood is 85% to 15%. With current staffing levels, output normally averages slightly over twenty five mantels per week. Demand for mantels has been rising for some time. Sales which were, in the past, based exclusively on single orders for individual customers have recently been supplemented by multiple orders from two local builders. In view of this trend, Ashburton's management is concerned about how best to meet the increase in demand. Unable to expand the current site because of planning restrictions, and reluctant to spend large sums on new equipment, the management is uncertain what to do.

Question
In terms of process types, what advice would you give to the operations manager at Ashburton Products?

The 1980's saw the emergence of the just-in-time (JIT) philosophy (chapter 13) from Japan which transformed the way businesses deliver goods and services.

Case studies are included with questions to encourage critical reflection on the key issues. Frequent examples provide additional real-life detail of operations concepts.

Reengineering (BPR) (chapter 17). Most recently the use of the internet to conduct transactions or E-Commerce (chapter 6) has changed the way operations management is performed.

WORKED EXAMPLE 2.1
Cost-Volume Profit Model

A manufacturer produces a product with the following parameters
Selling price (SP) = £7/unit
Variable cost (VC) = £4/unit
Fixed costs (FC) = £15,000/week

(a) What is the breakeven point?
(b) How many do they need to sell to make £ 15,000 profit a week?

● SOLUTION
(a) At breakeven point, P=0:

$$X = \frac{FC}{SP - FC}$$

$$= \frac{15,000}{7 - 4}$$

$$= 5,000 \text{ units/week}$$

(b) At P=15,000:

$$X = \frac{P + FC}{SP - FC}$$

$$= \frac{15,000 + 15,000}{7 - 4}$$

$$= 10,000 \text{ units/week}$$

Worked examples provide a step-by-step guide to the procedure to solve quantitative problems.

The Role of Operations Management
We will start by considering that the role of operations management is to manage the transformation of an organisation's inputs into finished goods and services (figure 2.1).

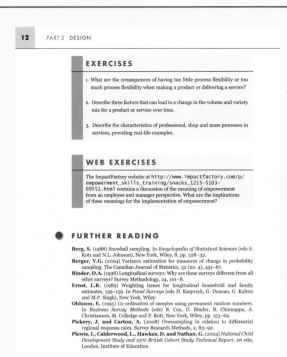

End-of-chapter exercises provide a review of the main concepts covered and examples to help develop practical skills.

References and **further reading** sections are supplied to enable students to explore topics in greater depth.

Lecturer Resources

Lecturers who adopt this text can obtain the following resources to support their teaching at the instructor companion site (**www.wileyeurope.com/college/greasley**):

- PowerPoint slides for each chapter
- Instructor's Manual with suggested solutions to case study questions, end-of-chapter exercises and teaching notes
- Test Bank, which is compatible with virtual learing environments such as Blackboard and WebCT.

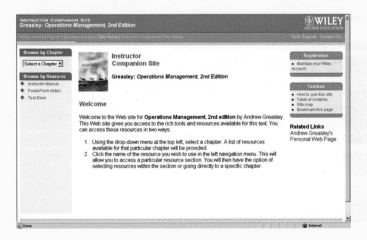

Student Resources

Students can also access the following resources at the student companion site: (**www.wileyeurope.com/college/greasley**):

- Multiple-Choice Self-Test Quizzes to review your understanding
- Online Glossary
- Web links to assist you in locating further materials.

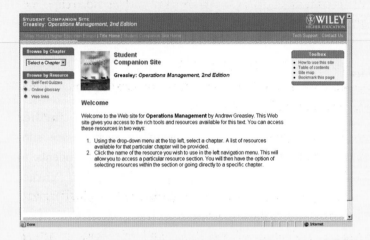

WileyPLUS

WileyPLUS is a powerful online tool that provides instructors and students with an integrated suite of teaching and learning resources, including an online version of the text, in one easy-to-use web site. To learn more about WileyPLUS and view a demo please visit **www.wileyplus.com**.

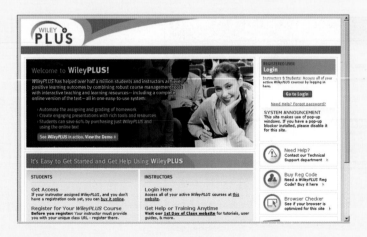

WileyPLUS Tools for Instructors

WileyPLUS enables you to:

- assign automatically graded practice questions from the test bank
- add your own questions to the test bank and create rules for each question
- track your students' progress in an instructor's grade book
- access all the teaching and learning resources in one easy-to-use web site
- create class presentations using Wiley provided resources, such as video clips and PowerPoint slides, with the ability to customize and add your own materials.

WileyPLUS Resources for Students

WileyPLUS features an online version of the book that is linked to the most useful resources for self-directed learning and practice, such as:

- animated demos of worked examples
- simulations demonstrating modelling techniques
- practice quizzes
- GO tutorial problems that present problems in a guided online (GO) format providing step-by-step interactive problem-solving guidance
- video clips that provide virtual tours of operations and role plays of actual situations.

ACKNOWLEDGEMENTS

The author would like to thank the team at John Wiley & Sons, Ltd for their assistance in the compilation of this book. Special thanks go to Sarah Booth, Deborah Egleton, Céline Durand and Claire Jardine. The author would also like to thank the team of reviewers for their constructive comments, which have helped to develop the book.

PART 1

INTRODUCTION

CHAPTER

1

Introduction

- Introduction
- What is operations management?
- The history of operations management
- The role of operations management
- Operations within the organization
- The process view of operations
- Service operations management
- The strategic role of operations
- Technology and operations management

LEARNING OBJECTIVES

- Define the term operations management
- Understand the role of operations in transforming the organization's inputs into finished goods and services
- Describe the process view of organizations
- Define the main types of service operations
- Understand the distinction between front-office and back-office tasks
- Understand the strategic role of operations
- Explain the relationship between technology and operations

INTRODUCTION

This chapter introduces the concept of operations management and describes some of the decision areas it covers. The operations activity is examined in terms of its components and its role in the organization. It is defined as a transformation process and as such occurs throughout the organization. The operations function itself is defined as being concerned with transformation processes that provide goods and services for customers. Some key themes of operations management are also explored, namely service operations management, the strategic role of operations and the use of technology in operations management.

WHAT IS OPERATIONS MANAGEMENT?

Operations management is about the management of the processes that produce or deliver goods and services. Not every organization will have a functional department called 'operations' but they will all undertake operations activities because every organization produces goods and/or delivers services.

> Operations management
> Operations management is about the management of the processes that produce or deliver goods and services.

Operations management has made a significant contribution to society by playing a role in areas such as increasing productivity, providing better quality goods and services and improving working conditions. Productivity has been increased through such measures as the use of technology (Chapter 6) and new production methods (Chapter 13). Increased productivity permits the more efficient production of goods and services and so helps raise living standards. Better quality goods and services are available through the use of quality initiatives such as total quality management (TQM) (Chapter 17). The rate of improvement in

quality levels is reflected in programmes such as Six-Sigma (Chapter 17). Improved working conditions are an outcome of the realization that the contribution of people is vital to an organization's success. Job design (Chapter 9) is used to help reach the full potential of employees.

The operations manager will have responsibility for managing resources involved in this process. Positions involved in operations have a variety of names, and may differ between the manufacturing and service sectors.

Examples of job titles involved in manufacturing include logistics manager and industrial engineer. Examples in the service industry include operations control manager (scheduling flights for an airline for example), quality manager, hotel manager and retail manager. An example job description for an operations role is shown in the box 'Job Description for Operations Director'.

Job Description for Operations Director (salary circa. £65,000)

Operations Director

This company has established itself as a leading manufacturer within an industry sector where growth is encouraging overseas competitors to venture into the UK market. Profitable, yet aware of the need to change, a plan has been put into place that will allow greater cohesiveness between manufacturing and commercial operations. Increased flexibility in production techniques is also on the corporate agenda with cost out and development of new products associated with initiatives in this area. This is a key position within the executive team carrying responsibility for all aspects of company activity with the exception of finance and commercial functions.

The Role
- Devise and implement a business operations strategy that secures the achievement of p&l objectives that are in line with the overall business plan.
- Management, motivation and development of the workforce (c. 120) through a period of change whilst ensuring continuous improvement in quality and operational efficiency.
- Create a culture of customer awareness that leads to collaborative product development and prompt resolution of issues that might affect perceptions of customer service.
- Influence the future direction of the business by being a fully participative member of the executive board.

The Candidate
- Graduate, operations or general manager of a customer-focused manufacturing business.
- Adept leader of change, able to devise innovative ways of working and ensure employee buy in.
- Has implemented, or at the very least explored the feasibility of, transferring some manufacturing activities to lower cost offshore alternatives.
- Clear communicator, numerate. Committed to achieving objectives and determined in overcoming obstacles.

People involved in operations participate in a wide variety of decision areas in the organization, examples of which are given in Table 1.1. The scale, importance and hopefully the excitement of operations management is indicated by the range of decision areas shown. Like many texts on the subject area of operations management, this book is structured around these decision areas (see chapter references in Table 1.1). The book is divided into sections on introducing operations and strategy (Chapters 1 to 2), design (Chapters 3 to 9) and management (Chapters 10 to 18) to aid clarity.

Chapter	Decision area	Example decision
2	Operations strategy	What strategy should be followed?
3	Process types	How do we configure the process that will deliver our service to customers?
4	Layout design	How do we organize the physical layout of our facilities and people?
5	Facility design and location	What is the location of our operations facilities?
6	Process technology	What role should technology have in the transformation of materials in the operations system?
7	Product and service design	What products and services should the organization provide?
8	Process design	How do we design the service delivery process?
9	Job and work design	How do we motivate our employees?
10	Planning and control	How do we deploy our staff day-to-day?
11	Capacity management	How do we ensure that our service is reliably available to our customers?
12	Inventory management	How can we keep track of our inventory?
13	Lean operations and JIT	How do we implement lean operations?
14	Enterprise resource planning	How do we organize the movement of goods across the supply chain?
15	Supply chain management	What benefits could e-procurement bring to our operations?
16	Project management	How do we ensure our projects finish on time and within budget?
17	Quality	How can we implement a TQM programme?
18	Improvement	What role could continuous improvement have in our operation?

Table 1.1: Decision Areas in Operations Management.

THE HISTORY OF OPERATIONS MANAGEMENT

Operations management did not emerge as a formal field until the 1950s and 1960s when textbooks specifically dealing with operations management were published. Major developments up to this point affecting the field of operations management start with the Industrial Revolution of the eighteenth century. Before this time products were made individually by skilled craftspeople in their homes and so were relatively expensive to produce. The use of inventions such as the steam engine (by

James Watt in England in 1764) and concepts such as the use of interchangeable parts (from Eli Whitney in 1790) and the division of labour (described by Adam Smith, 1776) led to the move to volume production. Here mechanization (provided by steam power) was combined with the use of low-skilled labour (people were given small, simple tasks using the concept of the division of labour) to produce standard parts in high volumes, which could be assembled into products. These ideas were refined and the use of scientific management, developed by Frederick W. Taylor and incorporating such elements as time study (Chapter 9), and the invention of the moving assembly line, first used by the car manufacturer Henry Ford in 1913, led to the era of mass production at the start of the twentieth century. This represented a major breakthrough in the ability of production systems to offer goods to a large amount of customers at a price they could afford.

An additional element in the makeup of operations management occurred during the First World War when the need to solve complex problems of logistics and weapons-system design led to the development of operations research. A number of the techniques developed then are still part of the operations management field today. As stated earlier, operations management as a discipline then began to emerge in the 1960s and has continued to develop since.

The 1970s saw the use of computers in materials requirements planning (MRP) software (Chapter 14) for inventory control and scheduling. The 1980s saw the emergence of the just-in-time (JIT) philosophy (Chapter 13) from Japan, which transformed the way businesses deliver goods and services. In response to the need to improve the quality of goods and service the ideas of total quality management (TQM) (Chapter 17) were widely adopted in the 1980s. The 1990s saw the emergence of such concepts as supply chain management (Chapter 15) and business process re-engineering (BPR) (Chapter 17). Most recently the use of the Internet to conduct transactions or e-Commerce (Chapter 6) has changed the way operations management is performed.

The history of operations shows how the field has adapted and continues to change as it tries to respond to an ever greater range of challenges, from the needs of customers who require high quality, low price goods delivered quickly to managing the impacts of global competition and addressing environmental concerns.

THE ROLE OF OPERATIONS MANAGEMENT

We will start by considering that the role of operations management is to manage the transformation of an organization's inputs into finished goods and services (Figure 1.1).

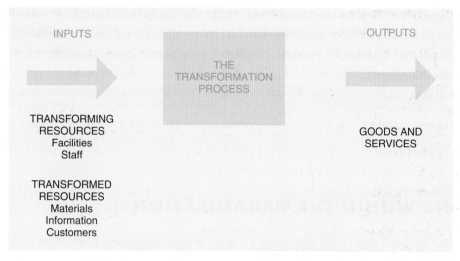

Figure 1.1: The Role of Operations Management.

The input activity involves two categories of resources. Transforming resources are the elements that act on, or carry out, the transformation process on other elements. The two main types of transforming resources are:

- Facilities, such as buildings, equipment and process technology. The management of these operations' resources is covered in Chapters 3 to 8.
- Staff, all the people involved in the operations process. In services the customer may well be involved as a transforming resource. Think of a fast-food restaurant where customers are expected to order the food and take it to their table and clear up afterwards. The management of human resources in operations is covered in Chapter 9.

The nature and mix of the transforming resources will differ between operations. The transformed resources, which are the elements acted on by the transforming resources, give the operations system its purpose or goal. The three main types of transformed resource, covered in Chapter 6, are:

- *Materials*. These can be transformed either physically (for example, manufacturing), by location (for example, transportation), by ownership (for example, retail) or by storage (for example, warehousing).
- *Information*. This can be transformed by property (for example, by accountants), by possession (for example, market research), by storage (for example, libraries), or by location (for example, telecommunications).

- *Customers*. They can be transformed either physically (for example, by hairdressers), by storage (for example, hotels), by location (for example, airlines), by physiological state (for example, hospitals), or by psychological state (for example, entertainment).

The transformation process itself will transform the material, information and customer resources in the way described above in order to produce goods and services.

OPERATIONS WITHIN THE ORGANIZATION

So far we have dealt with providing an overview of operations itself. This section discusses the role of operations in relation to other areas within the organization. Three of the most important functional areas in an organization can be classified as the operations, marketing and finance functions. The marketing function works to find and create demand for the company's goods and services by understanding customer needs and developing new markets. The need for marketing and operations to work closely together is particularly important as the marketing function will provide the forecast of demand from which operations can plan sufficient capacity in order to deliver goods and services on time. The finance function is responsible for obtaining and controlling funds and covering decisions such as investment in equipment and other operations resources such as personnel and materials.

Other functions that play a supporting role in the organization include the human resources (HR) function, which will play a role in regards to recruitment and labour relations; the research and development (R&D) function, which generates and investigates the potential of new ideas, and the information technology (IT) department, which supplies and coordinates the computer-based information needs of the organization.

The relationship between functions can be seen as a number of subsystems within the system called the 'organization'. Thus each function (such as marketing) can be treated using the same input/process/output transformation model as the operations function. In other words each function within the organization can be treated as performing an operations activity, as they are transforming inputs into outputs. This implies that every part of the organization is involved in the operations activity (to an internal or external customer) and indeed the topic of process management (Chapter 8) is an indication of how operations concepts are used across the organization.

THE PROCESS VIEW OF OPERATIONS

The view of the organization as a number of functions has been criticized. Melan (1993) considers the following conditions are usually built into the functional structure.

- Rewards systems that promote values and support the objectives of the functional department rather than the business in its entirety.
- Group behaviour, which encourages a strong loyalty within the department and an 'us-versus-them' attitude toward other departments within the firm.
- A high degree of decentralization, creating 'firms within the firm', each with its own agenda.

These and other deficiencies of the functional organization have led to a move away from considering business as a set of discrete functional areas and towards a view of the organization as consisting of sets of processes that link together in order to meet customer needs. Each process can be treated using the input/process/output transformation model as with the functional perspective, but there is a clear emphasis on breaking down the barriers between departments and ensuring that output meets customer requirements. Processes can be carried out by separate individuals (individual processes), contained within a department (functional processes) or can occur in several functional areas (cross-functional processes).

In functional terms the processes would be situated in areas such as operations, marketing and finance but from the customer's view the value they gain is dependent on the performance of the set of linked processes involved in the delivery of the product/service. The term 'value added' is used to denote the amount of value a process creates for its internal or external customer. The set of processes used to create value for a customer is often called the value chain (Porter and Millar, 1985). The value chain includes primary processes that directly create the value the customer perceives and support processes that assist the primary process in adding value. The key issue is that the configuration of the value chain should be aligned with the particular way the organization provides value to the customer. The design of operations from a process perspective is covered in Chapter 8.

> **Value chain**
> The value chain is the set of processes used to create value for a customer.

SERVICE OPERATIONS MANAGEMENT

Operations management has been historically associated with manufacturing industry but there has been a shift in its theory and practice to incorporate service systems. This is partly due to the importance of the service industry, which accounts for an

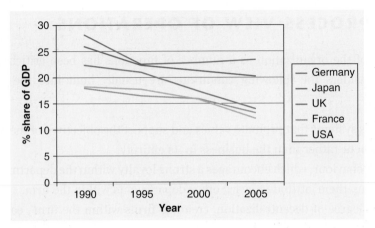

Figure 1.2: Manufacturing's Percentage Share of GDP in Period 1990 to 2005 in Selected Countries.
Source: United Nations Conference on Trade and Development (2008).

increasing proportion of the output of industrialized economies. In developed countries manufacturing output has generally fallen steadily as a proportion of GDP. This can be seen from Figure 1.2.

Case Study 1.2 at the end of the chapter outlines some of the reasons behind the shift from manufacturing to service output in the UK. The case study provides evidence that some of the decline in manufacturing output is not because these manufacturers have gone out of business but because they have reinvented themselves as service providers. The concept of **servitization** involves companies moving from being manufacturers with 'add-on' services to service companies whose output includes manufactured products.

It is difficult to measure the size of the service sector accurately because there is some disagreement about what constitutes the service sector but in the widest sense it can be seen as organizations that do not fall into what the economists call the primary sector (farming, forestry and fishing) or secondary sector (industries including manufacturing, mining and construction). Thus private-sector activities include retail, restaurants, hotels, transport and business services (this includes accounting, legal and computer services). Public sector service activities include health, defence, education and administration. Table 1.2 provides a classification of the service and nonservice sectors and indicates how their share of output, measured as gross value added (GVA), has changed in the UK over a 10-year period.

It can be seen from Table 1.2 that the service sector has risen as a share of output in the UK from around two-thirds in 1996 to three-quarters in 2006. The increasing prominence of the service sector in the economies of developed countries is due to an increase in what are termed consumer services and producer services.

Servitization
Servitization involves companies moving from being manufacturers with 'add-on' services to service companies whose output includes manufactured products.

Sector	Output (GVA) share (%)		Change in output (%)
	2006	**1996**	
Nonservices	24.9	33.2	− 8.3
Manufacturing	13.2	21.1	− 7.9
Mining and quarrying	2.4	2.9	− 0.4
Electricity, gas and water	2.7	2.3	0.4
Agriculture, forestry and fishing	0.9	1.8	− 0.8
Construction	5.7	5.1	0.6
Services	75	66.3	8.7
Real estate, renting and business services	24.8	19.1	5.7
Wholesale and retail trade	12.1	11.6	0.5
Financial intermediation (adjusted for FISIM)	4.4	3.2	1.2
Health and social work	7.3	6.4	0.9
Transport, storage and communications	7.2	7.8	− 0.6
Education	5.6	5.4	0.2
Other social and personal services	5.4	4.3	1.1
Public administration and defence	5.1	5.8	− 0.7
Hotels and restaurants	3.1	2.7	0.5

Table 1.2: Output (GVA) Share Percentage for Nonservices and Services in the UK.
Note: FISIM = financial intermediation services, independently measured, reported in Department for Business Enterprise and Regulatory Reform (BERR) (2008).
Source: Dye and Sosimi (2006).

Consumer services are services aimed at the final consumers and these have risen in line with people's increasing disposable income in developed countries. Once expenditure on essentials such as food and shelter has been accounted for, people will then spend on purchases such as travel, hotels, restaurants and other social and personal services.

Producer services are used in the production and delivery of goods and services and constitute firms providing services to other businesses such as consultancy advice, legal advice and IT support (classified under business services) and transportation and other facilities. The rise of producer services indicates that although the share of manufacturing is declining, it still plays an important part in a nation's economy. This is because many of the producer services are actually in business to provide services to manufacturers as well as other service providers. Many of the services that are now outsourced were once undertaken by manufacturers themselves and were thus formerly classified as part of the manufacturing sector.

The main reason for the decline in manufacturing in developed countries is often assumed to be competition from countries with lower labour costs. On the other hand services are often assumed to be required in the location they are consumed so cannot be outsourced overseas in the same way production activities are. Actually the provider and user of the service may not be required to move to the location of the consumption of the service as in 'separated services' such as the media channels of television and newspapers, Internet sites for downloading music and call-centre services. Generally, however, either the producer is required to move to the location of consumption in 'demand-located services' (for example management consultancy) or the user is required to move to the location of consumption in 'provider-located services' (for example hotels and hospitals). Some services, termed 'peripatetic services', require both the provider and user of the service to move their location to consume the service (for example trade shows and antique fairs). Users may be prepared to travel overseas for some services, such as medical treatments, but generally services need to be based near their users to be competitive and to meet local needs.

Types of Service Operation

In order to assess the challenges for operations in managing services it is useful to determine the characteristics of different services. It is useful to distinguish between the design of the service (Chapter 7) and the design of the system that delivers the service (Chapter 8). Services themselves can be classified by their tangibility, while the way they are delivered can be classified by their simultaneity.

Classifying Services by Tangibility

This is the most commonly used distinction between goods and services. Goods are tangible – they are physical things that you can touch. A service is intangible and can be seen as a process that is activated on demand. In reality, both goods and services have both tangible and intangible elements and can be placed on a continuum ranging from low to high intangibility. For example, the food in a fast-food restaurant is a major tangible element of the service. The food in a restaurant is still an important element, but other intangible elements such as waiter service and décor are important factors too. In fact most operations systems produce a mixture of goods and services. Most goods have some supporting service element (for example a maintenance contract with a new washing machine), called a facilitating service; many services will have support-ing goods (for example a report provided by a management consultant), termed a facilitating good. More information on the design of the service package (the bundle of goods and services) is given in Chapter 7 on product and service design.

The fact that services are intangible implies another important characteristic: perishability. A service is not a physical thing that can be stored, but is a process, so it must be consumed when it is produced or it will perish. The service provided by an empty seat in a restaurant or by an empty seat on an aircraft cannot be stored for use

---

Tangibility
If goods are tangible, they are physical things that you can touch. A service is intangible and can be seen as a process that is activated on demand.

Perishability
Perishability refers to the fact that because a service is not a physical thing that can be stored, but is a process, it must be consumed when it is produced or it will perish.

later. Thus revenue lost from these unused resources can never be recovered. This would not be a problem if the demand (in terms of volume and timing) for a service could be accurately determined and service capacity provided to match this. However, this is unlikely to be the case and unlike most goods, which can be stored if demand is lower than capacity to be used when demand is greater than capacity, services must always attempt to match supply and demand. This topic is considered in more detail in Chapter 11 on capacity management.

Classifying Service Delivery by Simultaneity

Simultaneity relates to the characteristic that services are produced and consumed simultaneously. This means the service provider and customer will interact during the service delivery process. The amount of interaction is termed the **degree of customer contact**. In fact the customer is unlikely to be a passive receiver of the service but will generally be involved to a greater or lesser extent in the actual delivery of the service itself. For instance a supermarket requires the customer to choose and transport the goods around the store and queue at an appropriate checkout till. However, it should not be assumed that all services are consumed at the point of production (for example, financial services) and that employees in a service operation have to deal directly with a customer. For the supermarket example, the checkout till is an example of high customer contact but stores' personnel may not have to deal directly with the customer at all.

A distinction in services is denoted by 'back-office' tasks, which add value to the inputs of the service operation, and 'front office' tasks, which deal with the customer both as an input and output of the operation (Figure 1.3).

Different organizations will have a different balance between front and back office operations. A front-office-based operation will be focused on the service experience of the customer and this is where most value will be added. Some

> **Simultaneity**
> Simultaneity relates to the characteristic that services are produced and consumed at the same time.

> **Degree of customer contact**
> The degree of customer contact relates to the amount of interaction between the service provider and customer during the service delivery process.

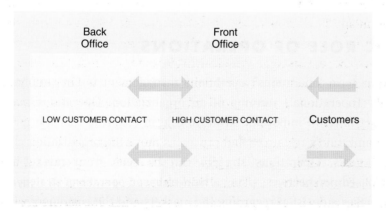

Figure 1.3: Front Office and Back Office in Operations Management.

traditional back-office focused organizations, such as manufacturers, are increasing the role of service experience and thus their front-office operations. This is because they judge that the ability to differentiate on the service aspect of their offering may provide a longer term source of competitive advantage than they can achieve by differentiating with the goods themselves. Some other organizations, however, are moving in the opposite direction and recognizing that customer value is being added by the tangible aspect of the service package delivered by the back office operations. For example budget airlines have eliminated many front-line service aspects of the flight experience and focused on the transportation of customer process itself.

Heterogeneity
Heterogeneity refers to the interaction of the customer, service provider and surroundings causing variability in the performance of the service.

The fact that services require simultaneity and are produced and consumed simultaneously implies another important characteristic: **heterogeneity**. This refers to the interaction of the customer, service provider and surroundings causing variability in the performance of the service. From the perspective of the service provider, humans, by their nature, are likely to vary their actions and sometimes makes mistakes. Individual customers will also perceive the quality of the service differently and the context of the service encounter (for example the existence of queues or weather conditions) may also impact on the service. This variability in performance and perceptions may lead to difficulties in maintaining a consistent level of service quality.

Some services, termed mass services, which operate at high volume and low variety of outcome, attempt to reduce variability due to heterogeneity by standardizing the service. This can be achieved by using approaches such as training staff to follow standard procedures and using equipment to support the service delivery process. This approach may not be appropriate for professional services, which operate at low volume and high variety, because here the customer requires high levels of contact with the service provider and a customized service. Service types such as mass service and professional service are covered in more detail in Chapter 3.

THE STRATEGIC ROLE OF OPERATIONS

Market-based operations strategy
In a market-based approach to operations strategy the organization makes a decision regarding the markets and the customers within those markets that it intends to target.

Despite the term 'operations', operations management is not simply about the day-to-day (operational) running of an organization. Operations management does in fact have an important strategic role in ensuring that the management of the organization's resources and processes move the organization closer to its long-term goals. Operations strategy can be seen from market-based and resource-based perspectives. Using a market-based operations strategy, the organization makes a decision regarding the markets and the customers within those markets that it intends to target. This market position is then translated into a list of criteria or objectives, which define what kind of performance is required in order to successfully compete in the markets chosen.

Some examples of criteria for performance are fast delivery, a wide range of services or a low price. A resource-based view works from the inside-out of the firm, rather than the outside-in perspective of the market-based approach. Here an assessment of the operation's tangible and intangible resources and processes leads to a view of the operation's capability. More detail on operations strategy is provided in Chapter 2.

> **Resource-based operations strategy**
> In a resource-based approach to operations strategy an assessment of the operation's tangible and intangible resources and processes leads to a view of the operation's capability.

TECHNOLOGY AND OPERATIONS MANAGEMENT

Technology plays a key role in the transformation process for which operations is responsible. **Process technology** is used to help transform the three main categories of transformed resources which are materials, customers and information. One of the most widely used and useful process technologies is computer-aided design (CAD), which allows testing of product and service designs using computer-based drawings. Customer processing technology such as automated teller machines can reduce or eliminate the need for employee contact in customer-facing operations. Information technologies such as e-Business systems are having a major effect on how firms organize their supply chains and use their capacity. More details on process technology are provided in Chapter 6.

> **Process technology**
> Process technology is used to help transform the three main categories of transformed resources, which are materials, customers and information.

CASE STUDY 1.1

'First Bank' PLC

'First Bank' has recently begun to offer Internet banking to extend its range of services to the customer and decrease the demand on branch personnel. However, the web site has been experiencing difficulties with a slow response rate to customer inquiries. Demand for the Internet service has also been much lower than expected. As operations manager the company requires your view on the following issues:

Questions

1. What are the competitive consequences of 'pulling out' of Internet banking for the company?

2. What impact will a decision to 'pull out' of Internet banking have on the company in terms of future technology-based initiatives.

3. How can the bank improve customer take-up of its Internet banking initiative?

SUMMARY

- Operations management is about the management of the processes that produce or deliver goods and services.

- The operations system can be seen as a transformation process. It converts inputs known as transformed resources (classified as materials, information and customers) using transforming resources (classified as staff and facilities) into finished goods and services.

- An alternative to the functional perspective of an organization is a process view in which the organization is seen as consisting of a set of processes that link together to meet customer needs.

- Service organizations can be classified by their tangibility (the extent that they incorporate a physical thing that you can touch). The way services are delivered can be classified by their simultaneity (the extent that the service is produced and consumed at the same time).

- Service operations can be denoted by front-office tasks, which deal directly with the customer, and back-office tasks, which add value to the inputs of the service operation.

- Operations management has an important strategic role in ensuring that the management of the organization's resources and processes direct the organization closer to its long-term goals.

- Technology plays a key role in the transformation of materials, customers and information for which operations is responsible.

CASE STUDY   1.2

Manufacturing's Decline Partly Due to Services Shift

Up to a fifth of the decline in manufacturing's share of the UK economy could be attributable to a shift by production companies towards service activities in place of turning out goods, according to UK government statisticians. The phenomenon of manufacturers undergoing a subtle metamorphosis so they become 'hybrid businesses' that combine production with services could explain why many individual companies regarded as manufacturers are performing a lot better than the sector's generally gloomy macroeconomic data. Lord Kumar Bhattacharyya, director of the Warwick Manufacturing Group at the University of Warwick, and a highly regarded observer of manufacturing trends, says: 'The fact that many more manufacturers in the UK have gone into services is one reason many have been able to survive.' Since 1995 the share of manufacturing in the economy has shrunk from 20% to less than 15%. This is a change generally linked to the faster growth of services plus productivity improvements in manufacturing reducing the value of factory output by making goods cheaper. Another factor is the growing share of global manufacturing output accounted for by countries with cheaper labour costs. UK data on the split between manufacturing and services are assembled by the government's Office for National Statistics. It does this by asking companies to classify their output between the two activities. If a manufacturer has abandoned most of its UK-based manufacturing – but continues to function in the UK as a distributor or provider of other services such as repair and maintenance. The company can be recategorized and may officially no longer be considered a manufacturer. According to a senior government statistician, no one has properly accounted for how much service activity is now being done by companies formerly considered as 100% manufacturers but today are classed either as hybrids or wholly service businesses. The official said it was 'quite plausible' that as much as a fifth of the apparent relative decline

in manufacturing in the past 10 years could be explained by this shift.

One of the best examples of companies making such a shift is Pace Micro Technology, a West Yorkshire business, which is a world leader in digital set-top boxes for televisions. In the late 1990s it employed 1500 at its main site in Shipley, most of them in manufacturing. Today the company's UK manufacturing output is non-existent – all its production being done by contractors in low-cost countries – but continues to employ 450 on the site, mainly in design engineering and software. Output from the site is categorized as a distribution activity – sales of set-top boxes to retailers – while the value of the engineering work is captured also in an unclassifiable part of these distribution sales. In a similar way Alstom, a French engineering company that in the 1990s operated large factories in the UK producing power turbines and trains, today employs 5000 in Britain – all but about 350 of whom are involved in services such as designing new power systems or maintaining railway equipment while it is being operated by customers. Indesit, an Italian white goods company formerly known as Merloni and which makes the Hotpoint brand of domestic appliances, has 5500 workers in the UK, only 2000 of them in conventional factory jobs. The rest are in activities such as servicing appliances in people's homes, distribution and logistics, sales and running a call centre in Peterborough for customer problems. Marco Milani, chief executive of Indesit, says: 'Services are an extremely important part of what we do.' UK company Dialight is a world leader in making light-emitting diodes – small electronic devices that can take the place of light bulbs and last a lot longer while providing more light. With most of its manufacturing in Mexico, it runs a plant in Newmarket, Cambridgeshire, employing 120. Most work is not in conventional manufacturing activities but jobs such as logistics and planning for the company's global operations. 'It's important to remember the work of a production company goes a lot further than what people regard as manufacturing,' says Roy Burton, chief executive.

Source: Peter Marsh, *Financial Times*, 22 May 2006. Reproduced with permission.

Question

Discuss the main reasons given for the growth in services in the case study.

EXERCISES

1.   Look at a recruitment web site or the recruitment section of a newspaper and locate three operations roles in job advertisements in the manufacturing industry and three in the service industry.

2.   How would you distinguish between the fields of operations management and operations research?

3.   Identify the main transformed and transforming resources for the types of organizations below:

- fast food restaurant
- hotel
- university
- food retailer
- car manufacturer.

4.   Explain the use of the process view of organizations.

5.   What are the implications of moving tasks between the front office and back office areas of a service operation?

6.   Explain the term heterogeneity as applied to service operations.

WEB EXERCISE

The UNCTAD web site (www.unctad.org) has a number of reports on the world economy. Visit the web site and from the UNCTAD handbook of statistics 2008 discover the value of the trade balance for developing and developed economies. Why do you think that the developed economies have such a high negative trade balance (imports are higher than exports)?

FURTHER READING

Johnston, R. and **Clark, G**. (2008) *Service Operations Management: Improving Service Delivery*, 3rd edn, Pearson Education Ltd.

Slack, N., Chambers, S. and **Johnston, R**. (2007) *Operations Management*, 5th edn, Pearson Education Ltd.

Slack, N. and **Lewis, M**. (2008) *Operations Strategy*, 2nd edn, Pearson Education Ltd.

Van Looy, B., Gemmel, P. and **Van Dierdonck, R.V**. (eds) (2003) *Services Management: An Integrated Approach*, 2nd edition, Pearson Education Ltd.

Vonderembse, M.A. and **White, G.P**. (2007) *Operations Management: Concepts, Methods and Strategies*, John Wiley & Sons, Ltd.

WEB LINKS

Selected List of Operations Management Web Sites

www.ame.org (accessed 23 September 2008). The Association for Manufacturing Excellence. Events and publications aimed at improving productivity.

www.apics.org (accessed 23 September 2008). The Association for Operations Management. Resources such as industry news in operations management.

www.brint.com (accessed 23 September 2008). An extensive search engine for business technology resources.

www.eiasm.org (accessed 23 September 2008). European Institute for Advanced Studies in Management (EIASM). International network for management research and teaching.

www.euroma-online.org (accessed 23 September 2008). European Operations Management Association (EUROMA). Leading association for operations managers. Contains information on conferences, workshops and publications.

www.informs.org (accessed 23 September 2008). Institute for Operations Research and Management Science. Resources such as web guides, journals and links to societies in the field of operations research.

www.iomnet.org.uk (accessed 23 September 2008). Institute of Operations Management. A professional body for those involved in operations management in the UK. Contains links to online resources.

www.manufacturinginstitute.co.uk (accessed 23 September 2008). The Manufacturing Institute contains news and events concerning manufacturing in the UK.

www.mas.berr.gov.uk (accessed 23 September 2008). Manufacturing Advisory Service. Department for Business Enterprise and Regulatory Reform (BERR) site for UK manufacturers.

www.mhhe.com/omc (accessed 23 September 2008). Operations Management Center. Resources regarding operations management for students and professionals.

www.poms.org (accessed 23 September 2008). Production and Operations Management Society. International society providing resources such as journals and encyclopedia of operations management terms.

www.sussex.ac.uk/Users/dt31/TOMI/ (accessed 23 September 2008). The Technology and Operations Management Index (TOMI) portal.

www.unctad.org (accessed 23 September 2008). United Nations Conference on Trade and Development. Provides links to a number of reports regarding world trade and economic development issues.

Selected List of Operations Management Academic Journals

http://jsr.sagepub.com/ (accessed 23 September 2008). *Journal of Service Research.*

www.emeraldinsight.com/ijopm.htm (accessed 23 September 2008). *International Journal of Operations and Production Management* (IJOPM).

www.poms.org/journal (accessed 23 September 2008). *Production and Operations Management* (POM).

www.sciencedirect.com/science/journal/01664972 (accessed 23 September 2008). *Technovation.*

www.sciencedirect.com/science/journal/02637863 (accessed 23 September 2008). *International Journal of Project Management.*

www.sciencedirect.com/science/journal/02726963 (accessed 23 September 2008). *Journal of Operations Management* (JOM).

www.sciencedirect.com/science/journal/07376782 (accessed 23 September 2008). *Journal of Product Innovation Management.*

www.sciencedirect.com/science/journal/09255273 (accessed 23 September 2008). *International Journal of Production Economics.*

www.sciencedirect.com/science/journal/09697012 (accessed 23 September 2008). *European Journal of Purchasing and Supply Management.*

● REFERENCES

Department for Business Enterprise and Regulatory Reform (BERR) (2008) *BERR Report 'Globalization and the Changing UK Economy'*, www.berr.gov.uk/files/file44332.pdf (accessed 22 September 2008).

Dye, J. and **Sosimi, J**. (eds) (2006), United Kingdom National Accounts: The Blue Book 2006, Office for National Statistics, HMSO, http://www.statistics.gov.uk/downloads/theme_economy/BlueBook2006.pdf (accessed 9 October 2008).

Melan, E.H. (1993) *Process Management: Methods for Improving Products and Services*, McGraw-Hill, New York.

Porter, M.E. and **Millar, V.E**. (1985) How information gives you competitive advantage, *Harvard Business Review* . July–August, 149–60.

UNCTAD (2008), UNCTAD Handbook of Statistics 2008, http://stats.unctad.org/handbook/ReportFolders/ReportFolders.aspx (accessed 9 October 2008).

CHAPTER 2

Operations Strategy

- **Introduction**
- **What is strategy?**
- **Judging the contribution of operations to strategy**
- **Measuring the contribution of operations to strategy**
- **Operations strategy approaches**
- **Operations strategy formulation**
- **Achieving strategic fit – trade-offs, focus and agility**

LEARNING OBJECTIVES

- Explain how strategy can exist at three levels within the organization

- Discuss the five performance objectives

- Contrast the market-based and resource-based approaches to operations strategy

- Discuss the Hill framework for operations strategy formulation

- Discuss two measurement systems to identify the relative importance of the competitive factors

- Explain the concept of trade-offs in operations

- Explain the concept of focus in operations

- Explain the concept of agile operations

INTRODUCTION

This chapter describes the role and formulation of operations strategy in the organization and discusses the increasing importance of the role of operations strategy. The purpose of operations in terms of an organization's strategy has often been seen as supportive, whereas functions such as marketing provide a competitive edge. Operations can, however, provide the basis of a firm's competitive strategy. The purpose of an operations strategy is to interpret the overall business strategy, which will be concerned with goals such as growth and profitability, into goals that direct how operations will be managed. These goals may be defined by the five operations performance objectives of quality, speed, dependability, flexibility and cost. In this chapter an approach to developing a strategy to achieve these goals is considered that is concerned with matching internal operations capability with external competitive market requirements.

WHAT IS STRATEGY?

Strategy can be defined as follows (Johnson, Scholes and Whittington, 2008):

> Strategy is the *direction* and *scope* of an organization over the *long term*, ideally, which matches its *resources* to its changing *environment* and in particular its *markets, customers* or *clients* so as to meet *stakeholder* expectations.

Thus strategic decisions occur as a result of an evaluation of the external and internal environment. The external evaluation may reveal market opportunities or threats from competitors. The evaluation of the internal environment may reveal limitations in capabilities relative to competitors. Strategy is seen as complex in nature due to factors such as the high level of uncertainty in future consequences arriving from decisions, the need for integration of long-term and day-to-day activities across the business and the fact that major change may have to be implemented as a consequence of strategic choices made.

Levels of Strategy

Strategy can be seen to exist at three main levels within the organization – corporate, business and functional (Figure 2.1).

Corporate Level Strategy

Highest or corporate level strategy provides long-range guidance for the whole organization, often expressed as a statement of its mission. The mission statement should define the key stakeholders whom the corporation will seek to satisfy and

Corporate level strategy
Provides long-range guidance on the direction of the whole organization.

Stakeholders
Anyone with an interest in the activities of an organization, such as employees, customers and government.

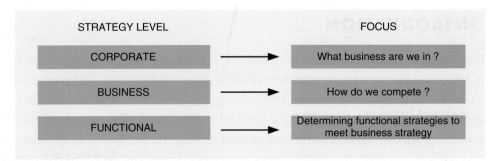

Figure 2.1: Levels of Strategy.

describe the overall strategy it will pursue to meet their objectives. Stakeholders can be defined as anyone with an interest in the activities of the organization. They can be divided into three main groups:

- *Internal stakeholders* include the organization's managers and employees. Employees will be concerned with issues such as job security, rewards, recognition and job satisfaction. In addition to these concerns one of the key roles of management is to try to reconcile the competing interests of stakeholder groups of customers, investors and employees.
- *Connected stakeholders* are parties with a direct connection with the organization such as customers, investors, shareholders, moneylenders, distributors and suppliers. These will all have a variety of needs from the organization. For example customers will be interested in the price, quality and service level of the goods and services that the organization delivers to the marketplace.
- *External stakeholders* cover other parties that can impact on the organization, the most important of which is usually the government. Governments are involved in such activities as setting regulations in areas such as health and safety and environmental policies. Government grants may be available in certain geographical areas which may affect the operations location decision. Other external stakeholders include the local community and pressure groups.

Using the stakeholder model the goal of the organization should be to satisfy the needs of stakeholders, which are necessary for the success of the organization in the long term.

Business Level Strategy

Business level strategy
Strategy at the organizational or SBU level in large companies. The strategy is concerned with the products and services that should be offered in the market defined at the corporate level.

The second level of strategy is termed a **business strategy** and may be for the organization or at the strategic business unit (SBU) level in larger diversified companies. Here the concern is with the products and services that should be offered in

CASE STUDY 2.1

Findus

Here is an example of a vision/mission statement from a company web site.

The Findus Vision

We have a common purpose within the Company to make the following 'Visions' a reality and these statements reflect the culture of the organization we are trying to develop. People make success, and so we want everyone to believe in our visions and work to achieve them.

Purpose

Findus will be one of the premier frozen food companies in Europe. Our consumers, employees, shareholders and communities will know us by the improvements we are making to their quality of life, through our superior products and the responsible way we create them.

Visions

- Findus products will be the consumer's first choice due to their superiority in taste, freshness and goodness.
- Findus will constantly lead the growth of the frozen food category at a pace never seen before.
- Findus will be the preferred supplier to all our customers.
- Findus will be a good place to work.
- Findus will set a new standard for corporate responsibility in the food industry.
- Findus will be organized to meet our business needs and will focus on the achievement of perfect customer and consumer service.
- Findus – The One Company.

Source: www.findus.co.uk. Reproduced by permission of Findus.

Question

Identify the stakeholder groups that are incorporated in the Findus vision statement.

---

the market defined at the corporate level. The SBU must develop a strategy at this level, which defines a competitive advantage for its products or services in the market. Competitive advantage may be achieved by strategies such as low cost, product innovation, or customization of a service to a niche market.

Functional Level Strategy

The third level of strategy is termed the operational or functional strategy where the functions of the business (for example, operations, marketing, finance) make long-range plans that support the competitive advantage being pursued by the business strategy.

The 'levels of strategy' model implies a 'top-down', structured approach to strategy formulation in which corporate goals are communicated down to business and

> **Functional level strategy**
> Where the functions of the business (such as operations, marketing, finance) make long-range plans that support the competitive advantage being pursued by the business-level strategy.

then functional areas. Although there has always been interaction within this hierarchy in both directions the role of functional areas such as operations in setting the framework for how a company can compete from the 'bottom up' is being recognized. For example the theory of emergent strategies (Mintzberg and Waters, 1995) shows how the implementation of strategy, rather than following a structure determined by a long-term plan, emerges from day-to-day experience at an operational level.

The contribution of operations to strategy development and its relationship to the levels in the organization where strategy is developed is the focus of discussion in this chapter.

JUDGING THE CONTRIBUTION OF OPERATIONS TO STRATEGY

As stated, the role that operations can play in strategy development and implementation is being recognized. Hayes and Wheelwright (1988) assert that the success of organizations depends on their overall operations capability and so provide a model which enables managers to identify operations' current strategic role and the changes needed in order to improve competitiveness. The four-stage model traces the contribution of the operations function from a largely reactive role in stage 1 to a proactive element in competitive success in stage 4 (Figure 2.2).

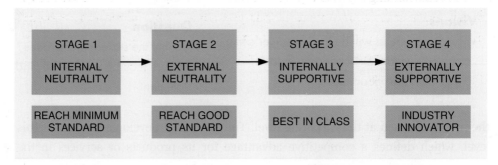

Figure 2.2: Four Stages of Judging Operations' Contribution to Strategy.

Stage 1: Internal Neutrality

Here the operations function has very little to contribute to competitive success and is seen as a barrier to better competitive performance by other functions. The operations function is simply attempting to reach a minimum acceptable standard required by the rest of the organization whilst avoiding any major mistakes, thus the term internal neutrality. However, a major mistake by operations could still have serious consequences for the rest of the organization (for example, product recall).

Stage 2: External Neutrality

Here the operations function begins to focus on comparing its performance with competitor organizations. Although it may not be innovative enough to be in the 'first division' of companies in its market, by taking the best ideas and attempting to match the performance of competitors it is attempting to be externally neutral.

Stage 3: Internally Supportive

Here the operations function is one of the best in its market area and aspires to be the best in market. The operations function will thus be organizing and developing the operations capabilities to meet the strategic requirements of the organization. Operations is taking a role in the implementation of strategy and being 'internally supportive'.

Stage 4: Externally Supportive

In stage 4 the operations function is becoming central to strategy making and providing the foundation for future competitive success. This may be delivered through the organization of resources in ways that are innovative and capable of adapting as markets change. When operations is in the role of the long-term driver of strategy it is being 'externally' supportive.

Figure 2.2 shows the four stages of judging operations' contribution to strategy and the corresponding role of the operations function in delivering the organization's strategy. As the organization moves from stage 1 to stage 4 its role moves from being reactive in response to strategic objectives passed down to it, to ensuring resources are developed to support the strategy, to (in Stage 4) providing the business with its competitive advantage.

MEASURING THE CONTRIBUTION OF OPERATIONS TO STRATEGY

The Performance Objectives

The five basic performance objectives (Slack, Chambers and Johnston, 2007) allow the organization to measure its operations' performance in achieving its strategic goals. The performance objectives are:

- quality
- speed
- dependability
- flexibility
- cost.

Performance objectives These allow the organization to measure its operations' performance in achieving its strategic goals. The performance objectives are quality, speed, dependability, flexibility and cost.

Each of these objectives will be discussed in terms of how it is measured and its significance to organizational competitiveness.

Quality

Quality (Chapter 17) covers both the quality of the design of the product or service itself (Chapter 7) and the quality of the process that delivers the product or service (Chapters 3, 6 and 8). From a customer perspective quality characteristics include reliability, performance and aesthetics. From an operations viewpoint quality is related to how closely the product or service meets the specification required by the design, termed the quality of conformance. In terms of measurement quality can be measured by the 'cost of quality' model covered in Chapter 17. Here quality costs are categorized as either the cost of achieving good quality (the cost of quality assurance) or the cost of poor quality products (the costs of not conforming to specifications). The advantages of good quality on competitiveness include:

- increased dependability – fewer problems due to poor quality means a more reliable delivery process
- reduced costs – if things are done correctly first time, expenditure is saved on scrap and correcting mistakes
- improved customer service – a consistently high quality product or service will lead to high customer satisfaction.

Speed

Speed is the time delay between a customer request for a product or service and then receiving that product or service. The activities triggered from a customer request for a product or service will be dependent on whether a make-to-stock or customer-to-order delivery system is in place. The concept of P:D ratios (Chapter 11) compares the demand time D (from customer request to receipt of goods or services) to the total throughput time P of the purchase, make and delivery stages. Thus in a make-to-stock system D is basically the delivery time, but for a customer-to-order system (for example a service system) the customer demand time is equal to the purchase, make and delivery stages (P). In this case the speed of the internal processes of purchase and make will directly effect the delivery time experienced by the customer.

Although the use of a make-to-stock system may reduce the delivery time as seen by the customer, it cannot be used for services and has disadvantages associated with producing for future demand in manufacturing. These include the risk of the products becoming obsolete, inaccurate forecasting of demand leading to stock-out or unwanted stock, the cost of any stock in terms of working capital and the decreased ability to react quickly to changes in customer requirements. Thus the advantage of speed is that it can be used to both reduce costs (by eliminating the costs associated with make-to-stock systems) and reduce delivery time leading to better customer service.

Dependability

Dependability refers to consistently meeting a promised delivery time for a product or service to a customer. Thus an increase in delivery speed may not lead to customer satisfaction if it is not produced in a consistent manner. Dependability can be measured by the percentage of customers that receive a product or service within the delivery time promised. In some instances it may even be important to deliver not too quickly, but only at the time required (for example a consignment of wet concrete for construction!). Dependability leads to better customer service when the customer can trust that the product or service will be delivered when expected. Dependability can also lead to lower cost, in that progress checking and other activities designed to ensure things happen on time can be reduced within the organization. Key activities needed to increase dependability include planning and control mechanisms to ensure problems are uncovered early, and making dependability a key performance measure.

> **Dependability**
> Dependability refers to consistently meeting a promised delivery time for a product or service to a customer.

Flexibility

Flexibility is the ability of the organization quickly to change what it does. This can mean the ability to offer a wide variety of products or services to the customer and to be able to change these products or services quickly. Flexibility is needed so the organization can adapt to changing customer needs in terms of product range and varying demand and to cope with capacity shortfalls due to equipment breakdown or component shortage. The following types of flexibility can be identified:

> **Flexibility**
> Flexibility is the ability of the organization to change what it does quickly. In terms of products or services this can relate to introducing new designs, changing the mix, changing the overall volume and changing the delivery timing.

- *Product or service* – to be able to act quickly in response to changing customer needs with new product or service designs;
- *Mix* – to be able to provide a wide range of products or services;
- *Volume* – to be able to decrease or increase output in response to changes in demand. Volume flexibility may be needed for seasonal changes in demand. Services may have to react to demand changes minute by minute.
- *Delivery* – this is the ability to react to changes in the timing of a delivery. This may involve the ability to change delivery priorities between orders and still deliver on time.

Flexibility can be measured in terms of range (the amount of the change) and response (the speed of the change). Table 2.1 outlines the range and response dimensions for the four flexibility types of product or service, mix, volume and delivery.

	Range flexibility	Response flexibility
Product or service flexibility	The range of products and services which the company has the capability to produce	The time necessary to develop or modify the products and services and processes which produce them to the point where regular delivery can start
Mix flexibility	The range of products and services which the company can deliver within a given time period	The time necessary to adjust the mix of products and services being delivered
Volume flexibility	The total output which the company can achieve for a given product and service mix	The time taken to change the total level of output
Delivery flexibility	The extent to which delivery dates can be changed	The time taken to reorganize the delivery system for the new delivery date

Table 2.1: The Range and Response Dimensions for the Four System Flexibility Types.

The range and response dimensions are connected in the sense that the more something is changed (range) the longer it will take (response). The relationship between the two can be observed by constructing range-response curves. In general the benefit of flexibility from the customer's point of view is that it speeds up response by being able to adapt to customer needs. The ability of the internal operation to react to changes will also help maintain the dependability objective.

CASE STUDY 2.2

Gecko

Jeff Sacreé turned his small, struggling, surfboard business into one of Europe's leading specialist helmet manufacturers on the basis of a casual conversation. His business was extremely seasonal and so he was looking to find a way of diversifying his products. Speaking to a lifeboat man, he found the Royal National Lifeboat Institute needed a lighter, more suitable helmet for use on the seas. It happened that he had been working on a helmet for surfers and so was well placed to supply the RNLI. After eventually securing the contract with RNLI, the question for Sacreé was where to take the business next.

Some potential markets sprang to mind immediately: specialist helmets could be usefully worn by river police, coastguard and customs officers – and a recent model has been designed specifically for helicopter winchmen. But, as the craze for new, extreme sports blossomed throughout the 1990s, a much wider market suddenly presented itself. Skateboarders, snowboarders, mountain bikers and powerboat racers all needed protection.

Prototype headgear was produced, tested and modified for each discipline and users were encouraged to respond with comments and suggested improvements. Gecko soon discovered that producing low-volume, handmade products was a distinct advantage when it comes to satisfying the niche markets of extreme sports. It involved less financial risk and allowed for the continual, minor improvements that customers wanted. 'We decided not to go down the automated production route,' says Sacreé 'and it seems to have paid off. Making everything by

hand gives us the crucial advantage of flexibility, so we can add altimeters and video cameras, torches and two-way radio systems – pretty well anything a customer asks for.'

Source: DTI web site (now Department for Business, Enterprise and Regulatory Reform).

Question

How has Gecko used flexibility to compete?

Cost

Cost is considered to be the finance required to obtain the inputs (transforming and transformed resources) and manage the transformation process that produces finished goods and services. If an organization is competing on price then it is essential that it keeps its cost base lower than the competition. Then it will either make more profit than rivals, if price is equal, or gain market share if price is lower. Cost is also important for a strategy of providing a product or service to a market niche, which competitors cannot provide. Thus cost proximity (to ensure costs are close to the market average) is important to maximize profits and deter competitors from entering the market.

> **Cost**
> Cost is considered to be the finance required to obtain the inputs and manage the transformation process that produces finished goods and services.

The major categories of cost are staff, facilities (including overheads) and material. The proportion of these costs will differ between operations but averages are staff 15%, facilities 30% and material 55%. Thus it can be seen that the greatest scope for reducing cost lies with a reduction in the cost of materials. A relatively small proportion of costs are usually assigned to direct labour.

The level and mix of these costs will be dependent on the volume and variety of output and the variation in demand. Increased volume means that the cost per unit will decrease as resources can be dedicated to the production or delivery of a particular service. However, diseconomies of scale (Chapter 5) can still occur due to increased organizational complexity, which can lead to poor communication. Increases in volume may be achieved with current resources or require significant investment in equipment and labour. The cost implications of increases in volume must therefore be considered carefully. Variety of output will increase complexity and thus costs. However, this complexity can be reduced by using such techniques as design simplification and standardization, increasing mix flexibility in moving from one product to another.

Finally cost is dependent on the other performance objectives. It was noted earlier that increased flexibility can lead to a decrease in the cost of the product or service design. In fact improvements in all the performance objectives can lead to a reduction in cost.

The Performance Objectives from an Internal and External Perspective

We can categorize the benefits of excelling at the performance objectives from an internal and external perspective (Table 2.2). This is useful because even though a performance objective may have little relevance in achieving performance that external stakeholders (such as customers) value it may bring benefits in improving the capability of operations from an internal perspective. When we look at approaches to strategy in the next section we find that competitiveness is not just a matter of simply improving performance along specific external competitive dimensions but incorporates the development of internal capabilities that provide specific operating advantages.

Performance objective	Internal (operations) benefits	External (market) benefits
Quality	Error-free processes	Satisfying customer needs
Dependability	Minimizes disruption	Meeting delivery commitments
Speed	Minimizes throughput	Get products and services to customers fast
Flexibility	Able to react to change	Offer frequent new products/services, a wide product/service range and cope with changing volume and delivery requirements
Cost	High productivity from low cost.	Market share and/or high margin.

Table 2.2: Internal and External Benefits of the Performance Objectives.

You might have noticed in the descriptions of the performance objectives in the previous section that improvement in the performance objective of cost derives from both lowering costs directly but also by improving the performance of the other performance objectives. Figure 2.3 shows this relationship.

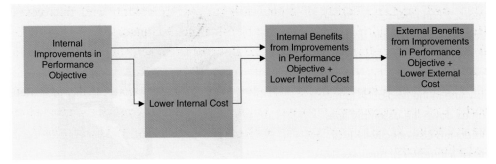

Figure 2.3: Internal Improvements in a Performance Objective also Lower Internal Costs.

Figure 2.3 shows how the internal improvements in the performance of a performance objective will show benefits for that performance objective but also lower costs. This can then be translated into external benefits from improvements in the performance objective as well as a reduction in costs. This relationship provides an indication of how operations can combine the performance criterion of low cost with criteria such as high quality and flexibility. It also shows that strategies that rely on immediate cost cutting (and thus risk damage to the operations capability) could be replaced by strategies that aim to improve performance on the other performance objectives, which will then lead to a reduction in cost. The issue of how to manage changes in the levels of performance objectives is discussed further in the later section on trade-offs.

CASE STUDY 2.3

Operations Strategy in Action

Almost every company seems to be restructuring itself to face the downturn, be it through financial engineering, or by retrenching to core activities. So they sell off foreign subsidiaries (Aviva), recent diversifications (ABB), or in desperate cases almost anything that's worth something and isn't nailed to the floor (Vivendi and Marconi). Oddly, few firms make a thing about going back to the real basics, which is manufacturing

or, more accurately, operations. Odd, because competing operationally – making and selling things better and more cheaply than the opposition – is the simplest and best strategy of all. In tough times like these, most other 'strategies' look like sorry substitutes for failing to get the basics right in the first place.

Schefenacker Vision Systems (formerly part of Britax) is a maker of car wing mirrors. Schefenacker has been improving its mirrors for more than 10 years. It can now satisfy the most demanding customers – for example, from its plant in the south of England it delivers a possible 420 permutations of mirror daily direct to Jaguar's assembly line in the Midlands to match each car that comes down the assembly line.

The ability to do this cost-effectively is an entry ticket to lots of international business. Less obviously, the company's virtuosity allows it to design and build better, more sophisticated parts – for instance, with lighting or electronics built in. That allows it to go upmarket, where margins are wider. At the same time, as with Dell, it also gives it the possibility of expanding up and down the value chain. Thanks to relentless emphasis on doing more with less . . . Schefenacker has freed up space on the factory floor for five new production cells. It uses these to manufacture simple parts which it had previously outsourced to others. Strategic result: Schefenacker no longer pays the other guy's profit margin, spreads overheads across a larger base, and can suck waste out of a larger section of the supply chain. Manufacturing director Mickey Love says: 'Lean production gives you an opportunity to make things that you can sell to customers you didn't have before.'

Of all the advantages of operations excellence as a strategy, its impact on people is the most momentous. In firms that take this route, improvement of every aspect of design,

manufacture, distribution, delivery and service is by definition strategic. Better product quality or a day sliced off delivery lead time is a strategic, not tactical, move. That means improvement is part of the day job for every individual; which also means 100 per cent participation, with no choice.

The secret is that operating excellence makes strategy easy. As Richard Schonberger, one of the original proselytizers for lean manufacturing, said: 'What makes a great team is the basics. Then almost anything the coach chooses to do makes the coach look like a shrewd strategist.'

Source: Excerpt from Caulkin, *The Observer*, (2002).

Questions

1. Read the article and discuss how operations can provide strategic advantage.
2. Discuss the performance of the company in terms of the five performance objectives.

OPERATIONS STRATEGY APPROACHES

The nature of the development of approaches to operations strategy has changed over time. For most of the twentieth century, market conditions were characterized by a mass-production era with an emphasis on high-volume and low-cost production.

Operations strategy was characterized by improving efficiency through aspects such as achieving a high utilization of equipment and having a closely supervised workforce undertaking standardized operations. This perspective was challenged by a new approach from Japan – lean operations (Chapter 13). Here the emphasis was not on low cost and high volume but on operations providing capabilities in areas such as reliability, speed and flexibility. This was achieved through such aspects as training staff in problem solving, using general purpose equipment for flexibility and eliminating waste in all its forms. Neither the 'mass' approach nor the 'lean' approach can be seen as a strategy in itself in that, to be successful, an operations strategy should support the competitive advantage being pursued by the business strategy. This means that the aim of the organization's operations strategy will be to seek a fit between the way it competes in the market and how operations is designed and managed. This 'fit' can be achieved in many ways and will in part be dependent on the operations current capabilities.

Market-Based Approach to Operations Strategy

Figure 2.4 shows the main elements of the market-based approach to operations strategy.

> **Market-based approach to operations strategy** Operations strategy is based on decisions regarding the markets and the customers within those markets that the organization intends to target.

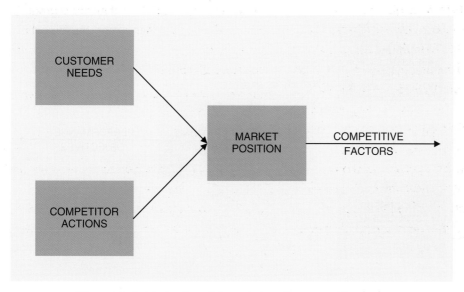

Figure 2.4: Market-Based Approach to Operations Strategy.

Using this approach an organization makes a decision regarding the markets and the customers within those markets that it intends to target. Along with meeting customer needs within a market the position the organization takes in that market will in part depend on the actions of its competitors. Thus the organization's market position is one in which its performance enables it to attract customers to its products or services in a more successful manner than its competitors. The next step is to translate the market position into a list of criteria or objectives which define what kind of performance is required in order to successfully compete in the markets chosen. Different authors use different terms for these measures, for example 'competitive criteria' (Hill, 2005) and 'competitive priorities' (Gaither and Frazier, 2002), but the term 'competitive factors' will be used here. Competitive factor is the term used to describe the dimension on which a product or service wins orders in the Hill methodology for operation strategy formulation described later in this chapter. Some examples of competitive factors are terms such as fast delivery, a wide range of services or a low price.

Resource-Based Approach to Operations Strategy

Resource-based approach to operations strategy
Operations strategy is based on an assessment of the operation's resources and processes.

A resource-based view of operations strategy works from the 'inside-out' of the firm, rather than the 'outside-in' perspective of the market-based approach. Here an assessment of the operation's resources and processes leads to a view of the operation's capability (Figure 2.5).

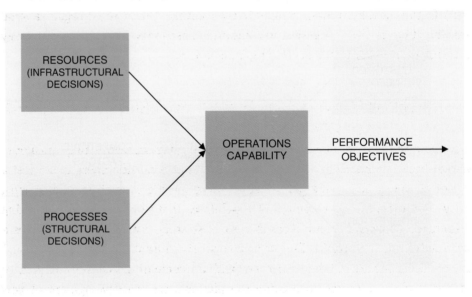

Figure 2.5: Resource-Based Approach to Operations Strategy.

The operations resources are categorized in Chapter 1 into transforming and transformed resources. Transforming resources are the facilities and staff that do the work on the transformed resources that deliver the goods or services to the customer. The transformed resources can be classified into materials, customers and information. However, even more important to the capability of an organization may be its intangible resources such as brand loyalty, supplier relationships, technological skills, design skills and a detailed understanding of customer markets. The important point to consider regarding an organization's intangible resources is that their value may not be recognized (they may not necessarily be included on the firm's balance sheet) and they are most likely to have been developed over time through experience and a process of learning. This second attribute makes them less easy to copy by competitors than tangible assets that can be bought in relatively rapidly. Processes are the way in which the firm operates its resources. Processes may follow formal rules laid down in company documentation, but informal processes are likely to form a large part of the way in which the organization operates. Informal processes are undertaken in a way that is dependent on factors such as the knowledge accumulated by staff, the relationships between staff members and the shared values and understandings of members of the organization. The nature and complexity of formal and informal processes and tangible and intangible resources is central to the resource-based view of strategy that the externally unobservable (within firm) factors are at least as important as observable industry market (between firm) factors in determining competitive advantage. The area of organizational learning (Chapter 18) is relevant to a resource-based view of operations strategy in terms of managing and developing capabilities.

Reconciling the Market-Based and Resource-Based Strategy Approaches

It has been found that not all companies pursue strategy in accordance with a pure market-based approach and it has been found that competitiveness is not just a matter of simply improving performance along specific competitive dimensions, but incorporates the development of capabilities that provide specific operating advantages. Thus the resource-based view of strategy is that operations takes a more active role in providing long-term competitive advantage. Thus resource and process decisions are not only concerned with implementing a chosen competitive strategy but are required to provide the platform for the development of new capabilities that are difficult for competitors to replicate. Thus the idea is that a resource-based view is not a substitute for a market position developed under a market-based view of strategy, but operation capabilities can allow a company to take up an attractive market position and can protect it from competitive threat (Figure 2.6).

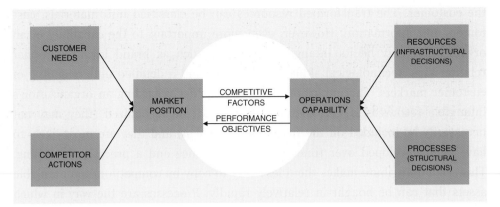

Figure 2.6: Reconciling the Market-Based and Resource-Based Approaches to Operations Strategy.

What makes the development of operations strategy particularly challenging is that not only should the market-based and resource-based views of strategy be considered at a point in time but the changing characteristics of markets and the need to develop operations capabilities over time means a dynamic as well as a static view of strategy is required. For example dynamic capabilities (Teece and Pisano, 1994) are built from the firm's resources and processes mediated by external market influences, but also driven by how managers make judgements about the firm and its future.

CASE STUDY   2.4

Texon

Sales of Texon jeans label material T484 continue to grow across the globe. Texon T484 cellulose material is available in eight different colour options, offering a distinct advantage over competitors who offer a very limited choice. Our product gauges run from 0.55 mm to 0.80 mm thick, and the material is available in rolls or sheets. Texon T484 was first introduced in 1991 when over 50 tons were sold. By 2003, the volume had increased to nearly 800 tons. From this quantity of almost 2 million m² of material, labels can be produced for around 460 million pairs of jeans. 2004 is expected to see a significant growth with sales going into 34 countries around the world. According to statistics, the world production of jeans is estimated at around 3 billion pairs, of which approximately 1.5 to 1.7 billion pairs feature a label made from cellulose material. In other words, one third of the world's production of jeans has a Texon jeans label. Texon continues to build on our shoemaking and innovative materials expertise to apply skills beyond footwear to other industries requiring high quality, high performance non-woven and cellulose products in apparel, automotive, furniture, luggage and filtration.

Source: Texon T484 'jeans label' success continues, www.texon.com/news/2004/

Reproduced by permission of Texon International Group Ltd (accessed 9 October 2008).

Question

Relate market-based and resource-based strategy approaches to Texon.

OPERATIONS STRATEGY FORMULATION

The following approach to operations strategy provides useful guidance in dealing with the issue of aligning operations to competitive needs. The emphasis within the Hill methodology (Hill, 2005) is that strategic decisions cannot be made based on information regarding customer and marketing opportunities addressed solely from a marketing-function perspective; the operations capability must also be taken into account. Hill proposes that the issue of the degree of 'fit' between the proposed marketing strategy and the operation's ability to support it is resolved at the business level in terms of meeting corporate (strategic) objectives. Thus Hill provides an iterative framework that links together the corporate objectives (which provide the organizational direction), the marketing strategy (which defines how the organization will compete in its chosen markets) and the operations strategy (which provides capability to compete in those markets). The framework consists of five steps:

1. Define corporate objectives
2. Determine marketing strategies to meet these objectives
3. Assess how different products win orders against competitors
4. Establish the most appropriate mode to deliver these sets of products
5. Provide the infrastructure required to support operations

In traditional strategy formulation the outcome of step 3 is 'passed on' to steps 4 and 5 and no further feedback occurs between steps in the process. The Hill methodology requires iteration between all five steps in order to link operations capability into decisions at a corporate level. This model is shown graphically in Table 2.3.

			Operations strategy	
1	**2**	**3**	**4**	**5**
Corporate objectives	**Marketing strategy**	**How do you qualify and win orders in the marketplace?**	**Delivery system choice**	**Infrastructure choice**
Sales revenue growth	Product/service markets and segments	Price	Choice of various delivery systems	Function support
Survival		Quality conformance		Operations planning and control systems
Profit	Range	Delivery: speed, reliability	Trade-offs embodied in these choices	Quality assurance and control
Return on investment	Mix	Demand increases		
	Volumes		Make-or-buy decisions	Systems engineering
Other financial measures	Standardization versus customization	Colour range	Capacity: size, timing, location	Clerical procedures
Environmental targets	Level of innovation	Product/service range	Role of inventory in the delivery system	Payment systems
	Leader versus follower alternatives	Design leadership		Work structuring
		Techical support supplied		Organizational structure
		Brand name		
		New products and services – time to market		

Table 2.3: Framework for Reflecting Operations Strategy Issues in Corporate Decisions.
Source: Terry Hill, Operations Management: Context and Managerial Analysis, 2000, Palgrave Macmillon, p. 39.

The steps in the Hill methodology are now described in more detail.

Step 1: Corporate Objectives

Step 1 involves establishing corporate objectives, which provide a direction for the organization, and performance indicators, which allow progress in achieving those objectives to be measured. The objectives will depend on the needs of external and internal stakeholders and so will include financial measures such as profit and growth rates as well as employee practices such as skills development and appropriate environmental policies.

Step 2: Marketing Strategy

Step 2 involves developing a marketing strategy to meet the corporate objectives defined in step 1. This involves identifying target markets and deciding how to compete in these markets. This will require the use of product/service characteristics such as range, mix and volume that the operations activity will be required to provide. Other issues considered will be the level of innovation and product development and the choice of 'leader' or 'follower' strategies in the chosen markets.

Step 3: How do you Qualify and Win Orders in the Marketplace?

This is the crucial stage in Hill's methodology where any mismatches between the requirements of the organization's strategy and the operations capability are revealed. This step provides the link between corporate marketing proposals and the operations processes and infrastructure necessary to support them. This is achieved by translating the marketing strategy into a range of competitive factors (for example, price, quality, delivery speed) on which the product or service wins orders. These external competitive factors provide the most important indicator as to the relative importance of the internal operations performance objectives discussed earlier in this chapter. Figure 2.7 provides examples of how different (external) competitive factors will require a focus on the corresponding (internal) performance objectives.

Competitive factors
A range of factors such as price, quality and delivery speed, derived from the marketing strategy, on which the product or service wins orders.

Figure 2.7 does not imply a one-to-one relationship between competitive factors and performance objectives. This is because of the interrelationships between the

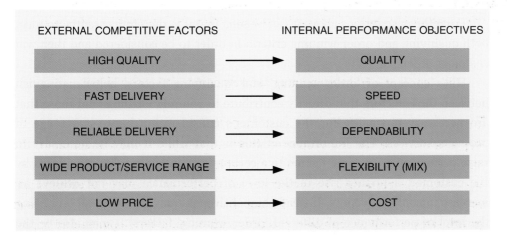

Figure 2.7: The Relationship between Competitive Factors and Performance Objectives.

performance objectives, for example speed will be partly dependent on other performance objectives such as cost and dependability. Thus the figure shows that a particular external competitive factor will provide an indication of the relative importance of the internal performance objective.

At this stage it is necessary to clarify the nature of the markets that operations will serve by identifying the relative importance of the range of competitive factors on which the product or service wins orders.

Influences on the Relative Importance of the Competitive Factors

Two main influences are considered, namely customers and competitors.

Customers

Customers will value a range of competitive factors for any particular product/service, thus it is necessary to identify the relative importance of a range of factors. Hill distinguishes between the following types of competitive factors which relate to securing customer orders in the marketplace.

- *Order-winning factors*. These are factors that contribute to winning business from customers. They are key reasons for customers purchasing the goods or services and raising the performance of the order-winning factor may secure more business
- *Qualifying factors*. These are factors that are required in order to be considered for business from customers. Performance of qualifying factors must be at a certain level to gain business from customers but performance above this level will not necessarily gain further competitive advantage.

From the descriptions above it can be seen that it is therefore essential to meet both qualifying and order-winning criteria in order to be considered and then win customer orders.

Hill's concept of 'order-winning' and 'qualifying factors' helps distinguish between those factors that directly contribute to winning business and those that are necessary to qualify for the customer's consideration between a range of products/services. The importance of this is that while it may be necessary to raise performance on some factors to a certain level in order to be considered by the customer, a further rise in the level of performance may not achieve an increase in competitiveness. Instead competitiveness may then depend on raising the level of performance of different 'order-winning' factors. It may also be the case that the order-winning and qualifying factors will differ for different customer groups that the organization may be serving. One strategy for dealing with divergent customer demands is to use the idea of the focused factory and to break the plant into units allocated on the basis of 'order-winner' and 'order-qualifying' criteria.

Competitors

Competitor actions will also influence the basis on which competition is based and may require a change in priorities of the competitive factors used by the organization. For example if an organization is competing on price and a competitor enters the market and takes market share by competing on faster delivery, the organization may need to consider that as a new competitive factor. The significance of this influence is that the initiative for change has been provided by a competitor, not the customer.

Slack (1991) uses a combination of customer and competitive factors using two dimensions – importance and performance – to help operations managers prioritize performance objectives. The relative *importance* of a competitive factor is assessed in terms of its importance to internal or external customers using a nine-point scale of degrees of order-winning, qualifying and less important customer viewed competitive factors (Table 2.4).

Order winner	Strong	1	Provides a crucial advantage
	Medium	2	Provides an important advantage
	Weak	3	Provides a useful advantage
Qualifier	Strong	4	Needs to be up to good industry standard
	Medium	5	Needs to be up to median industry standard
	Weak	6	Needs to be within close range of the rest of industry
Less important	Strong	7	Not usually of importance but could become more so
	Medium	8	Very rarely considered by customers
	Weak	9	Never considered by customers

Table 2.4: A Nine-Point Scale of Importance.
Source: Slack, Chambers and Johnston (2007, Fig. 18.6a, p. 590). Prentice Hall, reproduced with permission of Pearson Education.

The next step ranks the relative *performance* of a competitive factor against competitor achievement. Benchmarking in this way clarifies the competitive position of the organization and helps identify where performance should be improved. A nine-point performance scale (rating from consistently better than the nearest competitor to consistently worse than most competitors) is used for each performance objective (Table 2.5).

Better than competitors	Strong	1	Considerably better than competitors
	Medium	2	Clearly better than competitors
	Weak	3	Marginally better than competitors
Same as competitors	Strong	4	Sometimes marginally better than competitors
	Medium	5	About the same as most competitors
	Weak	6	Slightly lower than the average of most competitors
Worse than competitors	Strong	7	Usually marginally worse than most competitors
	Medium	8	Usually worse than competitors
	Weak	9	Consistently worse than competitors

Table 2.5: A Nine-Point Scale of Performance.
Source: Slack, Chambers and Johnston (2007, Fig. 18.6b, p. 590). Prentice Hall, reproduced with permission of Pearson Education.

The next step is to plot each importance rating and performance rating in an importance-performance matrix. This indicates what customers find important in achieved performance when compared with competitor performance. The importance-performance matrix is divided into four zones (Figure 2.8). The zones are defined as follows:

- Appropriate – performance objectives in this zone are satisfactory in the short to medium term, but there should be a wish to improve performance towards the upper boundary of the zone.
- Improve – performance objectives below the lower bound of the appropriate zone will be candidates for improvement.
- Urgent action – here performance objectives are far below what the customer requires and so should be improved to 'same as' or 'better than' competitor performance.
- Excess – here too many resources may be being used to achieve this level of performance. There is a possibility that they could be deployed to a less well performing area.

Although the main thrust of the operations function will be to move the performance objectives up the vertical scale and so outperform competitors, horizontal movement (changing customer perceptions of the relative importance of competitive factors) should be considered. The position of the performance objectives on the matrix will change, without any actions from the organization, as customer preferences change and competitor performance improves. Thus improvement strategies should take the dynamic nature of the variables into account.

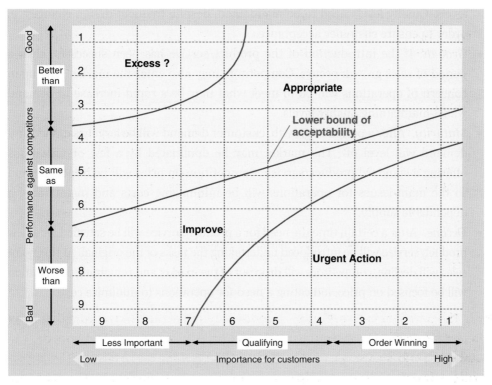

Figure 2.8: Priority Zones in the Importance-Performance Matrix.
Source: Slack, Chambers and Johnston (2007, Fig. 18.7, p. 591). Prentice Hall, reproduced with permission of Pearson Education.

Using the Product/Service Life Cycle to Describe Customer and Competitor Behaviour over Time

The product/service life cycle (PLC) provides one way of generalizing customer and competitor behaviour over time. The PLC is an attempt to describe the change in sales volume for a particular product or service from being introduced into a market until its withdrawal. The model shows sales volume passing through the four stages: introduction, growth, maturity and decline (Figure 2.9). The model is useful in that each stage in the life cycle requires a different approach from the operations function and thus emphasizes the need for a range of capabilities from the operations function. The drawback of the approach is that it may be difficult to predict when the product/service will enter the next stage of the cycle or even determine what stage of the cycle the product/service is currently in! The main stages of the PLC can be described as follows:

- *Introduction.* On introduction the product/service specification may frequently be changed as feedback is received from customers. Operations will need to maintain flexibility in terms of design changes and response to changes in demand levels. Quality levels need to be maintained, despite frequent design changes, in order to ensure customer acceptance.

- *Growth*. If the introduction of the product/service has been successful then a period of sales growth occurs. Competitors may also enter the market. The main concern of operations will be to meet what may be a rapid increase in demand whilst maintaining quality levels.

- *Maturity*. After a period of growth, customer demand will be largely satisfied and demand will level off. The market may be dominated by a few organizations offering a standard product/service. Competition on price will be important and so the main issues for operations will be minimizing costs and maintaining a dependable supply.

- *Decline*. After a certain time the need for a product/service will be satisfied, or a new product/service will be introduced undertaking the tasks of the original. At this point sales will decline, competitors will drop out of the market and remaining competition will be focused on price, indicating a need for operations to minimize costs.

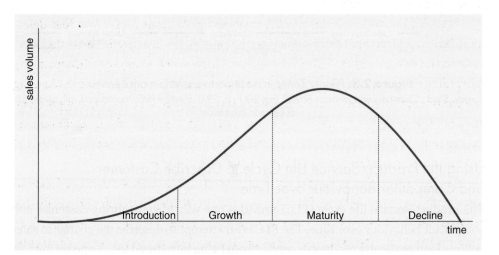

Figure 2.9: The Product/Service Life Cycle.

Step 4: Delivery System Choice (Structural Decisions) and Step 5: Infrastructure Choice (Infrastructural Decisions)

Steps 4 and 5 of Hill's methodology involve putting the processes and resources in place that provide the required performance as defined by the performance objectives. Hill categorizes operations decision areas into delivery system choice, which is often referred to as structural decisions, and infrastructure choice, commonly termed infrastructural decisions. These categories are useful because they indicate how the potential of the operation is limited by its structure, but it can only reach that potential if used with the appropriate infrastructure which governs the way it works on a day-to-day basis. It should be noted though that operations decision areas will have both a structural and infrastructural element to them. For example the implementation of process technology will affect both physical resources and systems and the policies and practices of the operation. The steps are now outlined, with references to the relevant chapters for decision areas within this text.

Delivery system choice, also termed **structural decisions**, concerns aspects of the organization's physical resources such as service delivery systems and capacity provision. This includes the choice of process type implemented in manufacturing (project, jobbing, batch, line or continuous) or services (professional, shop, mass) covered in Chapter 3 and the associated layout types covered in Chapter 4. Capacity issues include the volume, timing and location of capacity provision covered in Chapter 5. The provision of process technology for materials, information and customers is covered in Chapter 6.

Infrastructual decisions describe the systems, policies and practices that determine how the structural elements covered in step 4 are managed. These decisions include the design of jobs (Chapter 9), the management of capacity (Chapter 10), scheduling of operations (Chapter 11), inventory management (Chapter 12), planning and control systems such as JIT and ERP (Chapter 13 and Chapter 14), supply chain management (Chapter 15) and project management (Chapter 16). In addition performance improvement (Chapter 17) and performance measurement (Chapter 18) systems are also included under this heading.

It is important that structural and infrastructural decisions should be in alignment with one another and with the operations strategy in order to create the required capabilities defined by the performance objectives. This can be difficult as structural and infrastructural decisions are often taken at various points in time by people within different areas of the organization. This implies that the operations strategy needs to be clearly communicated across the organization if implementation of structural and infrastructural changes is to keep pace with changing competitive priorities. It should also be noted that there is no single solution to achieving a certain set of competitive priorities for the organization. For example, one firm may concentrate on structural elements such as process technology and another competing firm may concentrate on infrastructural elements such as a TQM programme. Slack and Lewis (2008) describe operations strategy as the intersection of a company's performance objectives with its decision areas. The process of reconciliation between the market-based and resource-based views of operations strategy takes place between these intersections. A strategy matrix (Slack and Lewis, 2008) can be used

---

Structural decisions
These concern aspects of the organization's physical resources such as service delivery systems and capacity provision.

Infrastructual decisions
These describe the systems, policies and practices that determine how the operations' structural elements are managed.

to show the intersections between what is required from the operations function (the relative priority given to each performance objective) and how the operation tries to achieve this through the set of choices made (and the capabilities which have been developed) in each decision area.

ACHIEVING STRATEGIC FIT – TRADE-OFFS, FOCUS AND AGILITY

Earlier in this chapter it was stated that the aim of the organization's operations strategy will be to seek a fit between the way it competes in the market and how operations is designed and managed. This 'fit' can be achieved in many ways and will in part be dependent on the operations' current capabilities. Step 3 of Hill's methodology involves providing a 'fit' between the external competitive factors derived from the market position and the internal performance objectives derived from the operations processes and resources (infrastructure). This section attempts to understand the relationship between the performance objectives and how we can approach changes in their absolute and relative performance.

The concept of trade-offs is first introduced as meaning that to excel in only one objective usually means poor performance in some or all of the others. Thus an attempt to be good at everything will lead to being mediocre at everything. Under this approach any pair of performance objectives potentially constitutes a trade-off and it is important to identify any trade-off relationships. A number of approaches to the trade-off issue are then explored including:

- the sandcone theory, which maintains that there is an ideal sequence in which operational capabilities should be developed, implying that certain operational capabilities enhance one another allowing improvements across multiple performance objectives
- the idea of focus to simplify competing demands
- the introduction of agile systems through the use of process technology and process design
- the development of flexibility through mass customization methods such as design for manufacture.

Trade-offs
A trade-off relationship means that to excel in one objective means poor performance in one or more other objectives.

Trade-offs

The idea of **trade-offs** (Skinner, 1985) provides a way of understanding the way in which the performance objectives relate to one another. The original idea of trade-offs is that there is a trade-off relationship between competitive objectives, such as cost, quality or delivery, which means that to excel in only one objective usually entails poor performance in some or all of the others. Thus an attempt to be good at everything will lead to being mediocre at everything. The existence of trade-offs means that optimum solutions must be sought within the inherent limits (constraints) of the operation. Any pair of performance measures potentially constitutes a trade-off and it is important to identify operations trade-off relationships. An example of a trade-off between customer service (which can be considered to constitute the four performance objectives of quality, speed, dependability and flexibility) and resource efficiency (which can be considered as determining the remaining performance objective of cost) is shown in Figure 2.10.

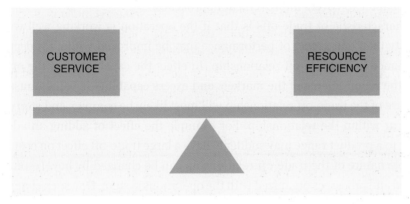

Figure 2.10: Trade-off Relationship between Customer Service and Resource Efficiency.

In order to analyse this trade-off it is necessary to understand that the resource efficiency of a system determines the cost of producing a product while customer service will influence selling price. Profitability is a function of both total production cost and sales revenue. The trade-off relationship means that to gain an improvement on one side of the profitability model, there will be a consequent penalty to be paid on the other. An example of this relationship is a trade-off between delivery performance and the cost of holding high stocks of materials. The better delivery performance is in a trade-off with the cost of material stocks. Alternatively the improvement and penalty may both lie on the same side of the model. An example of this is between overhead and material costs. Machine overheads can be reduced by increasing their utilization and by building stocks of materials; conversely reducing material stocks adversely affects utilization and increases overheads.

There are two basic approaches to managing trade-offs. The first approach is to manage the trade-off factors within the constraints of the operations system. This involves ensuring that an operation's relative achievement in each dimension of performance should be driven by the requirements of the market. This is not a straightforward process as there may be costs and risks involved in changing relative performance levels and the complexity of trade-off relationships can mean other trade-offs are affected. This approach is characterized by an acceptance of the constraints of the operations system but it can in itself lead to an improvement in overall performance.

The second approach is through improvement and loosening the constraints on the operations system. This involves increasing the capability of operations to enable improvement in both dimensions of performance or improvement in one dimension while preventing or limiting any deterioration in the other. This, again, is not a straightforward process and requires costs and risks in improving performance levels. Chapter 18 covers improvement approaches.

A characteristic of trade-offs is that if the operation is working well within its capability then one aspect of performance may be improved without a decrease in performance in its trade-off relationship. In effect the capabilities of the operation exceed the requirements of the markets and excess capability is being unused. Also the nature of the trade-off relationship will most likely be complex and step changes may occur within the relationship. For example the effect of adding an additional product to a product range may suddenly have a large trade-off effect on cost. Finally the whole nature of the trade-off relationship can be changed by how resources are deployed and processes organized with the operations system. One such change is the implementation of the idea of focus, considered in the next section.

The idea of trade-offs is challenged by the belief that performance can be improved simultaneously along multiple dimensions. Indeed Figure 2.3 shows how improvements in the performance objectives of quality, dependability, speed and flexibility can lead to both benefits from these improvements themselves as well as leading to an improvement in the performance objective of cost. Furthermore Ferdows and de Meyer (1990) state that operational excellence can be built in a cumulative fashion. Their sandcone theory maintains that there is an ideal sequence in which operational capabilities should be developed of quality, dependability, speed, flexibility and finally achieving excellence in cost. A cumulative effort to improve should begin with improvements in quality and when a minimum acceptable level of performance is reached, improvements are pursued in both quality and dependability. The full sequence of improvement is:

1. Quality.
2. Quality + dependability.
3. Quality + dependability + speed.
4. Quality + dependability + speed + flexibility.
5. Quality + dependability + speed + flexibility + cost.

This approach both highlights the need to only target reduction in costs after improvements in the other performance objectives have been secured and implies that certain operational capabilities enhance one another allowing improvements across multiple performance objectives.

Focus

The concept of focus (Skinner, 1974) is to align particular market demands with individual facilities to reduce the level of complexity generated when attempting to service a number of different market segments from an individual organization. This is because it is difficult and probably inadvisable for operations to try to offer superior performance over competitors across all of the performance objectives. Usually organizations succeed when they organize their resources and compete across one or two performance objectives. Also the capabilities of the organization will usually mean that it can do some things better than others and a strategy that uses inherent strengths will be more likely to offer a competitive advantage. This does not mean that capabilities cannot be changed over time, but it is likely that at any one time there are certain things that an organization can do well and certain things that it cannot do satisfactorily, if at all.

Focus
Focus aligns particular market demands with individual facilities to reduce the level of complexity generated when attempting to service a number of different market segments from an individual organization.

The idea of focus has been used by many firms to break up large and complex organizations into more simple and focused operations. Although many managers argue that the breakup of organizations leads to higher costs in terms of duplication of equipment, floor space and overheads, many companies have found that focusing has led to a decrease in operating and overhead costs. Many of the advantages of focus can be obtained without the subdivision of the organization using methods such as:

- Simplification through elimination of product or services that are seldom requested by customers.
- Operation-within-an-operation. This involves dividing a facility into separated work areas, with the advantage of reducing the considerable expense of setting up independent operations. (See JIT and focused-factory sections.)
- Cell layout – dedicating a small group of people and equipment to a subset of products or services (Chapter 4).
- Process design – using business process management to provide an integrated design for the processing steps involved in the manufacture of a product or delivery of a service (Chapter 8).

The implementation of a focus strategy requires a decision regarding both the dimension on which the focus is based and the level of focus that is required across this dimension. There are many different dimensions in which focus can be applied, including on a range of products or services (product focus), on market or customer groups (market focus) or on the process needs of products or services (process focus). Focus could also be based on competitive factors (such as low cost). This approach aims to ensure that the conditions are created where operations can excel at the criteria that are necessary for market success. Focus based in this way will need to reflect changes in the relative competitive factors of customer needs and competitor actions.

The level of focus can range from, say, separate cells producing each product or service at one extreme to producing all products and services from one operations facility at the other. The temptation is to add new products and service types to existing facilities over time in order to secure market share, adding complexity and losing focus. At some point a decision should be made on either simplifying the product or service range or subdividing the operation.

Benefits of the focus approach include increased clarity in the day-to-day management of operations resources and the ability to focus processes and resources for a specific subset of operations. Process improvement initiatives can also be more successful within a focused operation. However, the idea of focus, by definition, limits the scope of what the operations system can do and thus makes it vulnerable to shifts in the competitive environment. Focus also risks losing economy of scale advantages when resources that were once shared are now dedicated to separate departments (for example, discounts on high-volume purchasing may be lost).

Lean Operations and the Focused Factory

Just-in-time or lean production facilities often use the idea of the focused factory as outlined by Skinner (1974). These factories organize their functions around a relatively narrow range of products or a product family (a group of products that share similar production requirements) in order to ensure simple and consistent operations. This may be the outcome of splitting a large manufacturing plant that has developed a large product range over time into two or more focused plants. In terms of JIT flow, concentrating on a narrow range of products will simplify layout, reducing transportation time and reduce WIP inventories. To sustain flexibility in the focused factory there will be less automation than is generally associated with the focused factory. The concept of focus is connected with the JIT philosophy of keeping work methods simple and reducing system complexity. Lean operations and JIT are covered in more detail in Chapter 13.

Agile Operations

The aim of agile operations is to be able to respond quickly to changing market demand in order to retain current markets and gain new market share. Agile operations aim to serve fast-changing markets in which customers demand both high quality service and low cost. Thus an agile operations strategy aims to overcome trade-offs by developing the capability of its resources. Attempts to do this have included the use of process technology (Chapter 6) and process redesign (Chapter 8). An example of the use of process technology in order to overcome the trade-off of customer service and resource efficiency is the service offered by Amazon on the Internet. A vast array of books are offered to satisfy customer needs, but are not actually stocked by Amazon to keep costs low. Amazon is acting as an intermediary between customer and supplier and enabling the customer to obtain a high level of service without the costs usually associated with this. An example of the use of an agile operations strategy in the design process is that of mass customization.

> **Agile operations**
> These aim to respond quickly to changing market demand in order to retain current markets and gain new market share by developing the capability of resources.

Mass Customization

Mass customization (Pine, Best and Boynton, 1993) provides an alternative approach to the concept of focus in attempting to combine high-variety and high-volume output in order to provide the customer with customized products at a relatively low price. The expansion of options available in motor vehicles (for example engine size, engine type, body style) is an example of this approach. The ability to combine high volume and high variety can be achieved by excelling at the flexibility performance objective (Chapter 2) in order to provide high variety, without the costs usually involved in achieving this. One way of doing this is to incorporate the ideas related to design for manufacture, of simplification, standardization and modularization at the design stage.

> **Mass customization**
> An attempt to combine high-variety and high-volume output in order to provide the customer with customized products at a relatively low price.

Vonderembse and White (2004) describe three levels of customization:

- *Customer-contact customization* is where the product or service is tailored to individual needs. For example a haircut or bicycle can be designed and delivered to meet the specification provided by an individual customer.
- *Adaptive customization* is where a standard product or service can be customized to meet individual needs. For example a car can be customized by the customer by ordering from a list of options such as metallic and air conditioning. Here customization starts at the production rather than design stage.

- *Presentation customization* is where standard products are presented differently to different customers. This can be achieved through differences in elements such as packaging, delivery channel, terms and conditions of purchase and stated use. Here the level of customization occurs after the product is produced.

SUMMARY

- Strategy can be seen to exist at the corporate, business and functional levels of the organization. Operations may provide the organization with the basis for its competitive advantage.

- The five basic operations performance objectives are quality, speed, dependability, flexibility and cost. The performance objectives allow an operation to measure its performance in achieving strategic goals.

- The market-based approach selects a market position and defines a list of objectives in order to successfully compete in that market. A resource-based approach provides an assessment of the operations processes and resources, which leads to a view of a capability of operations.

- The Hill methodology for strategy development provides an iterative framework that links together corporate objectives, the marketing strategy and the operations strategy.

- Systems are used by operations managers to measure the influence of customers (Hill) and the influence of customers and competitors (Slack) on the relative importance of the competitive factors in securing customer orders.

- The idea of trade-offs can be used to help understand the way in which the performance objectives relate to one another.

- The concept of focus aligns particular market demands with individual facilities.

- Agile operations aim to respond quickly to changing market demand in order to retain current markets and gain new market share by developing the capability of resources.

- Mass customization is an attempt to combine high variety and high volume of output in order to provide the customer with customized products at a relatively low price.

Ryanair: Flying High in a Competitive Atmosphere

"Can we do what we are doing at a reduced cost? Can we achieve what we want to achieve a different way? How can we hand on those cost savings to the customer?"[1]

Michael Cawley, Commercial
Director and CFO, Ryanair

The airline industry in Europe was flooded with around 50 low cost carriers leading to severe competition among them. In fact the low cost carriers simplified airline travel by reducing luxury services thereby focusing on cheaper rates for air travel. They were exploiting the demand for cheap travel by saving on services, operation and overheads. To achieve this, they increased seats in their aircraft compared to full service airlines. Snacks served during flights and other auxiliary services were charged for and made optional. They reduced operating costs through low wages, low costs for maintenance, simple boarding processes and ticket sales through their websites. Many corporations who focused on reducing their air travel expenses shifted to low cost carrier services and saved 3–5% of costs in air travel. Through innovative branding and pricing strategies, they tapped the available opportunities in 'seat only' and charter traffic segments. The full service airlines could not reach the load factor[2] and operational margins of low cost carriers like Ryanair.

Ryanair was aggressively promoted as a low cost airline company with cheaper flights. It had become the leading low cost carrier in Ireland and UK. It accounted for 30% of seat capacity in Europe's low cost segment. It had an average load factor of 83% and it flew 35 million passengers in 2005. What were the strategies followed by Ryanair in cost cutting and branding to remain the leader among the European low cost airlines?

Low Cost Airline Industry in Europe

Low cost carriers (LCCs) in Europe emerged during the post liberalization era in the 1990s. A single European Aviation Market was created in 1993 which led to the growth in intra-European air travel. Their share of capacity increased from 1.4% in 1996 to 20.2% in 2003. Ryanair and easyJet[3] in Europe operated on similar lines to Southwest Airlines[4] in the US[5]. Although the market share growth of low cost carriers in Europe stabilized at 9.1% in 2003, it grew to 18% of all flights in September 2006 (Figure 2.11). The countries in which they had

---

[1] 'The Ryanair Success story: Price as Brand', http://www.ericsson.com/telecomreport/article.asp?aid=10&tid=85&ma=1&msa=3

[2] Load factor – The percentage of passengers who had travelled to total number of available seats.

[3] easyJet is a low cost airline officially known as easyJet Airline Company Limited, based at London Luton Airport. The airline operates frequent scheduled services for leisure and business passengers and serves more than 200 routes between more than 65 European airports.

[4] Southwest Airlines, Inc. based in Dallas, Texas, is a low-fare airline in the United States. It is the third-largest airline in the world by number of passengers carried and the largest in the United States by number of passengers carried domestically.

[5] Hyped Hopes for Europe, Binggeli Urs, Pompeo Luceo, The Economist, 2002.

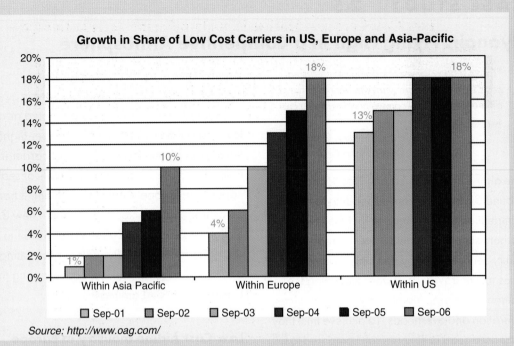

Figure 2.11: Growth in Share of Low Cost Carriers in US, Europe and Asia-Pacific.

greatest presence were Ireland (42%), Slovakia (41.4%) and UK (31.6%) as of May 2006 (Table 2.6).

The low cost carriers attracted people who travelled through charter airlines without an accompanying tour package and those who travelled to holiday homes. The passengers who travelled weekly and the cost conscious business passengers planned ahead and flew in low cost airlines. There was huge competition among low cost carriers, as a consequence of which their number in Europe decreased to 50 in 2006. From among them, there were 15 low cost carriers which had more than 50 flights/day compared to 13 (out of 100) in 2005[6]. But they added 2.4% to their market share during 2005–2006 (Table 2.7). Major development and growth for LCCs were happening in UK, Denmark and Finland (Figure 2.12). Ten of the top 25 low cost country–pair[7] flows involved the United Kingdom and these ten flows had 42% of all low cost flight movements. There was 17% growth in market share of low cost carriers in Finland and they had 9% growth in Denmark and Poland. The frequency of low cost carriers between Finland and Sweden had grown to 13% of all country pair flights. The low cost carriers accounted for 28% of passenger traffic in 2005. It was expected to grow to 37% by 2012 as they were on an expansion mode and building brand popularity. The major low cost

---

[6] Low Cost Carrier Market Update, May 2006, Eurocontrol.
[7] Country-pair – Agreement between two countries to allow aircraft flights between them.

Low Cost Carrier – Market Share in different states in Europe

Annex 1. Low-cost market share per State

Traffic Zone	Low-Cost Market Share: all IFR movements					Local Low-Cost Market Share: excluding overflights				
	2005 Jan-May		2006 Jan-May		Share Growth (% points)	2005 Jan-May		2006 Jan-May		Share Growth (% points)
	Daily Mvts	Share	Daily Mvts	Share		Daily Mvts	Share	Daily Mvts	Share	
Albania	21	8.0%	18	7.4%	-0.5%	.	.	0	0.7%	.
Austria	329	12.7%	369	13.8%	1.1%	85	9.5%	88	9.7%	0.2%
Belarus	5	1.6%	7	2.0%	0.5%	.	.	.	.	.
Belgium/Luxembourg	416	15.7%	458	16.7%	1.0%	87	8.8%	93	9.3%	0.5%
Bosnia-Herzegovina	23	6.5%	37	10.2%	3.7%	1	1.8%	0	0.8%	-1.0%
Bulgaria	60	7.0%	94	10.8%	3.8%	0	0.3%	4	2.9%	2.6%
Canary Islands	40	5.1%	56	6.8%	1.7%	40	5.9%	56	7.8%	2.0%
Croatia	55	7.3%	72	9.9%	2.6%	6	4.2%	12	8.0%	3.8%
Cyprus	8	1.4%	11	2.0%	0.5%	0	0.3%	2	1.8%	1.4%
Czech Republic	223	14.8%	257	16.9%	2.1%	46	11.1%	55	12.7%	1.7%
Denmark	139	8.8%	242	15.3%	6.5%	52	6.2%	115	14.6%	8.4%
Estonia	8	1.2%	14	4.4%	3.2%	5	2.3%	5	5.8%	3.5%
FYROM	22	9.3%	21	8.6%	-0.7%	3	9.1%	2	5.8%	-3.3%
Finland	22	3.3%	121	17.7%	14%	11	1.9%	111	19.1%	17%
France	1125	15.8%	1338	18.3%	2.5%	292	7.5%	373	9.2%	1.8%
Georgia	0	0.2%	0	0.2%	0.0%	0	1.1%	0	1.8%	0.7%
Germany	1112	15.0%	1391	18.2%	3.1%	775	15.7%	935	18.5%	2.9%
Greece	57	4.6%	69	5.6%	1.0%	38	5.6%	36	5.1%	-0.4%
Hungary	129	9.7%	156	10.9%	1.2%	58	18.0%	52	15.7%	-2.2%
Ireland	270	19.7%	310	21.5%	1.8%	263	39.9%	293	42.0%	2.1%
Italy	522	13.2%	613	15.1%	1.9%	384	13.0%	474	15.5%	2.4%
Latvia	14	3.5%	26	6.3%	2.7%	9	10.2%	16	18.3%	8.1%
Lisbon FIR	88	8.8%	127	12.0%	3.3%	56	10.5%	80	13.9%	3.3%
Lithuania	10	2.3%	23	5.5%	3.2%	0	0.0%	4	4.1%	4.0%
Malta	3	1.4%	2	1.3%	-0.1%	2	3.4%	2	3.1%	-0.4%
Moldova	0	0.6%	0	0.2%	-0.3%	.	.	.	.	.
Netherlands	409	15.6%	527	19.3%	3.8%	175	13.5%	210	15.7%	2.2%
Norway	104	8.1%	151	11.1%	3.0%	99	8.3%	147	11.6%	3.3%
Poland	88	8.4%	162	13.3%	4.9%	63	13.0%	125	21.4%	8.4%
Romania	61	6.4%	69	7.1%	0.7%	10	4.3%	16	6.2%	2.0%
Santa Maria FIR	0	0.1%	3	1.1%	1.0%	.	.	1	1.0%	.
Serbia&Montenegro	45	5.7%	78	9.2%	3.5%	6	4.2%	4	2.9%	-1.3%
Slovakia	109	14.8%	124	16.1%	1.2%	32	36.7%	37	41.4%	4.7%
Slovenia	47	8.0%	65	11.2%	3.2%	4	4.8%	3	3.8%	-1.0%
Spain	710	17.9%	830	19.9%	2.1%	602	19.5%	691	21.4%	1.9%
Sweden	215	11.9%	310	17.0%	5.1%	177	15.2%	213	18.8%	3.6%
Switzerland	401	15.1%	480	17.8%	2.7%	134	11.3%	147	12.5%	1.2%
Turkey	96	6.4%	137	8.4%	1.9%	89	10.1%	127	12.9%	2.8%
Ukraine	5	0.6%	4	0.4%	-0.2%	0	0.0%	.	.	.
United Kingdom	1530	24.8%	1818	28.4%	3.6%	1488	27.7%	1752	31.6%	3.9%
ESRA	3053	12.9%	3744	15.3%	2.4%	3051	13.0%	3741	15.4%	2.4%

Source: Low Cost Carrier Market Update May 2006, Eurocontrol.

Table 2.6: Low Cost Carrier Market Share in Different States in Europe.

Low Cost Carrier Performance—Jan-May 2006

Period	LCC	Others	Total	Share
Jan – May 2005	3,053	20,561	23,614	12.9%
Jan – May 2006	3,744	20,702	24,447	15.3%
Net Additional Movements	691	141	833	2.4%
% of all net additional movements	83%	17%		

Source: Low Cost Carrier Market Update May 2006, Eurocontrol

Table 2.7: Low Cost Carrier Performance, Jan–May 2006.

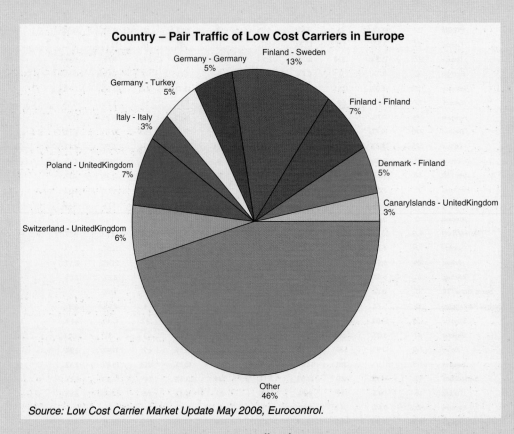

Country – Pair Traffic of Low Cost Carriers in Europe

Source: Low Cost Carrier Market Update May 2006, Eurocontrol.

Figure 2.12: Country-Pair Traffic of Low Cost Carriers in Europe.

carriers were Ryanair, easyJet, Virgin Express and there were emerging low cost carriers like Wizz Air,[8] Czech Airlines[9] and Air Berlin[10].

Background

Ryanair[11] was founded in 1985 by Christy Ryan, Liam Lonergan and Tony Ryan. Its initial flight was between Waterford in the southeast of Ireland to London Gatwick, using a 15 seat Embraer turboprop aircraft. Ryanair obtained permission in 1986 from regulatory authorities to operate between Dublin and London. The flights between the two airports were at a rate of just 99 pounds, but it broke the duopoly of British Airways[12] and Aer Lingus[13]. With two routes in operation, Ryanair carried 82000 passengers in 1986. In 1987, Ryanair increased its network with other flight routes from Dublin to Liverpool, Manchester, Glasgow and Cardiff and also from Luton to Cork, Shannon, Galway and Waterford.

In 1990, Ryanair decided to extend itself to the rest of Europe. Due to intense price competition from British Airways and Aer Lingus, Ryanair accumulated a £20 million loss. The Ryan family invested £20 million further and took many strategic decisions to reduce operational expenses and work as low cost airline(s). In 2001, Ryanair added a new base for operation in Charleroi in South Brussels. In 2002, Ryanair began flying to 26 new routes and established a hub[14] at Frankfurt-Hahn airport. In April 2003, Ryanair acquired Buzz[15] from KLM[16]. The revenue of Ryanair increased from 231 million euros in 1998 to 843 million euros in 2003 and its net profit was 239 million euros in 2003.The airline flew 127 routes and operated from 11 hubs, including two more bases at Rome and Barcelona in 2004. After 1 May 2004, Ryanair opened new routes to six new European Union member states. The company ordered 70 more Boeing aircraft in 2005, hoping that there would be greater demand with an increase in the number of routes.

Ryanair had sales growth of 28.3% between 2000 and 2005. It was reporting profit when other low cost airlines were struggling in bankruptcy and quitting the industry. It recorded a market capitalization of

---

[8] Wizz Air is a Polish/Hungarian low-cost airline focusing on the markets of Central Europe.

[9] CSA Czech Airlines is the Czech national airline company, and former carrier of Czechoslovakia based at Ruzyně International Airport, Prague. The airline connects to most major European destinations and to transit points in North America, Asia, Middle East and North Africa.

[10] Air Berlin is Europe's third largest low-cost airline based in Berlin, Germany. It operates scheduled services from a range of European airports.

[11] www.wikipedia.com

[12] British Airways is the largest airline of the United Kingdom and the third largest in Europe with flights from Europe across the Atlantic. Its main hubs are London Heathrow and London Gatwick, with wide-reaching European and domestic shorthaul networks, including smaller hubs at other UK airports including Manchester, from which some longer-haul flights are also operated.

[13] Aer Lingus is the national airline of Ireland. Based in Dublin, it operates over 30 aircraft serving Europe, the United States and recently Dubai, United Arab Emirates.

[14] Airline hub – an airport that serves as the base of operations for an airline.

[15] Buzz was a low-cost airline based at London Stansted operating services within Europe.

[16] KLM (in full: Koninklijke Luchtvaart Maatschappij, literally *Royal Aviation Company*; usual English: Royal Dutch Airlines) is a subsidiary of Air France-KLM. Before its merger with Air France, KLM was the national airline of the Netherlands.

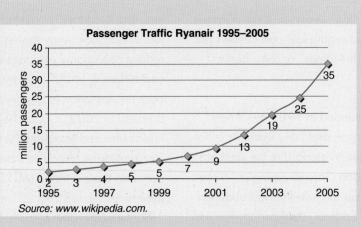

Source: www.wikipedia.com.

Figure 2.13: Passenger Traffic Ryanair 1995–2005.

Load Factor Pattern of Ryanair

	2005	2006	Rolling 12 months	2005	2006	Rolling 12months
Jan	2,041,575	2,538,371	33,865,381	74%	74%	83%
Feb	2,123,896	2,592,133	34,333,618	79%	78%	83%
Mar	2,565,706	3,000,901	34,768,813	80%	79%	83%
Apr	2,656,855	3,439,009	35,550,967	81%	85%	83%
May	2,904,939	3,556,113	36,202,141	82%	82%	83%
Jun	2,988,075	3,670,542	36,884,608	87%	87%	83%
Jul	3,198,977	3,940,792	37,626,423	90%	90%	83%
Aug	3,257,009	4,002,358	38,371,772	91%	91%	84%

Table 2.8: Load Factor Pattern of Ryanair.
Source: www.ryanair.com

11.82 billion euros and a profit margin of 20.09% in the first quarter of 2006. The passengers carried by Ryanair increased to 35 million in 2005 from 25 million in 2004 (Figure 2.13). It had a load factor of 84% in 2006 and the average fare for travel was 46 euros (Table 2.8). The Profit after Tax (PAT) of Ryanair increased from 64 million euros in 2005 to 116 million euros in 2006 (Figure 2.14). It had the highest operating margin among low cost airlines like Southwest Airlines and easyJet[17]. It was expanding to

---

[17] Airline Business, Association of European Airlines, US Department of Transportation, McKinsey Analysis 2002.

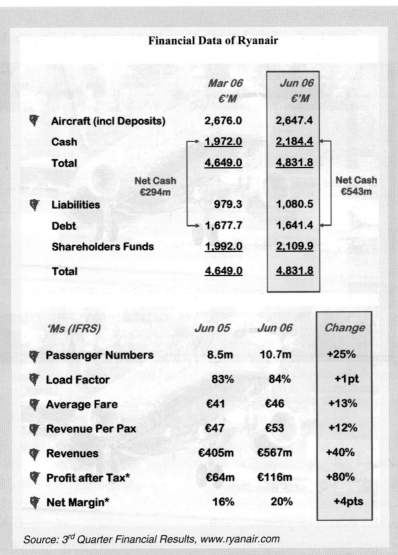

Figure 2.14: Financial Data of Ryanair.

new airport bases to cover the European continent and worked at minimal operating costs and fares (Figure 2.15).

Ryanair's Strategies

Ryanair, positioned aggressively as a low cost airline, had shown a profitable performance by implementing innovative strategies like common aircraft fleet, contracting online ticket booking and network expansion to secondary airports. Its strategies resulted in better operating margins, an increase in load factor, on time flight movements and fewer passenger complaints. Like Southwest Airlines in the US, it had only point to point flights[18], normal seats without pillows and no

---

[18] Point to point fight – the flights are arranged from one airport to another directly without landing and taking off from a hub. This reduces waiting time at a hub. But it is more suitable for short haul routes.

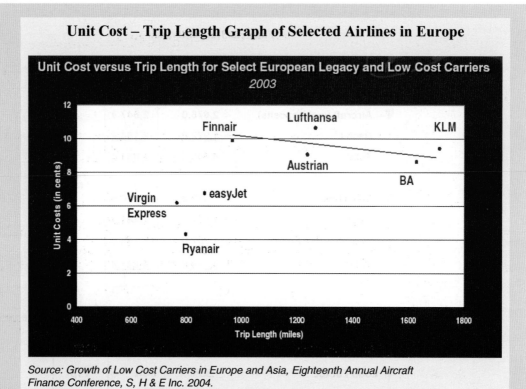

Figure 2.15: Unit Cost – Trip Length Graph of Selected Airlines in Europe.

frills during flights. It also had the first mover advantage in the Irish and European markets.

In spite of increasing competition, it had attracted attention through its advertising strategies which focused on promoting 'value for money' as the major advantage in comparison with other airlines. Its customers booked tickets online and rented apartments through its website without the help of travel agents. It acquired Buzz, one of its competitors, in 2002 to expand its network and increase market share. Its strategies to retain and develop loyal customers had been successful.

Marketing and Branding
Ryanair focused on spreading the idea of widely available lower fares on various routes.

It advertised its services in national and regional newspapers in Ireland and UK. Press conferences, publicity stunts, billboards and the local media were also utilized for promotional activities. The advertisements featured the slogan 'Ryanair.com, Fly Cheaper' to build a brand identity as the leading low cost carrier in Europe. The company conducted cooperative advertising campaigns with other travel agents and local tourist boards also. While it entered into new markets and inaugurated new services, Ryanair launched special advertising campaigns in the local media and its sales team visited pubs, shopping malls, factories, offices and universities to increase consumer awareness about the company (Figure 2.16).

Ryanair and other Low Cost Carriers – Branding

Criteria	Ryanair	easyJet	Go	Buzz	Virgin Express	Debonair[1]
Simple product ("no frills")	● Genuine no-frills offerings	● Genuine no-frills offerings	● Genuine no-frills offerings	● Use of KLM lounges, reservations possible	● Hybrid business design (low-cost, charter, wet lease)	● Two-class product ● FFP ● "High frills"
Low operating costs	● Sec. airports ● Homog. fleet ● Minimum cost base	● Services major airports, hence higher turnaround times and fees	● Services major airports, hence higher turnaround times and fees	● Major airports: higher turnaround times and fees ● 2 types of plane	● Services major airports, hence higher turnaround times and fees	● Complex processes ● No cost advantages
Positioning	● Straightforward, aggressive low-cost positioning	● Low-cost position except for major airports	● Low-cost position except for major airports	● Major airports ● Bulk customers ● Business focus	● Unclear position (low cost, code share SN, charter)	● Unclear position with "low cost, high frills"

Source: Mercer Management Consulting, www.mercermc.com

Figure 2.16: Ryanair and Other Low Cost Carriers – Branding.

Ryanair travel fares were lower and it hoped to attract price conscious passengers and business travellers who often used alternative transportation (Figure 2.17). It sold airline tickets on a one way basis which eliminated minimum stay requirements and did not compel the customer to book to and fro flights. The fares were set according to the demand for particular flights and although 70% of occupied seats were sold at a particular rate, the fares charged were higher if booking dates were closer to time of departure. On average 130 passengers were carried in a flight using Boeing 737 aircraft and the load factor for flights was more than 80%.

Ryanair's Dublin to London (Stansted) route had the largest passenger volume and the fare range was 0.99 to 199.9 euros[19]. It had point to point flights which had better punctuality and reported fewer cases of lost bags and cancellations according to the reports of the Association of European Airlines.

Secondary Airports and Third Party Contracts
Ryanair focused on airports like Barcelona in Spain, Pisa and Verona in Italy and London (Stansted), Luton and Glasgow in UK (Figure 2.18). These short haul routes were convenient for Ryanair to offer frequent service and avoid frills during travel. The concept of

Comparison of Ryanair fare with other LCCs and Scheduled Airlines

Ryanair Investor Day – 4 October 2005

		Av. Fare	% > Ryanair
Low	Ryanair	€41	
High	easyJet	€62	52%
	Air Berlin	€87	113%
	Iberia	€141	244%
	Alitalia	€186	353%
	Air France	€220	437%
	Lufthansa	€220	437%
	British Airways	€268	553%

Source: www.ryanair.com

Figure 2.17: Comparison of Ryanair Fare with Other LCCs and Scheduled Airlines.

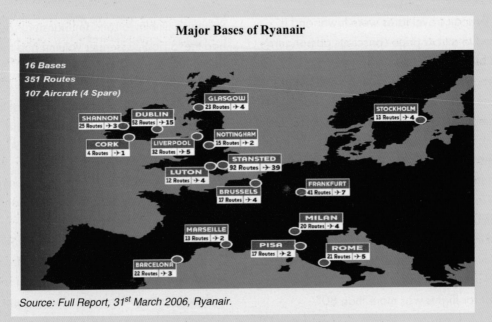

Source: Full Report, 31st March 2006, Ryanair.

Figure 2.18: Major Bases of Ryanair.

point to point flying allowed direct non stop routes leading to lower turnaround times and increased frequency of flights. It focused on secondary[20] and regional airports which resulted in less congestion, fewer terminal delays, easy airport access and lower handling costs and shorter turnaround times[21] compared to major airports. Secondary and regional airports often had fewer operating restrictions and slot requirements which would not limit the number of allowed take offs and landings.

Ryanair entered into agreements with third parties at airports for passenger and aircraft handling, ticketing and other services. The company negotiated with them for competitive rates and multi year contracts. This way, Ryanair reduced the need for additional staff and eliminated difficulties in luggage and traffic handling. Its engineering staff carried out routine maintenance and repair of aircraft but heavy maintenance was done through third party contracts. Ryanair staff supervised the operations of third parties to ensure the safety and quality of its operations.

Common Fleet

Ryanair had initially decided to buy used aircraft of a single type to reduce aircraft buying costs.

From 1994 to 1998, it purchased Boeing 737–200 aircraft which were 11 to 17 years old and its fleet had an average age of 23 years as of March 31, 2004. It changed this policy in 1998 and decided to buy Boeing 737–800 because used aircraft for sale were

scarce. The fleet of Boeing 737–800s had many common characteristics similar to the used aircraft fleet. It had placed an order for 100 Boeing 737-800 aircraft in 2002, expecting to expand its network and capacity. The idea of having a common fleet enabled it to limit costs associated with training of personnel, purchasing and replacement of spare parts and ensured flexibility in scheduling of crews and equipment. There were 107 aircraft with 189 seat capacity with Ryanair in 2006.

Increasing Productivity

For reduction in labour costs and improved productivity, Ryanair emphasized productivity-based pay incentives and a salary structure based on working hours and encouraged the labour force to join stock option programmes. Ryanair's pilots flew more hours and the cabin crew served more people compared to those in the traditional airlines. It imposed strict rules like banning the use of personal mobile phones and negotiated with employees regarding wages, work practices and conditions of employment in order to maintain employee productivity.

Ryanair changed its reservation system from the British Airways Booking System (BABS) to a new system called 'Flightspeed' by forming an agreement with Accenture Open Skies for ten years. An Internet booking facility called 'Skylight' was developed with the help of Accenture[22]. The Skylight system allowed Internet users to access Ryanair's reservation system to book, pay and confirm reservations

---

[20] Secondary airports – They are the regional airports which are second to major airports in a particular area.
[21] Turnaround Time – The time taken by a flight to land, unload passengers and take off.

in real time. As a result, 99% of all daily reservations were carried out through Internet bookings in September 2006. In March 2006, Ryanair introduced the 'Check 'N' Go' web based check-in service for passengers with EU passports travelling with hand luggage only, reducing the time for checking in before a flight. It also added online gaming and offers to attract more customers to book through its site directly.

Providing Ancillary Services for Additional Revenue

Ryanair provided several ancillary services like beverages, food and merchandise, hotel booking and vehicle rentals for its passengers. It sold bus and air tickets on its aircraft as well as through its web sites. It had a contract with the Hertz Corporation for automobile related services and car rentals. It charged a fixed fee from passengers for usage of credit and debit card payments for its services. In September 2006, it entered into a letter of intent with On Air, a provider of mobile voice communication services for aircraft. Ryanair had to bear the cost for equipment and its installation. It had also made a five year agreement with Inviseomedia to install seatback advertising in its current and new fleets. The 'Inviseo Table' was a custom-made, personal backrest tray-table which had an integrated advertising panel for printed advertisements. This gave an on-board advertising medium for the advertisers to attract mobile consumers in Europe. It also allowed advertisements on the wings and the body of the aircraft and promotions inside the aeroplane during flights.

Challenges

There were several challenges faced by low cost carriers in Europe like rising aviation fuel costs, ensuring staff productivity and maintaining a large fleet for expansion. As there were many low cost carriers on the European continent, the regional airports had become demanding in nature and gained more bargaining power. This would result in an increase in air traffic control charges. The customers had become price sensitive and Ryanair and easyJet were competing with each other on common routes. Although Ryanair maintained cheaper air fares, the increase in fuel costs and cost of expansion made its position more risky.

Fuel Costs

Aviation turbine fuel costs fluctuated owing to economic and political changes and increase in demand. The fuel charges were usually paid in US dollars and fluctuation in exchange rates caused subsequent variation in fuel costs. The fuel costs also fluctuated with the changing political scenario and the hostility between nations in the Middle East region. Ryanair's fuel prices during the year which ended in March 31, 2006 increased by 74.3% compared to those of 2005. The fuel costs accounted for 34.5% of Ryanair's total operating expenses compared to 26.3% in 2005. The fuel and oil costs included the direct

---

[22] Accenture is a global management, consulting, technology services and outsourcing company.

cost of fuel, cost of delivering fuel to aircraft and aircraft de- icing[23] costs. These costs had increased from just 17% of total operating costs in 2001 to 35% in 2006[24]. Ryanair had not added surcharges like other airlines so that it could maintain the low fares. But the rising fuel costs made it more risky for the company to operate at lower fares.

Competition

Ryanair faced stiff competition from other low cost carriers in Europe. Low cost airlines competed with each other with respect to fare levels, frequency and dependability of services and name recognition (Table 2.9). The state owned carriers could pose a threat to Ryanair because they would also fly at lower rates if they were provided government aid and subsidies. The major competitors of Ryanair were easyJet, bmibaby[25], Air Berlin, SkyEurope[26] and Wizz Air. Aer Lingus which moved to the low fares strategy in 2002 became a competitor on Irish routes. Go, a low cost carrier, attempted to compete with Ryanair by starting services from Dublin to Glasgow and Edinburgh. After a fierce battle for market share Go finally withdrew its services. EasyJet and Ryanair had also cancelled services from Gatwick out of competition from regional players. Ryanair had acquired Buzz, another low cost carrier, in 2002 and was negotiating with Aer Lingus to buy its shares in 2006. The

Ryanair vs easyJet –2005

Parameter	Ryanair	easyJet
Average fare	41€	62€
Total revenue per pax	48€	72€
Load factor	86.40%	84%
Fleet	**Airbus**–87	**Boeing 737–200**–9
	Boeing 737–800–32	**Boeing 737–800**–98
Seats Per Plane	189	130

Table 2.9: Ryanair vs easyJet, 2005.
Source: Compiled by the author referring to www.ryanair.com, www.easyJet.com

---

[23] De-icing – De-icing is the process of removing ice from a surface. De-icing can be accomplished by mechanical methods (scraping), through the application of heat, by use of chemicals designed to lower the freezing point of water (various salts or alcohols), or a combination of these different techniques.

[24] Ryanair Annual Report & Financial Statements 2001 to 2006, www.ryanair.com

[25] bmibaby is the low-cost airline subsidiary of bmi. It flies to destinations in Europe from its main bases at East Midlands, Manchester, Cardiff and Birmingham International.

[26] SkyEurope Airlines is a low-cost airline with its main base at M. R. Stefanik Airport (BTS) in Bratislava, Slovakia, and other bases in Kraków, Prague, Warsaw and Budapest.

airlines in the charter flight segment had entered into the low fares market. There were other low cost substitutes like train and tram services in some regions of Europe.

Risks of Expansion

Ryanair was looking forward to expanding on the European continent as it was becoming a popular tourist destination. It was planning to expand its network to North Africa also. The network expansion it had planned would require more aircraft, human resources and agreements with airport authorities and governments. The incidents of terrorism in UK and Europe resulted in increased security measures on all UK outbound flights in 2006. It cancelled 279 flights and refunded 2.7 million euros. The September 2001 terrorist attacks in the US also had severe impacts on the airline industry in Europe. It faced threat from airports in case they increased the rates for airport access and included policies like slot allocations. Each slot needed authorization to take off and land at particular airports at specific time periods. It would not be able to fly to those regions where it did not have the slot rights.

The Road Ahead

Ryanair added three more bases, viz. Madrid, Bremen and Marseille with direct routes to airports at London, Frankfurt, Dublin and Rome. It expanded its network to 20 new routes touching Dublin and was expecting to add 113

new routes in 2007. In total, it had 16 bases, 351 routes and 107 aircraft as of September 2006[27]. In order to become the leading airline in Ireland, it had acquired a 19.2% share of Aer Lingus for 254 million euros. It had a traffic growth of 22% and passenger traffic of 42.5 million as of September 2006. It was using fuel hedging practices to reduce fuel costs. As it had resorted to buying new Boeing aircraft which had better fuel efficiency and lower pollution levels, it complied with EU regulations on pollution control. Its operational efficiency and cost cutting strategies had been phenomenal and it was able to record profits when other low cost carriers were struggling to become financially feasible with rising fuel costs. It was the leader in Dublin – London (45% market share) and other routes like Rome–London (34%), London–Barcelona (30%) and Stockholm–Milan (50%). It was expecting a 35% increase in passenger traffic in UK, 15% in Italy and 12% in Ireland by 2007[28].

After the liberalization in air travel in Europe, the traditional airlines had become slower and many low cost carriers began flooding the continent with attractive packages. The passengers began to fly for leisure and business activities in and around Europe as the European Union opened up for intra European business with a common currency[29]. The flights between UK and US, UK and UAE, Germany and UK had grown significantly. Liberalization resulted in

---

[27] Ryanair's Annual Report 2006, www.ryanair.com
[28] ibid.
[29] 'The Economic Impact of Air Service Liberalisation', InterVISTAS-ga Consulting.Inc, www.intervistas.us

44 million additional passengers and an increase of 33% in total passenger traffic in Europe. The European GDP had grown by 85 billion US$ and added 1.4 million jobs. The European airports contributed 2.6% of Europe's GDP as of 2005. Liberalization resulted in favourable regulations for the growth of tourism and business not only on the European continent, but also between Europe, the Middle East and Africa. The expansion of Ryanair's network to North Africa and other European continents would augur well because there were many unexplored opportunities for flight development between Europe and Africa. Ryanair CEO, Michael O'Leary summed it up, *'Our strategy is like Wal-Mart: We pile it high and sell it cheap.'*

Source: Reproduced by permission of ICFAI IRC HQ Hyderabad.

Questions

1. How important is the role of operations in achieving competitive advantage at Ryanair?
2. What structural and infrastructural aspects are aligned with Ryanair's operations strategy?

EXERCISES

1. Evaluate strategy development at the corporate, business and functional levels of an organization.

2. Indicate how a major investment decision could be analysed in terms of its effect on the capability of the operations function.

3. How can the relative significance of the five performance objectives be determined in the formulation of the organization's strategic direction?

4. Discuss the main types of flexibility.

5. Explain the significance for management of linking operations strategy, marketing strategy and corporate objectives.

6. Evaluate the strategic role of the operations function.

7. Evaluate the potential advantages and disadvantages of focused manufacturing.

8. Compare and contrast the concepts of trade-offs and agile operations.

9. Does an improvement in one performance objective necessarily mean a reduction in the performance of others?

WEB EXERCISE

Visit the web site containing the annual reports for Marks and Spencer PLC at http://annualreport.marksandspencer.com/group/group_finance.html (accessed 24 September 2008). What role does operations have in supporting the company's strategy?

FURTHER READING

Brown, S., Lamming, R., Bessant, J. and Jones, P. (2005) *Strategic Operations Management*, 2nd edn, Elsevier Butterworth-Heinemann.

Fetzinger, E. and Hau, L.L. (1997) Mass customization at Hewlett Packard: the power of postponement. *Harvard Business Review*, **75** (1), 116–21.

Hayes, R., Pisano, G., Upton, D. and Wheelwright S. (2005) *Operations, Strategy, and Technology: Pursuing the Competitive Edge*, John Wiley & Sons, Ltd.

WEB LINKS

www.geckoheadgear.co.uk (accessed 24 September 2008). Gecko headgear site.

www.softwareceo.com (accessed 24 September 2008). Many articles available on operations strategy.

REFERENCES

Caulkin, S. (2002) Business: the basics that beat the world: making things better and cheaper is the best strategy of all. *Observer*, 3 November 2002.

Ferdows, K. and de Meyer, A. (1990) Lasting improvements in manufacturing. *Journal of Operations Management*, **9** (2), 168–84.

Gaither, N. and Frazier, G. (2002) *Operations Management*, 9th edn, South-Western.

Hayes, R.H. and Wheelwright, S.C. (1988) *Restoring Our Competitive Edge: Competing Through Manufacturing*, John Wiley & Sons, Ltd.

Hill, T. (2005) *Operations Management*, 2nd edn, Palgrave Macmillan.

Johnson, G., Scholes, K. and **Whittington, R.** (2008) *Exploring Corporate Strategy: Text and Cases*, 8th edn, FT Prentice Hall.

Mintzberg, H. and **Waters, J.A.** (1995) Of strategies: deliberate and emergent. *Strategic Management Journal*, **6** (3), 257–72.

Pine, B., Best, V. and **Boynton, A.** (1993) Making mass customisation work. *Harvard Business Review*, September–October, 108–19.

Skinner, W. (1974) The focused factory. *Harvard Business Review*, May–June, 113–21.

Skinner, W. (1985) *Manufacturing: The Formidable Competitive Weapon*, John Wiley & Sons, Ltd.

Slack, N. (1991) *Manufacturing Advantage: Achieving Competitive Manufacturing Operations*, Mercury.

Slack, N., Chambers, S. and **Johnston, R.** (2007) *Operations Management*, 5th edn, Pearson Education Limited.

Slack, N. and **Lewis, M.** (2008) *Operations Strategy*, 2nd edn, Pearson Education Ltd.

Teece, D.J. and **Pisano, G.** (1994) The dynamic capabilities of firms: an introduction. *Industrial and Corporate Change*, **3** (3), 537–56.

Vonderembse, M.A. and **White, G.P.** (2004) *Core Concepts of Operations Management*, John Wiley & Sons, Ltd.

PART 2

DESIGN

CHAPTER
3
Process Types

LEARNING OBJECTIVES

- Describe the main manufacturing process types

- Describe the main service process types

- Discuss an alternative service process type definition

- Explain the relationship between process type and the operations volume and variety of output

- Discuss the process type decision

INTRODUCTION

In operations, the design of the process is categorized into manufacturing and services. The choice of process design depends mostly on the volume and variety of the product or service that the organization offers. Manufacturing and services providers generally serve their customers on a continuum between a combination of low-variety and high-volume products and services to a combination of high-variety and low-volume products and services. The chapter provides categories for process designs, called process types, for different volume and variety combinations. The reasons for matching a particular volume and variety combination with a particular process type are then discussed.

MANUFACTURING PROCESS TYPES

In manufacturing, process types can be considered under five categories: project, jobbing, batch, mass and continuous (Figure 3.1). A description of each process type is followed by some examples of where each process type might be used.

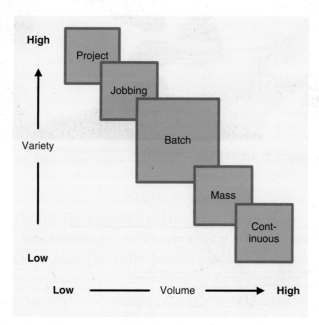

Figure 3.1: Manufacturing Process Types.

Project

Processes that produce high-variety and low-volume products are termed projects. Project processes are used to make one-off products to a customer specification. A feature of a project process is that the location of the product is stationary. This means that transforming resources such as staff and equipment that make the product must move or be moved to the location of the product. Other characteristics of projects are that they may require the coordination of many individuals and activities, demand a problem-solving approach to ensure they are completed on time and have a comparatively long duration of manufacture. The timescale of the completion of the project is an important performance measure. Because each project is unique it is likely that

Project process
A project process is used to make a one-off product to a customer specification. A feature of a project process is that the location of the product is stationary.

transforming resources will comprise general-purpose equipment that can be used on a number of projects. Examples of the use of a project process include building construction (Figure 3.2), movie film production and custom-built furniture.

Figure 3.2: A Construction Site: An Example of a Project Process.

Jobbing

Processes that produce high-variety and low-volume products are termed 'jobbing'. Jobbing processes are used to make a one-off (or low volume) product to a customer specification. A feature of a jobbing process is that the product moves to the location of transforming resources such as equipment. Thus resources such as staff and equipment can be shared between many products. Other characteristics of jobbing processes are the use of skilled labour in order to cope with the need for customization (variety) and the use of general purpose equipment which is shared between the products. There tends to be low utilization of equipment in jobbing processes due to the need to undertake frequent setting up of the machinery when moving from processing one product to another. Examples of the use of a jobbing process include bespoke tailors and precision engineers (Figure 3.3).

Batch

Processes that produce products of medium variety and medium volume are termed 'batch processes'. Batch processes cover a relatively wide range of volume and variety combinations. Products are grouped into batches whose batch size can range from two to hundreds. In a batch process the product moves to the location of transforming resources such as equipment and so resources are shared between

Jobbing process
Jobbing processes are used to make a one-off, or low-volume, product to a customer specification. The product moves to the location of transforming resources such as equipment.

Batch processes
Batch processes cover a relatively wide range of volume and variety combinations. Products are grouped into batches whose size can range from two to hundreds.

Figure 3.3: Precision Engineering: An Example of a Jobbing Process.
Source: http://gimp-savvy.com//cgi-bin/img.cgi?ailsy0rqhbLXCHU659 (accessed 30 September 2008).

the batches. Instead of setting up machinery between each product, as in a jobbing process, setups occur between batches, leading to greater utilization of equipment. Because of the relatively high volumes involved in batch, compared to project and jobbing, it can be cost-effective to use specialized labour and equipment dedicated

Figure 3.4: A Bakery: An Example of a Batch Process.

to certain product batches. A feature of batch processes is that, because it is difficult to predict when a batch of work will arrive at a machine, a lack of coordination can lead to many products waiting for that machine at any one time. These queues of work may dramatically increase the time the product takes to progress through the process. Examples of the use of a batch process include vehicle component assembly, clothing manufacture, bakeries (Figure 3.4), magazines and books.

Mass

Processes that produce high-volume and low-variety products are termed line or mass processes. Although there may be variants within the product design the production process will essentially be the same for all the products. Because of the high volumes of product it is cost-effective to use specialized labour and equipment. A feature of mass processes is that the movement of the product may be automated using a conveyor system and the production process broken down into a number of small, simple tasks. In order to ensure a smooth flow of product the process times per unit must be equalized at each stage of production using a technique called line balancing (Chapter 4). Because of the low product variety, setting up of equipment is minimized and utilization of equipment is high. Examples of the use of a mass process include vehicle manufacturing (Figure 3.5) and assembly of consumer durables such as televisions and computers.

Mass process
A mass or line process produces products of high volume and low variety. The process of production will essentially be the same for all the products and so it is cost-effective to use specialized labour and equipment.

Figure 3.5: Car Manufacturing: An Example of a Mass Process.

Continuous

Processes that operate continually to produce a very high volume of a standard product are termed 'continuous'. The products produced by a continuous operation are usually a continuous flow such as oil and gas. Continuous processes use a large amount of equipment, which is specialized and dedicated to producing a single product (such as an oil refinery for example). To make this large investment in dedicated equipment cost-effective continuous processes are often in constant operation, 24 hours a day. The role of labour in the operation of the processes is mainly one of monitoring and control of the process equipment with little contact with the product itself. Examples of a continuous process include an oil refinery (Figure 3.6), electricity production and steel making.

Continuous processes
A continuous process operates continually to produce a very high volume of a standard product. The products produced by a continuous operation are usually a continuous flow, such as oil and gas, rather than discrete items.

Figure 3.6: Oil Distribution: An Example of a Continuous Process.

SERVICE PROCESS TYPES

The classification of service process types is more recent and less standardized than the manufacturing process types outlined above. In this text three service process types – professional service, service shop and mass service – are categorized in terms of their ability to cope with different volume and variety characteristics (Figure 3.7).

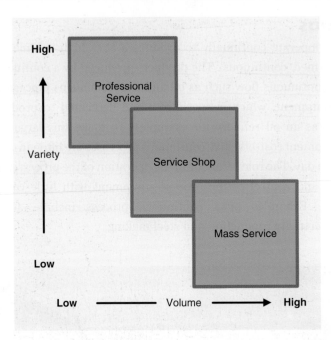

Figure 3.7: Service Process Types.

Professional Service

Professional service processes operate with high variety and low volume. They are characterized by high levels of customization in that each service delivery will be tailored to meet individual customer needs. This customization requires communication between the service provider and customer and so professional services are characterized by high levels of customer contact and a relatively high proportion of staff supplying the service in relation to customers. The emphasis in a professional service is on delivering a process rather than a tangible product associated with a process. An example of this is a management consultancy where the client is paying for the expertise and problem solving skills of the consultants. The physical report that is generated at the end of the consultancy assignment is a documentation of the process but it is the success of the process itself that is of interest to the client. Examples of a professional service include management consultancy, doctors (Figure 3.8) and health and safety inspectors.

Service Shop

Service shop processes operate with a medium amount of variety and volume. There will be a certain amount of customization of the service but not as extensive as in professional services. There will therefore be a mix of staff and equipment used to deliver the service. There is an emphasis both on the service delivery process itself and any tangible items that are associated with the service. For example, the success of a

Professional service
Professional services are characterized by high levels of customization, in that each service delivery will be tailored to meet individual customer needs. Professional services are characterized by high levels of customer contact and a relatively high proportion of staff supplying the service in relation to customers.

Service shop processes
Service shop processes operate with a medium amount of variety and volume. There will be therefore a mix of staff and equipment used to deliver the service.

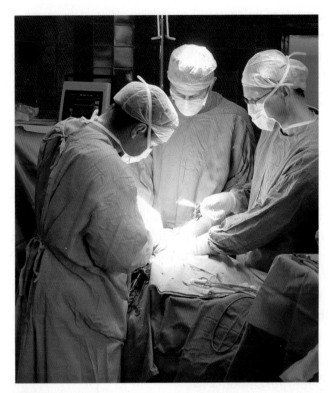

Figure 3.8: Surgery: An Example of a Professional Service.

Figure 3.9: A Delicatessen: An Example of a Service Shop.
Source: http://morguefile.com/archive/?display=155334 (accessed 24 September 2008).

restaurant is dependent on the level of service attained in terms of achieving an appropriate ambience but also the quality of the food itself. The variety of food offered provides a compromise between a personal chef who can cook meals to order (professional service) and a standard food item such as a hamburger (mass service). Examples of service shops include banks, shops (Figure 3.9), restaurants and travel agencies.

Mass Service

Mass service
Mass service processes operate with a low variety and high volume. There will be little customization of the service to individual customer needs and limited contact between the customer and people providing the service.

Mass service processes operate with a low variety and high volume. There will be little customization of the service to individual customer needs and limited contact between the customer and people providing the service. Because the service is standardized it is likely that equipment will be used to improve the efficiency of the service delivery process. The emphasis in a mass service is on the tangible item that is associated with the service delivery. For example supermarkets have certain differences in terms of layout and ambience but the major emphasis is on the provision of food items of the required price and quality. Examples of mass service providers are supermarkets, rail services and airports (Figure 3.10).

Figure 3.10: An Airport: An Example of a Mass Service.

Alternative Service Process Type Definitions

As mentioned earlier, the process type definitions for services are not standardized and in particular the definition of service shops may be subdivided into those that lie on the professional service boundary relating to professional services that have grown in volume and standardized their service and organizations that lie on the mass service boundary relating to mass services that have increased their service variety to differentiate them from competitors.

Another way to categorize service types is based on volume and variety against the degree of customer contact (Gaither and Frazier, 2002). Professional services can be distinguished by the fact that the service is provided through personal attention to the customer, the 'customer as product'. Service shops can be distinguished by a high degree of customer involvement in the process of generating the service, the 'customer as participant'. Mass services can be distinguished by the fact that there is almost no customer involvement in the production of the service, a 'quasi-manufacturing' process. These classifications are useful because the amount of customer contact in the service is significant when contemplating the design of the service. For example, a mass service with little customer contact can be automated using technology without affecting customer service, whereas a professional service relies on developing a personal relationship with all customers and customizing the service to their needs. The use of self-service facilities in service shops allows customers to specify the service elements they require.

Lovelock (1992) offers an alternative service process type classification based on the degree of labour intensity against the degree of interaction and customization. In this model labour intensity refers to the ratio of labour cost incurred in relation to the value of plant and equipment used to deliver the service. The degree of interaction and customization refers to a joint measure of the degree to which the customer interacts with the service process and the degree to which the service is customized. The interaction and customization variables are seen as generally showing similar

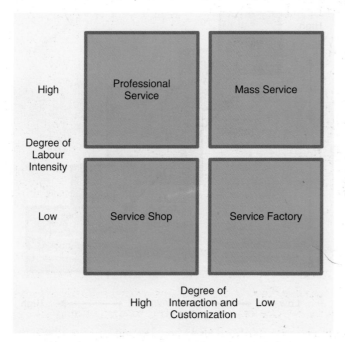

Figure 3.11: The Service Process Matrix (adapted from Lovelock, 1992, Pearson Education Ltd.).

behaviour – if interaction is high, so is customization. Lovelock feels this joint measure is an improvement on the sole use of customer contact as a variable. He states that the nature of the service also depends on irregularity and thus the need for customization in the service provision. An example is given of a hotel and hospital. Both services are classified as high customer contact but the irregularity and complexity of the service provision in a hospital makes the nature of its service provision different. There are four categories of service type in Lovelock's model, shown in Figure 3.11. Professional services are defined as having a high degree of both variables and include doctors, lawyers, accountants and architects. A service factory has low labour intensity and low interaction and customization and includes airlines and hotels. Mass service is defined as high labour intensity and low interaction and includes retailing, wholesaling and schools. The fourth category, service shop, is defined as high labour intensity and low interaction and includes hospitals and car-repair facilities.

MATCHING PROCESS TYPE WITH VOLUME AND VARIETY

For a certain volume and variety combination an organization needs to make a choice regarding which process type to use. Hayes and Wheelwright (1984) describe this choice in terms of a trade-off between cost and flexibility. In Figure 3.12 the volume

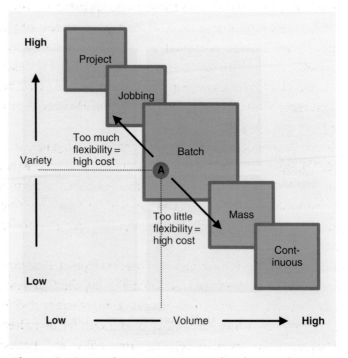

Figure 3.12: Matching Process Type with Volume and Variety.

and variety position shown by the dotted lines leads to a match for the production of product 'A' with a batch process type. This means for this particular volume and variety position a batch process provides what is termed the 'lowest cost' position.

If a jobbing process type was used in this position then operations would have too much flexibility for the amount of variety required. Thus they would have higher costs than another producer supplying the same market using a batch process type. This is due to the efficiencies made by moving from general purpose equipment and setting up for each individual item to the use of more specialized equipment and the need only to setup for a whole group or batch of products at a time. If a mass process type was used in this position then the operation would have too little flexibility for the amount of variety required. Thus they would have higher costs than another producer supplying the same market using a batch process type. This is due to the high changeover costs they would incur in moving from one product to another in order to meet the required variety of output required by the market. This concept can also be related to matching the volume and variety of service processes using Figure 3.7.

CHOOSING A PROCESS TYPE

A choice of process type must meet market needs in terms of the volume and variety requirements of customers and also the technical needs in terms of the configuration of resources to deliver a service or product. Process-type choice is strategic because it can represent a large amount of capital investment in terms of equipment and workforce and so sets a constraint around which the company can compete. The difficulty of process-type choice is that process decisions can take a relatively large amount of time and money to implement whereas market needs in a competitive environment can change rapidly.

Although the process type descriptions are quite distinct, in reality many operations blur these definitions. So, for example, there may be elements of batch processing in jobbing dominated processes and batching in mass processes. In practice, process types within an organization will lie on a continuum across the process types. Processes within a particular process-type category show different characteristics.

Companies may also use a combination of process types, for example jobbing and batch, for different product lines within a manufacturing plant. In services there may also be a mix of process types, with front-office customer-facing activities undertaken as a professional service, whilst back-office operations are organized as a service shop. See Chapter 1 for more details on front-office and back-office service operations.

The choice of process type for a process may also change over time. This may occur either at the level of the organization or at an individual product or service level.

At the level of the organization the company may be following a growth strategy, which involves standardization of its products or services, or a strategy for increasing the range of products and services to avoid competing on price alone.

A strategy for manufacturing companies who are successful and wish to grow is to standardize products and enter higher volume markets over time as they acquire more financial backing. This growth may take place gradually, however, so the point at which increased volumes necessitate a change in process type to match the volume/variety characteristics of the market may not be apparent. The choice of process type in these cases may be made using a break-even analysis that calculates profit at different volume levels (Russell and Taylor, 2008). One consequence of process choice is that for increasing volume, the level of investment in equipment required to ensure a cost-efficient operation increases. This requirement for capital investment can be a barrier for new companies entering a market and so many small companies with limited finances provide a customized service to a niche market, in which labour skills are more important than supporting infrastructure.

Many service companies operate in a niche market and the Web has provided a platform for many of them to market their services effectively. However, many service companies wish to grow and so may need to standardize their service. Thus in order to provide a consistent service level at higher volumes it may be necessary to 'package' the service the company provides to enable a lower skill base to deliver the service and to ensure consistent service quality. However, low-volume, professional-type services rely on the capability of the individuals working for them who provide tailored solutions for their clients. Thus a key factor in managing growth is that it may involve both a loss of autonomy of these existing staff and a need for training of additional staff to deliver the 'packaged' service.

At the level of the individual product or service there may be a repositioning of that product or service in the marketplace at a new volume/variety mix. Also, within the portfolio of products and services that an organization delivers, an individual product or service will progress through a lifecycle in terms of sales from introduction to maturity to decline, the process that best suits the needs of the firm will need to change to match the volume and variety of the output (Noori and Radford, 1995).

Two concepts that should be considered when designing an operations process to service volume and variety characteristics are 'focus' and 'mass customization'. The idea of 'focus' in manufacturing and services is used to help reduce the level of complexity involved when attempting to service a number of market segments and is covered in Chapter 2. The concept of 'mass customization', which attempts to provide the capability to produce both a high volume and high variety of products and services through the use of flexibility, is covered in Chapter 2.

SUMMARY

- The main manufacturing process types are project, jobbing, batch, line and continuous.

- The main service process types are professional, shop and mass.

- An alternative service process type definition is shop, factory, professional and mass.

- Each process type should be matched to a particular volume and variety of output to minimize cost.

CASE STUDY 3.1

Ashburton Products

Ashburton Products manufactures wooden fireplace mantels. They have a retail showroom in which various models are displayed. A small workshop close to the showroom was taken on a short-term lease and various items of second-hand woodworking machinery were acquired. Two joiners were taken on to build the mantels, which, for the most part, were custom built to customer requirements.

A mantel consists of three subassemblies comprising two legs and a shelf. Subassemblies are made from wood that has been cut, sawn, planed and routed. At the subassembly stage, the various items are brought together, glued and then clamped. The glue takes time to dry, so clamped subassemblies are left overnight. The assembly stage is similar. As with subassembly, assembly takes place on a specifically designed workbench. One person operates the cutting and planing machines, together with the saw. Another operates the router. Two people are employed in subassembly and final assembly

work. Two main categories of mantel are produced from hardwood and medium density fibreboard (MDF). The ratio of MDF mantels to hardwood is 85% to 15%. With current staffing levels, output normally averages slightly over 25 mantels per week. Demand for mantels has been rising for some time. Sales which were, in the past, based exclusively on single orders for individual customers have recently been supplemented by multiple orders from two local builders. In view of this trend, Ashburton's management is concerned about how best to meet the increase in demand. Unable to expand the current site because of planning restrictions, and reluctant to spend large sums on new equipment, the management is uncertain what to do.

Question

In terms of process types, what advice would you give to the operations manager at Ashburton Products?

CASE STUDY   3.2

Confident Bet on Instant Heritage

It takes a great deal of stamina to design, make and sell contemporary furniture. Moving just one product from sketchbook to store can take years of planning and vast injections of cash, and even then it can bomb. So I was intrigued to hear about a new company launching a new collection of British-designed, British-made furniture at the Salone del Mobile in Milan . . . How could it possibly hope to stand out – and establish a foothold – in this already crowded, competitive market? But confidence does not seem to be a problem for chief executive Alasdhair Willis, former publisher of *Wallpaper* magazine and husband to Stella McCartney. Just look at the name he picked for his company: Established & Sons.

The idea was 'to create immediate heritage and act as a reminder of the time when British manufacturing was buoyant', Willis explains. 'We feel strongly about creating a "home" for British designers who, too often, have to resort to an Italian or German manufacturer to have their products realized. [And] we believe we can generate significant sales, particularly at the top end.' Willis, whose creative consultancy Announcement advises brands including Adidas, Estée Lauder, and an Italian furniture manufacturer, has teamed up with four others in this venture: Mark Holmes, a Slade trained artist and product designer (lamps for the German manufacturer e15), designer and manufacturer Sebastian Wrong (Italian lighting specialist Flos recently bought the license to his Spun lamp) and Tamara Caspersz, general manager of the

London-based contemporary furniture retailer, Viaduct. Together they have commissioned a starry bunch of furniture designers – Barber Osgerby, Michael Marriott, Michael Young – plus the architects Zaha Hadid and Future Systems' Amanda Levete along with newcomer Alexander Taylor. Holmes and Wrong have also created products for the company's initial collection, which includes a sofa, coffee table, dining-cum-conference table, shelving, a desk, dining chair, lamps and a mirror. Prototypes will be on display in Milan, and products available in stores, such as Viaduct, in September.

The goal, says Willis, is for Established & Sons to be the British equivalent of pioneering Italian furniture manufacturer Cappellini. It's an interesting ambition considering that Cappellini was rescued from financial straits in a private equity buy-out just last year. If truly established players in niche furniture design are struggling, how can a new entrant succeed? 'If you've got a good product, properly marketed, it will sell,' Willis argues. 'We're going in at a tricky moment economically but we believe we'll be competitive. We see sales being very strong in the UK and good in the US and across Europe and in Japan . . . We're not in a gloomier period economically than any before.'

Sheridan Coakley of SCP, the London-based contemporary furniture manufacturer and retailer, agrees that there is still a market for 'high-end, small-batch production pieces' for Established & Sons to tap into. But Willis wants to go further, with a three-tier price structure on most items that makes Established & Sons accessible to a range of customers. Take the sofa. A handful of limited edition, bespoke models will carry a top price of around £30 000. A leather version with traditional hand-springing, will cost around £8000 – a price-tag equivalent to a sofa by Edra or B&B Italia – while a foam-based model will sell at around £3000. 'We're very aware of not limiting our audience,' Willis explains. 'It's like any brand. You need entry-level prices to buy into it.'

Much hangs, of course, on the quality of design and production. Established & Sons' manufacturing partner is Caparo, a UK-based company specializing in steel and engineering products, mainly for car makers, that is still controlled by the family of its founder, Lord Paul. It seems an odd choice. But Caparo can handle anything from aluminium cast components to steel nuts and bolts, woodworking to plastic injection blow-moulding, while specialist work, such as sofa springing and fabric sourcing, is contracted out. 'All the designers saw the manufacturing facilities before they began, [and] some were shocked . . . when they saw what the machines could do,' Holmes says. 'The facilities helped drive the creative process and are sowing the seeds for future designs.'

'The designs are not about style but substance,' adds Wrong. 'My mirror, for example, has instrument-quality glass normally used in aircraft, while Michael Young's desk has die-cast aluminium end sections.' Caparo, which last year generated sales of more than £55m, also backed Established & Sons with a 'significant financial investment'. And, says Willis, 'Angad Paul [Lord Paul's son] has a great passion for design. He's our age and has brought a lot to the party.' The party – and certainly Established & Sons' debut in Milan – will to some degree revolve around its high-profile founders and designers. The latter group was actually rather simple to put together, Willis says. After the four principals joined forces, they drew up a list of people they wanted to commission and got a positive response from everyone they approached.

Again, I'm sceptical, wondering how Established & Sons expects to create a unified collection with so many stars. And I'm not alone. 'It's terrific to see things being made in Britain, but the trouble with a conglomeration of talent is that it doesn't always add up to a particular vision,' says expert Sir Terence Conran. 'Why not go with one designer and get a continuity?' But Holmes responds: 'We wanted to portray the richness of talent in the UK at the moment, and it will be the quality of the manufacturing and of the products that will make the collection cohesive. We're building a family here.' The question is whether he is also building a successful business.

Source: by Nicole Swengley, 8 April 2005, The Financial Times Limited 2008. Reproduced by permission of Nicole Swengley.

Questions

1. What categories of operations process types do you think are required to meet the needs of Established & Sons?

2. How does operations management contribute to the success of Established & Sons?

EXERCISES

1. Describe the characteristics of project, jobbing, batch, line and continuous processes in manufacturing, providing real-life examples.

2. Describe the characteristics of professional, shop and mass processes in services, providing real-life examples.

3. Compare alternative service process type definitions using real-life examples.

4. What are the consequences of having too little process flexibility or too much process flexibility when making a product or delivering a service?

5. Describe three factors that can lead to a change in the volume and variety mix for a product or service over time.

6. Explain the concept of batch production.

WEB EXERCISE

Examine the tools used for layout design at http://www.mfgeng.com/fac.htm (accessed 25 September 2008).

FURTHER READING

Hill, T. (2005) *Operations Management*, 2nd edn, Palgrave Macmillan.

WEB LINKS

www.mas.berr.gov.uk (accessed 25 September 2008), UK Department for Business Enterprise and Regulatory Reform. Numerous case studies of operations concepts.

REFERENCES

Gaither, N. and **Frazier, G.** (2002) *Operations Management*, 9th edn, South-Western.

Hayes, R.H. and **Wheelwright, S.C.** (1984) *Restoring our Competitive Edge*, John Wiley & Sons, Ltd.

Lovelock, C.H. (1992) *Managing Services: Marketing, Operations and Human Resources*, 2nd edn, Pearson Education Ltd.

Noori, H. and **Radford, R.** (1995) *Production and Operations Management: Total Quality and Responsiveness*, McGraw-Hill, New York.

Russell, R.S. and **Taylor, B.W.** (2008) *Operations Management: Creating Value along the Supply Chain*, 6th edn, John Wiley & Sons, Ltd.

CHAPTER
4

- Introduction
- Layout design
- Detailed layout design

Layout Design

LEARNING OBJECTIVES

- Describe the basic layout types

- Evaluate the appropriateness of a layout type for a manufacturing or service process type

- Explain the concept of group technology

- Understand the concept of production flow analysis

- Understand the line-balancing technique

INTRODUCTION

Layout design concerns the physical placement of resources such as equipment and storage facilities. The layout is designed to facilitate the efficient flow of customers or materials through the manufacturing or service system. Layout design is important because it can have a significant effect on the cost and efficiency of an operation and can entail substantial investment in time and money. Layout design is important when designing manufacturing facilities but is also relevant to administrative activities such as the design of office layouts which can facilitate teamwork amongst groups of people. Layout design is relevant in service processes such as customer retail outlets where the placement of products can affect sales. In many operations the installation of a new layout, or redesign of an existing layout, can be difficult to alter once implemented due to the significant investment required on items such as equipment. This chapter describes the main categories of layout and techniques for detailed layout design.

LAYOUT DESIGN

Following the selection of the operations process type (see Chapter 3) it is necessary to select the layout (arrangement of facilities) of the operation. Figure 4.1 shows the relationship between manufacturing and service process types and layout types.

As can be seen from Figure 4.1, there are four basic layout types: fixed position, process, cell and product layout. As stated, the choice of layout type will follow from the process design choice. However, as can be seen from Figure 4.1, there is often a choice of layout types for a particular process type (such as a process layout or cell layout for batch process types). In this case the choice will depend on the characteristics of the layout type that are particularly relevant for the product or service that is to be delivered. An analysis may also be made using the trade-off between unit cost of production and variety of output that was used to determine process type in

Layout design
The arrangement of facilities in a service or manufacturing operation.

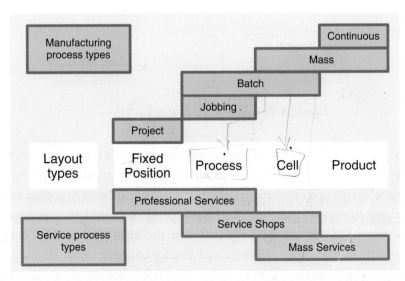

Figure 4.1: The Relationship between Process Type and Layout Type.

Chapter 3. For example, a cell layout is more likely to be relevant for relatively high volume batch systems where the cost of dedicated resources can be met by the lower unit cost of a high volume of product or service flowing through the cell.

The characteristics of each of the layout types will now be considered.

Fixed-Position Layout

This layout design is used when the product or service cannot be moved and so the transforming process must take place at the location of product creation or service delivery. Figure 4.2 shows an example of a fixed-position layout in a restaurant.

Fixed-position layout
This is used when the product or service cannot be moved and so the transforming process must take place at the location of product creation or service delivery.

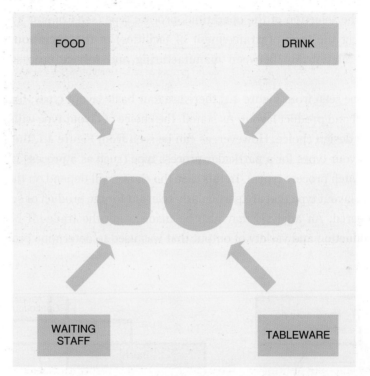

Figure 4.2: Fixed-Position Layout in a Restaurant.

In a fixed-position layout all resources for producing the product, such as equipment and labour must move to the site of the product or service. The emphasis when using a fixed-position layout is on the scheduling and coordination of resources to ensure that they are available in the required amounts at the required time. For example on a construction site most activities are dependent on the completion of other activities and cannot be undertaken simultaneously. The space available on the site may also constrain the amount of work activity that can take place at any one time. This means detailed scheduling of resources is required to minimize delays. In a restaurant it is important that the order is taken and food delivered to the table at the appropriate time. Chapter 16 examines planning techniques such as network analysis, which are used to assist in the scheduling of resources to a fixed-position layout.

From Figure 4.1, process types associated with a fixed-position layout are the project process type in manufacturing and the professional service type in services. Examples of fixed-position layouts include construction sites such as for buildings or for large ships, aircraft manufacture and full service restaurants (Figure 4.3).

Figure 4.3: A Meal at a Full-Service Restaurant: An Example of a Fixed-Position Layout.

Process/Functional Layout

A process layout, also termed a functional layout, is one in which resources (such as equipment and people) which have similar processes or functions are grouped together. Figure 4.4 shows a process layout in a manufacturing facility.

Process layouts are used when there is a large variety in the products or services being delivered and it may not be feasible to dedicate facilities to each individual product or service. A process layout allows the products or customers to move to each group of resources in turn, based on their individual requirements. Their flexibility means that process layouts are widely used. One advantage is that in service systems they allow a wide variety of routes that may be chosen by customers depending on their needs. Another advantage is that the product or service range may be extended and as long as no new resources are required may be accommodated within the current layout.

> **Process/functional layout**
> This is a layout in which resources (such as equipment and people) which have similar processes or functions are grouped together.

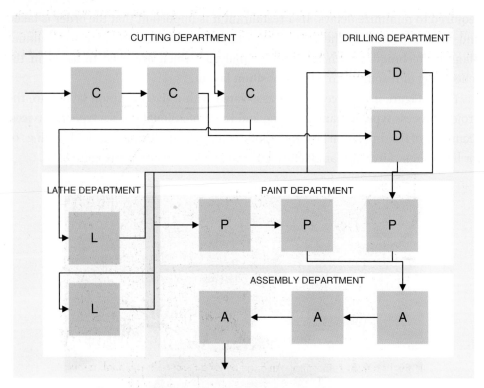

Figure 4.4: A Manufacturing Process or Functional Layout.

An important issue with process layouts is the management of the flow of products or services between the resource groups. One problem is that transportation between process groups can be a significant factor in terms of transportation time and handling costs. Another problem is the number of products or services involved and the fact that each product/service can follow an individual route between the process groups makes it difficult to predict when a particular product will be delivered or a service completed. This is because at certain times the number of customers or products arriving at a particular process group exceeds its capacity and so a queue forms until resources are available. This queuing time may take up a significant part of the time that the product or customer is in the process. This behaviour can lead to long throughput times (the time taken for a product or customer to progress through the layout). In a manufacturing organization a significant amount of time may be spent 'progress chasing' to give certain products priority to ensure they are delivered to customers on time. In a service system the customers may feel they are queuing in the system longer than they perceive is necessary for the service they require. However, in services there may be flexibility to add or remove staff to match the current arrival rate of customers to the service delivery point.

From Figure 4.1, process types associated with a process layout are jobbing and batch process types in manufacturing and service shops in services. Examples of process layouts include supermarkets, hospitals (Figure 4.5), department stores and component manufacturers.

Figure 4.5: A Hospital: An Example of a Process/Functional Layout.

Cell Layout

A cell layout attempts to combine the efficiency of a product layout with the flexibility of a process layout. Cells are created from placing together resources which service a subset of the total range of products or services. Figure 4.6 shows how a process layout with similar resources in departments has been redesigned as a series of three cells. Note how the routing of products is simplified using the cell layout format. The products are now processed in a single cell and need not be transported between departments.

When grouping products or services together in this way the grouping is termed a family. The process of grouping the products or services to create a family is termed group technology.

> **Cell layout**
> Cells are created from placing together resources that service a subset of the total range of products or services.

Group technology has three aspects:

> **Group technology**
> The process of grouping products for manufacture or services for delivery.

1. Grouping parts into families. Grouping parts or customers into families has the objective of reducing the changeover time between batches, allowing smaller batch sizes and thus improving flexibility. Parts family formation is based on the idea of grouping parts or customers together according to factors such as processing similarity.

2. Grouping physical facilities into cells to reduce transportation time between processes. Physical facilities are grouped into cells with the intention of reducing

material or customer movements. Whereas a process layout involves extensive movement of materials or customers between departments with common processes, a cell comprises all the facilities required to manufacture a family of components or deliver a service. Material and customer movement is therefore restricted to within the cell and throughput times are therefore reduced. Cells can be U-shaped (see Figure 4.9) to allow workers to work at more than one process while minimizing movement.

3. Creating groups of multiskilled workers. Creating groups of multiskilled workers enables increased autonomy and flexibility on the part of operators. This enables easier changeovers from one part to another and increases the job enrichment of members of the group. This in turn can improve motivation and have a beneficial effect on quality.

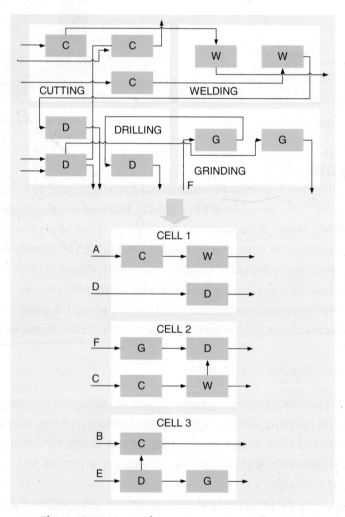

Figure 4.6: Moving from a Process to a Cell Layout.

Creating cells with dedicated resources can significantly reduce the time it takes for products and services to pass through the process by reducing queuing time. It also offers the opportunity for automation due to the close proximity of the process stages. Thus process technology can be used to replace a number of general purpose resources with a single dedicated multifunctional system such as a flexible manufacturing system (see Chapter 6). A disadvantage of cell layouts can be the extra expenditure due to the extra resources required in moving to a cell layout.

From Figure 4.1, process types associated with a cell layout are batch and mass process types in manufacturing and service shops and mass services in services. Examples of cell layouts include custom manufacture (Figure 4.7), a maternity unit in a hospital and a cafeteria with multiple serving areas. In services a cell layout could involve an insurance company organized by type of claim (such as car, home or travel).

Figure 4.7: A Retail Department Store: An Example of a Cell Layout.
Source: http://en.wikipedia.org/wiki/Image:Departmentstoreinterior.jpg (accessed 25 September 2008).

Product Layout

Product layouts, also termed line layouts, arrange the resources required for a product or service around the needs of that product or service. Figure 4.8 shows a configuration of a product layout. Here the material flows through four stages. The line may be automated or people may be assigned to one or more stages.

In manufacturing applications, such as assembly lines with a high volume of a standard product, the products will move in a flow from one processing station to the next. In contrast to the process layout, in which products move to the resources, here

> **Product layout**
> A layout with the resources required for a product or service arranged around the needs of that product or service.

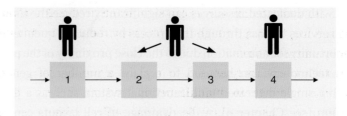

Figure 4.8: Product Layout.

the resources are arranged and dedicated to a particular product or service. The term product layout refers to the arrangement of the resources around the product or service. In services the requirements of a specific group of customers are identified and resources setup sequentially so the customers flow through the system, moving from one stage to another until the service is complete.

A key issue in product layouts is that the stages in the assembly line or flow line must be 'balanced'. This means that the time spent by components or customers should be approximately the same for each stage, otherwise queues will occur at the slowest stage. The topic of line balancing is considered later in this chapter.

The product or line layout is an efficient delivery system in that the use of dedicated equipment in a balanced line will allow a much faster throughput time than in a process layout. The major disadvantage of the approach is that it lacks the flexibility of a process layout and only produces a standard product or service. Another issue is that if any stage of the line fails, then in effect the output from the whole line is lost and so it lacks the robustness to loss of resources (for example equipment failure or staff illness) that the process layout can provide.

An alternative to the straight-line configuration shown in Figure 4.8 is to adopt a 'U-shape' design as in Figure 4.9. Here material flows through eight stages of

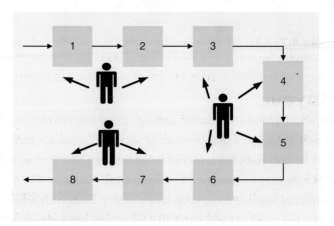

Figure 4.9: 'U-Shape' Product Layout.

production or assembly, which are assigned to three people. An advantage of the U shape is that it may allow people (or equipment) to be assigned to multiple stages and thus help balance the line.

From Figure 4.1 process types associated with a product layout are mass and continuous process types in manufacturing and mass services in services. Examples of product layouts include car assembly, self-service cafes (Figure 4.10) and car valeting.

Figure 4.10: A Self-Service Cafeteria: An Example of a Product Layout.
Source: http://en.wikipedia.org/wiki/Image:Infosys.Electronic.City.Cafeteria.JPG (accessed 25 September 2008).

Characteristics of Layout Types

Table 4.1 summarizes the main characteristics of operations systems using each of the four main layout types.

Although the main layout types can be adapted to meet the needs of a particular manufacturing or service system, it may be the case that a mix of layout types is required within a single operation. For example, hospitals are basically a process layout with people with similar needs (for example, intensive care) grouped together. However, the layout also shows characteristics of a fixed position layout in that staff, medicines and equipment are brought to the location of the customer.

Layout type	Characteristics of operations that use layout type
Fixed-position	Very high product and mix flexibility, but very high unit cost. Products or customers do not move; the resources are arranged around them. There can be a high variety of tasks for staff. A major issue for operations is the scheduling and coordination of activities over time.
Process *Functional*	High product and mix flexibility. Complex flow can lead to high levels of work-in-progress and high throughput times. Low utilization of resources. Flexible in terms of handling additions to the product/service mix. Robust in that nonavailability of resources does not stop delivery of product/service if other group resources remain.
Cell	Can provide flexibility of process layout and efficiency of product layout. Resources can be matched to product or service demand so work-in-progress and thus throughput times are much lower than for process layout. Variety of tasks offers opportunity for automation and more variation in duties for personnel. Can be costly to move and purchase additional plant — necessary to rearrange existing layout.
Product/line	Standard product or service in high volumes at low unit cost. Can specialize equipment to product or service needs. Allows relatively little variety in product or service. Line configuration leads to danger of failure of one process stage effectively stopping output from the whole line. Work can be repetitive if personnel are always based at one process stage.

Table 4.1: Characteristics of Operations for each Layout Type.

DETAILED LAYOUT DESIGN

Once the layout type has been chosen, its detailed configuration must be designed to meet the needs of a particular implementation.

In a fixed-position layout there will be a relatively low number of elements and there are no widely used techniques to help locate resources. The relative positioning of equipment and departments in a process layout can be analysed in terms of minimizing transportation costs or distances using an activity matrix. When a number of factors need to be taken into account, including qualitative aspects, relationship charts may be used. Process maps (described in Chapter 8) can also be used to show the flow of materials, customers and staff through the layout. In some instances, such as retail layout design, software is available that takes into consideration both financial aspects of layout design and customer requirements such as aesthetics and lighting (Hope and Mühlemann, 1997).

In this chapter the techniques of production-flow analysis for cell layouts and line balancing for product layouts will be covered.

Production Flow Analysis

A cell layout uses the concept of group technology to group resources into cells to process families of parts or customers. Production flow analysis (PFA) (Burbidge, 1996) is a group technology technique that can be used to identify families of parts with similar processing requirements. To show how PFA works, Figure 4.11 shows an example of a process layout.

> **Production flow analysis**
> This is a group technology technique that can be used to identify families of parts with similar processing requirements.

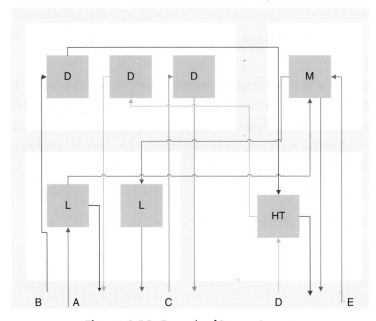

Figure 4.11: Example of Process Layout.

Five parts (A, B, C, D, E) are produced in a process layout consisting of a drill department with three drills (D), a lathe department with two lathes (L), a milling department with one mill (M) and a heat-treatment department with one-heat treatment machine (HT). The routings taken by the parts are shown in Table 4.2.

In order to identify families of parts, the first step in PFA is to draw a grid of parts against machines and mark which parts are processed on which machine (Table 4.3).

Part	Routing sequence
A	lathe, mill
B	drill, heat treatment
C	drill
D	heat treatment, drill
E	mill, lathe

Table 4.2: Part Routing Sequences for Machine Shop.

	Lathe	Mill	Heat treat	Drill
A	✓	✓		
B			✓	✓
C				✓
D			✓	✓
E	✓	✓		

Table 4.3: PFA Routing Matrix.

The next step is to observe which machines have parts in common. In this case it can be seen that lathe and heat treatment could form one cell and drill and mill could form another cell. Redraw the grid, rearranging the rows and columns to place parts using the machines in the adjacent cells. Two or more cells can be formed (Table 4.4).

	Lathe	Mill	Heat treat	Drill
A	✓	✓		
E	✓	✓		
C				✓
D			✓	✓
B			✓	✓
	CELL 1		CELL 2	

Table 4.4: Rearranged PFA Routing Matrix.

The cell layout can now be drawn, using the cells defined using the PFA analysis and referring back to the routing sequences in Table 4.2.

Figure 4.12 shows the cell layout routing. It is immediately apparent that the routing of parts is much clearer and routing distances are smaller than in the process layout (Figure 4.11).

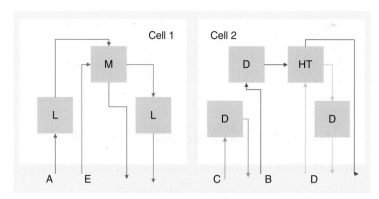

Figure 4.12: Cell Layout Routing.

Line Balancing

A product layout consists of a number of processes arranged one after another in a 'line' to produce a standard product or service in a relatively high volume. These systems which have a characteristic flow (product) layout use specialized equipment or staff dedicated to achieving an optimal flow of work through the system. This is important because all items follow virtually the same sequence of operations. A major aim of flow systems is to ensure that each stage of production is able to maintain production at an equal rate. The technique of line balancing is used to ensure that the output of each production stage is equal and maximum efficiency is attained.

Line balancing involves ensuring that the stages of production are co-ordinated and bottlenecks are avoided. The line flow configuration means that the tasks in the line must be undertaken in order (precedence) and the output of the whole line will be determined by the slowest or bottleneck process. The actual design of the line is thus guided by the order of the tasks which are involved in producing the product or delivering the service and the required output rate required to meet demand. This provides information that determines the number of stages and the output rate of each stage.

The steps in line balancing are as follows:

1 Draw a Precedence Diagram

The first step in line balancing is to identify the tasks involved in the process and the order in which these tasks must be undertaken. Once the tasks have been identified it is necessary to define their relationship to one another. There are some tasks that can only begin when other tasks have been completed. This is termed a serial relationship and is shown graphically in Figure 4.13.

> **Line balancing**
> This is used to ensure that the output of each production stage in a line layout is equal and maximum efficiency is attained.

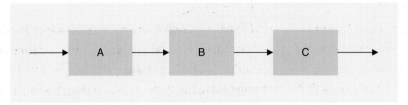

Figure 4.13: Serial Relationship of Tasks.

The execution of other tasks may be totally independent and thus they have a parallel relationship shown graphically in Figure 4.14.

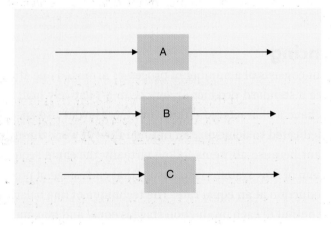

Figure 4.14: Parallel Relationship of Tasks.

Precedence diagrams are used to show the tasks undertaken in a line process and the dependencies between these tasks. Thus it is easy to see that task C for example can only take place when task A and task B have completed (see Figure 4.15).

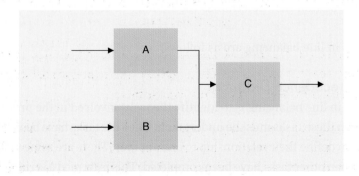

Figure 4.15: Precedence Diagram.

2 Determine the Cycle Time for the Line

For a particular line process we will wish to reach a desired rate of output for the line to meet projected demand. This is usually expressed in work items per time period, for example 30 parts per hour. Another way of expressing this output rate is that 30 parts per hour means that a part must leave the system every 2 minutes (60 minutes/ 30 parts). This measure, termed the cycle time, represents the longest time any part is allowed to spend at each task. Thus

$$\text{cycle time} = \text{available time/desired output}$$

Taking into consideration the discussion of bottleneck processes above, the cycle time for the line process is thus determined by the task with the highest cycle time or lowest output level.

3 Assign Tasks to Workstations

Once the cycle time for the line has been calculated we have the cycle time for each stage or workstation in the line process. We can now allocate tasks to each workstation based on their task times. As a rule of thumb it is more efficient to allocate eligible tasks to a workstation in the order of longest task times first. When the total task time would exceed the cycle time for a workstation then it is necessary to start a new workstation and repeat the allocation of tasks as before. If a task time is longer than the workstation cycle time then it is necessary either to allocate multiple tasks in parallel in order to meet the target time or to break the task down into smaller elements.

4 Calculate the Efficiency of the Line

When tasks are assigned to workstations it is very unlikely that their total task times at each workstation will match the cycle time exactly. A measure of how close these two values do meet for the whole line is called the line efficiency. To calculate the line efficiency:

$$\text{Line Efficiency \%} = (\text{Sum of the task times/(number of workstations * desired cycle time)}) * 100$$

It should be noted that the issue of line balancing will be complicated by constraints such as factory layout, material handling between stages and availability of worker skills. Other factors in designing product layouts include:

- *Variability in task times.* A major factor in achieving a proper line balance is to gather accurate estimates of task times in the line flow process. If timings are just based on an average of observations then there is a danger that the effect of variations on task times will not be considered. This can be limited somewhat by keeping a number of job elements in a task, which reduces variability and increases flexibility. Simulation modelling (Chapter 8) can be used to investigate these variations as well as the effect of random variations such as machine breakdown.

- *Mixed-model lines*. The use of a multimodel line (Chapter 13) to process a range of products, rather than a single product type, also increases the complexity of the line-balancing process.

- *Shape of the line*. Although the sequence of workstations in a product layout is linear, the actual shape of the line need not be straight. It can be an S shape, U shape, O shape or L shape. Factors that are used when deciding on a suitable shape include the ability of people to communicate, the ability of robots and people to reach parts and transportation distances between workstations.

- *Job enlargement*. After taking into consideration the constraints imposed by precedence and cycle time, a decision must be made regarding the level at which a task is broken down and how the elements of the task are allocated to personnel. For instance motivation can be improved by allocating the whole process to a single person instead of allocating smaller tasks to a number of people in a line.

SUMMARY

- There are four basic layout types: fixed position, process, cell and product.

- A fixed-position layout is used when the product or service cannot be moved. A process layout is one in which resources that have similar processes or functions are grouped together. A cell layout is created by placing together resources which serve a subset of the total range of products or services. A product layout arranges the resources required for a product or service around the needs of that product or service.

- Group technology has three aspects of grouping parts into families, grouping physical facilities into cells and creating multiskilled workers.

- Production flow analysis is a group technology technique that can be used to identify families of parts with similar processing requirements.

- The technique of line balancing is used to ensure that the output of each stage in a product line layout is equal and maximum utilization is attained.

CASE STUDY 4.1

Line Balancing in a Manufacturing Plant

This study concerns a former division of a major UK-based manufacturer of railway rolling stock and equipment. The plant manufactures a range of bogies, which are the supporting frames and wheel sets for rail vehicles. The company has a history of supplying the passenger train market in the UK but over a period of time low demand and increased competition had led it to enter new markets including European inner-city transport and the supply of freight bogies to Far East countries. The need to compete on a global basis led the company to re-evaluate its manufacturing facility with particular emphasis on the need to increase output, reduce lead times and increase flexibility. To meet these demands management had identified areas where substantial investment was required.

The Production Process

The facility layout is on a product-line basis with the manufacturing process consisting of six main stages of fabrication, welding, frame machining, paint, fitting and quality audit. Each stage must be completed in order before the next stage can begin. The stages are now briefly described:

- *Fabrication.* The fabrication stage prepares the bogie frame sections from sheet steel and bought-in castings. A custom template is designed from which the parts required are cut from sheet steel to standard batch sizes. Parts not needed immediately are held in storage. Processed parts and castings are

brought together to form a bogie 'kit', which is assembled on a jig and taken to the subsequent welding stage.

- *Welding.* A bogie subassembly is manually welded on a jig at a workstation to form a main bogie frame.
- *Frame machining.* The main bogie frame is then transferred to a CNC [computer numerically controlled machine] centre for the machining of any holes or bores needed for the fixing of subassemblies such as the braking and suspension systems. Bogies are fixed to a slave table and the machine processes the frame according to a preset operation sequence.
- *Paint.* The frame is then manually painted while being suspended from an overhead moving circular track.
- *Fitting.* Manufactured subassemblies and bought-in components such as motors are then assembled on the bogie frame. The frames are placed on supports and are moved along a line at different stages of assembly with overhead cranes.
- *Quality audit.* Final inspection is carried out to ensure all bogies meet the required specification. It is usual that a certain amount of paint touch-up work is required at this stage due to damage caused to the paint finish during the fitting stage.

The Line Balancing Study

The focus of the study was on product layout design with the main objective being to ensure that the performance of the whole manufacturing system would meet required output levels. The output level was converted into a target cycle time (time between manufacture of products or output rate). As stated, the product layout consists of six main stages with the product passing through each stage in turn. This means that the effective cycle time for the whole system is determined by the stage with the longest cycle time. The study objective was to obtain a balanced line (all cycle times equal), which would enable a smooth parts flow through the production stages facilitating the introduction of a pull-type just-in-time (JIT) production control system.

A simulation model (Chapter 8) was used to estimate the cycle time at the main manufacturing stages. The graph (Figure 4.16) shows clearly where management effort needed to be directed to achieve the target cycle time.

The quality audit stage was set at a nominal amount by management. Significant problems had occurred at this stage with the spray finish on the bogie frames being damaged during the subassembly fitting stage. This had to be rectified by a manual touch-up process, which could take longer than the original spray time. The paint area would also need to be reconfigured due to new environmental controls. Management had recognized the problems and an investment in an epoxy paint plant producing a hard-wearing finish was planned.

The bogie frame machining centre had previously been recognized by management as a bottleneck process. The bogie frame went through a number of preprogrammed steps on the machine and the cycle time was dependent on the capability of the machining centre itself. Consequently a major part of the planned investment was a new machining centre with a quoted cycle time below the target. An investigation of the fabrication processes revealed that although the cycle times were above target, the majority of this time was used for machine setup. Figure 4.17 shows the effect on cycle time of a reduction in setup time of 10% to 90%.

From Figure 4.17 it is clear that a setup reduction of 50% is required to achieve the

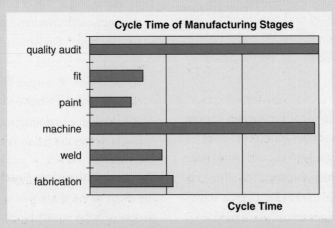

Figure 4.16: Cycle Time of Manufacturing Stages.

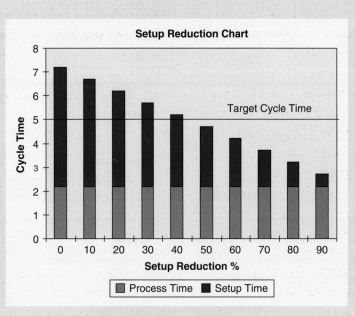

Figure 4.17: Setup Reduction.

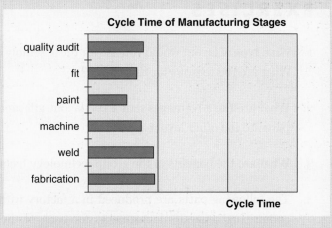

Figure 4.18: Cycle Time of Manufacturing Stages.

target cycle time. A team was assembled to achieve this target and it was met by the use of magnetic tables to hold parts ready for processing. The simulation was rerun and the results (Figure 4.18) show the system achieving the required performance. It can be seen that a further reduction in fabrication setup times and a reconfiguration of the welding line would reduce the overall cycle time further, producing a more balanced line and increasing capacity utilization.

By implementing the changes outlined in the study the simulation was able to predict the following improvements in performance (Table 4.5). In the table cycle efficiency $=100\% - \%$idle time where %idle time = idle time per cycle/total cycle time.

Performance measure	Change (%)
Cycle time	− 65
Lead time	− 19
Output per week	+220
Cycle efficiency	+29

Table 4.5: Line Balancing Study Results.

These are substantial improvements in performance and meet the output targets set by management. However, the results in Figure 4.18 show that further reductions in the cycle times for the fabrication and weld stages would lead to a further increase in cycle efficiency, reflecting a more balanced line, and thus a further increase in output.

Source: Excerpt from Greasley A. (2004). Reproduced by permission of Emerald Group Publishing Ltd.

Questions

1. What are the reasons given for the need to balance the line?
2. What strategies are used to balance the line?
3. Identify alternative strategies to balance the line.

EXERCISES

1. What type of layout would you use for the assembly of a television set? What are the reasons for this choice?

2. What are the advantages that a cell layout attempts to achieve compared to the other layout types?

3. What are the benefits of the group technology technique?

4. The following parts are produced in a factory with a process layout comprising separate departments for each of the four operations: lathe, grind, drill and machining.

Part no.	Routing sequence
24	Grind
12	Lathe, drill
67	Grind, machine
45	Lathe, drill
32	Lathe, drill
76	Grind, machine

Use production flow analysis (PFA) to show how the plant could be organized into cells using group technology to identify families of parts.

5. A company is currently organized with machines grouped into departments based on their function. The sequence of operations taken for each component is:

Part no.	Routing sequence
487	Lathe, mill, grind, drill
723	Shear, punch press, grind, deburr
245	Mill, drill, grind
29	Shear, p1aunch press, punch press, deburr

a) Draw a diagram of the plant and trace the routing sequence for each component.

b) Use PFA to analyse the routings and identify similarities between the components.

c) Group the components into families.

d) On the basis of the families identified in c), specify cells for producing the components and trace the flow of work through the reorganized plant.

e) If the company currently has one of each machine, how many additional machines are required?

6. Use PFA to indicate how the following plant could be reorganized into cells. Currently the process layout consists of a lathe department with two lathes, a grinder department with two grinders, with all other departments having a single machine each.

Part no.	Routing sequence
A1	Press, lathe
B2	Drill, mill, deburr
C3	Lathe, grinder, press
D4	Grinder, lathe
E5	Lathe, mill, drill
F6	Drill, grinder, deburr

7. Explain the need for line balancing.

8. What are the main techniques in determining capacity for a product layout and a process layout?

WEB EXERCISE

This chapter has focused on the layout of the operations facility in manufacturing or service systems primarily in the context of the efficient flow of materials and customers. Read the article at http://www.enotes.com/small-business-encyclopedia/facility-layout-design (accessed 25 September 2008) and note the additional factors that may be considered when designing factory and office layouts.

FURTHER READING

Chase, R.B., Jacobs, F.R. and **Aquilano, N.J.** (2005) *Operations Management for Competitive Advantage*, 11th edn, McGraw-Hill.
Slack, N., Chambers, S. and **Johnston, R.** (2007) *Operations Management*, 5th edn, Pearson Education Ltd.
Stevenson, W.J. (2006) *Operations Management*, 9th edn, McGraw-Hill.

WEB LINKS

www.proplanner.com/Product/Details/LineBalancing.aspx (accessed 26 September 2008). ProPlanner. Software for single- and mixed-model line-balancing applications.

www.protech-ie.com/flb.htm (accessed 26 September 2008). Production Techno logy. Software for line balancing applications.

www.sixsigmainstitute.com/training/plb_training.shtml (accessed 26 September 2008). Lean Sigma Institute. Training in line balancing.

REFERENCES

Burbidge, J.L. (1996) *Production Flow Analysis for Planning Group Technology*, Oxford University Press, Oxford.
Greasley, A. (2004) The case for the organisational use of simulation. *Journal of Manufacturing Technology Management*, **15** (7), 560–6.
Hope, C. and **Mühlemann, A.** (1997) *Service Operations Management: Strategy, Design and Delivery*, Prentice Hall, Hertfordshire.

CHAPTER
5

- Introduction
- Supply network design
- Long-term capacity planning
- Facility location
- Location selection techniques

Facility Design and Location

LEARNING OBJECTIVES

- Discuss the issue of supply network design

- Discuss the concept of economies of scale

- Discuss the concept of economies of scope

- Describe the approaches of lead capacity, match capacity and lag capacity

- Consider the facility location decision in terms of supply-side influences and demand-side influences

- Undertake the location selection techniques of weighted scoring, the centre-of-gravity method and locational cost-volume analysis

INTRODUCTION

The location decision is one of the key strategic decisions facing an organization. It involves business strategy (for example growth), marketing (entering new market segments) and operations (providing capability to meet customer needs) as well as other functions such as finance. The location decision may also involve a long-term commitment in terms of the purchase or lease of a building and a significant financial investment. For many service organizations, such as retail outlets, the location of the facility must be convenient for the potential customer base and location is thus an important factor in the success of the organization.

In this book facility design is taken in a broad sense to mean the decisions surrounding how capacity will be supplied by the organization to meet market demand. This may be achieved internally by the organization by the construction of facilities or externally by agreement with suppliers. There are three main issues involved in decisions regarding this area:

Supply network design
The configuration of the organization's relationship with its suppliers and the choice about what activities the organization should undertake internally and what should be subcontracted to other agencies.

1. How will the capacity be supplied (**supply network design**)? This includes decisions on the configurations of the organization's relationship with its suppliers and the choice about what activities the organization should undertake internally and what should be subcontracted to other agencies.
2. How much capacity should be supplied (long-term capacity planning)? This covers the question of how much long-term capacity should be supplied by the organization.
3. Where will the capacity be located (facility location)? This covers the question of the geographical location of capacity supplied by the organization.

SUPPLY NETWORK DESIGN

Every operation, as well as supplying capacity to the market in terms of goods and services, will require capacity in the form of inputs to the manufacturing and services process, such as materials, people and equipment. Thus, when designing an operations facility, consideration must be made regarding the relationship of the organization with its suppliers of the capacity required in order to provide the goods and services the facility is producing. Two aspects of this relationship with suppliers are considered. The configuration of all the suppliers, termed the supply network, and the choice regarding what the organization should do itself and what it should contract others to do.

For some organizations decisions may often be taken in the context of the integrated global strategy of an organization. While multinational companies can be classified as firms moving into more markets abroad, the **global organization** follows a business strategy where activities are coordinated on a worldwide basis. A global firm is organized into a network, which means that operations at several locations can perform tasks for a given customer group and/or a single facility can perform a task for several downstream (customer) groups. Networks can improve delivery and cost performance relative to fixed supply facilities because the network can pool demand and increase volume to reduce cost and choose different facilities to provide products for a given customer under different conditions. The use of a network should lead to a more robust system that avoids capacity bottlenecks through the use of close coordination facilitated by the use of communications technology. The aim of a global organization is to create a network of operations that will sell the same products in several countries, increase overall sales thereby reducing the cost per unit of development, coordinate the work of subsidiaries to provide a product/service to the global customer and shift production in response to exchange-rate fluctuations. An international network also requires an improvement of global supply chain performance that coordinates the location and capacity of plants as well as the purchasing function. The improvements will aim to secure economies of scale and scope by using a global supply chain to reduce unit costs through lower transportation expenses.

Global organization
Firms that follow a business strategy where activities are coordinated on a worldwide basis.

One of the main advantages of operating as a multinational company is reported to be the ability to learn and improve operations through knowledge transfer between the organization's units operating in different locations. The main difficulty in operating globally arises in the need to balance the needs of local markets, affected by factors such as different legislative environments and cultural differences, with achieving an efficient coordinated global operations capability. So how does an organization overcome the basic dilemma for a multinational company of aiming to integrate plants on a global scale to achieve maximum efficiency while at the same time having the flexibility to serve changing customer needs in different markets? Approaches have ranged from having companies manufacturing products close to their customers, tailoring regional operations at scattered plants to meet local needs to centralized manufacturing, offering a selection of standard, lower priced products to all the markets they serve

(McGrath and Hoole, 1992). Tom Peters (1994) argues that firms will achieve global reach not through the formal multinational structure but through the use of an informal decentralized network, facilitated by telecommunications technology, providing scale power without vertical integration. Asea Brown Boveri (ABB) is cited as a global manufacturing company attempting to combine the advantages of a global organization with the flexibility and innovation possible from small local units (see Case Study 5.1).

The issue of the design of the supply network is considered further in Chapter 15 on supply chain management. In particular the issues of supply chain integration and the use of e-Commerce are directly related to supply network decisions.

CASE STUDY 5.1

Asea Brown Boveri (ABB)

Asea Brown Boveri was created in 1987 through the merger of the Swedish firm Asea and the Swiss firm Brown Boveri. In 1991 ABB grossed $28.9 billion in revenue in 140 countries and employed 240 000 people worldwide. The company operated in eight business segments: power plants, power transmission, power distribution, industry, transportation, environmental control, financial services and various activities (such as robotics). The company aimed to resolve what it saw as three internal contradictions of a global firm; the need to be 'global and local', 'big and small' and 'radically decentralized with centralized reporting and control'. This was to be achieved through the framework of a matrix structure that was designed to enable business to be optimized on a global scale and maximize performance in each market location.

Along one dimension of the matrix the company is a distributed global network. Business area leaders around the world make decisions on product strategy and performance without regard to national borders. Along a second dimension country managers run a traditionally organized national company, serving its home markets as effectively as possible. Each national company is divided into profit centres of approximately 50 personnel, which are accountable to their own profit-and-loss account and serve external customers directly. Each profit centre manager reports to both the Business Area and Country manager who in turn refer to the Executive committee of 13 who decide global strategy and performance. Thus there are only three layers of management in total.

Most business area teams are pursuing economies of scale, but mostly learning scale, not production scale. Each local company is to think 'small', to worry about its home market and a handful of export markets, and to learn to make money on small volumes. Although economies of scale are possible at a global level to leverage suppliers on price, quantity and delivery schedules a greater advantage is perceived through the transfer of expertise between factories around the world, all facing the same problems and opportunities and providing solutions that are shared around the network.

Another feature of the matrix is that although the company is decentralized into small legally separate companies with their own profit and loss accounts, to ensure that the advantages of size are retained the company is simultaneously monitored by the 13 member executive committee, which is responsible for business segments, countries and staff functions. To achieve this a management information system collates monthly performance figures for all 4500 profit centres which is used to monitor trends and provide feedback to local managers.

Question

What lessons for global management could you derive from the case study?

LONG-TERM CAPACITY PLANNING

The level at which management sets the level of capacity is a key determinant of the competitiveness of the organization. This decision needs to be made within a long-term capacity plan, which provides a fit with the operations strategy of the organization. The operations strategy should define the nature of the markets that the organization intends to compete in, in terms of characteristics such as product mix, volume and geographic spread, which will impact on the amount and type of capacity required. Thus it is not simply a matter of attaining a sufficient amount of capacity to meet the expected demand, but the capacity must be available at the time needed and in the current format to ensure that targets are met. For example if it is required to meet sudden changes of demand in an overseas market, the transportation time for the capacity supplied in a local location may mean it cannot supply the market within the time required. There will also be constraints on overall capacity caused by a scarcity of certain types of capacity (such as employee skills). Thus the availability of different types of capacity must be considered in order to avoid bottlenecks occurring. This section will consider long-term capacity issues in terms of the volume of capacity required and the timing of when that capacity should be acquired. Short and medium term capacity planning issues in terms of meeting customer demand are covered in Chapter 11.

> **Long-term capacity planning**
> This covers the question of how much long-term capacity should be supplied by the organization. This decision needs to be made within a long-term plan that provides a fit with the operations strategy of the organization.

Capacity Volume

Economies of Scale

In determining the optimum capacity level for a facility the concept of **economies of scale** is considered. Economies of scale relate to the capital costs of building a new facility and the fixed costs of operating a facility.

> **Economies of scale**
> When a facility is expanded, fixed costs remain the same, and the average cost of producing each unit falls.

The capital costs of building a facility do not increase proportionally as its capacity increases, so for example a facility with twice the capacity of another facility will not have capital costs twice as high. This might suggest that the use of a single large facility that supplies all capacity needs is the most appropriate strategy. However, at a certain capacity level for a particular location, **diseconomies of scale** may set in. These may include the transportation costs incurred in supplying a large geographical area from a single location, the speed of delivery from a single location to the customer becomes too slow and the added complexity of a large organization may cause communication and coordination problems.

> **Diseconomies of scale**
> When a facility is expanded and the average cost of producing each unit rises.

As a facility is expanded and fixed costs remain the same the average cost of producing each unit will fall until the best operating level of the facility is reached and the lowest average unit cost met. Past a certain point, however, diseconomies of scale occur and average unit costs rise. This is due to the required capacity output of the facility being higher than it has been designed for. Operating at this level can cause loss of efficiency from factors such as poor decision-making due to management layers, congestion of materials and staff, complexity of combining many products and services, extensive use of (relatively expensive) shift working and overtime and reduced morale of staff due to working conditions. The relationship between average unit cost of output and volume for different facility sizes is shown in Figure 5.1.

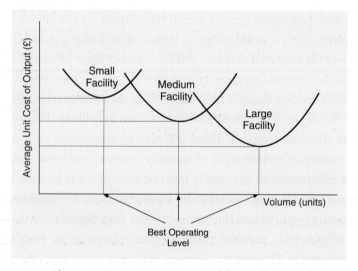

Figure 5.1: Best Operating Level for Facility Size.

The decision regarding the volume of capacity is complex because it is unlikely that the amount of capacity required from a facility will be fixed over the long term. Therefore there is a choice to be made between

- building a facility that provides more capacity than is currently needed but will provide sufficient capacity for planned growth in output; or
- matching the facility design to current capacity requirements, achieving maximum economies of scale, and then incurring the cost of expansion to meet any future increase in capacity requirements.

The expansion route is less risky, particularly when the forecast of future demand is uncertain as it requires less finance to be tied up in the facility infrastructure. However, construction costs can be considerably decreased if the complete facility is built in one phase. The decision will be based on the strategy of the firm and in particular the likely growth rate of the products or services the facility will supply.

When considering economies of scale it is important to understand that the rationalization of a number of facilities into a single large facility will achieve economies of scale only if the multiple facilities are doing the same type of work. Simply putting the work of a number of facilities doing different activities within one building is unlikely to achieve economy-of-scale benefits. There are also likely to be difficulties in achieving economies of scale in front-office service systems where contact with the customer and customization of the service offering may be required by the customer.

Economies of Scope

Traditionally, significant investment in process technology, such as automation, has only been justified for high-volume products where economies of scale provide a lowest average cost per unit. However, modern process technology, such as flexible manufacturing systems (FMS), described in Chapter 6, provide flexibility and allow a range of products to be produced quickly and efficiently. Thus economies of scope are created by the ability to produce many products in one highly flexible production facility more cheaply than in separate facilities.

> **Economies of scope**
> Economies of scope are created by the ability to produce many products in one highly flexible production facility more cheaply than in separate facilities.

Balancing Capacity

In calculating capacity volume another factor to take into account is that the total capacity of any system is dependent on the process with the smallest capacity, called the bottleneck. Thus in order for the system to operate at its most efficient it is necessary to equalize the capacity between processes. The capacity of sequential

> **Balancing capacity**
> This is the equalizing of the capacity of a number of sequential processes.

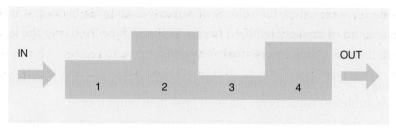

Figure 5.2: Diagram of the Capacity of Four Sequential Processes.

processes can be visualized as a series of pipes of varying capacity, with the smallest pipe limiting the capacity of the whole system (Figure 5.2).

In Figure 5.2 the total capacity of the system is limited by the capacity at process 3. Thus process 3 is the bottleneck process. One measure that can be used to assess the balance of the system is the cycle efficiency where:

cycle efficiency = 100% – %idle time

where

%idle time = idle time per cycle/total cycle time.

The cycle time is a measure of the time between output of each unit, and is related to output as follows:

cycle time = 1/output rate

Thus for an output rate of 30 products an hour the cycle time is 2 minutes (a unit is produced or a service delivered every 2 minutes).

See Chapter 4 for details of the line balancing technique for equalizing cycle times for sequential processes.

Subcontracting Networks

An alternative to obtaining capacity volume within the organization is to develop subcontractor and supplier networks. Here long-term contractual arrangements are made with suppliers to supply goods and services which means less capacity is required by the subcontracting organization. An advantage of this approach is that less capital is required for production and delivery facilities. There is also the flexibility to decrease capacity supplied to meet falling market demand without incurring the costs of under-utilization of resources or to increase capacity without the expense of additional resources. A disadvantage is the risk that subcontractors may not be able to meet changing capacity requirements. There is also a risk of the loss of skills inherent in outsourcing activities. Outsourcing is the term used when goods and services are obtained outside the organization. Business process outsourcing (BPO) refers to the outsourcing of processes, such as maintenance

---

Subcontracting networks:
Long-term contractual arrangements made with suppliers to supply goods and services.

Outsourcing
When goods and services are obtained outside the organization.

Business process outsourcing (BPO)
The outsourcing of processes.

processes for example. **Offshoring** is the term used to describe the transfer of activities to another country. This can be achieved by either moving activities to an overseas arm of a multinational firm or by outsourcing activities to a foreign supplier. Different forms of organizational relationships are covered in the supply chain integration section of Chapter 15.

> **Offshoring**
> The transfer of activities to another country.

CASE STUDY   5.2

The Supply Chains that Could Bind Unsuspecting Managers

Emma Maersk – and I don't think she would mind me saying this – is a very big girl indeed. She's as wide as a motorway. And at almost 400 m in length and 60 m in height she is probably the largest container ship the world has ever seen. When the *Emma Maersk* docked in Felixstowe in the south-east of England this month the sighs of relief from retailers, manufacturers and parents should have been audible all over the planet. Christmas, in the UK at least, had not been cancelled. An amazing 45 000 tonnes of Chinese manufactured goods have now been safely unloaded and despatched to shops and warehouses across the country. This is what it looks like when supply chains work. But the story does not always have such a happy ending. Globalization has led to the development of longer and at times more precarious supply chains. The drive for efficiency has often seen companies rationalize the number of suppliers

they use, leaving them more dependent on a smaller array of partners. As for suppliers, they find themselves under constant price pressure, with less slack or tolerance in the system. The suppliers' relationship with their customers is frequently less 'sticky' than it was in the past. There is the permanent risk of being substituted should problems – delays or quality concerns – arise. Supply chains, in other words, are both leaner and meaner than they used to be. And some observers suggest that this leaves many businesses exposed to much greater risks than perhaps they realize.

Source: By Stefan Stern, *Financial Times*, published 28 November 2006, (abridged version), reproduced with permission.

Question

Discuss the risks of operating in a global supply network.

Capacity Timing

An organization can adopt three main approaches to ensuring the correct amount of capacity is available at the right time to meet future plans. Three approaches of lead capacity, match capacity and lag capacity are outlined.

Lead Capacity

The first option is to obtain extra capacity above forecast demand – **lead capacity** – and so maintain a capacity 'cushion' to try to ensure capacity is sufficient if demand increases above forecast. This has the advantage of helping to maintain high levels of customer service and responding quickly to increases in customer demand, but has the disadvantage of the cost of maintaining the capacity cushion for all the different types of capacity (people, equipment, locations) required over time. An advantage of using a capacity cushion is that the cushion can be allocated to different products and services over time as the nature of demand fluctuates, although this is limited by specialization of resource, for example only certain trained people can do certain tasks.

A number of factors will impact on deciding the nature of the capacity cushion in a lead capacity strategy. The size of the cushion will be a trade-off between the costs of too much capacity in terms of unused resources against the costs of too little capacity in terms of using options such as overtime and outsourcing to meet customer demands, or losing customer orders through an inability to supply them quickly enough. The capacity cushion decision should also take into consideration the strategic context. For example, a new product or service in its growth phase may require a large capacity cushion to maximize customers, whereas for a product or service in the mature or decline stage of its lifecycle a smaller cushion may be more appropriate.

Match Capacity

The second option is to **match capacity** – simply obtain capacity to match forecasted demand. The advantage of this option is that it avoids the costs of a capacity cushion and the use of strategies such as outsourcing may be used to quickly fill capacity shortfalls. The disadvantage is the difficulty of forecasting future demand accurately enough in order that capacity can be obtained at the right time (not too early or too late) to meet that demand. Long project lead times for investments in capacity such as infrastructure projects means demand forecasts have to project further into the future and so are prone to greater error.

Lag Capacity

The third option is to only add capacity when extra demand is present that would use the additional resources (**lag capacity**). This has the advantage of delaying investments until it is certain they are needed and ensures a high utilization of capacity acquired. However, this option may mean customers are lost as they move to competitor products and services before the additional capacity has been acquired. There may also be a loss of flexibility as a consequence of the continual high utilization of resources using this strategy.

Timing the Capacity Increments

When undertaking a lead capacity or match capacity approach it is unlikely that the capacity cushion can be adjusted or the capacity matched smoothly, but adjustments will be made in increments (for example the purchase of new equipment or hiring of new staff). Thus there is a need to determine the timing of capacity increments.

In a lag capacity strategy the acquisition of new capacity is triggered by an increase in demand. One aspect of this strategy is that competitors also following a lag strategy will increase their capacity simultaneously, which may lead to an increase in the cost of capacity. This behaviour may also lead to overcapacity in the market, increasing competitive pressures. Organizations following a lead or match capacity strategy may avoid these problems by adding capacity when demand is low (at the low point of the business cycle). This strategy can reduce costs but carries the obvious risk that the demand planned for may not materialize.

An alternative approach is to build capacity, not simply for relatively short-term fluctuations in demand, but to a strategy of increasing market share over the long term. Again this approach is risky in the sense that it is not following a forecasted demand pattern. In order to reduce risk some organizations use the fact that their performance in the market is relative to the performance of their competitors. Thus capacity is added in response to the capacity expansion of the market leader. Whether it transpires that the capacity is needed or not, the relative position of the organization in respect to its competitors remains the same. These approaches have the disadvantage of being essentially reactive (either to demand or competitors) and do not take into account how capacity expansion can be used in a proactive manner as part of an operations strategy.

A number of companies have grown rapidly (for example Wal-Mart, easyJet) by continually adding new capacity and lowering costs in an attempt to freeze competitors out of the market. Retailing is an industry where quick expansion into geographical locations can freeze competitors out of these geographical locations that can only support a single retail outlet of a certain type. In some cases it may form part of the business strategy to build overcapacity to secure a locational presence or provide a higher level of performance of an objective such as delivery speed.

FACILITY LOCATION

There are three main reasons why a facility location decision is required. The first reason is that a new business has been created and requires facilities in order to manufacture its product or service its customers. The second reason is that there is a decision to relocate an existing business due to factors such as the need for larger premises or to be nearer a customer base. The third reason

Facility location
The geographical location of capacity supplied by the organization.

is to expand into new premises as part of a growth strategy. For each of these scenarios the facility location decision can be considered in terms of its effect on costs and customer service quality. Due to globalization the facility location decision made by an increasing number of manufacturing and service organizations means considering the option of locating their facilities outside their country of origin.

A company's competitiveness will be affected by its location, as the choice of location will impact on costs for elements such as transportation and labour. A location decision is costly and time consuming to change. The costs include the purchase of land and construction of buildings. An organization may be located inappropriately due to a previous poor location decision and an unwillingness to face the costs of a subsequent relocation. A change in input costs, such as materials or labour, may also lead to a need to change location.

The cost of establishing a new service facility may be relatively low compared to a manufacturing plant with its associated equipment. Service facilities also generally need to be in close contact with their customers. This has led to multiple service outlets being established in locations which serve a target market. Whereas manufacturing sites will often be located to minimize costs, services will be located to maximize income from customers. However, for services that process information, rather than customers, then telecommunications technology can be used to provide a service from a centralized facility.

The location decision can be considered in terms of factors that vary in such a way as to influence cost as location varies (supply-side factors) and factors that vary in such a way as to influence customer service as location varies (demand-side factors). The location decision can be seen as a trade-off between these factors. In service organizations a need for customer contact may mean that demand-side influences will dominate while in a manufacturing company labour and distribution costs may mean supply-side influences dominate.

Supply-side influences
When the location decision is considered in terms of factors that vary in such a way as to influence cost as location varies.

Supply-Side Influences

Distribution Costs

Distribution and transportation costs can be considerable, especially for a manufacturing organization that deals in tangible products. The sheer volume of the raw material involved in operations such as steel production means that a location decision will tend to favour areas near to raw materials. A manufacturer and seller of custom-built furniture, however, will need to be near potential customers. For service companies such as supermarkets and restaurants the need to be in a market-oriented location means that the cost of transportation of goods will not be a major factor in the location decision. However, many service organizations require distribution of stock from warehouses whose location should be considered carefully (Chapter 15).

Distribution across country borders means that a whole series of additional costs and delays must be taken into account, including import duties and delays in moving freight between different transportation methods (such as by air, rail, truck, sea). A site near to an airport or a rail link to an airport may be an important factor if delivery speed is important.

Labour Costs

Labour costs have generally become less important as the proportion of direct labour cost in high-volume manufacturing has fallen. What is becoming more important is the skills and flexibility of the labour force to adapt to new working methods and to engage in continuous improvement efforts. The wage rate of labour can be a factor in location decisions, especially when the service can be provided easily in alternative locations. Information technology companies involved in data entry can locate in alternative countries without the customer being aware.

Energy Costs

Some manufacturing companies use large amounts of power to operate production processes. Thus energy costs and the availability of enough energy to meet forecast demand can be important factors in the location decision.

Site and Construction Costs

Both the cost of the land and the cost of purchasing materials and building a facility are directly related to the location decision. These costs should be considered together as relatively low cost land may require substantial preparation to make it suitable for building development.

Intangible Factors

There are also a number of factors that are not financial but may have an effect on the location decision. These include the potential for objections to development on environmental grounds, local regulations regarding business developments and the necessary quality of life in the area needed to attract skilled employees.

Demand-Side Influences

The various demand-side influences are listed below.

Demand-side influences
When the location decision is considered in terms of factors that vary in such a way as to influence customer service as location varies.

Labour Skills

The need for a pool of skilled labour is becoming increasingly important. However, it may be possible in some instances to use skilled labour from a remote location, for example the use of computer programmers in India for American software companies.

Location Image

Retail outlets in particular will wish to locate in an area which 'fits' with the image they are trying to project. Often shopping districts will be associated with a particular type of retail outlet, such as designer clothing.

Customer Convenience

For many service organizations in particular, the location of the facility must be convenient for the potential customer. This can range from restaurants where customers may be prepared to travel a short distance, to hospitals where the speed of response is vital to the service. The physical link between customer and service provider can be in either direction. For example household goods such as gas ovens and central heating boilers will be serviced by staff at the customer's home.

CASE STUDY   5.3

Moving Textile Manufacturing Overseas

Due to global competitive pressures many garment manufacturers have scaled down or closed their operations in the UK and moved overseas. Production has increased in such areas as Asia due to lower labour costs in what is a labour-intensive industry. A textile manufacturer based in Leicester, UK produces a range of cotton and lycra textile mixes, which are used for garments such as t-shirts and women's tights. It has decided to supplement its UK operations and locate a textile production facility in Sri Lanka.

The move will permit the design of a more efficient layout in a purpose-built factory, as opposed to the current facilities, which are placed across a number of locations and buildings within the UK. An important part of the layout planning activity is the estimation of the quantity of work-in-progress inventory within the proposed facility. The estimation of inventory levels is critical because the relative bulk of inventory means the amount of floor-space required could be considerable. The need to sink drainage channels for effluent from the knit and dye machines and the size and weight of the machinery involved mean that it would be expensive and time-consuming to change the factory layout after construction.

Questions

1. Discuss the supply-side and demand-side influences on the facility location decision described in the case study.

2. Describe how the technique of business process simulation (Chapter 8) could help in the design of the new factory layout.

LOCATION SELECTION TECHNIQUES

The location selection process consists of identifying a suitable region/country, identifying an appropriate area within that region and finally comparing and selecting a suitable site from that area. A number of techniques for location selection are now described.

Weighted Scoring

In most situations cost will not be the only criterion for a location decision. Weighted scoring attempts to take a range of considerations into account. Weighted scoring, also referred to as factor rating or point rating, provides a rational basis for evaluation of alternative locations by establishing a composite value for each alternative. The ratings include factors based on qualitative as well as quantitative factors. The procedure consists of determining a list of factors that are relevant to the location decision. This may include such factors as convenience to customers, labour skills and transportation facilities. Each factor is then given a weighting that indicates its relative importance compared to the other factors. Each location is then scored on each factor and this score is multiplied by the factor value. The alternative with the highest score is then chosen. The usefulness of the method is dependent on identifying the appropriate location factors and devising a suitable weighting for each. One approach is to use the method to assess the intangible factors (such as quality of life) only and then determine if the difference between the intangible scores is worth the cost of the difference in tangible costs between the locations.

> **Weighted scoring**
> The procedure consists of determining a list of factors that are relevant to the location decision. Each factor is then given a weighting that indicates its relative importance compared to the other factors. Each location is then scored on each factor and this score is multiplied by the factor value. The alternative with the highest score is then chosen.

WORKED EXAMPLE 5.1
Weighted Scoring

New Technologies Ltd is an organization that specializes in simulation modelling consultancy. It has identified three sites on the west coast of the USA that have approximately equal initial and operating costs. The sites have been evaluated on a score of 1 to 10 (10 being best) against the following criteria and weighting assigned by management.

		City		
	Weight	Los Angeles	Portland	Seattle
Pool of skilled system modellers	0.5	6	4	5
University research in modelling	0.3	3	5	3
Recreational and cultural activities	0.2	5	3	4

Rank the three cities in order of their total weighted points score.

SOLUTION

Los Angeles $= (6 \times 0.5) + (3 \times 0.3) + (5 \times 0.2) = 4.9$

Seattle $= (5 \times 0.5) + (3 \times 0.3) + (4 \times 0.2) = 4.2$

Portland $= (4 \times 0.5) + (5 \times 0.3) + (3 \times 0.2) = 4.1$

The Centre of Gravity Method

The centre of gravity method
This can be used to determine the location of a distribution centre by minimizing distribution costs. The relative coordinates of the distribution points are placed on a map and the location of the distribution point should be at the centre of gravity of the coordinates.

The centre of gravity method can be used to determine the location of a distribution centre by minimizing distribution costs. In services when locating a retail outlet the gravity method can be used to maximize profit (Fitzsimmons and Fitzsimmons, 2008). The method assumes distribution costs change in a linear fashion with the distance and the quantity transported. The method also assumes the quantity transported is fixed for the duration of the journey. The relative coordinates of the distribution points are placed on a map and the location of the distribution point should be at the centre of gravity of the coordinates. To find this point the averages of the x co-ordinates and y co-ordinates are found using the following equations:

$$\bar{x} = \frac{\Sigma x_i Q_i}{\Sigma Q_i}$$

$$\bar{y} = \frac{\Sigma y_i Q_i}{\Sigma Q_i}$$

where

Q_i = quantity to be transported to destination i

x_i = x coordinate of destination i

y_i = y coordinate of destination i

x = x coordinate of centre of gravity

y = y coordinate of centre of gravity.

WORKED EXAMPLE 5.2
Centre of Gravity Method

A manufacturing organization wishes to build a centralized warehouse system that will serve a number of production facilities in Germany. The expected demand and relative grid references for the facility are given below.

Location	Demand (units/year)	Relative grid reference
Hamburg	40 000	(3,7)
Cologne	20 000	(1,4)
Stuttgart	35 000	(3,2)
Munich	70 000	(4,1)
Dresden	45 000	(6,5)
Berlin	110 000	(5,6)

At what location, in terms of grid reference, should the warehouse be situated?

SOLUTION

$$\bar{x} = \frac{(3 \times 40000)+(1 \times 20000)+(3 \times 35000)+(4 \times 70000)+(6 \times 45000)+(5 \times 110000)}{40000+20000+35000+70000+45000+110000}$$

$$\bar{y} = \frac{(7 \times 40000)+(4 \times 20000)+(2 \times 35000)+(1 \times 70000)+(5 \times 45000)+(6 \times 110000)}{40000+20000+35000+70000+45000+110000}$$

$$\bar{x} = 4.2$$

$$\bar{y} = 4.3$$

Locational Cost-Volume Analysis

Locational cost-volume analysis will indicate when a particular location is superior for a particular volume level by analysing the mix of fixed and variable costs. Some costs such as the costs of building the facility will be fixed, while others such as the level of demand will vary with the location. The relationship between both of these factors will vary for each location being considered. The procedure for graphical cost-volume analysis is as follows:

1. Determine the fixed and variable costs for each location.
2. Plot the total cost (fixed plus variable) lines for the location alternatives on the graph (Figure 5.3).
3. Choose the location with the lowest total cost line at the expected volume level.

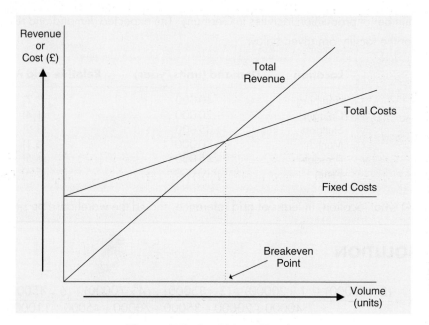

Figure 5.3: Cost-Volume Graph.

The equation for expressing costs in terms of location is:

$$TC = VC \times X + FC$$

where

 TC = total cost

 VC = variable cost per unit

 X = number of units produced

 FC = fixed costs

WORKED EXAMPLE 5.3
Locational Cost-Volume Analysis

A manufacturing organization is considering the following locations for its plant.

	Barcelona	Madrid
Variable costs	£1.75/unit	£1.25/unit
Annual fixed costs	200 000	180 000
Initial fixed costs	1 400 000	1 600 000

(a) Draw a cost-volume graph for both locations over a five-year period at a volume of 200 000 units per year.

(b) Which location has the lowest cost?

(c) At what volume do the locations have equal costs?

SOLUTION

Cost at year 0

Barcelona = 1 400 000

Madrid = 1 600 000

Cost at year 5

Barcelona = $1\,400\,000 + (5 \times 200{,}000) + (5 \times 200{,}000 \times 1.75) = £4\,150\,000$.

Madrid = $1\,600\,000 + (5 \times 180{,}000) + (5 \times 200{,}000 \times 1.25) = £3\,750\,000$.

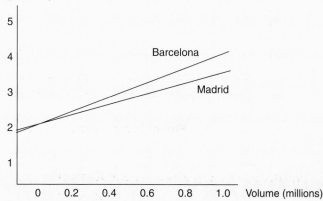

(a) From the graph Madrid has the lowest costs after 5 years.

(b) If X equals the number of years until costs are equal.

Using subscript B for Barcelona and M for Madrid.

$$TC_B = TC_M$$

$$1\,400\,000 + 200\,000X + (200\,000 \times 1.75)X = 1\,600\,000 + 180\,000X$$
$$+ (200\,000 \times 1.25)X$$
$$1\,600\,000 - 1\,400\,000 + 180\,000X - 200\,000X + 250\,000X - 350\,000X = 0$$
$$200\,000 - 120\,000X = 0$$

$$X = 200\,000/120\,000$$
$$= 1.6 \text{ years}$$

This method has assumed that fixed costs are constant for the volume range when in fact step changes may occur in fixed cost expenditure to meet certain volume levels. Variable costs are also assumed to have a linear (straight-line) relationship with volume, when this may not be so. Some cost-volume models may incorporate a nonlinear (curved) relationship. Another assumption is that output of the facility has also been aggregated into one product that may not reflect the complexity of how a mix of products affects costs over a range of volumes.

If the analysis includes the economics of the logistics activity for a range of volumes then it is possible to review make-or-buy issues and thus the mix between inhouse and the subcontracting of components. Again the decision will concern the relationship between fixed and variable costs through the product life cycle. The relationship between fixed and total costs, termed the operational gearing, is important in determining if production should be initiated and when it should cease. The operation with low fixed costs, and thus low operational gearing will have more flexibility in responding to changes in market demand over time. In other words if fixed costs are low the company does not require high volumes to break even and can thus reduce output to match demand more easily. A high-volume producer, however, invests in specialized equipment and thus increases operational gearing in order to reduce unit costs and thus create greater profit potential. An increase in volume for a high-volume producer will thereby only add a small amount of unit variable costs. This approach means the high-volume producer will prefer to operate as close to capacity limits as possible to maximize profit.

SUMMARY

- Supply network design concerns the relationship of the organization with its suppliers of capacity.

- Economies of scale refers to the characteristic that, as a facility is expanded and fixed costs remain the same, the average cost of producing each unit will fall.

- Economies of scope are created by the ability to produce many products in one highly flexible facility more cheaply than in separate facilities.

- A lead capacity strategy maintains a capacity cushion (extra capacity above forecast demand) in order to ensure sufficient capacity if demand increases. A match capacity strategy aims to obtain capacity to match forecast demand. A lag capacity strategy is to acquire additional capacity when extra demand is present.

- Facility location factors can be considered as influencing cost as location varies (supply-side factors) and influencing customer service as location varies (demand-side factors).

- Location selection techniques include the weighted scoring method, which attempts to take a range of considerations into account when choosing a location. The centre of gravity method determines location by minimizing distribution costs (or maximizing profits for a retail outlet). Locational cost-volume analysis indicates which location is suitable for a particular volume level by analysing the mix of fixed and variable costs.

CASE STUDY 5.4

Mom-and-Pop Companies Face Struggle for Survival

In 1999, Kachio Okuda left his job at a Tokyo printing company to set up his own small printing business. By 2000, he says, he was already regretting the move. 'As soon as a big company bids for a contract, the price plummets and we can't match it,' the 55-year-old entrepreneur says. 'More and more, we're living in a different world from the big firms.' Regrets aside, Mr Okuda has kept his 12-employee operation running for the past eight years. Many other small business owners are not so fortunate. Although bankruptcies declined from 19 000 in 2002 to 13 000 cases in 2006, the number of small firms has continued to fall steadily. 'These are family-run companies. They don't go bankrupt, they just close up shop,' Mr Okuda says.

Seven in 10 working Japanese are employed at small and medium-sized enterprises (SMEs), defined as having fewer than 50–300 workers, depending on the industry. In the US the ratio is five in 10, even though the small-business category there includes bigger companies. Toyota, Sony and other big exporters may carry Japan's flag abroad, but it is the vast pyramid of small suppliers on which they stand that gives the economy its muscle. Mr Okuda's 'different world' lament is supported by earnings data. Small firms' recurring profits grew an average of 2.4 percentage points more slowly in 2005 than those at big companies. In the 1990s the gap was a percentage point smaller.

Pessimism is widespread. Quarterly sentiment surveys by the Bank of Japan show that while business confidence has improved with Japan's five-year economic expansion, as a whole, managers of small businesses remain downbeat. This year they expect to cut capital investment by an average of 10.5 per cent, even as big companies spend almost 9 per cent more. Concerns about the plight of small businesses are tied to broader worries about social and economic inequality, which has increased slightly during the expansion. Promises of more small-business aid helped the opposition Democratic Party of Japan trounce the ruling Liberal Democrats in upper house elections in July.

A core problem for small companies has been their inability to pass on rising costs to their customers. 'The pattern we see is a high break-even point that makes it difficult for small and medium companies to absorb growth in costs such as raw materials and labour,' says Tetsufumi Yamakawa, senior economist at Goldman Sachs. In the auto industry, parts makers have groaned as Toyota and Nissan have pushed through aggressive cost-cutting programmes centred on rationalizing their supply lines and introducing more competition to procurement. Both auto giants are renowned for their ability to keep margins high by squeezing suppliers.

Every small business must contend with an inherent lack of economies of scale. In Japan, that handicap is being felt more keenly amid a general 'sizing up' of the economy, as big companies get bigger due to deregulation and a wave of mergers and acquisitions. In the retail sector, small shops that once dominated distribution of everything from televisions to bananas have been hurt by a relaxation of size restrictions. This has opened the way for large suburban shopping centres and 'big box' stores of the kind pioneered in the US.

'At first, supermarket-sized electronics stores took customers from the Mom-and-Pop dealers,' says a manager at a major electronics chain. 'Then, when the size limits went up again, we took over with huge outlets at the edge of town.'

As a result of this general bloating, sales at retailers with less than 500 m^2 of shop space shrank by a quarter between 1997 and 2004, accounting for the entire drop in Japanese retail sales during the period. Mr Okuda says his printing company could compete with bigger rivals if only banks would lend him enough cash to grow. 'Banks won't tell you "no" straight out, but the conditions they impose amount to the same thing,' he says. 'They don't understand small business.' Lenders remain cautious after writing off a mountain of bad loans to big and small companies alike over the last decade. Outstanding loans to small businesses fell to a low of Y245,000 billion in 2005 from about Y340,000 billion in 1998, although the total has picked up slightly in the last two years.

The higher margins associated with small-business loans mean big banks such as

Tokyo-Mitsubishi UFJ, Mizuho and Sumitomo Mitsui are in fact keen to offer credit, says Naoko Nemoto, analyst at Standard & Poor's. But they 'have no clear strategy for penetrating this market'. Small branch networks relative to their financial clout and a lack of staff trained to assess small companies' books have constrained the banks' ability to lend. Many small business owners want more help from the government, which already offers a range of support programmes. The Ministry of Economy, Trade and Industry's 2007 White Paper on small business includes 15 chapters on aid schemes, from preferential lending and tax breaks to help for ageing small business owners who are trying to recruit successors.

In truth, 'scaling up' the economy has brought gains for Japan as a whole, in the form of greater efficiency and productivity, economists say. That means government intervention is likely to focus on easing the growing pains rather than bringing back old restrictions. Mr Okuda appears resigned. 'It's the destiny of capitalism, I guess. But it doesn't leave you much room to enjoy what you're doing.'

Source: Jonathan Soble, *Financial Times*, 19 October 2007. Reproduced with permission.

Question

How can small companies try to overcome competition from large competitors with greater economies of scale?

EXERCISES

1. Outline how a strategy of globalization will impact on a policy of pursuing economies of scale advantages.

2. Evaluate the strategies of lead capacity, match capacity and lag capacity for a retail outlet.

3. Discuss the location decision of an organization with which you are familiar in terms of supply-side influences and demand-side influences.

4. A manufacturing organization is looking at the following two locations:

	Birmingham	Manchester
Variable costs	£14/unit	£16/unit
Annual fixed costs	£12 000 000	£15 000 000
Initial fixed costs	£165 000 000	£145 000 000

a) Draw a cost-volume graph for both locations over a 10-year period at a volume of 750,000 units per year.

b) Which location has the lowest cost at the end of the 10-year period?

c) At what volume do these locations have equal costs?

5. The following table lists the weightings representing the relative importance of factors for the location of a retail site. Four potential sites have been given a score out of 100 for each factor:

		Site			
Factor	**Weight**	**A**	**B**	**C**	**D**
Construction cost	0.1	90	60	80	70
Operating cost	0.1	90	80	90	85
Population density	0.4	70	90	80	75
Convenient access	0.2	75	80	90	90
Parking area	0.2	60	70	85	75

Rank the four sites in order of their total weighted points score for suitability for the proposed location.

6. A retail chain has four major stores in the East Midlands area which have the following monthly demand rates.

Store location	Monthly demand (units)
Derby	2000
Nottingham	1000
Leicester	1000
Sheffield	2000

The following map shows the relative coordinates of the four outlets.

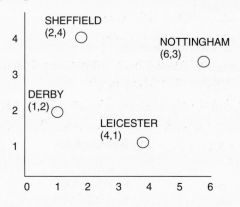

The organization has decided to find a 'central' location in which to build a warehouse. Find the coordinates of the centre that will minimize distribution costs.

7. A company has decided to relocate from three separate facilities: Plant A, Plant B and Plant C to a new facility: Plant D. Using the centre of gravity method determine the best location for Plant D to serve its customers using the facility locations and yearly demand shown below.

Facility	Location coordinates	Demand (per year)
A	(175, 280)	6000
B	(50, 200)	8200
C	(150, 75)	7000

8. The following provides the specification for a line process.

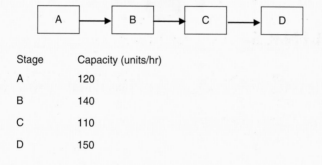

Stage	Capacity (units/hr)
A	120
B	140
C	110
D	150

a) What is the total system capacity?

b) Which stage is the bottleneck?

c) What is the level that system capacity can be increased to by increasing the bottleneck capacity only?

d) Calculate the current cycle efficiency.

e) Calculate the cycle efficiency when the bottleneck capacity is increased as in c).

WEB EXERCISE

Read the article at http://www.guardian.co.uk/business/2008/jun/
11/tesco.supermarkets (accessed 26 September 2008). How do
'economies of scale' in large organizations such as Tesco help protect it from
a business downturn?

FURTHER READING

Barnes, D. (2008) *Operations Management: An International Perspective,*
Thomson Learning.

Egelhoff, W.G. (1993) Great strategy or great strategy implementation – two ways
of competing in global markets. *Sloan Management Review,* Winter, 37–50.

Flaherty, M.T. (1996) *Global Operations Management,* McGraw-Hill.

Lei, D. and **Slocum, J.W.** (1992) Global strategy, competence building and strategic alliances. *California Management Review,* Fall, 81–97.

Mair, A. (1994) *Honda's Global Local Corporation,* Macmillan.

Schroeder, R.G. and **Flynn, B.B.** (2001) *High Performance Manufacturing:
Global Perspectives,* John Wiley & Sons, Inc.

WEB LINKS

www.bbc.co.uk/coventry/features/stories/2002/10/centre-of-england.
shtml (accessed 26 September 2008). BBC. How the BBC found the location of
the centre of England using the centre of gravity method!

www.bizhelp24.com/small_business/economies_of_scale.shtml (accessed 26
September 2008). BizHelp24. Outline of use of economies of scale for small
business.

www.ofcom.org.uk/static/archive/oftel/publications/about_oftel/
2002/smpg0802.htm (accessed 26 September 2008). Document 'Oftel's market
review guidelines: criteria for the assessment of significant market power.'
Contains definitions of economies of scope, economies of scale and vertical
integration.

REFERENCES

Fitzsimmons, J.A. and **Fitzsimmons, M.J.** (2008) *Service Management:
Operations, Strategy and Information Technology,* 6th edn, McGraw-Hill.

McGrath, M.E. and **Hoole, R.W.** (1992) Manufacturing's new economies of scale.
Harvard Business Review, May–June, 102–5.

Peters, T. (1994) *Liberation Management: Necessary Disorganization for the
Nanosecond Nineties,* Pan Books.

CHAPTER

6

Process Technology

LEARNING OBJECTIVES

- Explain the role of process technologies for materials processing

- Explain the role of information technology in the accumulation, organization and distribution of information

- Outline the distinguishing features of operational information systems and management information systems

- Define the terms e-Business and e-Commerce

- Discuss how technology can be used for customer processing in operations systems

INTRODUCTION

In Chapter 1 we defined the objective of an operations system as being to convert transformed resources from inputs into outputs in the form of goods and services. Transformed resources can be in the form of material, information and customers and this section will show the use of technology in the transformation of these resource categories. Technology is an important aspect of operations as it has led to a large growth in productivity in both manufacturing, where the emphasis is on technology for material and information transformation, and services, where the emphasis is on technology for information and customer transformations. In addition to the technologies described in this chapter, technologies relevant to operations are discussed throughout this text, including enterprise resource planning (ERP) (Chapter 14) and project-management software (Chapter 16).

PROCESS TECHNOLOGY FOR MATERIALS

There are many technological advances that are specific to a certain industrial sector (for example new material technologies used for construction). This section will describe some of the software systems and hardware technologies that have had a widespread impact on manufacturing firms in many industries.

Software Systems

Computer-aided design (CAD) is one of the most widespread technologies, used in even relatively small firms. A CAD system allows the designer to create drawings on a computer screen to assist in the visual design of a product or service (Figure 6.1). The

Computer-aided design
A CAD system allows the designer to create drawings on a computer screen to assist in the visual design of a product or service.

Figure 6.1: Computer-Aided Design Image.
Source: http://en.wikipedia.org/wiki/Image:UGS-NX-5-ActiveMockUp.JPG.

drawings can be viewed from any angle and drawings can be zoomed to allow inspection of a design in detail. Drawings are held in a database for future use and dissemination between designers and engineers across the company.

Computer-aided process planning (CAPP) extends CAD by transmitting a process plan of how parts will be manufactured to the machine tool. For example deciding on how individual pieces are to be cut from a sheet of metal. CAPP systems can also sequence parts through a number of process steps.

Computer-aided engineering (CAE) takes the drawings in a CAD system and subjects the designs to simulated tests. For example the behaviour of an engineering design for elements of a bridge can be observed under various amounts of stress. This allows various design options to be tested quickly and cheaply.

Computer-aided process planning
This transmits a process plan of how parts will be manufactured to a machine tool. It can also sequence parts through a number of process steps.

Computer-aided engineering
This takes the drawings in a CAD and subjects the designs to simulated tests.

CASE STUDY 6.1

Spencer Davis Engineering

Thanks to a carefully planned e-Business strategy, Spencer Davies Engineering has dramatically improved the efficiency of its production process and expanded the breadth of its offer.

Spencer Davies has introduced technology across the company, from a web site and customer database to CAD/CAM, an intranet and production control on the shop floor. Its strategy has been to balance bigger, structural investments in core functions – such as in CAD/CAM – with smaller applications that reduce employees' administrative burdens. The result of this approach is that each successive investment brings specific and cumulative benefits. For example, the original CAD/CAM investment improved the quality, speed and breadth of offer. When combined with email, which now accounts for 60% of client communications, designs can come directly from clients and go immediately to the shop floor, saving up to a week on every job. Handling the processes electronically makes them easier to review and the company can now hold less stock, ordering online from suppliers to secure the best deals.

The company intranet includes a research library, company documentation, job descriptions and a contact database of customers and suppliers. This has been integral in maintaining internal communications, giving staff the tools they need and improving customer service. Offsite engineers, meanwhile, are equipped with laptops, digital cameras and mobile phones so work can be budgeted, completed and approved on the spot. The company is also looking at integrating other aspects of its supply chain: it uses online procurement for office supplies and puts outsourcing enquiries on the Internet via engineering bulletin boards.

Spencer Davies's e-Business strategy has allowed it to expand while continuing to streamline its business. Its ICT investments have also produced greater auditing and management reporting facilities, giving the company the ability to evaluate future investments before committing financial resources. 'We've been able to quantify the benefits thanks to technology', says Owain Davies, Managing Director.

The time taken from design stage to the finished product has been dramatically reduced. Today, if the information is sent electronically by customers, the job can reach the production stage within 30 seconds. The company is now better equipped to tackle more complex engineering projects and consequently appeals to more potential customers. 'Our investment in technology has allowed us to develop the business and look at new markets', explains Owain.

The improvement in communications with suppliers has been due in large part to enthusiasm from Spencer Davies Engineering.

'Most of our suppliers are not eager to work electronically and that's a barrier', admits Owain. 'What I'm trying to do is show the benefits of technology and persuade them to come on board. Once they see the business benefits, we can usually win them over.'

In addition to the direct benefits of the company's investment in ICT, Owain has noticed some equally important but unexpected results. Spencer Davies's positive, forward-thinking attitude is producing a competitive advantage. 'We are getting some valuable customer referrals', explains Owain. 'Our use of technology gives them the confidence to recommend our services.' 'Technology has definitely allowed us to get more for our money. It's now easier for us to sell because of the information that we have.'

Source: DTI web site (now Department for Business, Enterprise and Regulatory Reform).

Question

What impact does the use of technology have on the competitive performance of Spencer Davies?

Computer numerically controlled machines (CNC)
These are machine tools that can be controlled by computer.

Robot
A programmable machine that can undertake tasks that may be dangerous, dirty or dull for people to carry out.

Hardware Technologies

Computer numerically controlled machines (CNC) are machine tools that can be controlled by computer. Machining centres (MC) are more complex technology and incorporate features such as the ability to carry tools that can be automatically changed depending on the requirements of the operation being undertaken.

A robot is a programmable machine that can undertake tasks that may be dangerous, dirty or dull for people to carry out. A robot may have an arm and end effector that are used to pick, hold and place items. Robots can generally undertake tasks quicker and more consistently than humans.

Automated material handling systems (AMH) are designed to improve efficiency in the movement, storage and retrieval of materials. Types of systems include *automated guided vehicle (AGV)* systems that transport material on driverless vehicles to various locations in the plant (Figure 6.2). *Automated storage and retrieval systems (AS/RS)* handle the storage and retrieval of materials using computers to direct automatic loaders to pick and place items in a storage facility.

Automated material handling systems
These are designed to improve efficiency in the movement, storage and retrieval of materials.

Figure 6.2: Laser-Guided AGV.
Source: http://en.wikipedia.org/wiki/Image:Unitload.jpg.

Flexible manufacturing cell (FMC) systems integrate individual items of automation described above to form an automated manufacturing system that can consist of two or more CNC machining centres, a robot and a cell computer that coordinates the various operations in the cell. The robot can be used to handle the parts that are being processed and also to perform tool-changing operations. The tool is the element of the CNC machine, for example the drill bit, which is

Flexible manufacturing cell
These are systems that integrate individual items of automation to form an automated manufacturing system.

used to process the part. The robot, under the direction of the cell computer, can sense when a tool needs changing either for processing requirements or if the tool is worn and needs replacing.

Flexible manufacturing systems (FMS) extend the facilities of an FMC by incorporating, in addition to several CNC machining centres and robots, automatic parts loading and unloading facilities and an automated guided vehicle system for parts movement. Flexible manufacturing systems held out the possibility of factories without people, where the robots and computers would perform all the material handling and processing tasks necessary. However, due to the complexities involved in producing a wide product range, fully automated plants have proved to be impractical. Flexibility (the production of a range of products at low cost that can be delivered quickly to customers) is a key strategic aim for operations. In terms of manufacturing this translates into the ability to perform rapid low cost switching from one product line to another. A flexible manufacturing system is designed to provide fast, low cost changes from one part to another, lower direct labour costs due to automation and achieve consistent and better quality due to automated control. However, the FMS machines may have a limited ability to adapt to changes in the product specification, a substantial amount of pre-planning is necessary before an FMS can be operated and the systems are very expensive in terms of capital investment. Due to these factors flexible manufacturing cells (FMC) are often used as an alternative due to their lower complexity and lower cost. Flexible manufacturing systems are most relevant to the production of items such as small batches of machined goods. Another option to achieve flexibility is to use the JIT philosophy of a flexible workforce and small simple machines.

Computer-Integrated Manufacture (CIM)

When the above technologies are integrated using a computer network and database system the resulting automated system is termed **computer-integrated manufacture (CIM)**. Whereas an FMS system is generally concerned with automation directly related to the transformation process, CIM is an automation of the product and process  design, planning and control and manufacture of the product. In a fully integrated system the areas of design, testing, fabrication, assembly, inspection and material handling are automated and integrated using technology. For example **computer-aided manufacturing (CAM)** extends the use of CAD by transmitting the design held in the CAD system electronically to computer controlled machine tools. Systems that

---

Flexible manufacturing systems
These extend the facilities of an FMC by incorporating automatic parts loading and unloading facilities and an automated guided vehicle system for parts movement.

Computer-integrated manufacture
This is the automation of the product and process design, planning and control and manufacture of the product.

Computer-aided manufacturing (CAM)
This extends the use of CAD by transmitting the design held in the CAD system electronically to computer controlled machine tools.

combine these two functions are often referred to as CADCAM. CADCAM systems represent a major tool for operations in linking the design and manufacturing processes.

PROCESS TECHNOLOGY FOR INFORMATION

Most organizations use some form of computer-based technology to accumulate, organize and distribute information. Most computers are now connected together in some form of network. A local area network (LAN) is usually limited to a company occupying a single building or even several buildings across a large company site. A small-scale network such as this allows people to share information, communicate via systems such as email and share facilities such as printing and software applications. A wide area network (WAN) may connect people across a city, country or between different countries. If the WAN enables communication across the whole company, it is referred to as the 'enterprise network' or 'enterprise-wide' network. To minimize the size of investment in wide area communications a company can use a value-added network (VAN) which is a network rented out by a service provider.

In the 1960s the use of electronic data interchange (EDI) became established (Chapter 15). This allows the exchange of structured information, such as orders, invoices, delivery advices and payment instructions, over a network. It permits, for example, the automatic reordering and payment for stock from a supplier without human intervention. The automated transfer of money between organizations is referred to as Electronic Funds Transfer (EFT). The most common platform for networked IT is the Internet, which is a global network of millions of connected networks that uses a transmission method called TCP/IP to communicate with one another. There is no global control over transmissions using this method – these are governed by the requester and sender of the information.

The majority of Internet services are available to any business or consumer who has access to the Internet. However, if information is limited to those within the organization it is termed an *intranet*. If access is extended to some others, but not everyone beyond the organization, this is an *extranet*. The World Wide Web (WWW) provides a standard method for exchanging and publishing information on the Internet. It provides a graphical environment with hyperlinks which allow users to readily move from one document or web site to another by selecting an image or text highlighted by underlining and/or a different colour.

> **Electronic data interchange**
> This allows the exchange of structured information, such as orders, invoices, delivery advices and payment instructions, over a network.

In order to understand how the information technology is applied, it is useful to outline some of the types of information systems that use information technology in manufacturing and service organizations. Operational information systems are generally concerned with process control, transaction processing communications and productivity. Management information systems are concerned with assisting decision-making activities. Other types of information systems considered are e-Business systems, m-business systems and customer relationship management systems.

Operational Information Systems

Operational systems are used for the tasks involved in the daily running of a business. Their performance is often vital to an organization and they are sometimes described as mission-critical or strategic information systems. We consider three types of operational systems:

- *Transaction processing systems (TPS).* These systems involve recording and processing data that results from an organization's business transactions. Applications include real-time (online) processing of balance enquiries in a cash-point system and batch processing of customer bills for utilities. Transaction processing systems are generally for frequent and routine transactions at an operational level in the organization. See Case Study 6.3 for an example of the use of transaction processing systems.
- *Office automation systems (OAS).* These are used to manage the administrative functions in an office environment and are often critical to service-based industries. They include Groupware, which assists teams of people working together through facilities such as email and teleconferencing within or between companies. *Workflow Management Systems* (WFMS) automate a business process by providing a structured framework to support the process. They can assign tasks to people, allow collaboration between people sharing tasks and retrieve information needed to complete a task, such as customer details. They can also provide an overview of the status of each task which can be used in conjunction with *document image processing (DIP)* to provide automated routing of documents across a computer network. Also concerned with the design of business processes, but at a higher level of abstraction is the technique for business process management (BPM) covered in Chapter 8.
- *Process control systems.* These include systems such as CAD, CAM and FMS which are important in manufacturing industries for controlling the manufacture of goods. These systems have been covered earlier in this chapter.

Management Information Systems

Management information systems can be defined as systems used to support tactical and strategic decision making. Three types of management information systems are:

- *Decision support systems (DSS).* These provide information and models in a form to facilitate tactical and strategic decision making. Types of DSS include *Expert Systems (ES)* to represent the knowledge and decision-making skills of specialists and *neural networks* which learn problem solving skills by exposure to a wide range of problems.
- *Information reporting systems (IRS).* These provide prespecified reports for day-to-day decision making. They include periodic reports such as weekly sales summary and exception reports triggered by events such as production levels falling below normal.
- *Executive information systems (EIS).* These provide senior managers with systems to analyse, compare and highlight trends to help govern the strategic direction of a company. *Data warehouses* are large database systems containing detailed company data on sales transactions, which are analysed to assist in improving the marketing and financial performance of companies. They have to a large extent displaced EIS in software purchases for strategic and tactical decision making. *Data marts* are small-scale data warehouses that hold departmental information. The term *data mining* of data warehouses is used to refer to an attempt to identify relationships between variables in order to assist decision making.

E-Business
This can be seen as the transformation of business processes through the use of Internet technologies.

E-Business

E-Business can be seen as the transformation of business processes through the use of Internet technologies.

In general, e-Business is concerned with making day-to-day business activities more efficient by improving information exchanges within the organization and between the organization and its partners. E-Business opportunities can be classified in terms of whether an organization is using the Internet to transact with consumers, called **business-to-consumer (B2C)** or other businesses, called **business-to-business (B2B)**. Business-to-business transactions predominate over the Internet in terms of value if not frequency. This is explained by the fact that there are many more opportunities for B2B transactions than B2C, both between an organization and its suppliers, together with intermediaries, and through distributors such as

Business-to-consumer
Web-based commercial transactions between an organization and consumers.

Business-to-business
Web-based commercial transactions between an organization and other organizations.

agents and wholesalers with customers. Moreover, there is a higher level of access to the Internet among businesses than among consumers and a greater propensity to use it for purchasing.

There are two additional types of transaction: where consumers transact directly with consumers (C2C) and where they initiate trading with business (C2B). Note that the terms C2C and C2B are less widely used but they do highlight significant differences between Internet-based commerce and earlier forms of commerce. Consumer-to-consumer interactions were relatively rare but are now very common in the form of online auctions and communities. As well as the models described it has been suggested that employees should be considered as a separate type of interaction through the use of intranets (internal Internet-based networks) – this is sometimes referred to as employee-to-employee or E2E.

The benefit to business of adopting e-Business is a mix of cost reduction achieved through lower costs of information transfer and processing and the potential for increased revenue arising from increased reach to a larger audience. The benefits of e-Business for operations relate to areas such as supply chain integration using B2B and B2C interactions as well as the increased efficiency and effectiveness of internal business processes using E2E interactions. For an example of an e-Business system see the description of e-procurement in Chapter 15.

E-Commerce

Electronic commerce (e-Commerce) is often thought to simply refer to buying and selling using the Internet: people immediately think of consumer retail purchases from companies such as Amazon. However, e-Commerce involves much more than electronically mediated financial transactions between organizations and customers. Many commentators refer to e-Commerce as *all* electronically mediated transactions between an organization and any third party it deals with. By this definition, non-financial transactions such as customer requests for further information would also be considered to be part of e-Commerce. When evaluating the impact of e-Commerce on an organization, it is instructive to identify opportunities for buy-side and sell-side e-Commerce transactions as depicted in Figure 6.3, since business information systems with different functionality will need to be created to accommodate transactions with buyers and suppliers. Buy-side e-Commerce refers to transactions to procure resources needed by an organization from its suppliers. Sell-side e-Commerce refers to transactions involved with selling products to an organization's customers.

In addition to buy-side and sell-side transactions, Figure 6.3 also shows the internal (or inside) processes that are part of e-Business. They include transactions

Electronic commerce
All electronically mediated information exchanges between an organization and its external stakeholders.

Buy-side e-Commerce
E-commerce transactions between a purchasing organization and its suppliers.

Sell-side e-Commerce
E-commerce transactions between a supplier organization and its customers.

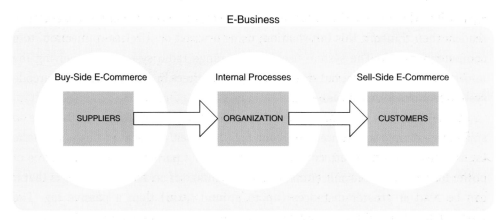

Figure 6.3: Buy-Side and Sell-Side E-Commerce.

related to the buy-side such as procurement and sell-side-related transactions such as dealing with customer enquiries as well as basic administrative functions related to employee leave and pay.

M-business

M-business can be defined as the integration of Internet and wireless communications technology. It is a result of mobile communications facilitated by broadband (high bandwidth) Internet connections and wireless technology (for example mobile phones using radio waves). Mobile computing allows people choice in how they communicate by offering multiple devices, applications and tools from which to select and it permits people to control the time and frequency with which they obtain information. Some of the applications for m-business include:

> **M-business**
> The integration of Internet and wireless communications technology.

- Procurement. The extension of e-procurement applications to enable orders to be taken using handheld devices (such as barcode readers and radio frequency identification devices).
- Order fulfilment and delivery management. Delivery information is input using a tablet and the customer can track their order immediately over the Internet.
- Asset tracking. The monitoring of materials internally will extend to the monitoring of highly mobile geographically dispersed assets.
- Service management. Service requests can be automatically dispatched to field personnel to ensure timely response and efficient scheduling.

Radio frequency identification (RFID) systems consist of a tag that can be attached to an item. The tag contains a microchip, which contains information about the item; its location is transmitted on request using radio signals to an RFID reader. The RFID readers then transmit this information, using a wired or wireless connection, to a computer network. The system uses a short-range radio system for receiving the information from the tag but does not require a direct line of sight that a barcode system requires for example.

Most RFID tags are 'passive' and do not contain a power source as they are so small (for example see Figure 6.4). Some tags, however, are 'active'; this is when the tag is equipped with a battery that can be used as a partial or complete source of power for the tag's electronic circuitry. The advantage of an active RFID tag is that it can be read at greater distances (up to around 30 m) than a passive tag. The disadvantage of the active tag is that because it cannot function without battery power it has a limited lifetime until the battery requires changing and it is typically more costly to buy.

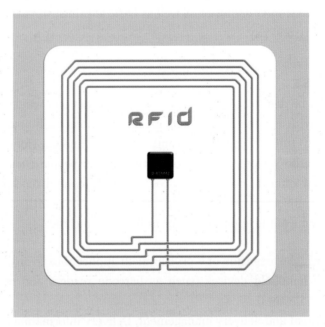

Figure 6.4: RFID Chip.

Radio frequency identification tags have many useful applications including keeping track of hold luggage on flights, tracking containers at sea ports, tracking inventory in the supply chain and tracking employees at work. More controversial applications include the use of RFID embedded in bank notes so that banks can instantly count large amounts of cash and even embedded tags under the skin of a child so they can be tracked if they get lost. The characteristic of RFID tags that causes concern is that they will continue to look for and respond to RFID readers even when their official use has been completed. Moreover RFID readers are freely available. This could mean someone being able to know how much cash you are carrying or tracking your movements by RFID tags embedded in your body or clothes without your knowledge.

CASE STUDY   6.2

Kennedys

With three international offices, seven associate offices and six different locations throughout the UK, supporting the mobility of key staff was an important consideration for Kennedys, a UK litigation firm.

Kennedys wanted to provide its employees with a way to access their work systems, for example their calendars, contacts and email inboxes, while on the move. The company decided a system whereby staff had remote access to its network would improve efficiency throughout the company and enable flexible working, vital in a business where staff are constantly 'in the field' and not necessarily working to strict office hours. The high-pressure world of litigation means that lawyers need regular access to their work systems to stay on top of their diaries and to manage 'time management' issues while outside the office.

Following a consultation on the company's communications services, Kennedys invested in BlackBerry devices – handheld devices for sending and receiving emails and accessing office features, like contacts and the corporate calendar, on the move. BlackBerry is a more advanced step from traditional personal digital assistants and also allows full access to the Internet. All data sent and received are fully encrypted. The device is made available to any employees who want to use it – to date 70 Kennedys partners have taken up the initiative, while the company claims to be one of the first businesses to take up this new technology.

Kennedys now has plans to roll out the device to a total of up to 200 employees. Kennedys' Carolyn Lees says BlackBerry has provided fast Internet access on the move, the ability to set up 'virtual private networks', which allow out-of-office access, making working practices far more efficient. Lees says: 'We can quantify the improvements only in terms of how much more productivity we see and the great accessibility to our work systems that we all now have.' She adds that the 'immediacy' of electronic communications is a key benefit of the new system, while accessibility to programmes across the Web has been improved greatly.

Key issues at Kennedys have been with educating users about the new systems. The speed of change, says Lees, means that users are often left behind and it is thus vital to train employees and other users such as suppliers effectively so that the new technologies can be exploited effectively. Initial increased complexity presents problems but the new technologies are designed to reduce complexity in terms of working practices. Training, she says, is the key. She says: 'People skills are still the key to success.' Also, Lees says, it is vital to build in contingency plans to cope with problems that may arise, adding that she has used IT publications and online forums on the Web to keep herself updated on the latest ICTs, while Kennedys relies on consultancy help on new technology projects.

While, Kennedys looks to enable more and more of its employees with the new BlackBerry devices, it continues to develop an ICT strategy 'geared towards retaining and acquiring new clients'. Overall, Lees says it intends 'to continue to remain competitive with our ICTs and to improve business efficiencies.'

Source: DTI web site (now Department for Business, Enterprise and Regulatory Reform).

Question

How does the use of the BlackBerry device help the effectiveness of the service Kennedys provides?

Customer Relationship Management (CRM)

Customer relationship management
These systems are designed to integrate the range of information systems that contain information regarding the customer.

Customer relationship management covers the whole process by which relationships with customers are built and maintained. Customer relationship management systems are designed to integrate the range of information systems that contain information regarding the customer. These include applications such as customer details and preference databases, sales order processing applications and sales force automation. The idea is to acquire customers, retain customers and increase customer involvement with the organization.

Customer relationship management systems are built around a database and when this database is accessed, by employees and customers, using a web site the technology is often referred to as eCRM. Common applications that would be integrated in a CRM system include:

- *Customer data collection.* This can include personal details such as age, sex and contact address. Also a record of purchase transactions undertaken in terms of factors such as location, date, time, quantity and price. This information can be used by call-centre staff to improve and tailor their services to individual customers.
- *Customer data analysis.* The captured data allows the categorization and targeting of customers according to criteria set by the firm. This information can be used to improve the effectiveness of marketing campaigns.
- *Sales force automation.* The entire sales cycle from lead generation to close of sale and after-sales service can be facilitated using CRM.

The technology must support all of these applications through whatever communications channel the customer and employee use. Communication channels include face-to-face, mail, phone, email as well as Web-based interaction. As with other technologies the implementation of CRM is a choice between attempting to integrate a number of legacy (existing) systems such as sales order processing or choosing a single-vendor supplier such as for ERP. Single-vendor systems from suppliers such as SAP and Oracle are able to provide better integration and thus potentially better customer service. However, they are relatively expensive to install and one firm is unlikely to supply the best-in-class applications in all aspects of the CRM implementation.

CASE STUDY   6.3

The Everyman Theatre

The Everyman Theatre developed a CRM system to maximize the marketing potential of the customer information it was receiving through its online ticketing system. It built a Web service programme that runs constantly, interrogating new bookings to retrieve specific information such as the person's email address, whether the tickets were bought as a result of a specific promotion, etc. This information is moved over to the marketing database, which continues to grow as more relevant information is added. The programme also builds a list of everyone who visited a show the previous evening. These customers are automatically emailed, thanked for their visit and invited to click on a link that takes them to the web site to fill in a survey on their experience at the theatre.

Source: DTI web site (now Department for Business, Enterprise and Regulatory Reform).

Question

What benefits does the Everyman Theatre gain from the use of their CRM system?

CASE STUDY   6.4

How to Click with your Customers

In the past ten years, customer relationship management, or CRM as it is known, has attained near mythical status within organizations. Some of the most successful companies in the world have built their operations around the notion that an ability to understand and deal directly with their customers helps to reduce costs and improve sales, but. most importantly in an age of radical competition, actually increases loyalty and profitability by providing a more personalized and responsive service. The model on which this virtuous circle relies is the notion that every transaction with an organization should improve your next experience. The world's greatest retailers, like Tesco and Amazon, view every shopping basket as not just a sale but as another opportunity to understand. These companies religiously study every interaction in the service of delivering better specification to their supplier and improved value to their customers.

This is not an easy job; in fact applying this model of continuous improvement is fiendishly difficult and relies not just on a complete devotion to the principle of putting the customer at the centre of how your organization thinks, but, most importantly, it stands and falls on the follow-through of the policies, processes and technologies used to support this vision. The notion of customer focus has so permeated organizational culture that even the public sector has embraced the concept that one size does not necessarily fit all. This wasn't always the case, in fact it wasn't more than ten years ago that databases were still a novel part of most organizations. So the idea of pulling together a single real-time view of a customer's history from information gleaned from both within (and sometimes beyond) their organization was still in the realm of science fiction.

The nirvana that the CRM travellers seek is a company where the extremities are perfectly attuned to the needs and realities of the customer. This is the world where all customer-facing employees have all the information they need at their fingertips, so when they interact with you they can appear as if they've known you forever, understand your issues and suggest solutions that at best will make you spend more and at worst will make sure you don't defect to the competition.

Chasing nirvana has always been a frustrating and expensive business. International Data Corporation predicts that $11.4 billion will be spent worldwide on CRM applications by 2008. But the bills don't stop with the software. The real money is being made by businesses like Accenture and IBM in services like CRM training and outsourcing which are expected by IDC to be worth $93 billion in 2005.

You'd think for all this expenditure and opportunity, we'd be stamping out more perfectly formed organizations. But the history of most CRM implementations has been nothing short of disastrous. Gartner reports that most businesses underestimate costs by as much as 75%. Large businesses will typically spend between $30 million and $90 million over a three-year period in technology, staff, consulting services and training related to CRM but Gartner suggests that over 50% of these implementations are considered a failure by the customers.

One of the great opportunities for ground-breaking CRM is in telecommunications. You would think with the intimate knowledge that phone companies have about our calling habits, coupled with the huge investments they have made in CRM systems, service and staff would have generated some world leaders. But today's operators have typically chosen a policy of sales over service. The operator who analyses calling habits for the purpose of letting its customers know not just that they could buy additional services but that by changing packages they could save money would win my loyalty for life and I'd tell anyone prepared to listen.

Source: excerpt from Klein (2004). Reproduced by permission of Saul Klein

Questions

1. How does the concept of CRM fit within a culture of continuous improvement?
2. Why do so many CRM implementations fail?

PROCESS TECHNOLOGY FOR CUSTOMERS

One approach to improving service delivery is the use of process technology in the service delivery process itself.

In an 'active' customer-technology interaction such as an automated teller machine (ATM) at a bank the technology can enable the customers to avail themselves of the

service at a time of their choosing and to make choices regarding that service. From a service provider viewpoint this has the advantage of reducing staffing requirements and empowering customers by giving them a greater sense of control over the type of service they require. However, customers have different preferences and many facilities may well need both customer-driven and traditional people-based service delivery systems such as a

call centre or physical outlet. For example it is common to see a customer using an ATM while another customer prefers to enter the bank and queue to see a clerk for exactly the same service! While ATM technology has allowed banks to significantly reduce their number of branches and staffing requirement there is still a need to provide customer contact for some services and some customers. The ATM is an example of a wider use of technology to provide self-service facilities with Internet services such as travel (for example www.expedia.co.uk) and books (for example www.amazon.co.uk) widely used.

Process technology also exists for 'passive' customer-technology interactions such as transportation systems, for example moving walkways for directing people at an airport or an underground tube system in a city. Because of the lack of interaction between the customer and technology customers will need clear instruction in the use of the technology to avoid confusion.

In a 'supported' customer-technology interaction there is a human server who acts as an intermediary between the customer and the technology itself. This means that advice and guidance can be given to the customer by the server in making their choices (for example booking a holiday in a travel agency). There may also be instances when the use of the technology requires skills and experience the customer could not be expected to have (for example a transportation system). Some organizations encourage their customers to use active rather than supported technology to reduce staffing costs. For example Ryanair (www.ryanair.com) charges customers extra if they wish to check in at the airport rather than undertaking the task online.

SUMMARY

- Process technologies for material processing cover a wide range of facilities such as design, engineering and manufacture.

- Information technology such as computer network systems can be used to accumulate, organize and distribute information.

- Operational information systems are used for tasks involved in the daily running of the business. Management information systems are used to support tactical and strategic decision making.

- E-Business can be seen as the transformation of business processes through the use of Internet technologies. E-Commerce can be seen as electronically mediated transactions between an organization and any third party it deals with.

- Technology such as automated teller machines can be used to provide assistance when the customer is present in the service delivery process.

CASE STUDY 6.5

Retail Applications of Transaction Processing Systems by Sainsbury's

This case study of UK retailer Sainsbury's considers the different ways in which a retailer may make use of transaction processing systems (TPS).

The Company and its Customer Service Objectives
- Seventeen thousand commodities.
- Aim is for no more than five commodities to be unavailable at any one time.

- Order lead time 24 to 48 hours.
- Distribution centres manage deliveries of 11 million cases to 335 stores.

How is Sainsbury's helped by TPS technology?

- Improved customer service through more choice, lower prices, better quality of produce and full shelves.
- Improved operational efficiency by automatic links to suppliers and better information on product demand and availability.
- Assessment of the effectiveness of product promotions through availability of better information.
- Marketing through customer loyalty schemes.

How does Sainsbury's Use Technologies?

- At the till – EPOS and EFTPOS.
- On shelves – auto-price-changing LCDs.
- On trolleys – 'self-scanning systems'.
- At home – direct wine sales from the Internet BarclaySquare site.

- At warehouses – EDI links between stores, warehouses, suppliers and banks.
- For banking – TPS are vital to providing customer statements and cash withdrawals.
- In the marketing department – the effectiveness of marketing campaigns and loyalty card schemes can be assessed using information on transactions stored in data warehouses. This type of system is covered in more detail later in the chapter.

Source: Bocij, P., Greasley, A. and Hickie, S. (2008) *Business Information Systems*, Pearson Education Ltd.

Questions

1. Draw a diagram summarizing the links between all the parties who access Sainsbury's TPS.

2. What benefits will Sainsbury's gain compared to the time before the introduction of TPS?

3. Can you think of any problems with using TPS so extensively? What can be done to counter these problems?

EXERCISES

1. What are the advantages of using computer-aided design (CAD) technology?

2. Describe the major elements of FMS and evaluate the concept.

3. Discuss how CIM could provide strategic advantage.

4. What is the relevance of process technology to service organizations?

5. Identify process technology that may be found in a large retail organization.

6. Describe the categories of operational information systems and management information systems and provide business examples of their use for each category.

7. Describe the purpose of workflow management systems throughout the organization.

8. Explain the relationship between the concepts of e-Commerce and e-Business.

WEB EXERCISE

Discuss ethical issues associated with RFID tags. In order to help you think of ideas this web site at `http://www.rfidgazette.org/2007/04/top_15_weirdest.html` (28 September 2008) provides some unusual examples of their use.

● FURTHER READING

Cannon, A.R., Reyes, P.M., Frazier, G.V. and Prater, E.L. (2008) RFID in the contemporary supply chain: multiple perspectives on its benefits and risks, *International Journal of Operations and Production Management*, **28** (5), 433–54.

Hayes, R., Pisano, G., Upton, D. and **Wheelwright, S.** (2005) *Pursuing the Competitive Edge: Operations, Strategy, and Technology*, John Wiley & Sons, Ltd.

● WEB LINKS

www.abb.com (accessed 28 September 2008). ABB. Supplier of many automation devices, such as robotic systems.

www.autodesk.co.uk (accessed 28 September 2008). AutoDesk Inc. AutoCAD software for product design.

www.e-consultancy.com (accessed 28 September 2008). Online digest of consultant and analyst reports in e-Business.

www.graphisoft.com (accessed 28 September 2008). Graphisoft Inc. ArchiCAD software for product design.

www.gsmworld.com/index.shtml (accessed 28 September 2008). GSM Association. Global trade association for GSM mobile operators.

www.wfmc.org (accessed 28 September 2008). Workflow Management Coalition. Contains introductory papers on the purpose and components of workflow systems.

www.wired.com (accessed 28 September 2008). Wired Magazine. News and articles on e-Business topics.

● REFERENCES

Bocij, P., Greasley, A. and Hickie, S. (2008) *Business Information Systems: Technology, Development and Management*, 4th edn, Pearson Education Limited, Harlow.

Klein, S. (2004) How to click with your customers. *Guardian*, 6 September.

CHAPTER

7

Product and Service Design

- Introduction
- The design process
- Service design
- Improving design

LEARNING OBJECTIVES

- Understand issues involved in the design of services

- Describe the main steps in the design process

- Discuss the use of concurrent design

- Understand the term 'mass customization'

- Describe the role of DFM, QFD and Taguchi methods in improving design

INTRODUCTION

Good design of products and services is an essential element in satisfying customer needs and therefore ensuring the long-term success of the organization. Due to competitive pressures most organizations will need to generate new products and services and improvements to existing products and services to remain successful. In addition organizations operating in international markets will need to consider the differing requirements of customers in different countries during the design stage.

An important issue is the connection between product and service design and the design of the processes that deliver these products and services to customers. For example the choice of materials used in a product design may have important consequences for process design in terms of the equipment and skills required to make the product. In service design the service and the process used to deliver it to the customer may be all but indistinguishable. Process design is covered in Chapter 8.

The success of the design process primarily depends on the relationship between the marketing, design and operations functions of the organization. These functions need to cooperate in order to identify customer needs and produce a cost-effective and quality design that meets these needs. The marketing function will undertake tasks such as conducting market research to evaluate consumer needs and provide a forecast of demand in the marketplace taking into account competitive pressures and the external environment. The design function will undertake the design of the product or service. It is operations' role to efficiently produce the product or deliver the service as designed using a specified process design (process design is covered in Chapter 8). The role of suppliers is becoming increasingly important in product design due to the practice of outsourcing or contracting to another company part of the design or production of the product itself. The finance function will also be involved in providing capital for development costs and facilities. It will need to evaluate the success of any products introduced into the marketplace and provide estimates of when the investment made to bring the product to market will be paid back. Communication between all of these functions can be facilitated by the use of accounting and information systems that allow up-to-date and accurate information to be available across the organization.

The chapter will first outline the steps involved in the design of a product or service before addressing some of the specific attributes of service design. There is then a discussion of some of the techniques that may be used to improve the results of the design process. Many of the techniques are concerned with ensuring that final quality is high by taking appropriate action at the design stage.

THE DESIGN PROCESS

The design process involves the following steps shown in Figure 7.1.

Traditionally the design process is undertaken as a number of sequential steps, shown in Figure 7.1, with work undertaken within functional areas (such as marketing, design and engineering). The problem with the traditional approach is the cost

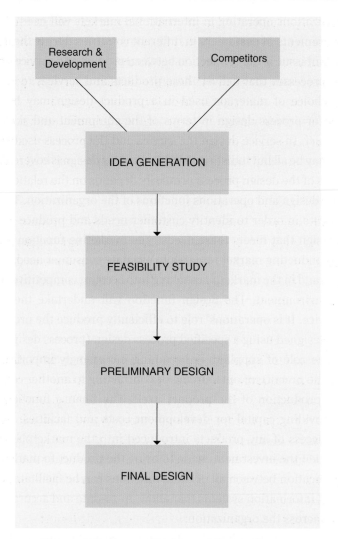

Figure 7.1: Steps in Product and Service Design.

and time involved in bringing the product to market. In some business sectors (such as information technology) shrinking product life cycles have meant that new products or improvements to existing products are required in an ever shorter timescale. Another problem with the traditional approach to design is the lack of communication between functional specialists involved in the different stages of design. This can lead to an attitude of passing the design to the next department without any consideration of problems that may be encountered at later design stages. An example of this is decisions made at the preliminary design stage that adversely affect choices at the product build stage. This can cause the design to be repeatedly passed between departments to satisfy everyone's needs, increasing time and costs.

Alternative approaches to design called 'concurrent design' or 'simultaneous engineering' involve contributors to the stages of the design effort providing their expertise throughout the design process, as a team. Concurrent design reduces the time wasted when each stage in the design process waits for the previous stage to finish completely before it can commence. By facilitating communication through the establishment of a project team the problem of a lack of communication between functions can be reduced. Concurrent design is discussed in more detail later in this chapter. The steps involved in the design process are now outlined in detail.

Idea Generation

Ideas for new products and services can come from a variety of sources, including the organization's research and development (R&D) department, suggestions from customers, market research data, salespeople, competitor actions or developments in new technology. The major source of new ideas or innovations will be dependent largely on the organization's strategy.

The Research and Development Function

For an organization that has a strategy of being first to the market with a new product or service, ideas will be devised principally from the organization's own R&D department. For an organization with a similar product to their competitors, innovation may be primarily in the design and manufacture stages to attain lower production costs. Successful product innovation comes from understanding the customer and identifying their needs. Various data collection methods such as questionnaires, focus groups and interviews should be used to gain sufficient understanding of customer requirements.

Research and development can take on the following forms:

- *pure research* – knowledge-oriented research to develop new ideas with no specific product in mind
- *applied research* – problem-oriented research to discover new ideas with specific commercial applications
- *development* – product-oriented research concerned with turning research ideas into products.

Pure research is often based in universities and funded by government agencies and so it is necessary for organizations to maintain close contact with the relevant institutions. Applied research will be undertaken by most organizations. The cost of undertaking research and development is high and there will be many failed projects but the payoff from the small number of successes may be vital to the organization's continued profitability.

CASE STUDY   7.1

R&D at Toyota

Toyota uses a multiphase development process. Synergy between these phases helps assure Toyota can consistently bring forward-thinking, high-quality, attractive products quickly to our customers.

1. Basic research and development. This phase defines the basic direction of development. It entails developing basic parts, the building blocks of a vehicle.
2. Advanced engineering development. This phase is where breakthroughs in technology occur. In order to keep one step ahead of our competitors, this phase focuses on new components and systems research.
3. Product development. This phase centres around developing new vehicle models.

Source: http://www.toyota.co.jp/en/pdf/toyota_world/2005/chap3.pdf (accessed 10 October 2008).

Question

What do you consider are the benefits of the multiphase approach adopted by Toyota?

Competitors

Competitors can provide a good source of ideas and it is important that the organization analyses any new products or services as they are introduced to the market and makes an appropriate response. **Reverse engineering** is a systematic approach to dismantling and inspecting a competitor's product to look for aspects of design that could be incorporated into the organization's own product. This is especially prevalent when the product is a complex assembly such as a car, where design choices are myriad.

Benchmarking compares a product or service against what is considered the best in that market segment and then makes recommendations on how the product or service can be improved to meet that standard. Although a reactive strategy, benchmarking can be useful to organizations that have lost ground to innovative competitors. More details on benchmarking are given in Chapter 18.

Reverse engineering
A systematic approach to dismantling and inspecting a competitor's product to look for aspects of design that could be incorporated into the organization's own product.

Benchmarking
Comparing a product or service against what is considered the best in that market segment and then making recommendations on how the product or service can be improved to meet that standard.

Feasibility Study

The marketing function will take the ideas created in the idea generation stage and form a series of alternative concepts on which a feasibility study is undertaken. The concept refers not to the physical product or specification of the service that the person is buying but the overall set of expected benefits that a customer is receiving. For instance a restaurant meal consists not only of the meal itself but the level of attention and the general surroundings. Thus the concept is referring to the combination of physical product and service, referred to as the package, which delivers a set of expected benefits to the customer. Once a concept has been formulated it must then be submitted to market, economic and technical analysis in order to assess its feasibility.

Market Analysis

A market analysis consists of evaluating the design concept with potential customers through interviews, focus groups and other data collection methods. A physical product may be tested by supplying a sample for customer evaluation. The market analysis should identify whether sufficient demand for the proposed product or service exists and its fit with the existing marketing strategy.

Market analysis
This consists of evaluating the design concept with potential customers through interviews, focus groups and other data-collection methods.

At a strategic level the organization can use the product life cycle (PLC) to determine the likely cost and volume characteristics of the product or service. The life cycle describes the volume sales over time in four phases of introduction, growth, maturity and decline (more details on stages in the PLC are given in Chapter 2).

In relating the PLC to the design process in the *introduction* phase production costs are high and design changes may be frequent. However, there may be little or no competition for the new product or service and so it may be possible to charge a premium price to customers. The *growth* phase sees a rapid increase in volume and the possibility of competitors entering the market. At this stage it is important to establish the product or service in the market as firmly as possible in order to secure future sales. Costs should be declining as process improvements and standardization take place. In the *mature* phase competitive pressures will increase and it is important that sales are secured through a brand image to differentiate it from competitors. There should be a continued effort at design improvement to the product or service itself and the process that delivers it. Some products, such as consumer durables, may stay in the mature phase almost indefinitely and techniques such as advertising are used to maintain interest and market share. Many services can be improved by the exploitation of technological developments such as Internet banking. In the *decline* phase, before the product or service is discontinued or modified to meet customer needs, the focus should be on optimizing profits while minimizing new investment.

The PLC is a useful tool in developing a portfolio of products and services to different stages of the life cycle, although it can be difficult to identify when they will enter the next stage of the life cycle or even what stage of the life cycle they are now in.

Economic Analysis

Economic analysis consists of developing estimates of production and delivery costs and comparing them with estimates of demand. In order to perform the analysis an accurate estimate of demand is required, possibly derived from statistical forecasts of industry sales and estimates of market share in the sector the product or service is competing in. These estimates will be based on a predicted price range for the product or service, which

is compatible with its position in the market. In order to assess the feasibility of the product or service, estimates of costs in terms of such factors as staffing, materials and equipment must be obtained. Techniques such as cost/benefit analysis, decision theory and accounting measures such as net present value (NPV) and internal rate of return (IRR) may be used to calculate the profitability of a product. Another tool that can be used is the cost-volume-profit model.

The Cost-Volume-Profit Model

The cost-volume-profit (CVP) model, which was used in Chapter 5 for location decisions (see Figure 5.3), can also be used to provide an estimate of the profit level generated by a product at a certain product volume. The model assumes a linear relationship of cost and revenue to volume.

If revenue is given by the following formula:

$$TR = SP \times X_S$$

where TR = total revenue, SP = selling price, X_S = units sold

And cost is given by the following formula:

$$TC = FC + VC \times X_P$$

where TC = total cost, FC = fixed cost, VC = variable cost per unit, X_P = number of units produced then profit can be given by the following formula:

$$P = TR - TC$$

where P = profit, TR = total revenue, TC = total cost

Assuming $X_S = X_P$ (all products made are sold) then the volume for a certain profit can be given by the following formula:

$$X = \frac{(P + FC)}{(SP - VC)}$$

where X = volume (units), P = profit, FC = fixed costs, SP = selling price, VC = variable costs

When profit = 0 (selling costs = production costs), the break-even point, volume can be calculated by the following formula:

$$X = \frac{FC}{(SP - VC)}$$

WORKED EXAMPLE 7.1
Cost-Volume-Profit Model

A manufacturer produces a product with the following parameters:

Selling price (SP) = £7/unit
Variable cost (VC) = £4/unit
Fixed costs (FC) = £15 000/week

a) What is the break-even point?
b) How many do they need to sell to make £15 000 profit a week?

SOLUTION

a) At break-even point, $P = 0$

$$X = \frac{FC}{(SP - VC)}$$

$$= \frac{15\,000}{(7 - 4)} = 5000 \text{ units/week}$$

b) At $P = 15\,000$

$$X = \frac{(P + FC)}{(SP - VC)}$$

$$= \frac{(15\,000 + 15\,000)}{(7 - 4)}$$

$$= 10\,000 \text{ units/week}$$

Using the CVP Model for Multiple Products

If a firm produces more than one product using the same fixed costs the total profit can be calculated. The weighted contribution (selling price – variable cost) is calculated as follows:

$$WC = \sum_{i=1}^{n} M_i (SP_i - VC_i)$$

where WC = weighted contribution, M_i = product mix as a percentage of the total sales for product i (where i = 1 to n, n = number of products), SP_i = selling price for product i, VC_i = variable cost for product i.

The volume for a certain profit level is given by the following formula:

$$X = \frac{(P + FC)}{WC}$$

where X = volume (units), P = profit, FC = fixed costs, WC = weighted contribution.

WORKED EXAMPLE 7.2
CVP Model for Multiple Products

The following product mix is planned.

	Pliers	Saws
Product mix	0.75	0.25
Selling price/unit	£1.50	£3.20
Variable cost	£1.20	£1.80

Annual fixed cost = £20 000

What is the break-even point?

SOLUTION

$$WC = \sum_{i=1}^{n} M_i(SP_i - VC_i)$$

$$
\begin{aligned}
WC &= 0.75 \times (1.50 - 1.20) + 0.25 \times (3.2 - 1.8) \\
&= 0.75 \times 0.3 + 0.25 \times 1.4 \\
&= 0.575
\end{aligned}
$$

At profit = 0

$$X = \frac{FC}{WC}$$

X = 20 000/0.575 = 34 783 units.

Technical Analysis

Technical analysis involves determining whether the technical capability to manufacture the product or deliver the service exists. This covers such issues as ensuring materials are available to make the product to the specification required, ensuring the appropriate machinery and skills are available to work with these materials and securing staff skills necessary to deliver a service. The technical analysis must take into account the target market and so designers have to consider the costs of reaching the customer with the product or service in order to ensure it can be sold at a competitive price.

> **Technical analysis**
> This consists of determining whether the technical capability to manufacture the product or deliver the service exists.

Preliminary Design

Design concepts that pass the feasibility stage enter preliminary design. The specification of the concept – what the product or service should do to satisfy customer needs – is translated into a technical specification of the components of the package (the product and service components that satisfy the customer needs defined in the concept) and the process by which the package is created. The specification of the components of the package requires a product and service structure which describes the relationship between the components and a bill of materials (BOM) or list of component quantities derived from the product structure. The process by which the package is created is considered under process design (Chapter 8).

Final Design

The final design stage involves refining the preliminary design through the use of a prototype until a viable final design can be made. Computer-aided design (CAD) (Chapter 6) and simulation modelling (Chapter 8) can be used at this stage to build a computer-based prototype and refine the product and process design. The final design will be assessed in three main areas of functional design, form design and production design

> **Functional design**
> This ensures that the design meets the performance characteristics that are specified in the product concept.

Functional Design

Functional design is ensuring that the design meets the performance characteristics that are specified in the product concept. Two aspects of functional design are reliability and maintainability.

> **Reliability**
> This measures the probability that a product or service will perform its intended function for a specified period of time under normal conditions of use.

Reliability

Reliability is an important performance characteristic and measures the probability that a product or service will perform its intended function for a specified period of time under normal conditions of use. The reliability of each part of the product or service must be determined by reference to the criteria of 'failure' and 'normal' service. These criteria are determined by reference to customer expectations and cost levels. Reliability can be determined by either the probability of failure during a given test or the probability of failure during a given time. Strategies for improving product or service reliability include simplified design (for example less parts in a product), improved reliability of individual elements of the product or service and the adoption of backup product or service elements.

The probability of failure during a given test is a function of the reliability of component parts and the relationship of those parts. For a product of two component parts the reliability is the product of the probabilities (Figure 7.2).

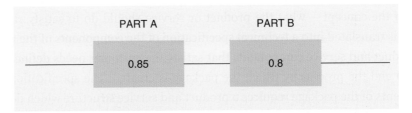

Figure 7.2: Product Reliability (Serial).

Reliability $= 0.85 \times 0.8 = 0.68$

Note that the product reliability (0.68) is much less than the component parts and will continue to decline as the number of parts increases. For a product with backup components Figure 7.3 applies.

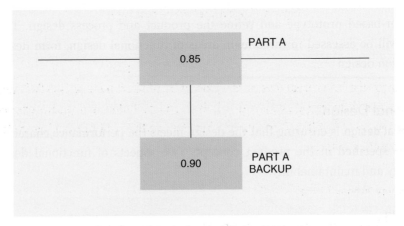

Figure 7.3: Product Reliability (Backup).

Reliability $= 0.9 + 0.85 \times (1 - 0.9) = 0.985$

Note that the product reliability (0.985) is much higher than the component part but the cost of providing a backup makes its use relevant in only critical components.

The probability of failure during a given time is expressed as a distribution pattern of failures over time. Failure rates tend to follow the pattern shown in Figure 7.4 where defective parts fail early and then the failure rate rises again towards the end of a product's life. A small number of random failures occur between these points.

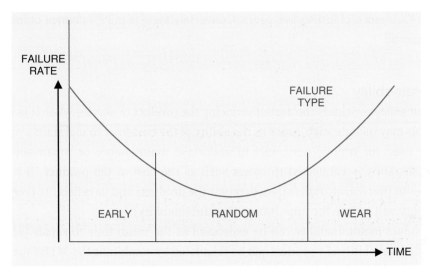

Figure 7.4: Failure Pattern over Time.

The reciprocal of the actual failure rate, found by product testing, is called the mean time between failures (MTBF) and if it is found to follow a negative exponential distribution the reliability (probability that the product will not fail before time T) can be found as follows:

$$P \text{ (no failure before T)} = e^{-T/\text{MTBF}}$$

where $e = 2.7183$, T = time period, MTBF = mean time between failures

WORKED EXAMPLE 7.3
Mean Time Between Failures (MTBF)

If the life of a product follows a negative exponential distribution and the average lifespan = 10 years, what is the probability that the product will fail after 5 years?

SOLUTION

MTBF=10

T=5

$P() = e^{-5/10} = 0.61$

Thus there is a 61% chance of lasting five years. Conversely there is a 39% chance of failure during this time period.

Maintainability

> **Maintainability**
> This considers the cost of servicing the product or service when it is in use.

Maintainability considers the cost of servicing the product or service when it is in use.

This may include such issues as the ability of the customer to maintain a product or the need for trained personnel to undertake maintenance or repair activities. Maintainability is connected to issues such as the cost of the product (it may be cheaper to throw away rather than to repair the product) and its reliability (very high reliability will reduce the importance of maintainability).

Product maintainability can be expressed as the mean time to repair (MTTR). Thus the availability of a product can be calculated by combining the MTBF measure, along with the time taken to repair these failures (MTTR).

$$Availability = MTBF/(MTBF + MTTR)$$

Maintainability can be improved by modular design to enable whole modules to be replaced rather than the lengthy investigation of faults. Maintenance schedules should also be specified to help prevent problems from occurring. An improved ability to perform under adverse conditions (termed the design robustness) will improve maintainability.

Form Design

> **Form design**
> This refers to the product aesthetics such as look, feel and sound if applicable.

Form design refers to the product aesthetics such as look, feel and sound if applicable. This is particularly important for consumer durables but even industrial appliances should at least project an image of quality. In services the design of the supporting facility, such as the room décor, lighting and music in a restaurant provide an important element of the service design.

Production Design

Production design involves ensuring that the design takes into consideration the ease and cost of manufacture of a product. Good design will take into consideration the present manufacturing capabilities in terms of material supplies, equipment and personnel skills available. The cost of production can be reduced by the following methods:

> **Production design**
> This involves ensuring that the design takes into consideration the ease and cost of manufacture of a product.

- *simplification* – reducing the number of assemblies
- *standardization* – enabling the use of components for different products and modules
- *modularization* – combining standardized building blocks in different ways to create a range of products.

CASE STUDY 7.2

Product Development at Fracino

By getting designers, engineers and marketers to work closely together, Fracino has been able to establish itself in an incredibly competitive market. Close collaboration means Fracino's coffee machines meet its customers' requirements exactly. The business decided to create project teams of designers, engineers and marketers who could work together at all stages of the process to assure the quality of the final project. Now, a three- or four-strong team sees each project from original concept, through prototyping and testing, to component supply and assembly. This creates real dedication and focus and means that modifications can be made quickly and seamlessly. Fracino also involves key customers in the prototyping phase to make sure the final product meets their needs.

Source: DTI web site (now Department for Business, Enterprise and Regulatory Reform).

Question

Explain the advantages of the collaborative approach to product development adopted by Fracino.

SERVICE DESIGN

The design process outlined in the previous section of this chapter is relevant both to products and services. This section outlines issues relevant to the design of services in particular. In service design the overall set of expected benefits that the customer is buying is termed the service concept. The service will usually consist of a combination of goods and services and is termed the service package. Fitzsimmons and

> **Service package**
> The combination of goods and services that comprise a service.

Fitzsimmons (2008) define the service package as a bundle of goods and services consisting of the following four features.

- Supporting facility – the physical resources that must be in place before a service can be offered.
- Facilitating goods – the material purchased or consumed by the buyer or items provided by the customer.
- Explicit services – the benefits that are readily observable by the senses and consist of the essential or intrinsic features of the service.
- Implicit services – psychological benefits that the customer may sense only vaguely or extrinsic features of the service.

The idea of the service package shows that although service design is often primarily related to the design of the process of the delivery of the service (process design is covered in Chapter 8) it can be seen that the service package will also require the design of physical aspects such as the supporting facility and facilitating goods. In terms of the design of the service element, the service package emphasizes the point that the providers of the service should not simply focus on the delivery of the explicit service and neglect the other components of the service package. Thus it is important to recognize the effect on the level of service that all the elements of the service package have.

A service is an experience, not simply the receiving of a good, so the customer will be in contact with the service as it is delivered. This means the service design must take into account how the individual customer will react to the service as it is delivered. This is not easy as all customers are different and have different expectations of what the service will provide. This requires close cooperation between operations and marketing to identify a target customer market and ensure that the service design is meeting their needs.

Another feature of service design is that because the service is intangible it is often difficult to test quality levels before the service is provided. From the customer's point of view quality may only be assessed when the service is provided or perhaps an indication of service quality may be gained by seeking the views of others who have experience of the service required. Quality can be

designed into the service by taking the design features and implementing a quality system to maintain conformance to design requirements. The techniques of QFD and Taguchi discussed later in this chapter are relevant in ensuring service design quality.

Finally it should be remembered that most products are accompanied by some sort of service (a one-year warranty for a washing machine for example) and most services are accompanied by some sort of product (a consultancy report presented at the end of a consultancy project) so generally product and service design will be considered together as part of the whole design concept.

CASE STUDY   7.3

Benugo

Taking its name from cofounders Ben and Hugo Warner, Benugo cafes opened for business in 1998. They offered customers a new style of cafe with 'pizzazz', in an environment where people could relax and enjoy their food. With 11 cafe shops in and around London, 150 staff employed throughout the business and annual revenues of over £6 million, Benugo has proved to be a big hit with customers. 'At Benugo we know that the customer always has a choice', says Tim Parfitt, Finance Director, 'We want Benugo to be that choice as often as possible.'

But in today's market margins are low and competition is fierce. Business survival depends on sustaining profitability and maintaining customer satisfaction. This is why Tim was intrigued by the proposition from technology solutions provider, Broadscape. The proposal was to provide Benugo's customers with high-speed Internet access over a Wireless LAN with a WiFi access point. This would effectively mean that customers could come into a Benugo cafe, open up their laptop and have instant access to the Internet without having to plug in any cables. Benugo trialled the idea in two of their cafes. They offered wireless Internet connections free of charge as long as customers spent £2 or over on food or coffee for every 30 minutes of use. A short flyer tells customers how to set up the WiFi access on their laptop and within minutes they're online. Broadscape's installation also included Bluetooth which allowed compatible PDAs to connect to the Internet as well. The innovative aspect of the system is that customers are not charged directly for Internet access. Which in turn means that there are no billing issues and nothing complicated to consider with billing updates.

Source: DTI web site (now Department for Business, Enterprise and Regulatory Reform).

Question

Relate the concept of the service package to the facilities offered by Benugo.

IMPROVING DESIGN

This chapter will now explore a number of techniques that have been developed in an attempt to improve the design process. Although they have a greater applicability to product design than to service design, they do have some relevance to service design.

Concurrent Design

Concurrent design, also known as simultaneous development, is when contributors to the stages of the design effort provide their expertise together throughout the design process as a team. This contrasts with the traditional sequential design process when work is undertaken within functional departments. The problem with the traditional approach is the cost and time involved in bringing the product to market. In some business sectors (such as consumer electronics) shrinking product life cycles have meant that new products or improvements to existing products are required in an ever shorter time scale. Concurrent design reduces the time wasted when each stage in the design process waits for the previous stage to finish completely before it can commence. For example critical equipment, some of which may take an extended time to purchase and install, is identified and procured early in the design process in order to reduce the overall development time.

Another problem of the traditional approach to design is the lack of communication between functional specialists involved in the different stages of design. This can lead to an attitude of 'throwing the design over the wall' without any consideration of problems that may be encountered by later stages. An example of this is decisions made at the preliminary design stage that adversely affect choices at the product build stage. This can cause the design to be repeatedly passed between departments to satisfy everyone's needs, increasing time and costs. Problems of this type can be reduced by facilitating communication through the establishment of a project team.

Design for Manufacture (DFM)

An important aspect of good design is that the product designed can be produced easily and at low cost. Design for manufacture is a concept that views product design as the first step in the manufacture of that product. It incorporates guidelines on such aspects as simplification, standardization and modularization but also techniques such as failure mode and effect analysis (FMEA) and value engineering (VE).

Failure Mode and Effect Analysis

Failure mode and effect analysis is a systematic approach to identifying the cause and effect of product failures. The approach involves the following:

- list the functions of the component parts of the product
- define the failure modes (such as leakage or fatigue) for all parts

- rank the failures in order of likelihood and seriousness
- address each failure in rank order, making design changes where necessary.

The idea of FMEA is to anticipate failures and deal with them at the design stage. The ranking of failures is achieved by calculating the product of the following three values on a scale of 1 to 10, termed the risk priority number (RPN).

O (occurrence) = probability of failure occurring (1 = almost never, 10 = often)
S (severity) = the effect the failure has if the failure takes place (1 = hardly noticeable, 10 = serious effect)
D (detectability) = the difficulty of detection (1 = absolutely obvious, 10 = undetectable)

The risk priority number (RPN) is thus = $O \times S \times D$ and can be used as a guide to prioritizing the most serious quality problems.

Value Engineering (VE)

Value engineering aims to eliminate unnecessary features and functions that do not contribute to the value or performance of the product. It is derived from the idea of value analysis (VA) which was developed to improve the actual design, particularly taking into account the use of new technology. The technique uses a team approach and follows a formal procedure which has the following core activities:

Define function. This involves defining each function of the product and its cost.
Gather alternatives. A team will brainstorm new ways to accomplish the functions.
Evaluate alternatives. Each idea generated is evaluated for feasibility and cost.

The technique can be used during design or as a continuous improvement tool during production when a flexible design specification is needed to accommodate suggestions at the production stage.

> **Value engineering**
> This aims to eliminate unnecessary features and functions that do not contribute to the value or performance of the product.

Quality Functional Deployment (QFD)

Quality functional deployment is a structured process that translates the voice of the customer (what the customer needs) into technical design requirements (how these needs are met). It is particularly relevant to the concept of concurrent design as it complements the use of teams in attempting to coordinate design objectives. The technique consists of a series of tables that translate requirements at successive design stages as follows:

> **Quality functional deployment**
> A structured process that translates the voice of the customer (what the customer needs) into technical design requirements (how these needs are met).

The House of Quality
Customer Requirements → Product Characteristics

Parts Deployment
Product Characteristics → Part Characteristics

Process Planning
Part Characteristics → Process Characteristics

Operating Requirements
Process Characteristics → Operations

The most used matrix is the House of Quality that converts customer requirements into product characteristics. The House of Quality matrix is shown in Figure 7.5.

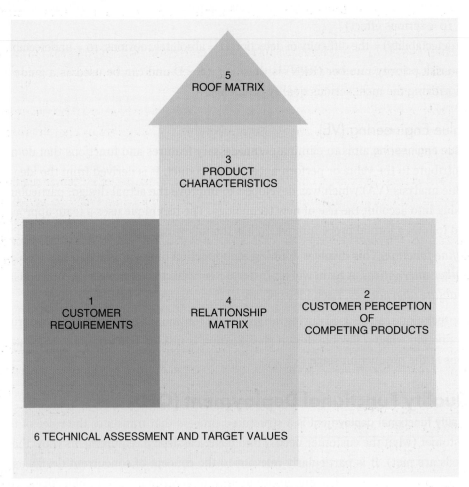

Figure 7.5: House of Quality Matrix.

The elements of the House of Quality are described below:

- *Customer requirements.* This element links the attributes of the product that are important to the customer along with their relative importance.
- *Customer perceptions of competitive products.* This compares customer perceptions of the organization and competitors' performance for each of the customer

requirements. It provides information on relative performance and also identifies where competitive advantage can be attained by improving relative performance on a highly ranked customer requirement.

- *Product characteristics.* This lists the product characteristics, expressed in engineering terms and grouped where appropriate.
- *Relationship matrix.* The matrix correlates the attributes of customer requirements with product characteristics. The relationship may be a positive or negative one and assists in identifying design changes to product characteristics to meet customer requirements.
- *Roof matrix.* This explores the interaction between product characteristics. This assists identification of an adverse change in product characteristic as a consequence of a change in another characteristic.
- *Technical assessment and target values.* This section includes performance measures to compare the product with competitors. It also contains chosen critical design factors such as cost and importance.

Any change in product characteristic as a result of analysis of customer requirements is then carried forward to the parts deployment matrix and then converted to the process planning and finally operating requirements matrix. In this way QFD enables the full consequences of any design change to be assessed and operationalized. The technology provides a method of communicating the effect of change quickly amongst all the members of the design team.

Taguchi Methods

Genichi Taguchi suggests that product failure is mainly a function of design. Taguchi argues that quality must be designed into a product and that it cannot be inspected in later if the design is not good. Techniques that Taguchi has provided for improving product and process quality are robust design, the quality loss function (QLF), target-oriented quality and design of experiments (DOE).

The robustness of a product is defined by its ability to withstand variations in environmental and operating conditions. **Robust design** is the process of designing in the ability of the product to perform under a variety of conditions and so reducing the chance of product failure. In order to achieve this Taguchi suggests a focus on consistency of parts rather than just requiring manufacture within a tolerance. The tolerance arbitrarily defines a cut-off point between poor quality and good quality which may not be recognized by the customer. Taguchi has formalized the effect on customer dissatisfaction as the actual value deviates from the target value (i.e. the distance from the tolerance limit) called the **quality loss function (QLF)**. Taguchi argues that consistency is especially important in assembled products where parts

> **Robust design**
> The process of designing in the ability of the product to perform under a variety of conditions and so reducing the chance of product failure.

> **Quality loss function**
> A simple cost estimate that shows how customer preferences are oriented towards consistently meeting quality expectations and that a customer's dissatisfaction (quality loss) increases geometrically as the actual value deviates from the target value.

at either end of their tolerance limit can result in a poor quality product. Thus the ability to produce a part to a consistent specification through design is important. The QLF is a simple cost estimate which shows how customer preferences are oriented towards consistently meeting quality expectations and that a customer's dissatisfaction (quality loss) increases geometrically as the actual value deviates from the target value (Figure 7.6).

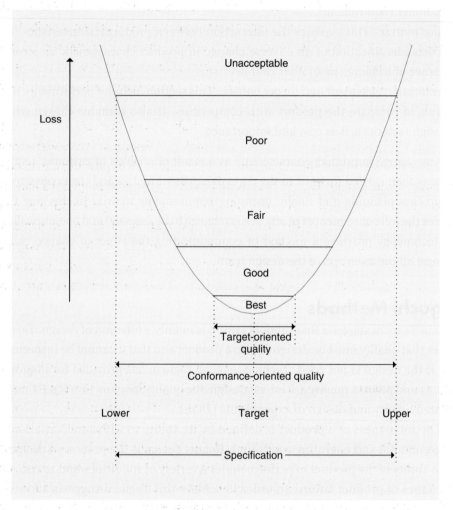

Figure 7.6: Quality Loss Function.

The Quality Loss Function can be expressed mathematically:

$$L = C \times d^2$$

where

L = quality loss
C = cost of the deviation from the specification limit
d = deviation from target value

Costs can be consumer loss factors, such as the cost of repair, the cost of correcting the results of a failure and the cost of not being able to use the product while it is being repaired, and functional tolerance factors when the deviation from the target value is when most customers will demand a repair or replacement. The QLF shows the quality loss that occurs when an organization simply aims to achieve quality levels between the upper and lower specification limits, termed conformance-oriented quality. Taguchi's **target-oriented quality** strives through a process of continuous improvement to keep as close as possible to the target specification and so losses are much lower (see Figure 7.6).

Design of experiments (DOE) aims to identify factors that affect a product's performance by providing a way of testing a number of design options under various operating and environmental conditions. In other words DOE provides a method of achieving robust design. The conditions that cause a poor product performance are separated into controllable and uncontrollable factors. In a design situation controllable factors are design parameters such as material type or dimensions. Uncontrollable factors derive from the wear of the product, such as the length of use or settings, or are environmental such as heat and humidity. A good design will have variables that act in a robust fashion to the possible occurrence of uncontrollable factors.

Cause-and-Effect Diagrams

The idea of a **cause-and-effect diagram** (sometimes referred to as a fishbone or Ishikawa diagram) is to work back from the quality problem and identify individual causes on lines radiating from each category branch, associated with the problem in each major category (Figure 7.7). Categories are often referred to as the 4Ms of Manpower, Machines, Materials and Method. Other categories can be used, for example the 4Ps of People, Products, Price and Promotions. Individual causes associated with each category are then tied to separate 'bones' along the category branch. This method often uses group processes such as brainstorming sessions to generate the ideas for causes.

Pareto Analysis

Pareto analysis is used to organize information and quality problems and help focus problem solving effort on the most important aspects. A Pareto chart is used to

---

Target-oriented quality
An approach that strives through the process of continuous improvement to keep as close as possible to the target specification.

Design of experiments
These aim to identify factors that affect a product's performance by providing a way of testing a number of design options under various operating and environmental conditions.

Cause-and-effect diagrams
A technique for identifying the causes of quality problems.

Pareto analysis
A technique used to organize information and quality problems and help focus problem solving effort on the most important aspects.

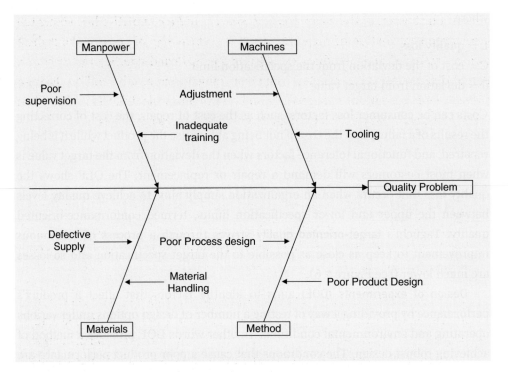

Figure 7.7: Cause-and-Effect Diagram.

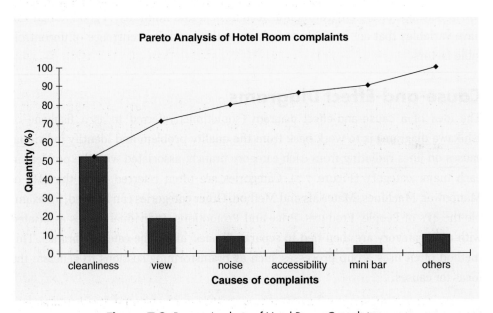

Figure 7.8: Pareto Analysis of Hotel Room Complaints.

display a histogram of the major areas of concern and a cumulative line shows the percentage contribution of each category. The data is organized with the highest category to the left and the 'others' category on the right hand side. Figure 7.8 shows a Pareto diagram for data collected using complaint forms in a hotel. The diagram shows a large amount of data visually and allows quick identification of problem areas which when tackled will have the largest effect on quality levels.

SUMMARY

- Service design relates to the combination of goods and service elements termed the service package.

- The steps in the design process are idea generation, feasibility study, preliminary design and final design. Ideas for new products can come from the organization's research and development (R&D) function, customers, market research data, competitors or technological development. The feasibility study consists of a market, economic and technical analysis. Preliminary design consists of forming a technical specification of the components of the package. The final design will be assessed in the three main areas of functional design, form design and production design.

- Concurrent design can reduce the time and cost involved in the product design process.

- Design for manufacture aims to ensure a product design can be produced easily and at low cost through guidelines on such aspects as simplification, standardization and modularization.

- Quality functional deployment (QFD) is a structured process that translates customer needs into technical design requirements.

- Taguchi methods for improving design quality include robust design, the quality loss function (QLF), target-oriented quality and design of experiments (DOE).

- Two further techniques for improving quality are cause-and-effect diagrams and Pareto analysis.

CASE STUDY   7.4

Nanyang Optical: Beyond Product Design – from Idea to Launch

Wee Beng Geok and Nigel Goodwin*
This case illustrates the process and challenges of designing a new product and then making it a reality.

Yang Wah Kiang had innovative ideas for spectacle frames and created two unique new product designs. But Yang was not just a product designer – he was also a practical, hands-on entrepreneur who owned and operated a medium-sized company. He was not content to leave his ideas on the drawing board; instead, he would do whatever it would take to make his designs become real products, ready for the market.

Yang was the managing director of Nanyang Optical, one of Singapore's largest optical retailers. In June 2006, he was ready to test his new eyewear designs in the retail market. Over the years, he had worked on a number of new concepts for spectacle frames, which he felt would offer unique value to consumers. His burning ambition was to test these new frame innovations in the international eyewear market.

In 2002, he and his Australian Chinese business partner set up a product design studio in Shenzhen, China. They spent the next three years designing and developing two new types of eyeglasses based on the new frame design concepts. When the prototypes were ready, Yang collaborated with French fashion designers who created contemporary styles, branding and packaging. The new frames were branded as Urband and Link. He and his French partners would work together to launch and eventually sell the frames, first in Europe and later in North America and Asia-Pacific.

Yang's next challenge was to produce enough of these frames to meet the orders that had already begun to flow in. Although outsourced manufacturing was a common practice in the eyewear industry, Yang was having difficulties finding outsourcing factories that could produce the frames at an acceptable level of quality. This was due to the uniqueness of the frame design and construction.

The case examines a myriad of product development, manufacturing and launch issues. It does this from two perspectives: that of a product designer and that of an entrepreneur and business owner. Thus, the issues are both creative and practical.

*Wee Beng Geok and Nigel Goodwin prepared this case based on public sources and interviews with Mr. Yang Wah Kiang. As the case is not intended to illustrate either effective or ineffective practices or policies, the information presented reflects the authors' interpretation of events and serves merely to provide opportunities for class discussion.

URBAND

Unique Eyewear...

Urband presented a revolutionary new concept in eyewear which defied convention: frames constructed without any springs, screws or soldering.[1] Urband had a simple, minimalist design. It consisted of three main parts: the

degrees without breaking. The titanium Urband had a sleek, urban style. The second variation was constructed of acetate, making it thicker and giving it a hipper, more youthful appearance. The titanium design was completed in April 2004 and the acetate design followed soon after.

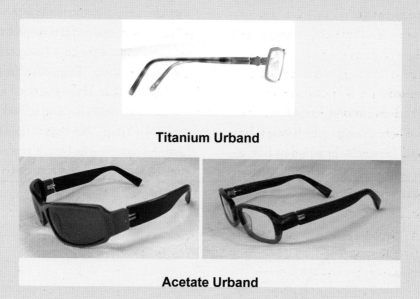

Titanium Urband

Acetate Urband

front portion, which held the lenses, and the two temple portions. These three parts were held together by two S-shaped clips near the hinges. The 'S-clips' were made of high-tensile strength stainless steel measuring 0.2 mm in thickness.

There were two variations of Urband. The original was constructed of titanium, making it light and virtually indestructible. In fact, the temples could bend outward nearly 180

...Offering Value Innovation

In Yang's opinion, Urband was functionally and aesthetically superior to conventional frames. Functionally, it was stronger. 'Without the soldering,' he explained, 'the structure becomes stronger. It's almost indestructible.' Also, the frames could be disassembled and reassembled easily, without the use of any tools, making it easier for optometrists to replace the lenses.

---

[1] A typical pair of eyeglasses required three sets of screws: two holding the nose pads, two locking the lenses in place and two joining the front piece to the temple pieces. A typical pair also had two springs allowing the temple pieces to open and had several points of soldering.

Aesthetically, Urband had a distinctive look. The frames were light and modern, and the brand had been described as subtle, elegant and sophisticated. The eyepiece was curved to follow eye movement and suit facial contour. 'There is nothing else like it on the market,' Yang declared. 'When you see Urband, you know it's Urband. It's beautiful. It's a very sexy design.'

LINK

A Hip Design ...

While working on Urband, Yang had an idea for a second frame design which would be even simpler. Eventually branded as Link, it featured small buckles which fastened the front portion to the temples. The front portion was

... *With Special Casing*

Yang also designed a case to specifically fit Link frames. The case was shaped as an oval with the centre cut out, like a stretched donut. When the temple portions of the glasses were folded inward, the frame would fit into the case and wrap around the hole. The case could be fastened to a shoulder 'sling' bag, with the shoulder strap running through the hole. The case could be opened and the frames stowed or removed without the case being removed from the shoulder strap. 'This makes the glasses easily accessible, since you don't have to dig around inside your bag to find the case,' explained Yang. 'The case is right there, fastened outside your bag. It's more convenient, it's hip, and it makes a fashion statement.'

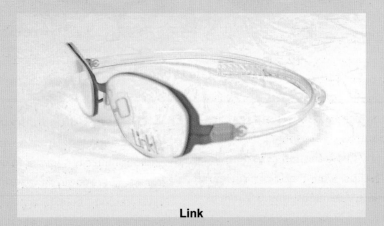

Link

made of stainless steel with silicone nose pads and the temples were made of TR90, an injection moulded plastic material. While the front portion was available in a variety of shapes, colours and styles, the temple pieces were consistent between models.

FROM CONCEPT TO DESIGN TO MARKET

Singapore-based entrepreneur Yang Wah Kiang worked with his business partners to develop, manufacture and launch two new fashion eyewear frames, branded as Urband

and Link. Yang viewed product development as a twofold process of product design and fashion design, and recognized that those two processes required different abilities. Yang and his partners had therefore combined their skills to develop frames that were both functional and stylish.

By June 2006, the product development phase was nearly complete and Yang reflected on the lessons he had learned. He also grappled with the new challenges of mass producing the frames and preparing for a full-scale market launch.

FASHION EYEWEAR INDUSTRY

A pair of eyeglasses had once been viewed as a tool, and often as an embarrassing or undesirable one. However, things began to change in the 1980s, with more emphasis placed on fashion. Consumers increasingly demanded eyeglass frames that were both functional and fashionable, and the world's top clothing designers responded with their own eyewear designs. By the 1990s, what had once been a necessity had become an accessory and glasses had become eyewear. Many consumers chose frames to express their identity, spent several hundred dollars per pair and changed them more often. Some consumers even purchased eyewear without prescriptions simply to achieve a desired look.

The total market for eyewear could be divided into two broad segments: mass and high-end. The high-end segment could be further divided into two sub-categories: mainstream fashion and niche. The mainstream fashion segment was served by (predominantly European) clothing designers

who had turned to eyewear in recent years. These designers included Armani, Gucci and dozens of others. Frames by these designers had actually become quite common, and some consumers wanted frames that were more distinctive and exclusive. This had given rise to the niche segment, which was served by designers specializing only in eyewear, such as Alain Mikli. The niche segment was smaller and the frames were typically more expensive.

In the fashion industry, product development consisted of two streams of work: product design, or the creation of a physical product; and fashion design, or the use of colour, materials, embellishments, packaging and branding to give the product more consumer appeal.

> Product Development = Product Design + Fashion Design
> where
> Product Design = Research & Development
> and
> Fashion Design = Style, Packaging & Branding

YANG: ENTREPRENEUR AND SELF-TAUGHT DESIGNER

Yang Wah Kiang, born in 1947, was the founder and managing director of Singapore-based Nanyang Optical. Nanyang Optical prepared prescription lenses and carried frames from mainstream fashion designers at eleven retail outlets in Singapore. These outlets generally catered to the mainstream fashion market segment. Nanyang Optical also included the Alexis Eyewear boutiques, carrying frames from exclusive designers and generally catering to the niche segment. Yang had opened two Alexis Eyewear boutiques in Singapore and six in Beijing, China.

(See Figure 7.9 for a timeline of key events for Yang's companies.)

> 'When you are in wholesale, your mind will have to work toward [original product development]. Because, you see, copying is not the way to go anymore.'

Opening the Alexis boutiques in Beijing exposed Yang to the market beyond Singapore retail and showed him the vast possibilities. In 1999, he turned his attention to wholesale activities and founded Eye-Biz. Eye-Biz was originally established to produce low-cost copies of popular European frames at factories in China, and to distribute the copies on a wholesale basis online through www.eye-biz.com. The venture failed, but it taught Yang a valuable lesson: if a small/ medium enterprise (SME) has any chance of breaking into the wholesale business, it must have a unique and differentiated product. Otherwise, the company would get lost among the bigger players. (See Tables 7.1 and 7.2 for Yang's assessment of three business strategies for wholesale eyewear.)

> 'I look at product design as a hobby. I enjoy it, it's my pastime. I'll take out a piece of paper and just start sketching.'

Meanwhile, Yang was discovering his own passion for product design. After three decades of retailing, he was no longer satisfied by selling other designers' products and engaging in customer service. He wanted to create something of his own. He had no formal training in product design, but realized he had a natural talent for it. By 2002, Yang had re-invented Eye-Biz as his product development arm.

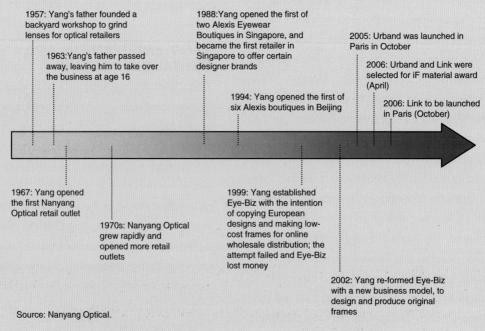

1957: Yang's father founded a backyard workshop to grind lenses for optical retailers

1963:Yang's father passed away, leaving him to take over the business at age 16

1988:Yang opened the first of two Alexis Eyewear Boutiques in Singapore, and became the first retailer in Singapore to offer certain designer brands

2005: Urband was launched in Paris in October

2006: Urband and Link were selected for iF material award (April)

1994: Yang opened the first of six Alexis boutiques in Beijing

2006: Link to be launched in Paris (October)

1967: Yang opened the first Nanyang Optical retail outlet

1970s: Nanyang Optical grew rapidly and opened more retail outlets

1999: Yang established Eye-Biz with the intention of copying European designs and making low-cost frames for online wholesale distribution; the attempt failed and Eye-Biz lost money

2002: Yang re-formed Eye-Biz with a new business model, to design and produce original frames

Source: Nanyang Optical.

Figure 7.9: History of Yang's Eyewear Companies.

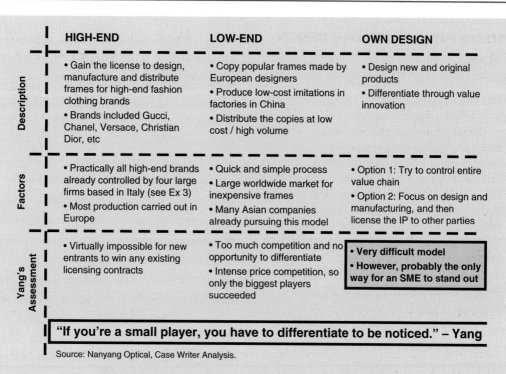

	HIGH-END	LOW-END	OWN DESIGN
Description	• Gain the license to design, manufacture and distribute frames for high-end fashion clothing brands • Brands included Gucci, Chanel, Versace, Christian Dior, etc	• Copy popular frames made by European designers • Produce low-cost imitations in factories in China • Distribute the copies at low cost / high volume	• Design new and original products • Differentiate through value innovation
Factors	• Practically all high-end brands already controlled by four large firms based in Italy (see Ex 3) • Most production carried out in Europe	• Quick and simple process • Large worldwide market for inexpensive frames • Many Asian companies already pursuing this model	• Option 1: Try to control entire value chain • Option 2: Focus on design and manufacturing, and then license the IP to other parties
Yang's Assessment	• Virtually impossible for new entrants to win any existing licensing contracts	• Too much competition and no opportunity to differentiate • Intense price competition, so only the biggest players succeeded	• Very difficult model • However, probably the only way for an SME to stand out

"If you're a small player, you have to differentiate to be noticed." – Yang

Source: Nanyang Optical, Case Writer Analysis.

Table 7.1: Three Business Models for Wholesale Eyewear.

Firm	Licensed Brands
Luxottica	Versace, Prada, Ferragamo, Bulgari, Moschino, Chanel, Donna Karan, Dolce & Gabbana and Anne Klein
Safilo	Armani, Polo Ralph Lauren, Max Mara, Liz Claiborne, Christian Dior, Valentino and Burberry, plus Gucci and Gucci-controlled brands like Yves Saint Laurent and Bottega Veneta
De Rigo	Celine, Givenchy, Loewe, Fendi, La Perla and Furla *Also, developing in-house brands like Police, Sting and Lozza*
Marcolin	Roberto Cavalli, Miss Sixty

Table 7.2: Leading Italian Eyewear Design and Manufacturing Firms.

Note: Luxottica also owned LensCrafters, Pearle Vision and Sunglass Hut for a network of 5,500 retail stores worldwide, making it the largest optical retailer in the US, Canada, Australia, New Zealand and Hong Kong. Also, in 1999, Luxottica purchased Ray-Ban.
Source: Sylvers, E. (2005, September 28). Eyewear taking the long view. *International Herald Tribune.* Kaiser, A. (2004, March 1). Eye drama. *Women's Wear Daily.*

CRITERIA FOR A SUCCESSFUL DESIGN

Yang was driven by a desire to create unique, distinctive eyewear. He thought the high-end frames from the mainstream fashion designers all looked the same. As he said:

> You try to look at people who wear Christian Dior, a pair of Max Mara, those brands of frames. You ask them to cover the label and you will never be able to guess. The brand is there because the brand is being stamped there, being printed there, being silk-screened there. You pay for top brands like that, there is no identity.

Furthermore, without unique design or positioning, it was hard to retain customer loyalty. 'The customer has too many choices, and those choices are all too similar,' he observed. 'If another designer or store sells it cheaper, the customer will go next door.'

Yang on Product Design

'Some people think product design is for the young and the hip, but you can design at any age as long as you are young-at-heart and creative. It doesn't matter if you're old – just don't think of yourself as being old!'

~

'Being a product designer is like being a chef. You must taste all the flavours and see what works before you can make a good meal.'

~

'Most importantly, you must believe in what you're doing, you must be confident and you must enjoy the work. You will have to solve many problems, and your attitude is what will get you through all of the ups and downs.'

Yang therefore wanted to create eyewear with its own identity and character. The frames should be instantly identifiable without the need for an obvious logo that 'shouted out the brand'. In his opinion, the need for a logo was an inherent design failure.

Yang also wanted to design eyewear that would offer value innovation. 'This is not innovation for the sake of innovation,' he explained. 'You must be able to see the *value* of this innovative function.' If retailers, opticians and consumers could see that value, they would favour the new product. Conversely, new features without real value were merely 'gimmicks'. For example, one high-end designer offered a frame with temple pieces that could swing 360 degrees. Yang thought that feature was interesting, but pointless.

Yang created two unique designs – one which used his innovative S-clips to attach the (side) temple pieces to the (front) eye piece, and one which used small buckles. The S-clips presented a revolutionary design without any screws, springs or soldering. This followed the industry trend toward simplification and minimalism, and made frames both strong and aesthetically pleasing.

PRODUCT DESIGN STUDIO

'In order to deliver . . . concept design and value innovation, you need a unit that can actually create and deliver, like a brain centre.'

PRODUCT DESIGN STUDIO

Next, Yang needed to transform his ideas into working prototypes. He did this with the help of an Australian-Chinese business partner living in Shenzhen, China. The two men established a product design studio in a rented 1,000-square foot apartment in Shenzhen. They assembled a team of ten research & design professionals and trained product designers. 'We hand-picked our staff,' Yang said. 'They are smart and skilled professionals.' The staff members were local Chinese, but since they were professionally trained, Yang and his partner paid them good wages. The two partners worked hand-in-hand with the design team, directing the work and adding their own input.

INSPIRATION

Yang found inspiration in objects from everyday living. In fact, the buckle design was inspired by the buckles on his infant grandson's car seat.

The product design phase took nearly three years – and significant financial investment – from conception until product launch. The work began with the S-clip design and the buckle design was added later. The team tested various designs and materials and encountered many obstacles. For example, it was discovered that titanium could not be used for the S-clips because friction caused titanium to discolour from grey to black. Stainless steel was subsequently adopted for the S-clips. Also, as the team quickly learned, the frame components had to be very precise.

The design team went through several iterations of each product before finally settling on three basic models: an S-clip frame with titanium front and temple pieces; an S-clip frame with acetate front and temple pieces; and a buckle frame with a stainless steel front piece and TR90 temple pieces.

Eye-Biz was not the only company in the world designing eyewear free of screws, springs and soldering. Yang knew of at least two companies in Europe that were pursuing the same goal. Eye-Biz was just trying to do it better than anyone else. Yang noted that one of the rival designs required a set of special tools to disassemble the frames, add the lenses and reassemble the frames, and he considered this a serious limitation. The Eye-Biz frames, by comparison, were much simpler and could be manipulated without any tools. Yang also thought the models from both of his competitors were too heavy and bulky. He therefore believed his own models were functionally and aesthetically superior.

FASHION DESIGN PARTNERSHIPS

Although Yang had passion and natural talent for product design, he admitted a lack of expertise in fashion design. To fill this gap, he formed partnerships with three French fashion eyewear designers whom he had met at international eyewear industry fairs.[2]

'Small details are crucial in the fashion world and can mean the difference between failure or success, and between a high retail price and a low retail price.'

---

[2] Eyewear industry players gathered twice each year, at the MIDO optical fair in Milan in May and at the SILMO fair in Paris in October.

Yang's new partners were up-and-coming designers who had worked for top names in the past and had recently ventured out independently. Two of them had worked for Alain Mikli and for Prada before forming their own partnership. The third was similarly experienced and was now working alone. Yang decided to work with them because they were skilled, entrepreneurial and well known in the optical trade. They were also ambitious, or in Yang's words, 'young and hungry'. He partnered with the first two designers for the S-clip frame and with the third designer for the buckle frames.

Equally important, the designers were French, and that image was a key point in Yang's strategy. Yang and his Shenzhen partner retained the patents on the frames, but sold the product licenses to the French partners and gave them control of the fashion design, packaging, branding and marketing aspects. As he explained:

> All around the world, French fashion is perceived to be the best – even better than Italian. Eyewear is fashion, so I need to work with the best. If consumers see the product as French, with French flair, it will have a much better chance of succeeding internationally. Also, consumers are willing to pay more for European brands than for Asian or even American brands, and higher retail prices will justify all the time and effort we spent creating our own products.

> 'We can take the backseat and let our French partners take the lead. They can have the profile. I don't need to be the front man as long as the product succeeds.'

The fashion designers created two brands for the frames: the S-clip frame was branded as Urband while the buckle frame became Link. They chose fashionable colour combinations and even advised Yang on product design changes to give the frames stronger identities. As Yang explained, 'Our French partners really have an eye for colour. They know what looks good and they know what works.' The partners also designed distinctive logos and attractive packaging.

The combined product design and fashion design efforts were validated when Urband and Link were selected as winners of the 2006 iF material award. The Hanover, Germany-based award recognized the best design work from virtually all product categories. With such a broad field and so many active designers around the world, recognition from iF was extremely significant.

BRANDING AND MARKETING

The plan was for both Urband and Link to be launched from Europe. Yang and his partners believed the brands should be identified as European so as to gain the associated cachet. They could be extended into America and brought back to Asia-Pacific later, with higher prestige and greater pricing power.

URBAND LAUNCH

For professionals in their 20s, 30s and 40s, with a strong sense of style

Launched October 2005 at SILMO Optical Fair

Retailing for ~ 200 Euros (both titanium & acetate)

Urband was launched at the SILMO industry fair in Paris in October 2005. The fair was a glamorous and stylish affair featuring over 1,000 exhibitor booths. Out of all the products on display, the French national newspaper Le Figaro chose the titanium Urband as the industry's #1 new design and the acetate Urband as #3. Urband received a great deal of additional positive media coverage, with one publication placing Urband alongside mega-brand Oakley in its reviews.

Urband was positioned for the high-end market. It would sell at a premium price of approximately 200 Euros, but would still be priced much lower than luxury brands like Cartier. Also, Yang was careful not to position Urband as 'fashion eyewear' because he felt that was an overused term and a saturated target market already. Instead, Urband was positioned as 'innovation eyewear' with distinct identity.

LINK LAUNCH

Fun eyewear for the young and young-at-heart

To be launched October 2006 at SILMO

Retailing for ~ 130 to 150 Euros

Yang and his two Urband partners divided the world into three sales regions. One of the partners would be responsible for sales in Europe, the other would be responsible for North America and Yang himself would take ownership of Asia-Pacific. The French partners would purchase large quantities of frames from

Yang at wholesale prices and use their own sales representatives to distribute the frames to optical retailers. Some sales representatives were in place already and more would be added as demand increased. Meanwhile, in Asia-Pacific, Yang would develop his own sales network. Although he would produce the frames, he would identify himself as the regional distributor for the French brand. The frames would feature standard packaging across all three regions.

Yang and his other French partner would follow a similar strategy in launching Link one year later. Link would be launched at SILMO in October 2006. That partner would distribute the product in both Europe and North America, and Yang would again be responsible for distribution in Asia-Pacific.

MANUFACTURING AND FULL-SCALE LAUNCH

Yang's greatest remaining challenge was to produce high quality Urband and Link frames for market distribution. He set quality as his top priority, ahead of production speed and quantity. He believed that even if he started slowly, he could build momentum over time as long as the brands had solid reputations among both retailers and consumers.

Yang did not want to own and operate a factory of his own. Even if Urband and Link production volumes could eventually justify a dedicated factory, there were too many duties, details and complications that would distract him from his true passion – design. As he said,

To me, owning a factory is a burden ... you are bogged down with realities that every month, you have to sell so much to cover all these expenses. That kills your innovation spirit [and the] creative aspect of the design.

> 'There are three elements in producing something. I call them the 3 Qs: quality, quantity and quickness. It's hard to have all three. I'm focusing on delivering high quality frames, even if it's in low quantities and it's slow at first.'

He therefore planned to outsource frame production and wanted to choose his component suppliers and ramp up production in the second half of 2006. Component manufacturing would be the most difficult part of the production process; assembly would be easier, but it would still require strict quality control.

Yang initially scouted for suitable factories in Shenzhen. A well-developed cluster of eyewear production facilities operated there and China was responsible for much of the world's eyewear frame output. However, Yang found that his options were limited. Few factory managers were willing to manufacture Urband or Link frames due to their unusual designs. Much of the work would have to be performed by hand and there would be much variation between styles and colours. Factory employees would have to be given special training, and since turnover was high at most of those factories, new employees would have to be trained on an ongoing basis. The high turnover would also lead to quality control problems, rework and low yields. Most Chinese factory managers would rather make copies of simple, conventional designs, which involved no learning curve.

'I need a responsible, reliable factory that will deliver what I ask for,' he said. 'That is very hard to find in China, especially when the parts are complex.' He also considered outsourcing to Taiwan, Korea and Japan, where quality would be better, but costs would be higher. (See Table 7.3 for Yang's assessment of these countries in terms of outsourced production.)

10,000 titanium Urband frames had already been produced in China in a test run. The components had been outsourced to several factories and the frames had later been assembled by hand by the Eye-Biz employees at the Shenzhen design studio. The factories had been unreliable, the assembly process had been tedious and the quality had suffered. Yang had initially ordered enough components for 4,000 frames, but only 1,300 assembled frames passed the quality inspection. Yang ordered more parts, and eventually 10,000 finished frames were assembled and approved. 'It was a production nightmare,' Yang said. 'We went through a lot of pain.'

The 10,000 frames were distributed in Europe to gather consumer feedback and generate industry buzz. The frames sold well, but some consumers later returned them to the retailers. As Yang discovered, the colour that had been painted onto the titanium faded after several months. Yang had since resolved the issue with a better colour plating technique.

> 'Probably eight out of ten entrepreneurs abandon their projects before becoming successful, but I keep pushing ahead through the obstacles because I truly believe this will work.'

Country	Yang's Assessment
Mainland China	• No language / cultural barrier • Labour cheaper than in other countries, but rising • High worker turnover, resulting in constant training of new staff • High worker turnover also leading to inconsistent quality • Lagging behind Taiwan for injection moulding, but catching up
Taiwan	• No language / cultural barrier • Good injection moulding factories • More expensive than China
Korea	• Language / cultural barrier • More expensive than China • Frames industry in decline
Japan	• Very orderly factories and infrastructure • 'By far the best, most reliable factories' • Most expensive option; costs too high for Yang to absorb • Language / cultural barrier

Table 7.3: Yang's Assessment of Various Countries in Terms of Outsourcing Potential.
Source: Yang Wah Kiang, Case Writer Analysis.

It would be even harder to produce the acetate Urband frames. The component pieces would have to be cut by hand and the acetate itself was prone to shrinkage due to temperature changes during the manufacturing process. Yang thought it would be easier to make the acetate Urband frames through the process of injection moulding. However, the moulds would be very expensuive, and many different moulds would be required to produce the range of frame variations.

Fortunately, it would be much easier to produce Link since the design was simpler. It would be easier to find factory managers willing to produce Link and the quality control process would be much easier. Injection moulding could also be used for the Link temple pieces, and this would be cost effective since all the temple pieces would be the same.

'We're just an SME doing what we like to do.'

Yang had made a shortlist of factories that might be appropriate for Urband and for Link, but he knew he'd have to work closely with the factories to provide technical support and oversee quality control.

THE FINAL PUSH

Yang had made an uncommon move by relinquishing some control of his intellectual property to his business partners. Most entrepreneurs and designers would rather take the lead in all decisions and activities themselves. By doing this, Yang had leveraged his partners' expertise and given himself more time to focus on the issues that were better suited to his own skill set. However, the production issues now facing Yang were very challenging and he had to resolve them as quickly as possible to support the products' worldwide launch campaigns.

Questions

1. Relate the case study to the main stages of product design.
2. Identify the key success factors in product design at Nanyang optical.

EXERCISES

1. A manufacturer produces a product with the following specification.
Selling price = £15.00/unit
Variable cost = £10.00/unit
Fixed costs = £10 000/week
a) What is the break-even point?
b) How many do they need to sell to make £20 000 profit a week?

2. The following product mix is planned.

	Knives	Forks	Spoons
Product mix	0.4	0.4	0.2
Selling price (£/unit)	0.07	0.08	0.05
Variable cost (£/unit)	0.05	0.06	0.03

Annual fixed cost = £1000

a) What is the break-even point?
b) At what volume will profit = £5000, given the current product mix?
c) If the price of a spoon is reduced by £0.01, what volume is required to make a profit of £5000?

3. An assembly is made up of four components arranged as follows:

B
|
———— A ———— C ———— D ————

The components can be purchased from three different suppliers with the following reliability ratings:

	Supplier		
Component	1	2	3
A	0.94	0.95	0.92
B	0.86	0.80	0.90
C	0.90	0.93	0.95
D	0.93	0.95	0.95

a) If only one supplier is chosen to supply all four components, which should be selected?

b) What supplier should be selected for the following configuration?

```
_____  A  _____  B  ____  C  ____  D  ____
```

4. Discuss the objectives of functional design, form design and production design.

5. Explain the role of standardization, simplification and modularization in design.

6. Outline the objectives of FMEA.

7. What is the purpose of QFD?

8. How would you implement a concurrent design programme?

WEB EXERCISE

Compare the design process steps outlined in this chapter with the 'double-diamond' design process model described by the Design Council at http://www.designcouncil.org.uk/en/About-Design/managingdesign/The-Study-of-the-Design-Process/ (28 September 2008).

FURTHER READING

Berman, B. (2002) Should your firm adopt a mass customisation strategy? *Business Horizons*, July–August, 51–60.

Hope, C. and **Mühlemann, A.** (1997) *Service Operations Management: Strategy, Design and Delivery*, Prentice Hall.

Taguchi, G. and **Clausing, D.** (1990) Robust quality, *Harvard Business Review*, January–February, 65–75.

● WEB LINKS

www.autocad.com (accessed 28 September 2008). AutoCAD. One of the most popular software packages for designing new products.

www.design-council.org.uk (accessed 28 September 2008). Design Council. Wide-ranging site including information on all aspects of design.

www.design-iv.com (accessed 28 September 2008). Design IV. Consultancy specializing in design for manufacture and assembly (DFMA). Site has information on conferences, software and training.

www.roundtable.com (accessed 28 September 2008). A variety of resources for product and technology development.

● REFERENCES

Fitzsimmons, J.A. and **Fitzsimmons, M.J.** (2008) *Service Management: Operations, Strategy, and Information Technology*, 6th edn, McGraw-Hill.

Kaiser, A. (2004) Eye drama, *Women's Wear Daily*, 1 March.

Sylvers, E. (2005) Eyewear taking the long view, *International Herald Tribune*, 28 September.

CHAPTER
8
Process Design

- Introduction
- Process design levels
- Business process management (BPM)
- Steps in process design
- Tools for process design

LEARNING OBJECTIVES

- Understand the role of business process management

- Describe the steps in process design

- Evaluate the use of process design techniques such as process activity charts, process mapping and service blueprinting

- Describe the relevance of using business process simulation to study manufacturing and service processes

INTRODUCTION

Historically, operations management has been concerned with the design of the flow of people and products through manufacturing and service processes once a process type and layout have been chosen. However, the term operations can now be seen to cover all aspects of an organization when the organization is considered to consist of a number of processes (the process view of operations is covered in Chapter 1). This means process design will not just be considered at the level of individual activities within manufacturing and service processes but at the level of processes across functional areas such as operations, marketing and finance and at the level of processes across organizations in the supply chain. The concept of business process management (BPM) is introduced as an approach to designing processes at all levels within and between organizations. The design of processes is complex and so the steps in a structured approach to process design are covered as are the use of tools to assist process design activities.

PROCESS DESIGN LEVELS

As stated in the introduction, processes are present in all parts of the organization and across organizations in the supply chain, so operations management is relevant in all these areas. Figure 8.1 shows processes at three levels in a textile-plant operation. Individual processes (knit, preparation and dye) make up part of the manufacturing process, which in turn with other areas such as engineering and warehousing makes up part of the organizational process. This organizational

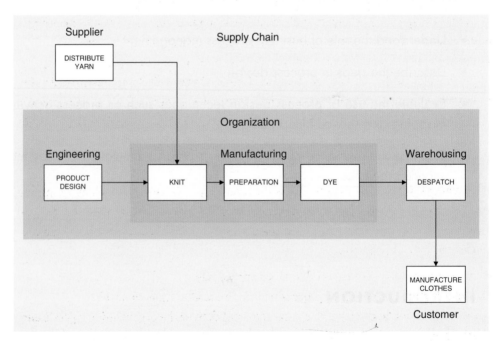

Figure 8.1: Process Design at the Three Levels of Process, Organization and Supply Chain for a Textile Manufacturing Plant.

process is in turn part of a process that spans across the supply chain. Thus personnel in all the areas shown in Figure 8.1 are operations managers in the sense that they are involved with the design and management of the processes in their area. Figure 8.1 also implies that to design and measure the performance of a process requires an understanding of the whole process across the supply chain. This can be approached, firstly, by measuring the whole process across the supply chain in terms of delivering customer satisfaction to the end user, then ensuring that organizational processes link together across functional areas and finally measuring individual process performance.

BUSINESS PROCESS MANAGEMENT (BPM)

Business process management is the term used to refer to the analysis and improvement of business processes. A process is a set of activities designed to produce a desired output from a specified input. The process orientation matches the idea of the main objectives of the operations function as the management of the transformation process of inputs (resources) into outputs (goods and services) covered in Chapter 1. Although BPM is usually used in the broad sense it is also used more narrowly to refer to software technologies for automating the management of specific processes. In its widest sense, however, BPM brings together aspects such as:

Business process management
This is the term used to refer to the analysis and improvement of business processes.

- process mapping techniques such as process mapping and service blueprinting;
- simulation modelling techniques such as business process simulation;
- the software design approach of service-oriented architecture (SOA);
- performance measurement systems such as business activity monitoring (BAM);
- implementation of information technologies such as workflow systems (Chapter 6);
- improvement approaches such as business process reengineering (BPR) (Chapter 18);
- assessment models such as ISO9000 (Chapter 17).

Business process management has been developed by authors such as Rummler and Brache (1995) who provide a method of undertaking the technique using organizational analysis and process analysis and design. Business process management is concerned with the following:

- linking corporate strategy and business processes;
- providing measurement of process performance at a strategic level;
- design and management of the processes that deliver the organization's goods and services;
- implementation of process change, both manually by employees and by the use of IT systems.

For implementation of processes that are performed by employees, consideration is made of such factors as job descriptions, motivation systems, supervision, training and evaluation of performance. A Six Sigma approach (Chapter 17) may be used in this area. For the implementation of processes automated by IT systems consideration is made of such factors as software development and maintenance. Use is made of software tools such as workflow (Chapter 6), business process simulation (Chapter 8) and packaged enterprise applications such as ERP (Chapter 14).

There is evidence that the full potential of business process management is not being realized. Fingar (2006) states that most BPM projects are tactical and about streamlining individual functions within a company. BPM's full potential offers a strategic capability through process innovation at the three levels of process design discussed earlier. The reason this has not occurred may be due to the fact, as Fingar (2006) notes, that the scope and complexity of process design increases as companies progress from the individual process level (termed point-solution BPM) to the organizational level (enterprise BPM) to the supply-chain level (value-chain BPM). Another feature of BPM projects is that they have been most successful in relation to the design of information systems such as workflow systems, but there are few examples of process design incorporating human interactions, for example of work teams working across organizations. This suggests the need for more understanding of human-driven processes, which requires knowledge of how people actually work and how these work processes change over time.

STEPS IN PROCESS DESIGN

The task of designing processes should be undertaken in a structured manner and the steps involved can be described as:

1. Identifying and documenting the process activities.
2. Identifying processes for improvement.
3. Evaluating process design alternatives.

1. Identifying and Documenting the Process Activities

The identification of activities in a current process design is a data-collection exercise using methods such as examination of current documentation, interviews and observation.

For the design of new processes, techniques such as *functional analysis* exist. This technique for mapping service processes starts by defining a high-level description of the service and then successively breaking down that description into a number of functions. Processes are then created by arranging the functions in the sequence in which the activities defined by the functions are performed.

In service processes it is useful to have a customer at the start and end of the process in order to evaluate the impact of the quality of the process on the customer. Another aspect of service process design is the important role that customers play in the delivery of the service. In order to incorporate the interactions between the customer and the service provider during service, processes can be classified into *operational activities*, which are the steps needed to deliver the service to the customer, and *customer service activities*, which are the customer and service-provider interactions.

Customer service activities tend to be overlooked in process design because they are measured by attributes such as responsiveness and friendliness, which are attributes of people and thus more difficult to measure. The key here is to design procedures around customer and service-provider interactions that maximize the reliability of the quality of service.

In order to provide a framework for the design and improvement of service processes the techniques of process mapping and service blueprinting can be used and are described later in this chapter.

2. Identifying Processes for Improvement

Once step one has been completed it is necessary to prioritize the process elements that will be allocated resources for improvement.

The identification of the relevant business processes for improvement can be undertaken using a scoring system such as the performance/importance matrix (Martilla and James, 1977) on which processes can be plotted in terms of how well the organization performs them and how important they are. Slack and Lewis (2008) outline a model in which prioritization is governed by importance to customers and performance against competitors. Greasley (2004a) presents a scoring system developed in conjunction with a public sector organization in which it is necessary to take into consideration a number of stakeholder views. The system consists of a two-dimensional marking guide based on the impact of the process on the critical success factors determined in a balanced scorecard review and an assessment of the scope for innovation (the amount of improvement possible) to the current process design. Processes that are strategically important and offer the largest scope for improvement are prioritized under this model (see Case Study 18.4).

3. Evaluating Process Design Alternatives

There are many ways in which a process can be designed to meet particular objectives and so it is necessary to generate a range of innovative solutions for evaluation. Three approaches that can be used to generate new ideas are:

- Generating new designs through brainstorming. This approach offers the greatest scope for radical improvements to the process design but represents a risk in the implementation of a totally new approach. A deep understanding of the process is required in order that the design will be feasible.
- Modifying existing designs. This approach is less risky than a blue-skies approach but may mean the opportunity for a radical improvement in process design is missed.
- Using an established 'benchmark' design. This approach applies the idea of identifying the best-in-class performer for the particular process in question and adopting that design. Disadvantages with this approach may be that the process design of the best-in-class performer may not be available or the context of the best-in-class performer may not match the context for the new design.

The process map or service blueprint provides an overall view of the current or expected process design and this should be used in order that an overall view is taken when process design options are generated. This helps to ensure that design solutions proposed in a specific area do not have a detrimental effect in other areas of the process and thus affect overall process performance.

The design of service processes in particular is a key factor in meeting the needs of the customer. In services the process incorporates employees, customers and facilitating goods in a dynamic event that may be undertaken in a different manner each time, according to the demands of the individual customer. The interaction between the customer and service provider can be analysed using the service blueprint diagrams described in this chapter.

In designing services Shostack (1987) categorizes services by their complexity – the number and interdependency of process elements – and divergency – how many different ways they can be performed. Once a service has been documented it can be analysed for opportunities either to increase or decrease one or both of these variables.

Peppard and Rowland (1995) provide a number of areas for the potential design of processes under the headings of Eliminate, Simplify, Integrate and Automate (ESIA) (Table 8.1).

Eliminate	Simplify	Integrate	Automate
Over-production	Forms	Jobs	Dirty
Waiting time	Procedures	Teams	Difficult
Transport	Communication	Customers	Dangerous
Processing	Technology	Suppliers	Boring
Inventory	Problem areas		Data capture
Defects/failures	Flows		Data transfer
Duplication	Processes		Data analysis
Reformatting			
Inspection			
Reconciling			

Table 8.1: ESIA Areas for Potential Redesign.
Source: Peppard and Rowland (1995). The Essence of Business Process Re-engineering, Prentice Hall. Reproduced by permission of Pearson Education.

It will be necessary to reduce the number of design alternatives generated and this can be achieved by a rating scheme that scores each design solution against key performance dimensions such as response time and cost of operation. The outcome of this analysis will be a reduced number of design solutions, which can then be subjected to more detailed analysis.

This analysis is often undertaken using mathematical models such as queuing theory (Chapter 11) and techniques such as business process simulation (BPS) (Chapter 8). The BPS technique allows the predicted variability in a process design to be incorporated in a computer model and thus the robustness of the design over time can be assessed.

TOOLS FOR PROCESS DESIGN

A number of tools are available to assist in the task of redesigning processes. These tools can help in all stages of the design process including documentation of processes, identification of processes for redesign and for evaluating design alternatives.

Process Activity Charts

A process activity chart (also called a process chart) is often used to analyse the steps of a job or how a set of jobs fit together into the overall flow of a process. For example the steps involved in processing a customer order received by telephone. There are five main symbols in a process activity chart, as shown in Figure 8.2. An example process chart for a generic administration process is shown in Figure 8.3.

> Process activity chart
> This is a charting device that is often used to analyse the steps of a job or how a set of jobs fit together into the overall flow of a process.

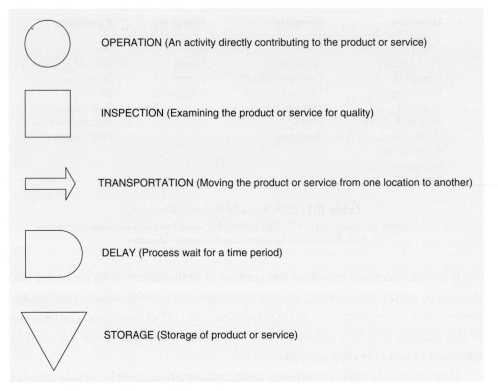

Figure 8.2: Symbols for a Process Activity Chart.

The process activity chart performs a number of functions including identifying the task sequence, task relationships, task delays (by including average task times), task movements and worker assignment to tasks. The charts can be used in conjunction with a written job description to form a detailed outline of a job. The charts can also be useful in the first stage of a job improvement scheme. There are, however, a number of limitations to the charts. Processes with decision points and parallel processes cannot be shown on a process activity chart. Process mapping can be used to incorporate these aspects. Only average task times are used to calculate the process time and variability in task times is not taken into account. Business process simulation can be used to incorporate variability.

Process Mapping

Documenting the process can be undertaken by the construction of a process map, also called a flow chart. This is a useful way of understanding any business process and showing the interrelationships between activities in a process. This can help in identifying and fixing problems with the process, assisting the development of new

Process Description   **Process Symbol**

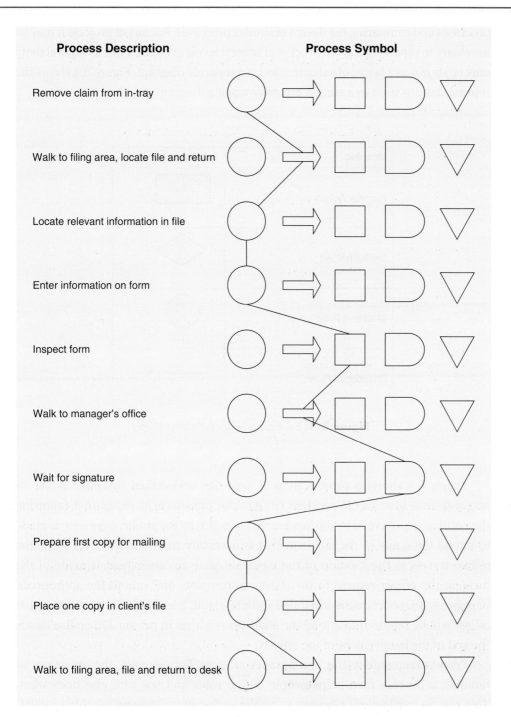

Remove claim from in-tray

Walk to filing area, locate file and return

Locate relevant information in file

Enter information on form

Inspect form

Walk to manager's office

Wait for signature

Prepare first copy for mailing

Place one copy in client's file

Walk to filing area, file and return to desk

Figure 8.3: Process Chart for Generic Administration Process.

processes and comparing the design of similar processes. For larger projects it may be necessary to represent a given process at several levels of detail. Thus a single activity may be shown as a series of subactivities on a separate diagram. Figure 8.4 shows the representations used in a simple **process mapping** diagram.

Process mapping
The use of a flow chart to document the process incorporating process activities and decision points.

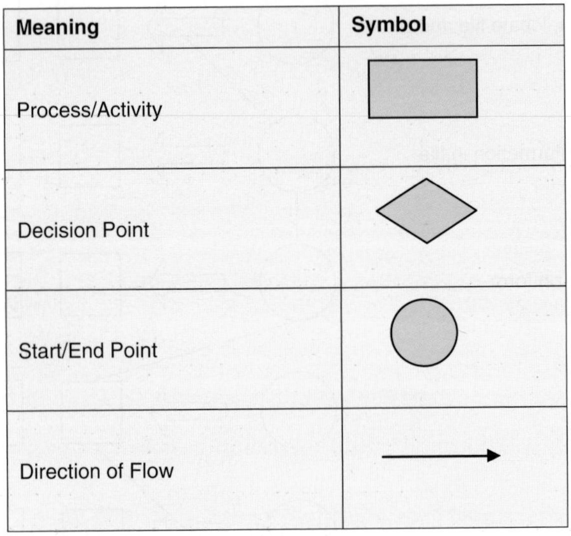

Meaning	Symbol
Process/Activity	▭
Decision Point	◇
Start/End Point	◯
Direction of Flow	→

Figure 8.4: Symbols used for a Process Map.

Figure 8.5 shows a process map of activities undertaken by traffic police in response to a road traffic accident (RTA). The process map shows that following the notification of a road traffic incident to the police by the public, a decision is made to attend the scene of the incident. If it is necessary to attend the RTA scene the officer travels to the location of the incident. After an assessment is made of the incident the officer returns to the station to complete and submit the appropriate paperwork. If a court case is scheduled and a not guilty plea has been entered then the officer will be required to attend the court proceedings in person. Otherwise this is the end of the involvement of the officer.

Process maps are useful in a number of ways. For example, the procedure of building a process map helps people define roles and see who else does what. This can be particularly relevant to public sector organizations in which modelling existing processes can be used to build consensus on what currently happens. The process map can also serve as a first step in using business process simulation as it identifies the processes and decision points required to build the model.

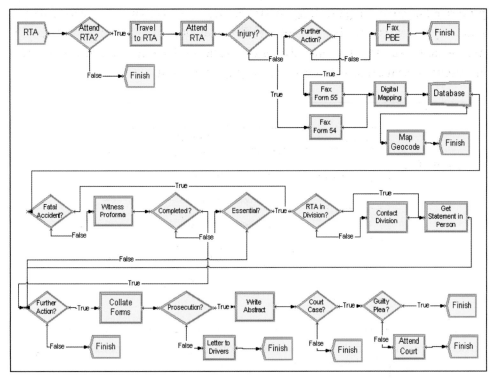

Figure 8.5: A Road Traffic Accident Reporting Process Map.

Service Blueprinting

Process maps are widely used in manufacturing to design the flow of a number of linked processes that produce an output. In services, however, process maps may be less relevant when a service consists of a number of subprocesses that are not linked and the service 'output' is a number of customer-employee interactions. In this case the process design may first focus on the design of the customer-employee interactions and then identify external performance measures such as customer satisfaction.

To assist in the analysis of customer-employee interactions process maps can be extended to show how a business interacts with customers. One system is called *service system mapping (SSM)* (Laguna and Marklund, 2005). Shostack (1984) has developed a flow chart (termed a blueprint) which structures the process activities either side of a customer 'line of visibility' (Figure 8.6). The activities above the line are visible to the customer and those below the line are operations that the customer does not see. Activities above the line of visibility are subdivided into two fields separated by the 'line of interaction', this divides activities undertaken by the customer and the service provider. Below the line of visibility a line of internal interaction

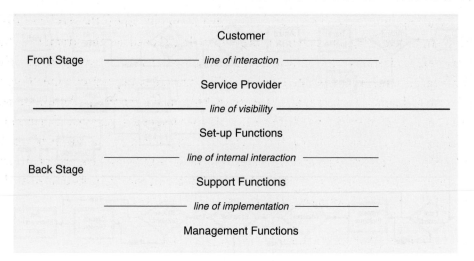

Figure 8.6: Service Blueprint Template.

separates the activities of front-line personnel who carry out setting-up actions prior to service provision (not in view of the customer) and support personnel who contribute materials or services required for the provision of the service. Finally the 'line of implementation' separates support activities from management activities such as planning, controlling and decision making.

Figure 8.7 shows an example service blueprint for a restaurant.

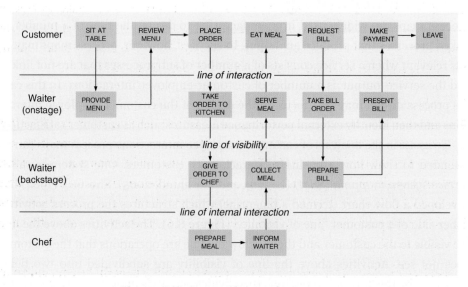

Figure 8.7: Service Blueprint for Restaurant.

The objective of the **service blueprint** is that it not only charts the service process flow (from left to right) as does a process map, but also shows the structure of the service organization on the vertical axis, showing relationships between, for example, internal customers, support staff and front-line providers. In particular the diagram aims to highlight the interactions between the customer and process where customer services can be affected. The diagrams can also be used as a design tool to determine staffing levels, job descriptions and selection of equipment and as a control tool to identify gaps in service provision through the analysis of fail points. Fail points are potential service system shortfalls between what the service delivers and what the targeted customers have been led to expect.

> **Service blueprintng**
> A charting device for processes, which documents the interaction between the customer and the service provider.

Business Process Simulation (BPS)

Defining Business Process Simulation

The use of a simulation model on a computer to mimic the operation of a business means that the performance of the business over an extended time period can be observed quickly and under a number of different scenarios. Simulation in general covers a large area of interest and so a short explanation is given of common terms used. Simulation can refer to a range of model types from spreadsheet models, system dynamic simulations and discrete-event simulation. **Business process simulation** is usually implemented using discrete-event simulation systems that move through time in (discrete) steps. Most simulation modelling software is now implemented using graphical user interfaces employing objects or icons that are placed on the screen to produce a model. These are often referred to as visual interactive modelling (VIM) systems. When a discrete-event simulation system using a visual interactive modelling interface is used in the context of a process-based change method it is commonly referred to as a business process simulation.

> **Business process simulation**
> The use of computer software, in the context of a process-based change, that allows operation of a business to be simulated.

Why Use Business Process Simulation?

The ease of use and usefulness of process design techniques such as process mapping has meant their use is widespread. Business process simulation requires a significant investment in time and skills but it is able to provide a more realistic assessment of the behaviour of manufacturing and service processes than most other process design tools. This is due to its ability to incorporate the dynamic (time-dependent) behaviour of operations systems. There are two aspects of dynamic systems that need to be addressed:

- *Variability.* Most business systems contain variability in both the demand on the system (for example, customer arrivals) and the durations (for instance, customer service times) of activities within the system. The use of fixed (for example, average) values will provide some indication of performance but simulation permits the incorporation of statistical distributions and thus provides an indication of both the range and variability of the performance of the system. This is important in customer-based systems when not only is the average performance relevant but performance should not drop below a certain level (for example, customer service time) or customers will be lost. In service systems, two widely used performance measures are an estimate of the maximum queuing time for customers and the utilization (percentage time occupied) of the staff serving the customer.

- *Interdependence.* Most systems contain a number of decision points that affect the overall performance of the system. The simulation technique can incorporate statistical distributions to model the likely decision options taken. The 'knock-on' effect of many interdependent decisions over time can also be assessed given the simulation's ability to show system behaviour over a time period.

WORKED EXAMPLE 8.1
Variability in Service Systems

A manager of a small shop wishes to predict how long customers wait for service during a typical day. The owner has identified two types of customer, who have different amounts of shopping and so take different amounts of time to serve. Type A customers account for 70% of custom and take on average ten minutes to serve. Type B customers account for 30% of custom and take on average five minutes to serve. The owner has estimated that during an eight hour day, on average the shop will serve 40 customers.

SOLUTION 1

The owner calculates the serve time during a particular day:

Customer A $= 0.7 \times 40 \times 10$ minutes $= 280$ minutes
Customer B $= 0.3 \times 40 \times 5$ minutes $= 60$ minutes
Therefore the total service time $= 340$ minutes and gives a utilization of the shop till of $340/480 \times 100 = 71\%$.

Thus the owner is confident all customers can be served promptly during a typical day.

A simulation model was constructed of this system to estimate the service time for customers. Using a fixed time between customer arrivals of $480/40 = 12$ minutes and with a 70% probability of a ten minutes' service time and a 30% probability of a five minutes' service time, the overall service time for customers has a range of between five to ten minutes and no queues are present in this system.

Service time for customer (minutes)

Average: 8.5

Minimum: 5

Maximum: 10

● SOLUTION 2

In reality customers will not arrive equally spaced at 12-minute intervals, but will arrive randomly with an average interval of 12 minutes. A simulation is used to simulate a time between arrivals of customers, which follows an exponential distribution (the exponential distribution is often used to mimic the behaviour of customer arrivals) with a mean of 12 minutes. The owner was surprised by the simulation results:

Service time for customer (minutes)

Average: 17

Minimum: 5

Maximum: 46

The average service time for a customer had doubled to 17 minutes, with a maximum of 46 minutes!

Example 8.1 demonstrates how the performance of even simple systems can be affected by randomness. Variability would also be present in this system in other areas such as customer service times and the mix of customer types over time. The simulation method is able to incorporate all of these sources of variability to provide a more realistic picture of system performance.

Using Business Process Simulation for Business Process Management

In order to undertake a successful simulation study a number of steps must be followed. The main steps in developing a simulation model outlined in Greasley (2004b) are:

Define the Study Objectives

A number of specific study objectives should be derived which will provide a guide to the data needs of the model, set the boundaries of the study (scope), the level of modelling detail and define the experimentation analysis required. It is necessary to refine the study objectives until specific scenarios defined by input variables and measures that can be defined by output variables can be specified. General improvement areas for a process design project include aspects such as the following:

- changes in process logic – changes to routing, decision points and layout
- changes in resource availability – shift patterns, equipment failure
- changes in demand – forecast pattern of demand on the process.

Many projects will study a combination of the above but it is important to study each area in turn to establish potential subjects for investigation at the project proposal stage.

Data Collection and Process Mapping

Once the simulation project objectives have been defined, and the scope and level of detail set, the modeller should prepare a specification of the data required for the model build. It is useful at this stage to identify the source of the information, its form (for example, documentation, observation, interview) and any personnel responsible for supplying the relevant information. A process map specification should define what processes will be mapped. The process map should provide a medium for obtaining information from a variety of viewpoints regarding the system being organized. In particular, issues of system boundaries (what to include and what to omit from the analysis) can be addressed.

Modelling Input Data

A specification of the type of statistical analysis used for modelling input variables and process durations should be made. A trace-driven model will require no statistical analysis of input data but a forecasting model may require the data to be fitted to a suitable probability distribution. The level of data analysis will depend on the study objectives, time constraints and the amount of raw data available.

Building the Model

A number of vendors offer business process simulation software packages. An example of a BPS is the ARENA™ system shown in Figure 8.8. The simulation is represented by symbols that closely relate to the standard process mapping symbols. The simulation is constructed by dragging the appropriate symbol from the window on the left-hand side of the screen and placing it on the main view window. The symbols are then connected together to represent the process flow. Each symbol is then double clicked with the mouse to reveal a menu that allows entry of parameters such as process times. When all the simulation data are entered, the 'run' button is

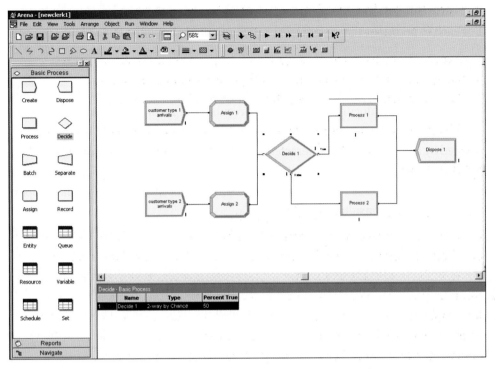

Figure 8.8: Screen Display of a Business Process Simulation.

clicked and the simulation moves through time. Animation features can be added as required and reports provide information on performance measures such as resource utilization and queuing times.

Validation and Verification

Verification or debugging time can be difficult to predict but some estimation of verification time can be made from the estimated complexity and size of the proposed model. Validation will require the analyst to spend time with people who are familiar with the model being studied to ensure model behaviour is appropriate. A number of meetings may be necessary to ensure that the simulation model has sufficient credibility with potential users. Sensitivity analysis may be required to validate a model of a system that does not currently exist. The type of sensitivity analysis envisaged should be defined in the project proposal.

Experimentation and Analysis

Experimentation and analysis aims to study the effects which changes in input variables (scenarios defined in the objectives) have on output variables (performance measures defined in the objectives) in the model. The number of experiments should be clearly defined as each experiment may take a substantial amount of analysis time. For each experiment the statistical analysis required should be defined.

Implementation

The results of the simulation study must be presented in report form, which should include full model documentation, study results and recommendations for further studies. An implementation plan may also be specified. The report can be supplemented by a presentation to interested parties. The duration and cost of both of these activities should be estimated. Further allocation of time and money may be required for aspects such as user training, run-time software licence and telephone support from an external consultant.

In terms of the process design steps outlined at the start of this chapter BPS is particularly relevant to the evaluation of process design alternatives. It should also be noted that the process mapping technique, often used to identify and document process activities, represents the basis for the simulation model design. After the use of the process map a decision can be made if the more in-depth analysis provided by the business process simulation is required. Case Study 8.2 provides an example of the use of BPS in a process-centred change project.

Business Activity Monitoring (BAM)

> **Business activity monitoring**
> Software that is designed to monitor, capture and analyse business performance data in real time and present them visually in order that rapid and effective decisions can be taken.

Business activity monitoring software provides an application that provides real-time or fast response information to decision makers. The software is in response to the need to manage increasingly complex business processes that can occur at several different locations. BAM software is designed to monitor, capture and analyse business performance data in real time and present them visually in order that rapid and effective decisions can be taken. BAM systems can be categorized into three levels of implementation: alert and dashboard, automatic response and predictive and adaptive:

- *Alert and dashboard.* These systems capture data from various applications and internal and external data sources, which are then filtered and analysed to provide an alert of unusual performance. A dashboard display is a graphical display on the computer presented to the decision maker, which includes graphical images such as meters, bar graphs, trace plots and text fields, to convey real-time information.
- *Automatic response.* In a standard alert and dashboard system any decisions made on the basis of the information supplied by the BAM are made using traditional telephone, email or alternative communication systems. Automatic response systems add the ability to automatically handle business exceptions.

They could do this, for example, by matching any exceptions with a repository of known error fixes and then initiating an appropriate business process, which can trigger a number of automated and manual events.

- *Predictive and adaptive.* This implementation of BAM not only provides alerts in response to exception events but also suggests alternative actions that could be taken and allows the exploration of future scenarios based on alternative responses. Business process simulation (BPS) could be used to predict future events and help explore future scenarios. In addition adaptive systems can adapt to and learn from changing business conditions.

Service-Oriented Architecture (SOA)

The use of information systems is a key element in process design. Enterprise resource systems (ERP) used in manufacturing processes are covered in Chapter 14 and many service processes use software systems that gather and distribute information to facilitate customer interactions. The concept of **service-oriented architecture** is the development of a number of reusable business-aligned IT services that span multiple applications across the organization. Service-oriented architecture defines the services in such a way as to be utilized in a manner that is independent of the underlying application and technology platforms. A collection of standardized services forms the basis of a **service inventory**. Individual services from the service inventory can be deployed in multiple business processes. Each collection of services used in a particular business process is termed a **service composition**. The advantage of this approach for business process management is that a business process can link with the business services which are activated by the business processes without the need to know about the underlying application and technology platforms. SOA will most often be implemented on the Web platform. The term **Web services** describes the technology that is most associated with the formation of an SOA. For more details on SOA see Bocij, Greasley and Hickie (2008).

Service-oriented architecture
An approach that incorporates reusable business-aligned IT services that can be utilized in a manner that is independent of the underlying application and technology platforms.

Service inventory
A collection of standardized services that are designed for use in a number of business processes.

Service composition
A selection of services from the service inventory that are allocated to a particular business process.

Web services
A collection of industry standards which represents the most likely technology connecting services together to form a service-oriented architecture.

SUMMARY

- Process design involves understanding the whole process and involves everyone in the organization as 'operations managers', managing the process.

- Business process management provides a method of undertaking the analysis and improvement of business processes.

- The steps in process design are: identify and document process activities, identify processes for improvement, evaluate process design alternatives.

- A process activity chart can be used to analyse the steps of a job.

- A process map can be used to show the interrelationships between activities in a process.

- A service blueprint is a flow chart that documents the interaction between the customer and the service provider.

- Business process simulation is a technique that can be used to measure the performance of processes over time by taking into consideration variability and interdependence factors.

- Business activity monitoring is software that is designed to monitor, capture and analyse business performance data.

- Service-oriented architecture is an approach that incorporates reusable business-aligned IT services that can be utilized in a manner that is independent of the underlying application and technology platforms.

CASE STUDY   8.1

Why the Bunker Mentality has become a Corporate Liability

Sir Howard Stringer, the Welsh-born boss of Sony, has declared war on them. At Morgan Stanley, new chief executive John Mack has vowed to smash them. The US intelligence system is, infamously, riddled with them. It is a fair bet that your organization is too. The objects of all this executive ire? Silos – divisions or departments that would rather burn in hell than cooperate with anyone on anything at any time.

The phenomenon is not new. Turf wars and internecine rivalries have been around since our ancestors first tried to work in teams. But silos thrive in large, modern organizations. Multinational companies, public sector bureaucracies and universities seem to be especially vulnerable. Before you ask, newspapers are not immune. Most of the time, silos are just another obstacle to be overcome or, more often, to be circumvented. Occasionally, however, silos become so powerful that an organization is rendered dysfunctional. Thus the bipartisan commission into the terrorist attacks of September 11 2001 concluded that the assault might have been averted if US intelligence agencies had been willing to share information among themselves. Similarly, the initially chaotic, uncoordinated response to Hurricane Katrina was symptomatic of silos at work. In the memorable words of Ray Nagin, the mayor of New Orleans, there were 'too many frickin' cooks'.

The irony is that silos arise from the quest for efficiency. As Adam Smith pointed out, work gets done more quickly when it is divided into chunks and done by specialists. In the modern firm, confident, outgoing types handle sales. Number crunchers look after finance. Engineers are drawn to product development and manufacturing. But, while division of labour is good for productivity it also breeds a complex sociology. One big-company chief executive complained to me this week that her company's design engineers rarely talk to the frontline sales force. As a result, they rarely visit customers. Getting these reticent silos to communicate – and, ultimately, cooperate – is high on her list of priorities.

Up to a point, this kind of institutional politics is nothing to get steamed up about. But it is worth remembering that organizations achieve their ultimate goals – whether manufacturing pins, countering terrorism or delivering aid to flood victims – only if specialists share information and work together. In the jargon of management, work mostly gets done in functional departments, but value is delivered to customers via 'cross-functional processes' – for example, the flow of a purchase order from sales to manufacturing to fulfilment to finance. Senior executives are getting worried about silos because the costs of

noncooperation are rising. In an increasingly competitive global economy, companies across all industries are under pressure to improve efficiency, year after year. The easy cost cuts have already been made. Further progress requires redesigning products and processes from first principles – something that can be achieved only if every department gets with the programme.

Large, multidivisional companies such as Sony and Morgan Stanley face the further challenge of trying to find cross-selling opportunities and synergies between business units. Without these economies of scope, what other reason do they have to exist? The public sector is hardly immune from these pressures. Governments are reluctant to raise taxes. Voters are demanding higher standards from public services. The only answer is more efficient delivery of services, achieved by getting government departments to work together more effectively – what Tony Blair likes to call 'joined-up government'. In public and private sectors alike, meanwhile, the rise of outsourcing and partnering gives a potential competitive edge to organizations that work well with others. Corporate strategy wonks, always quick to coin a buzz phrase, have dubbed this 'relational capital'. Needless to say, organizations characterized by silos and internal rivalries make for lousy partners. Dismiss it as nonsense if you will. But this line of thinking is being taken very seriously among the managers of corporate America.

If silos are such a liability, why do they persist? Because, like viruses, they occur naturally. Ask any large group of normally defensive, insecure people to work together on a project. Then stand back and watch the silos emerge. Our society of large, complex organizations is a perfect breeding ground. This is not to say that managers are powerless to combat them. The experience of General Electric suggests that a concerted effort to encourage cross-company cooperation can yield results. Jack Welch's 'boundarylessness' initiative of the mid-1990s got the message out in no uncertain terms. GE's subsequent adoption of Six Sigma, the process improvement methodology, is credited with further breaking down barriers by giving managers from across the organization a common language.

Like so much of what goes on within organizations, however, the kind of defensive, political behaviour that encourages silos is a function of corporate culture. A quick flirtation with Six Sigma or any other management technique is unlikely

to change the tacit 'way we do things around here'. More important is the steady flow of signals about the types of people who will do well in an organization and the attitudes that are frowned upon. Ultimately, then, the tone is set from the top. Chief executives who demonstrate an uncompromising, all-or-nothing management style can hardly complain when their subordinates are reluctant to cooperate with one another. Sir Howard, Mr Mack – and President George W. Bush – take note.

Source: by Simon London, *Financial Times*, 14 September 2005. Reproduced with permission.

Question

What barriers does the case study identify in moving to a process-oriented approach and what steps can be made to overcome these barriers?

CASE STUDY   8.2

Designing a Custody-of-Prisoner Process at a Police Force

The custody process under investigation includes the arrest process, from actual apprehension of a suspect, to processing through a custody suite (which contains booking-in, interview and detention facilities) to a possible court appearance. A number of different police roles are involved in the custody process including arrests by a police constable (PC), taking of personal details by a custody officer and supervision of persons in detention by a jailer. The first objective of the study was to identify staff costs involved in

arresting a person for a particular offence under the current design. The second objective of the study was to predict the change in utilization of staff as a result of redesigning the allocation of staff to activities within the custody process. The main stages of the investigation are now outlined:

Identify and Document the Process Activities

A process map (Figure 8.9) was constructed after discussions with police staff involved in

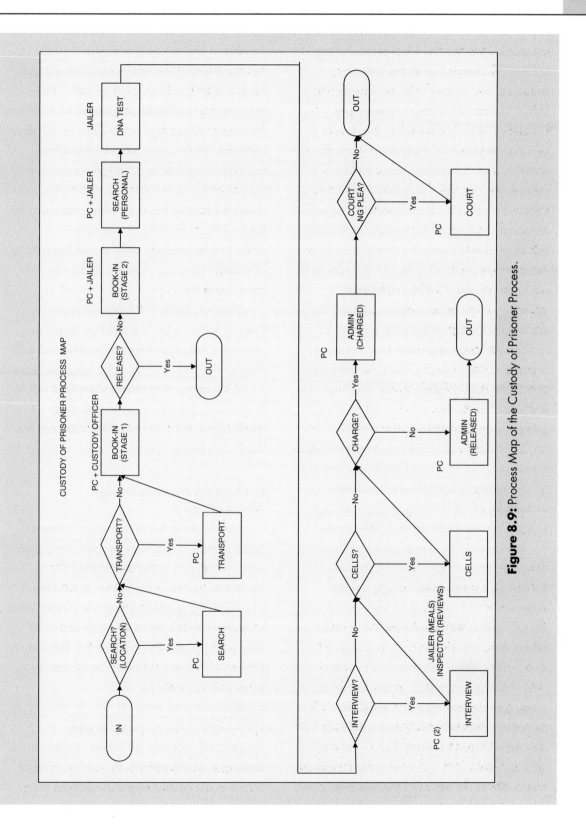

Figure 8.9: Process Map of the Custody of Prisoner Process.

the custody process. As this process was legally bound, documentation on the order of processes and certain requirements such as meals, visits and booking-in details was collated. The main activities in the arrest process are shown in the process map. Each decision point (diamond shape) will have a probability for a yes/no option. The first decision point in the arrest process is whether to conduct a search of the location of the arrest. For all decisions during the arrest process an independent probability distribution is used for each type of arrest (for example, theft, violence, drugs) at each decision point. The staffing rank required for each process is indicated above the process box. Personnel involved in the arrest process include the police constable, custody officer, jailer and inspector. The role of each rank is indicated on the process map for each activity.

To model the variability in process times, a number of estimated times were collected from a number of custody officers. In addition videotapes of the booking-in and interview procedures were viewed and timings taken.

The demand level of each arrival type is estimated from which a statistical distribution for the 'time between arrivals' is usually determined. In this case data were gathered on the timing of arrests over a period of time from information contained within booking-in sheets. From these data the demand pattern was analysed for a typical police station during a day and for each day in a week. As expected, demand both fluctuated during the day and differed between days in the week. It was decided to use historical data to drive the model due to the nature of the demand, with a number of arrests occasionally occurring simultaneously (as a result of a late-night brawl for example!), which would be difficult to reflect using an arrival distribution. Additionally the use of actual data would assist in model validation as model performance could be compared to actual performance over the period simulated. This approach was feasible because the focus of the study was on the investigation of the comparative performance between different configurations of custody operation rather than for use as a forecasting tool.

Most processes will consume resource time, which may be of a machine or person, and these resources need to be identified and their availability defined. If the resource is not available at any time, then the process will not commence until the resource becomes available. In this case the main resources are police constable, custody officer and jailer.

Evaluating Process Design Alternatives

In order to measure and analyse process performance, a business process simulation was constructed using the ARENA™ simulation system. This system uses icons (representing processes) that are placed on a screen area. The icons are connected by links to represent the logic of the process. Process duration and resource allocation to processes is made by double-clicking a process icon and entering data in the pop-up menu dialog. An animated display is constructed by using an inbuilt graphics package, which permits the construction of background (static) elements such as the

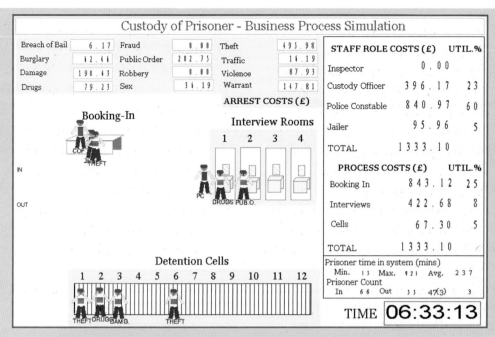

Figure 8.10: Custody of Prisoner – Business Process Simulation Display.

process layout schematic and animated (dynamic) elements which move across the screen. Figure 8.10 shows the custody display that consists of representations of the main custody area facilities (booking-in desk, interview rooms and cells) and the dynamic elements (arrested persons and police staff) that move between the custody facilities.

Before the model results are recorded model behaviour must be checked to ensure that the model is providing valid results. Verification is analogous to the practice of 'debugging' a computer program. This is accomplished by techniques such as a structured walkthrough of the model code, test runs and checking of the animation display. Validation is about ensuring that model behaviour is close enough to the real-world system for the purposes of the simulation study.

To achieve this the model builder should discuss and obtain information from people familiar with the real-world system including operating personnel, industrial engineers, management, vendors and documentation. Also the technique of sensitivity analysis, to test the behaviour of the model under various scenarios and compare results with real-world behaviour, can be used.

Once the model had been validated, it was run over a set time period and results collected. At this stage the model is simply reproducing the behaviour of the current process. This 'As-Is' model provided a visual representation of the whole process, which was important to provide a consensus that the model provides a convincing representation of the process. Demonstration of the model between interested parties provided a forum for communication of model behaviour and helped identify any anomalies.

In this study the aim of the model was to identify the main sources of cost in the system and thus provide strategies that would enable cost to be reduced. At present a budget-based approach meant that costs were not allocated to activities within the process. Each time a process was activated in the model by an arrested person being processed through the custody system a cost was calculated by multiplying the activity duration by the cost per time unit for the resource allocated to that process. The initial analysis aimed to identify the cost incurred for each type of arrest incorporated in the model. The cost for each arrest type is a function not only of the number of arrests but the likelihood of an arrest leading to interview, detention and court procedures. In this case relatively trivial theft offences (usually involving children shoplifting) are causing a heavy workload and thus a high cost. Thus a driving factor behind the overall cost structure has been identified. A possible way of reducing cost could be to decrease the theft activity through crime prevention activities for example.

In this case the 'to-be' model was used to explore the reduction of staffing cost by reallocating staff roles to processes. By estimating resource costs, in this case staff wages, it was possible to estimate the effects and feasibility of proposals to reallocate and civilianize staffing duties within the custody process.

Once a future process design has been decided, the simulation helps to implement this change in a number of ways. The graphical display provides an excellent tool with which to communicate the process to stakeholders such as management, customers and the workforce. The 'before' and 'after' graphic displays can be used to show how the changes will affect the process in practice. Also the display of the new process design can be used to train staff in the new operation and provide them with an overview of process behaviour, which enables them to see the relationship between a particular process activity and the overall process behaviour.

The graphics are complemented by performance measures to quantify before and after performance and thus demonstrate potential improvement. In the custody of prisoner case, measures of staff utilization were important in demonstrating the feasibility of the reallocation of tasks between staff. The figures also quantify potential savings in the utilization of police staff time, enabling plans to be made for the reallocation of staff time to other duties. In the analysis of workload in terms of arrest types, cost was used as a measure of the aggregated staff resource allocated to each arrest type that is serviced by the police. The simulation analysis could take account, not only of the number of arrests of each type, but the variable number of processes (for example, interview, court appearances by police constables) that each arrest triggered. The modelling of the complexity of interdependencies between arrest processes and the variability of arrest demand allowed an accurate picture of where cost/effort was being spent. These figures provided an impetus to focus expenditure on programmes, such as crime prevention, which could have a substantial effect on cost/effort and could free resources to provide an improved overall performance.

Source: Adapted from Greasley (2003). Reproduced by permission of Emerald Group Publishing Ltd.

Questions

1. What benefits does the case study demonstrate can be gained from using business process simulation for process design?

2. Can you identify any disadvantages of using business process simulation?

EXERCISES

1. Evaluate the technique of business process management.

2. What are the challenges when undertaking process design of service systems?

3. Draw a process activity chart for the processing of a book order from an Internet site.

4. Draw a process map for a potential property buyer making a telephone enquiry to a residential housing estate agency

5. Draw a service blueprint for servicing a car. Include in your diagram the customer, the supervisor who takes the bookings and schedules them, the mechanics and the car parts suppliers.

6. Past proceedings of the Winter Simulation Conference can be found at www.informs-cs.org/wscpapers.html (accessed 29 September 2008). Browse the Web and find case studies, noting the number of simulation applications by industry sector.

7. Describe how variability and interdependence affect the operation of a railway system.

● FURTHER READING

Anupindi, R., Chopra, S., Deshmukh, S.D. *et al.* (2008) *Managing Business Process Flows: Principles of Operations Management*, Pearson Education.

Greasley, A. (2008) *Building a Simulation Capability in the Organization*, Springer-Verlag Ltd.

Harrison-Broninski, K. (2005) *Human Interactions: The Heart and Soul of Business Process Management*, Meghan-Kiffer Press.

Kalakota, R. and **Robinson, M.** (2003) *Services Blueprint: Roadmap for Execution*, Addison-Wesley.

Kelton, W.D., Sadowski, R.P. and **Sadowski, D.A.** (2007) *Simulation with Arena*, 4th edn, McGraw Hill, New York.

Ramaswamy, R. (1996) *Design and Management of Service Processes*, Addison-Wesley Publishing Company.

Smith, H. and **Fingar, P.** (2003) *Business Process Management: The Third Wave*, Meghan-Kiffer Press, Tampa.

● WEB LINKS

www.bptrends.com (accessed 29 September 2008). Business Process Trends. Excellent portal with numerous resources regarding business process management.

● SIMULATION ORGANIZATIONS

www.iasted.org (accessed 29 September 2008). The International Association of Science and Technology for Development. Contains links to simulation conferences and journal.

www.informs-cs.org (accessed 29 September 2008). Institute for Operations Research and Management Science: Simulation Society. Contains links to conferences and conference papers.

www.scs.org (accessed 29 September 2008). The Society for Modeling and Simulation International. Conference details and links to journal and publications.

www.scs-europe.net (accessed 29 September 2008). The Society for Modelling and Simulation: European Council. European Conference details and links to journal and publications.

● SIMULATION SOFTWARE VENDORS

www.arenasimulation.com (accessed 29 September 2008). Rockwell Software (ARENA).

www.lanner.com (accessed 29 September 2008). Lanner Group Inc. (WITNESS).

www.maad.com (accessed 29 September 2008). Micro Analysis and Design (Micro Saint).

www.promodel.com (accessed 29 September 2008). Promodel Corporation (Promodel).

www.simul8.com (accessed 29 September 2008). Simul8 Corporation (SIMUL8).

● REFERENCES

Bocij, P., Greasley, A. and **Hickie, S.** (2008) *Business Information Systems*, 4th edn, Pearson Education Limited.

Fingar, P. (2006) *Extreme Competition: Innovation and the Great Twenty-First Century Business Reformation*, Meghan-Kiffer Press.

Greasley, A. (2003) Using business process simulation within a business process reengineering approach. *Business Process Management Journal*, **9** (4), 408–20.

Greasley, A. (2004a) Process improvement within a HR Division at a UK Police Force. *International Journal of Operations and Production Management*, **24** (2/3), 230–40.

Greasley, A. (2004b) *Simulation Modelling for Business*, Ashgate Publishing Ltd.

Laguna, M. and **Marklund, J.** (2005) *Business Process Modeling, Simulation and Design*, Pearson Education.

Martilla, J.A. and **James, J.C.** (1977) Importance-performance analysis, *Journal of Marketing*, January, 77–9.

Peppard, J. and **Rowland, P.** (1995) *The Essence of Business Process Re-engineering*, Prentice Hall.

Rummler, G.A. and **Brache, A.P.** (1995) *Improving Performance: How to Manage the White Space on the Organization Chart*, Jossey Bass Wiley.

Shostack, L.G. (1984) Designing services that deliver. *Harvard Business Review*, **62** (1), 133–9.

Shostack, L.G. (1987) Service positioning through structural change. *Journal of Marketing*, **51**, 34–43.

Slack, N. and **Lewis, M.** (2008) *Operations Strategy*, 2nd edn, Pearson Education Limited, Harlow.

CHAPTER

9

- Introduction
- Behavioural aspects of job design
- Physical aspects of job design
- Work study

Job and Work Design

LEARNING OBJECTIVES

- Describe the elements of the job characteristics model

- Discuss the role of empowerment

- Describe the sociotechnical systems approach

- Describe the use of ergonomics in terms of physical and environmental design

- Understand work study techniques

INTRODUCTION

Operations management deals with the management of personnel who create or deliver an organization's goods and services. Job and work design consists of the formal specifications and informal expectations of an employee's work-related activities and should try to meet the needs of both the jobholder and the organization. The main elements of job and work design are behavioural aspects, which impact on employee motivation and the physical effects of work. Work study represents an attempt to measure the performance of work and thus to create better designed jobs.

BEHAVIOURAL ASPECTS OF JOB DESIGN

In Chapter 1 it was explained that one of the key differences between manufacturing and services was the fact that in services it is likely that the producer of the service will come into contact with the customer. The customer may indeed be to a greater or lesser extent involved in the actual delivery of the service. This means service employees and customers frequently work together and thus the behaviour of employees is likely to have a major effect on the customer's perceived level of service quality. The level of satisfaction of service employees in turn has been found to have an impact on the quality of the service delivered (Schneider and Bowen, 1993).

The implication is that employees that are not motivated (due to factors such as low wages, boring tasks and inadequate training) will be dissatisfied and this will lead to a poor perception of service quality by customers. Technology is often used as a way of 'controlling' employee behaviour in these circumstances, but in services, in particular, it is difficult to replace the element of human interaction completely. The reasons why organizations have dissatisfied employees may be partly due to external factors such as an underinvestment in education and training by government, but also by a short-term focus on minimizing easily quantifiable costs such as for training. The long-term benefits of employee satisfaction leading to customer satisfaction are much harder to quantify and will achieve a payback over a relatively long time period.

Three theories that have had a significant impact on the behavioural aspects of job design are the job characteristics model, empowerment and sociotechnical systems.

The Job Characteristics Model

The Hackman and Oldham (1980) job characteristics model is useful in providing suggestions of how to structure jobs to include more motivators. The model links job characteristics with the desired psychological state of the individual and the outcomes in terms of motivation and job performance. The model takes into account

Job characteristics model
Links job characteristics with the desired psychological state of the individual and the outcomes in terms of motivation and job performance.

individual differences and provides a structure for analysing motivational problems at work and to predict the effects of change on people's jobs and to help plan new work systems. The model proposes five desirable characteristics for a job:

- Skill variety (SV) – the extent to which a job makes use of different skills and abilities.
- Task identity (TI) – the extent to which a job involves completing a whole identifiable piece of work rather than simply a part.
- Task significance (TS) – the extent to which a job has an impact on other people, both inside and outside the organization.
- Autonomy (AU) – the extent to which the job allows the jobholder to exercise choice and discretion in their work.
- Feedback (FB) – the extent to which the job itself (as opposed to other people) provides the jobholder with information on their performance.

The model proposes that the presence of these characteristics will lead to desirable mental states in terms of meaningful work (CV, TI, TS), responsibility for outcomes of work (AU) and knowledge of the results of work (FB). These mental states will in turn lead to higher motivation and quality of work performance. The effects predicted by the model are moderated by factors such as the importance an individual attaches to challenge and personal development.

The five core job characteristics can be combined to provide a 'motivating potential score' (MPS) using the following formula:

$$MPS = \left[\frac{(SV + TI + TS)}{3} \right] \times AU \times FB$$

The formula shows that the addition of skill variety (SV), task identity (TI) and task significance (TS) means that a low score on one of these variables can be compensated by a high score on another. The formula also shows that the combined effect of these three variables (which are divided by 3) is only equal to the other two job characteristics (autonomy and feedback) on their own.

The following are examples of approaches to job design that have been used in an attempt to bring these desirable job characteristics to people's work leading to an improved mental state and thus increased performance.

Job Rotation

Job rotation
A form of job enlargement that involves a worker changing job roles with another worker on a periodic basis.

Job rotation involves a worker changing job roles with another worker on a periodic basis. If successfully implemented this can help increase task identity, skill variety and autonomy through involvement in a wider range of work tasks, with discretion about when these mixes of tasks can be undertaken. However, this method does not actually improve the design of jobs and it can mean that people gravitate to jobs that suit them and are not interested in initiating rotation with colleagues. At worst it can mean rotation between a number of boring jobs with no acquisition of new skills.

Job Enlargement

Job enlargement involves the horizontal integration of tasks to expand the range of tasks involved in a particular job. If successfully implemented this can increase task identity, task significance and skill variety by involving the worker in the whole work task either individually or within the context of a group.

> **Job enlargement**
> This involves the horizontal integration of tasks to expand the range of tasks involved in a particular job.

Job Enrichment

Job enrichment involves the vertical integration of tasks and the integration of responsibility and decision making. If successfully implemented this can increase all five of the desirable job characteristics by involving the worker in a wider range of tasks and providing responsibility for the successful execution of these tasks. This technique does require feedback so that the success of the work can be judged. The managerial and staff responsibilities potentially given to an employee through enrichment can be seen as a form of empowerment. This should in turn lead to improved productivity and product quality.

> **Job enrichment**
> This involves the vertical integration of tasks and the integration of responsibility and decision making.

There are a number of factors that account for the fact that job rotation, job enlargement and job enrichment are not more widely implemented.

Firstly the scope for using different forms of work organization will be dependent to a large extent on the type of operation in which the work is organized. Job shop manufacturing will require skilled workers who will be involved in a variety of tasks and will have some discretion in how they undertake these tasks. Sales personnel may also have a high level of discretion in how they undertake their job duties. The amount of variety in a batch manufacturing environment will to a large extent depend on the length of the production runs used. Firms producing large batches of a single item will obviously have less scope for job enrichment than firms producing small batches on a make-to-order basis. One method for providing job enlargement is to use a cellular manufacturing system, which can permit a worker to undertake a range of tasks on a part. When combined with responsibility for cell performance this can lead to job enrichment. Jobs in mass production industries may be more difficult to enlarge. Car plants must work at a certain rate in order to meet production targets and on a moving line it is only viable for each worker to spend a few minutes on a task before the next worker on the line must take over. A way of overcoming this problem is to use teams. Here tasks are exchanged between team members and performance measurements are supplied for the team as a whole. This provides workers with greater variety and feedback, but also some autonomy and participation in the decisions of the team.

Secondly financial factors may be a constraint on further use. These may include the performance of individuals who actually prefer simple jobs, higher wage rates paid for the higher skills of employees increasing average wage costs and the capital costs of introducing the approaches. The problem is that many of the benefits associated with the technique, such as an increase in creativity, may be difficult to measure financially.

Finally the political aspects of job design changes have little effect on organizational structures and the role of management. Although job enrichment may affect supervisory levels of management, by replacement of a supervisor with a team leader for example, the power structure which is used to justify management decisions for personal objectives remains intact.

Empowerment

Empowerment
Empowerment is
characterized by an
organization in which
employees are given
more autonomy,
discretion and
responsibility in
decision making.

The ideas of job enrichment have led to the concept of empowerment. Empowerment is characterized by an organization in which employees are given more autonomy, discretion and responsibility in decision making. Autonomy can be defined as the degree to which people can and do make decisions on their own within their working context (Van Looy, Gemmel and Van Dierdonck, 2003).

Empowerment is especially relevant to service operations as customers and employees interact in the service delivery process. Because the customer is involved in the service delivery process and may require a response to individual requests the process may differ each time it is performed. This implies that the employee will require a certain level of autonomy in order to satisfy customer needs. This level of autonomy, however, will differ between operations. Bowen and Lawler (1992) describe a continuum of service operations from a 'production-line' approach characterized by the simplification of tasks, use of equipment and little discretion in decision making to an 'empowered' approach characterized by more discretion and autonomy and less emphasis on the systems surrounding service employees. The reason for this continuum is that the benefits of empowerment in terms of employee and customer satisfaction need to be weighed against the costs of selection and training and potential poor decisions made by empowered workers. However, it could be argued that all workers need empowerment to some extent, even in 'production-line' type environments as it is easy to underestimate the autonomy that can be exercised even in what may seem simple tasks.

In terms of implementing empowerment at the level of an individual employee, the approach is that providing more autonomy to employees will increase their motivation and thus satisfy customer needs. However, individual motivation will depend on a combination of autonomy and other dimensions which relate to the individual and task in hand. These dimensions are as follows (Van Looy, Gemmel and Van Dierdonck, 2003):

- *Meaning* – which can be seen as the value of a work goal, as perceived by the individual in relation to his or her own ideals and standards.
- *Competence* – the individual's belief that he or she is able to perform the required activities adequately.
- *Self-determination* – the individual's sense of having a say in initiatives and regulating work actions.
- *Strategic autonomy* – which refers to the extent to which people can influence the content of the job.
- *Impact* – the degree to which employees can influence outcomes of their direct work environment.

Figure 9.1 outlines the relationship between the five dimensions described above. The figure shows that the meaning and competence dimensions seem to be necessary for the dimensions of self-determination, impact and strategic autonomy. The implication of this is that when attempting to implement empowerment, in addition to examining the degree of autonomy present, a degree of meaningfulness and competence should be present. Empowerment can be seen as a process that starts with the creation of meaning and feelings of competence and evolves towards levels of self-determination, impact and even strategic autonomy.

One way of achieving empowerment is through the use of **self-directed work teams**, which may have responsibility for decision making including areas such as

Self-directed work teams
Teams in which workers are empowered to take many of the decisions concerning their work.

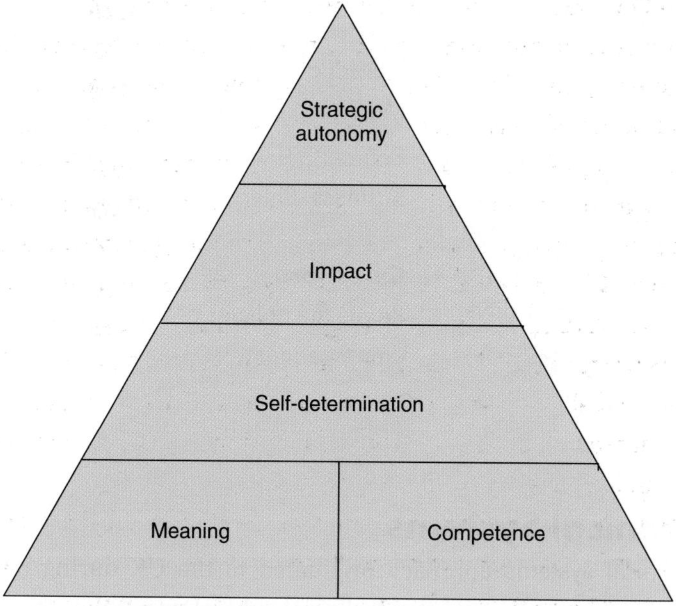

Figure 9.1: Empowerment as a Pyramid.
Source: Van Looy, Gemmel and Van Dierdonck, 2003, p. 234. Reproduced by permission of Pearson Education.

process design. Improvements in performance will usually be awarded at a team level to encourage team working. Self-directed teams can encourage a high level of motivation within team members but their performance can be affected by inadequate training of individual team members and conflict between team members when taking on extra responsibilities.

CASE STUDY 9.1

Innocent

Set up in 1998, fruit smoothies company Innocent (www.innocentdrinks.co.uk) sells its drinks in 3000 outlets throughout the UK, Ireland and Paris. The company attributes its success to allowing each member of staff to work in the way that suits them best. Because the company believes that individuals work optimally in different ways, it allows them to design their own work-life balance. In practice, this means that people who like getting up at the crack of dawn get in early and leave early, whereas others choose to come in a bit later and stay later, without any need for a formal flexitime system.

Staff are encouraged to work from home on days when they need some peace and quiet. And they are also able to pursue other interests, which means that Innocent retains skilled people rather than losing them. For example, the company's youngest employee works four days a week to allow him to do a college design course on Fridays. Another employee wanted to go travelling, so Innocent gave him six weeks off in order to fulfil his ambition. People are also given time off for hobbies and the company offers a hobby fund, workplace yoga and free fruit in the office. The company has won several awards including the Shell Live Wire Award for Best London Entrepreneurs and the National Business Award for Best Investor in People from SMEs 2002, and is the fastest growing food and drinks company in the UK. 'The success of Innocent is down to the performance of each individual within the company.' Richard Reed, Managing Director.

Source: DTI web site (now Department for Business, Enterprise and Regulatory Reform).

Question

Relate the policies at Innocent to the concept of empowerment.

Sociotechnical systems
A job design approach that suggests that the social and technical subsystems within the organization should be designed in parallel to achieve an overall optimum system.

Sociotechnical Systems

The sociotechnical systems approach originated in the UK during the 1950s and distinguishes between the social and technical subsystems within the organization. The idea is that these two aspects should be designed in parallel to achieve an overall optimum system. The approach is focused on group or team work and proposes the use of **autonomous work groups**, which would be able to decide on their own methods of working and should be responsible for handling problems as they arise. This focus on the redesign of work at the group level is the major way in which autonomous work groups can be distinguished from job enrichment. Typically an autonomous work group will be responsible for the whole delivery of a product or service and they are often associated with the use of cell layouts (Chapter 5). An early high-profile adopter of the autonomous work group approach, based on sociotechnical systems theory, is the car manufacturer Volvo.

> **Autonomous work groups**
> These are groups of people who are able to decide on their own methods of working and should be responsible for handling problems as they arise. They will typically be responsible for the whole delivery of a product or service.

PHYSICAL ASPECTS OF JOB DESIGN

In addition to behavioural factors, job design should consider the physical effects of work. The term **ergonomics** is used to describe the collection of information about human characteristics and behaviour to understand the effect of design, methods and environment. Two areas of major concern are the interaction with physical devices, such as computer terminals, and with the environment, such as the office.

> **Ergonomics**
> The collection of information about human characteristics and behaviour to understand the effect of design, methods and environment.

Physical Design

When required to operate a physical device a worker must be able to reach the controls and apply the necessary force to them. Although the average person is capable of a variety of tasks, the speed and accuracy of any actions can be affected by the location of a device. Because the human part of this system cannot be designed, considerable thought must be placed into the location of the device taking into account human capabilities.

Anthropometric Data

Anthropometric data are information concerning factors related to the physical attributes of a human being, such as the size, weight and strength of various parts of the human body. From this information it is possible to gather data on the range of motion, sitting height, strength, working height and other variables. The data can then be used to ensure that the vast majority, say 95% of the population, has the capability to use the device efficiently. For instance the reach required to operate equipment should be no greater than the shortest reach of all the persons required to operate it. In some cases equipment may need adjustment devices built in to cater for different needs. The adjustable car seat is an example of this. Other designs are more subtle. For instance the

> **Anthropometric data**
> Information concerning factors related to the physical attributes of a human being.

arrangement of a number of dials so they all point in the same direction during normal operation enables much speedier checking by an operative.

Environmental Design

This involves the immediate environment in which the job takes place. Some environmental variables to consider include the following.

Noise

Excessive noise levels can not only be distracting but can lead to damage to the workers' hearing. Noise is measured in decibels (dB) on a logarithmic scale that means that a 10 dB increase in noise equates to an increase of ten times in noise intensity. Extended periods of exposure above 90 dB have been judged to be permanently damaging to hearing. Higher sound intensities may be permitted for short exposures but no sound as high as 130 dB should be experienced.

Illumination

The level of illumination depends on the level of work being performed. Jobs requiring precise movements will generally require a higher level of illumination. Other lighting factors such as contrast, glare and shadows are also important.

Temperature and Humidity

Although humans can perform under various combinations of temperature, humidity and air movement, performance will suffer outside of an individual 'comfort zone'. Obviously the nature of the task will affect the temperature range under which work can be undertaken.

CASE STUDY   9.2

Rare

The first seeds of the company that would one day become the internationally renowned Rare were sown way back in the late 1970s, amidst a clutter of arcade boards in a terraced house in Leicestershire, UK. Momentum was building for the first great home gaming boom of the early 1980s, and Tim and Chris Stamper were determined to be ready for it. Thus was Ultimate – Play The Game born. Ultimate was to attain a near-legendary status in the European 8-bit world during its relatively brief existence, kicking off with the launch of Jetpac on its platform of choice, the Sinclair Spectrum, in the summer of 1983. But as the mid-80s drifted by, the home computer market began to wane and the Stampers became keenly aware that the future of the industry lay elsewhere – in the emerging breed of international consoles. Ultimate finally ground to a halt, and from its ashes rose the phoenix of Rare, based now in a farmhouse in the nearby village of Twycross, set up primarily to study and develop for the Nintendo Entertainment System. Rare went on to produce a total of around 60 games for the NES and Game Boy (with occasional dabblings in the Mega Drive/Genesis and Game Gear markets) over the next few years, from Slalom to Marble Madness, RC Pro-Am to Battletoads. But it was Donkey Kong Country on the SNES, released in late 1994, which was to suddenly hurl Rare back into the limelight. One of the biggest-selling videogames of all time, DKC was the beginning of a multiplatform franchise that has seen sales of well over 30 million copies to date. During 1999 Rare underwent another massive change, finally making the move from its long-time headquarters of a converted farmhouse to a custom-built centre of operations more suited to the business of creating cutting-edge videogames. The multimillion pound development at Manor Park, just down the road from Twycross, was designed and constructed over the course of five years to strict guidelines that ensured the preservation of the area's rural charm. Featuring fully landscaped grounds, a state-of-the-art internal climate management system and, vitally, much more free space to house the ever-increasing body of staff, this new HQ offered the perfect environment for Rare's production teams to go on creating the highly regarded titles for which they had become known. If nature is not your thing then there is also an outside five-a-side football pitch, basketball hoop and golfing nets. Further still, if sport is not your niche, there are meeting rooms for gaming and a football table resides in the canteen. On top of a competitive starting salary, Rare offer an annual bonus, private healthcare for employees and their families, life assurance, critical illness cover, use of the employee assistance programme and discounted Microsoft products from the company store for all new employees.

Source: www.rare.co.uk.

Question

Discuss the appropriateness of the work environment offered by Rare for its employees.

WORK STUDY

Work study, which has been developed to measure the performance of jobs, consists of two elements, method study and work measurement. To use this approach work should be sufficiently routine and repetitive to make it feasible to derive an average time from a sample of operators and operations. It must also be possible for the worker to vary their rate of work voluntarily in a measurable way. Therefore it can be

Work study
Measures the performance of jobs and consists of two elements. method study and work measurement.

applied quite readily to routine manual or clerical work but lends itself less well to indirect work such as maintenance or non-repetitive work such as professional and managerial duties.

Method study

Method study
Dividing and analysing
a job in order to reduce
waste, time and effort.

Dividing and analysing a job is called **method study** and was pioneered by Gilbreth (1911). The method takes a systematic approach to reducing waste, time and effort. The approach can be analysed in a six-step procedure:

1. *Select.* The tasks that are most suitable will probably be repetitive, require extensive labour input and be critical to overall performance.
2. *Record.* This involves observation and documentation of the correct method of performing the selected tasks. Process charts are often used to represent a sequence of events graphically. They are intended to highlight unnecessary material movements and unnecessary delay periods.
3. *Examine.* This involves examination of the current method, looking for ways in which tasks can be eliminated, combined, rearranged and simplified. This can be achieved by looking at the process chart and redesigning the sequence of tasks necessary to perform the activity.
4. *Develop.* Developing the best method and obtaining approval for this method. This means choosing the best alternative considered taking into account the constraints of the system such as the performance of the firm's equipment. The new method will require adequate documentation in order that procedures can be followed. Specifications may include tooling, operator skill level and working conditions.
5. *Install.* Implement the new method. Changes such as installation of new equipment and operator training will need to be undertaken.
6. *Maintain.* Routinely verify that the new method is being followed correctly.

New methods may not be followed due to inadequate training or support. On the other hand people may find ways to gradually improve the method over time. Learning curves can be used to analyse these effects.

Motion study
The study of the
individual human
motions that are used
in a job task with the
purpose of trying to
ensure that the job
does not include any
unnecessary motion or
movement by the
worker.

Motion Study

Motion study is the study of the individual human motions that are used in a job task. The purpose of motion study is to try to ensure that the job does not include any unnecessary motion or movement by the worker and to select the sequence of motions that ensure that the job is being carried out in the most efficient manner possible. The technique was originated by Gilbreth who studied many workers at their jobs and from among them picked the best way to perform each activity. He then combined these elements to form the best way to perform a task.

For even more detail, videotapes can be used to study individual work motions in slow motion and analyse them to find improvement – a technique termed micromotion analysis. Gilbreth's motion study research and analysis has evolved into a set of widely adopted principles of motion study, which are used by organizations as general guidelines for the efficient design of work. The principles are generally categorized according to the efficient use of the human body, efficient arrangement of the workplace and the efficient use of equipment and machinery. Table 9.1 summarizes these principles into general guidelines.

- **Efficient use of the human body**
Work should be rhythmic, symmetrical and simplified
The full capabilities of the human body should be employed
Energy should be conserved by letting machines perform tasks when possible

- **Efficient arrangement of the workplace**
Tools, materials and controls should have a defined place and be located to minimize the motions needed to get to them
The workplace should be comfortable and healthy

- **Efficient use of equipment**
Equipment and mechanized tools enhance worker abilities
Controls and foot-operated devices that can relieve the hand/arms of work should be maximized
Equipment should be constructed and arranged to fit worker use

Table 9.1: Summary of Guidelines of Motion Study.

Motion study is seen as one of the fundamental aspects of scientific management and indeed it was effective in the design of repetitive, simplified jobs with the task specialization that was a feature of the mass production system. The use of motion study has declined as there as been a movement towards greater job responsibility and a wider range of tasks within a job. However, the technique is still a useful analysis tool and, particularly in the service industries, can help improve process performance.

Work Measurement

The second element of work study is **work measurement**, which determines the length of time it will take to undertake a particular task. This is important not only to determine pay rates but also to ensure that each stage in a production line system is of an equal duration (i.e. 'balanced', see Chapter 4) thus ensuring maximum output. Usually the method study and work measurement activities are undertaken together to develop time as well as method standards. Setting time standards in a structured

Work measurement
This determines the length of time it will take to undertake a particular task.

manner permits the use of benchmarks against which to measure a range of variables such as cost of the product and share of work between team members. However, the work measurement technique has been criticized for being misused by management in determining worker compensation. The time needed to perform each work element can be determined by the use of historical data, work sampling or most usually time study.

Time Study

Time study
The use of statistical techniques to arrive at a standard time for performing one cycle of a repetitive job.

The purpose of time study is to use statistical techniques to determine a standard time for performing one cycle of a repetitive job. This is arrived at by observing a task a number of times. The standard time refers to the time allowed for the job under specific circumstances, taking into account allowances for rest and relaxation. The basic steps in a time study are indicated below:

1. Establish the standard job method. It is essential that the best method of undertaking the job is determined using method study before a time study is undertaken. If a better method for the job is found then the time study analysis will need to be repeated.
2. Break down the job into elements. The job should be broken down into a number of easily measurable tasks. This will permit a more accurate calculation of standard time as varying proficiencies at different parts of the whole job can be taken into account.
3. Study the job. This has traditionally been undertaken by observation of the task with a stopwatch, or electronic timer. Each time element is recorded on an observation sheet. A video camera can be used for observation, which permits study away from the workplace, and in slow motion, which permits a higher degree of accuracy of measurement.
4. Rate the worker's performance. As the time study is being conducted a rating of the worker's performance is also taken in order to achieve a true time rating for the task. Rating factors are usually between 80% and 120% of normal. This is an important but subjective element in the procedure and is best done if the observer is familiar with the job itself.
5. Compute the average time. Once a sufficient sample of job cycles has been undertaken an average is taken of the observed times called the cycle time. The sample size can be determined statistically, but is often around five to 15 due to cost restrictions.

6. Compute the normal time. Adjust the cycle time for the efficiency and speed of the worker who was observed. The normal time is calculated by multiplying the cycle time by the performance rating factors.

$$\text{normal time(NT)} = \text{cycle time(CT)} \times \text{rating factor(RF)}$$

7. Compute the standard time. The standard time is computed by adjusting the normal time by an allowance factor to take account of unavoidable delays such as machine breakdown and rest periods. The standard time is calculated as follows:

$$\text{standard time(ST)} = \text{normal time(NT)} \times \text{allowance}$$

WORKED EXAMPLE 9.1
Time Study

PCB Limited wants to determine the standard time for a manual solder operation on one of their new circuit boards. From the following task times observed during a time study exercise calculate the standard time for the job. Assume the worker who has been observed is 10% slower than average at this task. Assume an allowance factor of 20%.

Sample No.	1	2	3	4	5	6	7	8	9	10
Time (sec.)	6.7	7.1	7.3	7.0	7.1	6.8	6.9	6.8	7.1	7.0

● SOLUTION

Cycle time (CT) = average of samples = $\frac{69.8}{10}$ = 6.98

Normal time (NT) = CT × RF = 6.98 × 0.9 = 6.282

Standard time (ST) = NT × allowance = 6.282 × 1.2 = 7.54 seconds

Predetermined Motion Times

One problem with time studies is that workers will not always cooperate with their use, especially if they know the results will be used to set wage rates. Combined with the costs of undertaking a time study, a company may use historical data in the form of time files to construct a new standard job time from a previous job element.

Another method for calculating standard times without a time study is to use the predetermined motion time system (PMTS), which provides generic times for standard micromotions such as reach, move and release, which are common to many jobs. The standard item for the job is then constructed by breaking down the job into a series of micromotions that can then be assigned a time from the motion time database. The standard time for the job is the sum of these micromotion times. Factors such as load weight for move operations are included in the time motion database.

> **Predetermined motion times**
> These provide generic times for standard micromotions such as reach, move and release, which are common to many jobs.

The advantages of this approach are that standard times can be developed for jobs before they are introduced to the workplace without causing disruption and needing worker compliance. Also performance ratings are factored into the motion times and so the subjective part of the study is eliminated. The timings should also be much more consistent than historical data for instance. Disadvantages include the fact that these times ignore the context of the job in which they are undertaken – the timings are provided for the micromotion in isolation and are not part of a range of movements. The sample is from a broad range of workers in different industries with different skill levels, which may lead to an unrepresentative time. The timings are also only available for simple repetitious work which is becoming less common in industry.

Work Sampling

Work sampling is useful for analysing the increasing proportion of nonrepetitive tasks that are performed in most jobs. It is a method for determining the proportion of time a worker or machine spends on various activities and as such can be very useful in job redesign and estimating levels of worker output. The basic steps in work sampling are indicated below:

> **Work sampling**
> A method for determining the proportion of time a worker or machine spends on various activities and as such can be very useful in job redesign and estimating levels of worker output.

1. *Define the job activities.* All possible activities must be categorized for a particular job, for example 'worker idle' and 'worker busy' states could be used to define all possible activities.
2. *Determine the number of observations in the work sample.* The accuracy of the proportion of time the worker is in a particular state is determined by the observation sample size. Assuming the sample is approximately normally distributed the sample size can be estimated using the following formula:

$$n = \left(\frac{z}{e}\right)^2 \times p(1-p)$$

where

n = sample size

z = number of standard deviations from the mean for the desired level of confidence e = the degree of allowable error in the sample estimate

p = the estimated proportion of time spent on a work activity.

The accuracy of the estimated proportion p is usually expressed in terms of an allowable degree of error e (for example, for a 2% degree of error, e = 0.02). The degree of confidence would normally be 95% (giving a z value of 1.96) or 99% (giving a z value of 2.58).

3. *Determine the length of the sampling period.* There must be sufficient time in order for a random sample of the number of observations given by the equation in Step 2 to be collected. A random number generator can be used to generate the time between observations in order to achieve a random sample.

4. *Conduct the work sampling study and record the observations.* Calculate the sample and calculate the proportion (p) by dividing the number of observations for a particular activity by the total number of observations.

5. *Periodically recompute the sample size required.* It may be that the actual proportion for an activity is different from the proportion used to calculate the sample size in Step 2. Therefore as sampling progresses it is useful to recompute the sample size based on the proportions actually observed.

WORKED EXAMPLE 9.2
Work Sampling

The FastCabs Company has a complement of 25 cabs on duty at any one time. The manager of the company wishes to determine the amount of time a cab driver is sitting idle which he estimates at 35%. The cabs were called over a period of a week at random to determine their status. If the manager wants the estimate to be within +/− 5% of the actual proportion with a confidence level of 95%, estimate the sample size required.

SOLUTION

$$n = \left(\frac{z}{e}\right)^2 \times p(1-p)$$

At 95% confidence z = 1.96 (from normal table)

e = 0.05

p = 0.35

thus
$$n = (1.96/0.05)^2 \times 0.35(1 - 0.35)$$
$$n = 350$$
Thus 350 samples are required.

Learning Curves

Learning curves
Provide an organization with the ability to predict the improvement in productivity that can occur as experience is gained of a process.

Organizations have often used learning curves to predict the improvement in productivity that can occur as experience is gained of a process. Thus learning curves can give an organization a method of measuring continuous improvement activities. If a firm can estimate the rate at which an operation time will decrease then it can predict the impact on cost and increase in effective capacity over time.

The learning curve is based on the concept that when productivity doubles, the decrease in time per unit is the rate of the learning curve. Thus if the learning curve is at a rate of 85%, the second unit takes 85% of the time of the first unit, the fourth unit takes 85% of the second unit and the eighth unit takes 85% of the fourth and so on.

Figure 9.2 shows the general shape of a learning curve, where the process time per unit falls in an exponential like fashion as the units produced increase. Mathematically the learning curve is represented by the function

$$y = ax^{-b}$$

where
x = number of units produced
a = time required to produce the first unit
y = time to produce the xth unit
$b = $ constant equal to $\dfrac{-(\ln p)}{(\ln 2)}$

where
$\ln = \log_{10}$
p = learning rate (for example, 80% = 0.8)

Thus for an 80% learning curve:
$$b = \frac{-(\ln 0.8)}{(\ln (2))} = \frac{-(-0.233)}{(0.693)} = 0.322$$

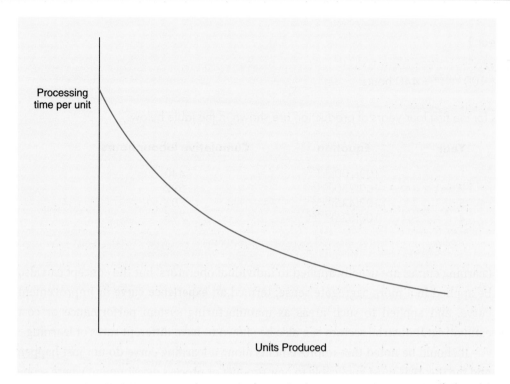

Figure 9.2: A Learning Curve.

WORKED EXAMPLE 9.3
Learning Curves

A company is introducing a new product and has determined that an 80% learning curve is applicable. Estimates of demand for the first four years of production are 100, 150, 175 and 200. The time to produce the first unit is estimated at 100 hours. Estimate the cumulative labour hours required for each of the first four years of production.

SOLUTION

$y = ax^{-b}$ where $b = \dfrac{-(\ln p)}{(\ln 2)}$

$a = 100$

$p = 0.8$

$b = -\dfrac{\ln 0.8}{\ln 2} = 0.322$

Thus for year 1

$x = 100$

$y = 100 \times 100^{0.322} = 440$ hours

The results for the first four years of production are shown in the table below:

Year	Equation	Cumulative labour hours
1	$100(100)^{0.322}$	440
2	$100(250)^{0.322}$	592
3	$100(425)^{0.322}$	702
4	$100(625)^{0.322}$	795

Experience curves
These provide an organization with the ability to predict the improvement in productivity that can occur as experience is gained in a market segment.

Learning curves are usually applied to individual operators, but the concept can also be applied in a more aggregate sense, termed an **experience curve** or improvement curve, and applied to such areas as manufacturing system performance or cost estimating. Industrial sectors can also be shown to have different rates of learning.

It should be noted that improvements along a learning curve do not just happen and the theory is most applicable to new product or process development where scope for improvement is greatest or businesses that include complex repetitive operations where the work pace is determined mostly by people, not machines. Examples of industries that use learning curves are construction, defence, aerospace and electronics. The learning curve effect in simple routine processes such as mass production may only show improvement for a short time and so their use is more limited.

When using learning curves it must be remembered that step changes can occur that can slow or accelerate the rate of learning, such as organizational change, changes in technology or quality improvement programmes. Learning effects also take place as the result of action. To ensure learning occurs the organization must invest in factors such as research and development, advanced technology, people and continuous improvement efforts (Chapter 17).

CASE STUDY 9.3

Experience Curves

Experience curve advantages have often been pursued by a strategy of dominating global market segments by aggressive sales and acquisition tactics. This is based on the assumption that, in a given industry, the producer with the largest volume and corresponding market share should have the lowest marginal cost. The market share leader should then be able to underprice competitors, discourage potential new entrants and thus achieve respectable profits. However, by the mid 1980s the simplified techniques of market-share leadership had become widely discredited as companies found that the premises behind the theories often did not hold. Michael Porter (1987) outlined the failure of portfolio planning where conglomerates had divested and acquired companies based on their position on a market share matrix. Over 50% of acquisitions and joint ventures had been subsequently divested by a sample of large companies in the USA in the period 1950–80. It seems that the market share of a company does not necessarily relate to profitability but is simply an element in a range of factors that should be considered. Porter argues for a detailed assessment of the industry attractiveness and the company's competitive strengths and weaknesses relative to competitors as the basis for a business plan aimed at sustaining competitive advantage.

Question
Why is the strategy of pursuing experience curve advantages not always successful?

SUMMARY

- The job characteristics model links job characteristics to performance through an intervening variable: motivation. Approaches to job design that have attempted to increase motivation (and thus performance) are job rotation, job enlargement and job enrichment.

- Empowerment has been developed in response to an individual need for challenging and meaningful work and the expectations of employers in a marketplace characterized by rapid change and new technologies.

- Sociotechnical systems theory distinguishes between the social and technical subsystems within the organization and states that these two aspects should be designed in parallel to achieve an overall optimum system.

- Ergonomics uses information about human characteristics and behaviour to understand the effect of physical and environmental design.

- Work study consists of two elements: method study and work measurement. Method study consists of dividing and analysing a task in a systematic manner in order to improve the method of carrying out that task. Work measurement consists of determining the length of time it will take to undertake a task in order to establish a benchmark against which performance can be measured.

CASE STUDY 9.4

The Importance of the Management of People

A policy based on improving management practices must be adopted by the government if it is to raise productivity, according to a report published today. In the report, published in February 2006, the Chartered Institute of Personnel and Development (CIPD) stated that a focus on investment, innovation and skills had failed to raise Britain's rate of productivity growth, despite it being a central plank of policy of the Labour government since 1997. The report anticipated the Office for National Statistics report that the UK output per hour in 2004 lagged behind France, the US and Germany. The CIPD stated that productivity growth would continue to disappoint without big improvements in the way that people are managed. The report states that management practices are 'more powerful predictors of company performance than strategy, technology or research and development'. It

identified 'team cohesion within organizations as a significant factor in translating higher productivity into higher performance and higher profits'. The CIPD called on the government to make improved working practices central to productivity policy. It called for measures such as improved benchmarking of the degree to which staff are multiskilled and given discretion and autonomy; increased emphasis on work-related training rather than qualifications, and a limit on working hours to urge employers to focus on encouraging staff to achieve more.

Questions

1. Discuss the comment that 'management practices are more powerful predictors of company performance than strategy, technology or research and development'.

2. Discuss the measures to improve productivity put forward by the CIPD.

EXERCISES

1. Evaluate the job design approaches of job rotation, job enlargement and job enrichment.

2. Discuss the major approaches to job design as they relate to the operations function.

3. Compare the job characteristics model with the concept of empowerment.

4. What is the difference between empowerment and autonomy?

5. Discuss the relevance of empowerment to successful operations management.

6. The following cycle times have been observed for a job consisting of five elements. A performance rating factor has been calculated for each element. Assume an allowance factor of 15%.

Element	Cycle time	Ratings factor
1	3.6	1.05
2	4.8	0.9
3	2.9	1.0
4	4.9	1.1
5	1.7	0.95

a) Determine the normal time (NT) for each element.
b) Determine the overall normal time.
c) Determine the standard time.

7. The following cycle times have been observed for a job consisting of four elements. A performance rating factor has been calculated for each element. Assume an allowance factor of 20%.

Element	Cycle time	Ratings factor
1	6.3	1.05
2	8.4	0.9
3	9.2	1.0
4	9.4	1.1

a) Determine the normal time (NT) for each element.
b) Determine the overall normal time.
c) Determine the standard time.

8. Calculate the sample size required to estimate the time a supervisor spends in a maintenance department. Management believe that 50% of the supervisor's time is spent in maintenance. They require an estimate to be within +/− 5% of the actual proportion with a 95% degree of confidence.

9. A call centre has a complement of 40 staff on duty at any one time. The manager of the company wishes to determine the amount of time an employee is sitting idle, which he estimates at 25%. The employees

were observed over a period of a week at random to determine their status. If the manager wants the estimate to be within $+/-$ 5% of the actual proportion with a confidence level of 95%, estimate the sample size required.

10. An electrical goods manufacturer is producing an electronic component for a washing machine. It is estimated that it will take 150 hours to produce the first unit. The standard learning curve for this type of component is 90%. What are the cumulative labour hours required for 500 units produced?

11. An electronics maker has estimated an 87% learning curve for a component with a time of 1600 hours to produce the first assembly. What are the cumulative labour hours required to produce the 30th and 60th units.

WEB EXERCISE

The ImpactFactory web site at `http://www.impactfactory.com/p/empowerment_skills_training/snacks_1215-5103-69551.html` (accessed 30 September 2008) contains a discussion of the meaning of empowerment from an employee and manager perspective. What are the implications of these meanings for the implementation of empowerment?

● FURTHER READING

Bailey, J. (1993) *Managing People and Technological Change*, FT Prentice Hall.

Bessant, J. (2003) *High Involvement Innovation: Building and Sustaining Competitive Advantage Through Continuous Change*, John Wiley & Sons, Ltd.

Daft, R.L. (2003) *Organization Theory and Design*, 8th edn, South Western College Publishing Co.

Mullins, L.J. (2007) *Management and Organizational Behaviour*, 8th edn, Prentice Hall.

Mundel, M.E. and **Danner, D.L.** (1994) *Motion and Time Study: Improving Productivity*, 7th edn, Prentice Hall.

Parker, S.K. and **Wall, T.D.** (1998) *Job and Work Design: Organizing Work to Promote Well-Being and Effectiveness*, Sage Publications Inc.

WEB LINKS

www.acsco.com/tseng.htm (accessed 30 September 2008). Applied Computer Services Inc. Software for time and motion studies.

www.eee.bham.ac.uk/eiac (accessed 30 September 2008). Ergonomics Information Analysis Centre. Contains over 170 000 abstracts in the area of ergonomics.

www.ergonomics.org.uk (accessed 30 September 2008). The Ergonomics Society. News, Information and conferences concerning ergonomics and human factors.

www.rostima.com/ (accessed 30 September 2008). Supplier of workforce management and scheduling software.

REFERENCES

Bowen, D. and **Lawler, E.** (1992) The empowerment of service workers: What, why, how and when, *Sloan Management Review*, Spring, 31–9.

Gilbreth, F. (1911), *Motion Study*, D. Van Nostrand Co, New York.

Hackman, J.R. and **Oldham, G.R.** (1980), *Work Redesign*, Prentice Hall.

Porter, M. (1987) From competitive advantage to corporate strategy, *Harvard Business Review*, May/June, 43–59.

Schneider, B. and **Bowen, D.E.** (1993) The service organization: human resources management is crucial. *Organizational Dynamics*, **21**(4), 39–52.

Van Looy, B., Gemmel, P. and Van Dierdonck, R. (eds) (2003) *Services Management: An Integrated Approach*, 2nd edn, Pearson Education, Harlow.

PART 3

MANAGEMENT

CHAPTER
10

Planning and Control

LEARNING OBJECTIVES

- Evaluate resource-to-order, make-to-order and make-to-stock planning policies
- Describe the principal approaches to the operations control task of loading
- Describe the use of priority rules for the operations control task of sequencing
- Discuss the operations control task of scheduling
- Identify techniques for scheduling in manufacturing and service operations
- Describe the operations control system of OPT

INTRODUCTION

Planning and control is about matching customer demand to the operations capacity. In the long term this can be considered as a design issue and is covered in Chapter 5. This chapter is concerned with short-term planning and control in order to meet estimated demand. This task is made challenging because of the unstable nature of market demand, which works against the execution of an efficient and effective operations system. In organizations with international operations there is a further difficulty in coordinating planning and control activities across different locations.

One way of dealing with unstable demand is to produce the product or service (or elements of the product or service) in advance. The first part of this chapter evaluates the use of make-to-stock, make-to-order and resource-to-order planning policies.

The second part of this chapter examines the activities that form operations control tasks. These generally consist of loading (determining capacity and volumes), sequencing (deciding on the order of execution of work) and scheduling (allocating a start and finish time to a customer order). A number of techniques for operations control are then described and the OPT operations control system is described. Further operations control systems that are discussed in this text include JIT and lean operations (Chapter 13), ERP (Chapter 14), supply chain management (Chapter 15) and project management (Chapter 16).

OPERATIONS PLANNING

Operations planning is concerned with taking actions, such as ensuring resources are in place, in anticipation of future events. The nature of the planning task is determined by how accurately future events can be predicted. The predictability of demand for goods and services can range from a situation of what is essentially dependent demand (demand can be predicted) to a high level of unpredictability (independent demand). Planning policies to meet this continuum are shown in Table 10.1.

> **Operations planning**
> This is concerned with taking actions, such as ensuring resources are in place, in anticipation of future events.

Demand type	Planning policy	Resources required in stock
Dependent	Resource-to-order	None
Independent (low variability)	Make-to-order	Transforming
Independent (high variability)	Make-to-stock	Transforming Transformed

Table 10.1: Planning Policies for Demand Types.

Thus in a dependent, demand-type situation it is not necessary to activate a planning system and acquire resources until a delivery date for an order is received. Both transforming resources (for example, staff, machinery) and transformed resources (for example, bricks for a house) may be acquired at the appropriate time for delivery. This is termed a **resource-to-order** planning policy. In an independent demand situation when demand is relatively predictable the transforming resources such as staff and machinery may be in place on a permanent basis. However, the

> **Resource-to-order**
> When it is not necessary to activate a planning system and acquire resources until a delivery date for an order is received.

transformed resources – the raw material that is used to construct the product – may be acquired on the receipt of a customer order. This is termed a make-to-order planning policy. Finally if demand is unpredictable, the organization will use a make-to-stock planning policy which produces to a forecast of demand for the product.

Two implications arise from the planning policy used by the organization. In a make-to-stock system each order must be small compared to total capacity or the risk of making to stock, and not finding a customer for the order, will be too high. Also a resource-to-order system implies each order is large compared to total system capacity to make the organization of resources worthwhile. The other implication is that of customer delivery time performance. Whilst the customer will only 'see' the delivery time from stock in a make-to-stock system, in a make-to-order system the delivery cycle will include the purchase, make and delivery stages. This effect is examined using P:D ratios.

P:D Ratios

The P:D ratio is a concept derived by Shingo (1989) and compares the demand time D (from customer request to receipt of goods/services) to the total throughput time P of the purchase, make and delivery stages. The purchase stage involves acquiring necessary resources from internal and external suppliers, the make stage includes the processing of resources through the operations system and the deliver stage involves packing and distribution of the finished good to the customer. The relationship between the planning and control systems and the P:D ratio is shown in Figure 10.1.

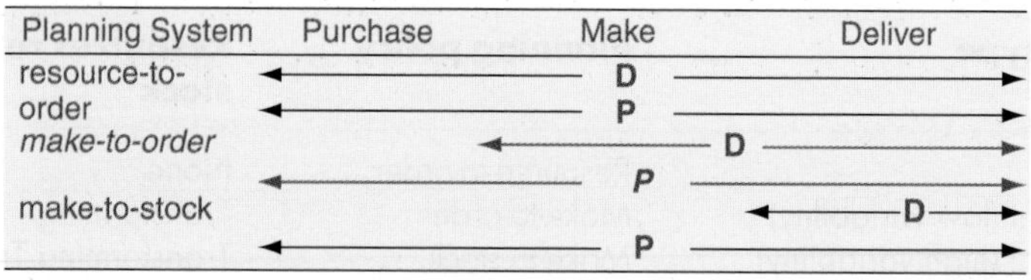

Planning System	Purchase	Make	Deliver
resource-to-order	← ————————————— D ————————————— →		
	← ————————————— P ————————————— →		
make-to-order		← ——————— D ——————— →	
	← ————————————— P ————————————— →		
make-to-stock			← ——— D ——→
	← ————————————— P ————————————— →		

Figure 10.1: The Relationship between the P:D Ratio and the Planning Policy.

Thus in a resource-to-order system the demand time and throughput time are essentially the same. The purchase-make-deliver cycle is not triggered until a customer order is received. In a make-to-stock system the demand time is essentially the time of delivery from stock to the customer.

The P:D ratio makes the implications for the delivery time to the customer explicit. In a resource-to-order system the purchase, make and deliver stages all affect delivery performance. In a make-to-stock system, however, the customer only

Make-to-order
A planning policy that acquires the raw material which is used to construct the product on the receipt of a customer order.

Make-to-stock
A planning policy that produces to a forecast of demand for the product.

P:D ratio
Compares the demand time D (from customer request to receipt of goods/services) to the total throughput time P of the purchase, make and delivery stages.

'sees' the delivery time. Although delivery performance is improved in a make-to-stock system, the item is being produced to a forecast demand, which is subject to error. The risk of producing to this forecast increases with the ratio of P:D, as an increase in throughput times means that the item must be produced to a demand further into the future. Thus reducing the P:D ratio will reduce the risk inherent in the planning policy.

OPERATIONS CONTROL

Although operations planning will attempt to anticipate events, there may be a mismatch between current actions and what actually is required due to unforeseen events or behaviours. An example would be an unforeseen change in customer demand in terms of total output or in the mix of goods and services. Operations control is concerned with ensuring that the current behaviour of the operations system conforms with the required behaviour. This section examines the activities that form operations control tasks. These generally consist of loading (determining the current capacity and volumes), sequencing (deciding on the order of execution of work) and scheduling (allocating start and finish times to a customer order).

> **Operations control**
> This is concerned with ensuring that the current behaviour of the operations system conforms with the required behaviour.

Loading

Loading involves determining the available capacity for each stage in a process and allocating a work task to that stage. The calculation of available capacity must take account of both planned factors such as machine maintenance and unplanned factors such as machine breakdowns and worker absenteeism. These issues are dealt with in more detail in Chapter 11. There are two principal approaches to loading.

> **Loading**
> Loading involves determining the available capacity for each stage in a process and allocating a work task to that stage.

Finite Loading

Finite loading allocates work up to an agreed fixed (finite) upper limit. This may be because:

- the upper limit of capacity is fixed, for example seats on a aircraft (although this does not rule out the policy of overbooking to ensure that all capacity is actually utilized!)
- the upper limit can be fixed through a policy such as using an appointment system
- there is a policy of limiting availability to the market (a limited edition of an expensive watch may enhance demand).

Infinite Loading

Infinite loading does not place a limit on the work loaded onto a stage. This may be because:

- It is not possible to limit demand. For example emergency hospital treatment should not be refused.
- It is acceptable to have a drop in performance. In manufacturing or services if demand exceeds capacity a queue will form. This may be acceptable in some instances, for example shopping outlets, when the customer understands the cost of always providing instant service is too high.

Sequencing

Sequencing (also known as dispatching) is the sequential assignment of tasks or jobs to individual processes. In order to attempt to control the progress of a job through a process a job priority system is used. The priority of jobs queuing at a process determines the order in which they are processed. The difficulty lies in determining an appropriate priority rule to obtain the best performance. Priority rules include:

Sequencing
Sequencing is the sequential assignment of tasks or jobs to individual processes.

- DDS (customer due date) – job with nearest customer due date to the current date
- FCFS (first come, first served) – job arriving first at a process (in order of arrival)
- SPT/SOT – (shortest process time/ shortest operating time) job with shortest process/operating time among waiting jobs
- LPT (longest process time) – job with longest process time among waiting jobs.

All the rules have different advantages and disadvantages. The SPT rule ensures that jobs with the shortest process time progress rapidly, thus the number of jobs processed should be high. This rule will generally give the best performance. However, a disadvantage of the SPT rule is that when the demand on the process is high this may mean a job with a longer process time may have an unacceptably long wait and is always at the end of the queue.

Rules can also use a combination of factors to determine the sequence, such as the critical ratio (CR) which is the ratio of the time left until the job's due date to the expected elapsed time for the job to be processed through the remaining processes to its completion. If the ratio is less than 1 the job is behind schedule and should receive priority.

Critical Ratio (CR) = (due date – current date) / days required to complete job

Gantt charts (Chapter 16) can be employed to show the effect of different job sequencing strategies on the performance of the process.

WORKED EXAMPLE 10.1
Sequencing

A copyshop offers a photocopying service to customers. Currently it uses an FCFS system because this seems the fairest way of working for the customers. However, the manager of the shop suspects that an alternative sequencing rule may improve performance. Using the data collected below try the FCFS, DDS and SPT sequences and state which rule provides the best performance using the measure of average lateness.

Job arrival sequence	Processing time (days)	Customer due date (days)
A	5	7
B	4	6
C	2	5
D	2	6
E	1	3

● SOLUTION

Trying the FCFS rule:

Job arrival sequence	Processing time (days)	Customer due date (days)	Process time (FCFS) (days)	Lateness (days)
A	5	7	$0 + 5 = 5$	0
B	4	6	$5 + 4 = 9$	3
C	2	5	$9 + 2 = 11$	6
D	2	6	$11 + 2 = 13$	7
E	1	3	$13 + 1 = 14$	11

$$\text{Average lateness} = \frac{(0 + 3 + 6 + 7 + 11)}{5} = \frac{27}{5}$$

$$= 5.4 \text{ days}$$

Trying the DDS rule:

Job arrival sequence	Processing time (days)	Customer due date (days)	Process time (DDS) (days)	Lateness (days)
A	5	7	$9 + 5 = 14$	7
B	4	6	$3 + 4 = 7$	1
C	2	5	$1 + 2 = 3$	0
D	2	6	$7 + 2 = 9$	3
E	1	3	$0 + 1 = 1$	0

$$\text{Average lateness} = \frac{(7+1+0+3+0)}{5} = \frac{11}{5}$$

$$= 2.2 \text{ days}$$

Trying the SPT rule:

Job arrival sequence	Processing time (days)	Customer due date (days)	Process time (SPT) (days)	Lateness (days)
A	5	7	9 + 5 = 14	7
B	4	6	5 + 4 = 9	3
C	2	5	3 + 2 = 5	0
D	2	6	1 + 2 = 3	0
E	1	3	0 + 1 = 1	0

$$\text{Average lateness} = \frac{(7+3+0+0+0)}{5} = \frac{10}{5}$$

$$= 2.0 \text{ days}$$

Of the three rules the SPT rule provides the best performance with an average job lateness of two days.

Johnson's Rule

An optimal solution to the job-sequencing problem has been found for the special case in which all jobs flow through two work centres or processes in the same order. Johnson's rule (Johnson, 1954) minimizes the overall lead time (start of first job to end of last job) in this case, assuming other costs (such as machine setup costs moving from one product to another) are not dependent on the job sequence chosen. Setup times are included in job process times.

The following steps should be followed:

1. List the processing time for all jobs for both stages of production.
2. For unscheduled jobs select the job with the shortest time in either stage.
3. If the shortest time is for the first processing stage, put the job as early as possible in the job sequence. If the shortest time is for the second processing stage, put the job as late as possible in the job sequence. If the time on the first stage for one job equals the time on the second stage for some other job then fill the earliest slot with the job having this amount of time for the first stage and fill the latest slot with the job having this amount of time for the second stage. If both jobs have the same time for both stages they can be placed at either end of the sequence.
4. Delete the job selected and repeat the steps until all jobs have been sequenced.

WORKED EXAMPLE 10.2
Johnson's Rule

A manufacturing department has five jobs, which must be processed on the sand process and then on the varnish process. Determine the sequence that will allow the set of five jobs to be completed in the minimum time.

Job	Process time (minutes)	
	Sand	Varnish
A	6	3
B	4	5
C	2	3
D	6	6
E	3	7

● SOLUTION

1. Shortest time is 2 for C in sand stage, therefore put as early as possible in job sequence.

C			

2. Next shortest time is 3 for A in varnish stage and 3 for E in sand stage. Therefore put E as early as possible in job sequence and A as late as possible in job sequence.

C	E			A

3. Next shortest is 4 for B in sand stage 1. Thus put B as early as possible in job sequence.

C	E	B		A

4. The only job remaining is job D, therefore final sequence is as follows.

C	E	B	D	A

    To find the completion time a Gantt chart is used to total the job completion time.

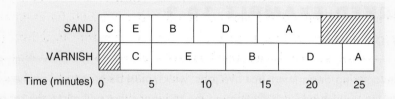

Thus the total completion time is 26 minutes.

It should be emphasized that the rule is only applicable to a flow through two work centres in the same order and does not consider individual job due dates in constructing the schedule.

Scheduling

Scheduling is the allocation of a start and finish time to each order while taking into account the loading and sequencing policies employed. The scheduling process is usually driven by the need to manage a number of jobs or customers in the system and ensure they are completed or receive their order by a target due date. This often necessitates the rescheduling of orders, termed **expediting**, in order to ensure targets are actually met. In theory expediting should not be necessary if planning and control activities have been undertaken correctly. However, in reality due to the complexity of the task and unexpected events (for example poor quality material in the process leading to rework or machine breakdown events) expediting on a day-to-day basis may be needed.

Scheduling issues in services and manufacturing are now discussed before a number of scheduling techniques are described.

Scheduling in Services

What makes scheduling particularly challenging in service systems is that services are generally produced and delivered by people, whose performance may be less predictable and more variable than manufacturing processes. A major factor in scheduling in services is varying the size of the workforce to meet variations in demand. This area is covered in the workforce scheduling technique section later in this chapter. Another issue in service scheduling is the fact that services are not only delivered by people but are also consumed by people. In fact that customer may be part of the

service itself or require the service on request. The combination of the difficulty in predicting when demand will occur (when people will arrive at a bank for example) and the short lead time between requesting the service and requiring its delivery (a few minutes for bank service for example) brings a challenge to scheduling in services. In practice a trade-off is made between providing enough capacity (staff) to provide customer satisfaction (no wait for service) and the cost of providing that capacity when it is not needed.

Scheduling in Manufacturing

In manufacturing systems the issue of scheduling is about ensuring that the capacity available is directed towards activities that will ensure that performance targets for delivery and lead times are met. The approach to scheduling in manufacturing is largely dependent on the volume and variety mix of the manufacturing system itself and so scheduling approaches will be considered under the headings of line, batch and jobbing process types (see Chapter 3 for an explanation of these process types).

Mass Process-Type Scheduling

Mass process-type systems produce a standard product in a relatively high volume. These systems which have a characteristic flow (product) layout use specialized equipment dedicated to achieving an optimal flow of work through the system. This is important because all items follow virtually the same sequence of operations. A major aim of flow systems is to ensure that each stage of production is able to maintain production at an equal rate. The technique of line balancing is used to ensure that the output of each production stage is equal and maximum utilization is attained.

Batch Process-Type Scheduling

Batch systems process a range of product types in batches (groups) thus combining some of the economics of repetitive production with the variety of a job shop. Scheduling in these configurations is a matter of ensuring that the batch of work introduced to the process will be completed to meet customer due dates. Two issues that affect the job completion time and thus the ability to meet due dates are the transfer batch size and the job sequence. The transfer batch size refers to the size of the batch of parts that is processed at a work station before progressing to the next work station. The actual order size may be greater than this, but is divided into a number of transfer batches to decrease the time the jobs take to pass through the production process. The job sequence is the order in which jobs are entered in to the production process. This will not, however, be the order in which they are completed as different jobs will pass through different work stations and will have different process times.

The material requirements planning (MRP) approach (Chapter 14) is often used to determine the batch size and timing (job sequence) of jobs to meet a projected demand expressed in the form of a master production schedule (MPS) that is developed from customer orders and demand forecasts. A closed-loop MRP system will check the feasibility of any schedule against the capacity available over the planning period. An OPT system (see under scheduling techniques) will focus on ensuring that the bottle-neck processes are kept busy as they determine the output of the whole process.

A problem with batch production control is the tendency for managers to try to keep all work stations busy at all times, which leads to work-in-progress (WIP) queues at heavily loaded work stations. Excessive WIP can seriously impede the ability to schedule batch systems successfully by creating long lead times and by making it difficult to determine the correct job priority for new work entering the system. An aim of the JIT system (Chapter 13) is to eliminate this inventory and make the production control process more transparent. Material requirements planning systems use a technique called production activity control to try to ensure that the production system is working to plan. The technique consists of two main components – Input/ Output Control and Priority Control – which are covered later in this chapter.

Jobbing Process-Type Scheduling

A jobbing system deals with a number of low-volume, high-variety products. Each product is customized to a customer order and so the production planning and control system must deal with a changing mix of jobs. The job may not have been produced before so it might be difficult to estimate the elements of lead time for each job. Because each product has a unique routing and component structure it is also difficult to use systems such as MRP for production planning and control. The pattern of flow through a job shop consists of a number of work stations with queues of work in front of them and what approaches a random flow path connecting the work stations. The technique of job sequencing is used to schedule in jobbing type systems.

Workforce Scheduling

Workforce scheduling aims to ensure that available staff are deployed to maximize the quality of service delivery to the customer. The amount of staff available will have been determined by long-term and more strategic decisions taken on the amount of staff required, often termed manpower planning policies. For day-to-day operations, how-ever, the problem is how to deploy the staff available to best effect. This may be done with the use of a workforce schedule, which determines the daily workload for each member of staff. This daily workload may cover a normal eight-hour day or two- or

Workforce schedule
The workforce schedule determines the daily workload for each member of staff.

three-shift working for certain service providers such as hospitals and police. The allocation of staff available must take into consideration a number of factors such as the number of staff available (taking into account absentees), the skills the individual staff possess, the demand over time for the services the staff supply and the working preferences of the staff themselves.

As mentioned earlier, the need to provide a service for immediate consumption by the customer and the inability to store a service delivery as inventory means that the capacity provided in the schedule needs to meet customer demand closely. If sufficient capacity is not provided, this can lead to overworked staff and delays in service provision, both leading to a fall in the quality of service. The flexibility to undertake a number of tasks can be used to provide a strategy for responding to short-term fluctuation in demand. For example you have probably witnessed the reallocation of staff from replenishing goods in a supermarket to working on a till in response to a sudden increase in customers checking out.

Workforce scheduling can be undertaken by estimating the demand for the operation and then scheduling staff to meet this demand. The use of Gantt charts (Chapter 16) or specialized computer software (for example project management software such as Microsoft Project^{TM}) can be used to facilitate this process.

CASE STUDY 10.1

Car Mechanics Ltd

Car Mechanics Ltd currently offer an express service for car exhaust repair and replacement. It is envisaged to widen the range of services offered to the customer by also performing a tyre change service. Many of the current customers tend to wait until the exhaust has failed and thus arrive at the premises requiring a new exhaust immediately! They also usually wait at the premises while the repair takes place and don't in general like to have to wait for more than 30 minutes for the service to be completed.

Question

What steps could you take to ensure customer satisfaction of the exhaust service is not affected by adding the new tyre change service?

Line Balancing

The issue of line balancing is important in a line-flow process in a service or manufacturing operation that is broken down into a number of stages. Line balancing involves ensuring that the stages of the process are coordinated and bottlenecks are avoided. Because of the line-flow configuration the output of the whole line is

Line balancing
Line balancing aims to ensure that the stages of a line process are coordinated and bottlenecks are avoided.

determined by the slowest or bottleneck stage. This means a reduction in process time at a nonbottleneck will have no effect on the overall output rate. The actual design of the line is guided by the tasks that are involved in producing the product or delivering the service and the required output rate required to meet demand. This provides information that determines the number of stages and the output rate of each stage. The output rate is usually expressed in terms of the cycle time, which is the time taken to produce or deliver one unit of output.

Cycle time
The cycle time is the time taken to produce or deliver one unit of output.

$$\text{cycle time} = \frac{1}{\text{output rate}}$$

Thus an output rate of 30 units/hour gives a cycle time of $1/30/60 = 2$ minutes. Thus a unit of output is delivered every 2 minutes. This means that each stage of the line process must be able to undertake its process within 2 minutes. If the process time is greater than 2 minutes, then it must be reduced by either splitting the stage into multiple stages or assigning more resources (for example assigning two people or running two machines in parallel) to reach the desired output rate. Note that the stage will be idle if its process time is less than the target cycle time of 2 minutes. Thus in order to achieve maximum efficiency each stage must match the target cycle time as closely as possible.

Once the target cycle is calculated, derived from the output rate, it is necessary to decide on the number of workstations and allocate tasks to them. This can be achieved by using computer software, but heuristic or rule-of-thumb methods can usually give good results. The heuristic methods involve allocating tasks, in process order, to each process stage until the stage process time reaches the target cycle time. Remaining tasks are allocated to further stages. In general if there is a choice of tasks to allocate to a stage then the task with the longest process time is allocated first to provide more flexibility in providing a balanced line.

A major factor in achieving a proper line balance is to gather accurate estimates of task times in the line-flow process. If timings are just based on an average of observations then there is a danger that the effect of variations on task times will not be considered. This can be limited somewhat by keeping a number of job elements in a task which reduces variability and increases flexibility. Simulation modelling (Chapter 8) can be used to investigate these variations as well as the effect of random variations such as machine breakdown. It should also be noted that the issue of line balancing will be complicated by constraints such as layout design, material handling between stages and availability of people skills. The use of a line to produce a range of products or services, rather than a single product or service type, also increases the complexity of the line balancing process. Further details of line balancing are given in Chapter 4.

Input/Output Control

Input/output control helps to control the length of queues in front of processes and thus the process lead time (process time + queue time). The queue time is the most variable and usually the largest factor in determining process lead time. Typical values for the breakdown of process lead times in small batch manufacturing are:

Transportation Time: 20%
Setup Time: 10%
Process Time: 15%
Queue Time: 55%

Queue time can in fact be as high as 80% to 95% of the total lead time in some instances. Each of the above factors can be reduced. Setup time can be reduced by a setup reduction programme, which involves separating internal and external operations (Chapter 13). Process time can be reduced through the use of process technology (Chapter 16) or learning curve effects (Chapter 9). Transportation time can be reduced by improved layout (Chapter 4) or increased use of material-handling equipment such as conveyors (Chapter 6). However, lead time is most affected by queue time. It is not just the length of the queuing time but the variability which affects the ability to successfully undertake planning and control activities. If the queue time is not known then the lead time cannot be estimated and so it is not known whether the item will meet its scheduled completion.

Input/output control attempts to control the size of the queues at processes in order that queue times are more consistent and predictable. The method measures the actual flow of work into a work centre and the actual flow of work from that work station. The difference is the amount of work-in-progress (WIP) at that process. By monitoring these figures using input/output reports, capacity is adjusted in order to ensure queues do not become too large and average actual lead time equals planned lead time as closely as possible. It is particularly important to provide control at each process in manufacturing assembly operations as a delay of a component at one process may affect the progress of a whole assembly at a subsequent process.

Priority Control

Priority control also takes an overall view of the production process so that if an assembly is waiting for one delayed part this part will get priority over jobs arriving earlier at that work station. The priority rule is implemented at each work station by issuing a dispatch list (schedule) for that work station, listing jobs for that operation in order of completion date. Thus jobs further over completion date will get priority. Each time a component leaves a work station it will be added to the dispatch list for the next work station.

OPTIMIZED PRODUCTION TECHNOLOGY (OPT)

Optimized production technology
This is an operations control system that is based on the identification of bottlenecks within the production process.

Optimized production technology is an operations control system that is based on the identification of bottlenecks within the production process. Goldratt and Cox (2004) define these bottlenecks as 'any resource whose capacity is less than or equal to the demand placed on it'. This approach attempts to avoid much of the complexity of scheduling by focusing on bottlenecks. The idea is that system output is determined by bottlenecks so it is essential to schedule nonbottleneck resources to ensure maximum use of the bottleneck resources themselves.

In identifying bottlenecks, OPT views the production process as a whole with respect to the market and the business within which it operates. It assumes that all manufacturers aim to make money as their overriding objective. This 'goal' is defined in terms of three performance measures (Goldratt and Cox, 2004):

- throughput
- inventory
- operational expense.

Throughput is the rate at which the production system generates money through sales. Throughput, however, does not equal manufacturing output as any output not sold is seen as waste in the long run. Optimized production technology therefore does not consider 'finished goods' stocks as assets. Inventory is defined as all the money that the system has invested in goods that it intends to sell. OPT excludes labour costs and indirect expenses from inventory valuation. Operational expense is that which the system spends in order to turn inventory into throughput. This includes all expenses, both direct and indirect. Goldratt and Cox (2004) use these performance criteria to restate the goal of a manufacturing organization as: 'To reduce operational expense and reduce inventory whilst simultaneously increasing throughput.'

To understand why OPT focuses on bottlenecks it is necessary to understand how OPT differs from traditional approaches to production planning. The traditional approach is to balance (make equal) capacity at all the work stations in response to anticipated demand from the master production schedule. However, there are two reasons why a production facility cannot be balanced to the demands of production.

These are nondeterminance and interdependence and they relate to the issues of variability and interdependence covered in Chapter 8.

Nondeterminance simply refers to the fact that the information used to derive the production schedule may not be of a fixed nature. For example the process time for an activity will vary each time it is performed. The rate usually quoted will be the average of these times. However, it can be shown that statistical fluctuations around the average can have a significant bearing on plant performance. Interdependence refers to the fact that most stages in production are connected in some way to other stages. For example stage A cannot start until stage B has finished, which cannot start until stages C and D have finished etc. The effect of interdependence is to accumulate the fluctuations caused by nondeterminance from stage to stage downstream of the production process. This is because the ability to go faster than average depends on the ability of all others in front of the process while there is no limit to go slower. Therefore fluctuations don't average out but accumulate and the end of the line has to make up for the accumulation of all the slowness. This behaviour has led Goldratt (1981) to suggest the following recommendations for dealing with an unbalanced plant:

- Bottlenecks must be identified and since they determine the rate of throughput for the whole plant, must be carefully protected from disturbances and potential delays to assure full utilization.
- The resources must be organized so the bottleneck resource is used primarily at one of the earliest stages of production.
- Instead of trying to eliminate overcapacity of nonbottlenecks at random, we must strive to arrange some resources such that one has sufficient overcapacity to support the bottleneck fully. Ideally this would involve a gradual increase of overcapacity as we go downstream.

These recommendations move away from trying to match capacity with demand to managing the whole system to the pace set by the bottlenecks. The principles underlying this approach are as follows:

1. Balance the flow, not capacity. Trying to maintain flow in a balanced capacity plant means that all stages are expected to work to full capacity. In a nonbalanced system (all systems) inventory will accumulate at bottleneck resources. Thus capacity should be used only when necessary, as in JIT control systems (Chapter 13).
2. Constraints determine nonbottleneck utilization. Bottlenecks should pace production and determine the level of utilization for nonbottleneck resources. The only machine to be working at 100% capacity is the bottleneck.

3. Activation is not always equal to utilization. To activate a resource not needed at the bottleneck is a waste.

4. An hour lost at a bottleneck is an hour lost for the entire system. In effect an hour lost at the bottleneck is an hour lost of factory output, as it can never be made up.

5. An hour saved at a nonbottleneck is a mirage. An hour saved at a nonbottleneck will not actually increase output of the whole system.

6. Bottlenecks govern throughput and inventory. Inventory will accumulate at the bottleneck. There is no point in inventory after this stage because throughput is determined by the rate of production at the bottleneck.

7. The transfer batch size should not always equal a process batch size at nonbottlenecks, transfer batches can be small to speed the flow of WIP as an increase in total setup time is not critical. At bottleneck resources these transfer batches then accumulate into larger process batches to save setups and maximize output.

8. Process batches should be variable, not fixed. The process batch should not be determined by some fixed lot-sizing rule for instance but should be varied to balance the flow of the manufacturing cycle.

9. Set the schedule by examining all the constraints simultaneously.

MRP II systems predetermine batch size, lead times and set schedules accordingly. Optimized production technology suggests that all the constraints of a complex network are considered simultaneously using the simulation capabilities of the OPT software. The OPT planning and control approach uses the terminology of the drum, buffer and rope.

The Drum

The drum determines the rate of production. In MRP and JIT control systems the rate of production is determined primarily from market demand but with OPT the bottleneck resources are used to develop the schedule ensuring that bottleneck capacity is not exceeded. Other nonbottleneck resources are scheduled to serve the bottlenecks by varying process batch and transfer batch sizes. Thus the bottleneck resource sets the drumbeat for the entire process.

The Buffer

Buffers are placed at certain locations to prevent unforeseen events disrupting output of finished goods. There are two types of inventory buffer. Time buffers are determined by the amount of output the system could produce during the period of time it takes to correct a disruption. They are generally placed before bottleneck resources.

Stock buffers are inventories of finished goods determined by forecasts of possible demand fluctuations.

The Rope

The rate of the operation of processes that come after the bottleneck is determined by the rate of output from the bottleneck machine. To control the rate of processes before the bottleneck there is a linkage between the bottleneck and the processes that feed it, termed the 'rope'. The rope can take the form of a planned production schedule or an informal discussion between employees at the bottleneck and employees at other work stations.

Figure 10.2 shows the use of the drum, buffer and rope control system. There is a flow of material from process A to process E, with a bottleneck resource being process C. Normally, without any control mechanism excess inventory will build up in front of the bottleneck process C. What is required is an inventory buffer in front of C, so that as the bottleneck resource it is always busy (despite variations in supply) but does not experience the build up of too much inventory. This is achieved by the use of a communication link (the rope) between process C and the upstream process A. This communication could be in the form of a schedule or an informal discussion between personnel. The buffer in front of process C is called a time buffer and ensures work is always present for process C, no matter what the schedule.

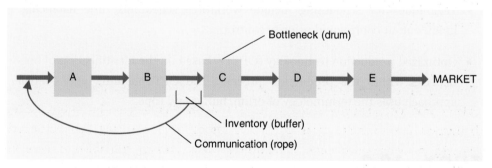

Figure 10.2: Drum, Buffer and Rope in an OPT Control System.

Although OPT can be relatively quickly implemented it needs expertise for correct implementation, which may not be available for small organizations. The OPT software may also be expensive for some organizations. OPT could also be criticized for not containing continuous improvement activities of JIT although these could be incorporated and the two approaches could be used in combination to form a continuous improvement effort.

SUMMARY

- In a make-to-stock system each order must be small compared to total capacity or the risk of making to stock and not finding a customer for the order will be too high. A resource-to-order system means that each order is large compared to total system capacity to make the organization of resources worthwhile. Whilst the customer will only 'see' the delivery time from stock in a make-to-stock system, in a make-to-order system the delivery cycle will include the purchase, make and delivery stages.

- Loading involves determining the available capacity for each stage in a process and allocating a task to that stage. The two principal approaches to loading are 'finite loading', which allocates works up to a fixed limit, and 'infinite loading', which does not place a limit on the work loaded onto a stage.

- Sequencing is the sequential assignment of tasks or jobs to individual processes. Sequencing can be undertaken using priority rules such as DDS (customer due date), FCFS (first-come first-served) and SPT (shortest processing time).

- For services, scheduling involves varying the size of the workforce to meet variations in demand. The approach to scheduling in manufacturing is largely dependent on the volume and variety mix of the manufacturing system.

- Techniques for scheduling include workforce scheduling, line balancing, input/output control and priority control.

- Optimized production technology (OPT) is based on the identification of bottlenecks within the production process. The OPT planning and control approach uses the terminology of drum, buffer and rope.

CASE STUDY 10.2

Using Workforce Scheduling to Lower Labour Costs

As a consequence of the credit crunch and the downturn in many economies, companies are finding it increasingly difficult to increase prices to consumers. This is a problem as many firms are experiencing increased costs in resources such as raw materials and energy. However, in the USA businesses have been able to demand that fewer employees do more work for less pay. Industrial output has continued to increase, even as employers have laid off workers. Companies, including retail giant Wal-Mart, are using new flexible scheduling technology to ensure fewer employees work at times when store customer traffic is low. Accordingly, labour costs, which account for about 70% of US corporate costs, have so far remained in check, in stark contrast to escalating wage inflation in countries such as Vietnam and China.

Question

Why is workforce scheduling technology particularly suitable to large organizations such as Wal-Mart?

EXERCISES

1. What are the implications of the P:D ratio for a manufacturing organization?

2. A job shop has five jobs which must be processed on machine 1 and then on machine 2 (times in minutes). Determine the sequence that will allow the set of five jobs to be completed in the minimum time. State the total job completion time.

Job	Machine 1	Machine 2
A	8	3
B	4	5
C	7	6
D	5	10
E	9	3

3. The following six jobs are to be scheduled on a piece of equipment.

Job	1	2	3	4	5	6
Duration (days)	6	4	2	8	1	5
Due date	6	20	22	24	2	10

a) Prepare a Gantt chart that will provide a schedule showing when jobs are to be undertaken on the machine. Use the FCFS rule.
b) Using FCFS how long will it take to complete all the jobs?
c) Given the due dates shown, calculate the average job lateness when FCFS is used.
d) Given the due dates shown, calculate the average job lateness when SPT is used.
e) What disadvantage is SPT likely to exhibit in a heavily loaded jobs shop?

4. Evaluate the use of the SPT/SOT in a retail and a manufacturing environment.

5. A small manufacturer produces custom parts that first require a shearing operation and then a punch operation. There are five jobs to be processed and the processing times (minutes) are estimated as the following.

Job	Shear	Punch
1	4	5
2	4	1
3	10	4
4	6	10
5	2	3

Use Johnson's algorithm to identify the processing sequence that will give the lowest overall throughput time. Use a Gantt chart to illustrate the sequence and state the total job completion time.

6. What are the main issues in the scheduling of jobbing, batch and line systems?

7. Discuss the advantages and disadvantages of the OPT approach to production planning.

8. Define the terms 'drum', 'buffer' and 'rope' as used in OPT terminology.

WEB EXERCISE

Reading the White Paper at http://www.goldratt.com/toctpwp1.htm (accessed 1 October 2008) why does the OPT approach claim to be so widely applicable?

● FURTHER READING

Chase, R.B., Jacobs, F.R. and **Aquilano, N.J.** (2005) *Operations Management for Competitive Advantage*, 11th edn, McGraw-Hill.
Goldratt, E.M. (2002) *It's Not Luck*, Gower.

Goldratt, E.M. and **Fox, R.** (1994) *The Race*, Gower.
Srikanth, M.L. and **Cavallaro, H.E.** (1995) *Regaining Competitiveness: Putting the Goal to Work*, 2nd revised edn, Spectrum Publications.

WEB LINKS

www.goldratt.com/ (accessed 1 October 2008). The Goldratt Institute home page.
www.production-scheduling.com (accessed 1 October 2008). Advice on scheduling using spreadsheets.
www.toyota.co.uk (accessed 1 October 2008). Web site containing detailed information on world car production.

REFERENCES

Goldratt, E.M. (1981) The unbalanced plant, *APICS 1981 International Conference Proceedings*, pp. 195–9.
Goldratt, E.M. and **Cox, J.** (2004) *The Goal: A Process of Ongoing Improvement*, 3rd edn, Gower.
Johnson, S.M. (1954) Optimal two- and three-stage production with setup times included. *Naval Research Quarterly*, **1**, 61–8.
Shingo, S. (1989) *A Study of Toyota Production System*, Productivity Press.

CHAPTER
11

Capacity Management

- Introduction
- Measuring demand
- Measuring capacity
- Reconciling capacity and demand
- Evaluating alternatives and making a choice
- Appendix: Forecasting

LEARNING OBJECTIVES

- Describe the elements in medium-term capacity planning

- Understand the effects of product mix on capacity

- Evaluate the three pure strategies for reconciling capacity and demand

- Understand approaches to demand management in services

- Understand the use of cumulative representatives to evaluate a level capacity planning approach

- Discuss the use of queuing theory to explore the trade-off between the amount of capacity and level of demand

- Discuss the relevance of propositions about the psychology of customer waiting time

- Understand qualitative and quantitative techniques for forecasting

INTRODUCTION

In operations management a definition of capacity should take into account both the volume and the time over which capacity is available. Thus capacity management is not just about providing customers with services or goods in the amount requested but involves providing them at the time they are requested too.

Capacity issues can be considered as long term and form part of the operations strategy. For example a strategy of capacity expansion may be used to provide a presence in geographical locations before competitors can gain access to a market. These long-term capacity issues are considered in Chapter 5. In this chapter, short- to medium-term capacity issues are considered. These are mainly concerned with ensuring sufficient capacity of the right type is available at the right time to meet demand for the planning period.

Setting capacity to meet the demands of the organization is termed 'capacity planning and control'. The capacity planning and control activity should be taken using a systematic approach using the following steps:

- measuring demand
- measuring capacity
- reconciling capacity and demand
- evaluating alternatives and making a choice.

The 'measuring demand' step requires that future demand be estimated; the 'measuring' step requires the measurement of present capacity; 'reconciling capacity and demand' requires analysis of capacity planning approaches and the final step requires a method of choosing a suitable capacity planning approach. This chapter is structured around these steps in capacity planning and control.

MEASURING DEMAND

For a long-term estimate of demand the strategic planning process will define the markets in which the organization will compete and such factors as the range and volume of products and services in these market segments. The marketing strategy will be evaluated in terms of corporate objectives. Corporate objectives are usually expressed in terms of financial measures such as growth or profitability. The role of marketing strategy and operations strategy in meeting corporate objectives is discussed in Chapter 2.

Based on the marketing strategy and forecasts of demand (see the appendix to this chapter) the organization can formulate a long-range business plan that will include capital budgets for expanding facilities and major equipment investment. Because of the relatively long lead time of acquiring these facilities they are considered in the short- to medium-term planning horizon to represent the effective capacity limit of the organization. Thus long-range demand factors are covered in the design section of this book in Chapter 5 under the heading of Long-term capacity planning.

In the medium term (approximately 2–18 months) planning is undertaken by various functions (manufacturing, marketing, finance and so forth) in order to coordinate efforts to achieve the business plan within the constraints of the long-term decisions made in that plan. The planning process can be described as working in cycles, with each cycle confirming detailed plans for the next time period and sketching more tentative plans for the following period. At the next planning meeting these tentative plans are now considered in more detail and the cycle repeats. This process means that the organization can build on previous plans instead of attempting to devise new plans at each planning cycle. This reduces planning time and leads to more continuity in decision making. The aggregate planning process will evaluate the production plan in order to ensure sufficient capacity is available to undertake the output targets.

The production plan (or operations plan in a service organization) states the amount of output which will be delivered from the operations function over the medium term business plan. The output can be expressed in terms of volume, currency or units. For example a retail outlet may commit to sales of clothes in terms of sales value or units sold  during the next 12-month period. The production plan provides an overall guide to the level of output from the manufacturing/operations department, which will be coordinated with other functions such as marketing and finance.

It is necessary to break the production plan down into a level of detail required for procurement and operational purposes. This means that the demand for each individual product and thus the materials, components and work tasks required to produce it, must be specified. The master production schedule (MPS) states the volume and timing of all products that have a significant demand on manufacturing resources. Further details of the MPS in relation to a materials requirements planning system are provided in Chapter 14.

MEASURING CAPACITY

Measuring capacity may at first seem straightforward, especially when compared to the uncertainty inherent in estimating demand. However, capacity is not fixed but is a variable that depends on a number of factors including:

- Capacity takes many different forms such as storage space, availability of employee skills, equipment numbers and transportation facilities.
- Any of these types of capacity may be the limiting factor or bottleneck on the capacity of a process. The actual bottleneck, and thus capacity, may also change over time.
- Working practices such as hours worked and holiday entitlement can also affect capacity calculations and may change over time. For example a change in company policy may decrease the hours a week of employees and thus reduce capacity.
- The amount of capacity required to deliver a particular process at a particular level may change over time due to the experience gained and improvements made to process design.
- Capacity available in multiple locations may not be simply totalled as transportation time and costs may make available capacity in a particular location unsuitable.
- Capacity is time-based and so capacity underutilized due to a drop in demand cannot be used later when demand increases. Thus the actual capacity available will be less the more demand fluctuates. Process time fluctuations will also affect capacity. Queuing theory (later in this chapter) and simulation modelling (Chapter 8) can be used to analyse this time-based behaviour.

Measuring capacity in services is a particular challenge. Generally services need to be more custom-designed and involve more personal contact in order to meet specific customer needs. Thus customer contact has a number of impacts on the way the service can be run. Customer involvement tends to provide an opportunity for special requests and instructions to be issued by the customer, which tends to disrupt routine procedures and thus efficiency. Capacity may be lost in providing conversation to the customer in addition to delivering the actual service. Quality is closely related to the customer's perception of satisfactory service. Operations employees employed where high levels of customer contact occur must be skilled in interpreting what the customer really wants. Thus the level of customer/client contact can have a direct effect on the efficiency and thus capacity availability that an operation can achieve.

There are a variety of methods to achieve efficiency and still provide the customer with good service. One way to limit the disruption from unusual requests is to standardize the service – for example in a fast-food restaurant. A common strategy to improve the overall efficiency of the operation is to keep separate those parts of the operation that do not require direct customer contact. Operations are divided into front office, where interaction with the customer takes place, and back office, where directions are primarily taken from managers, not customers (see Chapter 1).

Two further issues to consider when measuring capacity are product mix and the definitions of design and effective capacity.

Product Mix

Only when a narrow product (or service) range is involved can capacity be measured reasonably accurately and in this case be quoted in terms of output volume. The effect of product mix on capacity is shown in the Worked Example 11.1.

WORKED EXAMPLE 11.1
The Effect of Product Mix on Capacity

The following assembly times are given for three models of a washing machine.

	Assembly time (minutes)
Washer (basic)	50
Washer (deluxe)	150
Washer (dryer)	250

The target weekly output is given as 100 units. Calculate the total output for a product ratio of 4:2:1 for washer (basic), washer (deluxe) and washer (dryer) and total output for a product ratio of 3:2:2.

SOLUTION

For a product mix ratio of 4:2:1 the total output is as follows:

Ratio = 4:2:1
Assembly time for 7 units = $(4 \times 50) + (2 \times 150) + (1 \times 250) = 750$ minutes
Assembly minutes available = 9000
Therefore weekly output = $\dfrac{9000}{750} \times 7 = 84$ units

For a product mix ratio of 3:2:2 the output is as follows:

Ratio = 3:2:2
Assembly time for 7 units = $(3 \times 50) + (2 \times 150) + (2 \times 250) = 950$ minutes
Assembly minutes available = 9000
Therefore weekly output = $\dfrac{9000}{950} \times 7 = 66$ units

Thus a change in product mix from 4:2:1 to 3:2:2 alters the weekly capacity output from 84 to 66 units.

With a changing product mix therefore it may be more useful to measure capacity in terms of input measures, which provide some indication of the potential output. Also for planning purposes, when demand is stated in output terms it is necessary to convert input measures to an estimated output measure. For example in hospitals that undertake a range of activities, capacity is often measured in terms of beds available, an input measure. An output measure such as number of patients treated per week will be highly dependent on the mix of activities the hospital performs. Estimates of capacity based on output can also be misleading as part of this output may be accounted for by either inventory (for example, patients) part way through the process or the use of additional resources (for example, overtime, equipment rental, contracting out) that could not normally be treated as part of the organization's capacity. Examples of input and output measures of capacity are given in Table 11.1.

Operation	Input measure	Output measure
Hospital	Beds available	Patients treated
Airline	Seats available	Passengers flown
Manufacturer	Equipment available	Goods delivered
Retail outlet	Floor space available	Goods sold
Restaurant	Seating available	Meals served

Table 11.1: Examples of Input and Output Measures of Capacity.

Design, Effective and Actual Capacity

The design capacity of an operation represents the theoretical output of a process as it was designed. However, this level of capacity is rarely met due to occurrences that prevent the operation producing its full output. These occurrences are termed planned and unplanned factors (Figure 11.1).

Planned factors are activities whose timing can be determined in advance. They include such items as maintenance, training and machine setup time. During these activities the output from the operation is lost. One of the ways to reduce this loss of output for manufacturing processes is to use the technique of setup reduction (Chapter 13), which attempts to undertake as much of the setup process as possible while the operation is still in use. In services training of personnel may take place during the year when seasonal demand is low.

The capacity remaining after loss of output due to planned factors is termed the effective capacity of the process. However, this will also be above the level of capacity which is available due to unplanned occurrences such as machine

Design capacity
The capacity of an operation that represents the theoretical output of a process as it was designed.

Effective capacity
The capacity remaining after loss of output due to planned factors such as maintenance and training.

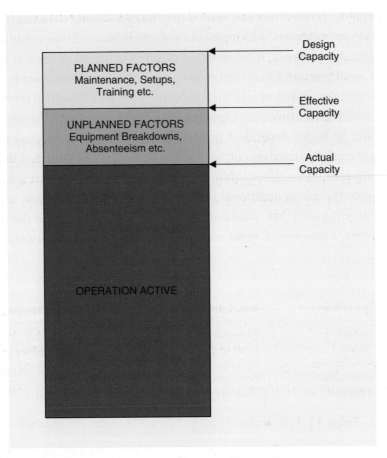

Figure 11.1: Design, Effective and Actual Capacity.

breakdowns and worker absenteeism. These are more difficult to deal with than planned factors, because by definition their timing cannot be predicted. In order to minimize these disturbances action should be taken such as preventative maintenance (Chapter 13). This involves undertaking planned maintenance activities, if possible when demand is low. These activities can include replacing equipment parts before they fail, in order to reduce unplanned breakdowns. Worker absenteeism could be reduced by improving motivation. This could be achieved by changing the job design using the ideas of the job characteristics model described in Chapter 9.

After taking both planned and unplanned factors into account there remains the capacity available for processing, termed the **actual capacity** of the operation.

Two measures that you often see used in relation to these capacity measures are utilization and efficiency. **Utilization** gives the proportion of time a process is in actual

Actual capacity
The capacity remaining after loss of output due to both planned factors and unplanned factors. Unplanned factors include equipment breakdown and absenteeism.

Utilization
This is the proportion of time a process is in actual use compared with its design capacity.

use compared to its design capacity and **efficiency** gives the proportion of time that a process is in use compared to its effective capacity. Thus:

$$\text{utilization} = \frac{\text{actual output}}{\text{design capacity}}$$

$$\text{efficiency} = \frac{\text{actual output}}{\text{effective capacity}}$$

Both measures are usually given in terms of percentages. A utilization of 60% means that a process was producing output for 60% of a time period. An efficiency rating of 60% denotes that a process was producing output for 60% of a time period in which it was available to produce output (it was not being used for maintenance or other planned activities).

Efficiency
This gives the proportion of time a process is in use compared to its effective capacity.

RECONCILING CAPACITY AND DEMAND

Methods for reconciling capacity and demand can be classified into three 'pure' strategies: level capacity, chase demand and demand management. Due to the complexity of capacity management and the need to optimize a range of performance objectives it is usually necessary to combine the three pure strategies described and form a mixed capacity planning strategy. The three strategies are now described.

Level Capacity

The **level capacity** strategy sets the processing capacity at a uniform level throughout the planning period regardless of fluctuations in forecast demand. This means output is set at a fixed rate, usually to meet average demand. Inventory is used to absorb variations in demand. During periods of low demand any overproduction can be transferred to finished goods inventory in anticipation of sales at a later time period (Figure 11.2). The disadvantage of this strategy is the cost of holding inventory and the cost of perishable items that may have to be discarded. To avoid producing obsolete items firms will try to create inventory for products which are relatively certain to be sold. This strategy is also of limited value for perishable goods.

For a service organization output cannot be stored as inventory so a level capacity plan involves running at a uniformly high level of capacity (Figure 11.3). The drawback of the approach is the cost of maintaining this high level of capacity, although it could be useful when the cost of lost sales is particularly high. In order to overcome this problem the concept of 'partitioning demand' is used, which involves keeping capacity in the customer contact area consistently high, so customers are not kept waiting, and keeping capacity in the noncontact areas at a more uniform level. Another strategy is for services to 'store' their output by performing part of their

Level capacity
This capacity planning strategy sets processing capacity at a uniform level throughout the planning period regardless of fluctuations in forecast demand. This means production is set at a fixed rate, usually to meet average demand and inventory is used to absorb variations in demand. For a service organization output cannot be stored as inventory so a level capacity plan involves running at a uniformly high level of capacity.

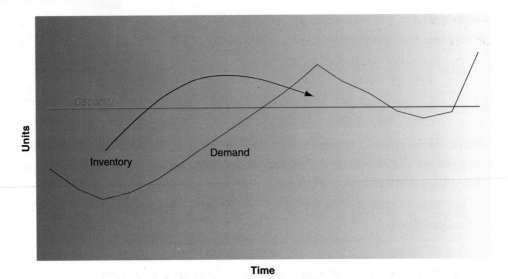

Figure 11.2: Level Capacity Plan.

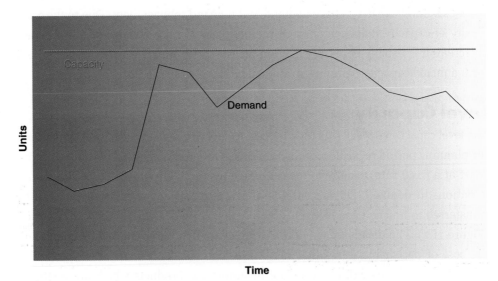

Figure 11.3: Level Capacity Plan at a High Level.

Chase demand
This capacity planning strategy seeks to match output to the demand pattern over time. Capacity is altered by such policies as changing the number of part-time staff, changing staff availability through overtime working, changing equipment levels and subcontracting.

work in anticipation of demand. An example is purchasing and displaying goods before actual customer demand occurs.

Chase Demand

The chase demand strategy seeks to match output to the demand pattern over time. Capacity is altered by such policies as changing the amount of part-time staff, changing the amount of staff availability through overtime working, changing equipment levels and subcontracting. The strategy is costly in terms of the costs of activities such as changing staffing levels and overtime payments. The costs may be particularly high in industries in which skills are scarce. Disadvantages of subcontracting include reduced profit margin lost to the subcontractor, loss of control, potentially longer lead times and the risk that the subcontractor may decide to enter the same market. For these reasons a pure chase demand strategy is more usually adopted by service operations which cannot store their output and so make a level capacity plan less attractive. A graphical representation of a chase demand plan is shown in Figure 11.4.

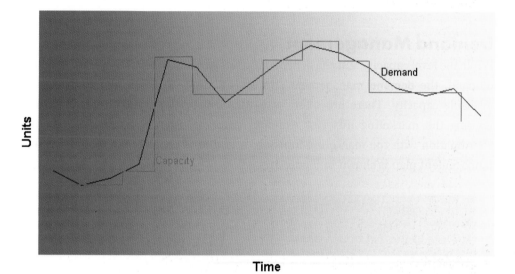

Figure 11.4: Chase Demand Plan.

In services, when the operation cannot usually match the demand rate with its capacity level, its objective becomes one of developing a capacity profile that matches its demand profile to the extent that this is feasible and economically viable. Strategies for achieving this include:

- *Staggered workshift schedules.* Scheduling the availability of capacity to cover demand involves constructing work shifts so that the number of operators available at any one time matches the demand profile – for example in a fast-food restaurant.
- *Part-time staff.* More flexibility to schedule and smooth the work demand is often available for those parts of a service where the customer is not present and the service is provided by working with some surrogate for the customer. A strategy of using part-time staff needs to trade the cost of not doing some work off against the extra cost of employing the staff.

- *Subcontractors*. If there is not enough capacity, additional capacity can be obtained from outside sources. For example, surgeries employing contract doctor services to cover weekends.
- *Multiskilled floating staff*. Having multiskilled staff increases flexibility in capacity decisions. For example in the case of a hospital it might be desirable to have some floating capacity that can be shifted from one department to another if the number of patients or the amount of nursing attention required in each department varies.
- *Customer self-service*. With this option, the service capacity arrives when the demand does. Customers at supermarkets and many department stores select most of their own merchandise.

Demand Management

While the level capacity and chase demand strategies aim to adjust capacity to match demand, the demand management strategy attempts to adjust demand to meet available capacity. There are many ways this can be done but most will involve altering the marketing mix (for example, price or promotion) and will require coordination with the marketing function. A graphical representation of a demand management plan is shown in Figure 11.5.

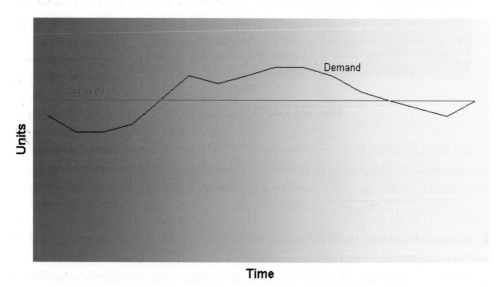

Figure 11.5: Demand Management Plan.

Demand management strategies include:

- *Varying the price*. During periods of low demand price discounts can be used to stimulate the demand level. Conversely when demand is higher than the capacity limit, price could be increased.

- *Advertising.* Advertising and other marketing activities can be used to increase sales during low demand periods.
- *Alternative products.* This is the use of existing processes to make or sell alternative products during low demand periods. An example is the way many garden centres use their premises to sell Christmas decorations during the winter months when gardening activity is low.
- *Maintenance of a fixed schedule.* Some services can schedule the times at which the service is available, for example airlines and rail services. Demand occurs as people purchase tickets to use some of the previously scheduled transportation capacity.
- *Use of an appointment system.* The pattern of demand variations over the longer term can also have a significant influence on the planning of efficient service operations. The ideal would be to achieve uniform utilization of service capacity but this is unlikely unless an appointment-only policy is operated. Some services are provided by appointment, for example a dentist or veterinary surgery. Use of an appointment system permits demand to be moved into available time. The delay between a request for an appointment and the time of the appointment may depend on the backlog or queue of waiting work.
- *Delayed delivery.* Delaying jobs until capacity is available serves to make the workload more uniform, for example a bank teller. In addition routine work may be set aside to make capacity available for rush jobs.
- *Providing economic incentives for off-peak demand.* Some operations have a high capital investment in the capacity they have to provide their services. The unit cost of capacity that is used only occasionally for peak demand is very high. These operations try to keep demand as uniform as possible by the use of economic inducements, for example off-peak electricity and off-peak telephone calls.

Yield Management

The use of demand management strategies is often particularly developed in service industries where capacity cannot be stored (output cannot be held as stock and used later) and demand is stochastic (there is variability in when customers request the service and how long it takes to service them). Yield management aims to maximize customer revenue in these service organizations and is particularly appropriate when the organization is operating with relatively fixed capacity and it is possible to segment the market into different types of customers.

The airline industry provides an example of the use of yield management. It has well-developed policies for ensuring as many seats as possible are occupied on its flights. Once a flight route has been scheduled and an aircraft has been allocated to

Yield management This is the use of demand management strategies aimed at maximizing customer revenue in service organizations. It is particularly appropriate when the organization is operating with relatively fixed capacity and it is possible to segment the market into different types of customers.

that route, the costs of operating the aircraft, including staffing, maintenance and fuel costs, are fixed and the variable cost in accommodating each additional passenger on a flight is very low. Moreover, capacity is lost once the flight takes place and cannot be stored for later use. The airline thus will want to fill as many seats as possible whilst max-

imizing the overall price the customers pay. One business model that airlines use to do this is to charge relatively high prices in advance to customers when the guarantee of a flight is more important than the price (for example, business customers) and then discount fares close to the flight time to maximize revenue (through such outlets as e-Commerce sites such as www.lastminute.com). An alternative strategy is to start prices low to ensure a proportion of capacity is sold and then increase the price as capacity becomes scarce as the flight fills. If the flight is not reaching its target for booked seats, discounts may be offered to customers to increase sales (budget airlines such as easyJet (www.easyjet.com) and Bmibaby (www.bmibaby.com) use this model).

As well as price-discounting other yield-management strategies include over-booking service provision, for example taking bookings from more people for a flight than there are seats on the plane. This strategy is based on the assumption that not all passengers will turn up for the flight and thus maximizes revenue. The obvious downside is that if everyone does arrive then passengers will need to be accommodated in some way (for example an upgrade to business class, financial compensation or a seat on a later plane or a combination of these) increasing costs. A further yield-management strategy is to vary the service type, for example different classes of ticket for a train journey. This allows a discounting strategy for price-sensitive customers but travel-time flexibility and higher service levels for higher paying business customers, maximizing overall revenue. Case study 11.2 provides further information on the sophistication of organizations' yield-management policies.

EVALUATING ALTERNATIVES AND MAKING A CHOICE

Capacity planning involves evaluating the capacity requirements and determining the best way to meet these using a feasible and low-cost capacity-planning approach. The term 'aggregate planning' is sometimes used to describe the process of aggregat-ing (grouping) capacity requirements over a medium term planning horizon to provide the best way to meet these requirements. In order to choose a capacity plan which meets the above criteria it is necessary to try to predict the consequences of that plan. This can be done with varying levels of accuracy and cost using the following methods:

- cumulative representations
- queuing theory
- the psychology of queuing.

Cumulative Representations

One method of evaluating a level capacity planning approach is to simply plot the cumulative demand and cumulative capacity for a product over the planning time period. As discussed earlier, capacity is required in the right volume, at the right time. When pursuing a level capacity plan, even though over time inventory levels may be sufficient to meet demand, this does not mean that inventory levels will be sufficient to meet demand at a particular point in time. Thus a running total or cumulative count of inventory, which should always meet or exceed cumulative demand, is used to ensure no stock-outs occur. An example of the use of cumulative representations is shown in Figure 11.6.

> **Cumulative representation**
> A running total or cumulative count of inventory, which should always meet or exceed cumulative demand. It is used to ensure no stock-outs occur when using a level capacity plan.

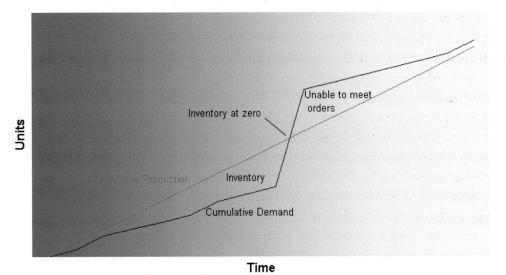

Figure 11.6: Cumulative Representations.

Figure 11.6 shows the relationship between capacity and demand over time and thus enables an assessment of the capacity plan. When the cumulative demand line is below the cumulative capacity, the distance between the lines is the level of inventory at that time. If the demand line lies above the capacity line then this represents a shortage of capacity at that time. The graph shows the cumulation of capacity and demand, so it takes into account the usage of any surplus inventory in periods when demand exceeds supply (when the graphs meet, inventory is zero). The cumulative representation graph can show if the capacity plan is meeting demand. This occurs when the capacity line is always along or above the demand line over the planning period.

Assessing the effect of capacity planning approaches on the capacity plan involves adjusting the gradient of the capacity (for chase demand approach) or demand (for demand management approach) line at the appropriate point at which the change is to take place. The ideal situation would be when the capacity and demand lines follow each other as closely as possible on the graph. However, the cost of changing the capacity or demand pattern must be taken into consideration. It should also be noted that it may be cost effective to only change capacity in certain blocks and the cost of the change may be dependent on the direction of that change. For example it may be cheaper to decrease capacity rather than increase capacity for a certain process.

Queuing Theory

Cumulative representations rely on the fact that when supply exceeds demand inventory can be stored for use when demand exceeds supply. In service situations, however, the output of the operation cannot be stored. Waiting time can only be eliminated when customers are asked to arrive at fixed intervals (an appointment system) and service times are fixed. Thus waiting time in queues is caused by fluctuations in arrival rates and variability in service times. Queuing theory can be used to explore the trade-off between the amount of capacity and the level of demand. Too much capacity and costs will be excessive, but too little capacity will cause long waiting for the customer and loss of service quality leading to loss of business. In a service context queuing theory can provide a useful guide in determining expected waiting time for an arriving customer and the average number of customers who will be waiting for service. This permits an estimate of the amount of capacity that will be needed to keep waiting time to a reasonable level taking into account the expected rate and variability of demand. Examples of queuing situations include customers at a bank, aeroplanes circling waiting to land, patients waiting to see a doctor and parts waiting for processing at a machining centre.

Uncertainty in arrival and service times means that, even although on average there may be adequate capacity to meet demand, queuing may still occur when a

Queuing theory
Waiting time in queues is caused by fluctuations in arrival rates and variability in service times. Queuing theory can be used to explore the trade-off between the amount of capacity and the level of demand.

number of successive arrivals or long service times occur. Conversely, idle time will occur when arrival rates or service time decreases. Although this behaviour means that full utilization will not be feasible for this type of system, queuing theory does allow analysis of how much capacity is needed to keep average or maximum queue length or waiting times to an acceptable level. This acceptable level or service-quality level will depend on the type of operation involved.

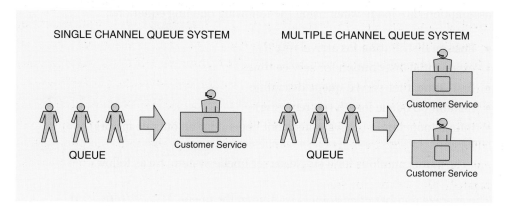

Figure 11.7: Single- and Multiple-Channel Queuing Systems.

Figure 11.7 shows how queue systems can be classified into a single-channel queuing systems consisting of a single queue of customers who wait until a service facility is available and a multiple-channel queuing systems that have parallel server facilities. Although a single queue system is increasingly popular and may be seen by customers as fairer in that it enforces the first-come, first-served (FCFS) rule, its operation may not always be practical; imagine a single line of customers with trolleys in a supermarket! Other disadvantages of a single queue system are that the length of the single queue may seem to imply a longer wait for customers than many short queues and a single-channel queue system assumes that all the servers can meet the needs of all the customers.

Arrivals, representing demand for the use of the facility, enter the system at a particular demand rate. If the service facility is already in use the arrival waits in a queue until capacity becomes available. Several factors determine the performance of a queuing system. The timing of customer arrivals into the system is usually assumed to occur randomly according to a probability distribution such as the Poisson distribution for arrival times and the exponential distribution for service times (Chase, Jacobs and Aquilano, 2005). A priority system may be used to select the next customer to receive service. In most systems the FCFS rule will apply. In some circumstances arrivals may not join the queue if it is too long when they arrive (balking), or they may wait for a time, become impatient and leave (reneging).

Queuing Theory Equations

There are several equations for different queuing structures but this text will consider the single server and multiple server models only (see Figure 11.7). The following assumptions are made when using the following queuing equations:

- Poisson distribution for arrival rate
- exponential distribution for service times
- first-come, first-served queue discipline
- no limit on queue length (no reneging)
- infinite population (arrival rate is not dependent on outside factors).

The main equations for a single server queue system are as follows:

The average number of customers waiting in the queue, $L_q = \lambda^2/(\mu(\mu - \lambda))$
The average time (in hours) that a customer spends in the queue, $W_q = \lambda/(\mu(\mu - \lambda))$
The probability that the server is busy (server utilization), $\rho = \lambda/\mu$

where

λ = average arrival rate of customers per hour
μ = average service rate of customers per hour

WORKED EXAMPLE 11.2
Single Server Queue

A local shop has a single counter/till at which customers are served. Customers arrive at an average rate of 24 per hour according to a Poisson distribution and service times are exponentially distributed with a average rate of 20 customers per hour.

a) What is the average number of customers waiting in the queue?
b) What is the average time a customer spends in the queue?
c) What is the probability that the till is busy?

SOLUTION

$\lambda = 20$

$\mu = 24$

a) $L_q = 20^2/(24 \times (24 - 20)) = 400/96 = 4.17$ customers

b) $W_q = 20/(24 \times (24 - 20)) = 20/96 = 0.2$ hours

c) $\rho = 20/24 = 0.83$

The main equations for a multiple server queue system are as follows:

The average number of customers waiting in the queue, $L_q = \dfrac{\lambda\mu(\lambda/\mu)^s}{(s-1)!(s\mu-\lambda)^2} \times P_0$

where $P_0 = 1 \Big/ \left(\displaystyle\sum_{n=0}^{s-1} \dfrac{(\lambda/\mu)^n}{n!} + \dfrac{(\lambda/\mu)^s}{s!(1-\lambda/s\mu)} \right)$

The average time (in hours) that a customer spends in the queue, $W_q = L_q/\lambda$

The probability that the server is busy (i.e. server utilization), $\rho = \lambda/s\mu$

where

$\lambda = $ average arrival rate of customers per hour

$\mu = $ average service rate of customers per hour

$s = $ number of servers

P_0 is most easily found by using a lookup table of values of λ/μ and s (see for example Stevenson, 2009).

WORKED EXAMPLE 11.3
Multiple Server Queue

Customers queue in a single line in a department store and are served at one of three tills on an FCFS basis. Customers arrive at a rate of 24 an hour (according to a Poisson distribution) and have a service time that is exponentially distributed with a mean rate of 10 customers served per hour.

a) What is the mean number of customers waiting in the queue?

b) What is the mean time a customer spends in the queue?

c) What is the probability that a till is busy?

SOLUTION

$\lambda = 24$

$\mu = 10$

$s = 3$

P_0 has been given as 0.056

a) $L_q = \dfrac{24 \times 10 \times (24/10)^3}{(3-1)! \times (3 \times 10 - 24)^2} \times 0.056 = \left(\dfrac{3317.76}{72}\right) \times 0.056 = 2.58$ customers

b) $W_q = \dfrac{L_q}{\lambda} = \dfrac{2.58}{24} = 0.1075$ hours

c) $\rho = \dfrac{24}{(3 \times 10)} = 0.8$

The mathematical equations used in queuing theory make a number of assumptions about the system. They assume steady-state conditions have been reached – that the effects of an empty system start-up phase have been overcome and the system has reached a steady state. This may never happen if the mean arrival rate is greater than the service rate. Also the system may shut down for breaks during the day or may not run long enough to reach equilibrium. The equations can also only be used to describe very simple systems. Business process simulation (Chapter 8) is often used to analyse situations that do not fit adequately the assumed conditions of queuing theory.

CASE STUDY   11.1

Lloyds Cameras Cut Time in Queues

Lloyds TSB has been using special video cameras to cut the amount of time its customers are spending queuing in branches. The UK's fifth-largest bank has installed special video cameras in 30 of its branches to monitor customer behaviour and track how long people spend queuing. As a result, the amount of time customers wait to be served in these branches has fallen from 1.86 minutes in November 2004 to 1.46 minutes in March as the bank redeploys key staff at busy times of the day. The number of customers who are served within two minutes of walking into these branches has risen from 72.4% last November to about 82.6% in March. The average time each customer spends in front of a cashier has remained stable at just over 2.2 minutes. Lloyds TSB has identified queuing time as a major gripe amongst customers.

Graham Lindsay, director of the branch network at Lloyds TSB, said: 'We have done customer research and two minutes is generally the gratification threshold. Customers resent waiting five minutes or more. Levels of customer satisfaction in branches are closely connected to waiting times and efficiency of service.' The technology has been developed by Brickstream, the US technology company. There are no comparable figures available from rival banks on how long customers spend queuing. However, at Barclays' annual meeting last month, Roger Davis, head of retail banking, said queuing times had fallen to three minutes at Barclays branches.

Source: by Jane Croft, FT.com, 9 May 2005. See www.ft.com/cms/s/0/3b4d1b30-c027-11d9-b376-00000e2511c8.html (accessed 11 October 2008). Reproduced with permission.

Question

How has the use of video cameras enabled Lloyds to cut queue times in its bank branches?

The Psychology of Queues

Maister (1985) suggests that although queuing theory has been used successfully to analyse waiting times it does not take into account customer perception of the waiting time itself. Thus depending on the situation a customer may or may not feel that a wait time of 10 minutes is acceptable for instance. Using the concepts of expectation and perception of service levels, Maister has developed a series of propositions about the psychology of queues, which can be used by service organizations to influence customer satisfaction with waiting times. The propositions are as follows:

Psychology of queues
A series of propositions that can be used by service organizations to instigate policies to influence customer satisfaction with waiting times.

- *Unoccupied time feels longer than occupied time.* The important point here is to try to ensure that unoccupied time is taken up with an activity that is seen as useful by the customer and is related in some way to the forthcoming service.
- *Pre-process waits feel longer than in-process waits.* It is important that human contact is made as soon as possible to convey that the service has started and reduce anxiety in the customer. For example handing out the menu in a restaurant immediately customers arrive ensures that they do not feel they have been overlooked.
- *Anxiety makes waits seem longer.* A particular form of this is when parallel queues are used for a service. What usually happens is that the queue you choose to enter suddenly stops moving while the other queues progress rapidly! Many service organizations (such as post offices) have a single queue system, which seems fairer to customers and reduces anxiety by operating a strict FCFS policy.

- *Uncertain waits are longer than known, finite waits.* It is important to inform the customer how long the wait will be. A particular problem with appointment systems is that they create a specific expectation about when a service should begin and if appointments begin to run behind, anxiety increases as the expectation is not met.
- *Unexplained waits are longer than explained waits.* If the customer understands the reason for a wait they will be more satisfied than if no explanation or an explanation which does not provide sufficient justification is given.
- *Unfair waits are longer than equitable waits.* One of the most irritating occurrences for a customer is when someone who has arrived at a later time is served first. This can be eliminated by a single queue system that operates on an FCFS basis.
- *The more valuable the service, the longer the customer will wait.* If the service is seen to be of little value, the tolerance for waiting will diminish greatly. In particular post-process waits, when the required service is over, feel longer than in-process or even pre-process waits.
- *Solo waits feel longer than group waits.* When there is group interaction in a waiting line, perhaps initiated by an announcement of a delay, then waiting becomes more tolerable.

Although the FCFS queue discipline has been mentioned as a possible solution to some of the above problems, it cannot always be applied due to factors such as the implications for available space (for instance, for a supermarket customer using a trolley). The single queue also eliminates the possibility of providing custom service points for different customer types (such as a customer with few items in a supermarket or first-class customers for an airline). Overall the propositions show that in addition to the actual wait or queue time the context of the waiting line will have a significant effect on the level of customer satisfaction.

APPENDIX: FORECASTING

Introduction

Accurate forecasts are an important factor in enabling organizations to deliver goods and services to the customer when required and thus achieve a quality service. Forecasting is important in relation to anticipating changing customer requirements and meeting them with new product and service designs (Chapter 7). The ability to measure demand is also a key part of the facility design (Chapter 5) capacity management process (Chapter 11) and supply-chain management (Chapter 15).

In order to produce accurate forecasts an organization must collect up-to-date data on relevant information such as prices and sales volumes and choose an appropriate forecasting technique. The accuracy of a forecast is also dependent on the time horizon over which the forecast is derived. Forecasts for short time horizons tend to be more accurate than for longer term forecasts, so one way of improving accuracy is shortening the lead time necessary for the organization to respond to a forecast. This might mean improving operations in terms of the flexibility performance objective.

Forecasting Techniques

Organizations must develop forecasts of the level of demand they should be prepared to meet. The forecast provides a basis for coordination of plans for activities in various parts of the organization, for example personnel employ the right amount of people, purchasing order the right amount of material and finance can estimate the capital required for the business. Forecasts can be developed either through a qualitative approach or a quantitative approach (Figure 11.8).

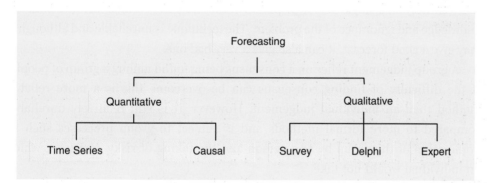

Figure 11.8: Forecasting Techniques.

Qualitative Forecasting Methods

Qualitative forecasting methods take a subjective approach and are based on estimates and opinions. The following qualitative techniques will be described: market surveys, the Delphi method and expert judgement.

Market Surveys

A market survey collects data from a sample of customers, analyses the responses and makes inferences about the population from which the sample is drawn. They are particularly useful before the launch of a new product when

Qualitative forecasting methods
Qualitative forecasting methods take a subjective approach and are based on estimates and opinions. They include market surveys, the Delphi method and expert judgement.

there is limited information on potential customer demand. For the survey to be statistically valid it is necessary to ensure that a correct sampling methodology is used and that questions are pertinent and unbiased. Care must also be taken with the analysis of responses. To achieve useful results can be an expensive and time-consuming activity.

Delphi Study

This is a formal procedure that aims to bring together the opinions of a group of experts. A questionnaire is completed by a panel of experts. It is then analysed and summaries are passed back to the experts. Each expert in the group can then compare their forecast with the summarized reply of the others. This process is repeated, maybe up to six times, until a consensus has emerged within the group on which decision to take. The accuracy of the Delphi method can be good, but the cost and effort of its use may be relatively high.

Expert Judgement

This can take the form of an individual or group judgement. An individual judgement relies entirely on a single person's opinion of the situation – which includes both the knowledge and ignorance of the problem. The technique is unreliable and although it may give a good forecast, it can also give a very bad one.

A group judgement relies on a consensus being found among a group of people. If the difficulty of finding consensus can be overcome this is a more reliable method than an individual judgement. However, it is still relatively unreliable compared to more formal methods and is subject to group processes such as domination of the group by one person and the taking of risky decisions, which an individual would not take.

Quantitative Forecasting Methods

Quantitative forecasting methods use a mathematical expression or model to show the relationship between demand and some independent variable or variables. The model that is appropriate for forecasting depends on the demand pattern to be projected and the forecaster's objectives for the model.

Quantitative forecasting methods
These use a mathematical expression or model to show the relationship between demand and some independent variable or variables. The methods include time series and causal forecasting models.

Time Series Analysis

A time series is a set of observations measured at successive points in time. Time series analysis attempts to discover a pattern and extrapolate this pattern into the future. There are four components of a time series: trend, cyclical, seasonal and irregular.

- Trend – a gradual movement to relatively higher or lower values over time (not random fluctuations).
- Cyclical – any recurring sequence of points above and below the trend line lasting for more than one year.
- Seasonal – any regularly repeating pattern that is less than one year in duration.
- Irregular – deviations from the time series values from those expected by the trend, cyclical and seasonal components. We cannot attempt to predict its impact on the time series.

To analyse a time series smoothing methods can be used. Smoothing methods 'smooth out' the random fluctuations caused by the irregular component of the time series. They are only appropriate for a stable time series – one that does not exhibit trend, cyclical or seasonal effects. The moving averages and exponential smoothing methods are described.

Moving Averages

A moving average is a procedure in which, as each new observation becomes available, a new average can be computed by dropping the oldest observation and including the new one. This moving average will then be the forecast for the next period. For example we might compute a three-week moving average at the end of each week to smooth out random fluctuations and obtain an estimate of the average sales per week. To compute a three-week moving average, at the end of each week we add sales for the latest 3 weeks and divide by 3. An example of a spreadsheet of a moving average forecast is given in Figure 11.9. An alternative approach is to use the Excel Data Analysis toolpak, which has a moving average function.

Averaging multiple periods helps smooth out random fluctuations so that the forecast or average has more stability or does not fluctuate erratically. A moving average will gain stability if a greater number of periods are used in the average. If the number of periods in the average is too great, however, the average will be so stable that it will be slow to respond to nonrandom changes in the demand data. Responsiveness is the ability of a forecast to adjust quickly to true changes in the base level of demand. Both responsiveness and stability are difficult to achieve with a forecasting method that looks only at the series of past demands without considering factors that may have caused a change in that pattern without taking into consideration external causative factors.

Exponential Smoothing

In practice the technique of moving averages as a forecasting technique is not used often because the method of exponential smoothing is generally superior. The most

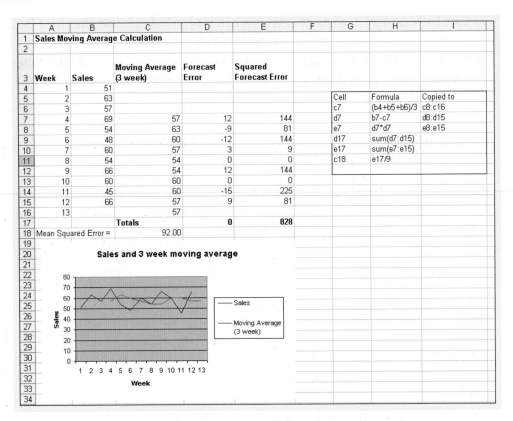

Figure 11.9: Spreadsheet of a Moving Average Forecast.

recent observations will usually provide the best guide to the future, so the exponential smoothing procedure uses exponentially decreasing weights as the observations get older. This method keeps a running average of demand and adjusts it for each period in proportion to the difference between the latest actual demand figure and the latest value of the average. The equation is:

$$SF_{t+1} = SF_t + \alpha(A_t - SF_t)$$

where

SF_{t+1} = smoothed forecast for time period following t

SF_t = smoothed forecast for period t

α = smoothing constant that determines weight given to previous data

A_t = actual demand in period t.

The smoothing constant is a decimal between 0 and 1 where 0 is most stable and 1 is most responsive. Values between 0.1 and 0.3 are often used in practice. A large value of α gives very little smoothing, while a small value gives considerable smoothing/damping. For a time series with little random variability, larger values of α are better as they react quicker to changes. For a time series with large random variability, lower values of α are best so they do not overreact and adjust the forecasts too quickly. Figure 11.10 provides an example of a spreadsheet of an exponential smoothing forecast. An alternative approach is to use the Excel data analysis toolpak, which has an exponential smoothing function.

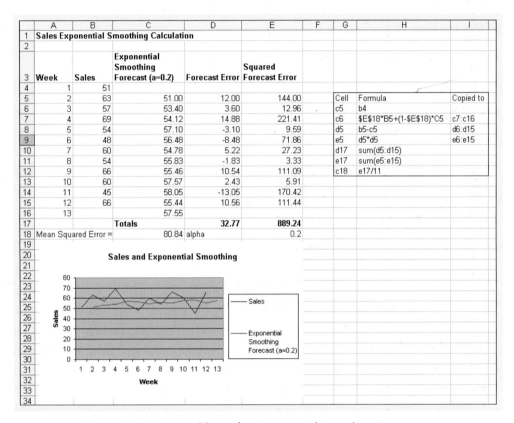

Figure 11.10: Spreadsheet of an Exponential Smoothing Forecast.

The major advantages of using the widely used smoothing methods described are their simplicity and low cost. More accuracy may be obtained with more sophisticated or decomposition methods. Smoothing methods are particularly appropriate for forecasts of thousands of items in inventory systems.

Time Series Decomposition

Often a pattern cannot be recognized in the raw data and so it must be decomposed into the four components of the time series (trend, seasonal, cyclical and random) that show a pattern that is helpful in projecting the data. Time series decomposition is appropriate if seasonal variation is evident in the demand pattern and the effect of seasonality is to be included in the forecast. The technique consists of smoothing past values to eliminate randomness so that the pattern can be projected into the future and used as a forecast. In many instances the patterns can be broken down (decomposed) into subpatterns that identify each component (for example, trend and seasonal) separately. Two common forms of the time series that can be used for decomposition are as follows:

additive form $Y_t = T_t + S_t + I_t$

multiplicative form $Y_t = T_t \times S_t \times I_t$

An additive model is appropriate if the magnitude of the seasonal fluctuation does not vary with the level of the series. Multiplicative decomposition is more prevalent with economic series because more seasonal economic series do have seasonal variation, which increases with the level of the series. Visual inspection of a plotted series is often used to determine the type of model that most appropriately represents the data. The steps involved in decomposing a series are to compute the seasonal indexes to deseasonalize the data and if a trend is apparent in the deseasonalized data then use regression analysis to estimate the trend.

To calculate the seasonal indexes a number of smoothing methods are available, the simplest being the moving average. To smooth a quarterly seasonal pattern we can use a four-period moving average. Assuming a multiplicative model, the moving average requires an odd number of observations to ensure the average is centred at the middle of the data values being averaged. For a four-period average the average for period 3 could be an average of periods 1–4 or 2–5 giving answers of 21.4 or 22.4. Thus we add another column, which is the average of the two successive values of the four-period average – the average of 21.4 and 22.4 = 21.9. The moving average graph smoothes out both the seasonal and irregular fluctuations in the time series. Divide the observation by the centred moving average to identify the seasonal-irregular effect in the time series.

The fluctuations over the three years can be assigned to the irregular influence, so we take an average value to compute the seasonal influence as below:

Q1 S-I values = 0.971, 0.918, 0.908 therefore

$$\text{seasonal index} = \frac{(0.971 + 0.918 + 0.908)}{3} = 0.93$$

Q2 seasonal index = 0.84
Q3 seasonal index = 1.09
Q4 seasonal index = 1.14

Thus the best sales are in Q4, 14% above average; the worst sales are in Q2, 16% below average.

For the multiplicative model, average seasonal indexes must equal 1.0 (average out over the year): $(0.93 + 0.84 + 1.09 + 1.14)/4 = 1.0$. In this case they do, otherwise adjust by multiplying each seasonal index by the number of seasons divided by the sum of the unadjusted seasonal indexes. In a multiplicative model we now divide each time series observation by the corresponding seasonal index. Thus in this case sales are divided by the seasonal index to get the deseasonalised sales figures (Figure 11.11).

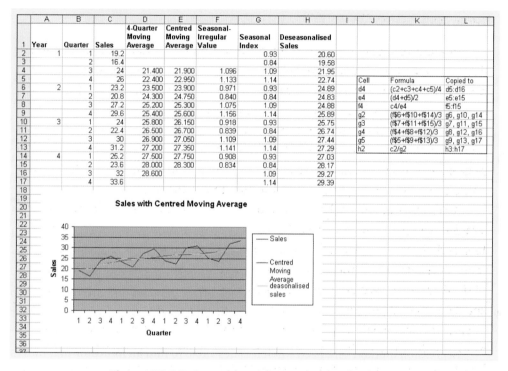

	A	B	C	D	E	F	G	H	I	J	K	L
1	Year	Quarter	Sales	4-Quarter Moving Average	Centred Moving Average	Seasonal-Irregular Value	Seasonal Index	Deseasonalised Sales				
2	1	1	19.2				0.93	20.60				
3		2	16.4				0.84	19.58				
4		3	24	21.400	21.900	1.096	1.09	21.95				
5		4	26	22.400	22.950	1.133	1.14	22.74		Cell	Formula	Copied to
6	2	1	23.2	23.500	23.900	0.971	0.93	24.89		d4	(c2+c3+c4+c5)/4	d5:d16
7		2	20.8	24.300	24.750	0.840	0.84	24.83		e4	(d4+d5)/2	e5:e15
8		3	27.2	25.200	25.300	1.075	1.09	24.88		f4	c4/e4	f5:f15
9		4	29.6	25.400	25.600	1.156	1.14	25.89		g2	(f$6+f$10+f$14)/3	g6, g10, g14
10	3	1	24	25.800	26.150	0.918	0.93	25.75		g3	(f$7+f$11+f$15)/3	g7, g11, g15
11		2	22.4	26.500	26.700	0.839	0.84	26.74		g4	(f$4+f$8+f$12)/3	g8, g12, g16
12		3	30	26.900	27.050	1.109	1.09	27.44		g5	(f$5+f$9+f$13)/3	g9, g13, g17
13		4	31.2	27.200	27.350	1.141	1.14	27.29		h2	c2/g2	h3:h17
14	4	1	25.2	27.500	27.750	0.908	0.93	27.03				
15		2	23.6	28.000	28.300	0.834	0.84	28.17				
16		3	32	28.600			1.09	29.27				
17		4	33.6				1.14	29.39				

Figure 11.11: Spreadsheet of Deseasonalized Sales.

To forecast sales a regression analysis (see next section 'causal models') can be undertaken using the Excel 'add trendline' function. In order to do this right click on the deaseasonalized sales plot on the centred moving average graph (Figure 11.12). A menu will appear, select the 'add trendline' option. Select the linear regression option and select the options tab. Enter a forward period value of 1 and check the 'display equation on chart' and 'display R-squared value on chart' options. The spreadsheet will now display the trendline projected forward one period (Figure 11.12). The use of the linear regression equation for forecasting is covered in the next section, 'causal models'.

There are many decomposition methods such as Census II and X-12-ARIMA but these work on the same principles as shown. In practice a straight-line trend model is

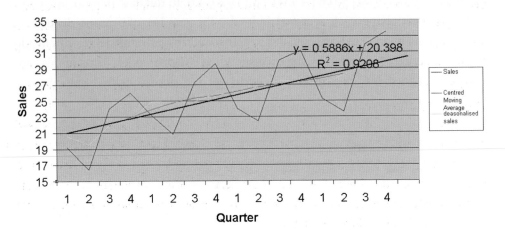

Sales with Centred Moving Average

$y = 0.5886x + 20.398$
$R^2 = 0.9208$

Figure 11.12: Graph of Deseasonalized Sales Showing Trendline.

rarely adequate. Decomposition is a useful tool for understanding the behaviour of a time series, before selection and application of a forecasting method.

Causal Models

Sometimes demand does not exhibit a consistent pattern over time because the level of one or more variables that have an effect on demand had changed during the period when the demand series was collected. Causal models are used to identify variables, or a combination of variables, which affect demand and are then used to predict future levels of demand. Models that may be used in this way include linear regression, curvilinear regression and multiple regression.

Regression methods are used when it is desirable to find an indicator that moves before the company's sales level changes (a leading indicator) and that has a significantly stable relationship with sales to be useful as a prediction tool. Linear regression is a means of finding and expressing a relationship. Regression analysis is the development of a mathematical equation that predicts the value of a dependent variable from single (simple regression) or multiple (multiple regression) independent variables. For example, sales (dependent) is related to advertising spend (independent). Note that, unlike using regression analysis for trend, project causal forecasting relates the forecasted variable to variables that are supposed to influence or explain that variable. It should be noted that causal forecasts are not necessarily time dependent. A model that relates inputs to outputs facilitates a better understanding of the situation and allows experimentation with different combinations of inputs to study their effects on the forecast (output). Thus the effect of decisions made today can be forecast in the future.

Causal Forecasting using Regression Analysis

Scatter graphs are a useful first step in investigating the relationships between two variables. They indicate the strength of the relationship (a small scatter indicates a string relationship) and the direction of a linear relationship (a positive relationship is when one variable gets larger the other variable gets larger, a negative relationship is when one variable gets larger the other variable gets smaller). They also may indicate any points that do not conform to the general pattern (called outliers).

To provide a measure of the degree of scatter the correlation coefficient (r) is used which is the ratio of variations in x and y compared to those of x and y separately; r is a value between -1 and $+1$, with -1 indicating perfect negative correlation, 0 indicating no correlation and +1 indicating perfect positive correlation. Please note that correlation does not mean causation. Just because a variable rises with another one does not imply a direct causation.

If a straight-line relationship is present then a simple linear regression method can be used. This is concerned with finding the straight line that best fits the data. The straight-line equation is used to formulate the relationship between the two variables.

$$\hat{Y}_i = b_0 + b_1 X_i$$

where

$\hat{Y}_i =$ predicted value of Y for observation i

$X_i =$ value of X for observation i

Thus the regression method determines the two regression coefficients, b_0 and b_1 and thus allows the value of Y to be predicted for a value of X.

The coefficient of determination (r^2) can be used to determine the proportion of variation that is explained by the independent variable in the regression model (0 = no prediction, 1 = perfect prediction). The adjusted r^2 gives better results for small samples and a value above 0.5 may be considered acceptable for forecasting purposes. Worked example 11.4 shows the procedure using the Microsoft Excel spreadsheet.

WORKED EXAMPLE 11.4
Regression Analysis

Over recent years a company has undertaken five separate advertising campaigns. The figures are as follows:

Advertising (£000)	Sales (£000)
2	60
5	100
4	70
6	90
3	80

You have been asked to establish whether there is a relationship (correlation) between advertising spend and sales income and derive a regression formula linking the two variables.

SOLUTION

1. *Draw the scatter graph.*

Select the insert, chart, XY (scatter) option, select format 1 that shows unconnected points (Figure 11.13), click next, and then enter the data range and select series by columns, click finish.

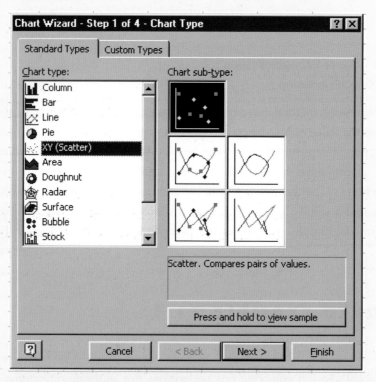

Figure 11.13: Dialog Box for Scatter Graph.

2. *Inspect the graph to see if there is a linear relationship between the variables.*

To insert the regression line click on the chart, with the mouse on a data point, click on the right-hand mouse button, choose Add Trendline from the options listed, select Linear (Figure 11.14) and in Options select Forecast Backward 2 units, then OK.

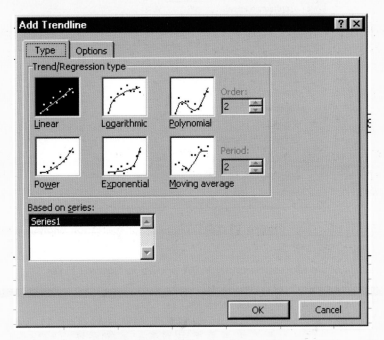

Figure 11.14: Dialog Box for Trendline.

A relative measure of the linear association between two variables is Pearson's coefficient of correlation (R). A value of $R = +1$ equals a perfect positive correlation, a value of $R = -1$ equals a perfect negative correlation and a value of $R = 0$ equals no correlation. The coefficient of determination (R^2) shows the proportion of the variation in Y that is explained by X. For example if $R^2 = 0.64$ then 64% of total variation can be accounted for by the regression line.

3. *Calculate the regression statistics.*

To calculate the regression statistics select Tools, Data Analysis, Regression, OK (Figure 11.15). Input the X and Y cell ranges. Select the Output Range where you wish the regression statistics to appear.

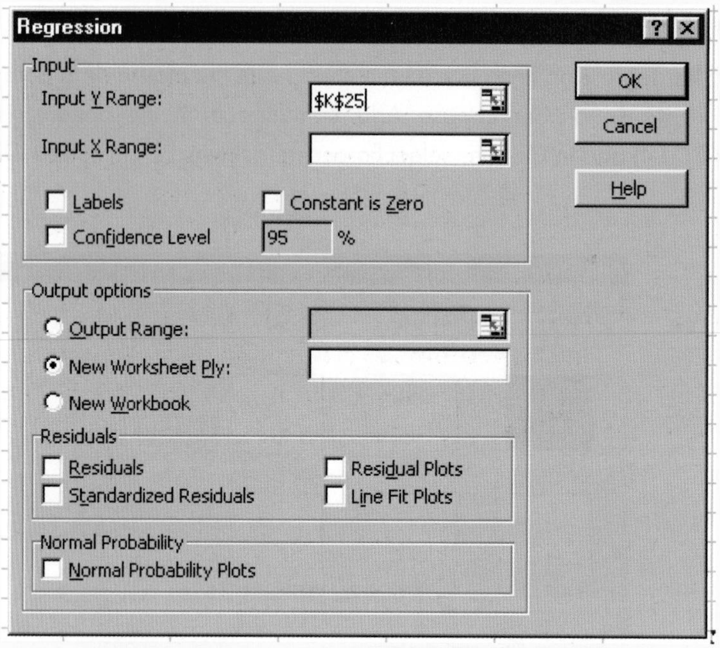

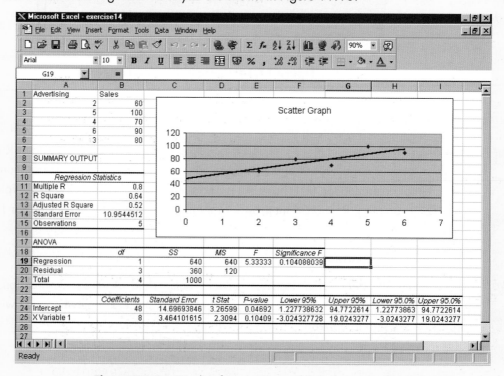

Figure 11.15: Dialog Box for Regression Analysis.

The results of the regression analysis are shown in Figure 11.16.

Figure 11.16: Results of Regression and Correlation Analysis.

4. *Interpret the results.*

- The adjusted R-square value (cell B13) gives a figure of 0.52, which is a weak positive relationship between the variables.
- The coefficients of the regression equation are given as intercept (b0) in cell B24 as 48 and the X variable 1 (b1) in cell B25 as 8. Thus the relationship between the variables could be shown by the formula $Y = 48 + 8 \times X$. For example, for an advertising spend of 4.5, sales $= 48 + 8 \times 4.5 + 84$.
- The strength of association between the variables is 0.8 (b11). Sixty-four per cent of the variation in sales can be explained by the variation in advertising (b12).
- The analysis does not provide evidence that one variable *causes* the other. For example the advertising budget could be based on last year's sales.

Simple regression is a special case of multiple regression, which has two or more independent variables. The general form of multiple regression is:

$$Y = b_0 + b_1X_1 + b_2X_2 + \cdots + b_kX_k$$

Thus if sales were the variable to be forecast, several factors such as advertising, prices, competition, R&D budget and time could be tested for their influence on sales. The coefficients in multiple regression can be calculated using the least squares method as for simple regression. R^2 can be used to show the proportion of the variation in Y which is explained by X. Multiple regression should be undertaken using the computer (for example, Excel).

Causal analysis allows the impact of decisions now to be forecast in the future. Correlation is not causation. For example the number of cola cans sold and the number of deaths by drowning could be correlated but the number of drownings do not cause the sales of cola. A pair of variables may be correlated because they are both caused by a third 'lurking' variable – for example, in summer both drownings and cola sales increase, thus temperature is a lurking variable.

SUMMARY

- The main elements in capacity planning decisions are the measurement of capacity and demand and the reconciling of the two to form a feasible plan.

- The product mix will affect the amount of capacity available as each product or service requires different amounts and different types of capacity at different times.

- A level capacity plan sets capacity at a uniform level throughout the planning period. A chase demand plan seeks to match production to demand over time. A demand management plan attempts to adjust demand to meet available capacity.

- Yield management is a collection of demand management approaches used to optimize the use of capacity in service operations where capacity is relatively fixed and the service cannot be stored in any way.

- Cumulative representations can be used to evaluate a level capacity planning approach by keeping a running total of inventory levels to ensure no stock-outs occur.

- Queuing theory can provide a useful guide in determining expected waiting time for an arriving customer by using statistical distributions of customer arrivals and service times.

- Propositions about the psychology of queues can be used by service organizations to influence customer satisfaction with waiting times.

- Qualitative forecasting techniques include market surveys, Delphi studies and expert judgement. Quantitative methods include time series and causal models.

CASE STUDY   11.2

Yield Management

When Megabus, the discount bus service, launched . . . in the UK, US and Canada, it stated that it was following the example of the no-frills airlines such as easyJet by running its business off the back of an online ticketing system. In fact, it showed its total commitment to the model by becoming the first UK travel operator to sell tickets exclusively over the Web. After four weeks of operation, Megabus had 20 000 hits per day on its site and a quarter of a million tickets had been sold for its 18 destinations. The company says that being Web-based has enabled its owners, Stagecoach, to go from initial idea to launch in only six months and to deliver a completely ticketless operation.

Online ticketing has been a dramatic success. EasyJet founder Stelios Haji-Ioannou initially said the Internet was 'just for geeks' but later he did a U-turn, launching the first UK online booking for an airline in April 1998. A year later, the site was selling 15% of all tickets online and today the figure is 98%. EasyJet's call centre now only takes bookings for flights less than two weeks ahead. The simplicity of online booking is partly responsible for its success. However, the way it integrates what are known as yield-management systems (or revenue-management systems) is the secret of how it is transforming the travel industry.

Yield management software, first devised by academics in the 1980s for American Airlines, allows operators to segment seats into scores of different price brackets, like steps on an escalator, with prices that change in relation to demand, the time remaining, and the flight date (which triggers seasonal differences). Such software has grown in sophistication to the extent that it is now commonplace for prices to be modified in real time and respond to subtle changes in buying patterns or sudden events that impact on demand. In essence, pricing is set by predicting demand from the previous year's travel patterns and modified whenever the operator believes that prices need to be shifted up or down.

Ian Tunnacliffe, an analyst with Meta Group, says that such software is transforming the travel industry: 'Traditionally, it was a massive investment: now it can be bought off the shelf for around £100,000 from a handful of suppliers. And the major airlines are taking it to the next level with systems that look at their whole network of routes and assign "bid prices" to each leg to gain the maximum revenue across the whole network. The systems are also finely honed to try to ensure that customers willing to pay at one level do not get tempted into paying less – it's about creating conditions to prevent them taking advantage of lower fares on the system.'

EasyJet, which recently took over rival Go, now sells 149 seats every 20 seconds and handles 20 million passengers a year. EasyJet Web manager Simon Pritchard says the aim is still about driving a higher level of Web sales: 'We look at what people do in a phone call and try to offer that online.' Last year, easyJet added the ability to look up booking details and make changes to a booking, succeeding in shifting 70% of such transactions online. Four staff run the Web operations, while 100 are needed in the call centre, which shows the cost savings of pushing activities online.

In a *Guardian* interview last year, Haji-Ioannou described how easyJet's yield management system works: 'We start with a low headline price that grabs attention, then raise it according to demand. But we won't tell you how high it will go, or how quickly.' Lack of visibility of the pricing model appears to be part of the secret of running such systems. So how do buyers behave on the Web? 'People do all kinds of weird and wonderful things,' says Pritchard, 'for example, many buyers trawl the site repeatedly to try and figure out pricing and get the best deal.' So why not make pricing more transparent? He says easyJet is looking at a range of options for improving the site but that its message is simple: 'book early for the best deals.'

EasyJet and the other no-frills airlines have the benefit of running simpler yield management systems than the larger airlines they threaten to engulf. They sell all or most of the tickets themselves, which makes it simpler for the systems to manage minute-to-minute changes. Large airlines sell direct and through huge worldwide reservation systems (Amadeus, Galileo, Sabre) that provide online services for a global network of travel agents and online travel agents such as eBookers, Lastminute.com, Expedia and Travelocity. The larger airlines usually allocate a set number of seats for online sales to ensure a spread across different distribution channels.

A further channel has been created by airlines banding together to form their own online agent sites such as Opodo and Orbitz. They also sometimes sell what are known as 'opaque tickets' on sites like Lastminute.com. These are offered cheaply to offload what might be called 'distressed stock'. The catch is that the customer must agree to buy the ticket before being told which airline they are flying. 'This allows airlines to offload seats without sending out a message to buyers that a particular flight is going cheap', said an industry insider.

Amadeus, which also provides online ticketing systems for airlines, says that when buyers surf the Web, only one in 300 visits to booking sites results in a sale. 'We call it the Look-to-Book ratio', says Ian Wheeler, managing director of Amadeus e-Travel. 'Most people look at four or five sites online before they buy. This is a sea change for the industry and the result is that operators with legacy systems experience crashes due to increased traffic when offers and promotions are available.

'A few years ago, buyers would call two to four travel agents and get a maximum of 12 quotes; now they go online and in the same time get about 600 quotes. A call centre just can't do that.' Meta Group's Tunnacliffe says the large airlines are now facing a fork in the road: 'They either think revenue management has gone too far and should be simplified or they are investing heavily in making it even more sophisticated. We advocate the latter. Only a handful of airlines have really implemented ticketing that takes account of the whole network they run because it involves structural change for the airline, because the system will override local pricing and sales incentives that may be in place. But the real revolution takes place when you tie these systems into the computers that organize scheduling. That is the long-term challenge.'

With hotel and car hire following the online sales trend, most observers believe that booking services in the travel industry will increasingly be Web based, leading to a radical shake up of distribution channels and the role of travel agents. Haji-Ioannou's ability to make a U-turn – and his faith in yield-management systems – looks like paying off many times over.

Source: Young (2004).

Questions

1. Discuss the impact of the Internet on yield-management systems.
2. What general capacity issues are evident within the case?

CASE STUDY 11.3

Queuing Theory

The debacle over the availability of tickets for the football World Cup in France in 1998 could have put lives in danger. English football fans, left hanging on the telephone while happy Frenchmen rejoiced over their tickets, felt the same sense of angry injustice that can lead to violent 'road rage' attacks, says the world's leading expert on queuing theory. Richard Larson of the Massachusetts Institute of Technology told a conference in Montreal . . . that road rage and related phenomena are an urgent new area for research. An electrical engineer by training, Larson is the leading exponent of a branch of science known as operations research. Operations research keeps the world moving and happy by employing science, maths and computer modelling to overcome the logistical and technical challenges associated with efficiently shifting people, commodities and information around the world.

Larson, who is known in his field as Dr Queue, acts as a consultant to major multinational companies and government agencies – satisfied customers include Coca-Cola, American Airlines, United Artists Cinemas and the US Department of Justice. Badly managed queues, he says, can tap into a reservoir of anger, hostility and frustration. He cites a new phenomenon: store rage. A fortnight ago, a woman had half her nose cut off by the woman behind her at the express checkout queue of a Milwaukee supermarket – her basket contained more than the permitted 12 items and she had refused to change queues.

Operations researchers manage queues in areas as diverse as air traffic control systems, passenger reservations and parcel delivery. 'There are billions of possibilities for this type of operation', says Larson. 'These things are too complex for any human mind – you need to employ mathematical modelling, observation, data analysis and computer science.' But, he admits, the most useful tool is still common sense: 'You need to formulate the problem correctly – if you get that wrong it doesn't matter how sophisticated the maths is.' His skill in combining common sense and computer modelling techniques was responsible for saving lives well before the advent of road rage. In the 1970s he pioneered a computer program for finding the most efficient distribution of fire and ambulance crews throughout a city. It has been widely employed throughout the US and Europe. The latest development – the Trauma Resource Allocation Model for Ambulances and Hospitals (Tramah) – was presented at the conference this week and showed how the right distribution of available resources can give a near-perfect emergency response. Using the 27 000 emergency cases in the state of Maryland between 1992 and 1994 as a model, researchers simulated various combinations of positions for trauma centres and helicopters. During this period, 95% of severely injured residents had received access to trauma system resources within 30 minutes and 70% had access within 15 minutes. Using the same amount of resources, but changing their locations, the Tramah program simulated access within 30 minutes for 99.97% of cases. They also found that taxpayers' money could be saved by cutting some helicopter depots and strategically placing the others – without losing any emergency response capability.

But Tramah's developers are aware that scientific advice doesn't always get acted on – local history and political expediency are often much more persuasive in the allocation of emergency resources. 'There will be some rural communities that spent 10 years selling brownies so they could buy a helicopter – there's no changing the location of that facility', says Charles Branas, who presented the report. Healthcare managers may not listen to the voice of reason, but in the airline industry the sound of ringing cash tills always catches the ear. United Airlines revealed at the conference that a computer program developed by their operations research office had saved the company $60 million in the past year. One hour before United's planes take off, the program analyses the latest weather reports and composes a flight plan that uses current wind conditions to the plane's advantage. 'There are millions of possible flight paths for flying from A to B – we came up with an

algorithm that searches all those options and gives us the best one', says Bob Bongiorno, the head of United Airlines' operations research department. 'It has saved us a huge amount in fuel costs and pilot time and shaved minutes off our flight times.'

According to Larson, queue management is easiest to implement in Britain and northern Europe, where there is an acknowledgement of the role of courtesy and 'first come, first served'. He told delegates to the conference that the best advice for avoiding road rage was to be found in a British driving manual. 'Wherever there's merging traffic, follow the rule: 'let one in and go' – this is the behaviour of fair standing queues and it seems to be the rule of the road in the UK', he said. Larson has not been to the UK since the 1970s – delegates with more recent experience of British driving no doubt took his observations with a pinch of salt.

Source: Brooks (1998). Reproduced with permission.

Question
Discuss the contribution of queuing theory and the psychology of queuing to queue management.

EXERCISES

1. Explain how capacity management affects organizational performance.

2. Evaluate ways of reconciling capacity and demand in a manufacturing organization.

3. Evaluate ways of reconciling capacity and demand in a service organization.

4. Evaluate the main issues in assessing capacity and demand in service organizations.

5. Customers arrive at an automated teller machine (ATM) at a rate of 20 per hour according to a Poisson distribution. The ATM serves customers at a mean rate of 15 customers per hour.

   a) What is the mean number of customers waiting in the queue?
   b) What is the mean time a customer spends in the queue?
   c) What is the probability that the till is busy?

6. Customers arrive at a Post Office counter a rate of 50 per hour according to a Poisson distribution. There are eight tills and the service time is at a mean rate of 10 customers per hour. P_0 has been given as 0.006.

   a) What is the mean number of customers waiting in the queue?
   b) What is the mean time a customer spends in the queue?
   c) What is the probability that the till is busy?

7. Discuss how the experience of waiting in a queue can be improved.

8. The following represents the annual number of employees in a bank for the years 1986–2005:

Year	Number	Year	Number	Year	Number
1986	1450	1994	2060	2002	1880
1987	1550	1995	1800	2003	2000
1988	1610	1996	1730	2004	2080
1989	1600	1997	1770	2005	1880
1990	1740	1998	1900		
1991	1920	1999	1820		
1992	1950	2000	1650		
1993	2040	2001	1730		

   a) Plot the data on a chart.
   b) Fit a three-year moving average to the data and plot the results on your chart.

c) Using a smoothing coefficient of 0.5, exponentially smooth the series and plot the results on your chart.

d) What is the exponentially smoothed forecast for the year 2006 (based on c)?

e) Using a smoothing coefficient of 0.25, exponentially smooth the series and plot the results on your chart.

f) What is the exponentially smoothed forecast for the year 2006 (based on e)?

g) Compare the results of d) and f).

9. The following represents the annual sales (in euros) for a small newsagent in the years 1980–2005:

Year	Sales	Year	Sales	Year	Sales
1980	41600	1989	53200	1998	36400
1981	48000	1990	53300	1999	38400
1982	51700	1991	51600	2000	42600
1983	55900	1992	49000	2001	34800
1984	51800	1993	38600	2002	28400
1985	57000	1994	37300	2003	23900
1986	64400	1995	43800	2004	27800
1987	60800	1996	41700	2005	42100
1988	56300	1997	38300		

a) Plot the data on a chart

b) Fit a seven-year moving average to the data and plot the results on your chart.

c) Using a smoothing coefficient of 0.25 exponentially smooth the series and plot the results on your chart.

d) What is the exponentially smoothed forecast for the year 2006 (based on c)?

e) Using a smoothing coefficient of 0.50 exponentially smooth the series and plot the results on your chart.

f) What is the exponentially smoothed forecast for the year 2006 (based on e)?

g) Compare the results of d) and f).

10. Assuming quarterly sales for dinghies for the past seven years are as in the table below, you are required to undertake the following analysis.

Year	Quarter 1	Quarter 2	Quarter 3	Quarter 4	Total sales
1	6	15	10	4	35
2	10	18	15	7	50
3	14	26	23	12	75
4	19	28	25	18	90
5	22	34	28	21	105
6	24	36	30	20	110
7	28	40	35	27	130

a) Show the four-quarter moving average values for this time series. Plot both the original time series and the moving averages on the same graph.

b) Compute the seasonal indexes for the four quarters.

c) Deseasonalize the data and use the deseasonalized time series to identify the trend.

d) Use the results of part c) to develop a quarterly forecast for next year based on trend.

e) Use the seasonal indexes to adjust the forecasts developed in part d) to take account of the effect of season.

11. A road traffic inspector believes that the number of accidents on a stretch of road is affected by the traffic speed. To test this theory records have produced the following data regarding accidents over a period of time related to estimated traffic speeds.

Traffic speed (mph)	Number of accidents
20	11
30	14
40	17
60	24
35	14
25	12

a) Develop the estimated regression equation that relates traffic speed to number of accidents.

b) Use the equation developed in a) to forecast the number of accidents at a traffic speed of 50 m.p.h.

12. The following data have been collected regarding the relationship between number of sales staff and sales.

Number of sales staff	Sales
1	19
4	44
6	40
10	52
14	53

a) Develop the estimated regression equation that relates number of sales staff to sales.

b) Use the equation developed in a) to forecast sales for eight sales staff.

WEB EXERCISE

Record the price for any flight with the airline Bmibaby (www.bmibaby.com) and British Airways (www.ba.com) repeatedly, once a week, over an eight-week period immediately before the flight departure date. What does the change in price demonstrate about the yield management policies of the airlines?

● FURTHER READING

Makridakis, S., Wheelwright, S.C. and **Hyndman, R.J.** (1998) *Forecasting: Methods and Applications*, 3rd edn, John Wiley & Sons, Ltd.

● WEB LINKS

http://go.to/forecasting/ (accessed 2 October 2008). Home page for Makridakis forecasting text.

● REFERENCES

Brooks, M. (1998) Science and technology: why are we waiting? *Guardian Online*, 1 May.

Chase, R.B., **Jacobs, F.R.** and **Aquilano, N.J.** (2005) *Operations Management for Competitive Advantage*, 11th edn, McGraw-Hill.

Maister, D.H. (1985) The psychology of waiting lines. In J.A. Czepiel, M.R. Solomon and C.F. Surprenant (eds) *The Service Encounter*, Lexington Press, pp. 113–23.

Stevenson, W.J. (2009) *Operations Management*, 10th edn, McGraw-Hill.

Young, K. (2004) Inside IT: just the ticket. *Guardian Life*, 8 April.

CHAPTER

12

Inventory Management

- **Introduction**
- **Types of inventory**
- **Managing inventory**
- **The ABC inventory classification system**
- **Inventory models**
- **Implementing inventory systems**

LEARNING OBJECTIVES

- Describe the different types of inventory.

- Discuss the purpose of the ABC inventory classification system.

- Discuss the role of the reorder point inventory model.

- Discuss the purpose of the EOQ model.

- Discuss the purpose of the FOI model.

- Understand the issues involved in implementing inventory systems.

INTRODUCTION

Inventory is present in all service and manufacturing processes. In manufacturing inventory consists of the components that go to make up the product being manufactured. In services inventory may be used as part of the service delivery system (for example disposable implements for a hospital operation) or it may be part of the tangible component of the service itself (for example the brochure for a car insurance policy). Inventory is important because although it is necessary for customer service it can also be a major cost to the organization. It has been estimated that a typical firm has about 30% of its current assets and perhaps as much as 90% of its working capital invested in inventory (Stevenson, 2009). Apart from the cost of inventory the use of excessive inventory can lead to other issues such as the disruption of workflow and hiding problems related to product quality and equipment breakdown. Addressing these issues is the focus of the concept of JIT and lean operations covered in Chapter 13.

Inventory management can be considered part of materials management in a service or manufacturing organization. Materials management includes the acquiring of inventory (see procurement section in Chapter 15), the organization of the movement of inventory (see physical distribution management section in Chapter 15) and the assessment of when inventory should be ordered and the amount of inventory that should be ordered, covered in this chapter. Inventory management systems calculate the volume and timing of independent demand items. Independent demand is when demand is not directly related to the demand for any other inventory item. Usually this demand comes from customers outside the company and so is not as predictable as dependent demand (the management of dependent demand items is covered in Chapter 14).

TYPES OF INVENTORY

All organizations will carry some inventory or stock of goods at any one time. This can range from items such as stationery to machinery parts or raw materials. Generally inventory is classified by its location or type.

Inventory Classified by Location

Inventory can be classified by location as raw materials (goods received from suppliers), work-in-progress (at some point within the operations process) or finished goods (goods ready for dispatch to the customer) (Figure 12.1).

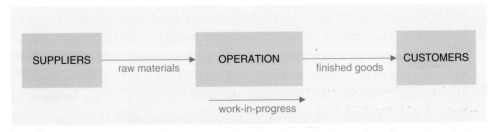

Figure 12.1: Inventory Classified by Location.

The proportions between these inventory types will vary but it is estimated that generally 30% are raw materials, 40% are work-in-progress and 30% finished goods. Waters (2002) indicates the arbitrary nature of these classifications as someone's finished goods are someone else's raw materials.

Raw materials inventory may be supplied in batches to secure quantity discounts and reduce material handling. However, smaller and more frequent order quantities translate into less inventory and may be achieved by negotiating smaller batches from suppliers. Variability in supplier lead times may be reduced by specifying longer but more reliable lead times from suppliers.

Work-in-progress inventory may help uncouple production stages and provide greater flexibility in production scheduling. It can be minimized by eliminating obsolete stock, improving the operation's processes and reducing the number of products or services.

Finished goods inventory may be used to ensure that important inventory items are always available to the customer or to avoid disruption caused by changing production output levels. It can be minimized by improving forecasts of customer demand and reducing fluctuations in demand caused by factors such as meeting end-of-period sales targets.

> **Raw materials inventory**
> Inventory received from suppliers.

> **Work-in-progress inventory**
> Inventory at some point within the operations process.

> **Finished goods inventory**
> Inventory ready for dispatch to the customer.

Inventory Classified by Type

The type of inventory can also be used to provide a method of identifying why inventory is being held and so suggest policies for reducing its level. Inventory types include:

- *Buffer/safety.* This is used to compensate for the uncertainties inherent in the timing or rate of supply and demand between two operational stages. Safety stock is often used to compensate for uncertainties in the timing of supplies from suppliers. It is also used to compensate for uncertainties in supply between operational stages in a process due to factors such as equipment breakdowns.
- *Cycle.* If it is required to produce multiple products from one operation in batches, there is a need to produce enough to keep a supply while the other batches are being produced. This is an example of how differences between the timing of supply and demand can lead to high levels of work-in-progress inventory.
- *Decoupling.* This permits stages in the manufacturing process to be managed and their performance measured independently, to run at their own speed and not match the rate of processing of departments at different points in the process.
- *Anticipation.* This includes producing to stock to anticipate an increase in demand due to seasonal factors. Also speculative policies such as buying in bulk to take advantage of price discounts may also increase inventory levels. Accurate

forecasting can help ensure anticipation inventory reflects any increase in demand. Bulk buying policies will need to take into account the full cost of storing inventory.

- *Pipeline/movement.* This is the inventory needed to compensate for the lack of stock while material is being transported between stages. For example the distribution time from the warehouse to a retail outlet. Thus pipeline inventory may be the result of delays in the supply chain between customer and supplier. If an alternative supplier can be found then pipeline inventory can be reduced.

Most organizations have a large amount of different types of inventory under their control and operations managers need to assess how they ensure that materials are available when needed, but inventory costs are not too high. Holding inventory reduces the risk of having no stock and can also reduce ordering costs by ordering larger, but fewer batches of materials, reducing stock-out costs by ensuring disruption to the manufacturing or service delivery system is avoided and reducing acquisition costs by securing quantity discounts. However, these costs need to be set against the costs of holding high levels of inventory. These include the cost of storing and handling inventory items, the lack of responsiveness to customer demands because of the large work-in-progress inventories, the increase in lead times due to inventory queuing, the use of inventory to provide a safety net to unreliable processes that need improving and the capital investment in inventory that will not be used for some time. These issues are explored further in Chapter 13.

The risk of having no stock is particularly important in service systems where the customer expects the immediate consumption of the service and its associated good. For example in a restaurant, customers will be dissatisfied if certain options are not available on the menu due to lack of produce. More importantly, hospitals need to ensure that inventory such as drugs are always available for patients.

MANAGING INVENTORY

One of the major issues in inventory management is the level of decentralization required in inventory distribution. Decentralized facilities offer a service closer to the customer and thus should provide a better service level in terms of knowledge of customer needs and speed of service. Centralization, however, offers the potential for less handling of goods between service points, less control costs and less overall inventory levels due to lower overall buffer levels required. The square-root law (Maister, 1975) states

that a firm currently operating out of five warehouses, which centralizes to one warehouse, can theoretically reduce inventory carried in stock by 55%. The overall demand pattern for a centralized facility will be an average of the variable demand patterns from a number of customers. This will decrease demand variability and thus require lower buffer stocks. Thus there is a trade-off between the customer service levels or effectiveness offered by a decentralized system and the lower costs or efficiency offered by a centralized system. One way of combining the advantages of a centralized facility with a high level of customer service is to reduce the delivery lead time between the centralized distribution centre and the customer outlet. This issue is discussed in more detail in the warehousing section of Chapter 15.

THE ABC INVENTORY CLASSIFICATION SYSTEM

ABC classification system
This system sorts inventory items into groups depending on the amount of annual expenditure or some other factor.

One way of deciding the importance of inventory items and thus an appropriate inventory management method for them is to use the ABC classification system. Depending on the classification of the inventory a fixed order quantity or fixed order period inventory system can be chosen for managing that system.

The ABC classification system sorts inventory items into groups depending on the amount of annual expenditure they incur which will depend on the estimated number of items used annually multiplied by the unit cost. To instigate an ABC system a table is produced listing the items in expenditure order (with largest expenditure at the top), and showing the percentage of total expenditure and cumulative percentage of the total expenditure for each item (Table 12.1).

Item	Annual expenditure (cost × usage) £000s	Percentage expenditure (%)	Cumulative expenditure (%)
D-76	800	24.1	24.1
A-25	650	19.6	43.7
C-40	475	14.3	58.1
C-22	450	13.6	71.6
B-18	300	9.0	80.7
G-44	200	8.0	86.7
A-42	150	5.4	91.3
D-21	100	3.0	94.3
H-67	75	2.3	96.5
E-88	65	2.0	98.5
F-23	50	1.5	100.0
TOTAL	3315		

Table 12.1: Example of an ABC Classification Table.

By reading the cumulative percentage figure it is usually found, following Pareto's law, that 10% to 20% of the items account for 60% to 80% of annual expenditure. These items are called A items and need to be controlled closely to reduce overall expenditure. Forecasting techniques may be used to improve the accuracy of demand forecasts for these items. It may also require a more strategic approach to management of these items, which may translate into closer buyer-supplier relationships. A items may be managed using a fixed order quantity system with perpetual inventory checks or a fixed order interval system employing a small time interval between review periods.

The B items account for the next 20% to 30% of items and usually account for a similar percentage of total expenditure. These items require fewer inventory level reviews than A items. A fixed order interval system with a minimum order level or a fixed order quantity system may be appropriate.

Finally C items represent the remaining 50% to 70% of items but only account for less than 25% of total expenditure. Here a fixed order quantity system may be appropriate or less rigorous inventory control methods can be used, as the cost of inventory tracking will outweigh the cost of holding additional stock. It is important to recognize that overall expenditure may not be the only appropriate basis on which to classify items. Other factors include the importance of a component part on the overall product, the variability in delivery time, the loss of value through deterioration and the disruption caused to the production process if a stock-out occurs. The fixed order quantity and fixed order interval systems for inventory management are now described.

INVENTORY MODELS

Inventory models are used to assess when inventory requires ordering and what quantity should be ordered at that point in time. In a fixed order quantity inventory system, inventory is ordered in response to some event, such as inventory falling to a particular level. The timing of the inventory order can be calculated using a reorder point (ROP) model. The quantity to order at this point in time may be calculated using the economic order quantity (EOQ) model. In a fixed order period inventory system, inventory is ordered at a fixed point in time (say once a month). A fixed order inventory (FOI) model can be used to determine the quantity to order at this point in time. These models are now described.

Fixed Order Quantity Inventory Systems

In fixed order quantity inventory systems the order quantity is the same each time the order is placed, but the time between orders varies according to the rate of use of the inventory item. When the inventory level has reduced to a certain amount, termed

Fixed order quantity inventory systems
In these systems the order quantity is the same each time the order is placed but the time between orders varies according to the rate of use of the inventory item.

the reorder point, an order for further inventory is made. The reorder point can be calculated by the use of a computer system that can also automate the ordering process. An alternative is the two-bin system. Here inventory is held in two containers, termed bins. When one bin is empty a replenishment order is made and inventory is taken from the other bin until the order arrives. These systems are termed perpetual systems to indicate that the inventory record of the amount of inventory is updated as inventory is used and replenished.

Some systems for less important items only check inventory levels at certain intervals (say once a week or once a month). When using a fixed order quantity system the point in time when an order should be placed can be determined using the reorder point or ROP model and the quantity to order at this time can be determined by the economic order quantity (EOQ) model. These inventory models are now described.

The Reorder Point (ROP) Model

The reorder point model identifies the time to order when the stock level drops to a predetermined amount. This amount will usually include a quantity of stock to cover for the delay between order and delivery (the delivery lead time) and an element of stock to reduce the risk of running out of stock when levels are low (the safety stock).

Safety stock is used in order to prevent a stock-out occurring. It provides an extra level of inventory above that needed to meet predicted demand, to cope with variations in demand over a time period. The level of safety stock used, if any, will vary for each inventory cycle but an average stock level above that needed to meet demand will be calculated. To calculate the safety stock level a number of factors should be taken into account including:

Reorder point model
The reorder point model identifies the time to order when the stock level drops to a predetermined amount.

- cost due to stock-out
- cost of holding safety stock
- variability in rate of demand
- variability in delivery lead time.

It is important to note that there is no stock-out risk between the maximum inventory level and the reorder level. The risk occurs due to variability in the rate of demand and due to variability in the delivery lead time between the reorder point and zero stock level.

The reorder level can, of course, be estimated by a rule of thumb, such as when stocks are at twice the expected level of demand during the delivery lead time. However, to consider the probability of stock-out, cost of inventory and cost of stock-out the idea of a service level is used.

The service level is a measure of the level of service, or how sure the organization is that it can supply inventory from stock. This can be expressed as the probability that the inventory on hand during the lead time is sufficient to meet expected demand (for example, a service level of 90% means that there is a 0.90 probability that demand will be met during the lead time period and the probability that a stock-out will occur is 10%). The service level set is dependent on a number of factors such as stockholding costs for the extra safety stock and the loss of sales if demand cannot be met.

The reorder problem is one of determining the level of safety stock that balances the expected holding costs with the costs of stock out. Equations will be derived for the following four scenarios of constant demand and constant lead time, variable demand and constant lead time, constant demand and variable lead time and variable demand and variable lead time.

1. Constant Demand and Constant Lead Time

Assuming that the delivery lead time and demand rate are constant there is no risk of stock-out, so no safety stock is required.

reorder point (units) $= d \times LT$

where
$d =$ daily demand
$LT =$ lead time

WORKED EXAMPLE 12.1
Constant Demand and Constant Lead Time ROP Model

A company has a demand for an item at a constant of 50 per week. The order delivery lead time is also constant at three weeks. What should the reorder point be?

 **SOLUTION**
$d = 50$, $LT = 3$
reorder point $= d \times LT = 3 \times 50 = 150$ units.

2. Variable Demand and Constant Lead Time

This model assumes that demand during the delivery lead time consists of a series of independent daily demands and thus can be described by a normal distribution. The average daily demand rate and its standard deviation (measure of variability) are used to determine the expected demand and standard deviation of demand for the lead time period. Thus the reorder point is:

reorder point (ROP) $=$ expected demand during lead time $+$ safety stock
$$= \bar{d} \times LT + z \times \sqrt{LT} \times \sigma_d$$

where

$\overline{d}$ = average demand rate

LT = delivery lead time

σ_d = standard deviation of demand rate

z = number of standard deviations from the mean

WORKED EXAMPLE 12.2
Variable Demand and Constant Lead Time ROP Model

An office supply company sells paper with a variable demand, which can be assumed to be normally distributed with a average of 800 boxes per week and a standard deviation of 250 boxes per week. The delivery lead time has been very consistent at three weeks. Determine the recommended reorder level if there is to be no more than a 1% chance that a stock-out will occur in any one replenishment period.

SOLUTION

$\overline{d} = 800/\text{week}$

$\sigma_d = 250/\text{week}.$

$LT = 3$

At 1% service level, $z = 2.33$ (from normal distribution table)

$$ROP = \overline{d} \times LT + z \times \sqrt{LT} \times \sigma_d$$
$$= 800 \times 3 + 2.33 \times \sqrt{3} \times 250$$
$$= 2400 + 2.33 \times 433$$
$$= 3409 \text{ units}$$

3. Constant Demand and Variable Lead Time

Here the lead time variation is described by a normal distribution and thus the expected lead time is normally distributed. Thus the reorder point is:

reorder point (ROP) = expected demand during lead time + safety stock

$$= d \times \overline{LT} + z \times d \times \sigma_{LT}$$

where

d = constant demand rate

$\overline{LT}$ = average lead time

σ_{LT} = standard deviation of lead time

z = number of standard deviations from the mean

4. Variable Demand Rate and Variable Lead Time

When both demand rate and lead time are variable, the expected demand during lead time is the average daily demand multiplied by average lead time. Both daily demand and lead time are assumed to be normally distributed.

reorder point (ROP) = expected demand during lead time + safety stock

$$= \bar{d} \times \overline{LT} + z \times \sqrt{\overline{LT} \times \sigma^2_d + \bar{d}^2 \times \sigma^2_{LT}}$$

The Economic Order Quantity (EOQ) Model

The economic order quantity (EOQ) model calculates the fixed inventory order volume required while seeking to minimize the sum of the annual costs of holding inventory and the annual costs of ordering inventory. The model makes a number of assumptions including:

- Stable or constant demand.
- Fixed and identifiable ordering cost.
- The relationship between the cost of holding inventory and number of items held is linear.
- The item cost does not vary with the order size.
- Delivery lead time does not vary.
- No quantity discounts are available.
- Annual demand exists.

> **The economic order quantity model** This model calculates the fixed inventory order volume required while seeking to minimize the sum of the annual costs of holding inventory and the annual costs of ordering inventory.

Brown, Lamming, Bessant and Jones (2005) are critical of the EOQ method because an approach of ordering a fixed quantity per order item is not seen as relevant in a complex and dynamic market. The assumption of one delivery per order, and then the use of that stock over time increases inventory levels and does not fit with the JIT approach. Annual demand will also not exist for products with a life cycle of less than a year. Another assumption made is that ordering costs are constant with no account taken of the method of ordering (for example email, fax, phone), the time spent placing the order, or the staffing costs of the person placing the order. However, the EOQ and other approaches in this chapter still have a role in inventory management in the right circumstances if their limitations are recognized.

Before the EOQ model is introduced it is useful to know that texts use a number of words to describe the cost of holding inventory and the cost of replacing that inventory. These include:

Inventory held	Inventory replaced
Holding cost	Order cost
Carrying cost	Replenishment cost
Storage cost	Delivery cost

Each order is assumed to be of Q units and is withdrawn at a constant rate over time until the quantity in stock is just sufficient to satisfy the demand during the order lead time (the time between placing an order and receiving the delivery). At this time an order for Q units is placed with the supplier. Assuming that the usage rate and lead time are constant the order will arrive when the stock level is at zero, thus eliminating excess stock or stock-outs. The order quantity must be set at a level which is not too small, leading to many orders and thus high order costs, but not too large leading to high average levels of inventory and thus high holding costs.

The annual holding cost is the average number of items in stock multiplied by the cost to hold an item for a year. If the amount in stock decreases at a constant rate from Q to 0 then the average in stock is Q/2 (Figure 12.2).

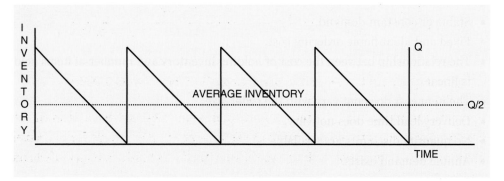

Figure 12.2: Inventory Level versus Time for the EOQ Model.

Thus if C_H is the average annual holding cost per unit, the total annual holding cost is:

$$\text{Annual Holding Cost} = \frac{Q}{2} \times C_H$$

The annual ordering cost is a function of the number of orders per year and the ordering cost per order. If D is the annual demand, then the number of orders per year is given by D/Q. Thus if C_O is the ordering cost per order then the total annual ordering cost is:

$$\text{Annual Ordering Cost} = \frac{D}{Q} \times C_O$$

Thus the total annual inventory cost is the sum of the total annual holding cost and the total annual ordering cost.

$$\text{Total Annual Cost} = \frac{Q}{2} \times C_H + \frac{D}{Q} \times C_O$$

where Q = order quantity, C_H = holding cost per unit, D = annual demand, C_O = ordering cost per order.

The total cost and its components of ordering and holding cost are shown graphically in Figure 12.3.

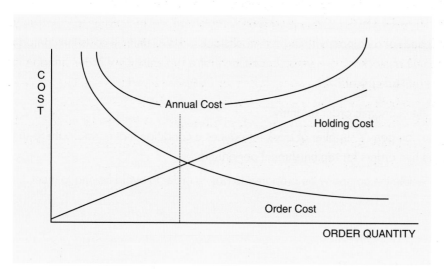

Figure 12.3: Inventory Cost versus Order Quantity for the EOQ Model.

From the graph it can be seen that the minimum total cost point is when the holding cost is equal to the ordering cost. Note, however, that in practice the actual order size may differ considerably from the calculated EOQ without major effects on total costs.

Mathematically, when holding costs = ordering costs:

$$\frac{Q}{2} \times C_H = \frac{D}{Q} \times C_O$$

Solving for Q gives

$$EOQ = \sqrt{\frac{2 \times D \times C_O}{C_H}}$$

The EOQ formula can also be used to calculate the optimum size of a batch to be manufactured.

$$EBS = \sqrt{\frac{2 \times S \times C_O}{C_H}}$$

Where EBS = economic batch size, C_H = holding cost per unit, S = cost per batch, C_O = ordering cost per order

In addition to the criticisms of the EOQ calculation, the calculation of the 'economic' batch size does not conform to the JIT aim of minimizing setup times in order to increase flexibility.

WORKED EXAMPLE 12.3
Economic Order Quantity Model

The annual demand for a company's single item of stock is 1000 units. It costs the company £6 to hold one unit of stock for one year. Each time that a replenishment order is made the company incurs a fixed cost of £75.

1.   Determine the economic order quantity.

Suppose that the company's supplier of stock introduces a condition that normally there shall be no more than five orders for replenishment per annum.

2.   How much would the company be prepared to pay in order to avoid having to meet this condition?

SOLUTION
1. $D = 1000$, $C_H = 6$, $C_O = 75$

$$EOQ = \sqrt{\frac{2 \times D \times C_O}{C_H}} = \sqrt{\frac{2 \times 1000 \times 75}{6}} = \sqrt{25000} = 158 \text{ units.}$$

2. Total cost at five orders per annum
Therefore $1000/5 = 200$ units delivered at one time.

$$\text{Total Annual Cost} = \frac{Q}{2} \times C_H + \frac{D}{Q} \times C_O$$

Total Annual Cost $= 200/2 \times 6 + 1000/200 \times 75 = 600 + 375 = £975$.
Total Annual Cost at EOQ
Total Annual Cost $= 158/2 \times 6 + 1000/158 \times 75 = 474 + 474 = £948$
Therefore company would be prepared to pay the difference £975 − £948 = £27.

The Economic Order Quantity (EOQ) with Quantity Discounts

Many firms provide discounts for large quantity orders for a number of reasons. These include economies of scale due to less setup times and other production efficiencies. Then the customer must balance the potential benefits of a reduced price against the holding costs incurred by the higher order quantity. The total annual cost with discounts is thus the sum of holding costs + ordering costs + purchasing costs. This can be expressed as the following equation:

$$TC = \frac{Q}{2} \times C_H + \frac{D}{Q} \times C_O + D \times C_P$$

where:

Q = quantity ordered

D = annual demand

C_O = order cost per order

C_H = holding cost per unit for Q being considered

C_P = unit price per unit for Q being considered

Both the unit price and thus holding cost vary with an order quantity that is at a different price point. Thus it may be necessary to calculate the total cost at each price point to find the lowest value. In addition we need to take into account the fact that we may not be permitted to order the quantity specified at the price discount set. It may also be that it would be more economical to purchase just a few more units and achieve a more generous price discount at the next price point.

There are two main scenarios that need to be considered. One is where holding costs are considered constant per unit. In this case there will be a single EOQ for all the cost curves at the different price point. In the second case holding costs are expressed as a percentage of purchase price and so each cost curve will increase the EOQ for each price point.

The procedure for finding the best order quantity is:

1. Begin with the lowest price and solve for the EOQ at this price.
2. If the EOQ is not within the quantity range for this price, go to step 3. Otherwise go to step 4.
3. Solve for the EOQ at the next highest price. Go to step 2.
4. Calculate the total cost for the EOQ that falls within the quantity range and for all the lower price points. Select the quantity with the lowest total cost.

WORKED EXAMPLE 12.4
The Economic Order Quantity Model with Discounts

A company is able to obtain quantity discounts on its order of material as follows:

Price per kg	Kg bought
6.00	less than 250
5.90	250 and less than 800
5.80	800 and less than 2000
5.70	2000 and less than 4000
5.60	4000 and over

The annual demand for the material is 4000 kilograms. Holding costs are 20% per year of material cost. The order cost per order is £6. Calculate the best quantity to order.

SOLUTION

Solving the EOQ at the lowest price (Q = 4000 and over)

$C_O = 6$, $C_H = 20/100 \times 5.6 = 1.12$, $C_P = 5.6$, $D = 4000$

$EOQ = SQRT (2 \times 4000 \times 6)/1.12$

$= 207$.

The EOQ is not in the quantity range (4000 and above). It is obvious that the EOQ is lower than the price ranges so skip to the highest price.

Solving the EOQ at the highest price. (Q = 250 and under)

$C_O = 6$, $C_H = 20/100 \times 6 = 1.2$, $C_P = 6$, $D = 4000$

$EOQ = SQRT(2 \times 4000 \times 6)/1.2$

$= 200$.

EOQ is in the quantity range so calculate the total cost at the EOQ and all lower price points.

Q	Order cost	Holding cost	Cost of goods	Total cost
200	120	120	24 000	24 240
250	96	147.5	23 600	23 843.5
800	30	464	23 200	23 694
2000	12	1140	22 800	23 952
4000	6	2240	22 400	24 646

Therefore the lowest cost and therefore best order quantity is 800.

Fixed Order Period Inventory Systems

Fixed order period inventory systems
In a fixed order period inventory system varying quantities are ordered at fixed time intervals.

For the fixed order quantity inventory systems, *fixed* quantities of items are ordered at varying time intervals. In a fixed order period inventory system *varying* quantities are ordered at fixed time intervals. This means that a higher than normal demand will mean a larger order size rather than a shorter time between orders as in a fixed quantity model. The main attribute of the fixed interval model is that it only requires a periodic review of inventory levels to determine the order quantity required. A graph of inventory level over time for a fixed order interval system is shown in Figure 12.4.

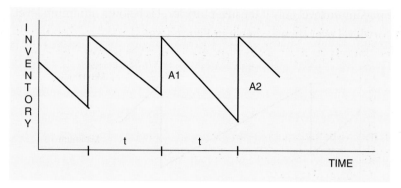

Figure 12.4: Inventory Level versus Time for the FOP Inventory System.

It can be seen that the amount ordered at the fixed interval time period t is determined by the rate of demand during that period. Thus the order amount, A2, is much greater than the order amount A1 due to the relatively high demand during the period leading up to A2. The main advantage of using this system is that it enables a group of related components to be ordered at any one time, saving the cost of repeat deliveries and simplifying stock control. In addition the need to continuously monitor stock, as in a fixed quantity system, is replaced by a periodic review and so saves monitoring duties.

Fixed Order Inventory (FOI) Model

The fixed order inventory model can be used to calculate the amount to order given a fixed interval between ordering. The calculation for the FOI model is dependent on whether demand and delivery lead time are treated as fixed or variable. If it is assumed that deliveries are relatively constant and demand levels are variable, the equation for the amount to order is given as follows:

> Fixed order
> inventory model
> This can be used to
> calculate the amount to
> order given a fixed
> interval between
> ordering.

amount to order = expected demand during protection interval + safety stock − amount on hand at reorder time

$$= \bar{d} \times (OI + LT) + z \times \sigma_d \times \sqrt{OI + LT} - A$$

where

$\bar{d}$ = average demand rate

OI = order interval (time between orders)

LT = delivery lead time

z = number of standard deviations from the mean

σ_d = standard deviation of demand rate

A = amount of units on hand at reorder time

A variation on the fixed order interval system is when minimum and maximum levels are set for inventory. Thus at a periodic interval review point inventory is replenished up to the maximum level only if the inventory level is below a minimum level. A graph of inventory level over time is shown in Figure 12.5.

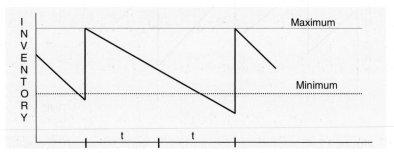

Figure 12.5: Inventory Level versus Time for the FOI Model with Minimum/Maximum Inventory Levels.

This system is suitable for low-cost items where the additional holding cost incurred when holding higher levels of inventory is offset by reductions in the need to order small amounts more frequently.

IMPLEMENTING INVENTORY SYSTEMS

In Chapter 15 the use of e-Business is discussed in its role of facilitating the outsourcing of supply chain activities to third parties. Inventory management can also be outsourced in this way and thus is sometimes referred to as vendor managed inventory. An example of this is when wholesalers hold stocks for a number of retailers. This allows the retailers to focus on selling activities and order stock from the wholesaler as needed. Several e-Business solutions are available in the area of inventory management and are usually provided as a module within a supply chain management or material management e-Business system (Figure 12.6).

SUMMARY

- Inventory management is important because it affects both customer service (inventory is needed to ensure goods and services are available) and costs (the purchase and holding costs of inventory items).

- Inventory can be classified into buffer/safety, cycle, decoupling, anticipation and pipeline/movement.

- The ABC classification system can be used in order to identify appropriate inventory control policies for stock items.

- The reorder point (ROP) model indicates the level of inventory at which point further inventory should be ordered to avoid a stock-out. The ROP model can take into consideration variable delivery lead time and variable demand characteristics for an item.

- The economic order quantity (EOQ) model may be used to calculate a fixed order volume that minimizes total inventory costs. Inventory costs are assumed to consist of holding and ordering costs.

- The fixed order inventory (FOI) model may be used to calculate inventory order volumes when orders are placed at fixed time intervals.

- Inventory management systems can be implemented using an e-Business platform and are usually supplied as part of an integrated supply chain management system.

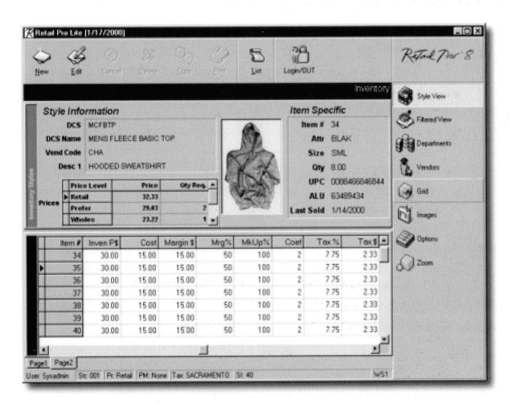

Figure 12.6: Example of Inventory Management E-Business Software.

CASE STUDY   12.1

Risk-taking on the Road to Faster Delivery

Every night at FedEx's Memphis hub, workers gather in teams to conduct the flex and stretch exercises required before anyone starts handling anything. The packages they will be shifting are heading for the airport on flights and in trucks from across the US. The smell of cardboard mixes with the heady aroma of jet fuel as everyone gears up for the night's big lift. However, behind the trucks and vans, the yard mules and dollies, the fleet of almost 700 aircraft and the mass of conveyor belts (300 miles of them at the Memphis hub alone) are sophisticated IT systems. For it is technology that underpins FedEx's business, helping the company shift an average of 6.5 million packages around the world every day.

'Go on FedEx.com – you'll see FedEx Ground, FedEx Express, FedEx Freight and it's a wonderful experience,' says Fred Smith, FedEx's founder and chairman. 'But there are all kinds of little hamsters running around to keep it going.' These 'little hamsters', as Mr Smith refers to the company's IT systems, are what get customers' packages to their destination on time and in good shape, and allow their progress to be tracked online.

Information technology was not at the forefront of Mr Smith's mind when he developed his idea for a business based on the overnight delivery by air of high-value shipments such as electronics, pharmaceuticals and luxury goods using a hub-and-spoke system. A graduate of Yale University, Mr Smith served as an officer in the US Marine Corps from 1966 to 1970. Just a year later, he founded what was then called Federal Express and on 17 April 1973, the company launched its first night of continuous operations. With 14 Dassault Falcon jets and 389 employees, Federal Express delivered 186 packages overnight to 25 cities in the US.

However, it soon became clear to the Mississippi-born entrepreneur that technology would become a critical part of the business. 'We were substituting this type of fast-cycle transportation for investment in inventory, and it became immediately apparent that, when you did that, you had to do it correctly every time.'

'The fact that you got bigger and bigger was irrelevant to the customers', he says. 'So we got very focused on technology as the only way to discretely manage every shipment in the enterprise.'

This, says Mr Smith, was his first epiphany, and by the late 1970s and early 1980s, FedEx was investing heavily in IT and had established a development centre in Colorado Springs to attract talented employees to that side of the business. It also acquired the IT division of a Memphis company that was being broken up, a deal that brought with it Jim Barksdale (the executive who would eventually head Netscape) as chief information officer. After several years in the position, Mr Barksdale became FedEx's chief operating officer. Crucially, at FedEx, the CIO was not part of the finance department – as so many 'computer divisions' were at the time – but was established as a senior position reporting to the chief executive. In addition to placing IT so prominently in the corporate hierarchy, a good deal of what Mr Smith calls 'evangelism' was needed to establish technology at the heart of the business. 'It wasn't understood how profound this requirement for information in terms of managing logistics would become', he says. By the late 1970s, Mr Smith had established his often-quoted principle that 'the information about the package is as important as the package itself', and through the 1980s, the IT innovations came thick and fast, with the introduction of an automated shipping system, barcode labelling, radio transmission systems and hand-held barcode scanners.

The second moment of truth was the recognition that customers needed to track their inventory whether at rest or in motion. In the early days, this information was delivered to customers using proprietary software on PCs supplied by FedEx. 'But in 1994 the Internet came on the scene and you had the potential to let people interface with you, not through proprietary networks or hardware and software we supplied', says Mr Smith. 'But from a screen anywhere.' The migration of package-tracking information to the Web was one of two big and risky decisions made early on in the company's development. The other had been the switch from using the ACP (airline control programme) applications developed for airline reservations systems to IMS, an inventory management system that was far more flexible. 'IMS was not nearly as robust and hardened – so that was a very difficult call in those days', says Mr Smith.

As FedEx was developing, so was the concept of just-in-time delivery. Instead of amassing inventory, companies were starting to produce goods only when the orders arrived. This, says Mr Smith, 'went hand in glove' with the evolution of FedEx's services, which met the demand for extremely fast transportation and the ability to track items on their journey. 'When we began to deploy the track-and-trace system, that changed the entire logistics world', he says. 'I knew it would change the game when you could keep up with a million items as discretely as you could keep up with a single item, and then migrate the visibility of that information to the customer. It was quite a project. But we definitely understood that it could change the landscape.'

Today, technology is critical to, and visible in, every corner of the company's operations. At the Global Operations Control centre in Memphis, a large screen displays the position of every aircraft in the sky. At the customers' end, handheld scanners capture the information about their packages through their barcodes and allow them to be tracked along their journey. Behind the scenes, technology determines the most efficient route for each shipment, while IMS applications track millions of packages on the move. So it comes as no surprise to find that FedEx still invests about $1.5 billion a year in its IT. Researchers at its FedEx Institute for Technology investigate everything from nanotechnology to artificial intelligence, while staff at FedEx Labs, located in EmergeMemphis, a business and IT incubator, keep the pipeline of technology innovations flowing. Mr Smith believes that the rapid increase in available processing power will continue to transform the organization – and not just for FedEx but also for its customers. He cites new services available over the Web such as FedEx Trade Manager, which allows customers to download customs forms, estimate duties and find regulatory information relating to shipments.

'With these vast databases and the ability to cut across the various information systems, you as a small customer in a small city in the US can have literally the market of the world available to you', he says. 'The development of these kinds of services over the Web completely changes the way businesses operate – it opens up the world to small companies.'

As a result, technology is not only the key to running Mr Smith's business, but through Web-based services allows his customers to manage their businesses more effectively – in the process binding their operations more closely to FedEx. 'It's the centrepiece of the whole fast cycle logistics revolution that's taken place over the past 25 years', he says.

Source: by Sarah Murray, *Financial Times*, 11 July 2007. Reproduced by permission of Sarah Murray.

Question

Discuss the role of IT in managing logistics.

CASE STUDY 12.2

Implementing Inventory Systems

Retailers face two big challenges. The first is anticipating what customers want; the second is making sure they have enough of what customers want. Running out of stock is a nightmare. It harms a company's reputation for competence and unhappy customers create a poor image for a company. Ian Dignum, sales director of Prolog, a marketing support-services company, said: 'Not all businesses need the same approach. But they all need access to good-quality data telling them which items are selling well, how many are in stock and whether they have enough to meet demand.'

Prolog, which handles order-processing and fulfilment for several government departments, as well as Corrs Brewers in the UK, uses the Mailbrain software package.

Dignum said: 'If a purchase order is raised on Mailbrain, you can give the order a due date so customer-service staff can tell a customer when the item is likely to be in stock. If you cannot supply this kind of information, you are taking a risk with customer goodwill.'

Michael Ross, managing director of Figleaves.com, an online lingerie retailer, agrees that collating sales data and interpreting them correctly is essential for any retailer's success. He said: 'In our company every item is barcode scanned in and out. We even monitor "pick fails" – when someone goes to pick something off the shelf but it's not there. Every aspect of the business is monitored.' Figleaves has its own analytical software, but most companies use established packages. For example, Matt Giles, commercial manager of I Want One Of Those, an online retailer of boys' toys, gadgets and gizmos, said: 'Our system is based on Elucid's software. It gives us great data. We can tell the top 20 sellers by hour, day or year. We even know when stock is getting low in relation to purchase frequency.'

But knowing which products are selling is one thing, predicting which ones will sell is another. Ross explained the difficulties in his business: 'There are two distinct types of lingerie. First you have your basics; long-running lines that are unlikely to go out of stock. We know how much we are selling each week, how long the deliveries take and the likelihood of deliveries arriving on time. Then there are the fashion items. You have to predict what demand is likely to be, what styles and sizes are likely to be the most popular. This is hard. It's complicated further by volatility of demand and supply.' Although making these decisions can be helped by software, a lot depends on knowing your customer intimately and having an instinct for market trends. That comes with experience and research.

A small, growing company must decide if it can handle inventory management and order fulfilment internally or whether outsourcing would make more sense. It is cheaper to do it internally, but more convenient to outsource. Businesses that keep logistics in-house face the hassle of needing to hire temporary staff at busy times. That cost becomes a millstone if you have overestimated demand. And if your systems cannot cope with increased orders you risk alienating new customers if service standards drop.

Whether outsourced or done in-house, the key to successful inventory management is integrated systems. Your warehouse and call-centre operations must be singing from the same hymn sheet and your processing system should be able to handle all types of order method – mail, telephone or Internet. These days, most warehouse systems incorporate some form of barcode scanning linked to an integrated order-handling database. You take a product off the shelf, scan it and the software automatically updates the figures on how much of that product remains in stock.

Managing suppliers and developing a close relationship with them is another crucial element of inventory management. The more you can share data, the earlier you will be aware of potential supply problems. This is becoming easier now that the computing language XML is becoming standard for database systems. Giles said: 'When a newspaper featured our remote-controlled plane, we sold 85 in two days. Until then we had been selling about 20 a week. Our supplier realized the importance of keeping the stock going and air-freighted them to us at no extra cost. It wouldn't have done that if we didn't have an excellent relationship with that company.'

Source: Wall (2004). Reproduced with permission.

Question

Discuss the major issues raised in the case study concerning the introduction of an inventory management system.

EXERCISES

1. Distinguish between the different types of inventory.

2. Evaluate the EOQ model for inventory control.

3. A typing pool requires 1000 boxes of typing paper each year. Each box is worth £20 and storage costs are 13.5% of stock value a year. The cost of placing an order is £15.

    a) For the order quantities 50, 100, 150, 200 and 250 calculate the storage cost, replenishment cost and total cost.
    b) Plot the costs in a) on a graph.
    c) Show algebraically that delivery costs and storage costs are equal when 105 boxes are ordered at a time.

4. A company has a demand of 2000 items per annum. Stock ordering costs are fixed at £100 irrespective of the scale of replenishment. It costs £2.50 to hold one item in stock for one year. Calculate the economic order quantity.

5. A company experiences annual demand for 2500 units of the single product that it stocks. The replenishment cost for inventory is fixed at £400 regardless of the size of replenishment. Annual holding costs are £8 per unit. What is the optimum number of replenishments per annum?

6. Computers Ltd. has expanded its range of computers and now requires each year, at a constant rate, 200 000 circuit boards which it obtains from an outside supplier. The order cost is £32. For any circuit board in stock it is estimated that the annual holding cost is equal to 10% of its cost. The circuit boards cost £8 each. No stock-outs are permitted.

    a) What is the optimal order size and how many orders should be placed in a year?
    b) What are the ordering and holding costs and hence what is the total relevant inventory cost per annum?
    c) If the demand has been underestimated and the true demand is 242,000 circuit boards per annum, what would be the effect to the

order quantity calculated in a) and still meeting demand, rather than using a new optimal level?

7. The purchasing manager of an electrical component retailer holds a regular stock of light bulbs. Over the past year he has sold, on average, 25 a week and he anticipates that this rate of sale will continue during the next year (which you may assume to be 50 weeks). He buys light bulbs from his supplier at the rate of £5 for 10 and every time he places an order it costs on average £10, bearing in mind the necessary secretarial expenses and the time involved in checking the order. As a guide to the stockholding costs involved, the company usually values its cost of capital at 20% and as the storage space required is negligible the manager decides that this figure is appropriate in this case. Furthermore, the prices charged to customers are determined by taking the purchasing and stockholding costs and applying a standard markup of 20%

    a) Currently the manager is reviewing the ordering and pricing policies and needs to know how many light bulbs should be ordered each time and what price he should charge. What would be your advice?

    b) If he now finds that he can obtain a discount of 5% for ordering in batches of 1000 would you advise him to amend the ordering and pricing policy that you have suggested and, if so, to what?

8. The manager of a large fishing-tackle shop opens for 50 weeks each year and holds a regular stock of fishing flies. Although the manager has to purchase boxes of these items for £9.60 per box containing 12 flies he is prepared to sell them as single items. Over the past year he has sold, on average, 12 boxes of fishing flies each week and it is likely that this level of sales will continue into the future. Due to telephone, secretarial and transport costs it is estimated that the cost of receiving each order is £16. The annual cost of storage is estimated at 20% of the stock item value and is based on the cost of storage space and the company's cost of capital. The manager of the shop sets a price for his goods by taking the sum of the purchase cost and the appropriately allocated holding cost (storage and delivery) and then applying a markup of 50%

    a) Determine the optimum number of boxes of fishing flies the shop manager should order at a time and the number of orders per year. Show that the selling price per fly that results from this optimum policy is £1.24

b) The supplier offers a discount of 4% on the price of each box of flies if the manager is prepared to purchase 500 boxes at a time. It can be assumed that there are no price effects on demand. Show whether or not this discount, assuming it is passed on, is advantageous or not to the customer in terms of shop price.

c) What percentage discount is required for the order quantity of 500 boxes to be beneficial to the customers?

WEB EXERCISE

Discuss how you could quantify the cost of inventory in an organization. Use the article at http://www.inventorymanagementreview.org/2005/09/dell_computers_.html (accessed 4 October 2008) to help your discussion.

FURTHER READING

Brown, S. (1996) *Strategic Manufacturing for Competitive Advantage*, Hemel Hempstead, Prentice Hall.

Kornafel, P. (2004) *Inventory Management and Purchasing: Tales and Techniques from the Automotive Aftermarket*, First Books Library.

Shingo, S. (1989) *A Study of Toyota Production Systems*, Productivity Press.

Waters, D. (2004) *Inventory Control and Management*, 2nd edn, John Wiley & Sons, Ltd.

WEB LINKS

www.inventoryops.com (accessed 4 October 2008). Guide containing extensive links to inventory articles and organizations.

http://logistics.about.com/od/inventorymanagement/ (accessed 4 October 2008). Links to inventory management resources including background to the Square Root Law.

www.mapics.com (accessed 4 October 2008) MAPICS SA manufacturing software, including inventory management features.

REFERENCES

Brown, S., Lamming, R., Bessant, J. and **Jones, P.** (2005) *Strategic Operations Management*, 2nd edn, Elsevier Butterworth-Heinemann Oxford.

Maister, D.H. (1975) Centralisation of Inventories and the square root law. *International Journal of Physical Distribution*, **6** (3), 124–34.

Stevenson, W.J. (2009) *Operations Management*, 10th edn, McGraw-Hill.

Wall, M. (2004) Keeping suppliers in order. *Sunday Times*, 25 July.

Waters, D. (2002) *Operations Management: Producing Goods and Services*, 2nd edn, FT Prentice Hall.

CHAPTER

13

Lean Operations and JIT

LEARNING OBJECTIVES

- Describe the two levels of JIT

- Explain the main elements of the lean philosophy

- Explain the need for JIT techniques

- Understand the relevance of the kanban production control system to JIT

- Discuss the concepts of levelled scheduling and mixed model scheduling

- Evaluate the use of JIT in service and administration systems

- Discuss the use of JIT and lean operations in service and administrative systems

- Evaluate when a JIT and lean implementation are appropriate

INTRODUCTION

Lean operations is a concept that involves eliminating nonvalue-added activities from the entire supply chain. The term was first used by Womack, Jones and Roos (2007) and is often used interchangeably with the concept of just-in-time (JIT). However, JIT traditionally only applies to the organization and its immediate suppliers, whereas lean encompasses the entire supply chain (supply chain management, or SCM, is covered in Chapter 15). The term 'lean' is meant to emphasize the concept of elimination of waste in all its forms. The concept continues to develop and Bicheno (2004) uses the term 'new lean' to describe an amalgam of traditional lean, theory of constraints (Chapter 11), Six Sigma (Chapter 18) and 'a range of relatively new concepts for measurements, analysis, and transformation'. In this chapter JIT and lean operations are considered interchangeably and as an integration of a philosophy and techniques designed to improve performance.

> **JIT and lean operations**
> An integration of a philosophy and techniques designed to improve performance.

THE PHILOSOPHY OF JIT AND LEAN OPERATIONS

Just-in-time and lean operations is a philosophy originating from the Japanese auto maker Toyota where Taiichi Ohno developed the Toyota Production System (Ohno, 1988). The basic idea behind JIT is to produce only what you need, when you need it. This may seem a simple idea but to deliver it requires a number of elements to be in place such as high quality and elimination of wasteful activities. Bicheno (1991) states that 'JIT aims to meet demand instantaneously, with perfect quality and no waste'. To achieve this aim requires a whole new approach, or philosophy, from the organization in how it operates. Three key issues identified by Harrison (1992) as the core of JIT philosophy are: eliminate waste, involve everyone and continuous improvement. They are used here to explain the main elements of the lean philosophy.

Eliminate Waste

Waste is considered in the widest sense as any activity which does not add value to the operation. Bicheno (2004) states that although waste is strongly linked to lean, waste elimination is a means to achieving the lean ideal, it is not an end in itself and waste prevention is at least as important as waste elimination. The seven types of waste identified by Ohno (1988) are as follows:

- *Over-production.* This is classified as the greatest source of waste and is an outcome of producing more than is needed by the next process.

- *Waiting time.* This is the time spent by labour or equipment waiting to add value to a product. This may be disguised by undertaking unnecessary operations – for example, generating work in progress (WIP) on a machine – which are not immediately needed (the waste is converted from time to WIP).
- *Transport.* Unnecessary transportation of WIP is another source of waste. Layout changes can substantially reduce transportation time.
- *Process.* Some operations do not add value to the product but are simply there because of poor design or machine maintenance. Improved design or preventative maintenance should eliminate these processes.
- *Inventory.* Inventory of all types (such as pipeline or cycle – see Chapter 12) is considered as waste and should be eliminated.
- *Motion.* Simplification of work movement will reduce waste caused by unnecessary motion of labour and equipment.
- *Defective goods.* The total costs of poor quality can be very high and will include scrap material, wasted labour time and time expediting orders and loss of goodwill through missed delivery dates.

From a customer, rather than an organizational, perspective the seven service wastes can be the basis for an improvement programme:

- *Delay* on the part of customers waiting for service, for delivery, in queues, for response, not arriving as promised.
- *Duplication.* Having to re-enter data, repeat details on forms and answering queries from several sources within the same organization.
- *Unnecessary movements.* Queuing several times, poor ergonomics in the service encounter.
- *Unclear communication* and the waste of seeking clarification.
- *Incorrect inventory.* Out-of-stock, unable to get exactly what is required, substitute products or services.
- *Opportunity lost* to retain or win customers, failure to establish rapport, ignoring customers, unfriendliness and rudeness.
- *Errors* in the service transaction, product defects in the product-service bundle, lost or damaged goods.

Involvement of Everyone

Just-in-time aims to create a new culture in which all employees are encouraged to contribute to continuous improvement efforts through generating ideas for improvements and perform a range of functions. In order to undertake this level of involvement the organization will provide training to staff in a wide range of areas, including techniques such as statistical process control (SPC) and more general problem solving techniques.

Continuous Improvement

Continuous improvement or *Kaizen*, the Japanese term, is a philosophy stating that it is possible to get to the ideals of JIT by a continuous stream of improvements over time. Russell and Taylor (2005) adapt the ten principles given in Hirano (1989) into the following principles for implementing a continuous improvement effort

> **Continuous improvement**
> This is a philosophy that believes that it is possible to get to the ideals of JIT by a continuous stream of improvements over time.

1. *Create a mind-set for improvement.* Do not accept that the present way of doing things is necessarily the best.
2. *Try and try again.* Don't seek immediate perfection but move to your goal by small improvements, checking for mistakes as you progress.
3. *THINK.* Get to the real cause of the problem – ask why? Five times.
4. *Work in teams.* Use the ideas from a number of people to brainstorm new ways.
5. *Recognize that improvement knows no limits.* Get in the habit of always looking for better ways of doing things.

Chapter 17 deals with the continuous improvement approach in more detail.

CASE STUDY   13.1

Quake Upsets Lean Supply Model

The latest natural disaster in north-western Japan has once again raised questions about the weaknesses of the vaunted lean production system pioneered by Toyota and practised to varying degrees by other automakers. The entire Japanese vehicle industry ground to a halt following an earthquake that stopped production of piston rings for engines provided by Riken, the industry leader in the domestic market. Toyota, in particular, was forced to stop operations at all 12 of its domestic plants. The situation has highlighted problems not only with lean manufacturing, which aims to reduce all waste, including inventories, to the minimum, but also with the Japanese industry's dependence on one manufacturer for a key product.

The earthquake had a larger than expected impact on Japanese auto manufacturers because they have aimed to reduce the inventory level of components, to reduce working capital, noted Tatsuya Miyamoto, analyst at Fitch in Tokyo. However, doing so 'enhances the risk of stalling the production in the event of a disruption of supply', he wrote in a report. Moreover, the latest setback has revealed that automakers were heavily dependent on one supplier for a key part. This was despite their stated policy of signing on multiple vendors to avoid disruptions to production in unexpected situations, like a natural disaster. Riken, with a 50% share of the domestic piston ring market, single-handedly disrupted the production of the entire Japanese auto industry.

Katsuaki Watanabe, president of Toyota, underlined the difficulty of diversifying procurement in an age when the quality of the parts is critical to the competitiveness of the finished product. 'Basically, we adhere to the principle of multiple procurement but for products where we work very closely with a supplier from an early stage in the development [of a vehicle] there is tremendous difficulty in transferring that technology itself or asking [another manufacturer] to make that product', he said. Riken has specialized technology that other suppliers have had difficulty emulating, making it difficult for carmakers to diversify their supplies, said Hirofumi Yokoi, industry analyst at CSM Worldwide. Mr Watanabe conceded that 'we must deepen our understanding of how to manage risk at suppliers that we rely on for specialized products.' With the increasingly important role parts makers play in determining the competitiveness of carmakers, Mr Mizuno at Fitch expected carmakers to 'put more emphasis on establishing closer relationships with key component suppliers and enclosing them within their group.'

However, analysts and industry officials believe that the advantages of the lean production system far outweigh any weaknesses it may have exposed in emergencies, such as the latest earthquake. Mr Yokoi said if you compared the long-term advantages of lower costs and efficiency that were the fruits of the lean production system with what was lost in a natural

disaster, there was no question that the former was of greater value. Indeed, Toyota officials said that having a low level of inventory helped them to assess quickly where the problems lay and address those problems promptly. Because lean producers kept inventory levels to a minimum, it was possible to grasp quickly the level of inventory at every stage of the supply chain. This made it possible to determine speedily where the missing parts were needed and in what quantities, the Toyota officials said. If inventory levels were high – as in the old days – it would be impossible to sort things out quickly and resume production as quickly as Toyota had been able to, they said. There was no going back on lean production, said Mr Yokoi. 'The key is how to recover quickly when an emergency strikes', he said. The rebound by Japanese vehicle makers a few days after the earthquake shows that they had been quick to master that task, he added.

Source: by Michiyo Nakamoto, 23 July 2007, Financial Times Limited 2008. Reproduced with permission.

Question
Use the case study to discuss the advantages and disadvantages of lean production.

JUST-IN-TIME AND LEAN TECHNIQUES

A wide variety of JIT techniques are considered to be within the lean philosophy. Concepts such as concurrent design, design for manufacture (DFM), mass customization, failure modes and effect analysis (FMEA) and value engineering (VE) are considered in Chapter 7. Additional techniques are considered below.

Cellular Manufacturing

In cellular manufacturing, to reduce transportation, machines are moved from functional departments (all similar machines are placed together) to a cell, which is a close grouping of different types of equipment, each of which performs a different operation. Cell layouts are particularly suited to JIT manufacturing when it is feasible to dedicate equipment to the production of specific products. Equipment can be arranged close together in a U-shaped line to reduce transportation and material handling costs and allow multiskilled workers to carry out a number of operations simultaneously. Chapter 4 covers cell layouts in more detail.

Cellular manufacturing When equipment is placed in a cell layout which is a close grouping of different types of equipment, each of which performs a different operation.

JIT Supplier Networks

The JIT system requires a continuous stream of small batch supplies to ensure inventory is minimized within the organization. To achieve this, close long-term relationships are formed with a small number of suppliers, forming supplier networks. Because of the frequency of deliveries in JIT supply, suppliers are usually situated relatively close to the organization. In order to facilitate design for manufacture (DFM) (Chapter 7) the organization will work with suppliers to improve component design and ensure quality. It is necessary for JIT suppliers to practice

JIT supplier networks A formation of close long-term relationships with a small number of suppliers.

CASE STUDY 13.2

Satair

Satair, a supplier of parts and hardware to the aerospace industry, decided to invest in JIT to differentiate itself from competitors, to streamline the supply chain and to cut both its own and its customers' costs. 'We wanted to offer customers and potential customers lean supply techniques', says Steve Reading, Managing Director. Used by customers or by Satair employees at the business's site, the JIT system handles stock control and fulfilment. Barcodes are swiped as parts are used and the information is relayed back to the system which triggers JIT resupply and invoicing. Full stock

usage history at each of the 15 off-site depots is recorded, and parts are also tracked through each stage of the supply chain. 'We can see on our computers where every part is at every stage', says Steve. Operations with Satair's biggest customer are completely paperless via links to the customer's MRP system.

Source: DTI web site (now Department for Business, Enterprise and Regulatory Reform).

Question

How is Satair helping its customers to implement lean operations?

JIT supply themselves or to avoid inventory being 'pushed' back to them. Supply chain issues such as these are dealt with in more detail in Chapter 15.

Total Preventative Maintenance (TPM)

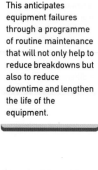

Total preventative maintenance
This anticipates equipment failures through a programme of routine maintenance that will not only help to reduce breakdowns but also to reduce downtime and lengthen the life of the equipment.

Total preventative maintenance ombines the practice of preventative maintenance with the ideas of total quality and employee involvement, which form part of the JIT and TQM philosophies. The idea behind preventative maintenance is to anticipate equipment failures through a programme of routine maintenance which will not only help to reduce breakdowns, but also to reduce downtime (time not in operation) and lengthen the life of the equipment. It has been realized that the cost of a maintenance programme can be outweighed by the more consistent output of a better quality product.

In a TPM programme all employees are encouraged to use their knowledge to improve equipment reliability and reduce variability in performance. When considering the cost implications of maintenance activities it is important to consider not just the cost of lost production due to poor maintenance but the costs associated with loss of business due to poor customer service.

Total preventative maintenance includes the following activities:

- Regular maintenance activities such as lubricating, painting, cleaning and inspection. These activities are normally carried out by the operator in order to prevent equipment deterioration.
- Periodic inspection to assess the condition of equipment in order to avoid breakdowns. These inspections are normally carried out at regular time intervals by either operators or maintenance personnel.
- Preventative repairs, due to deterioration but before a breakdown has occurred. Normally carried out by maintenance personnel but ideally by the operators.

Total preventative management thus emphasizes the equipment operator's role in maintenance and considers preventative maintenance to be more than preventative repairs but the execution of regular maintenance and inspection activities which ensures the equipment is in the best possible environment and is not allowed to deteriorate. This will require a programme of training operators to maintain equipment over its life span. The TPM approach embraces the philosophy of continuous improvement in that the idea is not just to keep equipment operational but to make improvements to eliminate breakdowns (zero defects). To do this requires the design of products to include aspects such as the ease of maintenance of equipment used to produce that product.

Preventative maintenance uses a system of routine inspection and replacement of parts. This may lead to the equipment being out of service for periods of inspection or even replacement of parts during what could be productive time. Predictive main-tenance uses a system of monitoring performance measures of equipment to predict failures, rather than a periodic check. Thus by predicting problems in advance the maintenance activity may take place when the machine is not in use, saving produc-tion output. Also overtime payments and component expediting costs may be saved.

Predictive maintenance is undertaken using sensors that monitor variables such as vibration at critical points. These readings are tracked by computer which identi-fies trends in performance. Analysis of particles in lubricants and examination of equipment parts by fibre optics, eliminating the need for disassembly, can also help to predict problems and thus help plan maintenance outputs in advance.

The amount of preventative maintenance undertaken can be considered as a trade-off between the cost of preventative maintenance and the cost of breakdown maintenance. The amount of preventative maintenance will depend on a variety of factors such as the age of equipment (see notes on reliability, Chapter 7) but there is a point when too much preventative maintenance (for example, rebuilding equipment every day) can be too costly. The relationship between cost and preventative main-tenance is shown graphically in Figure 13.1.

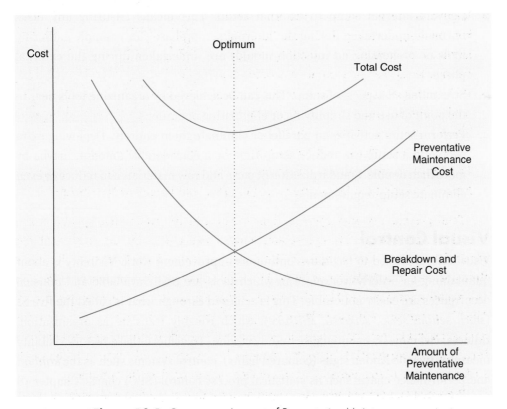

Figure 13.1: Cost versus Amount of Preventative Maintenance.

Setup Reduction (SUR)

In order to operate with the small batch sizes required by JIT it is necessary to reduce setup time (the time taken to adjust equipment to work on a different component) drastically because of the increased number of setups needed with small batches – this is known as **setup reduction**. Originally some operations such as stamping car door panels with a press die were done in very large batch sizes, and the output stored in inventory, because the setup time for the press could be measured in hours or even days. Shigeo Shingo was hired by Toyota to study how press die setup could be reduced and he achieved impressive results. For example he reduced the setup time on one 1000 ton press from six hours to only three minutes. The system he developed became known as the single minute exchange of dies (SMED) (Shingo, 1996) and is based on the following principles:

1. Separate internal setup from external setup. Setup tasks are classified as internal – they must be performed while the machine is stopped – and external – they can be performed in advance while the machine is running. Performing external setup tasks during operation and then delaying only for the internal setup tasks can reduce setup times by 30% to 50%.

2. Convert internal setup to external setup. This means ensuring any tasks normally undertaken during the internal setup phase (for example gathering tools or preheating an injection mould) are undertaken during the external phase.

3. Streamline all aspects of setup. This can be achieved by organizing tools near to the point of use and simplifying or eliminating operations.

4. Perform setup activities in parallel or eliminate them entirely. Deploying extra people to a setup can reduce setup time by a considerable amount, maybe by more than double. Standardization of parts and raw materials can reduce or even eliminate setup requirements.

Visual Control

Visual control is used to facilitate continuous improvement work. Visibility is about maintaining an orderly workplace in which tools are easily available and unusual occurrences are easily noticeable. This is achieved through what is called the five Ss (*seiri, seiton, seiso, seiketsu, shitsuke*), which roughly translate as organization, tidiness, cleanliness, maintenance and discipline. To achieve these factors visibility measures include Andon signs (coloured lights), control systems such as the *kanban* and performance charts such as statistical process control (SPC) charts. Chapter 18 covers the SPC method.

Setup reduction
The reduction of setup time (the time taken to adjust a machine to work on a different component).

Visual control
This is about maintaining an orderly workplace in which tools are easily available and unusual occurrences are easily noticeable.

Push and Pull Production Systems

In a push production system a schedule pushes work on to machines which is then passed through to the next work centre (Figure 13.2).

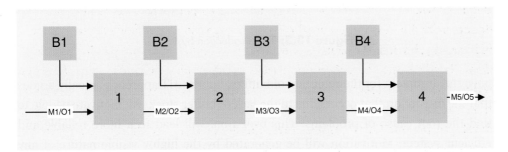

Figure 13.2: Push Production System.

In Figure 13.2 materials (M1) and orders for production (O1) are 'pushed' onto production stage 1. Production stage 1 then produces material for production stage 2 and the cycle repeats through the production stages. At each production stage a buffer stock (B1, B2 etc.) is kept to ensure that if any production stage fails then the subsequent production stage will not be starved of material. For example if there is a breakdown at stage 2 of the production line, stage 3 will be fed from a buffer stock (B3) until the problem is fixed. The higher the buffer stocks kept at each stage of the line, the more disruption can occur without the production line being halted by lack of material.

The pull system developed by Ohno (1988) comes from the idea of a supermarket in which items are purchased by a customer only when needed and are replenished as they are removed. Thus inventory coordination is controlled by a customer pulling items from the system, which are then replaced as needed.

In a pull system (Figure 13.3) the process starts by an order for the finished product (for example, car) at the end of the production line (O1). This then triggers an order for components of that item (O2), which in turn triggers an order for further subcomponents (O3). The process repeats until the initial stage of production and the material flows through the system as in the 'push' approach. Using the pull system the production system produces output at each stage only in response to demand and eliminates the need for buffer stock.

The aim of the elimination of buffers between production stages is to ensure a responsive system. However, the pull system does not overcome the basic characteristic of a line layout that if one stage fails, all subsequent stages will be starved of work and, in effect, output from the whole production line is lost. This would seem to be a

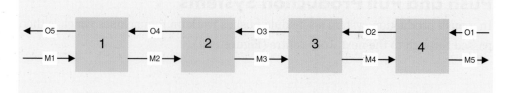

Figure 13.3: 'Pull' Production System.

powerful argument for the retention of buffers, but the JIT approach actually argues that the disruption that occurs due to the lack of buffer stock will motivate people to find the root cause of problems. This over time will lead to a more reliable and efficient system. Motivation will be generated by the highly visible nature of any problem occurring (it will bring the whole factory to a halt) and the fact that the problem is now everyone's problem and not just a local difficulty of which no one else is aware. In moving from a push to a pull system it is common practice to gradually reduce the buffer levels as the production system reliability is increased. An attempt to move directly to eliminate buffers is likely to cause severe disruption to a system formerly reliant on this safety net.

The pull approach is applied not just to internal production systems but to the relationship between customers and suppliers in the supply chain. Thus suppliers in a lean supply chain are required to only supply customers in response to demand and the customer will not keep buffer stocks 'just-in-case' the supplier fails to deliver on time. This reduces inventory and increases responsiveness in the supply chain but does require close cooperation between customer and supplier and reliability in the supplier operations (see Chapter 15).

CASE STUDY 13.3

Goodwin Steel Castings

Goodwin Steel Castings' use of JIT systems has increased profits, reduced timescales and helped develop more competitive products. Faced with an extremely competitive market, steel manufacturer Goodwin Steel Castings decided to introduce JIT working as part of an investment in technology aimed at improving the efficiency of their systems. Now, from taking orders and production through to process control and customer service, the company has integrated its systems. Since JIT is a demand-led process, Goodwin has worked with clients to ensure it can gauge their needs with maximum accuracy. Many of the company's clients now make their delivery schedules and requirements available on their web sites for Goodwin to retrieve. This information is then translated automatically into project updates which are available online for all customers. As orders are fed through to the foundry, electronic monitors place orders with the business's suppliers. Says General Manager Steven Birks, 'The latest stage of our investment in JIT telemetry technology enables us to access information on their web sites so we can get valuable management information like trends and historic usage.' The main business benefit of integrating JIT technology into Goodwin's supply chain has been faster response times, which has led to winning more orders and the business being able to quote more accurately. The company has also managed to improve efficiency through closer monitoring of manufacturing.

Source: DTI web site (now Department for Business, Enterprise and Regulatory Reform).

Question

Why are faster response times important in a JIT system?

Kanban Production System

There are a number of ways of implementing a pull production system including the drum buffer rope approach of OPT covered in Chapter 10. One system for implementing a pull system is called a *kanban* production system (kanban is Japanese for 'card' or 'sign'). Each *kanban* provides information on the part identification, quantity per container that the part is transported in and the preceding and next work station. *Kanbans*, in themselves, do not provide the schedule for production but without them production cannot take place as they authorize the production and movement of material through the pull system. *Kanbans* need not be a card, but should be something that can be used as a signal for production such as a marker, or coloured square area. There are two types of *kanban* system: the single card and two card.

The single-card system uses only one type of *kanban* card called the conveyance *kanban*, which authorizes the movement of parts. The number of containers at a work centre is limited by the number of *kanbans*. A signal to replace inventory at the work centre can only be sent when the container is emptied. Toyota use a dual card system which, in addition to the conveyance *kanban*, uses a production *kanban* to authorize the production of parts. This system permits greater control over production as well as inventory. If the processes are tightly linked (one always follows the other) then a single *kanban* can be used.

In order for a *kanban* system to be implemented it is important that the seven operational rules that govern the system are followed. These rules can be summarized as follows:

- Move a *kanban* only when the lot it represents is consumed. This means the whole of the batch of parts must be processed before the *kanban* is sent to the preceding process to ask for more parts.

> **Kanban production system**
> To implement a pull system a *kanban* is used to pass information such as the part identification, quantity per container that the part is transported in and the preceding and next work station.

- No withdrawal of parts without a *kanban* is allowed. No process can move parts without the authorization of a *kanban* request.
- The number of parts issued to the subsequent process must be the exact number specified by the *kanban*. This means a *kanban* must wait until sufficient parts are made before the lot of parts is moved.
- A *kanban* should always be attached to the physical product. The *kanban* should travel with the parts themselves and be visible.
- The preceding process should always produce its parts in the quantities withdrawn by the subsequent process. Processes should never overproduce parts in any quantity.
- Defective parts should never be conveyed to the subsequent process. A high level of quality must be maintained because of the lack of buffer inventory. A feedback mechanism, which reports quality problems quickly to the preceding process, must be implemented.
- Process the *kanbans* in every work centre strictly in the order in which they arrive at the work centre. If several *kanbans* are waiting for production they must be served in the order that they have arrived. If the rule is not followed there will be a gap in the production rate of one or more of the subsequent processes.

The operation for a dual card *kanban* system is outlined in Figure 13.4:

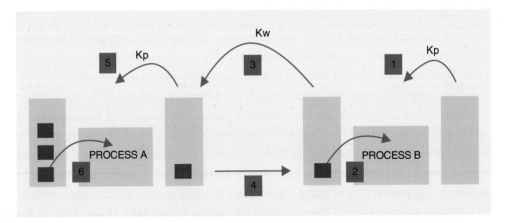

Figure 13.4: Dual-card *Kanban* System.

1. A production *kanban* arrives at process B, attached to an empty container. Process B is activated to fill the container.
2. Process B requests inputs, from process A, to fulfil 1.
3. A withdrawal *kanban* is sent to process A to fulfil 2.
4. A full container is sent from process A to process B.

5. The production *kanban*, which was attached to the container in 4 is placed on an empty container, activating process A.
6. Process A requests inputs to fulfil 5. A withdrawal *kanban* is not activated as sufficient stock is present.

The *kanban* system is similar to the reorder point inventory system but has the objective of the continual reduction of inventory. The amount of inventory can be reduced over time by reducing the number of *kanban*s in the system. The formula suggested by Hall (1989) for the number of *kanban*s at each production stage is given below:

$$y = \frac{D \times (T_W + T_P) \times (1 + X)}{a}$$

y = total number of *kanban*s (production and conveyance) for a part
D = planned usage rate (units/day)
T_W = average waiting time for replenishment of parts (fraction of a day)
T_P = average production time for a container of parts (fraction of a day)
X = a policy variable corresponding to possible inefficiencies in the system
a = capacity of a standard container in units (should usually be less than 10% of daily usage for that part)

Setting X to zero provides just enough inventory (y × a) to cover the time required to produce and move a container of parts.

The system is implemented with a given number of cards in order to obtain a smooth flow. The number of cards is then decreased, decreasing inventory and any problems that surface are tackled. Cards are decreased, one at a time, to continue the continuous improvement process. It is important to note that a successful implementation of a *kanban* system will require a stable and reliable production system to be in place. That requires prior introduction of many of the lean techniques described here, including setup reduction, total preventative maintenance and levelled scheduling.

CASE STUDY   13.4

Messier-Dowty

Messier-Dowty designs, develops, manufactures and supports landing gear systems for over 19 000 aircraft worldwide. Despite the firm's success, David Johnson, team leader for systems and supplier development says: 'We realized that we were not meeting our customers' expectations. We needed to reach 'zero defect' status, be cost competitive and deliver our products on time every time. To achieve the highest performance standards, we needed a systematic approach.' Crucially, the changes needed to be made along the supply chain, improving flow, reducing batch sizes and improving overall quality.

A structured solution was the key: Messier-Dowty introduced a programme of training, diagnostics, workshops and reviews for its own staff and its newly formed 'Supply Chain Group'. Lean systems were introduced to eliminate waste at each stage of production. Following an extensive analysis of production techniques, work flows and key suppliers, the manufacturing process was broken into logical blocks, using *kanban* – a production control system where components are supplied only when demanded and arrive 'just-in-time'. This creates a more accurate replenishment cycle, cuts lead time, makes inventories more precise and, ultimately, reduces costs.

Initially, the changes involved 19 of its suppliers. Rather than take on new staff, Messier-Dowty hired consultants to manage the change. The cost was £38 000, but the programme saved over £350 000 in operating costs in the first year, and £470 000 in the year after. Other members of the Supply Chain Group reported savings of up to £315 000 in the first year with minimal extra expenditure. These savings have then been shared with Messier-Dowty through price cuts. As David Johnson points out: 'While this was never intended to be a cost-saving initiative, it's clear that cutting waste and improving the quality of our performance has created considerable financial benefits.'

Dramatic changes have occurred in the speed and reliability of supplies. The *kanban* system means that over 200 supplies are now

delivered on time, 100% of the time. Suppliers have also responded positively. Paul Buckley of Ultra Electronics has noticed that: 'Our involvement in the Messier-Dowty supply chain group has focused our attention on improving our manufacturing process by significantly reducing waste. At Ultra we have been working on improvement activities with the aim of sustaining 100% on-time delivery and total customer satisfaction.'

At first not all the suppliers in the group were convinced that the changes would be mutually beneficial. Paul Foulds, from supply company Middlesex Group, says: 'Initially there was some scepticism. We'd made attempts at introducing change before, but these initiatives had not been followed through with sufficient conviction. Neither I nor my colleagues knew very much about these techniques at first, but it seemed a practical proposal that offered the opportunity to improve the business while working with one of our major customers.'

Central to Messier-Dowty's success was its programme of engagement with suppliers. It trained 57 advocates for the programme internally and 35 advocates among its suppliers to ensure the changes were communicated and managed effectively. Messier-Dowty intends to introduce new suppliers to the initiative at the outset of the business relationship. The firm will continue to work with existing suppliers to eliminate waste, and to monitor and report progress to ensure that the initiative grows with the business.

David Johnson thinks that the results have had a more far-reaching effect than his team at

Messier-Dowty could have predicted:
'Ultimately, it's a high standard of delivery that
satisfies the customer. Focusing on improving
our delivery performance has changed the way
we do business, and I think we'll be enjoying
the benefits for many years to come.'

Source: DTI web site (now Department for
Business, Enterprise and Regulatory Reform).

Question

How has the introduction of lean systems
succeeded in improving delivery performance?

Levelled Scheduling

The approach to scheduling which has been followed in traditional manufacturing
systems is to make a large number of one product before switching to another.
Unfortunately this approach will lead to high levels of finished goods inventory at
some times (the end of a production run) with the possibility of not being able to
satisfy customer demand at other times (when long production runs of other goods
are being manufactured). Levelled scheduling attempts to overcome this problem by
producing the smallest reasonable number of units of each product at a time.

> **Levelled scheduling**
> A level assembly schedule produces the smallest reasonable number of units of each product at a time.

Mixed Model Scheduling

Mixed model scheduling attempts to spread the production of several different end
items evenly throughout each day. This results in a constant rate of flow all day, rather
than in different rates for different products. If, say, three different products are to be
produced then the ideal schedule would be to produce the products in sequence
throughout the day. Usually, however, the products in the sequence will be needed
in different quantities so that the sequence will need to be adjusted to reflect that.

> **Mixed model scheduling**
> This attempts to spread the production of several different end items evenly throughout each day.

When a level assembly schedule has been achieved the production of each item
will closely match demand. However, because the flow of component parts must be
adjusted to match the rate at which finished goods will be produced, it is necessary to
match the cycle time (the rate of production) at the work centres with the demand rate.

WORKED EXAMPLE 13.1
Mixed Model Scheduling

If total demand for three products is 80 units a day and production is available for 8 hours (480
minutes) a day the cycle time is as follows:

cycle time = working time per day/units required per day
cycle time = 480/80 = 6 minutes /unit

Extending the cycle time calculation for each product, based on a mixed model sequence,
gives the figures shown in Table 13.1.

Product	Daily demand	Cycle time (minutes)
A	40	$\dfrac{480}{40} = 12$
B	10	$\dfrac{480}{10} = 48$
C	30	$\dfrac{480}{30} = 16$

Table 13.1: Cycle Times.

One possible assembly sequence could be ACACBACA. One unit of product A will be produced every 12 minutes on average throughout the day to a level assembly schedule. This means that components must be supplied to product A to match this cycle time. The system must also be coordinated to produce either A, B or C once every 6 minutes. To achieve these results requires that sufficient equipment and labour are configured and setup times minimized.

JUST-IN-TIME IN SERVICE SYSTEMS

Just-in-time is usually associated with manufacturing applications because this is the setting in which it was developed and has been applied most frequently. However, many of the ideas behind JIT can be employed in service settings. For example Schniederjans (1993) presents introductory JIT implementation strategies that can be applied to almost all administration organizations.

- Everybody in an administration department should serve as a customer-service agent. Service quality is everybody's responsibility in a JIT administration. When poor quality is observed in the delivery of an administration service that can be corrected the individual worker or department that is responsible should be made to implement the correction.
- Management should be willing to sacrifice production for improved quality and allow workers extra time for JIT activities such as quality control.

- All employees should be multifunctional to increase worker flexibility and help workers understand more of the operation.
- Walls and departmental barriers cause greater routing, filing, walking and proofing and should be restructured into various groups of workers

or group technology (GT) cell work stations with multifunctional skills. Multiple cells allow more than one channel through which work can flow, increasing flexibility to better balance work load with variable capacity. In a departmental system if one department is backlogged other offices will become idle and inefficiencies can occur. Elimination of departments also decreases much duplication and can substantially reduce the amount of commonly used equipment, filing cabinets and storage areas.

- Standardizing work procedures can save time in training and improve operational efficiency by removing job complexity. Standardizing order forms and routing systems can also reduce complexity and helps workers understand processes and thus suggest improvements.

Womack and Jones (2005) have developed lean thinking principles for the processes of consumption. This involves streamlining the systems for providing goods and services using six principles:

1. Solve the customer's problem completely by ensuring that all the goods and services work, and work together.
2. Don't waste the customer's time.
3. Provide exactly *what* the customer wants.
4. Provide what's wanted exactly *where* it's wanted.
5. Provide what's wanted where it's wanted exactly *when* it's wanted.
6. Continually aggregate solutions to reduce the customer's time and hassle.

IMPLEMENTING JIT AND LEAN OPERATIONS

Just-in-time and lean operations have been covered in this chapter both as a philosophy and as a set of techniques.

From the viewpoint of JIT as a philosophy of the elimination of waste it can be seen as applicable to all organizations, small or large, manufacturing or service. At this level JIT requires organizational systems to be developed around identifying and eliminating waste. The main implementation issues concern the requirement of a problem solving culture of trust and cooperation within the workforce. It is also likely that problem identification and problem solving activities will be more successful at a higher volume of output, which gives a better chance for learning to occur.

At the level of JIT as a collection of tools and techniques it is more likely to be applicable to medium to high volumes of products that have reached a mature development phase in the market. Just-in-time techniques include the *kanban* production control system. Prerequisites for the implementation of this type of system include aspects such as layout design (for example, cell manufacturing) (Chapter 5), setup time reduction (SUR) (Chapter 13), line balancing (Chapter 4) and total quality management (TQM) techniques (Chapter 17) such as statistical process control (SPC) (Chapter 18).

SUMMARY

- Just-in-time can be seen on one level as a philosophy and on a second level as a set of tools and techniques.

- The concepts of waste elimination, involvement of everyone and continuous improvement are the core of the JIT philosophy.

- Just-in-time tools and techniques are required to implement lean operations.

- Just-in-time tools and techniques include design for manufacture, value engineering and value analysis, cellular manufacturing, JIT supplier networks, total preventative maintenance, setup reduction and visual control.

- Just-in-time planning and control are based on the *kanban* production control system

- The techniques of levelled scheduling and mixed model scheduling attempt to match the production of each item with demand.

- Just-in-time and lean techniques may be applicable to service and administration systems.

- Just-in-time and lean operations require a problem-solving culture and are more likely to be applicable to medium- to high-volume organizations in mature markets.

CASE STUDY   13.5

It Pays to Cut Out Waste but Not to Trim All the Value Away

When Hoyt Buck started making hunting knives in the early years of the twentieth century, his competitors were other Kansas blacksmiths. One hundred years later, Buck Knives is up against companies from across the world, many of them based in countries where labour, utility and other costs are substantially below those in the US. Most companies in these circumstances send their manufacturing offshore. If you can't beat them, join them. But

Hoyt Buck's descendants were reluctant. Instead of exporting jobs to Asia, three years ago they started to import an Asian idea – the 'lean' manufacturing methods pioneered by Toyota.

The story shows, first, that the doctrines of the Toyota production system have spread far beyond the automotive sector. Fifteen years after the publication of *The Machine That Changed the World*, the book that popularized Toyota's management methods, the war against *muda* – Japanese for waste – is being fought across swaths of manufacturing industry and increasingly in services, too. Second, the experience of Buck Knives underlines that lean thinking can be a powerful weapon in the fight to keep manufacturing and other jobs in developed countries.

Lean thinking teaches managers to eradicate anything from the production process that does not add value for customers, including inventory. Instead of stockpiling goods in warehouses and praying that demand forecasts turn out to be accurate – the conventional 'push' model – lean manufacturers aim to produce only in response to firm orders. When an order is placed, raw materials are 'pulled' from the supply chain and down the production line as fast as possible. The result: high speed, no waste, low cost and a happy customer.

Irrespective of whether this ideal is achieved in practice, lean thinkers tend to be sceptical about the supposed benefits of sending jobs to low-wage economies. It is hard to run a low inventory, just-in-time supply chain when you are sourcing components from across the globe. What if the widgets required for tomorrow's production run are delayed by a typhoon or stuck for three days at the border? Besides, there is nothing lean about shipping steel, shoes or electronic components halfway around the world by container ship. Think of all that *muda* in time, capital and diesel fuel.

Another strand of lean thinking is the notion that frontline workers – whether on the production line or in customer service – are best placed to identify and solve problems. But they can do this only if they are very familiar with the products and can talk directly to the engineers and managers who are likely to be at the root cause of any problem. On this view, sending jobs offshore will result in fewer problems solved and unhappier customers in the long run.

James Womack and Daniel Jones, authors (with Daniel Roos) of *The Machine That Changed the World*, write in their new book, *Lean Solutions*, that the best location for service and support jobs is 'near the corporate technical centres that developed the products or near the operations centres of client firms'. Similarly, lean thinkers tend to be sceptical about the value of outsourcing jobs to contractors, even if the workers stay close by. Overheads may be reduced in the short term, but learning opportunities are likely to be lost.

At Buck Knives you can see these ideas in action. The old production line has been redesigned into a series of circular 'cells' that build knives from start to finish. The new layout minimizes the distance travelled by each product (less *muda*) and encourages communication among employees, allowing them to see the entire manufacturing process. This way of working makes it more likely that production bottlenecks or product defects will be recognized early and dealt with on the spot, says CJ Buck, chief executive and great-grandson of the founder. There is less need for expensive (and sometimes oppressive) supervision.

In true Toyota style, Buck Knives last month staged a symposium for its suppliers to explore ways of improving cooperation. Running a just-in-time supply chain requires a higher degree of collaboration – and trust – than is usual among manufacturers used to carrying weeks or months of surplus inventory. 'Much of what we are doing today is making the company more like it was when my grandfather was running the business and everything was done on a handshake', says Mr Buck.

To be sure, lean thinking is no panacea. It is hard to learn and even harder to sustain. It has limits. Going lean was not sufficient to get Buck Knives' unit costs down to competitive levels. After more than 50 years in California,

where Hoyt Buck moved in 1947, the company last year relocated to Idaho in search of lower overheads. While many of its products still carry a 'Made in USA' stamp, its less expensive models are now made in Taiwan. And as every chief executive knows, a world-class cost structure and commitment to continuous improvement is only table stakes these days. If Buck Knives wants to be around for another decade – let alone another century – it will have to come up with products that are consistently more desirable than the domestic and international competition. Innovation and inspiration must also be on the cutting edge.

Source: by Simon London, *Financial Times*, 12 October 2005. Reproduced with permission.

Question

Discuss how lean thinking can lead to the keeping of manufacturing jobs in developed countries.

EXERCISES

1. Explain the main elements of the JIT and lean philosophy.

2. Provide an analysis of the techniques used to implement a JIT philosophy in a manufacturing organization.

3. Distinguish between preventative and predictive maintenance.

4. Explain, using an example, how you would use the concepts of JIT in a service operations environment.

5. Evaluate the advantages and disadvantages of the JIT approach to production planning.

6. To gain efficiency it is essential to minimize the time it takes to make a car. Compare how this is achieved under traditional and lean operations approaches.

7. Why is the traditional approach to production control termed a 'buffered system'?

8. Discuss how JIT and lean operations can enhance flexibility.

WEB EXERCISE

Provide a definition of 'lean' using the history of lean at http://www.lean.org/WhatsLean/History.cfm (accessed 5 October 2008).

FURTHER READING

Bicheno, J. (2008) *The Lean Toolbox for Service Systems*, PICSIE Books.

Drew, J., McCallum, B. and **Roggenhofer, S.** (2004) *Journey to Lean: Making Operational Change Stick*, Palgrave Macmillan: Basingstoke.

Keyte, B. and **Locher, D.** (2005) *The Complete Lean Enterprise: Value Stream Mapping for Administration and Office Processes*, Productivity Press.

Krafcik, J.F. (1988) Triumph of the lean production system. *Sloan Management Review*, Fall, 41–52.

Parry, S., Barlow, S. and **Faulkner, M.** (2005) *Sense and Respond: The Journey to Customer Purpose*, Palgrave Macmillan.

Schonberger, R. (2008) *World Class Manufacturing: The Lessons of Simplicity Applied*, Free Press.

Womack, J.P. and **Jones, D.T.** (2007) *Lean Solutions: How Producers and Consumers Achieve Mutual Value and Create Wealth*, Simon & Schuster.

WEB LINKS

www.lean.org (accessed 5 October 2008). Lean Enterprise Institute. Details workshops and tools for lean implementation.

www.nummi.com (accessed 5 October 2008). New United Motor Manufacturing Inc. Joint venture of General Motors Corporation and Toyota Motor Corporation to introduce the Toyota Production System and a teamwork-based working environment to the United States.

www.shingoprize.com (accessed 5 October 2008). Shingo Prize for Excellence in Manufacturing.

www.toyota.com (accessed 5 October 2008). Toyota UK. News and information regarding Toyota.

REFERENCES

Bicheno, J. (1991) *Implementing Just-in-Time*, IFS.

Bicheno, J. (2004) *The New Lean Toolbox: Towards Fast, Flexible Flow*, PICSIE Books, Buckingham.

Hall, R.W. (1989) *Attaining Manufacturing Excellence*, IRWIN.

Harrison, A. (1992) *Just-in-time in Perspective*, Prentice Hall.

Hirano, H. (1989) *JIT Factory Revolution: A Pictorial Guide to Factory Design of the Future*, Productivity Press.

Ohno, T. (1988) *Toyota Production System: Beyond Large-Scale Production*, Productivity Press.

Russell, R.S. and **Taylor, B.W.** (2005) *Operations Management*, 5th edn, John Wiley & Sons, Inc.

Schniederjans, M.J. (1993) *Topics in Just-In-Time Management*, Allyn & Bacon.

Shingo, S. (1996) *Quick Changeover for Operators: The SMED System*, Productivity Press.

Womack, J.P. and **Jones, D.T.** (2005) Lean consumption. *Harvard Business Review*, March, 1–11.

Womack, J.P., Jones, D.T. and **Roos, D.** (2007) *The Machine that Changed the World*, Free Press.

CHAPTER

14

Enterprise Resource Planning

- **Introduction**
- **Enterprise resource planning (ERP) systems**
- **Resource planning**
- **Materials requirements planning**
- **Manufacturing resource planning (MRP II)**
- **Distribution requirements planning (DRP)**

LEARNING OBJECTIVES

- Understand the concept of enterprise resource planning (ERP)

- Describe the elements in resource planning

- Understand the concept of materials requirements planning (MRP)

- Describe the components of MRP

- Understand the concept of manufacturing resource planning (MRP II)

- Understand the concept of distribution requirements planning (DRP)

INTRODUCTION

This chapter covers the use of information systems that provide assistance to the operations manager in resource-planning activities. Enterprise resource planning (ERP) systems provide integration of software applications in different functional areas and provide links to external customers and suppliers in the supply chain. The elements of resource planning are then outlined before the use of MRP, manufacturing resource planning (MRP II) and distribution requirements planning (DRP) systems are discussed. Materials requirements planning systems are used to determine the timing and quantity of material requirements. Materials requirements planning aims to ensure that just the right quantity of each item is held at the right time in order to meet the needs of the production schedule taking into account ordering and manufacturing lead times. Manufacturing resource planning (MRP II) systems are a development of MRP and connect the system to other functional areas such as marketing and finance. Distribution requirements planning (DRP) widens the traditional acquisition, handling and production functions of MRP across the supply chain so that another form of dependent demand can be considered between the producer of goods, the regional distribution centre, the local distribution outlets or retailers and the customer.

ENTERPRISE RESOURCE PLANNING (ERP) SYSTEMS

Enterprise resource planning
These systems provide a single solution concerned with internal distribution and financial processes.

Enterprise resource planning systems (often termed enterprise systems) support the business processes of an organization across functional boundaries that exist within that organization. They usually use Internet technology to integrate information within the business and with external stakeholders such as customers, suppliers and partners. The main elements of an enterprise resource planning (ERP) system are concerned with internal production, distribution and financial processes but may also include elements such as customer relationship management (CRM), which is concerned with marketing and sales processes (Chapter 6), supply chain management (SCM) which is concerned with the flow of materials, information and customers through the supply chain (Chapter 15) and supplier relationship management (SRM), which is concerned with all activities involved with obtaining items from a supplier, which includes procurement, but also inbound logistics such as transportation, goods-in and warehousing before the item is used (Chapters 12–15). Other elements may include product lifecycle management (PLM), financial management and human capital management. Figure 14.1 shows a selection of enterprise software applications available from the SAP software vendor under the title of SAP Business Suite.

Enterprise resource planning systems are normally purchased as an off-the-shelf package, which is then tailored. Enterprise resource planning is particularly relevant in the integration of supply chains in enabling organizations in the supply chain to access one another's databases. ERP systems may access other members of the

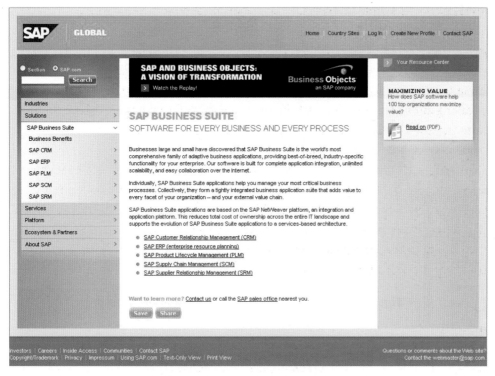

Figure 14.1: SAP Business Suite.
Source: www.sap.com (accessed 5 October 2008).

supply chain via electronic data interchange (EDI) facilities (Chapter 15) but usually use the Internet as a platform to allow secure access to information by members of the supply chain.

The main reason for implementing an ERP system is that it can replace a number of separate IT applications using incompatible data (sometimes known as 'information islands') in different functional parts of the company (Figure 14.2).

There are two main reasons for the existence of information islands. Firstly, some organizations have grown through the merger of firms, each with its own systems, which were incompatible with those of other firms. The second reason is that in many organizations the selection of software applications became devolved, with the end-users in individual departments making their own purchasing decisions. This often led to separate applications from different vendors in different departments, often with poor data transfer between applications. The goal of ERP is to achieve integration across the organization (Figure 14.3).

This integration of applications across the organization fits with the process view that organizations have used in improvement approaches such as business process management (Chapter 8). Using a process view, the organization is seen as a family of

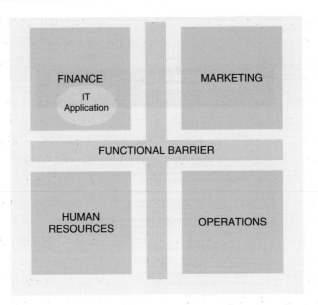

Figure 14.2: An IT Application within an Information Island.

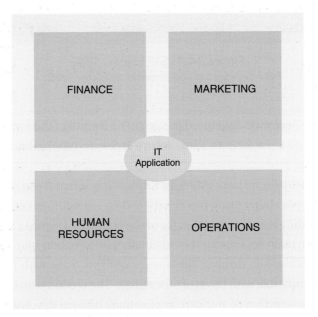

Figure 14.3: An IT Application Integrated across the Organization.

processes (such as order fulfilment), rather than as a set of departments. Enterprise resource planning is seen as a way of implementing a process view in the organization through the use of software.

Although many successful ERP implementations exist there are potential disadvantages to ERP systems, the most prominent of which is the potential high costs of installing a system which replaces all the previous departmental applications. The cost of an ERP system can be in the millions of euros and so it may not be a feasible option for many small and medium sized organizations. However, scaled-down versions of ERP software are appearing for small and medium sized enterprises. The move to an ERP system with a common database can also mean that working practices have to change. This has implications for the cost of training personnel in new ways of working and any loss of performance that may derive from the need to adapt to the ERP system, rather than use applications developed to departmental requirements.

In common with other investment decisions that operations managers have to make in terms of people and equipment, it is important that decisions are based on achieving strategic objectives. It is unlikely that one ERP software supplier will provide all the most current and relevant application software for a particular company. If alternative software is available that may provide a competitive advantage then a decision to forego the advantages of integration may have to be taken. It should also be considered that the main reason for ERP, in terms of achieving integration of systems, can usually be achieved at a price in terms of the time and cost of writing integration software. The major choice facing an organization is whether to renew IT systems in a number of 'big bangs' with the installation of detailed specified major systems or to develop systems that contain a mix of new and old (legacy) systems in a more incremental manner. Either of these choices may make sense and can incorporate the advantages of the other.

Enterprise resource planning systems may allow some customization (without requiring a whole new system) through the use of application programming interfaces (APIs), which allow programmers some access to the ERP software package. Mixed systems can provide compatibility by defining standards at the communications interface level. Thus the internal operation of software can be tailored to local needs but all software must work to a common interface. However, the choice made should be directed by the need to improve strategic performance, in regards to the performance objectives such as lower prices, higher quality, lower lead times that gives the organization a competitive advantage in the marketplace.

CASE STUDY 14.1

Small and Medium Enterprises: How Oracle and SAP are Moving Down 'The Tail'

Directors of small and mid-sized businesses can expect to be feted by two of the world's largest software vendors in coming months; if they have not already received their invitations. For enterprise software giants Oracle and SAP, the mid-sized and smaller company is not just the next sales opportunity. It is set to be the greatest driver of their growth. In June, SAP booked the

10 000th customer for its Business One package for smaller companies. It says sales to small and medium companies are contributing to its double-digit growth in turnover. Oracle has set itself tough targets for increasing sales to SMEs, executives say. Both software companies want to win custom for their enterprise resource planning, financial, supply-chain, customer relationship management and other business-critical software. They are hoping to draw smaller companies away from specialist local software vendors or away from business systems that might have been written in-house, in favour of highly functional software suites. To add appeal to smaller companies with specialist industry needs and limited in-house IT skills, both Oracle and SAP are investing heavily in their channel and partner networks, and in providing modules tailored for smaller companies that just want to install the software and go, without much customization.

Source: by Stephen Pritchard, FT.com, 18 October 2006. (Abridged version.) Reproduced with permission.

Question

What are the particular challenges for a small business in introducing an enterprise resource planning system?

RESOURCE PLANNING

Aggregate plan
This will specify aspects such as overall production rate, size of the workforce, the amount of subcontracting required to deliver the mix of products or service required to meet the demand profile.

Demand profile
This consists of the products and services required by the marketing plan, future customer orders and other demand factors such as the manufacture of items for spares.

This section outlines the steps in the resource-planning process that is at the core of any ERP system. This is an important activity in operations management as it ensures that appropriate resources are available to undertake the operations function. The elements involved in resource planning are shown in Figure 14.4.

The first step in resource planning is to generate an **aggregate plan** (also called the production plan) which identifies the resources required in the medium term (6–18 months). The **demand profile** consists of the products and services required by the marketing plan, future customer orders and other demand factors such as the manufacture of items for spares. The aggregate plan will specify aspects such as overall production rate, size of the workforce, the amount of subcontracting required to deliver the mix of products or service required to meet the demand profile. The plan will not normally detail the amount of resource necessary for a particular product or service but will provide figures aggregated at the level of product or service families. The plans may be updated on a monthly basis and can incorporate the concepts of lead capacity, lag capacity and the use of inventory to smooth demand (see the capacity timing section in Chapter 5). There are many different aggregate plans that can be formulated to produce a particular output, so each plan should be evaluated in terms of factors such as cost, customer service, operational effectiveness and effect on workforce morale.

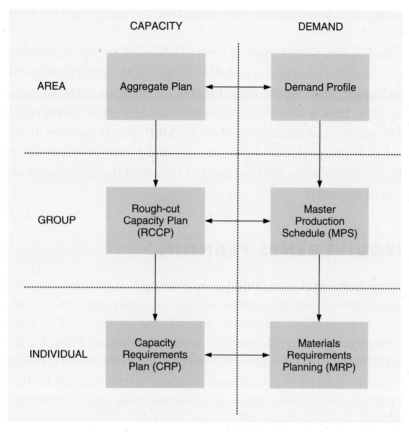

Figure 14.4: Elements in Resource Planning.

The next stage in the planning process is to develop the **master production schedule (MPS)**, which shows how many products or services are planned for each time period, based on the resources authorized in the aggregate plan. Thus the aggregate plan shows the number of products or services to be produced in a time period (say 500 a month) while the master production schedule specifies the actual products or services to be produced (say 200 of service A, 150 of service B and 150 of service C, making 500 in total). The MPS is based on information from the aggregate plan (based on the demand profile) and any other forms of demand that require capacity in the short term (for example new customer orders). The MPS is then used by the rough-cut capacity planning process to calculate rough estimates of the workload placed by the schedule on key resource constraints. Most operations will have bottleneck resources that constrain the overall production capacity. Checking at this level may save unnecessary detailed planning. If the capacity is not available to meet the MPS, either additional capacity must be secured or the MPS

Master production schedule
This shows how many products or services are planned for each time period, based on the resources authorized in the aggregate plan.

must be adjusted, although this may mean that the marketing plan may not be achieved.

As stated earlier, the aggregate plan takes information from the marketing plan to identify the resources required to deliver the products and services specified. The rough-cut capacity plan (RCCP) takes information from the MPS to evaluate the feasibility of the MPS. A third level of checking of capacity is the capacity requirements plan (CRP) which takes information from the MRP system (see next section for a discussion of MRP) to calculate workloads for critical work centres or workers. This allows the feasibility of the MRP system and the use of the critical work centres or workers to be evaluated.

Rough-cut capacity plan (RCCP)
This takes information from the MPS to evaluate the feasibility of the MPS.

Capacity requirements plan (CRP)
This takes information from the MRP system to calculate workloads for critical work centres or workers.

MATERIALS REQUIREMENTS PLANNING

Materials requirements planning
This is an information system used to calculate the requirements for component materials needed to produce end items.

Materials requirements planning (MRP) is an information system used to calculate the requirements for component materials needed to produce end items. These components have what is called dependent demand (the management of independent demand items is covered in Chapter 12). A dependent demand item has a demand that is relatively predictable because it is dependent on other factors. For example a fireplace mantel consists of two legs and one shelf. If daily demand for the mantel, derived from the production schedule, is 50 mantels, then a daily demand of 100 legs and 50 shelves can be predicted. Thus a dependent demand item can be classified as having a demand that can be calculated as the quantity of the item needed to produce a scheduled quantity of an assembly that uses that item. MRP systems manage dependent demand items by calculating the quantity needed and the timing required (taking into account purchasing and manufacturing lead times) of each item. The components of an MRP system that use and process this information are shown in Figure 14.5 and each component of the MRP system is now described.

Master Production Schedule (MPS)

Master production schedule
This provides a plan for the quantity and timing of when orders are required.

An ideal master production schedule (MPS) is one which most efficiently uses the organization's capacity while being able to meet customer due dates. The master schedule provides a plan for the quantity and timing of when orders are required. The MRP system will use this information and, taking into account delivery, production and supply lead times, will indicate when materials are needed to achieve the master schedule. The MPS will usually show plans based on time 'buckets' based on, for example, a day or a week. The length of the time bucket will generally be longer (for instance a month) for planning purposes and become shorter closer to the present time for detailed production planning tasks.

The MPS will usually contain a mix of both plans for customer ordered items and plans to produce to forecast sales. The forecast is a best estimate of what future

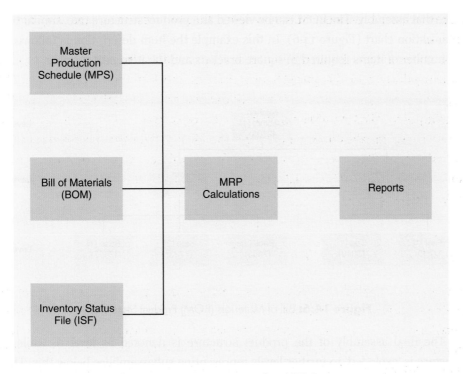

Figure 14.5: Components of an MRP System.

demand will be, which may be derived from past sales and contact with the customer. These forecasts should be replaced by firm orders as the expected order date approaches. If actual orders exceed the forecast then either the order will be delivered to the customer late or extra capacity must be obtained (for example, overtime, subcontracting) to meet the customer delivery date.

The mix of forecast and firm orders that a business can work to depends on the nature of the business. A resource-to-order company (such as a construction firm) will only allocate resources and materials to a firm order. Purchase-to-order organizations will not order materials until a firm order is made but will have labour and equipment permanently available. A make-to-stock business, however, will work mainly to forecast demand. Most operations will actually operate with different P:D ratios (Chapter 11) for different product or service types. The mix between firm orders and forecast demand may also vary over time for a certain business. For example seasonal effects may increase the number of firm orders taken in certain time periods.

Bill of Materials (BOM)

The bill of materials (BOM) identifies all the components required to produce a scheduled quantity of an assembly and the structure of how these components fit together to

Bill of materials (BOM)
This identifies all the components required to produce a scheduled quantity of an assembly and the structure of how these components fit together to make that assembly.

make that assembly. The BOM can be viewed as a product structure tree, similar to an organization chart (Figure 14.6). In this example the item description is followed by the number of items required in square brackets and the item part number.

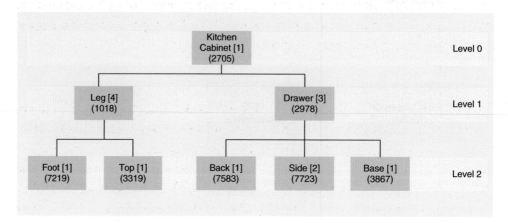

Figure 14.6: Bill of Materials (BOM) Product Structure.

The final assembly of the product structure is denoted as level 0, while the structure is 'exploded' to further levels representing subassemblies below this. These subassemblies are then broken down into further levels until the individual order components are reached. Individual order components can either be a single component item or subassemblies purchased from suppliers and thus treated as a single component. The tree structure shown in Figure 14.6 is useful to show the relationships among components but to present the structure in a format suitable for processing by the computerized MRP system an indented BOM is used (Table 14.1).

Level	Part no.	Quantity	Description
0	2705	1	Kitchen cabinet
1	1018	4	Leg
1	2978	3	Drawer
2	7219	1	Foot
2	3319	1	Top
2	7583	1	Back
2	7723	2	Side
2	3867	1	Base

Table 14.1: Indented Bill of Materials.

The MRP system holds information on the number required of any item in the structure and the 'parent' item of which it is a component. Usually the product structure is stored in a series of single-level bills of materials, each of which holds a component part number and a list of the part numbers and quantities of the next lower level. The computer will move through all component BOMs in the product structure to derive a total number of components required for the product. Note the same component may appear in different parts of the product structure if it is used more than once. What is needed is the total number required for each component to make the final assembly. The accuracy of the BOM is obviously vital in generating the correct schedule of parts at the right time.

Inventory Status File (ISF)

The BOM indicates the quantity of components needed from the product structure but this will not be directly translated into demand for components because it is likely that some of the components will be currently held in inventory. The inventory status file provides information on the identification and quantity of items in stock. The MRP system will determine if a sufficient quantity of an item is in stock or whether an order must be placed. The inventory status file will also contain the lead time, or time between order and availability, for each component.

> **Inventory status file**
> This provides information on the identification and quantity of items in stock.

As with the BOM, the accuracy of the inventory status file is vital and some organizations use perpetual physical inventory checking (PPI) to ensure that inventory records are accurate. This means a continuous check of inventory records against actual stock, instead of the traditional year end checks for accounting purposes.

Materials Requirements Planning Calculations

The time-phased inventory status record can be used to show the inventory data requirements for each stock item and to follow the calculations necessary by the MRP programme. A simplified status record is shown in Table 14.2.

Item: subassembly 1				Week			
	0	1	2	3	4	5	
Gross requirements		100	0	200	0	30	
Scheduled receipts				200			
Projected on hand	100	0	0	0	0	–30	

Table 14.2: Time-Phased Inventory Record

In this case weekly time buckets have been used, which is usual for short-term plans. Longer time buckets may be used for long-term planning purposes. The definition of each row is given below:

- *Gross requirements.* This row simply states the estimated requirements, in this case per week, for the item described. It is assumed that requirements occur during the time bucket (week) so that the scheduled receipts at the beginning of the week will cover them.

- *Scheduled receipts.* This row indicates when the item becomes available for use, from a previously released order. It is assumed that the receipt of the item occurs at the start of the time bucket period.
- *Projected on hand.* Numbers in this row show the number of units to be available at the end of each time bucket based on the balance of requirements and receipts. The formula for projected on hand is:

projected on hand = inventory on hand + scheduled receipts − gross requirements.

To account for a negative projected on hand, the time-phased inventory status record is extended as in Table 14.3.

Item: subassembly 1			Week			
	0	1	2	3	4	5
Gross requirements		100	0	200	0	30
Scheduled receipts				200		
Projected on hand	100	0	0	0	0	− 30
Net requirements						30
Planned order release				30		

Table 14.3: Inventory Status File Showing Net Requirements.

- *Net requirements* If the projected on hand is negative it is called a net requirement and means there will not be enough of this component to produce the quantities required to meet the master production schedule. Thus when a negative projected on hand is shown this will increase the net requirements row by a positive amount equal to the negative on hand.
- *Planned order release* (POR). The POR row indicates when an order should be released to ensure that the projected-on-hand figure does not become negative (that there are enough items to satisfy the MPS). The POR time must take into consideration the lead time between placing the order and the component becoming available (in the case of Figure 14.5 the lead time is two weeks). Thus the planned order release is offset by the required time amount to ensure enough items are available to cover net requirements and sometimes to also cover net requirements in future time buckets. It is important that the MRP programme works through all the levels of the assembly before calculating the net requirement for a time bucket as the same item may be needed at different levels of the same assembly or in different assemblies.

WORKED EXAMPLE 14.1

A dentist has scheduled appointments for the surgery over the next four weeks.

	Week			
	1	2	3	4
Appointments scheduled	30	60	55	60

Surgical gloves are ordered 100 pairs at a time and the ordering lead time is two weeks. There are 75 pairs of gloves in inventory at the start of week 1 with another 100 pairs expected to arrive during that week. Use MRP to schedule planned order releases for the gloves.

Item: gloves		Week			
	0	1	2	3	4
Gross requirements		30	80	75	60
Scheduled receipts		100		100	
Projected on hand	75	145	65	90	30
Net requirements					
Planned order release		100			

Thus there is a need for an order release in week 1 to ensure there is sufficient stock in week 3.

Materials Requirements Planning Reports

A number of reports can be generated by the MRP programme, which include information on the quantity of each item to order in the current and future time period, indication of which due dates cannot be met and showing when they can be met and showing changes to quantities of currently ordered items. The system can also show the results of simulation of scenarios for planning purposes. For instance by entering a customer order to the master schedule the effect of this extra work on overall customer due-date performance can be examined. If capacity restrictions mean that the order cannot be completed by the required due date, a new due date can be suggested.

Implementation of MRP

The use of MRP can reduce inventory by providing information on the actual inventory required for parent items (rather than stocking enough components for estimated parent demand). It can also help to prioritize orders to ensure delivery due dates are met, provide information on resource (labour and equipment) requirements for planning purposes and provide financial information on projected inventory expenditure. It is most useful in complex scheduling situations when the number of levels of subassemblies and components is high.

However, there are a number of limitations of MRP. For instance, when using MRP it is not always possible to assess the feasibility of meeting the due date quoted to a customer. Repeated changes to order due dates will entail new plans generated from the MRP system, which could lead to ever-changing schedules. The need to manufacture in batches negates the advantage of only scheduling inventory when needed. If batches are used extensively the component batch size will be a major factor in manufacturing lead time. If insufficient capacity is available, it is necessary to adjust planned order dates or make available additional resources. The knock-on effect may not be clear until the MRP schedule is regenerated. This may lead to a lengthy process of trying to find a feasible schedule. The MRP system has limited ability to assess the robustness of the schedule to random events (for example, machine breakdown). Changes to the inputs to the MRP system may be so rapid (customer needs change, design changes and so forth) that the planning function of MRP may be extremely limited. Many of the problems of MRP revolve around the problem of estimating capacity at various time frames. The aggregate plan, rough-cut capacity plan and the capacity requirements plan discussed earlier help with this.

MANUFACTURING RESOURCE PLANNING (MRP II)

Manufacturing resource planning (MRP II)
This extends the idea of MRP to other areas in the firm such as marketing and finance.

Manufacturing resource planning (MRP II) extends the idea of MRP to other areas in the firm such as marketing and finance (Wight, 1984). Thus central databases hold information on product structure (the BOM file), which can be updated due to design changes by engineering for example. By incorporating financial elements into item details, inventory cost information can be used by finance departments. At a wider level information provided by the MRP II system from simulations of business plans can be used to estimate plant investment needs and workforce requirements. This information can then be used to coordinate efforts across departments including marketing, finance, engineering and manufacturing.

Although MRP II overcame many of the problems of MRP systems, there are still problems with MRP II implementations. A major problem remains the issue of ensuring the accuracy of information such as inventory records and bills of materials to ensure a usable system. Some MRP II systems are so complex they often require installation by external agencies who may not understand the business needs of the company. Companies were also faced with expensive modifications to systems that did not provide all the functionality required for the business. The MRP systems are based around meeting performance targets in terms of meeting customer due dates. However, conflicting objectives, such as financial targets, may override these, so undermining the planning process defined by the MRP implementation.

DISTRIBUTION REQUIREMENTS PLANNING (DRP)

Traditionally, MRP is associated with managing dependent demand items which form an assembly which has as independent demand (the demand is not dependent on other items). However, if the concept of MRP is widened from the traditional acquisition, handling and production functions across the supply chain to the customer then another form of dependent demand can be considered between the producer of goods, the regional distribution centre, the local distribution outlets or retailers and the customer. Distribution requirements planning (DRP) manages these linkages between all these elements on the supply chain beginning with an analysis of demand at each customer service location. These demands are aggregated across distribution centres to form a gross requirement which is fed into the master production schedule. Independent demand items are incorporated into the MRP logic by having a safety stock level below which a replenishment order is triggered. The order amount is determined by a lot sizing calculation. This method is called time-phased order point.

> **Distribution requirements planning (DRP)** This manages linkages between elements of the supply chain beginning with an analysis of demand at each customer service location.

SUMMARY

- ERP provides an integrated solution to resource planning across the supply chain and across business functions such as production, distribution, sales, finance and human resources management.

- Resource planning involves developing an MPS, which is derived from the medium-term aggregate plan of resource requirements and the demand profile. The feasibility of the MPS is checked by the RCCP and the CRP.

- Materials requirements planning (MRP) is a computer software package that provides resource planning facilities. It is used to calculate demand for component materials needed to produce end items.

- Materials requirements planning calculations are based on how many products or services are planned, held in the MPS, the product structures, held in the BOM, and current inventory levels, held in the ISF.

- Manufacturing resource planning extends the concept of MRP to other areas in the organization such as marketing and finance to form an integrated business system.

- Distribution requirements planning extends the concept of MRP across the supply chain to producers and distributors of goods.

CASE STUDY   14.2

The Challenge of Changing Everything at Once

For Kolok, a South African distributor of printer consumables, such as ink cartridges and toner, meeting demand meant making changes. It moved premises, more than doubling warehouse space, added additional shifts and installed new warehouse and enterprise resource planning systems – all at the same time.

In southern Africa – Kolok's main market is South Africa but it also exports to neighbouring countries including Namibia and Botswana – customers expect quick delivery. Kolok, part of the Bidvest group, sells to retailers and directly to larger businesses. Neither set of customers wants to hold large stocks of supplies and many simply cannot afford to. 'The South African market is not like the US or Europe', says Allan Thompson, Kolok's managing director. 'We have persuaded our customers not to tie up their resources in stock,

but to use our resources. And corporate customers expect delivery within a couple of hours.'

The weakness of the rand and other southern African currencies against the dollar and euro adds to this pressure, but also puts pressure on margins at both Kolok and its customers. 'Inflation here is 14% and that affects customers' spending ability, even though IT markets are growing at 19%', says Mr Thompson. He adds that currency swings can quickly wipe out any margins. On the day Mr Thompson spoke to Digital Business, the rand fell 6% against the dollar. As a result, much of Kolok's recent investment has been aimed at improving stock control.

Within South Africa, Kolok's Johannesburg warehouse covers a territory that stretches 1200 km north and 1400 km south, to the

Cape. The company handles 4500 product lines from a 7000 m^2 warehouse with 8000 storage locations, some of which are 12 m high. It also has to manage a mix of long- and short-term products. Some stock turns over 16 times a year but other lines turn just twice a year. The existing infrastructure could not cope. 'In the past, we would take deliveries and it would take four to five days to unload the containers', admits Mr Thompson. 'Once we had put the stock away, we didn't know where it was. We had spreadsheets we were trying to update, which was impossible with the volumes we handle. We now have stock management on a 24-hour basis, instead of a nine hours a day basis, and our "pick and pack" operations run for 16 hours rather than eight. We are getting much better utilization of our assets.'

For the systems update, which took place alongside the relocation of the company's main Johannesburg warehouse, spending on software and IT infrastructure came to $3.5 million. This excluded costs such as training and management time. However, the changeover was as smooth as Kolok had hoped. The scale of the upgrade – bringing warehouse storage locations onstream; updating the warehouse system with software from Manhattan Associates; and installing a new ERP platform in the shape of Microsoft Dynamics AX – put the company under real strain. Some staff, used to the previous DOS-based systems, had never operated a computer with a mouse before.

Integrating the ERP and warehouse systems proved harder than the company, and its suppliers, had expected. Service standards fell and Mr Thompson says these are only now returning to a level he considers acceptable. 'I would not update both the ERP and warehouse management systems at the same time again, but we had no option', he explains. 'For a year, we could not find stock, and we had to find stock to sell it. We had a short period from inception to the go-live date to have all the software tested, so we could not do the ERP today and the warehouse tomorrow. We would have been totally in the dark.'

Integration was further hampered by the difficulty of taking staff away from the job for training. And the security situation and poor public transport in South Africa do not allow staff to stay late for training courses. But the systems have now been integrated, at least for larger customers. 'The big customers are now seeing the benefit, but for me, it's as important to serve the small and mid-sized companies who might grow into large ones', Mr Thompson says.

The results for the business overall have justified the investment. Volumes handled by Kolok are up 27% on February 2007, and capacity in the warehouse operations has doubled. 'We are more efficient, and have more control of our assets, both mechanical equipment and human resources. Now, we can see where the pressure points are and where resources are needed. Previously, we had to go on gut feeling.' An order can now be ready for customer collection or delivery 15 minutes after it reaches the warehouse.

Once the integration problems have been resolved, Mr Thompson expects to realize a full return on investment in the IT side of the project within 18 months, primarily through better visibility of stock levels. 'We need to move stock as quickly as possible', he says. 'If it is a

Monday, and we get 14 containers, we want to have none left by Friday.'

Source: by Stephen Pritchard, The Financial Times Limited 2008, 2 April 2008. Reproduced with permission.

Questions

1. What are the main advantages of the ERP system described in the case study?

2. Can you identify any risks involved with an organization implementing ERP?

EXERCISES

1. Discuss the advantages and disadvantages of implementing an ERP system.

2. Discuss the use of ERP software to replace software packages used in single areas of the organization, such as operations, marketing and accounting.

3. Identify and explain the role of the main components of an MRP system.

4. A company makes a product with a product code S40. Each S40 consists of two subassemblies A10 and B5. Subassembly A10 consists of part 1765 (two required) and part 1867 (one required). Part 1867 is in turn made from part 8644 (one required) and part 2888 (five required). Subassembly B5 consists of part 2887 (two required) and part 2888 (four required).

   a) Draw a tree diagram showing the product structure of product S40.
   b) Show an indented bill of materials for product S40.

5. A company has the following master schedule for its most popular dining table.

Week					
1	2	3	4	5	6
400	300	450	300	450	400

Each table has four legs which have a production lead time of two weeks. 3500 legs are available projected on-hand inventory. An order for 2000 legs has already been released and is scheduled to arrive in week 2. The legs may be produced in any quantity. Use MRP to schedule planned order releases.

6. What are the main factors in the successful implementation of a Materials Requirement Planning system?

7. Evaluate the advantages and disadvantages of the MRP approach to production planning.

8. An electrical retailer operates two regional warehouses both of which are supplied from a central distribution centre. Delivery time from the distribution centre to the warehouses is one week. A particular model of dishwasher has a production lead time to the distribution centre of two weeks. It is shipped in standard quantities of fifty units. Use DRP to determine planned order releases for each warehouse and for the distribution centre using the following data.

Warehouse 1

Week	0	1	2	3	4
Gross requirements		30	30	40	20
Scheduled receipts					
Projected on hand	10				

Warehouse 2

Week	0	1	2	3	4
Gross requirements		20	30	30	30
Scheduled receipts					
Projected on hand	40				

WEB EXERCISE

Investigate the functions of a commercial ERP system at http://www.sap.com/solutions/business-suite/erp/featuresfunctions/index.epx (accessed 5 October 2008).

● FURTHER READING

Bocij, P., **Greasley, A.** and **Hickie, S.** (2008) *Business Information Systems: Technology, Development and Management,* 4th edn , Pearson Education Ltd.

● WEB LINKS

www.bpic.co.uk (accessed 5 October 2008). Portal for resources for MRP and ERP installations.

www.manufacturingtalk.com (accessed 5 October 2008). Portal for resources for manufacturing, including MRP and ERP.

ERP Vendors

www.infor.com/solutions/erp/ (accessed 5 October 2008). Infor ERP Solutions.

www.oracle.com/applications/jdedwards-enterprise-one.html (accessed 5 October 2008). Oracle's JD Edwards Enterprise One ERP software.

www.sap.com (accessed 5 October 2008). SAP Business Suite.

● REFERENCES

Wight, O. (1984) *Manufacturing Resource Planning: MRP II*, Oliver Wight Ltd.

CHAPTER
15

Supply Chain Management

- **Introduction**
- **Supply chain design**
- **Activities in the supply chain**

LEARNING OBJECTIVES

- Identify the elements of a supply chain management system

- Understand how demand fluctuations can occur in supply chains

- Describe the varying degrees of cooperation and integration in the supply chain

- Understand the role of procurement in the supply chain

- Describe an e-procurement system

- Discuss the area of physical distribution management in terms of material handling, warehousing, packaging and transportation.

INTRODUCTION

The **supply chain** consists of the series of activities that moves materials from suppliers, through operations to customers. Each product or service will have its own supply chain, which may involve many organizations in processing, transportation, warehousing and retail. The set of relationships between a firm and its suppliers and customers in the supply chain is termed the supply network (Chapter 5).

Supply chain
This consists of the series of activities that moves materials from suppliers, through operations to customers.

A representation of the structure of a supply chain is shown in Figure 15.1. Activities on the input side to the organization are termed 'upstream' or 'supply' side and are divided into tiers of suppliers. Upstream suppliers that supply the organization directly are termed 'first tier' and suppliers that supply first tier organizations are termed 'second tier' and so on. Examples of upstream suppliers are component and subassembly suppliers.

Activities on the output side are termed 'downstream' or 'demand' side and are divided into tiers of customers. Examples of downstream customers are wholesalers and retailers. There will be a separate supply chain for each product or service that an organization produces and this structure is sometimes referred to as the 'supply network' or 'supply web'.

Upstream suppliers
Suppliers that supply the organization with goods or services.

Downstream customers
Customers of the organization such as wholesalers and retailers.

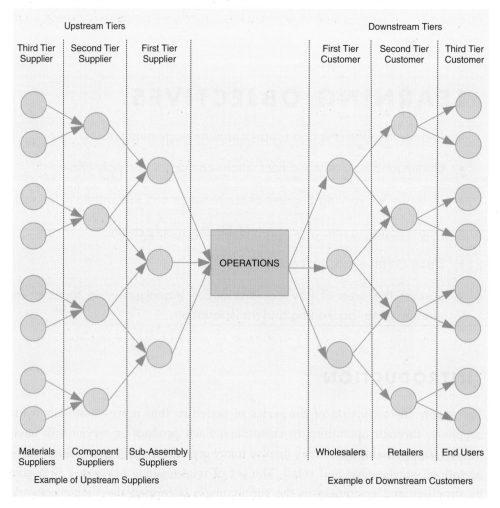

Figure 15.1: The Structure of a Supply Chain.

The terms used in the area of supply chain management are defined in a number of ways and so the most common terms are first defined as they will be used in this text (Figure 15.2). Supply chain management and logistics are terms used to refer to the management of the flow of materials through the entire supply chain. Sometimes logistics or business logistics refer to activities in the downstream portion of the chain. Inbound (or inward) logistics is used to describe the activity of moving material in from suppliers and outbound (or outward) logistics is used to describe the activity of moving materials out to customers. The movement of materials within the organization is termed materials management (materials management can also be used to refer to the management of upstream supply chain activities). Materials management activities are specifically addressed in this text in Chapters 12, 13 and 14. In this chapter, supply chain activities are presented around the areas of procurement, which is the operations interface with upstream activities, and physical distribution management, which deals with downstream activities such as warehousing and transportation.

Supply chain management
This is used to refer to the management of the flow of materials through the entire supply chain.

Inbound logistics
This is used to describe the activity of moving material in from suppliers.

Outbound logistics
This is used to describe the activity of moving materials out to customers.

Materials management
The movement of materials within the organization.

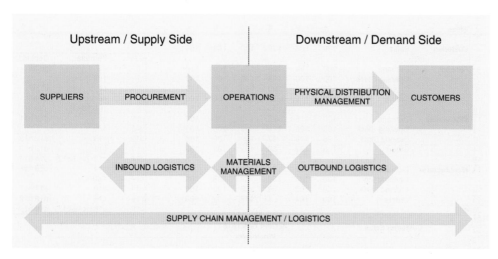

Figure 15.2: Terms used to Describe the Management of the Supply Chain.

SUPPLY CHAIN DESIGN

This section discusses the strategic issue of how the supply chain should be designed to optimize performance. Other strategic issues regarding supply chain design are facility location and long-term capacity planning, both covered in Chapter 5. One of the key issues in supply chain design is that organizations need to cooperate with one another in order to provide customer satisfaction. One of the reasons for that cooperation is to limit fluctuations in demand which occur in these networks and affect performance. The reasons behind those fluctuations will be discussed, before exploring the various ways in which the supply chain network can be configured to promote cooperation.

Fluctuations in the Supply Chain

The behaviour of supply chains that are subject to demand fluctuations has been described as the Forrester effect or bullwhip effect as described by Jay Forrester (1961). The effect occurs when there is a lack of synchronization in supply chain members, when even a slight change in consumer sales will ripple backwards in the form of magnified oscillations in demand upstream. To demonstrate this effect Figure 15.3 shows a spreadsheet of the relationship between four members of a supply chain, the customer, retailer, wholesaler and manufacturer. As can be seen a

Bullwhip effect
This effect occurs when there is a lack of synchronization in supply chain members. Even a slight change in consumer sales will ripple backwards in the form of magnified oscillations in demand upstream.

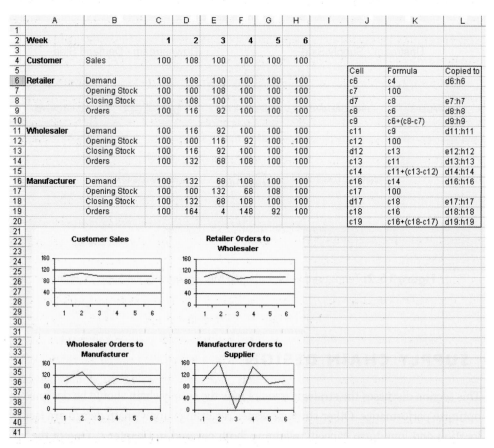

Figure 15.3: Spreadsheet Showing Effect of Varying Sales Demand on Supply Chain.

slight change in customer demand, rising from 100 units to 108 units in week 2, has an ever increasing effect on demand at each stage of the upstream demand. Note also that it takes until week 6 for the supply chain to revert to the stable pattern shown in week 1, despite customer demand reverting to 100 units from week 3 onwards.

The calculations used in the spreadsheet are as follows:

- demand = orders made by next tier in supply chain
- opening stock = closing stock from previous week
- closing stock = demand for that week
- orders = demand + (closing stock − opening stock).

The bullwhip effect occurs because each tier in the supply chain increases demand by the current amount but also assumes that demand is now at this new level, so increases demand to cover the next week too. Thus each member in the supply chain updates its demand forecast with every inventory review. Thus in week 2 an increase in customer demand of eight units is translated into an order from the retailer to the warehouse of 16 units (eight units to cover this week and eight units to cover next week's demand), who then orders 32 units from the manufacturer, who then orders 64 units from the supplier and so on. Thus each member in the supply chain is replenishing each level in the supply chain above it, rather than being linked directly to customer demand.

There are other factors that increase variability in the supply chain. These include a time lag between ordering materials and getting them delivered, leading to over-ordering in advance to ensure sufficient stock is available to meet customer demand. Also the use of order batching (when orders are not placed until they reach a prede-termined batch size) can cause a mismatch between demand and the order quantity. Price fluctuations such as price cuts and quantity discounts also lead to more demand variability in the supply chain as companies buy products before they need them.

In order to limit the bullwhip effect certain actions can be taken. The major aspect that can limit supply-chain variability is to share information amongst mem-bers of the supply chain. In particular it is useful for members to have access to the product demand to the final seller, so that all members in the chain are aware of the true customer demand. Information technology such as electronic point-of-sale (EPOS) systems can be used by retailers to collect customer demand information at cash registers which can be transmitted to warehouses and suppliers further down the supply chain. If information is available to all parts of the supply chain it will also help to reduce lead times between ordering and delivery by using a system of coordinated or synchronized material movements.

Using smaller batch sizes will also smooth the demand pattern. Often batch sizes are large because of the relative high cost of each order. Technologies such as e-procurement and electronic data interchange (EDI) can reduce the cost of placing an order and so help eliminate the need for large batch orders. Finally the use of a stable pricing policy can also help limit demand fluctuations.

Supply Chain Integration

Organizations in a supply chain can have varying degrees of cooperation and integration. In order of increasing ownership, the options are a market relationship, strategic partnerships and alliances, virtual organization and vertical integration (Figure 15.4).

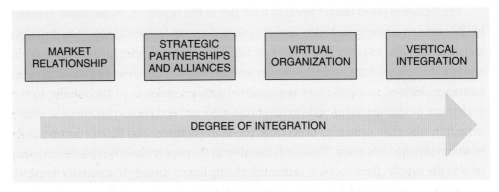

Figure 15.4: Supply Chain Relationships by Degree of Integration.

At the level of an individual product or service the amount of integration in the supply chain can be characterized as an analysis of the costs and risks in either making a component in-house or buying it from a supplier, termed a make-or-buy decision. However, this approach does not take into account what may be critical strategic issues involved in deciding what it should do itself and what can be done by others. At a strategic level supply chain integration decisions should be related to the way that the organization competes in the marketplace. For example if speed of delivery is an order winner then it may be necessary to make certain components in-house to ensure a fast and reliable supply.

One way of looking at supply-chain integration decisions is to use the technique of value-chain analysis (Porter and Millar, 1985), which views the decision in terms of which set of activities (for example, design, assembly) should be undertaken, rather than from the viewpoint of products or services. This approach allows consideration of the fact that the outsourcing of one product or service may have cost implications for other products and services, which are produced using the same resources. Thus the impact of economies of scope is taken into account, as well as economies of scale (see Chapter 5 for more information on economies of scale and economies of scope).

However, value-chain analysis aims to configure activities in order to minimize cost, given a firm's competitive strategy, and not specifically define where (inside or outside the firm) activities should occur. It is suggested that the degree of ownership should be directed by the capability or core competences (Chapter 2) that the organization requires to support the current and future strategy. This decision will need to be made within the constraints of the financial resources available to the organization in acquiring supply chain elements and the challenge of the coordination of activities within the supply chain.

The different degrees of integration in the supply chain are now discussed.

Market Relationships

Cooperation can simply mean the act of conducting a transaction between two organizations. Here each purchase is treated as a separate transaction and the market relationship between the buyer and seller lasts as long as this transaction takes. There can be some additional arrangements around this relationship such as the use of electronic data interchange (EDI) facilities to share information, combining orders in a single delivery to reduce transportation costs, agreements on packaging standards to improve materials handling and other factors. This approach does have a number of advantages in that it permits flexibility, in that suppliers can be changed or discontinued if demand drops or a supplier introduces a new product. Other advantages include the use of competition between suppliers to improve performance in aspects such as price, delivery and quality. However, there can be disadvantages in this arrangement in that either side can end the relationship at any time. A supplier withdrawal requires the often lengthy task of finding a new supplier. From a supplier perspective the withdrawal of a buyer may cause a sudden drop in demand on the operations facility leading to disruption and idle resources.

> **Market relationships**
> Here each purchase is treated as a separate transaction and the relationship between the buyer and seller lasts as long as this transaction takes.

CASE STUDY 15.1

Demands to Drop Prices Spark Building Resentment among the Subcontractors

Subcontractors are up in arms about housebuilders' demands for price reductions of between 2.5% and 10% as they seek to protect margins in the face of worsening conditions in the UK housing market. Taylor Wimpey, Persimmon, Barratt Developments and Bellway have all sent letters to suppliers requesting price cuts to maintain margins in the face of falling house prices and poor consumer sentiment. Industry watchers claim that squeezing suppliers will only bring short-term respite for the housebuilders and that they need to take a longer term view of costs in their supply chain. The Construction Federation has joined other contractor bodies to condemn the housebuilders, complaining about attempts to impose retrospective reductions on existing agreements.

Rupert Choat, construction specialist at CMS Cameron McKenna, said the housebuilders were unlikely to face legal problems demanding cuts for contracts not yet concluded but that they could face problems with contracts already agreed. 'Even if the other party expressly agrees to the price reduction, they might later rely upon the law of duress to set that agreement aside although it would not be easy to win such a case', he said. Subcontractors complained that the demands for them to absorb costs were symptomatic of 'outdated' business practices of the housebuilders.

Graham Wren, executive director of Balfour Beatty ground engineering, described the tactics used by the housebuilders as 'strong-arming'. 'This action is prehistoric and is completely counter to the environment in the wider construction industry that we are trying to work towards', he said. 'They are asking contractors to strip out the whole of their margins to maintain theirs.' He said he understood the need to cut costs but stressed that the housebuilders should work with their suppliers to find savings rather than make demands.

Pete Redfern, chief executive of Taylor Wimpey, dismissed the suggestion that housebuilder working practices were out of date and said that the letters were meant as the starting point for discussions rather than a blanket demand. 'Taylor Wimpey has good long-term relationships with its supplier base

and this is part of the natural process of reducing costs in the supply chain when general market conditions are tighter. We share the benefits when times are good and we want to talk about costs now that conditions are more difficult.'

Mr Wren said public statements that have followed the letters appeared to be backtracking on the tone of the original demands. Barratt Developments said: 'This is normal business practice in a tight market and we are duty bound to obtain the most competitive price possible. Kevin Cammack, housebuilding analyst at Kaupthing, dismissed the contractor objections and supported housebuilder attempts to cut costs. 'I would be horrified if the housebuilders were not trying to reduce labour rates in the current markets.' Jonathan Hook from PwC said housebuilders were right to look at costs but said they needed to change their working practices for a longer-term solution. 'Housebuilders' results have been flattered for years by the growth in house prices as they trade off land bought several years earlier', he said. 'I suspect many have had a very fragmented approach to the supply chain with a lot of inefficiency. But frankly it just hasn't been so important in a rising market. Renegotiating prices on work already completed has the most short-term impact, but seems at best out of step with the rest of the construction sector, which has made great strides to move towards a partnering culture.'

Source: by Tom Griggs, *Financial Times*, 29 January 2008. Reproduced with permission.

Question

Discuss the demand by housebuilders for a reduction in prices from their suppliers.

Strategic Partnerships and Alliances

When an organization and supplier are trading successfully they can decide to form a **strategic alliance or strategic partnership**. This involves a long-term relationship in which organizations work together and share information regarding aspects such as planning systems and development of products and processes. There may also be agreement on such aspects as product costs and product margins. The idea of a partnership or alliance is to combine the advantages of a marketplace relationship, which encourages flexibility and innovation, with the advantages of vertical integration, which allows close coordination and control of such aspects as quality.

> **Strategic partnerships and alliances**
> These involve long-term relationships in which organizations work together and share information regarding aspects such as planning systems and development of products and processes.

From a supplier viewpoint a long-term strategic partnership may give them the confidence to invest in resources and focus on a product line to serve a particular customer. Lambert *et al.* (1996) categorize the factors that make a successful partnership as:

- Drivers – these are compelling reasons for forming partnerships, such as cost reduction, better customer service or security.
- Facilitators – these are supportive corporate factors that encourage partnerships, such as compatibility of operations, similar management styles and common aims.
- Components – these are the joint activities and operations used to build and sustain a relationship, such as communication channels, joint planning, shared risk and rewards and investments.
- Some factors may mitigate against the formation of a partnership. For instance for low-value items the use of a partnership may not be worthwhile. Also a company may not want to share sensitive information or lose control of a particular product or process.

CASE STUDY 15.2

BASF and Aker Kvaerner

BASF and Aker Kvaerner benefit from an innovative alliance for maintaining one of the UK's largest chemical plants. BASF is the world's leading chemical company. It has production facilities in 39 countries and trades in 170 countries. Its strategy at its Seal Sands plant on Teesside in the UK has been to marry technological and commercial innovation through partnering. One of the ways it has done this is through a partnership with the maintenance arm of Aker Kvaerner, a provider of services to the engineering and construction sectors. Throughout the history of the Seal Sands plant the maintenance provision has been managed by BASF but outsourced to a number of different providers. Whilst the company names have changed, many of the employees had worked on the site for more than 20 years. Although the general belief for many years was that the service was world class, in reality an emphasis on cost control was stifling development and long-term improvements. BASF decided to shake things up by looking at partnering. Its first step was to define what it meant by a partnership – a long-term, mutually beneficial relationship where resources, knowledge, skills and values are shared with the purpose of enhancing each partner's competitive position.' When BASF settled on Aker Kvaerner to provide the whole maintenance service for the site, the main reason was the approach of its senior management team. BASF saw the team as having the ability to see beyond traditional approaches and to adopt the new ways of working enthusiastically. The core of the agreement is a performance-based contract whereby Aker Kvaerner is paid according to a set of Key Performance Indicators (KPIs). Where Aker Kvaerner achieves or exceeds performance, BASF's productivity and profitability are enhanced. BASF then shares its additional gains with Aker Kvaerner.

Source: DTI web site (now Department for Business, Enterprise and Regulatory Reform).

Question
What steps did BASF take to encourage a successful strategic partnership?

The Virtual Organization

The form of an organization's relationship within its supply chain is increasingly being affected by developments in e-Business systems. E-Business involves electronically mediated information exchanges, both within an organization and between organizations. Evans and Wurster (1997) describe how information can impact the value chain in three ways:

Virtual organization
An organization in which e-Business is used to outsource more and more supply chain activities to third parties so that the boundaries between and within organizations become blurred.

E-Business
This involves electronically mediated information exchanges, both within an organization and between organizations.

- Reach – a business can share information with more stakeholders or gain a larger audience at a relatively low cost
- Customization – information can be more readily tailored for sharing with a large number of partners.
- Dialogue – interaction between the parties is two-way rather than the traditional push of information. For example, it is possible for a supplier to anticipate a retailer's product requirements from examining their inventory forecast rather than awaiting a faxed order.

Thus the implication of e-Business developments is that it becomes easier to outsource more and more supply-chain activities to third parties and the boundaries between and within organizations become blurred. This development is known as virtualization and companies that follow this route are known as virtual organizations. The objective is that the absence of any rigid boundary or hierarchy within the organization should lead to a more responsive and flexible company with greater market orientation. Kraut *et al.* (1998) suggest that the features of a virtual organization are:

- processes transcend the boundaries of a single form and are not controlled by a single organizational hierarchy
- production processes are flexible with different parties involved at different times
- parties involved in the production of a single product are often geographically dispersed
- given this dispersion, coordination is heavily dependent on telecommunications and data networks.

E-Business can also be used to alter the supply chain structure by bypassing some of the tiers using a process known as **disintermediation**. Figure 15.5 shows a traditional demand side supply chain from operations through a wholesaler and retailer to the customer. Disintermediation is shown omitting both the wholesaler and retailer. This process is facilitated by the use of Web-based **e-Commerce** systems, which involve electronically mediated information exchanges between organizations. By omitting these stages in the supply chain, the producer is able to reduce their costs.

Disintermediation
Using e-Business to alter the supply chain structure by by-passing some of the tiers.

E-Commerce
This involves electronically mediated information exchanges between organizations.

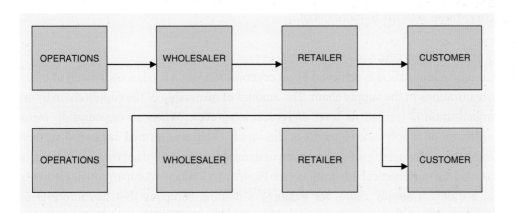

Figure 15.5: Disintermediation in the Supply Chain.

Perhaps a more significant phenomenon using e-Commerce systems is the use of **reintermediation** – the creation of new intermediaries between customers and suppliers in the supply chain. Figure 15.6 demonstrates the change in structure when an intermediary is placed between operations and suppliers in the supply chain.

Reintermediation
The creation of new intermediaries between customers and suppliers in the supply chain.

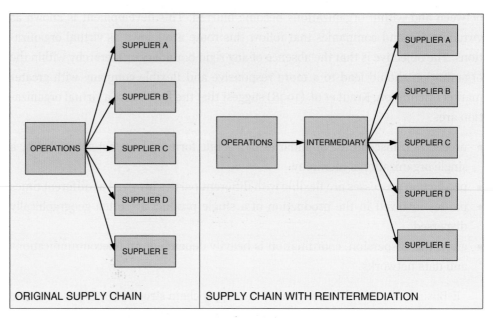

Figure 15.6: Reintermediation in the Supply Chain.

Reintermidiation removes the inefficiency of checking all the suppliers by placing an intermediary between purchaser and seller. This intermediary performs the price evaluation stage of fulfilment since its e-procurement or ERP system (Chapter 14) has links updated from the different suppliers. The next section on procurement will cover these systems in more detail.

Vertical Integration

Complete integration is achieved by an organization when it takes ownership of other organizations in the supply chain. The amount of ownership of the supply chain by an organization is termed its level of **vertical integration**. When an organization owns upstream or supply-side elements of the supply chain it is termed 'backward vertical integration'. Ownership of downstream or demand-side elements of the supply chain is termed 'forward vertical integration' (see Figure 15.7). When a company owns elements of a different supply chain, for example a holding company that has interests in organizations operating in various markets, the term used is 'horizontal integration'.

One potential advantage of vertical integration is the ability to secure a greater control of the competitive environment. Although a market-based economy is based on the idea of competition, many firms will attempt to reduce competition and thus provide an opportunity to increase profits. For example a manufacturer can use forward integration to buy retailers to limit the availability of competing product ranges. Backward integration, implemented by owning suppliers, can secure supplies

> **Vertical integration**
> The amount of ownership of the supply chain by an organization.

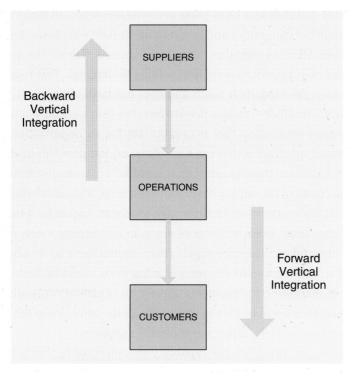

Figure 15.7: Types of Vertical Integration.

of components whose availability and price to competitors can be controlled. Another factor is that technological innovations in one part of the organization are available to other elements in the supply chain. Thus product and process improvements can be disseminated quickly. Also improved communication can help coordinate planning and control systems in the supply chain to improve delivery speed and dependability.

Another reason for vertical integration is to keep distinctive competence or capability in-house and not available to competitors. If an activity is seen as strategically important, or it uses specialized knowledge, or is in an area where the company has superior performance to competitors then it is likely that the company will want to keep that activity as part of its supply chain.

There are, however, a number of disadvantages of vertical integration and perhaps the major reason for outsourcing is the cost incurred in owning major elements of the supply chain. The resources required to own elements of the supply chain are resources that cannot be dedicated to the activities that represent the core tasks of the organization. This suggests that there is a risk, in that trying to do everything will mean that the company is not competitive against companies who are focusing their resources and skills on particular elements of the supply chain. For example the activity of warehousing may not be a core task for a manufacturer. By outsourcing this function the facilities of a third party are available who can share storage costs amongst a number of companies and invest in up-to-date warehouse technologies in order to increase efficiency. Another factor is the increased flexibility available when using a number of suppliers to meet fluctuations in demand. This means the organization only buys the capacity it needs and does not have idle capacity in-house.

In summary, a number of factors need to be taken into account when deciding the amount of vertical integration that is appropriate for an organization. Firstly, the amount of vertical integration that can feasibly be undertaken will be dependent on the financial resources of the organization. It is unlikely that smaller firms will be able to own large sections of the supply chain, but even large organizations may find this difficult. For example a car manufacturer may source an engine for a new car from a third party rather than invest millions of euros in developing a new design. Apart from cost, the time taken to acquire supply chain capabilities may be a barrier. It may also be felt that resources used for vertical integration could be better spent elsewhere (R&D or marketing for example). Finally an organization needs to consider that it is unlikely that it will be able to undertake all the activities in the supply chain well and it may leave certain aspects to specialist suppliers.

Even if the organization has the capability to undertake further activities in the supply chain it may not make sense to take ownership of them. The virtual organization concept using e-Business systems described earlier may allow efficient coordination of supply-chain activities without the need to own them. Disadvantages of nonownership of supply-chain elements include the potential high cost of switching partners, loss of intellectual property, which may provide the competitive advantage of the firm and the termination of partnerships if the strategic interests of the supply-chain partners diverge.

ACTIVITIES IN THE SUPPLY CHAIN

In this section supply-chain activities are presented around the areas of procurement, which is the operations interface with upstream activities, and physical distribution management, which deals with downstream activities such as warehousing and transportation.

Procurement

Procurement
The role of procurement is to acquire all the materials needed by an organization.

The role of **procurement** is to acquire all the materials needed by an organization in the form of purchases, rentals, contracts and other acquisition methods. The procurement process also includes activities such as selecting suppliers, approving orders and receiving goods from suppliers. The term 'purchasing' usually refers to the actual act of buying the raw materials, parts, equipment and all the other goods and services used in operations systems. However, the procurement process is often located in what is called the purchasing department.

Procurement is an important aspect of the operations function as the cost of materials can represent a substantial amount of the total cost of a product or service. There has recently been an enhanced focus on the procurement activity due to the increased use of process technology, both in terms of materials and information processing. In terms of materials processing the use of process technology such as flexible manufacturing systems (FMS) (Chapter 6) has meant a reduction in labour costs and thus a further increase in the relative cost of materials associated with a manufactured product. This means that the control of material costs becomes a major focus in the control of overall manufacturing costs for a product.

WORKED EXAMPLE 15.1
Procurement Costs

The simple example below demonstrates the importance of procurement costs on the profitability of the organization.

● SCENARIO 1

A company sells a product for €11, of which €6 is on raw materials and €4 on operations.
Profit $= 11 - (6 + 4) = €1$ per unit

● SCENARIO 2

The procurement function has negotiated a 10% discount on material costs.
Profit $= 11 - ((6 \times 0.9) + 4) = 11 - 9.4 = €1.6$ per unit

Thus a 10% drop in material costs has led to an increase in profit of 60%.

Another issue that has increased the importance of procurement is that the efficient use of automated systems requires a high quality and reliable source of materials to be available. This is also the case with the adoption of production planning systems such as JIT which require the delivery of materials of perfect quality, at the right time and the right quantity.

Steps in Procurement
Figure 15.8 outlines the main steps in the purchasing process and the relationship between operations, purchasing and suppliers in the process.

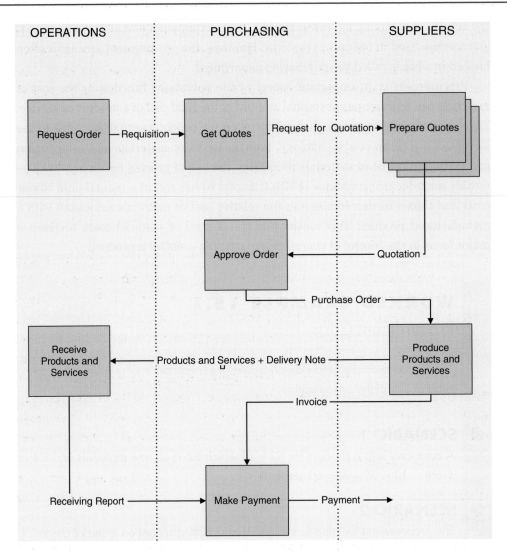

Figure 15.8: Steps in the Procurement Process.

The procurement process begins with the department requiring the goods or services issuing a purchase requisition, which authorizes the purchasing function to buy the goods or services. The requisition will usually include a description of what is to be purchased, the amount to be purchased and a requested date for delivery. Other information provided will be the account to which the purchase cost will be charged, the delivery address and the approval of an appropriate person for the transaction.

The purchasing department will receive the request and prepare a 'request for quotation' document to a suitable supplier or suppliers. The quotation will require a price, any other payment terms such as quantity discounts, a delivery date and any other conditions stipulated by the supplier. When a supplier has been chosen (see section 'choosing suppliers') then they are issued with a purchase order which represents a legal obligation by the buyer to pay for the items requested. The purchase order will usually include information specifying the item to be purchased, its price and delivery date.

The supplier will then produce the goods or service and deliver them to the relevant department and provide an invoice form requesting payment. When the organization is satisfied the good or services and the invoice details are satisfactory a payment will be issued to the supplier.

Choosing Suppliers

Before choosing a supplier, the organization must decide whether it is feasible and desirable to produce the good or service in-house. Buyers in purchasing departments, with assistance from operations, will regularly perform a make-or-buy analysis to determine the source of supply. Often goods can be sourced internally at a lower cost, with higher quality or faster delivery than from a supplier. On the other hand suppliers who focus on delivering a good or service can specialize their expertise and resources and thus provide better performance. Strategic issues may also need to be considered when contemplating the outsourcing of supplies. For instance internal skills required to offer a distinctive competence may be lost if certain activities are outsourced. It may also mean that distinctive competencies can be offered to competitors by the supplier.

If a decision is made to use an external supplier, the next decision relates to the choice of that supplier. Criteria for choosing suppliers for quotation and approval include the following:

- *Price* – as stated in the introduction, the cost of goods and services from suppliers is forming an increasingly large percentage of the cost of goods and services that are delivered to customers. Thus minimizing the price of purchased goods and services can provide a significant cost advantage to the organization.
- *Quality* – to be considered as a supplier, it is expected that a company will provide an assured level of quality of product or service. This is because poor quality goods and services can have a significant disruptive effect on the performance of the operations function. For example, resources may have to be deployed checking for quality before products can be used, poor quality products that get into the production system may be processed at expense before faults are found and poor quality goods and services that reach the customer will lead to returns and loss of goodwill.

- *Delivery* – in terms of delivery, suppliers who can deliver on time, every time, in other words show reliability, are required. The ability to deliver with a short lead time and respond quickly once an order has been placed, can also be an important aspect of performance.

The process of locating a supplier will depend on the nature of the good or service and its importance to the organization. If there are few suppliers capable of providing the service then they will most likely be well known to the organization. If there are a number of potential suppliers and the goods are important to the organization then a relatively lengthy process of searching for suppliers and the evaluation of quotations may take place.

Most organizations have a list of approved suppliers that they have used in the past, or that are otherwise known to be reliable. However, it is important to monitor suppliers in order to ensure that they continue to provide a satisfactory service. A system of supplier rating, or vendor rating is used to undertake this. One form of vendor rating is a checklist, which provides feedback to the supplier on their performance and suggestions for improvement. Another approach is to identify the important performance criteria required of the supplier, for example delivery reliability, product quality and price. The supplier can then be rated on each of these performance measures against historical performance and competitor performance.

When choosing suppliers, a decision is made whether to source each good or service from an individual supplier, termed single sourcing, or whether to use a number of suppliers, termed multisourcing. Although the trend toward alliances and partnerships between firms leads towards single sourcing, there are certain advantages to the multisourcing approach (Table 15.1).

Advantages of single sourcing	Advantages of multisourcing
Stronger relationship between parties, leading to greater commitment to success.	Reduces risk of loss of supply from single supplier.
Opportunities for savings due to economies of scale with larger order quantities.	Can be used to reduce price by encouraging competition between suppliers.
Facilitates better communication and reduces administration overhead.	Provides more flexibility in meeting changes in demand.
Easier to maintain confidential terms of business.	A range of suppliers can give access to a wider knowledge about goods and services.

Table 15.1: Advantages of Single Sourcing and Multisourcing.

CASE STUDY   15.3

Supplier Evaluation at EADS

On 8 March 2004, John Summers, head of the supply management strategy at EADS, a company based in Europe, got the assignment from the Procurement Directors Board (PDB) to make suggestions for improving the company's supplier evaluation system. The proposal was to be presented at the PDB meeting the following month.

EADS and the Aerospace Industry

EADS was one of the largest players in the aerospace industry. There were only a few other companies in the market and therefore the competition was characterized by oligopolistic structures.

EADS had a sales volume of approximately €30 billion while its biggest competitor sold aeroplanes and other products for the aerospace industry worth around €40 billion, followed by some other competitors with sales volumes of €10 billion to €20 billion. Due to its strong sales position in North America and Europe, but some weaknesses in Asia and South America, EADS was looking for new ways to improve its competitive position on the last-named continents.

EADS's main customers were airlines from all over the world, which were using their increasing purchasing power to get price reductions and flexible contracts.

Since EADS and its competitors had a degree of value added of only 25%–35%, the suppliers were an important source of competitive advantage and a potential leverage for cost reductions, revenue enhancements and risk reduction.

The Supply Situation in the Aerospace Industry

Due to long development cycles and extremely long product lives in the aerospace industry, the supplier situation in this industry was determined by some special requirements. The suppliers had to be able to guarantee the durability and quality of their products in a high-tech environment and under extreme conditions. EADS and its suppliers had to fulfil the needs of its global customers on the one hand and very demanding requirements from official bodies such as the Federal Aviation Administration (FAA) of the United States of America on the other hand. Therefore, every supplier for critical parts had to go through a tough and costly quality audit process and had to prove regularly that his products met the certification requirements.

Due to the outstanding product complexity, EADS and its competitors could not handle all requirements and necessary activities of aeroplane manufacturing on their own. Interdependent relationships occurred between EADS and its most important suppliers in terms of innovation and efficiency management. As a consequence, EADS had to buy most of its crucial manufacturing parts from single-source suppliers.

The Supply Organization of EADS

The final decision-making body for all supply management issues of EADS was the Procurement Directors Board. The PDB consisted of the procurement directors of the eight business units of EADS. On the second level, the corporate supply organization was divided into PDB subgroups that were responsible for different tasks such as the management of the specific lead-buyers within the organization, the e-procurement processes or the supply management strategy for which John Summers was responsible. On the third level, there were the different sourcing organizations of EADS's business units with about 1800 buyers.

The Supply Strategy of EADS

The supply vision of EADS was to achieve competitive advantage by winning, integrating and developing the world's best suppliers. Therefore, EADS had a supply strategy that aimed at getting the best suppliers possible in order to fulfil the following objectives:

- Procurement marketing: the supply activities of EADS needed to support its sales department because selling aeroplanes to certain countries required that the aeroplanes were produced in line with local content requirements.
- Risk and opportunity management: suppliers had to share the risks and opportunities of the aerospace industry with EADS.

The Supplier Evaluation System of EADS

When John Summer and his team analysed the supplier evaluation system at EADS they found five common criteria for evaluation:

- commercial performance (product cost, delivery cost, quality cost, etc.)
- logistics performance (reliability, delivery precision, etc.)

- customer support (geographical distribution of plants and service stations, etc.)
- quality performance (quality level, quality reliability, etc.)
- technical performance (product design and development, process development, etc.).

EADS had implemented a system that measured the different evaluation ratings for each supplier on the basis of the delivered commodities on business unit and corporate levels (see Figure 15.9). The supplier value was determined on the aggregated performance and future contracts were given to high scoring suppliers. However, the rating measures sometimes bore little relationship to the supply strategy requirements.

The Supplier Structure of EADS

In 2003, EADS had approximately 24 000 suppliers in total. However, it bought almost 65% of its supply volume from only about 250 suppliers. It sourced more than two-thirds of the products and services in Europe and only a fourth in North America. The supply volumes in Asia or South America were almost negligible. Therefore, the supply volume of EADS was even more unequally distributed than its sales volume.

John's Suggestions for Improvement

John knew that the current supplier evaluation system had worked smoothly for more than four years and was well implemented. However, he was not sure whether EADS was really measuring all important dimensions of the supplier value in order to achieve new competitive advantages in the relevant markets.

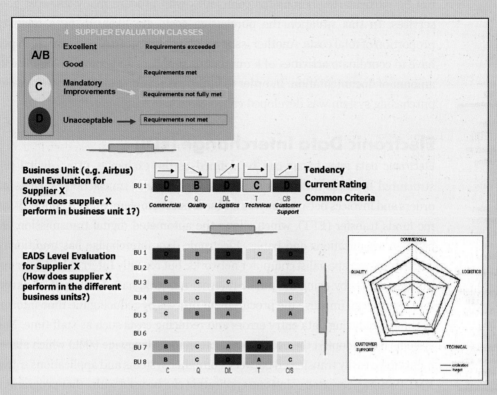

Figure 15.9: The Supplier Evaluation System at Eads.

This case was written by Roger Moser, Supply Management Institute SMI™, European Business School. It was prepared solely to provide material for class discussion and does not intend to illustrate either effective or ineffective handling of a managerial situation. The author may have disguised certain names and other identifying information to protect confidential data.

Source: Roger Moser, Supply Management Institute SMI, ebs European Business School.

Question

Identify the weaknesses in the EADS supplier evaluation system and suggest improvements to the system.

Procurement Information Systems

There are a number of steps in the procurement process, which has implications in terms of time, cost and reliability. One problem is the time lapse between a department requesting a good or service and receiving it. This is due to the time it takes to undertake all the steps involved, including supplier selection and the exchange of documentation. The cost involved in employing personnel to undertake these tasks can be particularly onerous for companies who procure many low-cost goods and services. In this situation the purchasing costs are likely to be a relatively high proportion of total costs. Another issue is the reliability of a process in which personnel have to coordinate activities of a number of suppliers and complete and track a large amount of documentation. In order to improve the procurement process an electronic purchasing system was developed called electronic data interchange (EDI).

Electronic Data Interchange (EDI)

Electronic data interchange can be defined as the exchange, using digital media, of structured business information, particularly for sales transactions such as purchase orders and invoices between buyers and sellers. A complementary technology is electronic funds transfer (EFT), which allows the automated digital transmission of money between organizations and banks. Electronic data interchange has traditionally been carried out over specialist computer networks, but recently Internet EDI systems, which can lower costs by using the public Internet network, have been used. Electronic data interchange can improve the procurement process by reducing the time information is in transit, reducing data entry errors and reducing costs such as staff time. Many EDI systems have adopted the use of extensible markup language (XML) which allows documents to be easily transferred between computer systems and applications software. An XML document created using one application can be used with other programs without

> **Electronic data interchange (EDI)**
> This can be defined as the exchange, using digital media, of structured business information, particularly for sales transactions such as purchase orders and invoices between buyers and sellers.

> **Extensible markup language (XML)**
> A data description language that allows documents to store any kind of information.

CASE STUDY 15.4

Chance & Hunt

Chance & Hunt has employed technology right across its business – including EDI – which has allowed an extensive degree of supply chain integration. The company, which markets and distributes chemicals, wanted to improve its telemetry system for managing its clients' inventories – with the aim of offering a better service and cutting costs. The idea was that automatic exchange of business information with clients could bring dramatic efficiency savings and help cement long-term relationships. The company's solution was to invest in the infrastructure to provide remote network access, online credit card purchasing – an industry first – and an integrated, EDI ordering system that

checks stock and links to the warehouse. The system constantly monitors client inventories checking stock levels against optimum levels. Should stocks fall below this level, the system delivers alerts to the client budget holders and relevant sales staff, before channelling orders back to Chance & Hunt's internal systems.

Source: DTI web site (now Department for Business, Enterprise and Regulatory Reform).

Question
What business benefits do you think would be gained from the use of EDI described in the case study?

the need to convert it or process it in any other way. XML lends itself to applications that include e-Commerce and e-procurement. The use of XML in e-procurement systems is likely to replace many EDI based applications over the coming years.

E-Procurement

E-procurement refers to the electronic integration and management of all procurement activities including purchase request, authorization, ordering, delivery and payment between purchaser and supplier. E-procurement can achieve significant savings and other benefits, which directly impact the customer.

- Faster purchase cycle times leading to a need for less material in inventory.
- Less staff time spent in searching and ordering products and reconciling deliveries with invoices.
- Savings also occur through automated validation of pre-approved spending budgets for individuals or departments, leading to fewer people processing each order, and in less time.
- A reduction in the cost of physical materials such as specially printed order forms and invoices.
- Enables greater flexibility in ordering goods from different suppliers according to best value.

E-procurement also tends to change the role of buyers in the purchasing department. By removing administrative tasks such as placing orders and reconciling deliveries and invoices with purchase orders, buyers can spend more time on value-adding activities. Such activities may include more time spent with key suppliers to improve product delivery and costs or analysis and control of purchasing behaviour.

E-procurement can be classified in terms of business and consumer models of Internet access. **Business-to-consumer (B2C)** transactions are between an organization and consumers, whilst **business-to-business (B2B)** is used to describe transactions between an organization and other organizations. Although the use of the Internet by consumers for purchases has received most media attention, the majority of commerce over the Internet is actually between businesses, using the B2B model and most e-procurement is undertaken in this way.

A risk of implementing an e-procurement system, typical of many e-Business implementations, is the difficulty in integrating information systems. Figure 15.10 shows how different types of information system cover different parts of the procurement cycle. The different types of systems are described below.

- *Stock control system* – this relates mainly to production-related procurement; the system highlights when reordering is required when the number in stock falls below reorder thresholds.

E-procurement
This refers to the electronic integration and management of all procurement activities including purchase request, authorization, ordering, delivery and payment between purchaser and supplier.

Business-to-consumer (B2C)
Transactions between an organization and consumers.

Business-to-business (B2B)
Transactions between an organization and other organizations.

- *CD- or Web-based catalogue* – paper catalogues have been replaced by electronic forms that make it quicker to find suppliers.
- *Email or database-based workflow systems* integrate the entry of the order by the originator, approval by manager and placement by buyer. The order is routed from one person to the next and will wait in their inbox for actioning. Such systems may be extended to accounting systems.
- *Order-entry on web site* – the buyer often has the opportunity to order directly on the supplier web site, but this will involve rekeying and there is no integration with systems for requisitioning or accounting.
- *Accounting systems* – networked accounting systems enable staff in the buying department to enter an order which can then be used by accounting staff to make payment when the invoice arrives.
- *Integrated e-procurement or ERP systems* – these aim to integrate all the facilities above and will also include integration with suppliers' systems.

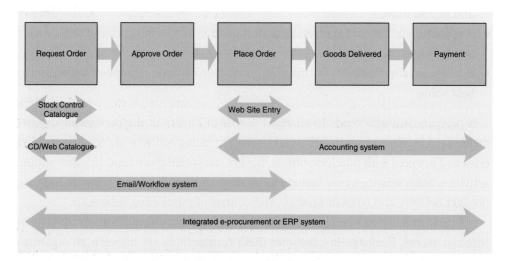

Figure 15.10: Use of Different Information Systems for Procurement.

Apart from the use of the appropriate technology the introduction of an information system should address change in terms of its implications for people and processes. The introduction of e-procurement will require people to change the way that they work in order to secure the benefits of the information system. It may also require changes to current supplier-customer relationships and both of these issues can lead to resistance and dissatisfaction. There is also a need to avoid replacing poor manual procurement processes with poor automated procurement processes. This may mean the use of a process-centred design effort, using techniques such as process mapping, as part of the e-procurement implementation. Another point to consider is that no matter how efficient the electronic e-procurement systems are, the success of the procurement process will still depend on the efficiency, derived from their operations capability, with which the suppliers in the supply chain can deliver the physical goods or services requested.

Perhaps the major barrier to the use of e-procurement is in the difficulty of linking systems with suppliers whose systems may be incompatible or nonexistent. It may be that small firms may find themselves increasingly excluded by buyers due to their lack of investment in the required information technology infrastructure. For organizations that are attempting to provide an integrated e-procurement or ERP implementation one of the main issues is gaining access to the price catalogues of suppliers. One approach is to house electronic catalogues from different suppliers inside the company and use a firewall for security. These catalogues can be updated by either an occasional link beyond the firewall or the delivery of a CD version from the supplier. An alternative approach is to 'punch out' through the firewall to access the catalogue either on a supplier's site or intermediary site such as a B2B market-place. A B2B marketplace provides a web site that connects buyers and sellers to enable trading in a private and secure environment.

Physical Distribution Management

Physical distribution management, sometimes called business logistics, refers to the movement of materials from the operation to the customer. Four main areas of physical distribution management are materials handling, warehousing, packaging and transportation.

> **Physical distribution management**
> This refers to the movement of materials from the operation to the customer.

Materials Handling

Materials handling relates to the movement of materials, either within warehouses or between storage area and transportation links. The aim of materials handling is to move materials as efficiently as possible. The type of materials handling systems available can be categorized as manual, mechanized and automated. A manual handling system uses people to move material. This provides a flexible system, but is only feasible when materials are movable using people with little assistance. An example is a supermarket where trolleys are used to assist with movement, but the presence of customers and the nature of the items make the use of mechanization or automation not feasible. Mechanized warehouses use equipment such as forklift trucks, cranes and conveyor systems to provide a more efficient handling system, which can also handle items too heavy for people. Automated warehouses use technology such as automated guided vehicles (AGVs) and loading/unloading machines to process high volumes of material efficiently. More information on process technologies is provided in Chapter 6.

> **Materials handling**
> This relates to the movement of materials, either within warehouses or between storage areas and transportation links.

Warehousing

Warehousing
The use of locations to hold a stock of incoming raw materials used in production or hold finished goods ready for distribution to customers. Warehousing is also used to store work-in-progress items or spares for equipment.

When producing a tangible item it is possible to provide a buffer between supply and demand by holding a stock of the item – **warehousing**. Many organizations have specific locations to hold this stock, termed a warehouse or distribution centre. Most warehouses are used to hold a stock of incoming raw materials used in production or hold finished goods ready for distribution to customers. Warehouses are also used to store work-in-progress items or spares for equipment.

Because of the need to process goods and services through the supply chain as quickly as possible to serve customer demand, warehouses are not simply seen as long-term storage areas for goods, but provide a useful staging post for activities such as sorting, consolidating and packing goods for distribution along the supply chain. Consolidation occurs by merging products from multiple suppliers over time, for transportation in a single load to the operations site. Finished goods sourced from a number of suppliers may also be grouped together for delivery to a customer in order to reduce the number of communication and transportation links between suppliers and customers. The opposite of consolidation is break-bulk where a supplier sends all the demand for a particular geographical area to a local warehouse. The warehouse then processes the goods and delivers the separate orders to the customers.

One of the major issues in warehouse management is the level of decentralization and thus the number and size of the warehouses required in inventory distribution. Decentralized facilities offer a service closer to the customer and thus should provide a better service level in terms of knowledge of customer needs and speed of service. Centralization, however, offers the potential for less handling of goods between service points, less control costs and less overall inventory levels due to lower overall buffer levels required. The overall demand pattern for a centralized facility will be an aggregation of a number of variable demand patterns from customer outlets and so will be a smoother overall demand pattern thus requiring lower buffer stocks (see Figure 15.11). Thus there is a trade-off between the customer service levels or effectiveness offered by a decentralized system and the lower costs or efficiency offered by a centralized system. One way of combining the advantages of a centralized facility with a high level of customer service is to reduce the delivery lead time between the centralized distribution centre and the customer outlet. This can be accomplished by using the facility of electronic data interchange (EDI) or e-procurement systems discussed in the procurement section.

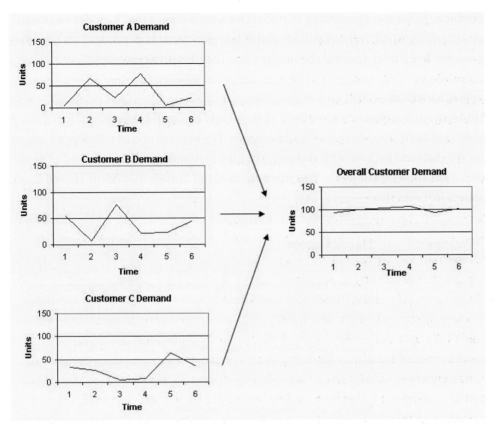

Figure 15.11: Aggregating Customer Demand in a Centralized Warehouse Facility.

The warehouse or distribution system can itself be outsourced and this will often be the only feasible option for small firms. The choice is between a single-user or private warehouse, which is owned or leased by the organization for its own use and a multiuser or public warehouse, which is run as an independent business. The choice of single-user or multiuser warehouse may be seen as a break-even analysis with a comparison of the lower fixed costs but higher operating costs of a multiuser warehouse, against the high fixed costs and lower operating cost of a single-user warehouse. However, the cost analysis should be put into a strategic context. For example, the warehouse and distribution system may enable a superior service to be offered to customers. It may also be seen as a barrier to entry to competitors due to the time and cost of setting up such a system.

Private or single-user warehouse
A warehouse owned or leased by the organization for its own use.

Public or multiuser warehouse
A warehouse run as an independent business.

Packaging

Packaging provides a number of functions including identifying the product, giving protection during transportation and storage, and making handling easier and providing information to customers. The emphasis put on each of these factors will depend on the nature of the product, with protection being a major factor for some products. In terms of packaging materials we have a choice that includes cardboard, plastic, glass, wood and metal. The choice between these is dependent on how they meet the functional needs of the product and their relative cost.

Transportation

Distribution is an important element of the supply chain and can account for as much as 20% of the total costs of goods and services. The amount of cost will depend largely on the distance between the company and its customers and the method of transportation chosen. There are five main methods of transportation to choose from, shown in Table 15.2.

Transport mode	Normal usage
Rail	Provides fast movement of bulky products, but total transportation time lengthened by the need to use alternative transport between train station nodes and destination point.
Road	Provides flexible point-to-point service for most products of any size. Most popular method of transportation but reliability of delivery time can be affected by traffic congestion.
Air Freight	All types of products can be moved long distances quickly. Most suited to lightweight products and overseas destinations. Requires handling facilities which slows overall transportation time.
Water	Can carry all types of products either inland on canal systems or by sea travel. Provides slow transportation, but relatively low cost and especially useful for carrying bulky items internationally.
Pipeline	Transportation of liquids and gases such as water, oil and gas. After high initial cost of laying pipeline provides a reliable transportation method with low operating costs.

Table 15.2: Transportation Methods.

SUMMARY

- A supply chain management system is made up of procurement, materials management and physical distribution management elements.

- Demand fluctuations occur in a supply chain when there is a lack of synchronization between supply chain members.

- Supply chain integration can range, in order of increasing integration, from a market relationship to a strategic partnership, to a virtual organization and to vertical integration. A market relationship permits flexibility but can be ended by either organization at any time. A strategic partnership or alliance involves a long-term relationship in which the organizations work together and share information. A virtual organization is where information technology is used to allow outsourcing of supply chain activities and the boundaries between and within organizations become blurred. Vertical integration is when an organization takes ownership of other organizations in the supply chain.

- The role of procurement is to acquire all the materials needed by an organization in the forms of purchases, rentals, contracts and other acquisition methods.

- E-procurement refers to the electronic integration and management of all procurement activities.

- Physical distribution management refers to the movement of materials from the operation to the customers. It covers the areas of materials handling, warehousing, packaging and transportation.

CASE STUDY 15.5

Supply Chain Practices of Three European Apparel Companies: Zara, H&M and Benetton

I. Zara

Zara, the flagship brand of the Spain-based Inditex Group, operated through 1058 stores located in 69 countries across the world as of March 2008. Zara pioneered the concept of customized retailing and was able to conceptualize the garment, develop it and deliver it to the stores within two to three weeks. The key to Zara's success was its vertically integrated supply chain where design, production, distribution and retailing were integrated.

Zara was founded by Amancio Ortega Gaona (Ortega), in La Coruña, Spain and the first store was opened in 1975. Between 1976 and 1984, Zara extended its presence to major Spanish cities. The first store outside Spain was opened in 1988 in Portugal. From then on, Zara expanded rapidly in international markets.

Design
Zara's design process began with spotting the trends across the world. The details of the trends in vogue were then passed on to the design and production centre at Zara's headquarters in Spain. Zara had a dedicated design team in Arteixo, A Coruña, in northern

Spain. Ideas for new designs or for modifications to be made in existing designs mainly came from Zara's stores. The store managers and sales staff updated the head office every day about the moving stock and provided inputs regarding the new lines, colours, styles, and fabrics that customers were demanding. Another source of inspiration for the new designs was the team of designers who travelled across the world looking for new designs and the emerging trends. Zara's employees kept scouting around at fashion shows, discotheques, universities, and watched movies and music videos to spot new trends.

The store managers across Zara's stores placed orders twice a week, on Wednesdays and Saturdays in southern Europe and Spain and on Tuesdays and Fridays in the other parts of the world. At the Zara headquarters, the store specialists collected the information gathered from different stores across the globe. Each of the store specialists was responsible for a group of stores. Most of the store specialists would have worked as store managers and possessed a deep knowledge about managing stores.

At the design and production centre, a team of 200 designers churned out about 60 styles each. The centre had three different units – one each for women's, men's, and children's clothing lines. The designers were encouraged to experiment, but within Zara's defined parameters. The store specialists provided the designers with an outline of the new styles, designs, and fabric as demanded by the stores. The procurement and production managers provided inputs regarding the capacity and manufacturing costs. The designers came out

with the design specifications and the technical brief. With all the teams working in tandem, the prototypes were ready within a few hours.

Production

Once the team came out with the final design, a prototype was made. It did not take much time as the fabric was already available with Zara. The teams decided on the sizes and the number of garments to be produced (Zara procured unprocessed and undyed fabric and coloured the product based on the need. Zara sourced undyed fabric from the Far East, Morocco and India). Fabric was then sent for cutting to Zara's own automated cutting facilities. Several layers of fabric, meant for garments of a particular design, were laid out on cutting tables, vacuum sealed, and cut by machines, based on a computer layout of the sample pieces. The layout was prepared so as to minimize wastage. The cut pieces were then barcoded and marked for sewing.

The pieces were distributed for sewing among 350 small workshops in Spain and northern Portugal (about 60% of Zara's total production was carried out in Portugal and Spain). These workshops, which were not owned by Zara, employed about 11 000 workers and were provided with a set of instructions on how to sew the garment. The garments were generally ready in around a week's time. After the stitched garments arrived at the production centres, they were checked twice for quality, pressed, tagged, wrapped in plastic bags and sent to the distribution centres.

Distribution

The distribution of garments was carried out at Zara's 500 000 m^2 distribution centre in

Arteixo. This centre was located centrally among 14 manufacturing plants in La Coruña. Zara had its own railway track of 211 km on which the goods moved to the distribution centre. In 2002, another distribution centre was opened at Zaragoza in Spain to complement the existing facility.

The merchandise was scanned by optical reading devices that sorted out more than 60 000 items every hour. The distribution centre had two levels and was fully automated. On one level folded apparel was packed into cardboard boxes. The boxes were dropped through a shaft according to their destination. On the lower level, garments – sorted based on their styles – were placed on hangers. There were two belt systems – one for folded and one for hung garments. The garments were then routed using automatic routing devices. All the garments were prepriced and the lots labelled according to their destination.

At the loading docks, fleets of trucks took the goods to their destinations. Twice a week, the garments were shipped out of the distribution centre. Non-European consignments were sent to the airport at Santiago di Compostela. For stores within Europe, the merchandise was sent on trucks. While the stores within Europe received the consignments within 24 to 36 hours, those located outside Europe received them within two days.

Once the trucks reached the stores, the pressed and labelled garments were put on display straight away. Zara was able to achieve an accuracy level of 98.9% in its shipments. A particular store received the items that its store manager had ordered and sometimes new items that were popular with stores at nearby locations. With new stock arriving twice a week, the stores always had something new to offer and the customers waited eagerly for the new arrivals. According to Zara, customers visited Zara's stores 17 times a year on an average, compared to the three to four times they visited Zara's competitors.

The display of clothes was given prominence in the stores. When the shipments arrived, there were codes on all the items which conveyed to the staff where exactly the items needed to be placed. In the stores, the clothes were organized by colour rather than type of garments. This was done in order to encourage customers to spend more time at the stores matching items.

Zara was very particular about the location of its stores. The stores were mostly located in prime locations across the world. For example, Zara outlets were located in 34th Street, Fifth Avenue, SoHo in New York, Regent Street in London and Champs Elysées in Paris. All of Zara's stores were uniform in outlay, including lighting, fixtures, window display and arrangement of garments. A typical store had a floor space of 1200 m^2 (See Figure 15.12 for an illustration of Zara's Supply Chain).

Most of the stores were company owned and in some markets, particularly in Asia, Zara went in for alliances and franchises. All the franchise operations were controlled by strict quality procedures laid out by Zara. It provided the franchise partners with extensive training on human resources and logistics. Even while entering into agreements with franchisees, Zara retained the right to open its own stores in

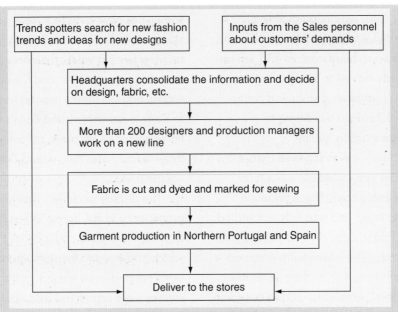

Figure 15.12: Zara's Supply Chain.
Adapted from www.fashionnet.org

the location and buy out franchised operations in case the franchise experienced any problems with running the stores.

Through its flexible supply chain Zara reaped several benefits. It was able to react swiftly to the emerging trends in the fashion industry. The company ensured that its stores were stocked with the products that the customers wanted. In contrast, other retailers took between eight and 12 months to forecast and arrive at a style and send it for production.

Producing a product in limited quantity had another advantage. If the style did not sell as expected, Zara did not lose much, as there was not much stock to be discounted. On an average, Zara sold only 18% of the clothes through discount sales twice a year, as against the industry average of 36% and constant markdowns. Analysts opined that Zara's main advantage was its ability to respond to demand shifts during the season. If any collection was not

doing well during the season, Zara could immediately realign its resources, whereas the other retailers had to resort to discounts and advertising to clear their stocks.

Defying conventional wisdom, Zara adopted practices that resulted in higher costs. These included three product lines, deliveries twice a week, using planes and trucks to transport its goods instead of cheaper alternatives like trains and ships, and shipping some of the garments on hangers, which occupied more space, thus increasing freight costs. However, these very practices helped Zara maintain a low inventory and higher profit margins. Analysts opined that Zara's supply chain did not minimize costs but worked towards maximizing revenues.

Analysts, however, cautioned Zara against aggressive expansion. They pointed out that the further Zara moved its operations from Spain the further away it would be from its centralized distribution system, which would lead to higher costs. Analysts warned that vertical integration, which was Zara's strength, could also turn out to be its weakness if it continued expanding to far-off locations in Asia and America. One of the disadvantages of vertical integration was the lack of economies of scale, where Zara was unable to reap the advantage of producing large quantities of products to sell them at competitive prices.

II. Hennes & Mauritz

Sweden based Hennes & Mauritz (H&M) was among the pioneers in fast fashion and, apart from introducing its own styles, it also scouted around the world for styles and fashion that could click among customers. The clothes from H&M were reasonably priced, stocks were replenished every day, and no item remained on the shelves for more than a month. The secret of H&M's success was a well-integrated supply chain where the clothes designed by the headquarters at Stockholm were made by more than 600 suppliers located in 22 countries across the world to be shipped to more than 1300 stores spread in 25 countries across the world.

H&M was founded by Erling Persson, a salesman from Västerås, Sweden in 1947 as Hennes. By 1967, Hennes had a presence in other Scandinavian countries, Norway and Denmark. In 1968, after the acquisition of Mauritz Widforss, Hennes became H&M. In 1976, a store was opened in the UK at Oxford Circus, London. By the end of the 1990s, H&M had become one of the top players in the apparel retail market in Europe. As of 2002, H&M's outlets were selling around 550 million items a year. By 2004, the number of stores had reached 1000.

Design

Initially, H&M sourced the products mostly from its agents in Asian countries and sold them through its stores. In the late 1980s, H&M began building a design team so that it could come out with products that met customers' tastes and requirements. Later, all of H&M's collections began to be planned and designed centrally by the company's purchase and design department in Sweden. The department had over 100 in-house designers, and cooperation from around 100 buyers and 50 pattern designers. While finalizing the designs, H&M essentially concentrated on three factors – fashion, quality, and price – and achieved a fine balance among the three. Themes, colours, fabrics, and designs were decided on the basis of customer demands. The designers had highly sophisticated design software and colour-matching tools at their disposal and used these to design new collections.

Each of H&M's concepts like Men, Women, Kids, Divided and Denim had its own team of designers, buyers, pattern makers, assistants and controllers who together produced the garments according to demand. The team of designers was required to constantly observe the trends in the fashion industry, street fashion, college fashion, visit exhibitions, flea markets, and watch films and attend events, travel, and keep an eye on television and the Internet. However, copying designs from fashion shows was not encouraged. The designers were required to have a good knowledge of the history of fashion and cyclical trends. They were required to come up with original designs and new concepts when needed.

Inputs from employees were also considered crucial for designing new garments and arriving at new trends. Feedback was obtained from the merchandise managers present in all countries where H&M had stores as they constantly interacted with the customers. They also reported on the new collections introduced by competitors.

Every year, H&M brought out two main collections, one during the spring and one during the autumn season. Within each season, several subcollections were released. Designing for each season started with a brainstorming session, involving all designers, buyers and pattern designers. They deliberated on the styles and designs that were successful the previous year and the designs that had failed to attract customers' attention. The design team then decided on the look for the year and the designers drew the sketches. The group of designers concentrated on designing clothes that were stylish but not too complicated. Not all the finished sketches received approval and most often, only half of the total sketches made it to the stores. They tried to arrive at a fine balance between clothes that were viable and those that presented the latest designs. Periodically H&M brought out collections in collaboration with renowned designers like Karl Lagerfeld, Stella McCartney, Viktor & Rolf and Roberto Cavalli.

Production

Initially, all the production activities of H&M took place in Sweden. In the 1960s, some of the production activities were shifted to other European countries and in the late 1970s to Far Eastern countries. As of 2006, H&M had 22 production offices, of which 10 were in Europe, 10 in the Far East, and one each in Central America and Africa. The buyers, who were part of the design process, were in contact with the production offices. The main responsibilities of the production office included identifying new suppliers, placing orders with the right suppliers, negotiating price, ensuring suppliers maintained quality, minimizing transport times and so forth. All the production offices had quality controllers who helped in checking the supplies in the factories and ensuring that they adhered to the company's quality standards. H&M did not own any factories or manufacturing units, and clothes were procured from more than 700 independent suppliers.

The buyers communicated to the production offices about the designs, number of garments required, material to be used and other specifications. The production offices browsed through the list of suppliers to decide on the ones who had the facilities to produce the required garments. The chosen suppliers were given the specifications and 24 hours to make the samples as specified by H&M and send them back. If a supplier was not able to meet the deadline, the order was given to another supplier.

The production offices provided the buyers at Stockholm with the list of suppliers who could deliver the specified garments along with the samples. The buyers then placed the order taking into consideration different factors, such as location of the factory, which determined the distance to the market, price, past record, etc. For clothes that were fashion sensitive and required to be replenished quickly, H&M used the suppliers in Europe. If there was a demand for some garments only from a particular country or store, suppliers located in close proximity to that country or store were given the order. H&M essentially operated through two supply chains in order to optimize time and cost. The first chain took care of the cost component and the manufacturing was done mainly in Asian countries. The second one, termed 'rapid reaction', was used for fashion-sensitive garments and was based in Europe.

Distribution

A large part of the finished products that were manufactured were shipped using external contract companies to the central warehouse in Hamburg, Germany, which served as the transit terminal. Most of the goods from the production centres across the world passed through this transit terminal on their way to the destination country.

In all the countries in which H&M operated, a distribution centre was set up. When goods arrived from the transit terminal to the distribution centre, they were sorted as per the stores, checked for quality and pressed. Depending on the demand, they were either sent to the stores or kept in a call-off warehouse, a centralized room that held the stock and was a part of the distribution centre. The merchandise was delivered to stores from the distribution centre in daily shipments. Items were replenished from the call-off warehouse as per the demand from the stores.

The goods from the Asian countries were shipped by sea in order to minimize costs. When the orders from a particular store were large, the shipment was sent directly to the stores. If the garments were in demand only in a particular country, then they were sent directly to the distribution centre in that country.

All the H&M stores were managed by the company. H&M was of the view that franchising and joint ventures would jeopardize the uniformity that was necessary, especially in the clothing retail and fashion sector. H&M chose the best available locations for its stores, in the main shopping districts of major cities and towns where it operated. All the stores were self-service stores and the garments were placed in a way that made it easy for customers to find the things they were looking for.

The stores were restocked every day. Most of the restocking was done between 7 a.m. and 9 a.m. In some of the stores, where demand was high, they were restocked three times a day. Sometimes, as in the case of new store openings when demand was very high, the store were restocked several times a day. No item stayed in the stores for more than a month, and so customers were keen on visiting the store more often. Items that did not sell quickly were marked down, to make way for new items. (See Figure 15.13 for an illustration of H&M's supply chain.)

Due to the short length of time it took for a garment to move from the designers' tables to the shelf (an average of 21 days), H&M was able to add the designs that were not a part of

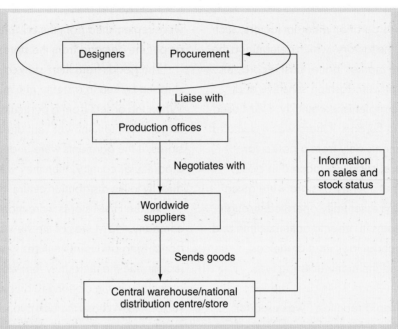

Figure 15.13: Supply Chain – H&M.
Source: www.eurofound.europa.eu

the collection it had released for the season. This enabled the company to reflect trends better as compared to its competitors. H&M was also able to produce garments that were in vogue and were selling well in the market and to stock them in the stores to meet demand. Though compared to its competitor Zara, H&M took more time to deliver the clothes, the extra time gave the company a cost advantage and clothes at H&M were 30%–50% cheaper compared to those at Zara.

III. Benetton

In 2004, Italy-based clothing company Benetton SpA (Benetton) formally adopted the 'Dual Supply Chain' system. The new system was a top down, pull driven supply chain, which enabled the company to bring more products on to the store shelves more often, in accordance with the growing demands of the customers and changing fashion trends.

Benetton was founded by Luciano Benetton after the Second World War in Italy. He started a small business producing sweaters with his brothers Carlo and Gilberto, and sister Giuliani. In 1956, the Benettons launched their own line of sweaters under the label Trés Jolie. They started Benetton Group as a partnership in March 1965. The first Benetton store was opened in 1968. The first store outside Italy was opened in Paris in 1969. In December 1985, the company adopted the name Benetton SpA, as a result of corporate reorganization. During the late 1980s, Benetton expanded into global markets, mainly in the Far East and China. By 1996, Benetton had a presence in over 100 countries. By 2005, Benetton was present in 120 countries around the world with 5000 stores.

Benetton operated a three-tier supply chain model. The first tier consisted of suppliers of raw materials and unfinished products, and production plants. The second tier had contractors and subcontractors, and the third tier had retail outlets (franchisees and agents) spread across several countries.

Design

The responsibility of designing, and keeping tabs on the innovations happening in the apparel retail sector, remained with the headquarters of Benetton. Benetton had a design centre at Ponziano, Italy. The design centre had several designers, from various backgrounds and cultures. The designers worked in three groups, with the first group taking care of the commercial aspect of the products, the second group carrying out research on the fabrics and the third responsible for graphics.

To understand customer preferences better, Benetton conducted in-store surveys and testing among customers. In order to keep up with the trends, Benetton hired top designers, and also had designers who essentially took clues from fashion shows across the world, and adapted some of them to clothes that would fit into Benetton's price range. Design samples were shown to the sales force as well. Benetton used CAD (Computer Aided Design) to design its garments [CAD is a combination of hardware and software used mainly by engineers and architects to design a wide range of products ranging from clothes and furniture, to automobiles and aeroplanes] and also used computer aided garment cutting and assembly. Once the designs were ready, fabric in neutral colours was then laid in layers and cut into the required pieces using a prototype.

The cut unstitched fabric was then sent to the contractors.

Production

Benetton manufactured garments using a vertically integrated model. While technically sophisticated parts of the garment manufacture process were retained in-house, labour intensive parts were outsourced. Benetton built close relationships with its contractors, and therefore could coordinate the activities among different contractors smoothly. Benetton also encouraged employees to become contractors as they were aware of the quality and other specifications of the company. This arrangement provided Benetton the flexibility to operate in a highly competitive environment and lower labour costs.

Contractors received production planning support, and technical assistance to maintain quality. In many cases, Benetton stepped in to provide contractors with financial assistance to procure the required machinery. However, the company never entered into formal contracts with any of the contractors as the need to do this was not felt by either party.

Benetton had more than 200 contractors and several subcontractors who worked to produce the garments as specified by the company. The tasks that were carried out by subcontractors included tasks like stitching, finishing, and ironing. The contractors were an integral part of Benetton's supply chain and had workshops employing anywhere between 30 to 200 people. They operated at a low volume and had low-cost processes. Every day, the contractors collected the material from the company, and each consignment was provided a specific order number. Once the order was executed, they returned the finished product to Benetton, which undertook quality checks.

Distribution

The clothes were distributed through a distribution centre located in Castrette, Italy. It was spread across 20 000 m^2, and could handle around 40 000 cartons, both incoming and outgoing, every day. From the distribution centre, the garments were sent to around 5000 Benetton outlets located across the world.

The distribution centre, built on two levels (below and above the ground), was 170 m long, 80 m wide and 20 m high, and could hold up to 250 000 cartons. The building had around 20 loading and unloading bays. The finished garments, packed, addressed and barcoded were collected at the receipt bays below ground level. At the receipt bays, they were scanned and using high-speed conveyors were transported to the storage area above ground level.

Benetton functioned through a licensor–licensee relationship, where the needs of the retail market were catered to by agents, who obtained a license from Benetton to sell its products. The agents were responsible for recruiting retailers, promoting Benetton's collections at fashion related events in different countries, processing retailer orders, selecting retailer locations, training, and letting the company know the latest trends in a particular region. The agents were paid a commission of around 4% of the total sales in that region.

The agents acted as intermediaries between the stores in their region and the company. As of 2002, Benetton had more than 80 agents, whose activities were supervised by seven area managers in the company. The area managers reported to the commercial director. The commercial director provided guidance about merchandising, product selection, store location, etc. This system helped Benetton to focus on designing, production and distribution and offered the retailers support in terms of publicity.

Benetton's franchise operations were quite different from other apparel manufacturers. The store owners did not have a formal agreement with the company, and they entered into agreements with the agents. There was no written contract between Benetton and the franchisees and there was no license fee, or royalty to be paid by the franchisees. But they needed to agree to stock and sell only products and accessories supplied by Benetton and also follow the guidelines provided by the company pertaining to merchandise display and pricing. In choosing the licensees, Benetton essentially looked for an ability to develop the market, and commitment. The company supplied clothes on a no-return basis. The outlets operated by the franchisees were also much smaller compared to those of Benetton's competitors. Initially, most of the stores were typically of 400 sq. feet area while the stores of competitors occupied around 1500 sq. feet. Even so, in the 1980s, Benetton's stores' turnover averaged twice as much as that of competing companies. In order to address the issue of growing competition, in 1999, Benetton decided to increase the size of its stores so that a wider range of garments and accessories could be displayed. In the main shopping districts of prominent cities across the world, Benetton decided to open its own retail outlets with area ranging between 10 000 and 20 000 sq. ft. The stores had large display areas, where display items were changed frequently reflecting the new collections and fashion trends.

The Dual Supply Chain

Each fashion season generally began with ten alternative colours of which only two or three recorded high demand. As Benetton delayed dyeing the garments, it provided the company an opportunity to respond to the demand on time. (See Figure 15.14 for more about manufacturing process at Benetton.) The agents provided Benetton information about the demand and, using this, replenishment schedules for the garments were drawn up and the colours were chosen. Since the popular colours were usually sold during the first ten days, Benetton was able to gain a competitive edge over the other players in the market.

However, while this model was highly successful in the 1980s and 1990s, it could not serve the fast changing demands of the customers by the turn of the century. Under the existing model Benetton required the stores to place most of the orders months in advance, when most of the stores did not have much idea about the upcoming fashion trends. Benetton was able to come out with only two collections a year, while competitors were bringing out several collections every year.

To address these problems, in 2004, Benetton began implementing its dual supply chain model. A dual supply chain had a better ability to respond to changes in demand and to balance activities like production, sales, and product design. Using this system, Benetton carried out production in different locations depending on the time required to market the product. Through the dual supply chain, Benetton brought out more collections per year and maintained the novelty of products by introducing new designs in accordance with the changes in demand.

The dual supply chain included the sequential dual supply chain and the integrated dual supply chain. A sequential dual supply chain acted on push focused demand. This was generally used for supplying garments that were ordered by the franchisees prior to the start of a season. An integrated dual supply chain was used for clothes that were delivered during the season; these items needed to be in the market within a

---

At Benetton, initially, garment manufacturing process began with spinning or purchasing the yarn. Then Benetton dyed the yarn in the required colours, and finished it to knit different parts of the garment. To develop the final product, different parts were joined. They were then stored to be sent to the retailers. This model had a disadvantage as any change in the demand could not be met immediately and the lead times for making the garments were long. In order to be more flexible, Benetton came up with a new manufacturing process, where it postponed dyeing of the garment. In 1964, Benetton arrived at a method of dyeing wool, where sweaters could be dyed after they were fully made. The new process also began with spinning or buying the yarn. Benetton manufactured the garment parts and then joined them. The garment was not dyed, but just stored as it was. Only after the final demand was assessed, the garment was dyed in the required colours and then shipped to the retailers.

Figure 15.14: Benetton – Manufacturing Process.
Compiled from various sources

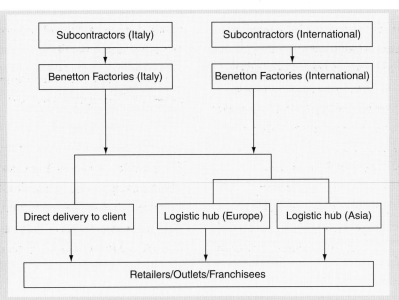

Figure 15.15: Benetton's Dual Supply Chain.
Source: www.cazenove.com

very short time frame. The integrated dual supply chain catered to pull focused demand. In this, the clothes were made taking into account the demand from customers and the inputs from the sales force. This was used mainly to top up the existing seasonal collections during the same season, and to keep up with the latest fashion trends. Here, the focus was not on minimizing the cost but on serving the customer with trendy wear.

After the implementation of the dual supply chain, Benetton came up with five collections in each season. The first collection called 'Contemporary 1' was made eight to six months before the season. This was based on the main trends as highlighted in various fashion shows and was sent to the stores at the beginning of the season. The second collection was known as 'Contemporary 2' and was made six to four months before the season. Through this collection, stores across the world could bring in new clothes to meet

the demands of customers. The third collection was called 'Trends' and was ready four to two months before the start of a season. New fashion trends were incorporated into the garments through minor adjustments. The 'just-in-time' collection, brought out between two months to two weeks before the sellout date, incorporated the latest trends. The last collection, 'Evergreen', was brought into stores one to two weeks before a season began and consisted of base items with recurring sales and season specific items. (See Figure 15.15 for a diagram explaining Benetton's Dual Supply Chain.)

The franchises were required to use an Internet-based platform to order items under the 'Evergreen' collection. Benetton ensured that the garments reached shops within a week in Italy and within 14 days in the other parts of the world. Benetton maintained higher inventories for the 'Evergreen' collection, so that it could ship them on time across the world.

The dual supply chain helped Benetton offer new products to its customers on a continuous basis. The company was able to maintain the sales momentum even after the season ended by minimizing the time to market and by offering products based on demand pull. With the dual supply chain system in place, Benetton divided the inventory shipments into smaller lots, and built the capacity to ship clothes every two weeks. It could also deliver garments in a week if the demand arose. Moreover, Benetton was able to balance time to market and cost, which had not been possible earlier.

Source: © ICFAI Center for Management Research. Reproduced with permission.

Questions

1. Describe how each company organises the design, production, distribution and retail elements of its supply chain.
2. Evaluate the level of supply chain integration for each organization.

EXERCISES

1. Describe the elements of a supply chain.

2. Explain the term 'bullwhip effect'. How can it be overcome?

3. Evaluate the main supply chain relationships in terms of their degree of integration.

4. Discuss the increasing importance of procurement.

5. What are the key factors in choosing suppliers?

6. What is the impact of e-Commerce on procurement activities?

7. Locate e-procurement software suppliers on the Internet and evaluate the benefits claimed for this software.

8. Discuss the relative merits of the centralization and decentralization of warehouse facilities.

WEB EXERCISE

Compare the distribution strategy of the online supermarket shopping company Ocado (`http://corporate.ocado.com/background.html`, accessed 7 October 2008) who deliver from a single warehouse across the UK and Sainsbury's (`http://www.sainsburys.co.uk/home`, accessed 7 October 2008) who deliver goods ordered online to the customer from a local supermarket.

● FURTHER READING

Gattorna, J. (2006) *Living Supply Chains: How to Mobilize the Enterprise Around Delivering What Your Customers Want*, Prentice Hall.

Kim, B. (2005) *Supply Chain Management*, John Wiley & Sons, Ltd.

Murray, E.A. and **Mahon, J.F.** (1993) 'Strategic alliances: gateway to the New Europe? *Long Range Planning*, **26** (4), 102–11.

Susaki, T. (1993) What the Japanese have learned from strategic alliances. *Long Range Planning*, **26** (6), 41–53.

● WEB LINKS

www.cips.org (accessed 7 October 2008). The Chartered Institute for Purchasing and Supply. Promotes best practice.

www.ism.ws (accessed 7 October 2008). Institute for Supply Management. Conferences, guides and tools in the area of supply chain management.

www.lmi.org (accessed 7 October 2008). Logistics Management Institute. Provides a database of reports regarding logistics issues.

www.steelauction.com (accessed 7 October 2008). Web auction site for the steel industry.

www.supply-chain.org (accessed 7 October 2008). The Supply Chain Council. Numerous papers and news items regarding supply chain management.

● REFERENCES

Evans, P. and **Wurster, T.S.** (1997) Strategy and the new economics of information. *Harvard Business Review*, September–October, 71–82.

Forrester, J.W. (1961) *Industrial Dynamics*, MIT Press.

Kraut, R., Chan, A., Butler, B. and **Hong, A.** (1998) Coordination and virtualisation: the role of electronic networks and personal relationships. *Journal of*

Computer Mediated Communications, **3** (4). Available online at http://jcmc.-indiana.edu/vol3/issue4/kraut.html (accessed 12 October 2008).

Lambert, D.M., Emmelhainz, M.A. and **Gardner, J.T.** (1996) Developing and implementing supply chain partnerships. *International Journal of Logistics Management*, **7** (2), 1–17.

Porter, M.E. and **Millar, V.E.** (1985) How information gives you competitive advantage. *Harvard Business Review*, July–August, 149–60.

CHAPTER

16

Project Management

- Introduction
- Project management activities
- Projects and organizational structure
- The role of the project manager
- Network analysis

LEARNING OBJECTIVES

- Provide a definition of a project

- Understand the main elements of the project-management approach

- Discuss how projects can relate to the structure of an organization

- Describe the role of the project manager

- Describe the steps in the network analysis technique

- Undertake the construction of a network diagram using the activity-on-node method

- Undertake the construction of a Gantt chart

- Describe methods of project risk analysis

- Understand the benefits and limitations of the network analysis approach

INTRODUCTION

Projects are unique, one-time operations designed to accomplish a specific set of objectives in a limited time frame. Examples of projects include a building construction or introducing a new service or product to the market. Large projects may consist of many activities and must therefore be carefully planned and coordinated if a project is to meet cost and time targets. However, not all aspects of implementation can be controlled or planned but the chance of success can be increased by anticipating potential problems and by applying corrective strategies. Network analysis can be used to assist the project planning and control activities.

PROJECT MANAGEMENT ACTIVITIES

The project management process includes the following main elements of estimate, plan and control.

Project Estimating

At the start of the project a broad plan is drawn up assuming unlimited resources. Once project estimates have been made of the resources required to undertake these activities it is then possible to compare overall project requirements with available resources. If highly specialized resources are required then the project completion date may have to be set to ensure these resources are not overloaded. This is a resource-constrained project. Alternatively there may be a need to complete a project in a specific time frame (for example, due date specified by customer). In this case alternative resources may have to be used (for example, subcontractors) to ensure timely project completion. This is a time-constrained project.

The next step is to generate estimates for the time and resources required to undertake each task defined in the project. This information can then be used to plan what resources are required and what activities should be undertaken over the life cycle of the project. Statistical methods should be used when the project is large (and therefore complex) or novel. This allows the project team to replace a single estimate of duration with a range within which they are confident the real duration will lie. This is particularly useful for the early stage of the project when uncertainty is greatest. The accuracy of the estimates can also be improved as their use changes from project evaluation purposes to approval and day-to-day project control. The project evaluation and review technique (PERT) approach described later in this chapter allows optimistic, pessimistic and most likely times to be specified for each task from which a probabilistic estimate of project completion time can be computed.

Project estimating
Estimating the type and amount of resources required to undertake a project.

Resource-constrained project
If highly specialized resources are required then the project completion date may have to be set to ensure these resources are not overloaded.

Time-constrained project
If there is a need to complete a project in a specific time frame alternative resources may have to be utilized to ensure timely project completion.

Once the activities have been identified and their resource requirements estimated it is necessary to define their relationship to one another. There are some activities that can only begin when other activities have been completed. This is termed a serial relationship. Other activities may be totally independent and thus they have a parallel relationship. These relationships are shown graphically in Figure 16.1 and Figure 16.2.

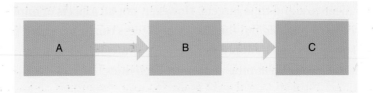

Figure 16.1: Serial Relationship of Activities.

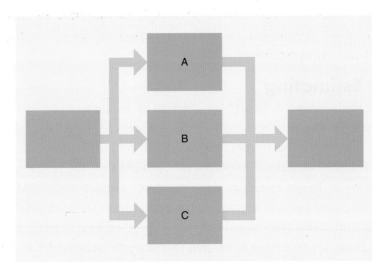

Figure 16.2: Parallel Relationship of Activities.

For a reasonable sized project there may be a range of alternative plans that may meet the project objectives. Project management software can be used to assist in choosing the most feasible schedule by recalculating resource requirements and timings for each operation.

Project Planning

The purpose of the project planning stage is to ensure that the project objectives of cost, time and quality are met. It does this by estimating both the level and timing of resources needed over the project duration. These steps may need to be undertaken repeatedly in a complex project due to uncertainties and to accommodate changes as the

Project planning
Project planning is to ensure that the project objectives of cost, time and quality are met. It does this by estimating both the level and timing of resources needed over the project duration.

project progresses. The planning process does not eradicate the need for the experience of the project manager in anticipating problems or the need for skill in dealing with unforeseen and novel incidences during project execution. However, the use of plans that can be executed sensibly will greatly improve the performance of the project.

The project management method uses a systems approach to deal with a complex task in that the components of the project are broken down repeatedly into smaller tasks until a manageable chunk is defined. Each task is given its own cost, time and quality objectives. It is then essential that responsibility is assigned to achieving these objectives for each particular task. This procedure should produce a work breakdown structure (WBS), which shows the hierarchical relationship between the project tasks (Figure 16.3). A typical WBS will have at the top level the project and at the bottom level the individual work package. A work package is an individual work element that can be accurately defined, budgeted, scheduled and controlled. Between the top and bottom levels various categories can be defined. These categories are usually organized in a product-oriented fashion but may be task oriented for service operations such as design or management.

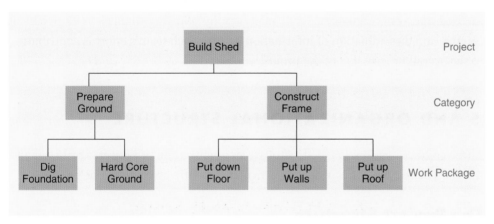

Figure 16.3: Work Breakdown Structure (WBS) for Building a Shed.

Project Control

Project control involves the monitoring of the project objectives of cost, time and quality as the project progresses. It is important to monitor and assess performance as the project progresses in order that the project does not deviate from plans to a large extent. Milestones or time events are defined during the project when performance against objectives can be measured. The amount of control will depend on the size of the project. Larger projects will require development of control activities from the project leader to team leaders. Computer project-management packages can be used to automate the collection of project progress data and production of progress reports.

Project control
This involves the monitoring of the project objectives of cost, time and quality as the project progresses.

The type of project structure required will depend on the size of the team undertaking the project. Projects with up to six team members can simply report directly to a project leader at appropriate intervals during project execution. For larger projects requiring up to 20 team members it is usual to implement an additional tier of management in the form of team leaders. The team leader could be responsible for either a phase of the development or a type of work. For any structure it is important that the project leader ensures consistency across development phases or development areas as appropriate. For projects with more than 20 members it is likely that additional management layers will be needed in order to ensure that no one person is involved with too much supervision.

The two main methods of reporting the progress of a project are by written reports and verbally at meetings of the project team. It is important that a formal statement of progress is made in written form, preferably in a standard report format, to ensure that everyone is aware of the current project situation. This is particularly important when changes to specifications are made during the project. In order to facilitate two-way communication between team members and team management, regular meetings should be arranged by the project manager. These meetings can increase the commitment of team members by allowing discussion of points of interest and dissemination of information on how each team's effort is contributing to the overall progression of the project.

PROJECTS AND ORGANIZATIONAL STRUCTURE

There are three main ways of structuring an organization of project, functional and matrix. The reasons for choosing a particular structure are outlined below.

The Project Structure

This consists of an organization that not only follows a team approach to projects but has an organizational structure based on teams formed specifically for projects. The approach delivers a high focus on completing project objectives but can involve duplication of resources across teams, an inhibition of diffusion of learning across teams, a lack of hierarchical career structure and less continuity of employment. Many professional service firms such as management consultancies use this approach.

The Functional Structure

Here a project is given to the most appropriate functional department. Thus the organizational structure remains in the standard hierarchical form. The approach ensures there is limited disruption to the normal organizational activities but can lead to a lack of focus on project objectives. A lack of coordination can result, especially if outside help is required. There can be a failure to meet customer needs if other departmental activities are taking priority over project work.

The Matrix Structure

Here several project teams are overlaid on a functional structure in an effort to provide a balance between functional and project needs. There are three different forms of matrix structure:

- *Functional matrix.* Here the project manager reports to functional heads to coordinate staff across departments.
- *Balanced matrix.* Here the project manager manages the project jointly with functional heads.
- *Project matrix.* Here functional staff join a project team for a fixed period of time.

THE ROLE OF THE PROJECT MANAGER

The project manager, sometimes known as a team leader or project coordinator, bears the ultimate responsibility for the success or failure of the project. Included in the functions of the project manager are providing clearly defined goals to project participants and ensuring that adequately skilled and experienced human resources are employed on the project. Throughout the project it is necessary to manage the elements of time, cost and quality. Because of the unique nature of projects and the potentially high number of interrelated tasks involved an effective way is needed to communicate project plans and progress across the project team. Network analysis methods can provide a valuable aid to the monitoring and control of projects and will be described below.

NETWORK ANALYSIS

Network analysis refers to the use of network-based techniques for the analysis and management of projects. This section describes two network analysis techniques of the critical path method (CPM) and PERT. The CPM method described here was developed by DuPont during the 1950s to manage plant construction. The PERT approach was developed by the US Navy during the development of the Polaris Submarine Launched Ballistic Missile System during the same decade (Sapolsky, 1972). The main difference between the approaches is the ability of PERT to take into consideration uncertainty in activity durations.

Network analysis
This refers to the use of network-based techniques for the analysis and management of projects.

In order to undertake network analysis it is necessary to break the project down into a number of identifiable activities or tasks. This enables individuals to be assigned responsibility to particular tasks that have a well-defined start and finish time. Performance objectives of time, cost and quality can be associated with each activity. The next stage is to retrieve information concerning the duration of the tasks involved in the project. This can be collated from a number of sources, such as documentation, observation and interviewing. The accuracy of the project plan will depend on the accuracy of these estimates. The next step is to identify any relationships between tasks in the project. For instance a particular task may not be able to begin until another task has finished. Thus the task waiting to begin depends on the former task. Other tasks may not have a dependent relationship and can thus occur simultaneously.

Critical Path Method (CPM)

Critical path method
This is used to show the activities undertaken during a project, the dependencies between these activities and the project duration.

Critical path diagrams are used extensively to show the activities undertaken during a project and the dependencies between these activities. Thus it is easy to see that activity C for example can only take place when activity A and activity B have completed. There are two methods of constructing critical path diagrams, activity on arrow (AOA), where the arrows represent the activities, and activity on node (AON), where the nodes represent the activities. The issues involved in which one to use will be discussed later. The following description on critical path analysis will use the AON method. For the activity-on-node notation each activity task is represented by a node with the format in Figure 16.4.

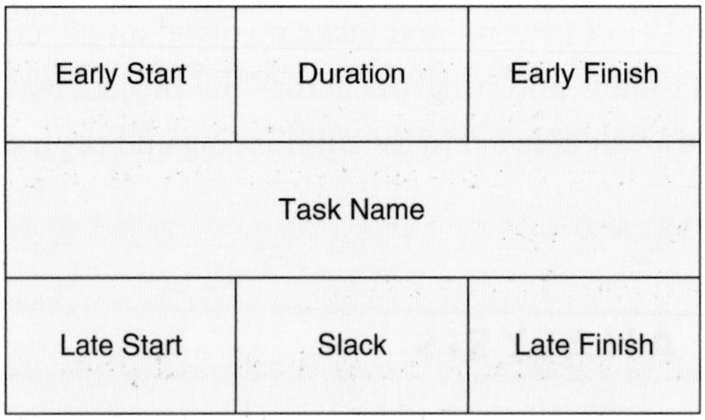

Early Start	Duration	Early Finish
	Task Name	
Late Start	Slack	Late Finish

Figure 16.4: Activity on Node Notation.

Thus a completed network will consist of a number of nodes connected by lines, one for each task, between a start and end node. An example of a completed network is shown in Figure 16.5.

Once the network diagram has been constructed it is possible to follow a sequence of activities, called a path, through the network from start to end. The length of time it takes to follow the path is the sum of all the durations of activities on

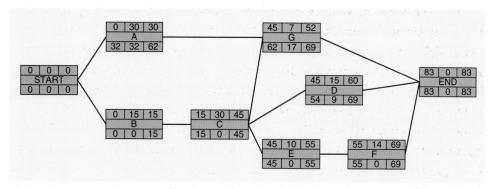

Figure 16.5: Activity on Node Network Diagram.

that path. The path with the longest duration gives the project completion time. This is called the critical path because any change in duration in any activities on this path will cause the whole project duration to either become shorter or longer. The following four steps show how to identify the critical path.

1. Calculate the earliest start/finish times (forward pass). From the duration of each task and the dependency relationship between the tasks it is possible to estimate the earliest start and finish time for each task as follows. You move left to right along the network, forward through time.

    1) Assume the start (first) task begins at time = 0.
    2) Calculate the earliest finish time where: earliest finish = earliest start + duration.
    3) Calculate the earliest start time of the next task where: earliest start = earliest finish of task immediately before. If there is more than one task immediately before, take the task with the latest finish time to calculate the earliest start time for the current task.
    4) Repeat steps 2) and 3) for all tasks.

2. Calculate the latest start/finish times (backward pass). It is now possible to estimate the latest start and finish time for each task as follows. You move right to left along the network, backward through time.

    1) Assume the end (last) task end time is the earliest finish time (unless the project end time is given).
    2) Calculate the latest start time where: latest start = latest finish − duration.
    3) Calculate the latest finish time of the previous task where: latest finish = latest start of task immediately after. If there is more than one task immediately

after take the task with the earliest start time to calculate the latest finish time for the current task.

   4) Repeat steps 2 and 3 for all tasks.

3. Calculate the slack/float times. The slack or float value is the difference between the earliest start and latest start (or earliest finish and latest finish) times for each task. To calculate the slack time

   1) Slack = latest start – earliest start OR slack = latest finish – earliest finish.
   2) Repeat step 1 for all tasks.

4. Identify the critical path.

   Any tasks with a slack time of 0 must obviously be undertaken on schedule at the earliest start time. The critical path is the pathway connecting all the nodes with a zero slack time. There must be at least one critical path through the network but there can be more than one. The significance of the critical path is that if any node on the path finishes later than the earliest finish time, the overall network time will increase by the same amount, putting the project behind schedule. Thus any planning and control activities should focus on ensuring tasks on the critical path remain within schedule.

WORKED EXAMPLE 16.1
Critical Path Method

A particular project comprises the following activities:

Activity	Duration (days)	Immediate predecessor(s)
A	30	–
B	15	–
C	30	B
D	15	C
E	10	C
F	14	E
G	7	A, C
H	14	D, F, G

a) Draw an AON diagram for this project.
b) Calculate the earliest start, earliest finish, latest start, latest finish and slack times for each activity.
c) Identify the critical path.

SOLUTION

(a) The AON diagram is constructed by using the predecessor information contained in the table to connect the nodes as appropriate. For instance activity G has two predecessors, A and C, so both these nodes must point to the start of activity G.

(b) The earliest start/finish times are calculated by a forward pass (left to right) through the network. For instance activity A earliest start $= 0$, duration $= 15$, therefore earliest end $= 15 - 0 = 15$. Activity G, earliest start $= 45$ ($=$ earliest finish of activities immediately before; A $= 30$, C $= 45$).

The latest start/finish times are calculated by a backward pass (right to left) through the network. For instance activity H latest end $= 83$, duration $= 14$, therefore latest start $= 83 - 14 = 69$. Activity C, latest end $= 45$ ($=$ latest start of task immediately after; G $= 62$, D $= 54$, E $= 45$).

The slack time is the difference between the earliest and latest start times for each activity. For instance slack for G $= 17$ ($=$ latest start $-$ earliest start $= 62 - 45 = 17$).

(c) The critical path is the path or paths through the network with all nodes having a zero slack time. In this case there is one critical path; B, C, E, F, H.

The Activity-On-Arrow Method

The format for the activity-on-arrow method will now be described. The symbol used in this method is shown in Figure 16.6.

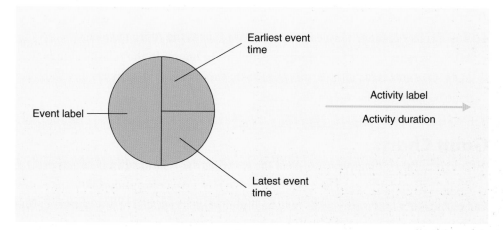

Figure 16.6: Activity-on-Arrow Notation.

Rather than considering the earliest and latest start and finish times of the activities directly, this method uses the earliest and latest event times as below:

- Earliest event time. This is determined by the earliest time at which any subsequent activity can start.
- Latest event time. This is determined by the latest time at which any subsequent activity can start.
- Thus for a single activity the format would be as shown in Figure 16.7.

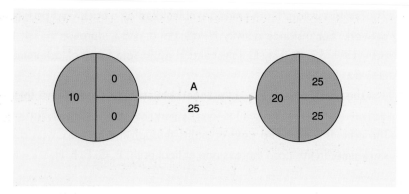

Figure 16.7: Calculating Event Times for an AOA Network.

As stated earlier there are two methods of constructing network diagrams. Historically there has been a greater use of the activity-on-arrow (AOA) method, but the activity-on-node (AON) method is now being recognized as having a number of advantages including:

- most project management computer software uses the AON approach
- AON diagrams do not need dummy activities to maintain the relationship logic
- AON diagrams have all the information on timings and identification within the node box, leading to clearer diagrams.

Gantt chart
These provide a view of which tasks are being undertaken over time. This allows monitoring of project progress against planned progress and so provides a valuable tool for project control.

Gantt Charts

Although network diagrams are ideal for showing the relationship between project tasks, they do not provide a clear view of which tasks are being undertaken over time and particularly how many tasks may be undertaken in parallel at any one time. The Gantt chart provides an overview for the project manager to allow them to monitor project progress against planned progress and so provides a valuable information source for project control.

To draw a Gantt chart manually undertake the following steps:

1. Draw a grid with the tasks along the vertical axis and the time scale (up to the project duration) along the horizontal axis.
2. Draw a horizontal bar across from the task identifier along the left of the chart starting at the earliest start time and ending at the earliest finish time.
3. Indicate the slack amount by drawing a line from the earliest finish time to the latest finish time.
4. Repeat steps 2 and 3 for each task.

A Gantt chart for the project network shown in Figure 16.5 is shown in Figure 16.8.

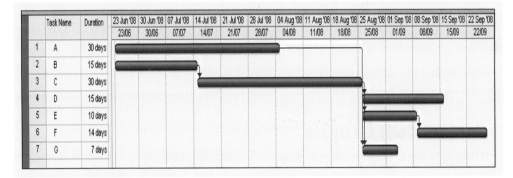

Figure 16.8: Microsoft Project Screen Showing Gantt Chart.

Capacity Loading Graphs

The basic network diagram assumes that all tasks can be undertaken at the earliest start times derived from the critical path calculations. However, the capacity available for what may be a number of parallel tasks requiring the same type of resource is usually limited. In order to calculate the capacity requirements of a project over time the capacity requirements associated with each task are indicated on the Gantt chart. From this a capacity loading graph can be developed by projecting the loading figures on a time graph (Figure 16.9). The resource graph in Figure 16.9 shows an area of over allocation of resource (shown in red). In order to remove this over allocation of resource either more resource would be required (in a time-constrained project) or the project tasks must be rescheduled and the project completion time extended (in a resource-constrained project).

Capacity loading graphs
Indicate the type and level of capacity required at a point in time.

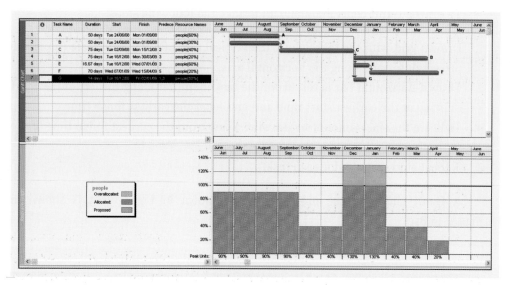

Figure 16.9: Microsoft Project Screen Showing Gantt Chart and Resource (Capacity Loading) Graph.

Project Cost Graphs

Project cost graphs
These provide an indication of the amount of cost incurred over the life of a project.

The previous discussion has concentrated on the need to schedule and control activities in order to complete the entire project within a minimum timespan. However, there are situations in which the project cost is an important factor. If the costs of each task are known then it is possible to produce a cost graph that will show the amount of cost incurred over the life of the project. This is useful in showing any periods when a number of parallel tasks are incurring significant costs leading to the need for additional cash-flow at key times. In large projects it may be necessary to aggregate the costs of a number of activities, particularly if they are the responsibility of one department or subcontractor. As a control mechanism the project manager can collect information on cost to date and percentage completion to date for each task to identify any cost above budget and take appropriate action without delay. Conversely costs below budget may be an indication of a project running late. The performance measures used to do this are called the **earned value** or budgeted cost of work performed (BCWP) and show, for any day in the project, how much work has actually been done in terms of budgeted costs. This measure can be compared with the budgeted cost of work scheduled (BCWS) to find the schedule variance (SV) (SV = BCWP – BCWS) and the actual cost of work performed (ACWP) to find the cost variance (CV) (CV = BCWP – ACWP).

Earned value
Also termed the budgeted cost of work performed (BCWP), shows, for any day in the project, how much work has actually been done in terms of budgeted costs.

Project Crashing

Within any project there will be a number of time-cost trade-offs to consider. Most projects will have tasks that can be completed with an injection of additional resources, such as equipment or people. Reasons to reduce project completion time include:

- reduce high indirect costs associated with equipment.
- reduce new product development time to market
- avoid penalties for late completion
- gain incentives for early completion
- release resources for other projects.

The use of additional resources to reduce project completion time is termed crashing the project. The idea is to reduce overall indirect project costs by increasing direct costs on a particular task. One of the most obvious ways of decreasing task duration is to allocate additional labour to a task. This can be either an additional team member or through overtime working. The following information is required to enable a decision to be made on the potential benefits of crashing a task:

> **Project crashing**
> The use of additional resources to reduce project completion time.

- the normal task duration
- the crash task duration
- The cost of crashing the task to the crash task duration per unit time.

A task is chosen for crashing by observing which task can be reduced for the required time for the lowest cost. As stated before, the overall project completion time is the sum of the task durations on the critical path. Thus it is always necessary to crash a task which is on the critical path. As the duration of tasks on the critical path are reduced, however, other paths in the network will also become critical. If this happens it will require the crashing process to be undertaken on all the paths that are critical at any one time.

WORKED EXAMPLE 16.2
Project Crashing

Software Ltd has established a project team to undertake some important market research work. It is possible to reduce the expected or 'normal' times for certain activities in units of one week (but not in fractions of a week) but at an extra cost. The relevant information is given below.

		Normal		Crash	
Activity	Predecessor	Duration (weeks)	Cost of weeks (£)	Duration (weeks)	Extra cost per week saved (£)
A	–	5	4000	3	2000
B	–	4	3000	4	–
C	A	2	6000	1	15 000
D	C	4	1000	4	–
E	B	5	4000	3	3000
F	B	5	7000	1	7000
G	B, C	4	4000	2	20 000
H	F	3	5000	2	10 000

In addition to the costs shown there is a cost of retainer fees and administration overheads of £10 000 for each week that the project lasts.

a) What is the normal expected duration of the project, and its total cost? What is the critical path?

b) What would be the cost of completing the project using the normal durations?

c) What would be the duration of the project if costs are to be minimized?

● SOLUTION

a) Construct the AON diagram by using the predecessor information in the table. From the diagram the duration of the project is 12 weeks. The critical path is B, F, H.

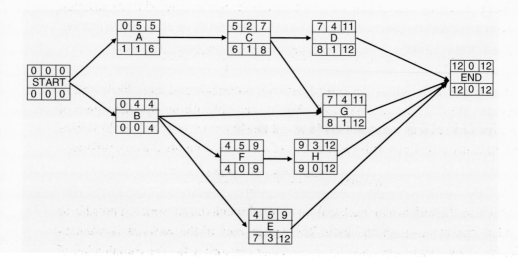

b) The total project cost = cost of activities + other costs = £34 000 + 12 × £10 000
    = £154 000

c) The minimum cost solution can be found by looking at the normal time solution.

Ignore B and D because they cannot be reduced.

Ignore C, G and H because it is too expensive to reduce these activities.

This leaves A, E and F.

F is the only activity on the critical path, so reduce this activity from 5 weeks to 4 weeks.

This costs £7000 but saves £10 000, net saving £3000.

Reduce E by 2 and A by 2, thus reducing the overall project duration to 9 weeks.

This costs 2 × £9,000 but saves 2 × £10 000, net saving of £2000.

No more time can be saved for less than the relevant cost.

Therefore the optimal duration is 9 weeks, optimal cost is £149 000.

Project Evaluation and Review Technique (PERT)

The PERT approach attempts to take into account the fact that most task durations are not fixed but vary when they are executed. Thus PERT provides a way of incorporating risk into project schedules. It does this by using a beta probability distribution to describe the variability inherent in the processes. The probabilistic approach involves three time estimates for each activity:

- Optimistic time – the task duration under the most optimistic conditions.
- Pessimistic time – the task duration under the most pessimistic conditions.
- Most likely time – the most likely task duration.

> **PERT**
> This network analysis approach attempts to take into account the fact that most task durations are not fixed by using a statistical distribution to describe the variability inherent in the tasks.

To derive the average or expected time for a task duration the following equation is used

$$\text{expected duration} = \frac{(\text{optimistic} + (4 \times \text{most likely}) + \text{pessimistic})}{4}$$

Greater risk is reflected in the spread between optimistic and most likely and in particular most likely and pessimistic. For an activity with no risk the values of optimistic, most likely and pessimistic would be the same. To calculate the degree of uncertainty associated with the duration of a task we compute the task variance.

$$\text{variance} = \frac{(\text{pessimistic} - \text{optimistic})^2}{36}$$

By summing the variance for each task on a path through the network it is possible to calculate the variance for the path. The square root of the variance is taken to calculate the standard deviation for a particular network path. The combination of the expected time and standard deviation for the network path allows managers to compute probabilistic estimates of project completion times. The probability of completing any path through the network in a specified time is calculated using the following equation:

$$z = \frac{(\text{specified time} - \text{expected time})}{\text{path standard deviation}}$$

Thus if the specified time = 20 and the expected time = 19, with a path standard deviation of 1.00, z = (20 − 19)/1.00 therefore z = 1. Looking up the value of z on a standardized normal curve gives an area under the curve of 0.8413. Thus the probability of finishing the project in 20 weeks is 84.13%. The project manager can then make an informed decision about the use of a time buffer or reserve to the project schedule to increase the likelihood of the project completing on time.

A point to bear in mind with these estimates is that they only take into consideration the tasks on the critical path and discount the fact that slack on tasks on a noncritical path could delay the project. Therefore the probability that the project will be completed by a specified date is the probability that all paths will be completed by that date, which is the product of the probabilities for all the paths.

WORKED EXAMPLE 16.3
Project Evaluation and Review Technique

Stone Ltd. has just accepted a project that can be broken down into the following eight activities.

Activity	Predecessor	Estimated duration (days)		
		Optimistic	Most likely	Pessimistic
A	—	4	11	12
B	—	45	48	63
C	B	13	33	35
D	B	25	29	39
E	A, C	14	21	22
F	D, E	18	32	34
G	A, C	17	19	27
H	G	15	20	25

The project must be completed in 141 days, otherwise severe penalties become payable. You are required to find the critical path and to estimate the probability of the critical path time exceeding 141 days.

SOLUTION

First calculate the mean and standard deviation for each activity.

$$\text{mean} = \frac{(\text{optimistic} + 4 \times \text{most likely} + \text{pessimistic})}{6}$$

$$\text{standard deviation} = \frac{(\text{pessimistic} - \text{optimistic})^2}{36}$$

Activity	Mean	Standard Deviation
A	10	1.33
B	50	3
C	30	3.67
D	30	2.33
E	20	1.33
F	30	2.67
G	20	1.67
H	20	1.67

Next draw the AON network diagram.

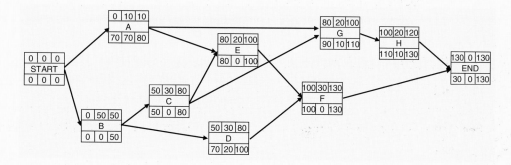

This gives a critical path of B, C, E, F giving an expected time of 130 days. Assuming that the distribution of the total project time is normal, the probability of the project time exceeding 141 days can be found as follows:

There are five routes through the network.

Route	Mean duration	Standard deviation	(141 – mean)	Z	Probability within 141 days
BCEF	130	5.6	11	1.96	97.5%
BDF	110	4.6	31	6.63	100%
BCGH	120	5.3	21	3.96	100%
AEF	60	3.3	81	24.55	100%
AGH	50	2.7	91	33.7	100%

The only route likely to exceed 141 days is BCEF, so the probability that the company will become liable to pay the penalties is (100 – 97.5) = 2.5%.

Project Network Simulation

In addition to the use of PERT another method for measuring the consequence of risk on project completion times is the use of project network simulation. In order to use the PERT approach it must be assumed that the paths of a project are independent and the same tasks are not on more than one path. If a task is on more than one path and its actual completion time was much larger than its expected time it is obvious that the paths are not independent. If the network consists of these paths and they are near the critical path time then the results will be invalid. Simulation can be used to develop estimates of a project's completion time by taking into account all the network paths. Probability distributions are constructed for each task derived from estimates provided by such data collection methods as observation and historical data. A simulation then generates a random number within the probability distribution for each task. The critical path is then determined and the project duration calculated. This procedure is repeated a number of times (maybe more than 100) until there is sufficient data in order to construct a frequency distribution of project times. This distribution can be used to make a probabilistic assessment of the actual project duration. If greater accuracy is required the process can be repeated to generate additional project completion estimates which can be added to the frequency distribution.

Apart from the use of PERT and simulation to provide a measure of the consequence of risk on project completion times other methods include decision trees and payoff tables. See Nicholas and Steyn (2008) for more details.

Benefits and Limitations of the Network Analysis Approach

A number of benefits can be attained by using the network analysis approach in project management. Firstly it requires a structured analysis of the number and sequence of tasks contained within a project, so aiding understanding of resource requirements for project completion, and it provides a number of useful graphical displays, which assist understanding of such factors as project dependencies and resource loading. It also gives a reasonable estimate of the project duration and the tasks which must be completed on time to meet this duration (the critical path). The network also acts as a control mechanism to monitor actual progress against planned progress on the Gantt chart. It also provides a means of estimating any decrease in overall project time by providing extra resources at any stage and finally it can be used to provide cost estimates for different project scenarios.

There are, however, a number of limitations to bear in mind when using network analysis. Its use is no substitute for good management judgement in such areas as prioritizing and selecting suppliers and personnel for the project. Any errors in the network such as incorrect dependency relationships or the omission of tasks may invalidate the results. The task times are forecasts and are thus estimates that are subject to error. The PERT and simulation techniques may reduce time estimation errors but at the cost of greater complexity, which may divert management time away from more important issues. Time estimates for tasks may be greater than necessary to provide managers with slack to ensure they meet deadlines ('sandbagging') or too short for a realistic estimate ('blue skies'). Also the method assumes activities are independent. Actually the duration of one activity may be dependent on the duration of another. The method assumes a precise breaking point between activities. In reality one activity may start before a predecessor activity has finished. Finally activities just off the critical path may become critical after it is too late to do anything about them.

SUMMARY

- Projects are unique, one-time operations designed to accomplish a specific set of objectives in a limited time frame.

- The main elements of project management are estimate, plan and control.

- There are three main ways of structuring an organization: project, functional and matrix.

- The role of the project manager is to provide clearly defined goals and ensure adequate resources are employed on the project.

- The steps in the network analysis technique briefly comprise identifying the project activities, estimating activity durations, identifying activity relationships, drawing the network diagram and identifying the critical path.

- Project risk analysis can be undertaken using methods such as PERT and simulation.

- The network analysis technique can provide an estimate of project performance under a number of scenarios. It is not, however, a substitute for good project management.

CASE STUDY 16.1

Fast Homes – Courtesy of Prefabrication

On a muddy building site in the flat Cambridgeshire countryside in the UK, a crane swings a prefabricated concrete slab over a half-finished house and a team of workers slots it in to form part of the ground floor ceiling. A three-storey house built using prefabricated methods employed by Bovis Homes in the new village of Cambourne can be weathertight within ten days compared with the five-and-a-half weeks required by conventional techniques. This allows electricians and plumbers to get to work sooner and means the house can be completed in less than half the 22 weeks normally needed, says David Lowther, Bovis's research and development director.

Bovis and a handful of other housebuilders see prefabrication as the way forward while the government is keen for the building industry to modernize its production techniques. But despite years of trials and the use of timber-frame construction methods in Scotland, Scandinavia and the US, prefabrication remains controversial. The home-buying public associates it with postwar austerity and with the draughty, condensation-prone, system-built

high-rises of the 1960s and 1970s. The verdict in the City is that prefabrication is a useful way of speeding up production and improving the housebuilders' return on capital. But the industry has yet to show that faster build times justify the higher costs and prefabrication is not a reason for giving a company a higher rating.

Malcolm Harris, Bovis chief executive, believes factory-finished components – a term he prefers to pre fabrication – is essential to overcome skill shortages among trades such as bricklayers and to boost quality. Units made in advance in a factory can be built to much tighter tolerances than are possible on a muddy, windy building site. This results in fewer complaints. After trials Bovis is using its modern techniques at Cambourne, a development that will grow to 3300 homes over the next 10 years. Houses are being built with inner walls made of 'aircrete' blocks that are stuck together with glue. The blocks, made from relatively light aerated concrete, are the size of about 10 bricks, allowing walls to be built more quickly. Unlike traditional mortar, the glue can be used in freezing conditions, which means construction can continue throughout the winter. The selling points of concrete over timber are that it feels more solid and is fire-proof, rot-proof and provides better insulation.

Once the walls and floors are up, the roof trusses can be fixed and covered with waterproof felt, allowing work on installing the

electrics, plumbing and internal finishes to be carried out. Bovis's plan is to build complete roof units on the ground – where work can go ahead faster and more safely than on the top of a house – and lift them into place. If the tiling industry can develop lightweight roof tiles, Bovis's aim is to fix the tiles as well before lifting the roof into position. With the roof in place, factory-made one-piece dormer windows are lifted by crane into position. Underneath, completed door and window units are fitted in the gaps left in the walls.

Once the inner wall is up and work is going on inside, the bricklayer can be brought in to build a brick outer 'skin' so the house looks just like its traditional counterparts. 'The beauty of this method is that it removes the bricklayer from the critical path of building the house', says Mr Harris.

Bovis is not alone in shifting to prefabrication although it buys the components rather than making them itself. Two other large housebuilders, Westbury and Wilson Connolly, have in-house operations making timber-frame units. But while Westbury is increasing production, Wilson Connolly is cutting back because it has not achieved savings. The problem with prefabrication is that it is more expensive than traditional methods – although costs should come down as more experience is gained and volumes increase. Faster build times mean a higher return on capital invested but, for companies with manufacturing arms, moving to factory production requires the housebuilders to forecast demand in a notoriously cyclical market, analysts warn.

Source: by Charles Batchelor, FT.com, 21 November 2001. Reproduced by permission.

Question

Discuss the strategies used in this case to reduce the project completion time of new homes.

CASE STUDY 16.2

The Concorde Project – A Technical and Engineering Triumph but a Commercial Disaster

On 5 November 1956, the Supersonic Transport Aircraft Committee (STAC) was established. The committee was made up of representatives of Britain's aircraft and engine manufacturers, as well as government officials and personnel from the Royal Aircraft Establishment (at Farnborough, England), to study the possibility of building a supersonic airliner. On 9 March 1959, STAC recommended design studies for two supersonic airliners, one to fly at a speed of Mach 1.2 and the other at Mach 2.0. In 1962, the French President Charles de Gaulle requested Britain and France to cooperate in building a civil aircraft that would fly at supersonic speed. Both the countries' aircraft industries would have to be involved in this project as the building of such an aircraft would be too expensive for Britain or France to fund alone. The British Minister of Aviation, Julian Amery, and the French ambassador, Jouffroy de Coursel, signed a draft treaty for collaborating on the construction of a supersonic aircraft. The treaty stipulated that Great Britain and France 'must in all aspects of the project make an equal contribution in both the costs to be taken on and the work to be carried out, and to share proceeds from sales equally.'

The building of this aircraft was assigned to four companies: The British Aircraft Corporation (Britain) and Sud Aviation (France) were responsible for building the airframe and Bristol Siddeley (Britain) and SNECMA (France), had to manufacture the Olympus 593 jet engines. On 11 September 1965, work commenced on the airframe at the British Aircraft Corporation's division at Filton. Only 40% of the airframe was to be built in Britain; the other 60% was the responsibility of the French. Although the agreement was for a 50/50 share in the production of the entire aircraft, Britain had a bigger share in the production of the Olympus 593 jet engine than France. On 11 December 1967, the first prototype of the supersonic jet was ceremonially rolled out in Toulouse. The aircraft was called Concorde 001. With the British Concorde prototype almost complete, the British Technology Minister, Anthony Wedgwood Benn, announced at Toulouse that from then on the British aircraft would also be called the Concorde. Concorde 002 (G-BSST) made its premiere in Germany at the Hanover Air Show on 22 and 23 April 1972. The Concorde aircraft can be regarded as a technical and engineering triumph.

The Concorde was the first of an important new breed of aerospace projects: those built through international collaboration. It was a huge technology-push 'spearhead' project, whose basic objective was to carry passengers safely at supersonic speed. Its development represented a continual struggle to reconcile two entirely different requirements: sustained supersonic flight and subsonic approach. Its cost-escalation and schedule delays were huge. This led to public criticism that embarrassed the government. The British government was so traumatized by this criticism that its response to suggestions for high-risk major projects for many decades following this was invariably one of nervous disinclination. However, the Concorde was an economic disaster not because of its huge developmental costs but because of the unexpectedly high cost of fuel and the inability to obtain authorization to fly it supersonically over land.

There was no break clause to the treaty, no performance requirements and no financial limits. Management structures and programmes (schedules) were proposed in the treaty but generally in imprecise terms. The management structure, for instance, comprised a series of hierarchical committees. The project was set up with little regard to the most basic rules of project management, such as a clearly identified owner organization; there was no owner and no one person in charge. The first prototype flight was scheduled for the second half of 1966, with the Certificate of Air-worthiness to be awarded at the end of 1969; in fact these were accomplished in October 1969 and December 1975 respectively. The project's financial estimate in November 1962 was £135.2 million; by 1979 the cost of the programme had grown more than eightfold to around £1129 million. Between 1964 and 1970, the Concorde's commercial prospects became increasingly doubtful. The pattern of air traffic began to change with the advent of wide-bodied aircraft; economy and price became the critical parameters rather than speed. The new Labour government of 1964 attempted to scrap the project, along with TSR-2, the P-1154 and HS-681 (other supersonic models), but the French threatened to sue the British government in the International Court of Justice if the Treaty was abrogated. The decision to start production was taken in 1968. Environmentalist opposition grew dramatically, particularly in the USA, where it effectively killed the US Supersonic Transport. With the rise in the price of fuel following the Yom Kippur War in 1973, the economics of operating the Concorde became even more unfavourable, especially as its economic speed was designed to be Mach 2 rather than subsonic. In 1973, most of the airliners took back the orders they had placed for buying Concorde. Obtaining permission to enter the US proved extremely difficult, and it was not until May 1976, 20 years after the project's inception, that the first flight landed in Washington DC. The Concorde did not touch New York until November 1977.

In the end, the Concorde proved to be a commercial disaster for its developers (the two governments), although not for its builders or operators: a technological triumph, yet a plane designed on a massive misconception that speed was the principal criterion for an airliner's success. An aircraft project that was set up without taking the basic rules of project management into account (such as a clearly identified owner organization) and one that experienced severe problems of design and technology management; a project whose chances of success were severely compromised by two external factors, changes in fuel prices and environmentalist opposition. Also, the cost of travel is very high.

Questions for Discussion

1. 'The Concorde project can be regarded as a technical and engineering triumph but a commercial disaster.' What is the criterion for judging the success of a project?

2. The case attributes the failure of the Concorde project to nonadherence to the most basic rules of project management. Comment.

3. What approach should the two governments have followed to make the project a success?

Source: © ICFAI Center for Management Research. Reproduced with permission.

EXERCISES

1. Discuss the project management activities of estimate, plan and control.

2. What assumptions does the network analysis method make?

3. A company has identified the following activities that will make up a project.

Activity	Duration (hours)	Immediate predecessor(s)
A	1	—
B	1	A
C	3	B
D	2	B
E	2	D
F	1	E
G	3	C
H	2	F, G
I	1	H
J	1	I
K	1	I
L	1	J, K

a) Draw an AON diagram for this project.

b) Calculate the earliest start, earliest finish, latest start, latest finish and slack times for each activity.

c) Identify the critical path.

4. A company has identified the following activities and resource requirements for the following project:

Activity	Duration (days)	Immediate predecessor	Members required (day)
A	3	—	4
B	4	—	3
C	9	—	4
D	4	A, B	7
E	5	B	8
F	6	D, C	9
G	6	E, C	5
H	10	F, G	2

a) Draw an AON diagram for this project.

b) Calculate the earliest start, earliest finish, latest start, latest finish and slack times for each activity.

c) Identify the critical path.

d) Draw a Gantt chart of the project indicating the slack times for each activity.

e) Draw a capacity loading graph based on the Gantt chart.

5. The following describes the introduction of a new product to be manufactured by a firm. The product has been developed and market tested by the R&D centre, but the manufacturing processes required to produce the product have yet to be developed. The process engineering group has been assigned the responsibility of the design project and have been given a target of 60 days to arrive at an overall process design. Although 60 days seemed very short to the process engineers at first, after some discussion it was concluded that they could probably pull it off because the product and its processes were so similar to the present processing technologies in use at their plant. These activities, their precedence relationships and their durations were estimated by the engineers as follows:

Activity	Description	Precedence	Duration (days)
A	Initial product design study	—	12
B	Preliminary product redesign for production	A	10
C	Preliminary facility redesign for product	A	15
D	Preliminary process technologies study	A	9
E	Facility modification for product redesign	B	6
F	Intermediate facility redesign	C, E	12
G	Intermediate product redesign	B	14
H	Specific process machinery design	B, D	21
I	Final facility, product and process design	F, G, H	10

a) Draw an AON diagram for this project.
b) Calculate the earliest start, earliest finish, latest start, latest finish and slack times for each activity.
c) Identify the critical path.

6. The HairCare company manufactures a range of hair-care products, including a range of hair styling gels. A competitor has recently introduced a new hair gel, which in the last six months has taken a significant share of the market, with adverse effects on HairCare's sales. The management at HairCare has decided that a competitive product must be introduced as quickly as possible and has asked Walter Dobie, the management accountant, to draw up a plan for developing and marketing the new product. As the first step in planning the project, Walter has identified the following major tasks, which will be involved in the new product launch. He has also estimated how long each task will take and what other tasks must precede each one.

Activity	Description	Precedence	Estimated duration (weeks)
A	Design new product	–	8
B	Design packaging	–	4
C	Organize production facilities	A	4
D	Obtain production materials	A	2
E	Manufacture trial batch	C, D	3
F	Obtain packaging	B	2
G	Decide on test market area	–	1
H	Package trial batch	E, F	2
I	Distribute product in test area	H, G	3
J	Conduct test market	I	4
K	Assess test market	J	3
L	Plan national launch	K	4

a) Draw an AON diagram for this project and determine how long it will be before the new product can be launched.
b) Calculate the slack time available for all the activities.
c) The time taken to complete tasks A, B, D, K and L is somewhat uncertain and so the following optimistic and pessimistic estimates

have also been made to supplement the most likely figure given above. The additional estimates are:

Activity	Optimistic time (weeks)	Pessimistic time (weeks)
A	5	13
B	2	6
D	1	4
K	2	6
L	2	8

What now is the expected time until the product can be launched and what is the probability of this time exceeding 35 weeks? (You should assume that the overall project duration follows a normal distribution.)

7. A computer system has recently been installed in the accounts department of a manufacturing company. The activities involved in introducing the system are listed below together with their normal durations and costs. It would be possible to shorten the overall project duration by crashing certain activities at extra cost, so the relevant details are also included. In addition there will be a weekly charge of £2500 to cover overheads.

		Normal		Crash	
Activity	Predecessor	Duration (weeks)	Cost	Duration (weeks)	Cost
A	–	3	3000	2	4000
B	–	6	6000	–	–
C	A	4	8000	1	11 000
D	B	2	1500	–	–
E	A	8	4000	5	5000
F	B	4	3000	2	5000
G	C, D	2	2000	–	–
H	F	3	3000	1	6000

The crash time represents the shortest time in which the activity can be completed given the use of more costly methods of completion. Assume that it is possible to reduce the normal time to the crash time in steps of one week and that the extra cost will be proportional to the time saved.

a) Using the normal durations and costs construct an activity network for the introduction of the new computer system. Determine the critical path and associated cost.

b) Activities E and F have to be supervised by the chief accountant who will not be available for the first seven weeks of the project period. Both activities, however, can be supervised simultaneously. Determine whether or not this will affect the completion date and, if so, state how it will be affected.

c) Assuming that the chief accountant will be available whenever required and that all resources necessary to implement the crashing procedures will also be available, determine the minimum cost of undertaking the project.

8. Explain the following terms associated with project management.

a) Critical path.

b) Slack time.

c) Crashing.

d) PERT.

WEB EXERCISE

Identify elements that led to project failure by locating reports on the BBC news web site (http://news.bbc.co.uk, accessed 7 October 2008) such as hospital construction http://news.bbc.co.uk/1/hi/health/436046.stm (accessed 7 October 2008) and the Princess Diana memorial http://news.bbc.co.uk/1/hi/england/london/4826020.stm (accessed 7 October 2008).

● FURTHER READING

Cadle, J. and **Yeates, D.** (2008) *Project Management for Information Systems*, 5th edn, Pearson Education, Harlow.

Hughes, B. and **Cotterell, M.** (2006) *Software Project Management*, 4th edn, McGraw-Hill.

Lock, D. (2008) *Project Management*, 9th edn, Gower, Aldershot.

Maylor, H. (2005) *Project Management*, 3rd edn, FT Prentice Hall.

Moser, S., Henderson-Sellers, B. and **Misic, V.B.** (1999) Cost estimation based on business models. *Journal of Systems and Software*, **49** (1), 33–42.

● WEB LINKS

`www.comp.glam.ac.uk/pages/staff/dwfarthi/projman.htm` (accessed 7 October 2008). Dave W Farthing's Software Project Management web link page – contains many links to project management resources.

`www.pmi.org` (accessed 7 October 2008). Project Management Institute. Contains information regarding news and events in the area of project management.

`www.primavera.com` (accessed 7 October 2008). Primavera Systems Inc. Software product Primavera Project Planner.

`www.projectmanagement.com` (accessed 7 October 2008). Contains many articles regarding project management.

`www.projectnet.co.uk` Project Manager Today (accessed 7 October 2008). Links to books and events in the area of project management.

● REFERENCES

Nicholas, J.M. and **Steyn, H**. (2008) *Project Management for Business, Engineering, and Technology: Principles and Practice*, 3rd edn, Elsevier Butterworth-Heinemann, Oxford.

Sapolsky, H.M. (1972) *The Polaris System Development: Bureaucratic and Programmatic Success in Government*, Harvard University Press, pp. 118–19.

CHAPTER

17

Quality

- Introduction
- Defining quality
- Measuring quality
- Improving quality
- Methodologies for quality improvement
- Six sigma quality
- Statistical process control (SPC)
- Acceptance sampling

LEARNING OBJECTIVES

- Explore the definition of quality

- Understand operational, financial and customer based measures of quality

- Understand techniques for quality improvement from operational, financial and customer perspectives

- Understand the philosophy of total quality management (TQM)

- Describe the concept of Six Sigma improvement

- Understand the objectives of the ISO 9000 quality standard

- Understand the use of statistical process control and acceptance sampling

INTRODUCTION

Quality is one of the five performance objectives and having a high quality product or service often represents an essential element when being considered by the customer.

Quality is a particular challenge for service organizations in that both the tangible and intangible aspects of the service (for example the food and the service at a restaurant) must meet quality standards in order to earn repeat customers. The quality of the intangible aspect of the service may be difficult to measure and often depends on an unpredictable interaction between the service provider and customer.

Quality is a concept that can be viewed from a variety of perspectives and so the chapter begins by discussing various ways in which the concept of quality has been defined for products and services. The task of measuring quality is then discussed using operational, financial and customer quality measures. The chapter then considers techniques relevant to the pursuit of quality improvement from these three perspectives.

Various methodologies are then discussed for quality improvement. Total quality management (TQM) is a philosophy and approach that aims to ensure that high quality is a primary concern throughout the organization. The realization that a high level of quality can deliver competitive advantage is reflected in the widening use of Six Sigma initiatives.

Finally two operational oriented quality improvement techniques are covered in detail. Statistical process control is a particularly important technique in ensuring that the process of delivering the product/service is performing satisfactorily and acceptance sampling is relevant to organizations when the cost of inspection is high relative to the cost of a defect being identified

DEFINING QUALITY

Quality can actually mean quite different things to different people. This section starts by looking at different perspectives of what we mean by quality. Most definitions of quality will recognize the role of the customer in judging the quality of a product or service, so we will then look at the dimensions that customers may use in judging the quality of products and services.

What Does Quality Mean?

Garvin (1988) provides a model that presents five different perspectives on a definition of quality:

- *Transcendent*. This views quality with excellence or the best available. An Aston Martin sports car or a seven-star hotel would wish to be seen in this way. This view implies that customers will be able to recognize excellence when they see it.

- *Product based.* This views quality as a precise and measurable variable that is made up of a number of characteristics. This implies quality can be measured as a number of attributes making up a product or service. Thus, the quality of a car could be measured by its acceleration, top speed, engine size, etc. The assessment of product variables may vary considerably amongst individuals.

- *User based.* This views quality as the level of satisfaction held by an individual customer. This implies that quality is a subjective concept and will vary with the needs of individual customers. This means a car with a large range of options for engine sizes and accessories that can be customized to an individual customer's needs. Quality using this perception is defined as how well the product performs its intended function according to the customer.

- *Operations based.* This views quality as conformance to internally developed specifications in service operations or manufacturing. This implies that quality will be defined in terms of productivity targets. Thus a car produced consistently over time with no defective components and matching the design specification would be considered of high quality.

- *Value based.* This views quality in terms of best price for a given purpose. This implies quality is viewed from a customer perspective in terms of 'value for money'. Thus a Ford Fiesta could be seen to be as a better quality product than a BMW if it can meet customer's needs for a lower price. Thus a quality product is seen to be as useful as competing products but cheaper or offers greater satisfaction than products sold at a comparable price.

These five perspectives demonstrate that there is no single 'correct' view of how to define quality and all of these perspectives may be relevant but have their limitations if taken in isolation. For example the product-based and operations-based views may fail to take into account customer views. A product-based approach may have an over focus on internal design attributes and an operations-based approach may have an over focus on conformance to the design specification. On the other hand the transcendent, user-based and value-based approaches may find it difficult to operationalize the many individual customer expectations into viable products and services. A transcendent approach relies on the subjective judgement of individual potential customers as to what is the 'best'. The user-based approach may lead to unprofitable offerings in an attempt to please as many customers as possible. A value-based approach has the difficulty of determining how customers might trade off aspects of quality with cost considerations.

Slack, Chambers and Johnston (2007) attempt to reconcile these different views with the following definition of quality: *quality is consistent conformance to customers' expectations.*

Consistent implies that conformance to specification is not an *ad hoc* event but the product or service delivery process has been designed so that the product or service meets the specification using a set of measurable characteristics (product-based view). *Conformance* implies there that is a need to meet a clear specification (operations-based view). *Customers' expectations* implies that the customer receives a product or service with attributes that they can reasonably expect (user based) at a reasonable cost (value based).

Finally the perspectives are also useful in relating responsibility for quality to areas within the organization. For example the marketing department would have a large responsibility for quality defined in the customer-oriented perspectives of transcendent-based, product-based and user-based. Operations would be largely responsible for the conformance to specification viewpoint of the operations-based perspective of quality. The design function would be largely responsible for achieving a value-based perspective through low cost product and process design.

How Do Customers Define Product Quality?

Whatever the perspectives of quality taken in the previous section it is clear that an important aspect when considering quality is understanding and meeting customer requirements. However, since different customers will have different product needs and requirements it follows that they will have different quality expectations. In an attempt to understand the criteria that customers use to judge quality, Garvin (1984) breaks the concept of quality down into eight dimensions or elements:

- performance
- features
- reliability
- conformance
- durability
- serviceability
- aesthetics
- other perceptions

Each of these dimensions is self-contained and distinct and each provides an independent basis for ranking products. For example, in some markets customers will equate quality with superior performance, while in others they base their ratings on reliability. This view of quality implies there is no one way to superior quality; different organizations may choose to focus on different aspects of quality and they may all be successful; but an understanding of customer needs is important in determining a quality strategy.

How Do Customers Define Service Quality?

For services, the assessment of quality is made during the service delivery process. The nature of services in terms of their intangibility, the fact that they often involve customer contact and the customized nature of professional services means that defining quality is difficult. One approach to the definition of quality in services is given by Parasuraman, Zeithaml and Berry (1985) in terms of five principal dimensions that customers use to judge service quality:

- Reliability. This relates to the ability to perform a service dependably and accurately. Customers expect reliable service – that is, a service that is delivered on time, in the same manner and without errors every time.
- Responsiveness. This relates to the willingness to help customers and to provide prompt service. Customers in particular dislike waiting for a service especially if there is no apparent reason for the wait. A quick recovery if a service failure occurs is also important if achieving a favourable customer experience.
- Assurance. This relates to the abilities of employees delivering the service to the customer. They should demonstrate competence, respect for the customer and be able to effectively communicate with the customer.
- Empathy. This also concerns the abilities of employees and relates to the provision of a caring, individualized service requiring approachability, sensitivity and to demonstrate an effort to understand the customer's needs.
- Tangibles. This relates to the physical aspects of the service delivery environment such as the condition of the physical surroundings. Clean and tidy physical surroundings provide the customer with evidence of the care and attention to detail shown by the service provider.

The concept is that customers use these five dimensions to form their judgement of service quality, which are based on a comparison between expectations and perceptions of that service quality. These measurements are gathered from customers using the survey research instrument SERVQUAL described in the measuring quality section of this chapter. The difference between the expected and perceived service level is termed the 'service quality gap' and can be used to identify areas for improvement in service quality. The service quality gap model is also considered in more detail in the improving quality section of this chapter.

MEASURING QUALITY

In order to control quality it needs to be measured. However, we have just seen different perspectives on how to define quality so it follows there will be different approaches to its measurement. Three main categories of measures are operational, financial and customer based.

Operational Quality Measures

These measures cover operational performance indicators that are not financial or customer-based measures. Operational quality measures include scrap rates which measure the proportion of parts and materials that have been damaged by movement or manufacture and are not possible to be reused after rework. Another operational performance measure is defect rates for parts and materials that fail to meet design specifications. Performance indicators can also include service operational quality measures such as the on-time delivery performance of suppliers. Tools for improving operational quality measures include statistical process quality and quality acceptance sampling discussed later in this chapter.

Financial Quality Measures

Quality gurus such as Juran and Crosby argue that the costs of poor quality and thus the benefits of improvements in quality should be identified. Quality costs are defined as any expenditures in excess of those that would have occurred had the product been manufactured or the service been delivered right first time. These quality costs can be categorized as either the cost of achieving good quality – the cost of quality assurance or the cost of poor quality products – the cost of not conforming to specifications.

The Cost of Achieving Good Quality

The costs of maintaining an effective quality management programme can be categorized into prevention costs and appraisal costs. Prevention costs reflect the quality philosophy of 'doing it right the first time' and include those costs incurred in trying to prevent problems occurring in the first place. Examples of prevention costs include:

- the cost of designing products with quality control characteristics
- the cost of designing processes which conform to quality specifications
- the cost of the implementation of staff training programmes.

Prevention costs
These reflect the quality philosophy of 'doing it right the first time' and include those costs incurred in trying to prevent problems occurring in the first place.

Appraisal costs
These are the costs associated with controlling quality through the use of measuring and testing products and processes to ensure conformance to quality specifications.

Appraisal costs are the costs associated with controlling quality through the use of measuring and testing products and processes to ensure conformance to quality specifications. Examples of appraisal costs include:

- the cost of testing and inspecting products;
- the costs of maintaining testing equipment;
- the time spent in gathering data for testing;
- the time spent adjusting equipment to maintain quality.

Tools for improving financial quality measures include the zero defects approach discussed later in this chapter.

The Cost of Poor Quality

This can be seen as the difference between what it actually costs to provide a good or service and what it would cost if there was no poor quality or failures. This can account for 70% to 90% of total quality costs and can be categorized into internal failure costs and external failure costs. Internal failure costs occur before the good is delivered to the customer. Examples of internal failure costs include:

- the scrap cost of poor quality parts that must be discarded
- the rework cost of fixing defective products
- the downtime cost of machine time lost due to fixing equipment or replacing defective product.

External failure costs occur after the customer has received the product and primarily relate to customer service. Examples of external failure costs include:

- the cost of responding to customer complaints
- the cost of handling and replacing poor-quality products
- the litigation cost resulting from product liability
- the lost sales incurred because of customer goodwill affecting future business.

The Quality-Cost Trade-Off

The classical economic trade-off between costs shows that when the cost of achieving good quality (prevention and appraisal costs) increases, the cost of poor quality (internal and external failure costs) declines. This relationship is shown graphically in Figure 17.1.

Adding the two costs together produces the total cost curve. The optimal quality level is thus at the point when quality costs are minimized. This implies that prevention costs should be increased until this point is reached.

However, many Japanese organizations did not accept assumptions behind the traditional model and aimed for a zero-defect performance instead. The two views on the costs of quality can be seen by comparing the 'Traditional' (Figure 17.1) and 'Zero Defect' (Figure 17.2) cost-of-quality graphs. According to the traditional view the costs

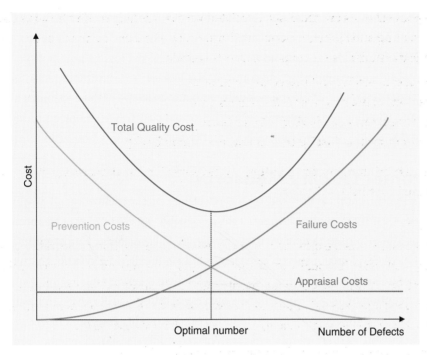

Figure 17.1: The Traditional Quality-Cost Trade-Off.

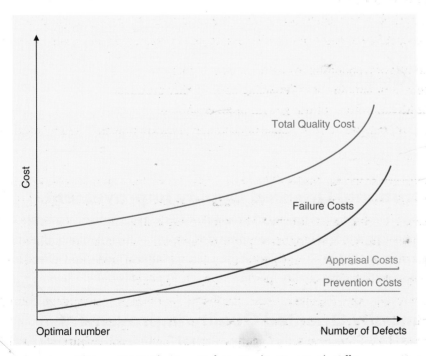

Figure 17.2: The Zero Defects Quality-Cost Trade-Off.

of prevention rise substantially as the zero-defect level is approached. This is based on the assumption that the last errors are the hardest to find and correct. The zero-defect approach assumes that it costs no more to remove the last error than the first. It may take longer to determine what the source of the last error is but the steps to correct it are likely to be simple. While there is debate about the shape of the cost-quality curves and about whether zero defects is really the lowest cost way to make a product, it is beyond doubt that the new approach to quality performance is beneficial.

Customer Quality Measures

Earlier in this chapter the role of the customer in the definition of quality was outlined. Customer quality measures move beyond operational and financial measures and incorporate the customer perspective. Parasuraman, Zeithaml and Berry (1988) have developed a survey research instrument called SERVQUAL that is based on the premise that customers can measure a firm's service quality by comparing their perception of its service with their own expectations. SERVQUAL measures the five dimensions that customers use to judge service quality (outlined in the 'defining quality' section earlier in this chapter) of reliability, responsiveness, assurance, empathy and tangibles. The survey has an initial section that records customer expectations of a service followed by a second section to record a customer's perceptions for a particular service firm offering this service. SERVQUAL can be used either to track service quality over a period of time by repeatedly administering the survey or by conducting a multisite survey to identify poor-performing units.

SERVQUAL
A survey research instrument that is based on the premise that customers can measure a firm's service quality by comparing their perception of its service with their own expectations.

IMPROVING QUALITY

In this section the techniques for quality improvement are categorized as for the quality measures in the previous section into operational, financial and customer oriented techniques.

Operational Oriented Quality Improvement

The operational oriented quality improvement methods of statistical process control (SPC) and acceptance sampling are covered at the end of this chapter. Other methods of ensuring quality at the design stage such as failure mode and effect analysis (FMEA) and Taguchi's quality loss function (QLF) are covered in Chapter 7.

Cost of quality
A concept that is intended to highlight and define the cost of quality and enable quality improvement efforts.

Financially Oriented Quality Improvement

This section will cover the financially oriented quality improvement approach of the cost of quality (COQ). The identification and measurements of the costs of quality began in the 1950s as an extension to the standard financial reporting used by organizations to control and improve organizational performance. When an attempt to measure costs was undertaken it was found that the costs of quality were much larger than previously thought, were incurred across the organization (not just in manufacturing) and most of these costs were avoidable. The measurement of these costs in financial terms alerted senior management to their significance and enabled responsibility for their reduction to be assigned.

As a first step in identifying quality costs they can be organized into the categories defined in the 'financial quality measures' section earlier in this chapter. These categories are prevention costs, appraisal costs, internal failure costs and external failure costs. Costs can be further analysed by location in terms of product line, process or department. Once the type and location of the quality costs has been determined then techniques such as Pareto analysis (Chapter 7) can be used to identify the small number of causes of the majority of costs, which will provide the greatest return on corrective action taken.

It is usual that organizations find that the highest quality costs are found in the external failure category followed by internal failure, appraisal and then prevention. The aim should be to reverse this order and eliminate external and internal failure costs as much as possible. This will mean investing in appraisal activities to identify failure costs and then when failure costs decrease the amount of appraisal can be reduced and the emphasis can shift to prevention activities.

Other financially oriented approaches to quality improvement include the need to ensure that quality is designed into the product to eliminate costly problems later at the manufacturing stage. Techniques such as value engineering (Chapter 7) can be used to do this.

Customer Oriented Quality Improvement

This section will cover the customer-oriented quality improvement technique of the **quality gap approach**. This model uses customer-based information from the SERVQUAL survey instrument (see 'measuring quality' section) and attempts to identify the nature and the location of quality problem areas. The approach was developed by Parasuraman, Zeithaml and Berry (1985) to devise a way of improving quality by identifying the gap between what customers expect from a service and what they perceive they are actually getting. The difference between the two is termed the 'quality gap' and the size of this gap determines customer dissatisfaction. Although the concept was originally devised for service operations it can be used to assess quality failures in manufactured products.

There are five possible quality gaps in the model (Figure 17.3).

Quality gap approach
This approach aims to improve quality by identifying the gap between what customers expect from a service and what they perceive they are actually getting. The difference between the two is termed the quality gap and the size of this gap determines customer dissatisfaction.

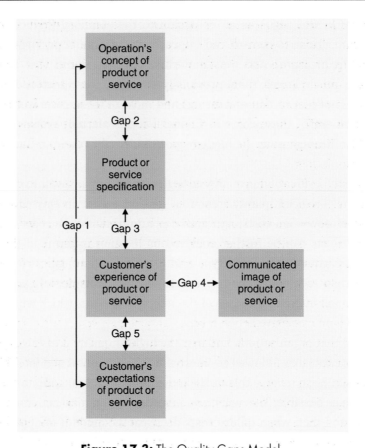

Figure 17.3: The Quality Gaps Model.
Source: Adapted from Parasuraman, Zeithaml and Berry, 1985, with permission of the American Marketing Association.

The gaps are described in turn:

- *Gap 1: operation's concept of product or service – customer's expectations of product or service.* This is when the operation's concept of the product or service does not meet customer expectations. For example a customer may expect a breakfast as part of their hotel room booking but it is not included in the specification. This gap can be closed by operations gaining a close understanding of customer expectations of the product or service.

- *Gap 2: operation's concept of product or service – product or service specification.* This is when the operation's concept of the product or service is not followed by the product or service specification. This could be due to a poorly detailed product specification or a lack of detailed plans for undertaking the service delivery process. For example the concept of a luxury hotel could be undermined by a poorly defined room cleaning process. This gap can be closed by ensuring the product or service specification is aligned with the concept.

- *Gap 3: customer's experience of product or service – product or service specification.* This is when there is a gap between the customer's experience of a product or service and the service specification. For example a customer requests a 'quiet' room in a hotel and is given a room with a connecting door to the adjacent room which permits noise to travel. This service failure could be due to poor staff training in room allocation or a lack of resource, i.e. room availability. This gap can be closed by ensuring that the product or service specification is met.

- *Gap 4: customer's experience of product or service – communicated image of product or service.* This is when there is a gap between the customer's experience of a product or service and claims made in any promotional activity concerning that product or service. For example promotional material for a hotel shows pictures of fitness equipment that is only available to hotel guests for a fee. This gap can be closed by making sure promotional materials do not imply a level of service that is not available.

- *Gap 5: customer's experience of product or service – customer's expectations of product or service.* This is when there is a gap between a customer's experience of a product or service and their expectation of that product or service. This gap is a consequence of gaps 1 to 4 and can be closed by identifying and closing the other relevant gaps. For example a customer may be disappointed at the size of their 'large' hotel room. Their expectation of what constitutes a 'large' hotel room size could have been affected by their previous experience of similar hotels or the same chain of hotels (gap 1), incorrectly specified room sizes when the hotel was designed (gap 2), incorrect allocation of a family to a standard room (gap 3) or images on the hotel web site giving a false impression of room size (gap 4).

METHODOLOGIES FOR QUALITY IMPROVEMENT

This section covers methodologies for organization wide quality improvement. The methodologies covered are total quality management (TQM), Six Sigma, the ISO 9000 quality standards and quality award programmes.

Total Quality Management (TQM)

Total quality management is a philosophy and approach that aims to ensure that high quality, as defined by the customer, is a primary concern throughout the organization and all parts of the organization work towards this goal. Total quality management does not prescribe a number of steps that must be followed in order to achieve high quality but rather should be considered a framework within which

> **Total quality management**
> A philosophy and approach which aims to ensure that high quality, as defined by the customer, is a primary concern throughout the organization and all parts of the organization work towards this goal.

organizations can work. The TQM process will be dependent on factors such as customer needs, employee skills and the current state of quality management within the organization.

The Principles of Total Quality Management

Total quality management has evolved over a number of years from ideas presented by a number of experts in the field, known as quality gurus. The original approach to ensuring quality was by the method of quality inspection, which involves detection of a quality problem by a quality inspector leading to either rejection or repair of the product. People such as W. Shewhart (1980) developed many of the technical methods of statistical control such as control charts and sampling methods which formed the basis of quality assurance and allowed a more preventative approach to be established. In the early 1970s, however, this technical focus was subsumed by more of a managerial philosophy. A.V. Feigenbaum (2007) introduced the concept of total quality control to reflect a commitment of effort on the part of management and employees throughout an organization to improving quality. There is a particular emphasis on strong leadership to ensure everyone takes responsibility for control and there is an emphasis on quality improvement as a continual process – giving rise to the term 'continuous improvement' (Chapter 18). Total quality management encompasses both the techniques of quality assurance and the approach of total quality control. A number of implementation models have been put forward by the quality gurus, who include Crosby (1996), Deming (1985) and Juran (2001).

Deming (1985) proposed an implementation plan consisting of 14 steps, which emphasizes continuous improvement of the production process to achieve conformance to specification and reduce variability. This is achieved by eliminating common causes of quality problems such as poor design and insufficient training and special causes such as a specific machine or operator. He also places great emphasis on statistical quality control techniques and promotes extensive employee involvement in the quality improvement programme. Deming's 14 steps are summarized as follows:

1. Create a constancy of purpose toward product improvement to achieve long-term organizational goals.
2. Adopt a philosophy of preventing poor-quality products instead of acceptable levels of poor quality as necessary to compete internationally.

Quality inspection
This involves detection of a quality problem by a quality inspector leading to either rejection or repair of the product.

Quality assurance
An approach to prevention rather than correction and the use of statistical tools to ensure the quality of processes.

Total quality control
An approach that emphasizes a commitment of effort on the part of management and employees throughout an organization to improving quality.

3. Eliminate the need for inspection to achieve quality by relying instead on statistical quality control to improve product and process design.

4. Select a few suppliers or vendors based on quality commitment rather than competitive prices.

5. Constantly improve the production process by focusing on the two primary sources of quality problems, the system and workers, thus increasing productivity and reducing costs.

6. Institute worker training that focuses on the prevention of quality problems and the use of statistical control techniques.

7. Instil leadership among supervisors to help workers perform better.

8. Encourage employee involvement by eliminating the fear of reprisal for asking questions or identifying quality problems.

9. Eliminate barriers between departments and promote cooperation and a team approach to working together.

10. Eliminate slogans and numerical targets that urge workers to achieve higher performance levels without first showing them how to do it.

11. Eliminate numerical quotas that employees attempt to meet at any cost without regard for quality.

12. Enhance worker pride, artisanry and self-esteem by improving supervision and the production process so that workers can perform to their capabilities.

13. Institute vigorous education and training programmes in methods of quality improvement throughout the organization, from top management down, so that continuous improvement can occur.

14. Develop a commitment from top management to implement the previous thirteen points.

Juran (2001) put forward a ten-step plan in which he emphasizes the elements of

- quality planning – designing the product quality level and ensuring the process can meet this;
- quality control – using statistical process control methods to ensure quality levels are kept during the production process; and
- quality improvement – tackling quality problems through improvement projects.

Crosby (1996) suggested a 14-step programme for the implementation of TQM. He is known for changing people's perceptions of the cost of quality when he pointed out that the costs of poor quality far outweigh the cost of preventing poor quality, a view not traditionally accepted at the time.

Oakland (2003) sees the approaches of the quality gurus as essentially complementary and has suggested his own 11-step process.

The main principles of TQM covered in these plans can be summarized in the following three statements:

1. Customers define quality and thus their needs must be met. Earlier it was stated that the organization must consider quality both from the producer and customer point of view. Thus the product design must take into consideration the production process in order that the design specification can be met. A customer perspective is required so that the implications for customers are considered at all stages in corporate decision making.

2. Quality is the responsibility of all employees in all parts of the organization. In order to ensure the complete involvement of the whole organization in quality issues, TQM uses the concept of the internal customer and internal supplier. This recognizes that everyone in the organization consumes goods and services provided by other organizational members or internal suppliers. In turn every service provided by an organizational member will have an internal customer. The implication is that poor quality provided within an organization will, if allowed to go unchecked along the chain of customer/supplier relationships, eventually lead to the external customer. Therefore it is essential that each internal customer's needs are satisfied. This requires a definition for each internal customer about what constitutes an acceptable quality of service. It is a principle of TQM that the responsibility for quality should rest with the people undertaking the tasks that can either directly or indirectly affect the quality of customer service. It requires not only a commitment to avoid mistakes but actually a capability to improve the ways in which they undertake their jobs. This requires management to adopt an approach of empowerment. It also involves providing people with training and the decision-making authority necessary in order that they can take responsibility for the work they are involved in and learn from their experiences.

3. A 'continuous improvement' culture must be developed to instil a culture that recognizes the importance of quality to performance. Continuous improvement is discussed later in this chapter.

SIX SIGMA QUALITY

Six Sigma
A company-wide initiative to reduce costs through process efficiency and increase revenues through process effectiveness.

Six Sigma is a quality improvement initiative launched by Motorola in the USA in the 1980s. The initiative was originally conceived by Motorola to achieve quality levels that are within Six-Sigma control limits, corresponding to a rate of 3.4 defective parts per million (PPM). However, Six Sigma has developed beyond a defect-elimination programme to become a company-wide initiative to reduce costs through process efficiency and increase revenues through process effectiveness. The relationship between efficiency, effectiveness and organizational performance measured by revenue is shown in Figure 17.4.

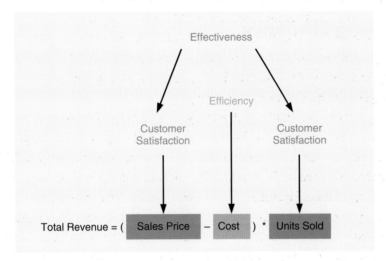

Figure 17.4: The Relationship between Effectiveness, Efficiency and Revenue.

Revenue is given by the difference between the sales price and cost of the good or service (the profit margin) multiplied by the volume of the units sold or services delivered (the market share). The model shows how an increase in effectiveness leads to an increase in customer satisfaction, which enables an increase in sales price (increasing profit margin) and an increase in units sold (increasing market share). An increase in efficiency will allow a reduction in cost (increasing profit margin) and again increasing total revenue. An increase in efficiency can also allow sales price to be reduced, keeping profit margin constant but leading to an increase in market share. Six Sigma contains plans for both increasing effectiveness and efficiency so leading to increased revenues and thus improving company performance.

Improving Effectiveness

The level of effectiveness of the organization is reflected in the level of customer satisfaction. This means that efforts to improve effectiveness will focus on identifying and meeting internal and external customer requirements. In order to identify customer requirements and translate them into product and service characteristics Six Sigma advocates the use of quality functional deployment (QFD). QFD asks customers not only about their critical requirements but also about the desired target values and limits for these requirements. Internal customer requirements must be aligned with those of the external customer. This is because external customers ultimately generate the revenues by being prepared to pay for a good or service at a price and at a volume that generates sufficient revenues. More details on QFD are given in Chapter 7.

Improving Efficiency

The aim of every process improvement approach using Six Sigma is to achieve measurable cost savings through a focus on decreasing process variation in terms of dispersion, predictability and centring. Dispersion relates to the amount (or width) of the variation in the process. Predictability means that the measured characteristic belongs to the same statistical distribution over time. Centring refers to how well the mean of the distribution is aligned with the target value over time. An ideal process would be predictable, with a low dispersion and well centred.

Process variation is inherent in any process and needs to be analysed and the source identified in order to reduce its effect and thereby increase quality and reduce costs. One tool for reducing process variation is statistical process control (SPC), which is covered later in this chapter. Once identified, the variation is usually divided into two types; common cause or random variation, which is inherent in the design of the process itself and special cause or nonrandom variation, which can be attributed to identifiable causes (for example poor material entering the process). The first step in reducing overall variation is to eliminate the special cause variation and then if necessary reduce the common cause variation by a new process design. A five-step methodology of define, measure, analyse, improve and control (DMAIC) is used for both improving process performance and for improving process or product design.

The DMAIC Methodology

**DMAIC
methodology**
This emphasizes the
use of statistical tools to
gather data at each of
the five stages of
define, measure,
analyse, improve and
control.

DMAIC methodology emphasizes the use of statistical tools to gather data at each of the five stages of define, measure, analyse, improve and control.

- *Define* – identify a potential area of improvement and define the project scope and processes involved. Assign a project team.
- *Measure* – decide which characteristics of the process require improvement. Identify the critical input variables that can be controlled and affect the output. Define what constitutes unacceptable performance or a defect. Collect sufficient data on process performance.
- *Analyse* – use the data collected in the measure phase to document current performance. Use control charts to judge whether the process is in control. The process performance can be benchmarked against similar internal or external processes.

- *Improve* – eliminate the root causes of nonrandom variation to achieve improvements in predictability, dispersion and centring. If no special causes can be found the improvement effort may need to focus on the design of the product or process.
- *Control* – verify and embed the change through the use of techniques such as control charts. Share experiences to transfer knowledge between process improvement teams.

Implementing Six Sigma

The DMAIC methodology is one aspect of a framework for implementation of the Six Sigma concept. Other aspects of this framework include top management commitment, stakeholder involvement and training and measurement. Top management commitment is required in order to implement Six Sigma in all parts of the organization. Six Sigma requires the involvement of stakeholders such as employees, suppliers and customers. Employees are required to be trained and implement the concept and suppliers must deliver high-quality inputs to the organization. The whole rationale behind Six Sigma is to understand and meet the needs of customers, so their involvement is also vital. Training is important in order to implement the statistical tools necessary for Six Sigma and is based on various levels of expertise. These levels are often denoted by the terms White Belts, Green Belts, Black Belts, Master Black Belts and Champions in order of increasing training duration and level. In terms of measurement Six Sigma focuses on the measure of variation and uses the metric of defects per million opportunities (dpmo). As stated earlier the goal is to reduce variation to within Six-Sigma control limits, corresponding to a rate of 3.4 defective parts per million (PPM).

To summarize, the Six Sigma approach emphasizes a measurable improvement in revenues through increasing effectiveness and efficiency. It uses the DMAIC methodology to ensure process improvement efforts are based on factual data. It uses customer focused improvements to ensure change increases revenue and uses training to ensure the appropriate tools are used for specific improvement projects.

CASE STUDY 17.1

Adventures in Six Sigma: How the Problem-solving Technique helped Xerox

Like many other US companies, Xerox was introduced to Six Sigma through its interactions with General Electric. The financial services to biotechnology conglomerate adopted the metrics-mad process improvement technique in the mid-1990s. Thanks to its size and influence, it has served as an effective missionary. Anne Mulcahy's conversion came as she was negotiating the outsourcing of Xerox's troubled billing and collections operation to GE Capital. She recalls: 'I remember sitting there and watching the discipline with which [the GE team] defined the problem, scoped the problem and attacked it from a Six Sigma perspective. I remember feeling for the first time that the problem would be fixed.'

The precise definition of Six Sigma quality is an error rate of 3.4 per million. More important than the exact number, however, is an approach to problem solving that emphasizes small teams, measurement and economic return. Quality improvement techniques were by no means new to Xerox. In the 1980s, it was one of the first US companies to adopt Total Quality Management (TQM) as it fought to turn back the tide of Japanese competition. As an up-and-coming manager, Ms Mulcahy experienced TQM first hand. 'The financial metrics were not as precise with TQM,' she recalls. 'Six Sigma is very rigid and very disciplined by comparison. Every project is managed with economic profit metrics. There is none of the squishy stuff.' The 'squishy stuff' is the emphasis in TQM on consensus building that, while part of an earnest desire to replicate the best of Japanese management, did not always play well at US companies.

Ms Mulcahy is also at pains to point out that Xerox practises Lean Six Sigma, a variation that asks managers to think not only how processes can be improved but also how waste can be reduced: 'Lean is an important nuance. The leaning process begins with taking out waste, working out where value gets added and where it does not. For big companies, this is very important.' While companies generally adopt Six Sigma to improve efficiency, converts insist that there are other benefits. The introduction of a company-wide approach to project management is reckoned to break down barriers between departments, and make it easier to work with suppliers and customers. Ms Mulcahy says: 'The reality of our business is that in order to compete you have to find ways to deliver 8, 9, 10% productivity improvements every single year. You only get there if you have a systemic approach.'

Source: *Financial Times*, 23 September 2005. Reproduced with permission.

Question

Discuss the advantages of Six Sigma outlined in the case study.

The ISO 9000 Quality Standard

ISO 9000
A group of quality management standards laid down by the International Organization for Standardization.

ISO 9000 provides a quality standard between suppliers and a customer developed by the International Organization for Standardization (www.iso.ch). Having a predefined quality standard reduces the complexity of managing a number of different quality standards when a customer has many suppliers. Many countries have adopted ISO 9000 and so it is particularly useful in standardizing the relationship between customers and suppliers on a global basis. The ISO 9000 model contains eight quality management principles on which to base a quality management system (QMS):

1. Customer focus.
2. Leadership.
3. Involvement of people.
4. Process approach.
5. Systems approach to management.
6. Continual improvement.
7. Factual approach to decision making.
8. Mutually beneficial supplier relationships.

The most recent ISO 9000 series of standards for quality management systems comprises the following:

- ISO 9000:2000 – fundamentals and vocabulary of quality management systems.
- ISO 9001:2000 – requirements of quality management systems.
- ISO 9004:2000 – detailed guidelines for performance improvement in quality management systems.

The standard is general enough to apply to almost any good or service but it is the specific organization or facility that is registered or certified to the standard. A facility must document its procedures for every element in the standard to achieve certification. These procedures are then audited by a third party periodically. The system thus ensures that the organization is following a documented, and thus consistent, procedure, which makes errors easier to find and correct.

Quality Awards

Programmes which provide national and international standards for quality are the European Quality Award (EQA), the EFQM Excellence Model®, Baldrige Award and the Deming Prize. The EQA was launched in 1992 by members of the European Foundation for Quality Management (EFQM) and is a yearly competition in which companies are scored in various categories such as leadership, processes and key performance results. The EFQM has also developed an Excellence Model®, which allows a company to compare the way it runs its business to best practice. A checklist is provided covering the areas of leadership, policy and strategy, people, partnerships and resources, processes, customer results, people results, society results and key performance results. The Baldrige Award was established in the USA in 1987 and seeks to recognize and encourage quality improvements. It measures performance in the seven areas of leadership, strategic planning, customer and market focus, measurement, analysis and knowledge management, human resource focus, process management and business results. The Deming Prize was established in 1951 in Japan and is awarded annually to companies that have distinguished quality management programmes.

STATISTICAL PROCESS CONTROL (SPC)

Statistical process control
This is a sampling technique that checks the quality of an item engaged in a process.

Statistical process control is an operational-oriented technique for quality improvement. It involves taking a sample that checks the quality of an item that is engaged in a process. Thus SPC should be seen as a quality check for process rather than product design. Statistical process control works by identifying the nature of variations in a process, which are classified as being caused by 'chance' causes or 'assignable' causes.

Chance Causes of Variation

Chance causes of variation
The inherent variability in processes due to factors such as ambient temperature, wear of moving parts or slight variations in the composition of the material that is being processed.

All processes will have some inherent variability due to factors such as ambient temperature, wear of moving parts or slight variations in the composition of the material that is being processed. The technique of SPC involves calculating the limits of these chance-cause variations for a stable system, so any problems with the process can be identified quickly. The limits of the chance causes of variations are called control limits and are shown on a control chart, which also shows sample data of the measured characteristic over time. There are control limits above and below the target value for the measurement, termed the upper control limit (UCL) and lower control limit (LCL) respectively. An example control chart is shown in Figure 17.5.

The behaviour of the process can thus be observed by studying the control chart. If the sample data plotted on the chart shows a random pattern within the upper and lower control limits then the process is 'in-control'. However, if a sample falls outside the control limits or the plot shows a nonrandom pattern then the process is 'out-of-control'.

Assignable causes of variation
These are variations in the process which are not due to random variation but can be attributed to some change in the process, which needs to be investigated and rectified.

Assignable Causes of Variation

If an 'out-of-control' process is discovered, then it is assumed to have been caused by an assignable cause of variation. This is a variation in the process that is not due to random variation but can be attributed to some change in the process, which needs to be investigated and rectified. However, in some instances the process could actually be working properly and the results could have been caused by

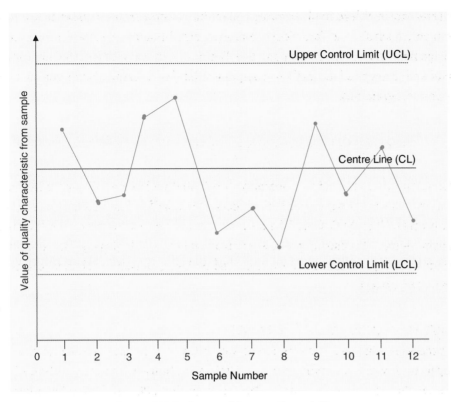

Figure 17.5: Statistical Process Control Chart.

sampling error. There are two types of error that can occur when sampling from a population:

- Type-I error – an error is indicated from the sample output when none actually occurs. The probability of a type I error is termed α.
- Type-II error – an error is occurring but has not been indicated by the sample output. The probability of a type II error is termed β.

Thus type I errors may lead to some costly investigation and rectification work, which is unnecessary. They may even lead to an unnecessary recall of 'faulty' products. Type II errors will lead to defective products as a result of an out-of-control process going unnoticed. Customer compensation and loss of sales may result if defective products reach the marketplace. The sampling methodology should ensure that the probability of type I and type II errors should be kept as low as reasonably possible.

Control Charts for Variable Data

Control charts for variable data display samples of a measurement that can take a value from a range of possible values. Values will fall in or out of a range around a specified

Control charts for variable data
Control charts for variable data display samples of a measurement that can take a value from a range of possible values. Values will fall in or out of a range around a specified target value.

target value. Examples of variable data could be a customer transaction time in a bank or the width of an assembly component. Two control charts are used in measuring variable data. The $\overline{X}$ chart shows the distance of sample values from the target value (central tendency) and the R chart shows the variability of sample values (dispersion).

$\overline{X}$ Chart

The $\overline{X}$ (X-bar) chart consists of a series of tests on a sample of data to check that the mean value of the process aligns with the target value. The sample size tends to be small, four or five. The $\overline{X}$ chart uses the central limit theorem, which states that the sample means will be normally distributed if the process distribution is also normal. Otherwise if the process does not follow a normal distribution the distribution of the sample means will be normally distributed if the sample size is sufficiently large. Thus to construct control limits for an $\overline{X}$ chart the following calculations can be used:

$$UCL = \mu + z \times \sigma_x$$
$$LCL = \mu - z \times \sigma_x$$

where

μ = process average
$\sigma_x = \sigma/\sqrt{n}$
σ = process standard deviation
n = sample size
$z = 3$ (for a three-sigma chart)

When the process mean, μ, is not known, the average of the sample means, $\overline{\overline{X}}$, can be used instead and substituted in the previous equation.

A z value of 3 corresponds to a normal probability of 99.74%. Sometimes the z value is 2, giving a probability of 95%, thus giving more narrow control limits. A smaller value of z increases the risk that the process sample will fall outside the control limits due to normal random variations. Conversely a large value of z means that nonrandom changes may not be discovered. Traditionally control charts use $z = 3$, called three-sigma (3σ) or three standard deviation limits.

Using $\overline{X}$ with R Charts

Usually the $\overline{X}$ and R charts are used together and in this case the sample range is used as a measure of process variability. Thus the control limits can be calculated as follows:

$$CV = \overline{\overline{X}}$$
$$UCL = \overline{\overline{X}} + A_2 \times \overline{R}$$
$$LCL = \overline{\overline{X}} - A_2 \times \overline{R}$$

where

$\overline{\overline{X}}$ = average of sample means

R = average sample range

values of A_2 vary with the sample size and are shown in Table 17.1.

Sample size n	Factor for $\overline{X}$ chart A_2	Factor for R chart D_3	Factor for R chart D_4
2	1.88	0	3.27
3	1.02	0	2.57
4	0.73	0	2.28
5	0.58	0	2.11
6	0.48	0	2.00
7	0.42	0.08	1.92
8	0.37	0.14	1.86
9	0.34	0.18	1.82
10	0.31	0.22	1.78
11	0.29	0.26	1.74
12	0.27	0.28	1.72
13	0.25	0.31	1.69
14	0.24	0.33	1.67
15	0.22	0.35	1.65
16	0.21	0.36	1.64
17	0.20	0.38	1.62
18	0.19	0.39	1.61
19	0.19	0.40	1.60
20	0.18	0.41	1.59
21	0.17	0.43	1.58
22	0.17	0.43	1.57
23	0.16	0.44	1.56
24	0.16	0.45	1.55
25	0.15	0.46	1.54

Table 17.1: Factors for Determining Control Limits for $\overline{X}$ and R Charts.

R Chart

Control limits for range limits are found using the following calculations:

$CV = \overline{R}$

$UCL = D_4 \overline{R}$

$LCL = D_3 \overline{R}$

R = average sample range

values of D_3 and D_4 vary with the sample size and can be found in Table 17.1.

It is usual to plot both an $\overline{X}$ and a separate R chart for a process to provide perspectives on both movements in the process mean and movements in process dispersion respectively.

WORKED EXAMPLE 17.1
Control Charts for Variable Data

As part of its process control activities a bakery wishes to monitor the weight of dough portions being measured out prior to baking. Below are given the weight of thirteen samples each of five portions. Plot these data onto the appropriate charts and comment on the stability or otherwise of the process.

Sample/weight (grams)

1	2	3	4	5	6	7	8	9	10	11	12	13
375	375	375	373	375	378	375	379	378	374	378	374	379
378	374	375	376	379	373	373	374	378	376	376	379	380
376	376	378	377	376	376	377	376	375	373	380	379	379
378	379	377	376	378	375	376	376	377	376	379	376	377
377	376	376	375	376	378	377	379	378	377	377	379	379

SOLUTION

The first step is to calculate the mean ($\overline{X}$) and range (R) for each sample.

Sample	1	2	3	4	5	6	7	8	9	10	11	12	13
$\overline{X}$	376.8	376	376.2	375.4	376.8	376	375.6	376.8	377.2	375.2	378	377.4	378.8
R	3	5	3	4	4	5	4	5	3	4	4	5	3

Then calculate the mean of the means:

$\overline{\overline{X}} = 376.6$ and $\overline{R} = 4$

For the means chart:
Sample size is 5 therefore A_2 is 0.58 (lookup value in Table 17.1).

$LCL = 376.6 - 0.58 \times 4 = 374.28$
$CV = 376.6$
$UCL = 376.6 + 0.58 \times 4 = 378.92$

For the ranges chart:
Sample size is 5 therefore $D_3 = 0$ and $D_4 = 2.11$ (lookup values in Table 17.1).

$LCL = 4 \times 0 = 0$
$CV = 4$
$UCL = 4 \times 2.11 = 8.44$

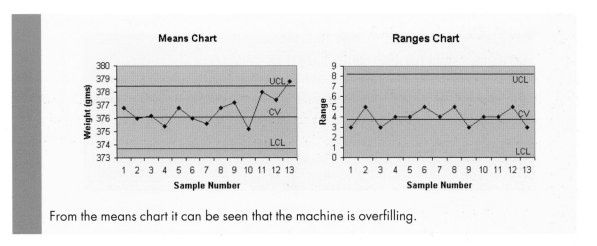

From the means chart it can be seen that the machine is overfilling.

Control Charts for Attribute Data

Attribute control charts measure discrete values such as if a component is defective or not. Thus there are no values, as in a variable control chart, from which a mean and range can be calculated. The data will simply provide a count of how many items conform to a specification and how many do not. Two control charts will be described for attribute data. The p-chart shows the proportion of defectives in a sample; the c-chart shows the number of defectives in a sample.

> **Control charts for attribute data**
> These measure discrete values such as if a component is defective or not. Thus there are no values, as in a variable control chart, from which a mean and range can be calculated. The data will simply provide a count of how many items conform to a specification and how many do not.

p-chart

The p-chart is used when it is possible to distinguish between defectives and non-defectives for each sample item, and thus calculate the number of defectives as a percentage of the whole (i.e. the proportion).

A p-chart takes samples from a process over time and the proportion of defective items is calculated to see if it falls within the control limits on the chart. Assuming a significant sample size and a three-sigma chart, the calculations can be based on a normal distribution to calculate the control limits as follows:

$$CV = p$$

$$UCL = p + 3\sqrt{\left(\frac{(p(1-p))}{n}\right)}$$

$$LCL = p - 3\sqrt{\left(\frac{(p(1-p))}{n}\right)}$$

where

p = population proportion defective (process mean)

n = sample size

When the process mean, p, is not known the proportion defective, $\bar{p}$, can be calculated from the samples and substituted in the previous equation.

WORKED EXAMPLE 17.2
Control Charts for Attribute Data

The following table gives the results of daily inspections of 500 units of a standard-design electronic device produced during the month of June 1998.

Date in June	3	4	5	6	7	10	11	12	13	14
Rejects	10	14	18	10	14	21	17	12	15	16
Date in June	17	18	19	20	21	24	25	26	27	28
Rejects	16	25	26	12	14	17	15	9	10	14

(a) Estimate the total proportion of rejects during this month.
(b) Establish a single set of control limits for the daily fraction of rejects based on these figures and plot a control chart, showing the daily results.
(c) Comment on the stability of the manufacturing process. What appears to have happened to cause the sudden change between 19 and 20 June?
(d) Based on the records of this month, what would you recommend as the central value, p, to use for the following month's control chart for fraction rejects?

● SOLUTION

The number of inspections in June 1998 is 500 units per day for 20 days, totalling 10 000 units. During this month a total of 305 units are rejected. Hence the proportion rejected, p, is:

$$p = \frac{305}{10\,000}$$
$$= 0.0305 \ (3.05\%)$$

(a) The control limits are as follows:

$p = 0.0305$
$n = 500$

$UCL = 0.0305 + 0.02306 = 0.0536$
$CV = 0.0305$
$LCL = 0.0305 - 0.02306 = 0.0074$

The proportion of rejects over the 20 working days of June 1998 is as follows:

Date	3	4	5	6	7	10	11	12	13	14
Proportion Defective	0.02	0.028	0.036	0.02	0.028	0.042	0.034	0.024	0.030	0.032
Date	17	18	19	20	21	24	25	26	27	28
Proportion Defective	0.032	0.050	0.052	0.024	0.028	0.034	0.030	0.018	0.020	0.028

p Chart

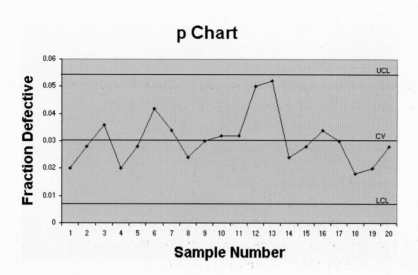

(b) The manufacturing process appears to be under control for the first half of June, and again over the last few days of the month. However, it seems clear that the process was interrupted between the 19 and 20 of June. It seems likely that the process controller decided that the process had gone out of control during the 18 and 19 June, with two consecutive observations so close to the upper control limit. This fault was rectified so that the later results were an improvement.

(c) When recommending a central value for the following month it would seem sensible to only use those days in June when the process was stable. Hence the results of the 18 and 19 June would be ignored. The recommended value for p for the following month is:

$$p = \frac{305 - (25 + 26)}{10000 - 1000} = \frac{254}{9000} = 0.0282$$

Alternatively we might use the results of just the last seven days of June (the days after adjustment) to form the basis of the recommendation. This gives:

$$p = 91/3500 = 0.026$$

c-Chart

A c-chart counts the actual number of defects when the proportion cannot be calculated. For example if the quality of paint on a car body panel is being inspected, the number of blemishes (defects) can be counted but the proportion cannot be calculated because the total number is not known. The Poisson distribution is theoretically used to represent the probability of a defect from an extremely large population, but the normal distribution is used as a substitute for the c-chart. Assuming a three-sigma chart the control limits can be calculated as follows:

$$CV = c$$
$$UCL = c + 3 \times \sqrt{c}$$
$$LCL = c - 3 \times \sqrt{c}$$

where

c = mean number of defects per sample

When the process mean, c, is not known the sample mean, $\bar{c}$, can be estimated by dividing the number of defects by the number of samples and substituting in the previous equation.

Investigating Control Chart Patterns

Apart from the plots on the control charts that lie outside the control limits, it is still possible that the process may be out of control due to nonrandom behaviour within the control limits. If the behaviour is random then the plots should follow no discernible pattern and occur either side of the centre line. There are several guidelines for identifying nonrandom behaviour. Several of these guidelines are shown in Figure 17.6.

Run Patterns

It is possible to use a z pattern test or run test to determine the probability of certain plot patterns occurring. The general form of the calculation for the z test is as follows:

$$z_{TEST} = \frac{\text{observed runs} - \text{expected runs}}{\sigma}$$

where σ = standard deviation. From this the following calculation is derived for a run of sample values that consistently go up or down within the control limits:

$$Z_{U/D} = \frac{r - [(2N - 1)/3]}{\sqrt{(16N - 29)/90}}$$

where

r = observed number of runs

N = sample sise

For a run of sample values which are above or below the centre line, the calculation is as follows:

$$Z_{A/B} = \frac{r - [(N/2) + 1]}{\sqrt{(N - 1)/4}}$$

where

r = observed number of runs

N = sample size

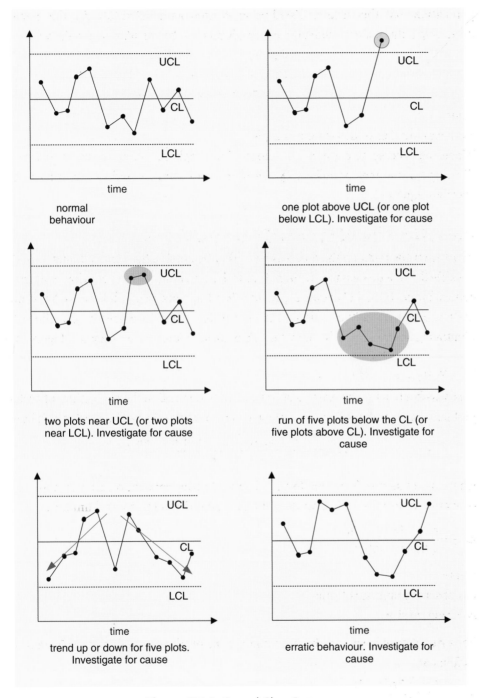

Figure 17.6: Control Chart Patterns.

The z test values are compared to a z value for a particular level of variability. Thus at a 95% probability level the z value will be $+/-1.96$. This means if the $Z_{A/B}$ or $Z_{U/D}$ is not within $+/-1.96$ then there is a 95% chance that the variability is not due to random variation.

WORKED EXAMPLE 17.3
Control Chart Patterns

A company wants to perform run tests to see if there is a pattern of nonrandomness exhibited within the control limits. It wants to use a test statistic consistent with a 95% probability that the nonrandom patterns exist. The following run pattern has been identified.

Sample	Above/below	Up/down
1	B	—
2	A	U
3	B	D
4	A	U
5	B	D
6	B	D
7	A	U
8	B	D
9	A	U
10	B	D

SOLUTION

$r = 9, N = 10$

$$Z_{A/B} = \frac{9 - ((10/2) + 1)}{\sqrt{((10 - 1)/4)}} = 2.00$$

$r = 8, N = 10$

$$Z_{U/D} = \frac{8 - ((20 - 1)/3)}{\sqrt{((160 - 29)/90)}}$$

$$= 1.38$$

At a 95% probability $z = +/-1.96$. The above/below test is slightly over this limit at $+2.00$, indicating that there may be some nonrandom pattern in the samples and the process should be checked.

Determining the Sample Size for Variable and Attribute Control Charts

It is important to note that the required sample size for each plot for a variable or attribute control chart is quite different. For $\bar{x}$ and $\bar{r}$ charts, sample sizes are usually four or five and can be as low as two. This is because even two observations should provide a reasonable measure of the sample range and sample average. For p-charts and c-charts sample size is usually in the hundreds to achieve a useful quality measure. For example, a defective proportion of 5% would require five defective items from 100. In practice sample size is also kept to a minimum to save operator time in observation. This will also permit more observation points to be implemented, which will assist in finding the cause of any quality problem. Also observations of output from a mix of machines may make it difficult to identify which machine is the source of the error.

Tolerances, Control Limits and Process Capability

It is important to distinguish between the above terms, referring to the variability of process output. They can be defined as follows:

- Tolerance – a specified range of values (for example, from customer needs) in which individual units of output must fall in order to be acceptable.
- Control limits – statistical limits on how sample statistics (such as mean or range) can vary due to randomness alone.
- Process capability – the inherent variability in a process.

The relationship between control limits and process capability can be expressed in the following formula:

$$\text{Control Limits} = \text{Process Mean} +/- z \times \frac{\text{Process Capability}}{\sqrt{n}}$$

where

z = number of standard deviations from the mean

n = sample size

Thus it can be seen that control limits are based on the variability of samples of process output whose variability is a function of the process capability. Tolerances, however, are product/service specifications and are not specified in terms of the process by which the product/service is generated. Thus a process that is performing statistically 'in control' may not necessarily be conforming to the external tolerance specifications imposed. Therefore it is essential to ensure that the process is capable of meeting the required specifications and then ensure that it can meet this tolerance consistently over time using process control. Conversely, if the natural variation of the process exceeds the designed tolerances of the product, the process cannot produce the product according to specifications as the process variations which occur naturally, at random, are greater than the designed variation. To avoid this situation it is important that process capability studies are undertaken during the product/service design stage.

ACCEPTANCE SAMPLING

Acceptance sampling
This consists of taking a random sample from a larger batch or lot of material to be inspected. The quality of the sample is assumed to reflect the overall quality of the lot.

Acceptance sampling, like SPC, is an operational-oriented quality improvement technique. It involves taking a random sample from a larger batch or lot of material to be inspected. The quality of the sample is assumed to reflect the overall quality of the lot. If the sample has an unacceptable amount of defects the whole lot will be rejected. The point at which the defect level becomes unacceptable is based on an agreement between the customer and supplier of the goods. Because acceptance sampling is based on the traditional approach which assumes that a number of defects will be produced by a process, it is usually associated with the receiving inspection process from external suppliers.

Although the acceptable defect rate may be quoted as a percentage the comments on Six-Sigma quality levels in the SPC section also apply here. Thus many organizations that take a TQM approach would expect defect levels measured in the parts per million (PPM). Indeed, if suppliers have successfully achieved a TQM philosophy and are in a stable partnership with the supplier the receiving inspection process may be eliminated.

Acceptance sampling is, however, still relevant to organizations that have not yet achieved TQM quality levels and has also been traditionally used when the cost of inspection (for example, destructive testing or sampling food) is high relative to the cost of the defect being identified. As in SPC when the product is inspected to see if it conforms to a specification the measurement can be variable or in the form of an attribute.

The sampling design includes the following aspects.

- the operating characteristic curve
- producer's and consumer's risk
- average outgoing quality.

The Operating Characteristic Curve

We are only using a sample to estimate the actual number of defects in the lot, so this may lead to errors in accepting or rejecting a lot due to sampling error. For example, if there is a target of 2% fraction defectives in a lot, a particular sample may contain a higher percentage than this even though the whole lot may not. Therefore the lot will be incorrectly rejected.

The operating characteristic (OC) curve indicates how effective the sampling plan is in discriminating between good and bad lots by showing the probability of accepting a lot for different quality levels for a given sample size and acceptance level. The shape and location of the OC curve is determined by the sample size (n) and the acceptance level (c) for the sampling plan. A selection of OC curves for different values of n and c is shown in Figure 17.7. Note when the sample size is the same as the lot size the curve is a vertical line indicating 100% inspection with no risk.

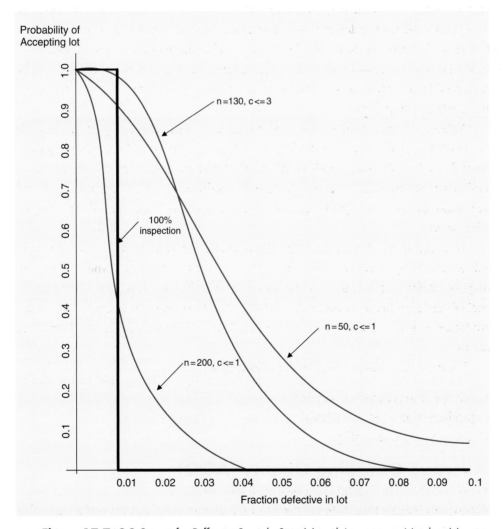

Figure 17.7: OC Curves for Different Sample Size (n) and Acceptance Number (c).

Producer's and Consumer's Risk

As discerned for the OC curve sampling error may mean either that a good lot is rejected (type I sample error) or that a bad lot is accepted (type II sample error). The acceptable quality level (AQL) is the maximum percentage (fraction defective) that is considered acceptable. The probability of rejecting a lot that has an acceptable quality level is termed the producer's risk and is related to α, the probability of a type I error. Due to sampling error there may be a sample taken that does not accurately reflect the quality level of the lot and thus a lot that does not meet the AQL is passed on to the customer. The upper limit of defective items which the customer will accept is termed the lot tolerance percent defective (LTPD). The probability of accepting a lot in which the quality level (fraction defective) exceeds the LTPD is termed the consumer's risk and relates to β, the probability of a type II error.

Usually the customer will prefer the quality of lots to be as good or better than the AQL but is willing to accept some lots with quality levels no worse than the LTPD. A common scenario is to have a producer's risk (α) at 5% and consumer's risk (β) at 10%. This means the customer expects to reject lots that are good or better than the AQL about 5% of the time and to accept lots that exceed the LTPD about 10% of the time.

A sampling plan is devised from these measures by using the OC curve. The α and AQL measures specify a point on the probability of acceptance axis and the β and LTPD measures define a point on the proportion defective axis. However, a trial-and-error process is required to determine the sample size (n) and acceptance number (c) to achieve these performance measures. This involves determining the probabilities of accepting a lot for various lot percentage defective values. A typical OC curve is shown in Figure 17.8.

From Figure 17.8, it can be seen in this case that if a lot has 3% defective items, for example, the probability of accepting a lot is 0.95. If management defines the AQL at 3%, then the probability that the lot will be rejected (α) is 1 minus the probability of accepting a lot ($1 - 0.95 = 0.05$). If management is willing to accept lots with a percentage defective up to 15% (LTPD), this corresponds to a probability (β) of 0.10 that the lot will be accepted.

To avoid the time-consuming task of using a trial-and-error method to construct OC curves, standardized tables, called the Dodge–Romig Inspection tables, can be used based on a given set of risks. Computer software is also available, which will develop sampling plans based on values for AQL, LTPD, α and β.

Average Outgoing Quality (AOQ)

Even though the probability of accepting a lot containing defects may be very small, all lots, whether they are accepted or not, will pass on some defects to the customer. The expected number of these defective items is measured by the AOQ. Assuming

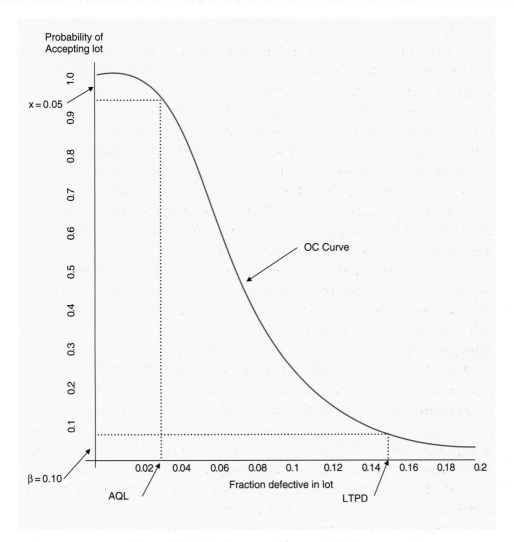

Figure 17.8: An Operating Characteristic Curve.

that defective items rejected (and thus completely inspected) lots are replaced the defective items that are passed on to the customer are contained in the lots that are accepted. Thus

$$AOQ = pP_a\left(\frac{(N - n)}{N}\right)$$

where

p = percentage defectives (horizontal axis in OC chart)

P_a = possibility of accepting a lot (vertical axis in OC chart)

N = lot size

n = sample size

Values for AOQ against fraction defectives are shown in Figure 17.9.

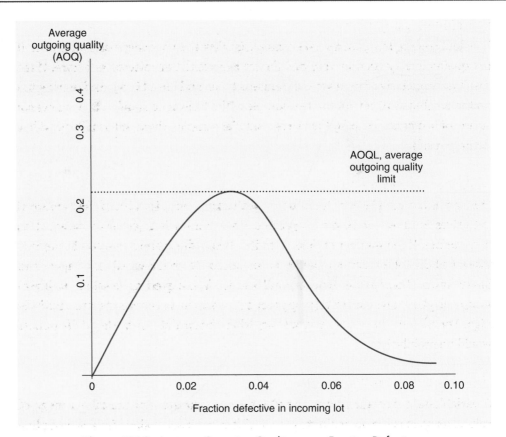

Figure 17.9: Average Outgoing Quality versus Fraction Defectives.

From Figure 17.9 it can be seen that the AOQ rises to a point from the origin and then falls back again. The peak is termed the average outgoing quality limit (AOQL) and represents when the sampling plan does its worst job of upgrading quality, i.e. below this there are few defects accepted, above this there are more defects, but they are rejected and replaced. Each sampling plan will have a different AOQ curve and the AOQL can be used to select a suitable sampling plan.

Sampling Plans

The method of sampling or sampling plan can take a number of forms including the following.

Single-Sampling Plan

For a single sample attribute plan the method consists of selecting a sample at random from a larger lot and determining if the goods are defective or not (a discrete decision).

factory in Indonesia and aims to globalize its business over the next few years. The scenario before and after TQM reflects how far TVS has come in nearly two decades. Productivity, quality and sales have improved dramatically. Previously, the rate of 're-work' – parts plagued by faults – was 15%. That figure has fallen to 100 parts per million. The factory used to make four deliveries a month to customers compared with two daily now.

It was no easy task to overhaul the family-owned company that was founded in 1911 by Mr Srinivasan's grandfather, TV Sundaram Iyengar. For three decades after 1960, India closed its markets to global competition. Imports were restricted and licences were required to start businesses, creating little incentive to improve or strive for quality. After earning a degree in engineering from Madras University in today's Chennai, Mr Srinivasan went to the US for graduate studies, like many scions of India's business families. In 1979 he earned a master's in science and management at Purdue University in Indiana – the degree became known as an MBA in 2001 – where he received a 'strong dose' of industrial engineering.

He visited factories of US automakers such as General Motors but was unimpressed. 'US factories did not have that exactness,' he recalls. A trip to Japan in 1981 and visits to the Suzuki and Honda factories proved pivotal. 'Even the bullet train aligned exactly on the platform. People were highly motivated and committed.' He was inspired by 'a country that could create this kind of excellence' and sought to restore the high quality for which TVS was known in the 1940s when it ran a highly efficient bus network and General Motors dealership.

Mr Srinivasan began reading books about TQM and 'desperately tried to get hold of Japanese professors, but India was not on the radar' in the early 1980s. The mission to restructure TVS grew more urgent in the 1980s when profits slipped although sales grew. 'That triggered the need for change. I knew that if we continued like that we wouldn't be in business.' Mr Srinivasan introduced TQM to the company in 1989 and implemented and improved it over the next nine years. Experts from Japan still visit the company.

TVS's adaptation of TQM rests on five pillars. They include policy deployment; involving every person at the company; *kaizen*, or continuous improvement; standardization of processes; and new product development. Seated at a long boardroom table at the TVS office, Mr Srinivasan takes a pen and draws a series of boxes to illustrate the 'silos' that hobbled the company before. There were six layers of management. With little cooperation or communication between divisions, 'most meetings were full of fault-finding and finger pointing'. Under the new regime, silos were broken down. For instance, different teams collaborated on design of new motorcycles so staff from R&D worked jointly with production and assembly. As a result, innovation has been boosted. TVS rolled out its first 20 models in 21 years but it has produced 10 new products in the past three years alone. This year TVS expects to roll out six new models.

On the factory floor, inefficiencies were identified and weeded out. TVS used to keep ten weeks of inventory at its factory compared with two weeks now. The assembly line suffered frequent delays. 'We couldn't predict what we could supply to customers', says Mr Srinivasan. 'It used to be a real mess.' Mr Srinivasan recalls that previously the factory floor was haphazardly organized. 'One man operated one machine with another man doing inspections. Relative to today it would be dirty.' Today employees are trained to operate different machines, allowing for a leaner workforce. In traditionally hierarchical India, Mr Srinivasan shocked employees by picking up cigarette butts from the factory floor in keeping with one of the pillars of involving every employee.

He started tracking all the company's statistics and breaking them down, line by line. Figures were conveyed to employees through charts displayed in the factory. 'Everybody could see the actual graph. Before, people would fudge', says Mr Srinivasan. 'But every hour productivity is displayed. We created a feedback loop.' Changing an entrenched mindset was a difficult task. 'It requires a high degree of understanding between employees and management', says C. Narasimhan,

formerly president of Sundaram-Clayton, the auto-components firm and sister company of TVS. But employees were encouraged to offer suggestions for improvement. 'Some employees give 200 suggestions a year', says Mr Narasimhan. 'Awards are given for the best suggestion.' Roles of each employee are now clarified and targets clearly assigned. Results are displayed for everyone to see in order 'to hold the gains'. Changing his own role at TVS was also a challenge for Mr Srinivasan, whose position as family trustee shifted as the company's president became more empowered. 'For me to move back and change my role took a lot of change myself', admits Mr Srinivasan. 'You've got to look at yourself in the mirror honestly. But you have to make the change to get other people to make the changes you expect of them.'

Source: by Amy Yee, The Financial Times, 28 January 2008. Reproduced with permission.

Question
How do the principles of TQM relate to the management of the TVS motorbike factory?

CASE STUDY   17.3

Yell

With some 3400 employees, Yell is an international directories business operating in the classified advertising market. Its vision is to be the best business information bridge between buyers and sellers, regardless of

channel, time or location in the markets in which they operate. The company aims to put buyers in touch with sellers through an integrated portfolio of simple to use advertising solutions – including printed

(Yellow Pages), on-line (Yell.com) phone products and services.

Yell started introducing quality management in the late 1980s by adopting a TQM approach, and this approach became integrated into the way Yell manages its business. The company has used tools such as the EFQM Excellence Model®, Six Sigma, ISO 9001:2000, ISO 14001:1996, OHSAS 18001:1999 and Investors in People (IiP) to review and refine its overall management approach. A critical enabler of activities has been Yell's commitment to effective leadership, involvement and communication. Its focus is now on becoming the best in everything the company does.

Yell sets the scope and direction for its system of management through its vision and business purpose. It also defines the way this will be achieved through strong and clear values. Together these provide the framework for all their activities. Yell brings this alive for people, through a structured approach that focuses on both the process and the people:

- alignment of goals and objectives through a systematic planning process
- integration of policies and processes through a key process framework
- enablement of activity through effective leadership, involvement and communication.

Senior managers generate the policy and strategy through an annual planning process. They work closely with members of the strategic planning team to ensure alignment with vision, purpose and strategic goals. All managers and their people are involved in the effective deployment of strategy by agreeing business initiatives and departmental plans and budgets. This is a highly interactive process with managers using a scorecard approach to help them to align objectives with strategy.

Policy and strategy are delivered through a key process framework, which provides the top-level architecture for their process management system. It consists of a value chain of customer facing processes supported by five internal management processes. 'Providing Strategic Direction' is the first part of the Key Process Framework.

Strategy is communicated via face-to-face presentations to managers, and they then communicate to their team. This is supported by an 'objectives' intranet site where people can trace their progress. In addition, the theme for objectives is revised each year, to provide renewed focus – in the 'You make us unique' objectives brochure every employees name was featured in the design. Other themes have included 'Breaking Boundaries', 'Superbrand-Superfuture' and 'Accelerating Performance'

Against the backdrop of regulatory conditions and the changing economy between 2001 and 2004, Yell has achieved consistent annual UK revenue growth of approximately 5%. This is matched in its growth in customer base by approximately 5% and by continuous improvement in processes and customer services. The company has achieved positive trends, sustained high performance and good comparisons with other organizations, for example errors in over 1 million individually produced adverts have been reduced by several per cent over the past 10 years to just 0.1%.

Yell UK is considered to be a benchmark in its approach to engaging with its people. For example, the objectives communication process is supported by a communication approach called 'Storytellers', which is highly interactive and encourages all employees to think strategically about their contribution to Yell. The company also runs an 'Uncles Programme', where senior managers meet with geographically dispersed teams and talk about business strategy and individual concerns. Senior managers go outside their own function and it keeps them in touch with front line issues as well as enabling them to explain strategic decisions.

Yell is very proud of its record on communicating individual responsibilities, and carries out a census survey amongst its employees once a year. The most recent survey achieved a 94% response rate. Since 1998 they have averaged over 97% for people saying that they clearly understand what is expected of them.

In 1999 Yell won the European Quality Award, and in 2004 became the first company to win the award for a second time. Yell also received two Special Prizes for 'Leadership' and 'People Development and Management.'

One of the challenges the company has faced was the proliferation of Areas for Improvement (AFIs). When Yell began its quality journey, and following any of its many assessments, it highlighted a daunting number of AFIs. This led to the introduction of a prioritizing approach, with improvement activities that are followed through until completed – with the focus clearly on actions and outcomes. Achievements are always recognized and this is communicated throughout the organization.

The company has also been very careful not to establish a 'flavour of the month'. The focus of the approach was placed upon improvement and not introducing 'another' initiative. This was also achieved by integrating tools such as the EFQM Excellence Model®, ISO 9001 and IiP into the overall management system.

Source: excerpt from DTI web site (now Department for Business, Enterprise and Regulatory Reform).

Question

What is Yell trying to achieve with its use of quality management standards and techniques?

EXERCISES

1. How do customers define product and service quality?

2. Contrast the traditional quality/cost trade-off with the zero defects quality/cost trade-off.

3. How can the quality gap approach be used to improve quality?

4. What is the purpose of TQM?

5. Explain the relationship between Six Sigma and process management.

6. Use the Web to compare the Baldrige Award and the European Quality Award.

7. The following table gives the number of defectives in successive samples of 100 final assemblies removed at random from that day's production.

Day	Number of defectives	Day	Number of defectives
1	6	11	11
2	8	12	8
3	7	13	13
4	10	14	14
5	11	15	15
6	5	16	12
7	13	17	7
8	9	18	34
9	9	19	29
10	10	20	8

a) Estimate the total proportion of rejects.
b) Establish a single set of control limits for the daily fraction of rejects based on these figures and plot a control chart, showing the daily results.
c) Comment on the stability of the manufacturing process.

8. The following table gives the means and ranges, from a sample size of 10, for the diameter of a machined part.

Mean	Range R	Mean	Range R	Mean	Range R
0.52	0.03	0.5	0.11	0.57	0.1
0.53	0.1	0.53	0.08	0.52	0.07
0.57	0.09	0.52	0.05	0.52	0.12
0.49	0.08	0.48	0.09	0.51	0.11
0.48	0.12	0.54	0.03	0.49	0.09

Use the data to set up a control chart for means and for ranges.

9. A machine produces components to a specified average length of 9.03 cm. Every hour a random sample of five components is selected from the process and their lengths measured. After 10 hours the data given below have been collected.

Sample number	Measurements (cm)				
1	9.00	9.10	9.00	9.05	8.95
2	9.10	9.10	9.00	9.05	9.05
3	9.00	9.05	9.00	9.05	9.00
4	9.00	9.00	8.95	9.00	9.05
5	9.00	9.10	9.05	9.05	9.00
6	9.00	9.10	9.10	9.05	9.00
7	9.00	9.10	9.05	9.15	9.05
8	9.00	9.10	9.10	9.00	9.05
9	9.00	9.00	8.95	9.00	9.00
10	9.00	9.05	9.00	9.10	8.95

Use the data to set up a control chart for means and for ranges.

10. Explain the concepts of producer's risk and consumer's risk in acceptance sampling.

WEB EXERCISE

Write a description of the EFQM excellence model using information from the EFQM web site at `http://www.efqm.org/Default.aspx?tabid=35` (accessed 9 October 2008).

FURTHER READING

Besterfield, D.H. (2008) *Quality Control*, 8th edn, Prentice Hall.
Dale, B.G. (2008) *Managing Quality*, 5th edn, Wiley Blackwell Publishers Inc.
Dodge, H.F. and **Romig, H.G.** (1998) *Sampling Inspection Tables – Single and Double Sampling*, 2nd edn, John Wiley & Sons, Inc.
Rummler, G.A. (2007) *Serious Performance Consulting: According to Rummler*, Jossey Bass.
Taguchi, G., **Chowdhury, S.** and **Wu, Y.** (2005) *Taguchi's Quality Engineering Handbook*, John Wiley & Sons, Inc.
Wheeler, D.J. (2000) *Understanding Variation: The Key to Managing Chaos*, 2nd edn, SPC Press Inc.

● WEB LINKS

www.asq.org (accessed 9 October 2008). American Society for Quality. Publications and courses in the area of quality management.

www.baldrige.nist.gov (accessed 9 October 2008). National Institute of Standards and Technology. Details of the Baldrige Award.

www.efqm.org (accessed 9 October 2008). European Foundation for Quality Management. Details of the European Quality Award.

www.iso.ch (accessed 9 October 2008). International Organization for Standardization (ISO). Site providing details on ISO 9000 and other standards.

www.qfdi.org (accessed 9 October 2008). QFD Institute. Contains newsletters and forums in the area of QFD.

www.quality.co.uk (accessed 9 October 2008). Quality Network. Resources on benchmarking, ISO 9000 and environmental management.

www.qualitydigest.com (accessed 9 October 2008). Quality Digest. Access to magazine, news and tips on quality management.

www.quality-foundation.co.uk (accessed 9 October 2008). British Quality Foundation. A not for profit organization that promotes business excellence to the private, public and voluntary sectors.

www.ukas.com (accessed 9 October 2008). UK Accreditation Service. Accredits the certification bodies which oversee the implementation of quality management systems based on ISO 9001:2000.

● REFERENCES

Crosby, P.B. (1996) *Quality is Still Free: Making Quality Certain in Uncertain Times*, McGraw-Hill.

Deming, W.E. (1985) Transformation of Western-style management. *Interfaces*, **15**(3), 6–11.

Feigenbaum, A.V. (2007) *Total Quality Control*, 4th edn, McGraw-Hill.

Garvin, D.A. (1984) What does quality really mean. *Sloan Management Review*, **26**(1), 25–43.

Garvin, D.A. (1988) *Managing Quality*, Free Press.

Juran, J.M. (2001) *Juran's Quality Handbook*, 5th edn, McGraw-Hill.

Oakland, J.S. (2003) *TQM: Text with Cases*, 3rd edn, Butterworth Heinemann.

Parasuraman, A., Zeithaml, V.A. and **Berry, L.L.** (1985) A conceptual model of service quality and its implications for future research. *Journal of Marketing*, **49**(4), 41–50.

Parasuraman, A., Zeithaml, V.A. and **Berry, L.L.** (1988) SERVQUAL: a multiple item scale for measuring consumer perceptions of service quality. *Journal of Retailing*, **64**(1), 12–40.

Shewhart, W. (1980) *Economic Control of Quality of Manufactured Product*, ASQC/Quality Press.

Slack, N., Chambers, S. and **Johnston, R.** (2007) *Operations Management*, Prentice Hall: Harlow.

CHAPTER 18

Performance Measurement and Improvement

LEARNING OBJECTIVES

- Understand the use of performance measures

- Understand how areas for improvement are identified using performance measures

- Evaluate the use of discontinuous and incremental approaches to performance improvement

- Describe the use of activity-based costing

- Describe the use of the balanced scorecard

- Understand the concept of benchmarking

- Understand the concept of business process re-engineering (BPR)

- Understand the role of environment, involvement and problem solving in the implementation of continuous improvement

- Understand the need for organizational learning

INTRODUCTION

This chapter covers the topic of performance measurement and improvement. Before improvement can take place we need to identify suitable measures of performance. Traditional measures of performance such as productivity and efficiency are covered and then measures associated with operations' five performance objectives are discussed. The measure of cost is explored further and the use of activity-based costing is covered. The need to incorporate measures from a number of perspectives and link strategic measures to operational targets is discussed in the context of the balanced scorecard measurement system.

The next step, once measures of performance have been identified, is to compare each performance measure against a performance standard in order to identify areas for improvement. This standard can be internal to the organization, such as a comparison against previous performance or against targets for future performance. External targets include comparison to competitor performance, best practice or 'best-in-class' performance or market requirements. Internal targets are often based on comparing past financial and sales performance with targets for future performance. This section also covers the use of benchmarking and the methods covered in Chapter 2 for identifying performance objectives that require improvement.

Once priorities for improvement have been identified then an improvement programme can be implemented. In this chapter the improvement approaches of business process re-engineering (BPR) and continuous improvement (CI) are discussed.

HOW DO WE MEASURE PERFORMANCE?

Performance measurement involves both choosing the measures that will be used to identify where improvements should take place and also determining if improvement has taken place after change has been implemented. This section looks at a variety of performance measures that are used in operations management.

Traditionally performance measures in operations have focused on indicators such as **productivity**, which divides the value of the output by the value of the input resources consumed:

$$\text{productivity} = \frac{\text{output}}{\text{input}}$$

Productivity
This divides the value of the output by the value of the input resources consumed.

Productivity is used at both the organizational and national level as a comparative measure of performance. From the equation it can be seen that productivity can be increased by either increasing output without a proportionate increase in input or decreasing input without a proportionate decrease in output. Productivity can be a valid tool for the operations manager and provides an indication of the level of utilization of resources. However, it can be difficult to find appropriate input and output parameters for the calculation and the measure also fails to consider performance from a wider viewpoint encompassing customer and other stakeholder needs.

Other performance measures include **efficiency**:

Efficiency
The use of a resource in terms of availability

$$\text{efficiency} = \frac{\text{actual output}}{\text{effective capacity}}$$

In Chapter 11 efficiency is defined as a measure of the use of capacity remaining after the loss of output due to planned factors such as maintenance and training. In other words efficiency relates to the use of a resource in terms of availability. However, a high level of efficiency does not necessarily imply that resources are being used effectively in improving overall performance. **Effectiveness** can be defined as the extent to which the output of a process meets the requirements of its customers. This is more difficult to measure quantitatively than productivity or efficiency. In service operations effectiveness is often measured by surveys of customer satisfaction. As was discussed in Chapter 17, however, customer satisfaction will be dependent on the perceptions and expectations of individual customers. Other indicators of effectiveness could be sales volume and sales margin figures for products and services.

Effectiveness
The extent to which the outputs of a process meet the requirements of its customers.

Chapter 2 (strategy) considers that the focus of improvement should be directed towards appropriate areas of the operation where any increase in performance will help the organization meet its strategic goals. In this text the **five performance objectives** of quality, speed, dependability, flexibility and cost are used to measure operations performance in relation to its strategy. It also shows that strategies that rely on immediate cost cutting (achieving **economy** by lowering the costs of inputs into the operations transformation process) should be replaced by strategies that aim to improve performance on the other performance objectives which will then lead to a reduction in cost. Measures for each of the performance objectives are shown in Table 18.1.

Five performance objectives
These are used to measure operations performance in relation to its strategy.

Economy
Lowering the cost of inputs into the operations transformation process.

Cost is traditionally calculated by estimating in terms of staff, facilities and material the resources that are required for the input and transformation processes in an operation. However, the way these costs are allocated to products and services is often arbitrary. For example the actual costs of producing a product in a factory where hundreds of other products are also being made is dependent on an accurate allocation of direct costs (staff, equipment and material costs directly connected to the product) and indirect costs (for example overheads such as factory space, energy, administration and central staffing costs). The aim of performance measurement is to identify where cost is being incurred within an operation so improvement efforts can be focused in the correct areas. As an alternative to the usual overhead based

Performance objectives	Measures
Quality	Operational, financial and customer measures (see Chapter 17).
Dependability	Percentage of customers that receive the product or service when promised.
Speed	Time delay between request and receiving product or service.
Flexibility	The amount of change (range) or speed of change (response) in product/service, mix, volume or delivery (see Chapter 2)
Cost	Staff, facilities and material costs for product or service. Cost of activities undertaken to produce product or service (see activity-based costing in Chapter 18).

Table 18.1: Performance Measures for the Performance Objectives.

costing methods **activity-based costing** provides a way of allocating costs to manufacturing and service activities in order that a company can determine how much it costs to make a certain product or deliver a service. In ABC there are three main drivers of cost: the cost driver, the resource driver and the activity driver.

- The cost driver relates to the amount of resources needed to perform an activity and can be reduced by, for example, redesigning the process.
- The resource driver relates to the type of resources needed for an activity and can be reduced, for example, by using different personnel, information technology or equipment.
- The activity driver relates to the number of times the process occurs and can be reduced, for example, by training to improve the reliability of a process.

Turney (1996) outlines an ABC model, which has two main views (Figure 18.1):

The cost assignment view of ABC allocates costs to activities by identifying *resource drivers*, which determine the cost of resources, and *activity drivers*, which determine the use of these resources. The process view of ABC provides information about the effort needed for the activity termed the *cost driver* and provides performance measures of the outcome of the activities. The cost assignment view can be used to reduce the activity cost by either reconfiguring the resources needed for an activity (resource driver) or reducing the amount of resource required (activity driver). The process view provides a link between the inputs needed to perform an activity (cost driver) and the outputs required by the internal or external customer of that activity (performance measure). Thus an investigation of a combination of resource drivers, activity drivers and cost drivers for an activity can improve process performance by identifying why cost has been incurred. Case Study 18.1 shows the advantages of being able to identify where cost is being incurred.

Activity-based costing
Provides a way of allocating costs to manufacturing and service activities in order that a company can determine how much it costs to make a certain product or deliver a service.

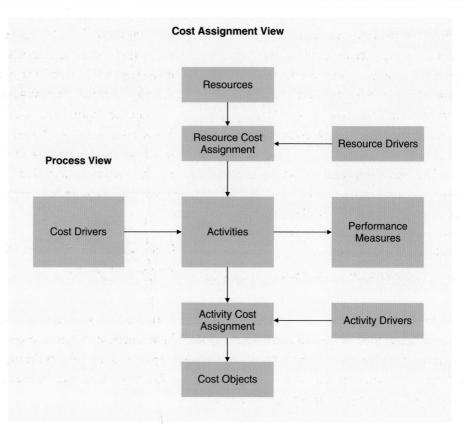

Figure 18.1: The Two Perspectives of Activity-Based Costing.

CASE STUDY   18.1

Activity-Based Costing at a Police Service

A study was undertaken of the costs involved in operating a custody suite at a police service in the UK. The custody suite is involved in the processing of arrested persons and their subsequent release, interview or detention. Like most service operations the custody operation is characterized by having a large part of its resources in the form of labour. Unfortunately this often leads to a situation of management of resources by inputs (budgets). Thus the amount of resources (for example,

people and capital) deployed is based on historical budgets with a large proportion classified as overhead and fixed with an annual addition for inflation. Departments are then managed by tracking variances in expenditure from budgeted amounts. In this case an ABC approach was taken in order to identify where cost was being incurred, as a first step to improving performance.

In terms of cost drivers, a major source of cost was found to be the time taken to undertake the paper-based booking-in process, which occurs for all arrested persons. In order to reduce the amount of resource needed for this the booking-in process was redesigned using BPR and a proposal for computerization put in place.

The resource drivers in this case relate primarily to the pay rates of personnel involved in the arrest process. A civilianization programme, which involves using trained civilians for activities formerly undertaken by police personnel, was proposed.

In this case the activity driver relates to the timing and frequency of arrests. The activity driver depends on environmental factors such as the crime rate and government policy on crime as well as factors under the control of the police. It was found, however, that a high proportion of arrests were for minor theft offences involving children, which could possibly be processed using alternative methods.

Question

What are the benefits of the ABC analysis of the custody suite?

Another approach to performance measurement has been the use of the **balanced scorecard** developed by Kaplan and Norton (1996). The balanced scorecard approach is an attempt to incorporate the interests of a broader range of stakeholders through performance measures across four perspectives of financial, customer, business process and learning and growth (Figure 18.2).

Balanced scorecard
A measurement system that incorporates performance measures across the four perspectives of financial, stakeholder, business process and innovation and learning.

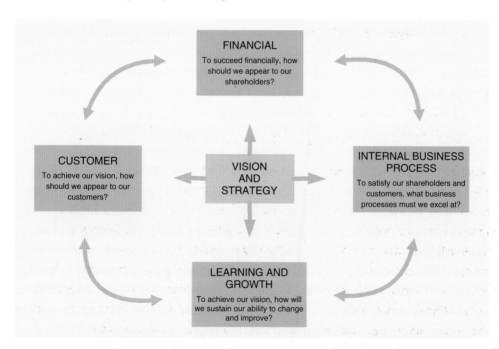

Figure 18.2: The Balanced Scorecard.
Source: Adapted from Kaplan and Norton (1996), Harvard Business School Press, used with permission.

The idea of the scorecard is to provide managers with a multiple perspective of the goals that need to be met for organizational success. Although designed for performance measurement at a strategic level its relevance to operations is that it provides a direction for the organization that will impact on and be impacted by operations (see the Hill methodology for operations strategy in Chapter 2). The balanced scorecard also provides a way of translating strategy into action. It does this by translating performance measures at a strategic level into operational performance measures. Case Study 18.4 shows how strategic targets on absence at a UK Police Service were translated into measures at an operational level.

WHERE SHOULD WE IMPROVE PERFORMANCE?

Performance standard
A target value for a performance measure.

In order to identify where performance improvement should take place it is necessary to compare the performance measure against a performance standard. This standard can be internal to the organization such as comparing against previous performance or against targets for future performance. External targets include comparison to competitor performance, best practice or 'best-in-class' performance or market requirements.

Internal targets are often based on a comparison between past financial and sales performance and targets for future performance. The advantage of these measures is that they are widely used and comparable across organizations and use data that are readily available. However, they may be of limited value in identifying why performance is above or below a target value.

External performance targets have the advantage of providing a comparison of performance against competitors operating in similar competitive markets. This approach is often termed benchmarking. Benchmarking can be defined as the continuous measurement of an organization's products and processes against a company recognized as a leader in that industry. The analysis of competitor products is an older technique, which forms part of the product design process (Chapter 7). Benchmarking was initially restricted to the comparison of direct competitors in the manufacturing sector. Now it is practised in the service sector (for example, banks), in all functional areas (such as marketing) and in comparison with a wide variety of competitors from which lessons can be learnt (not just the best in class). Because of the widespread use of the technique and the requests by many organizations to visit the same high performance firms, much benchmarking data is held in databases for general use. A number of models for implementing a benchmarking

Benchmarking
The continuous measurement of an organization's products and processes against a company recognized as a leader in that industry.

programme have been developed. The main activities involved in benchmarking are summarized below:

- *Planning*. Understand your own processes, identify key processes and form benchmarking teams.
- *Analysis*. Conduct research on possible competitors and formulate questions to elicit the required information. Establish a relationship with a partner organization and collect and share information.
- *Implementation*. Implement and monitor improvements suggested by analysis.

It is important that the relevant processes in the organization are benchmarked before comparison with a competitor. Processes are benchmarked in terms of metrics (numeric measurements) and procedures (process flows). For example a payment process could be measured by the time taken from receiving the request to delivery of the payment. The technique would also measure the type and amount of personnel involved in each step of the process. One problem with some benchmarking programmes has been the focus on developing metrics and the lack of energy put into implementing changes suggested by the benchmarking process. Other problems are the difficulty in obtaining competitor information and the fact that if the process is simply used to emulate a competitor, competitive advantage may be short-lived as the competitor makes further improvements.

In terms of the measures associated with the five operations performance objectives, Chapter 2 identifies two models that can be used to identify where performance should be improved.

The Hill model (Hill, 2005) is based on market requirements. The concepts of 'order winning' and 'qualifying factors' are used to distinguish between those factors that directly contribute to winning business and those that are necessary to qualify for the customer's consideration between a range of products/services. The importance of this is that while it may be necessary to raise performance on some factors to a certain level in order to be considered by the customer, a further rise in the level of performance may not achieve an increase in competitiveness. Instead competitiveness may then depend on raising the level of performance of different 'order-winning' factors.

The second model of Slack (1991) uses a combination of market and competitive factors and two dimensions – importance and performance – to help operations managers prioritize performance objectives. The relative importance of a competitive factor is assessed in terms of its importance to internal or external customers using a nine-point scale of degrees of order winning, qualifying and less important customer viewed competitive factors. The next step ranks the relative *performance* of a competitive factor against competitor achievement. A nine-point performance scale (rating from consistently better than the nearest competitor to consistently worse than most competitors) is used for each performance objective. The next step is to plot each importance rating and performance rating in an importance-performance matrix. This indicates what customers find important in achieved performance when compared with competitor performance.

HOW DO WE IMPROVE PERFORMANCE?

There are two main approaches to improving performance in organizations. One is the concept of discontinuous (a major 'step') change in the way of working and the other is a gradual or incremental approach. These two approaches will be discussed using their associated methods of business process re-engineering and continuous improvement respectively. Note that both of these performance improvement techniques are often subsumed under the term 'business process management' (BPM), which refers generally to the analysis and improvement of business processes. Business process management is covered in Chapter 8.

BUSINESS PROCESS RE-ENGINEERING

In the early-to-mid 1990s, organization-wide transformational change was advocated under the label of BPR. It was popularized through the pronouncements of Hammer and Champy (1993) and Davenport (1993). The essence of BPR is the assertion that business processes, organizational structures, team structures and employee responsibilities can be fundamentally altered to improve business performance. Hammer and Champy (1993) defined BPR as 'the fundamental rethinking and radical redesign of business processes to achieve dramatic improvements in critical, contemporary measures of performance, such as cost, quality, service, and speed.'

The key words from this definition that encapsulate the BPR concept are:

- *Fundamental rethinking* – re-engineering usually refers to the changing of significant business processes such as customer service, sales order processing or manufacturing;
- *Radical redesign* – re-engineering is not involved with minor, incremental change or automation of existing ways of working. It involves a complete rethinking about the way business processes operate;
- *Dramatic improvements* – the aim of BPR is to achieve improvements measured in tens or hundreds of per cent. With automation of existing processes only single-figure improvements may be possible;
- *Critical contemporary measures of performance* – this point refers to the importance of measuring how well the processes operate in terms of the four important measures of cost, quality, service and speed.

Willcocks and Smith (1995) characterize the typical changes that arise in an organization with process innovation as:

- work units changing from functional departments to process teams;
- jobs change from simple tasks to multidimensional work;
- people's roles change from controlled to empowered;
- focus of performance changes from activities to results;
- values change from protective to productive.

Many re-engineering projects were launched in the 1990s and failed due to their ambitious scale and the problems of managing large information systems projects. Furthermore, BPR was also often linked to downsizing in many organizations, leading to an outflow of staff and knowledge from businesses. As a result BPR as a concept has fallen out of favour and more caution is advocated in attempting to achieve change.

Less radical approaches to organizational transformation are referred to as **business process improvement (BPI)** or by Davenport (1993) as 'business process innovation'. Taking the example of supply-chain management, an organization would have to decide on the scope of change. For instance, do all supply chain activities need to be revised simultaneously or can certain activities such as procurement or outbound logistics be targeted initially? Modern thinking would suggest that the latter approach is preferable. A five-step approach to the introduction of BPR has been suggested by Davenport (1993).

> **Business process improvement**
> Optimizing existing processes typically coupled with enhancements in information technology.

1. Identifying processes for innovation. The organization should select a process or processes that are critical to the organization and so provide a potentially large increase in performance in return for the re-engineering effort. The scope and number of process redesign projects must be compatible with the organization's ability and experience to undertake them.
2. Identifying change levers. The three main enablers or levers of change are information technology (IT), information and organizational/human resource. Davenport provides categories in which IT can provide process innovation (Table 18.2).

    Much information is not manipulated by IT resources in the organization but may still be a powerful lever in making process innovation possible. Examples include the visible display of information on the shop floor in lean production organizations and the market information used by executives in making strategic decisions.

    The need to align the organizational culture with technological change is discussed in Chapter 9 on Job Design. For example many process innovations will lead to increased worker empowerment which may require an adjustment in

Category of IT	Process innovation
Automational	For example, robotics in manufacturing, workflow in services.
Informational	The ability of IT to provide additional information about a process that can be used for improvement (see Zuboff, 1988).
Sequential	Transform process execution (such as concurrent engineering).
Tracking	Knowing the status of components (such as mail delivery systems).
Analytical	Providing additional information for decision making.
Geographical	Using worldwide communications system (for example, linked CAD).
Integrative	Case management approach – needs database of information from around the organization.
Intellectual	Database of company knowledge of processes.
Disintermediating	Connects buyers and sellers without intermediaries.

Table 18.2: Categories in which IT can provide Process Innovation.

organizational culture to ensure successful implementation. The successful use of teams is also essential in implementing cross-functional processes.

3. Developing process vision. It is essential that the process innovation effort is consistent with the organization's strategy. A process vision consists of measurable objectives and provides the link between strategy and action. A shared vision is essential to ensure true innovation, rather than standard improvement efforts such as simplification and rationalization. A vision allows conventional wisdom about how processes are undertaken to be questioned. Key activities in developing a process vision include assessing existing business strategy for process direction, consulting with process customers, benchmarking process performance targets and developing process performance objectives and attributes.

4. Understanding existing processes. This step is necessary to enable those involved in the innovation activities to develop a common understanding of the existing processes, understand complexities, avoid duplicating current problems and provide a benchmark against which improvement can be measured. Traditional process-oriented approaches such as flow charting can be used for this task but do not contain the elements necessary for the implementation of radical change.

5. Designing and prototyping the new processes. The design of new processes requires a team with a mix of members who can deliver creative and innovative process solutions and ensure that they are implemented. Key activities in the design and prototype phase are the brainstorming of design activities, assessing the feasibility of these alternatives, prototyping the new process design,

developing a migration strategy and implementation of the new organizational structure and systems. Simulation modelling can be a valuable tool in assessing new process design (Chapter 8).

CONTINUOUS IMPROVEMENT

Continuous improvement programmes are associated with incremental changes within the organization whose cumulative effect is to deliver an increased rate of performance improvement. Continuous improvement is associated with the JIT and lean philosophy, where it is referred to as *Kaizen*, a Japanese term, meaning a way of getting to the ideals of JIT by a continuous stream of improvements over time (see Chapter 13).

> **Continuous improvement**
> Continuous improvement concerns incremental changes within the organization whose cumulative effect is to deliver an increased rate of performance improvement.

Continuous improvement requires creating the right environment in which the importance of the approach is recognized and rewarded. This means ensuring the involvement of all the members of the organization and ensuring that these members have the problem-solving skills necessary to achieve worthwhile improvements. The issues of environment, involvement and problem-solving skills will now be explored in relation to continuous improvement implementation.

Environment

In order to create the right environment in which improvement can take place it is important to have a set of procedures for the improvement process, which formalizes actions so that progress can be monitored and measured. A procedure for an improvement study could follow the steps of the Plan-Do-Check-Act (PDCA) cycle (Figure 18.3) as follows:

1. What changes are needed in order to gain continual improvement?
2. Analyse appropriate data. Carry out suggested changes to the process.
3. Evaluate the results of the changes to the process.
4. Make the changes permanent, or try another step (go to step 1).

The PDCA was developed by Deming and Shewhart (see Gabor, 1992) for improving production processes and separates the process creation and execution phases ('plan' and 'do') from the process checking and improvement ('check' and 'act') phases. Thus a continuous feedback loop is created between process operation and process improvement.

Involvement

The idea behind continuous improvement is to use the skills and knowledge of all the workforce in a sustained attempt to improve every aspect of how the organization

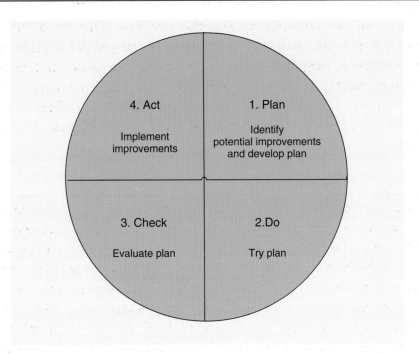

Figure 18.3: The Plan-Do-Check-Act (PDCA) Cycle.

operates. It is useful to disseminate information around the organization regarding progress on various performance measures in order to emphasize the importance of the improvement effort. This can be done using meetings, newsletters and boards displaying charts. The most common objectives used are the QCDSM measures of Quality, Cost, Delivery, Safety and Morale. Suggestion schemes offer the person closest to the work activity the opportunity to suggest improvements to the process. Suggestions by employees are evaluated and if they are assessed as providing a significant saving then a cash award may be paid to the employee. The award could be a fixed amount for all suggestions or a percentage of net savings over a specific time period. Suggestion schemes are most likely to be successful when employees are given training in aspects such as data collection and the scheme is promoted, rather than the size of any award payments. Process improvement teams or quality circles are using the different skills and experiences of a group of people in order to solve problems and thus provide a basis for continual improvement. In order to do this the team should be aware of the tools available for measuring and thus improving performance such as statistical

process control (SPC) (Chapter 17). Expertise outside the group can also be used to contribute to group effectiveness. A quality circle is a small group of people (6–12) who meet voluntarily on a regular basis. Process improvement teams are usually made up of experienced problem solvers from departments affected by the process and are appointed by management. The use of a group can be particularly effective at working through a cause-and-effect diagram (Chapter 7) to find the root cause of a particular problem.

Problem Solving Skills

Information technology has had a particular impact on the level of problem solving and thus decision making skills required in the organization. The decision-making activity is often classified in order that different decision processes and methods can be adopted for the common features of decisions within these choices. Decision types can be classified into strategic, tactical and operational relating to top, middle and supervisory management levels. The main variables across these levels being the time-span over which decisions are taken and the amount of money involved in the choice of option. However, these classifications fail to recognize the changes that are taking place with the introduction of information systems (see Case Study 18.2).

CASE STUDY 18.2

In the Age of the Smart Machine

Shoshana Zuboff in her book *In the Age of the Smart Machine* (Zuboff, 1988) describes the changes that took place within continuous process factories in the United States which changed to computer controlled systems. The extra information produced by these systems required a different kind of conceptual grasp by the person concerned in order to recognize patterns and understand the consequences of actions on the overall process. This represents a major change from just the monitoring of information on a computer screen. In other words these more sophisticated computer applications, rather than simply replacing repetitive and mechanical tasks, often serve as a sophisticated decision support tool that is most valuable in the hands of a sophisticated user with broad responsibilities. This implies that the link between information and management level may become increasingly inappropriate as the job scope and responsibility of many people within the organization increases with the advent of information systems.

Question

What are the implications of the findings in the case study for operations managers?

Learning organization
This aims to create an environment that builds knowledge within the organization and can use that to improve performance.

Continuous improvement is associated with the concept of the **learning organization**, which aims to create an environment which builds knowledge within the organization and can use that to improve performance. The need for organizational learning has been identified as a consequence of the need for organizations to continually produce innovations in order to maintain a competitive edge. The ability to generate a continuous stream of ideas for improvement and implement them is seen as a sustainable competitive advantage for organizations. To consider how an organization learns is really to consider how learning of individuals within that organization takes place and how the results of that learning are integrated into the practices, procedures and processes of the organization. The transfer of knowledge from individual to organizational system means that the knowledge becomes independent of the individual and is possessed by the organization and is replicable by individuals within that organization. Probst and Büchel (1997) state that the outcome of an organizational learning process is qualitatively different from the sum of the individual learning processes. This is because learning is the outcome of human interactions and the sharing of experiences between individuals. For example a decision made by a group can have outcomes which are totally different from the outcomes of the sum of individual decisions. There are a range of definitions of the levels of organizational learning. Probst and Büchel distinguish between 3 different levels of adaptive, reconstructive and process learning which are now described.

- *Adaptive learning* is when an organization adapts to its environment by means of members of that organization identifying problems in the environment, developing strategies for dealing with them and implementing these strategies. Thus the organization is making a correction in order to align behaviour towards existing goals.
- *Reconstructive learning* or double-loop learning occurs when there is a more significant change in the relationship between the organization and its environment for which a process of adaptation is insufficient. Here changes at the more fundamental level of the values of individuals or groups within the organization must be changed in order to align behaviour towards attainment of an organization's goals. In fact this questioning of the organization's 'theories of action' leads to a questioning of the original organizational goals, which are then changed.
- *Process learning.* Defensive routines that individuals, groups and organizations have built up to protect them from the threat of change can be formidable obstacles to a successful learning process (Argyris, 1999). This means that even if individuals recognize the need for learning, these defensive routines prevent this

from occurring. Thus a process of 'learning to learn' – the study of the process of learning itself – must take place. This process is the highest level of learning and is in fact the act of learning to understand adaptive and reconstructive learning.

CASE STUDY 18.3

Managers Disrupt Learning with their 'Great Ideas'

It is all too easy for businesses to underestimate how much learning is taking place via the informal networks that become established in large organizations – networks that are often invisible to managers. These networks, says Peter Senge, a senior lecturer at the MIT Sloan School of Management, are delicate and can end up being destroyed when senior managers try to introduce new systems. 'A lot of learning is going on in organizations but management is screwing it up with their great ideas on how to do things more efficiently or their great ideas for reorganizing', he warns. 'In any healthy organization, there's a lot of learning going on. But 90% of it is informal and is going on well below the radar screen of the management structure', says Professor Senge. 'So you need to help managers become more aware.' He says that it is important to question assumptions when seeking to raise skill levels in the workplace or to introduce new technology: the rigid hierarchical structure found in many organizations needs to be turned on its head.

Professor Senge, who is founding chair of the Society for Organizational Learning and author of *The Fifth Discipline: The Art and Practice of the Learning Organization*, believes the learning process begins by taking a fresh look at the way the organization operates – and this applies to the implementation of IT systems.

'There's a very understandable life cycle you go through, when you first start using IT, to do what you've always done', he says. 'Someone thinks there's an efficiency gain or the potential for cost reduction or maybe you could do something more reliably – but you rarely think about doing something that you have never done before.' Part of the problem, he says, is that there is usually a disproportionate amount of power at the top of the organization. 'That almost always means a bunch of people with 25 to 30 years' experience', he says. 'That can make them impervious to seeing the significance of developments that a 25-year-old might see.' Companies also suffer because of the persistent belief that learning goes on only in a classroom. Often, however, when employees have been given the formal training on a new system, as much is learnt back at their desk where they can lean over and ask a colleague the best way to carry out a particular function they need at that particular moment. There will always be people within an organization who are better than others at learning how to use IT systems and explaining it to others. Professor Senge believes these people can and should play a big part in IT training. What training specialists provide, he says, is usually often delivered out of context of the workplace. 'No one ever learnt anything in a final sense in a classroom. It's all contextual –

it's not the tool. It's how you use the tool in a particular setting with particular people and under particular pressures.'

What Professor Senge is advocating is a grass-roots approach to learning. Rather than spreading technical knowledge from above through leaders that have decided what people need to know, he suggests starting at the other end, where some people may be more adept than others at learning and operating IT systems. 'Sample both ends of the spectrum', he says. 'Start by looking at the really good stuff that is working today – and then what's keeping that from spreading.' At higher levels of an organization, this dissemination is just as crucial. After all, for senior managers to be able to make strategic decisions about IT, they need to have an understanding of the systems being used throughout the organization. However, there is often resistance by these people to taking a training course they might see as below them. 'That's a big problem – the executives want the 30-minute summary and want everyone else to spend days on it', says Professor Senge. He suggests starting at the 'shallow end of the pool' by seeking out managers who are more motivated than others and focusing initial attention on them. Most important when introducing any new system, he says: 'Go to the most sophisticated users to first get it working well and then figure out how to help other people get it working well – don't just hand it over to the training department.'

Source: by Sarah Murray, published: 19 September 2006. Copyright The Financial Times Limited, 2008.

Question

Discuss how the learning of individuals can be integrated into the practices, procedures and processes of the organization.

THE RELATIONSHIP BETWEEN BPR AND CI APPROACHES

Continuous improvement programmes are associated with incremental changes within the organization whose cumulative effect is to deliver an increased rate of performance improvement. The important point about continuous improvement is that it can deliver improvements that are difficult to copy by competitors. For instance, a culture that recognizes and delivers quality and reliability is a long-term project that may not show immediate financial benefit. In order to catch up or overtake competitors it has been realized that continuous improvements may not be enough, but step changes in performance are required. These are associated with innovations in areas such as product design or process design. The BPR technique has been widely cited as an approach that locates suitable areas for change and delivers improvements to them.

These two approaches share orientation to process as the unit of improvement, orientation to strategy execution rather than strategy itself, belief in the importance

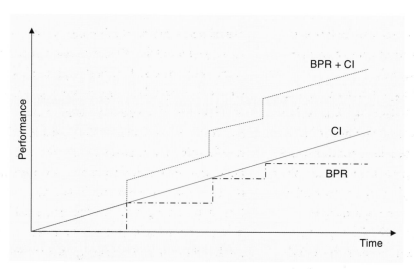

Figure 18.4: Combining BPR and CI initiatives.

of measurement and analysis and focus on external criteria (for example, bench-marking) as the basis for judging improvement. When BPR and CI coexist within an organization they should be perceived as being related aspects of an overall perfor-mance improvement initiative. Figure 18.4 shows how the two approaches could be combined in an improvement initiative to outperform an organization using only one of the approaches.

In the 1990s many organizations attempted major or breakthrough change by attempting to implement radical process redesigns under the banner of BPR. It was found that many of these efforts failed but the use of a process perspective was seen as useful and so companies are now more likely to try process improvement to enable more limited changes. The concept of business process management (BPM) (Chapter 8) is used to refer to the various methods and technologies that are used to enable a process oriented change using both incremental and breakthrough approaches.

SUMMARY

- Performance measurement involves choosing both the measures that will be used to identify where improvements should take place and also to determine if improvement has taken place after change has been implemented.

- Activity-based costing assists in determining how much it costs to make a certain product or deliver a service.

- The balanced scorecard incorporates performance measures for improvement across the perspectives of financial, customer, business process and innovation and learning.

- In order to identify where performance improvement should take place it is necessary to compare the performance measure against a performance standard.

- Benchmarking can be defined as the continuous measurement of an organization's products and processes against a company recognized as a leader in that industry.

- There are two main approaches to improving performance in organizations. One is the concept of discontinuous change in the way of working (associated with business process re-engineering) and the other is a gradual or incremental approach (associated with continuous improvement).

- Business process re-engineering calls for an analysis of a business from a process rather than functional perspective and then the re-engineering of these processes to optimize performance.

- Implementation of continuous improvement requires attention to the organizational environment, involvement of organizational members and development of problem solving skills.

- Organizational learning has been identified as a consequence of the need for organizations to continually produce innovations in order to maintain a competitive edge.

CASE STUDY 18.4

Process Improvement at a UK Police Service

The nature of the Police Service as a service industry means that a central task is the management and deployment of human resources. As part of a re-engineering study covering all aspects of police duties an investigation of the human resources division and its information technology infrastructure was undertaken. One particular area selected for redesign was the sickness and absence process located in the HR division. This is of particular interest as the issue of illicit absenteeism from work in the UK Police Service has attracted publicity. It has been estimated that it was costing Police Services in England

and Wales £250 million a year, losing an average of 11 working days per officer annually (Sheehan, 2000).

The following steps were undertaken in the process improvement exercise.

1. Derive the critical success factors.
2. Process mapping.
3. Identify processes for improvement.

4. Process redesign.
5. Measure performance.

Step 1: Derive the Critical Success Factors

Critical success factors (CSF) can provide a guide to determine 'what needs doing well' in order to implement a strategy and fulfil the organizational vision. The critical success

Perspective	Critical success factor
Innovation and learning	**Increase individual performance** This CSF needs positive improvement and measures to improve individual performance. For example, health and welfare of staff, rewards/penalties, attract quality applicants, retain staff, staff relations, development and training of staff.
Business process	**Increase effectiveness of strategic management.** This CSF will provide accurate management information on which to base strategic development and policies and decisions. For example, improve service to public, develop policies, support and advise on organizational change, empowerment.
	Improve staff communications This CSF will ensure that staff are better informed of and are aware of new legislation, policies and procedures, where to obtain relevant management information and expert advice and set up procedures to enforce policies particularly those mandated by legislation or otherwise.
Stakeholder/ customer	**Meet legislative requirements** Failure to meet this CSF will result in penalties including financial penalties and dismissal . . .
	Increase effectiveness of service in its delivery to external customers This CSF will require HR to provide accurate management information to the service on which the service can base both strategic and tactical responses to the needs of external customers and agencies.
	Increase effectiveness in delivery to internal customers This CSF will require HR to provide accurate management information and professional advice to heads of departments and line managers (all levels) on which heads of departments and line managers can base both strategic and tactical responses to the needs of their own staff and other internal customers.
Financial	**Improve value for money (of HR to the organization)** This CSF will require HR management to develop strategic and tactical plans and policies to guide service strategic development in HR aspects and make the most effective use of resources and systems to provide a high quality service

Table 18.3: The CSFs for the Balanced Scorecard Perspectives.

factors can be placed within the four perspectives of the balanced scorecard, which provides a balanced set of performance indicators to reflect the views of the wide range of stakeholder groups involved. A balanced scorecard can be constructed at the organizational or departmental level at which a focused strategy can be adopted. The critical success factors for the HR organization were based on the strategic plan developed by the Police Service at a divisional level. The objectives were then passed to the heads of the various departments within the HR division (for example, head of personnel or head of training) for discussion. The CSFs are shown in Table 18.3.

Step 2: Process Mapping

In order to identify activities within the sickness and absence process the technique of process mapping was used. Process mapping involves a study of how activities link together to form a process. The technique involves interviewing personnel and observation of the relevant process which provides information which is used to draw a process map. The analysis shows the interrelationships between activities and identifies the elements and roles involved in process execution (more details on process mapping are given in Chapter 8).

Step 3: Identify Processes for Improvement

Once the process mapping has been completed it is necessary to prioritize the process elements, which will be allocated resources for improvement. The following example presents a measurement system developed in conjunction with the service. The system consists of a two-dimensional marking guide based on the impact of the process on the critical success factors determined in the balanced scorecard review and an assessment of the scope for innovation (the amount of improvement possible) to the current process design. Processes which are strategically important and offer the largest scope for improvement are prioritized under this model. The marking guide marks each process on a scale of 0 to 5 against 2 measures:

IMPACT – the extent to which the achievement of the CSF depends on the process.
INNOVATION – the extent of the change required to the process in order to meet the CSF.

The marking guides for each measure are shown in Table 18.4 and Table 18.5.

In terms of the balanced scorecard the IMPACT measure relates to the achievement of the CSF from the stakeholder and financial (external) perspectives of the balanced scorecard. The INNOVATION measure relates to the amount of change required from the learning and business process (internal) perspectives (Figure 18.5).

Each process element is scored (0–5) against each CSF for the impact and innovation measures. The score for each measure is multiplied to provide a composite score (0–25) for each CSF. An overall composite score for each process is calculated by adding the composite score for each CSF. A spreadsheet sort by composite score identifies a priority list of processes for improvement.

Mark	IMPACT (External Perspective) Marking Guide
0	This individual process has minimal or no effect on the individual CSF
1	This individual process is dependent on another process, in to order for it to have an effect on this CSF
2	This individual process has a marked influence on this CSF
3	The individual process has substantial impact on whether another process can maximize its beneficial effects on this CSF
4	The individual process has substantial influence on this CSF
5	The individual process is a critical part of being able to achieve the individual CSF

Table 18.4: IMPACT (External Perspective) Marking Guide.

Mark	INNOVATION (Internal Perspective) Marking Guide
0	This process cannot be improved for this CSF
1	This process achieves its objective but could be improved even further.
2	This process achieves its objective but could be improved by review of both automation and process improvement.
3	This process does not effectively achieve all its objectives and could be improved by review of both automation and process improvement.
4	The process exists and functions but needs substantial alteration to meet its objectives.
5	The process either does not exist or only partially exists and fails to meet any objectives.

Table 18.5: INNOVATION (Internal Perspective) Marking Guide.

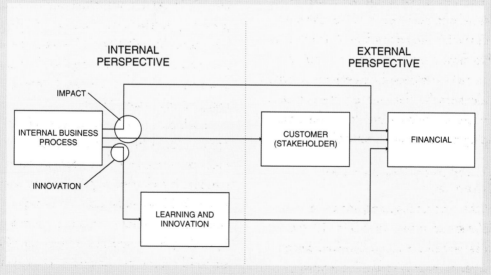

Figure 18.5: Relationship between the Scoring Systems and the Balanced Scorecard Perspectives.

Step 4: Process Redesign

Once suitable processes have been identified for improvement, the next stage was to redesign these processes to improve their performance. Peppard and Rowland (1995) provide a number of areas of potential redesign under the headings of Eliminate, Simplify, Integrate and Automate (ESIA) (see Chapter 8 for more details on ESIA).

In the case of the 'sickness-and-absence' process, this involved integration of the present 30 separate process maps into a single process. Some duplication of activities was found, primarily due to functions included with the sickness process being based both at Headquarters and Divisional level. The redesign improved performance both internally and externally. Internally process efficiency was increased with an estimated saving per sickness/absence event of between 45 minutes to 60 minutes of staff time, representing a significant resource saving which can be re-deployed to improve performance. External process effectiveness has been increased by increasing the speed of follow-up checks to absent officers and new innovations such as requiring earlier checks by the police doctor.

Step 5: Measure Performance

In this case, in order that progress is maintained towards strategic objectives, it was considered important to relate performance of the process at an operational level to strategic targets. The 'sickness and absence' process is related to the CSF identified in the balanced scorecard initiative of increasing individual performance. At a strategic level, the measure of staff productivity was chosen with a target to increase availability of police officers by 5%. In order to meet this strategic target, measures and targets are needed at an operational level. These are derived both from the strategic measure and an understanding of the relevant business process. The measure chosen for the sickness and absence process was 'average days lost per year'. The target for this measure is 11.9 days lost per year per employee for sickness and absence. This benchmark was derived from the national average performance. The current performance was at 14.1 days lost per year per employee (Figure 18.6).

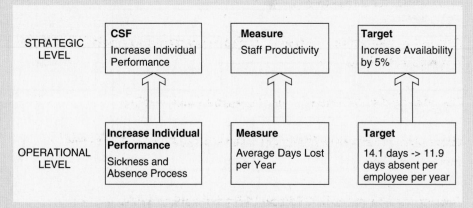

Figure 18.6: Deriving Operational Measures from Strategic Objectives.

Slack and Lewis (2008) state that the strategic management of any operation cannot be separated from how resources and processes are managed at a detailed and day-to-day level. The case study presents one way of ensuring the correct processes are identified and redesigned at an operational level in such a way as to support the organization's strategic aims. In addition a performance measurement system is used to attempt to ensure that the changes implemented do actually achieve the desired effect over time.

Source: Adapted from Greasley (2004). Reproduced by permission of Emerald Group Publishing Ltd.

Questions

1. Discuss the choice of performance measures, how areas of improvement are identified and the method of improvement chosen in the case study.

2. How were the strategic targets linked to operational change in the case study?

EXERCISES

1. Distinguish between the terms efficiency, effectiveness and economy.

2. Why is activity-based costing a useful tool for the operations manager?

3. Identify the need for using a balanced scorecard rather than measuring performance using a measure such as productivity.

4. Discuss the role of benchmarking.

5. Discuss the main issues involved in the implementation of a continuous improvement effort.

6. Describe the three different levels of organizational learning.

7. Discuss the factors behind the integration of the BPR and CI improvement approaches.

8. Compare and contrast the BPR and CI improvement approaches.

WEB EXERCISE

Using the company profiles at `http://www.apqc.org/portal/apqc/site/?path=/research/profiles/index.html` (accessed 10 October 2008), provide a summary of the features of a successful benchmarking effort.

FURTHER READING

Greasley, A. (2000) A simulation analysis of arrest costs. *Journal of the Operational Research Society*, **51**, 162–7.

Harmon, P. (2003) *Business Process Change: A Manager's Guide to Improving, Redesigning, and Automating Processes*, Morgan Kaufman.

Holloway, J., Lewis, J. and Mallory, G. (eds) (1995) *Performance Measurement and Evaluation*, Sage Publications.

Imai, M. (1996) *Kaizen: The Key to Japan's Competitive Success*, McGraw-Hill.

Kaplan, R.S. and Norton, D.P. (2006) *Alignment*, Harvard Business School Press.

Senge, P.M. (1990) *The Fifth Discipline: The Art and Practice of the Learning Organization*, Century Business.

Shingo, S. (2008) *Kaizen and the Art of Creative Thinking*, Norman Bodek.

Zuboff, S. and Maxmin, J. (2004) *The Support Economy*, Penguin Books Ltd.

WEB LINKS

`www.apqc.org` (accessed 12 October 2008). Amercian Productivity and Quality Center. This site provides information on such topics as benchmarking and performance measurement.

`www.kaizen-institute.com` (accessed 12 October 2008). Kaizen Institute. Contains tips for implementing continuous improvement.

`www.prosci.com` (accessed 12 October 2008). BPR Online Learning Centre. Contains tutorials and many articles on BPR.

REFERENCES

Argyris, C. (1999) *On Organizational Learning*, 2nd edn, Blackwell Publishers.

Davenport, T.H. (1993) *Process Innovation: Re-engineering Work through Information Technology*, Harvard Business School Press.

Gabor, A. (1992) *The Man who Discovered Quality*, Penguin.

Greasley, A. (2004) Process Improvement within a HR Division at a UK Police Force. *International Journal of Operations and Production Management,* **24** (2/3), 230–40.

Hammer, M. and **Champy, J.** (1993) *Re-engineering the Corporation: A Manifesto for Business Revolution,* Harper Business, New York.

Hill, T. (2005) *Operations Management,* 2nd edn, Palgrave Macmillan.

Kaplan, R.S. and **Norton, D.P.** (1996) *The Balanced Scorecard: Translating Strategy into Action,* Harvard Business School Press, Boston.

Peppard, J. and **Rowland, P.** (1995) *The Essence of Business Process Re-engineering,* Prentice Hall.

Probst, G. and **Büchel, B.** (1997) *Organizational Learning: The Competitive Advantage of the Future,* Prentice Hall.

Sheehan, M. (2000) Police chiefs crack down on shirkers. *Sunday Times,* 27 February, p. 9.

Slack, N. (1991) *Manufacturing Advantage: Achieving Competitive Manufacturing Operations,* Mercury.

Slack, N. and **Lewis, M.** (2008) *Operations Strategy,* 2nd edn, Pearson Education Ltd, Harlow.

Turney, P.B.B. (1996) *Activity-based Costing: The Performance Breakthrough,* Kogan Page.

Willcocks, L. and **Smith, G.** (1995) IT enabled business process re-engineering: organizational and human resource dimension. *Strategic Information Systems,* **4**(3), 279–301.

Zuboff, S. (1988) *In the Age of the Smart Machine: The Future of Work and Power,* Heinemann.

GLOSSARY

ABC classification system   Sorts inventory items into groups depending on factors such as the amount of annual expenditure.

Acceptance sampling   Consists of taking a random sample from a larger batch or lot of material to be inspected. The quality of the sample is assumed to reflect the overall quality of the lot.

Activity-based costing (ABC)   A way of allocating costs to manufacturing and service activities in order to determine how much a company spends to make a certain product or deliver a service.

Actual capacity   The capacity remaining after loss of output due to both planned and unplanned factors. Unplanned factors include equipment breakdown and absenteeism. See also effective capacity.

Aggregate plan   A plan that specifies aspects such as overall production rate, size of the workforce and the amount of subcontracting required to deliver the mix of products or services required to meet the demand profile.

Agile operations   The ability to respond quickly to changing market demand in order to retain current markets and gain new market share by developing the capability of resources.

Anthropometric data   Information concerning factors related to the physical attributes of a human being, such as the size, weight and strength of various parts of the human body.

Appraisal costs   Costs associated with controlling quality through the use of measuring and testing products and processes to ensure conformance to quality specifications.

Assignable causes of variation   Variations in the process that are not due to random variation but can be attributed to some change in the process, which needs to be investigated and rectified. See also chance causes of variation.

Automated material handling (AMH) systems   Systems designed to improve efficiency in the movement, storage and retrieval of materials.

Autonomous work groups   Groups that are able to decide on their own working methods and handle problems as they arise. They will typically be responsible for the whole delivery of a product or service.

Balanced scorecard   A measurement system that incorporates performance measures across four perspectives: financial, stakeholder, business process and innovation and learning.

Balancing capacity   Equalizing the capacity of a number of sequential processes.

Batch process   A process that covers a relatively wide range of volume and variety combinations. Products are grouped into batches whose batch size can range from two to hundreds. See also continuous process, jobbing process, mass process, project process.

Benchmarking   The continuous measurement of an organization's products and processes against a company recognized as a leader in that industry.

Bill of materials (BOM)   A document that identifies all the components required to produce a scheduled quantity of an assembly and the structure of how these components fit together to make that assembly.

Budgeted cost of work performed (BCWP)   See earned value.

Bullwhip effect   The results of a lack of synchronization between supply chain members, where even a slight change in consumer sales will ripple backwards in the form of magnified oscillations in demand upstream.

Business activity monitoring   Software that is designed to monitor, capture and analyse business performance data in real time and present them visually in order that rapid and effective decisions can be taken.

Business level strategy   Strategy at the organizational or strategic business unit (SBU) level in large companies, which is concerned with the products and services that should be offered in the market defined at the corporate level. See also functional level strategy.

Business process improvement   Optimizing existing processes typically coupled with enhancements in information technology.

Business process management (BPM)   The analysis and improvement of business processes.

Business process outsourcing (BPO)   The outsourcing of processes.

Business process re-engineering (BPR)   The analysis of a business from a process rather than a functional perspective and the redesign of processes to optimize performance.

Business process simulation   The use of computer software, in the context of a process-based change, to simulate the operation of a business.

Business-to-business (B2B)   Transactions between an organization and other organizations.

Business-to-consumer (B2C)   Transactions between an organization and consumers.

Buy-side e-commerce   Web-based transactions between a purchasing organization and its suppliers. See also sell-side e-commerce.

Capacity loading graph   A graph showing the type and level of capacity required at a point in time.

Capacity requirements plan (CRP)   The calculation of workloads for critical work centres or workers based on information from the MRP system.

Cause-and-effect diagrams   A technique for identifying the causes of quality problems.

Cell layout   Cells are created from placing together resources which service a subset of the total range of products or services.

Cellular manufacturing   The placing of equipment in a cell layout that is a close grouping of different types of equipment, each of which performs a different operation.

Centre of gravity method   A way of determining the location of a distribution centre by minimizing distribution costs. The relative coordinates of the distribution points are placed on a map and the location of the distribution centre should be at the centre of gravity of the coordinates.

Chance causes of variation   The inherent variability in processes due to factors such as ambient temperature, wear of moving parts or slight variations in the composition of the material that is being processed. See also assignable causes of variation.

Chase demand   A capacity-planning strategy that seeks to match output to the demand pattern over time. Capacity is altered by such policies as changing the number of part-time staff, increasing staff availability through overtime working, changing equipment levels and subcontracting.

Competitive factors A range of factors such as price, quality and delivery speed, derived from the marketing strategy on which the product or service wins orders.

Computer numerically controlled (CNC) machines Machine tools that can be controlled by computer.

Computer-aided design (CAD) The ability to create drawings on a computer screen to assist in the visual design of a product or service.

Computer-aided engineering (CAE) The ability to design simulated tests and run them on drawings in a CAD system.

Computer-aided manufacturing (CAM) An extension of the use of CAD, which electronically transmits the design held in the CAD system to computer-controlled machine tools.

Computer-aided process planning (CAPP) An extension of the use of CAD, which electronically transmits a process plan of how parts will be manufactured to a machine tool. It can also sequence parts through a number of process steps.

Computer-integrated manufacture (CIM) The automation of the product and process design, planning and control, and manufacture of the product.

Concurrent design When contributors to the stages of the design effort provide their expertise together throughout the design process as a team.

Continuous improvement Incremental changes within the organization whose cumulative effect is to deliver an increased rate of performance improvement.

Continuous process An operation that produces a very high volume of a standard product, usually by a continuous flow, rather than in discrete items, such as oil and gas. See also batch process, jobbing process, mass process, project process.

Control chart for attribute data Measures discrete values such as whether a component is defective or not. Thus, there are no values, as in a control chart for variable data, from which a mean and range can be calculated. The data will simply provide a count of how many items conform to a specification and how many do not.

Control chart for variable data Displays samples of a measurement that can take a value from a range of possible values. Values will fall in or out of a range around a specified target value.

Corporate level strategy Long-range guidance on the direction of the whole organization.

Cost The finance required to obtain the inputs and manage the transformation process, which produces finished goods and services.

Cost of quality A concept that is intended to highlight and define the cost of quality and enable quality improvement efforts.

Critical path method (CPM) A way of mapping the activities undertaken during a project, the dependencies between these activities and the project duration.

Cumulative representation A running total of inventory, which should always meet or exceed cumulative demand. It is used to ensure no stock-outs occur when using a level capacity plan.

Customer relationship management (CRM) Systems designed to integrate the range of information systems that contain data about the customer.

Cycle time The time taken to produce or deliver one unit of output.

Degree of customer contact The amount of interaction between the service provider and customer during the service delivery process.

Demand management A capacity-planning strategy that attempts to adjust demand to meet available capacity. This can be achieved by strategies such as varying price of goods and services, advertising and using appointment systems. See also level capacity.

Demand profile Consists of the products and services required by the marketing plan, future customer orders and other demand factors such as the manufacture of items for spares.

Demand-side influences Factors influencing customer services that vary according to location and are, therefore, taken into account when making the location decision. See also supply-side influences.

Dependability Consistently meeting a promised delivery time for a product or service to a customer.

Design capacity The theoretical output of a process as it was designed.

Design for manufacture (DFM) A concept that views product design as the first step in the manufacture of that product.

Design of experiments (DOE) A way of testing a number of design options under various operating and environmental conditions in order to identify which factors affect a product's performance.

Diseconomies of scale When a facility is expanded and the average cost of producing each unit rises.

Disintermediation Using e-Business to alter the supply chain structure by bypassing some of the tiers. See also reintermediation.

Distribution requirements planning (DRP) The management of linkages between elements of the supply chain, beginning with an analysis of demand at each customer service location.

DMAIC methodology The use of statistical tools to gather data at each of the five stages: define, measure, analyse, improve and control.

Downstream customers Customers of the organization such as wholesalers and retailers. See also upstream suppliers.

Earned value How much work has actually been done in terms of budgeted costs for any day in the project. Also termed 'budgeted cost of work performed' (BCWP).

E-Business Electronically mediated information exchanges, both within an organization and between organizations.

E-Commerce Electronically mediated information exchanges between organizations.

Economic analysis The comparison of estimates of production and delivery costs with estimates of demand.

Economic order quantity (EOQ) model A model that calculates the fixed inventory order volume required while seeking to minimize the sum of the annual costs of holding inventory and the annual costs of ordering inventory.

Economies of scale Savings that result if a facility is expanded and fixed costs remain the same, so that the average cost of producing each unit will fall until the best operating level of the facility is reached and the lowest average unit cost met.

Economies of scope Savings that result from the ability to produce many products in one highly flexible production facility more cheaply than in separate facilities.

Economy Lowering the cost of inputs into the operations transformation process.

Effective capacity The capacity remaining after loss of output due to planned factors such as maintenance and training. See also actual capacity.

Effectiveness   The extent to which the outputs of a process meet the requirements of its customers.

Efficiency   The proportion of time a process is in use compared with its effective capacity. See also utilization.

Electronic commerce   See E-Commerce.

Electronic data interchange (EDI)   The exchange, using digital media, of structured business information, particularly for sales transactions such as purchase orders and invoices between buyers and sellers.

Empowerment   When employees of an organization are given more autonomy, discretion and responsibility for decision making.

Enterprise resource planning (ERP)   A system that provides a single solution from a single supplier with integrated functions for the major business areas.

E-procurement   The electronic integration and management of all procurement activities, including purchase request, authorization, ordering, delivery and payment between purchaser and supplier.

Ergonomics   The collection of information about human characteristics and behaviour in order to understand the effect of design, methods and environment.

Expediting   The short-term rescheduling of orders in order to ensure targets are met.

Experience curves   These provide an organization with the ability to predict the improvement in productivity that can occur as experience is gained in a market segment.

Extensible markup language (XML)   A data description language that allows documents to store any kind of information.

Facility location   The geographical location of capacity supplied by the organization.

Failure mode and effect analysis (FMEA)   A systematic approach to identifying the cause and effect of product failures. The idea of FMEA is to anticipate failures and deal with them at the design stage.

Finished goods inventory   Inventory ready for dispatch to the customer.

Five performance objectives   These are used to measure operations performance in relation to its strategy.

Fixed order inventory model   A way of calculating the amount to order based on a fixed interval between ordering.

Fixed order period inventory system   A system in which orders for varying quantities are placed at fixed time intervals.

Fixed order quantity inventory system   A system in which orders for the same quantity are placed, but the time between orders varies according to the rate of use of the inventory item.

Fixed-position layout   Used when the product or service cannot be moved and so the transforming process must take place at the location of product creation or service delivery.

Flexibility   The ability of the organization to change what it does quickly. In terms of products or services this can relate to introducing new designs, changing the mix, changing the overall volume and changing the delivery timing.

Flexible manufacturing cell (FMC)   Systems that integrate individual items of automation to form an automated manufacturing system.

Flexible manufacturing systems (FMS)   These extend the facilities of an FMC by incorporating automatic parts loading and unloading facilities and an automated guided vehicle system for parts movement.

Focus   The alignment of particular market demands with individual facilities to reduce the level of complexity generated when attempting to service a number of different market segments from an individual organization.

Form design   The product aesthetics, such as look, feel and sound.

Functional design   Design that meets the performance characteristics specified in the product concept.

Functional level strategy   Long-range plans made by the functions of the business (for example, operations, marketing, finance), which support the competitive advantage being pursued by the business-level strategy.

Gantt chart   A valuable tool for project control, which allows monitoring of project progress against plan by providing a view of which tasks are being undertaken over time.

Global organization   Firms that follow a business strategy where activities are coordinated on a worldwide basis.

Group technology   The process of grouping products for manufacture or services for delivery.

Heterogeneity   The interaction of the customer, service provider and surroundings causing variability in the performance of the service.

Human capital management system (HCMS)   A Web-based software application that manages human resource functions such as payroll, recruitment and staff deployment across the organization.

Inbound logistics   The activity of moving material in from suppliers.

Infrastructural decisions   The systems, policies and practices that determine how the operation's structural elements are managed.

Input/output control   Attempt to make queue times more consistent and predictable by managing the size of the queues at processes.

Inventory status file (ISF)   Information on the identification and quantity of items in stock.

ISO 9000   A group of quality management standards laid down by the International Organization for Standardization.

JIT and lean operations   An integration of a philosophy and techniques designed to improve performance.

JIT supplier network   A formation of close, long-term relationships with a small number of suppliers.

Job characteristics model   Linking job characteristics with the desired psychological state of the individual and the outcomes in terms of motivation and job performance.

Job enlargement   The horizontal integration of tasks to expand the range of tasks involved in a particular job.

Job enrichment   The vertical integration of tasks and the integration of responsibility and decision making.

Job rotation   A form of job enlargement that involves a worker changing job roles with another worker on a periodic basis.

Jobbing process   The process for making a one-off, or low volume, product to a customer specification. The product moves to the location of transforming resources such as equipment. See also batch process, continuous process, mass process, project process.

Just-in-time   See JIT and lean operations.

Kanban **production system** To implement a pull system, a *kanban* is used to pass information such as the part identification, quantity per container that the part is transported in and the preceding and next workstation.

Lag capacity Capacity that is added only when there is extra demand that would use the additional resources. See also lead capacity.

Layout design The arrangement of facilities in a service or manufacturing operation.

Lead capacity Extra capacity above forecast demand, which allows an operation to maintain a capacity 'cushion'. This tries to ensure that capacity is sufficient even if demand increases above forecast. See also lag capacity.

Lean operations See JIT and lean operations.

Learning curves Provide an organization with the ability to predict the improvement in productivity that can occur as experience of a process is gained.

Learning organization A working environment that builds knowledge within the organization and uses that knowledge to improve performance.

Level capacity A capacity-planning strategy that sets processing capacity at a uniform level throughout the planning period regardless of fluctuations in forecast demand. This means production is set at a fixed rate, usually to meet average demand, and inventory is used to absorb variations in demand. For a service organization, output cannot be stored as inventory so a level capacity plan involves running at a uniformly high level of capacity. See also demand management.

Levelled scheduling Producing the smallest reasonable number of units of each product at a time.

Line balancing Aims to ensure that the output of each production stage in a line layout is equal and maximum efficiency is attained.

Loading Determining the available capacity for each stage in a process and allocating a work task to that stage.

Locational cost–volume analysis Identifying when a particular location is superior for a particular volume level by analysing the mix of fixed and variable costs.

Long-term capacity planning Determining how much long-term capacity should be supplied by the organization. This decision needs to be made within a long-term plan, which provides a fit with the operations strategy of the organization.

Maintainability The cost of servicing the product or service when it is in use.

Make-to-order A planning policy that acquires the raw material used to construct the product on the receipt of a customer order. See also make-to-stock.

Make-to-stock A planning policy that produces to a forecast of demand for the product. See also make-to-order.

Manufacturing resource planning (MRP II) Extends the idea of materials requirements planning to other areas in the firm such as marketing and finance.

Market analysis Evaluating the design concept with potential customers through interviews, focus groups and other data-collection methods.

Market relationships Where each purchase is treated as a separate transaction and the relationship between the buyer and seller lasts as long as this transaction takes.

Market-based operations strategy A method of determining organizational strategy based on decisions regarding the markets and the customers within those markets that it intends to target. See also resource-based operations strategy.

Mass customization An attempt to combine high-variety and high-volume output in order to provide the customer with customized products at a relatively low price.

Mass process   A process that produces products of high volume and low variety. The process of production will essentially be the same for all the products and so it is cost-effective to use specialized labour and equipment. See also batch process, continuous process, jobbing process, project process.

Mass service   Processes that operate with a low variety and high volume. There will be little customization of the service to individual customer needs and limited contact between the customer and people providing the service.

Master production schedule (MPS)   Shows how many products or services are planned for each time period, based on the resources authorized in the aggregate plan.

Match capacity   Obtaining capacity to match forecasted demand.

Materials handling   The movement of materials, either within warehouses or between storage areas and transportation links.

Materials management   The movement of materials within the organization.

Materials requirements planning (MRP)   An information system used to calculate the requirements for component materials needed to produce end items.

M-business   The integration of Internet and wireless communications technology.

Method study   Dividing and analysing a job in order to reduce waste, time and effort.

Mixed model scheduling   Spreading the production of several different end items evenly throughout each day.

Motion study   The study of the individual human motions that are used in a job task with the purpose of trying to ensure that the job does not include any unnecessary motion or movement by the worker.

Network analysis   The use of network-based techniques for the analysis and management of projects.

Offshoring   The transfer of activities to another country.

Operations control   This is concerned with ensuring that the current behaviour of the operations system conforms with the required behaviour.

Operations management   The management of the processes that produce or deliver goods and services.

Operations performance objectives   The five objectives by which operations performance is measured: quality, speed, dependability, flexibility and cost.

Operations planning   This is concerned with taking actions, such as ensuring resources are in place, in anticipation of future events.

Optimized production technology (OPT)   An operations control system that is based on the identification of bottlenecks within the production process.

Outbound logistics   The activity of moving materials out to customers.

Outsourcing   When goods and services are obtained outside the organization.

Pareto analysis   A technique used to organize information and quality problems and help focus problem solving effort on the most important aspects.

P:D ratio   The comparison of the demand time D (from customer request to receipt of goods/services) with the total throughput time P of the purchase, make and delivery stages.

Performance objectives   These allow the organization to measure its operations performance in achieving its strategic goals. The performance objectives are quality, speed, dependability, flexibility and cost.

Performance standard   A target value for a performance measure.

Perishability   This refers to the fact that because a service is a process, not a physical thing that can be stored, it must be consumed when it is produced.

PERT   See project evaluation and review technique.

Physical distribution management   The movement of materials from the operation to the customer.

Predetermined motion times   Generic times for standard micromotions such as reach, move and release, which are common to many jobs.

Prevention costs   Costs arising from the quality philosophy of 'doing it right the first time', such as those incurred by trying to prevent problems occurring.

Private or single-user warehouse   A warehouse owned or leased by the organization for its own use. See also **public or multiuser warehouse**.

Process activity chart   A device used to analyse the steps of a job or how a set of jobs fit together into the overall flow of a process.

Process layout   A layout in which resources (such as equipment and people) that have similar processes or functions are grouped together.

Process mapping   The use of a flow chart to document the process, incorporating process activities and decision points.

Process technology   Used to help transform the three main categories of transformed resources: materials, customers and information.

Procurement   The acquisition of all the materials needed by an organization.

Product layout   A layout in which the resources required for a product or service are arranged around the needs of that product or service.

Production design   Design that takes into consideration the ease and cost of manufacture of a product.

Production flow analysis (PFA)   A group technology technique that can be used to identify families of parts with similar processing requirements.

Productivity   The value of the output divided by the value of the input resources consumed.

Professional service   Professional services are characterized by high levels of customization, in that each service delivery will be tailored to meet individual customer needs. Professional services are characterized by high levels of customer contact and a relatively high proportion of staff supplying the service in relation to customers.

Project control   The monitoring of the project objectives of cost, time and quality as the project progresses.

Project cost graph   Provides an indication of the amount of cost incurred over the life of a project.

Project crashing   The use of additional resources to reduce project completion time.

Project estimating   Estimating the type and amount of resources required to undertake a project.

Project evaluation and review technique (PERT)   A form of network analysis that takes into account the fact that most task durations are not fixed by using a statistical distribution to describe the variability inherent in the tasks.

Project network simulation   A method of estimating a project's completion time without the assumptions that all paths of a project are independent and the same tasks are not on more than one path.

Project planning   Ensuring that the project objectives of cost, time and quality are met by estimating both the level and timing of resources needed over the project duration.

Project process Used to make a one-off product to a customer specification. A feature of a project process is that the location of the product is stationary. See also batch process, continuous process, jobbing process, mass process.

Psychology of queues A series of propositions that can be used by service organizations to instigate policies to influence customer satisfaction with waiting times.

Public or multiuser warehouse A warehouse run as an independent business. See also private or single-user warehouse.

Qualitative forecasting methods Methods that take a subjective approach and are based on estimates and opinions. They include market surveys, the Delphi method and expert judgement. See also quantitative forecasting methods.

Quality Quality covers both the product or service itself and the processes that produce the product or service.

Quality assurance An approach to prevention rather than correction and the use of statistical tools to ensure the quality of processes.

Quality functional deployment A structured process that translates the voice of the customer (what the customer needs) into technical design requirements (how these needs are met).

Quality gap approach This approach aims to improve quality by identifying the gap between what customers expect from a service and what they perceive they are actually getting. The difference between the two is termed the quality gap and the size of this gap determines customer dissatisfaction.

Quality inspection This involves detection of a quality problem by a quality inspector leading to either rejection or repair of the product.

Quality loss function A simple cost estimate, which shows how customer preferences are oriented towards consistently meeting quality expectations and that a customer's dissatisfaction (quality loss) increases geometrically as the actual value deviates from the target value.

Quality of conformance How closely the product meets the specification required by the design.

Quantitative forecasting methods Methods that use a mathematical expression or model to show the relationship between demand and some independent variable or variables. They include time series and causal forecasting models. See also qualitative forecasting methods.

Queuing theory Waiting time in queues is caused by fluctuations in arrival rates and variability in service times. Queuing theory can be used to explore the trade-off between the amount of capacity and the level of demand.

Raw materials inventory Inventory received from suppliers.

Reintermediation The creation of new intermediaries between customers and suppliers in the supply chain. See also disintermediation.

Reliability The probability that a product or service will perform its intended function for a specified period of time under normal conditions of use.

Reorder point (ROP) model Identifying the time to order when the stock level drops to a predetermined amount.

Resource-based operations strategy A method of evaluating operations capability based on an assessment of the operation's tangible and intangible resources and processes. See also market-based operations strategy.

Resource-constrained project A project requiring highly specialized resources, meaning that the completion date will have to be set to ensure these resources are not overloaded. See also time-constrained project.

Resource-to-order When it is not necessary to activate a planning system and acquire resources until a delivery date for an order is received.

Reverse engineering A systematic approach to dismantling and inspecting a competitor's product to look for aspects of design that could be incorporated into the organization's own product.

Robot A programmable machine that can undertake tasks that may be dangerous, dirty or dull for people to carry out.

Robust design The process of designing in the ability of the product to perform under a variety of conditions and so reducing the chance of product failure.

Rough-cut capacity plan (RCCP) This takes information from the master production schedule to evaluate its feasibility.

Scheduling The allocation of a start and finish time to each order while taking into account the loading and sequencing policies employed.

Self-directed work teams Teams in which workers are empowered to take many of the decisions concerning their work.

Sell-side e-commerce E-Commerce transactions between a supplier organization and its customers. See also buy-side e-Commerce.

Sequencing The sequential assignment of tasks or jobs to individual processes.

Service blueprinting A charting device for processes, which documents the interaction between the customer and the service provider.

Service composition A selection of services from the service inventory that are allocated to a particular business process.

Service inventory A collection of standardized services that are designed for use in a number of business processes.

Service-oriented architecture An approach that incorporates reusable business-aligned IT services that can be utilized in a manner that is independent of the underlying application and technology platforms.

Service package The combination of goods and services that comprise a service.

Service shop process A process that operates with a medium amount of variety and volume. There will be, therefore, a mix of staff and equipment used to deliver the service.

Servitization Servitization involves companies moving from being manufacturers with 'add-on' services to service companies whose output includes manufactured products.

SERVQUAL A survey research instrument that is based on the premise that customers can measure a firm's service quality by comparing their perception of its service with their own expectations.

Setup reduction (SUR) The reduction of the time taken to adjust a machine to work on a different component.

Simultaneity Describes services that are produced and consumed at the same time.

Six Sigma A company-wide initiative to reduce costs through process efficiency and increase revenues through process effectiveness.

Sociotechnical systems A job design approach that suggests that the social and technical subsystems within the organization should be designed in parallel to achieve an overall optimum system.

Speed The time delay between a customer request for a product or service and receipt of that product or service.

Stakeholder Anyone with an interest in the activities of an organization, such as employees, customers and government.

Statistical process control (SPC) A sampling technique that checks the quality of an item that is engaged in a process.

Strategic partnerships and alliances Long-term relationships in which organizations work together and share information regarding aspects such as planning systems and development of products and processes.

Structural decisions Decisions that concern aspects of the organization's physical resources such as service delivery systems and capacity provision.

Subcontracting networks Long-term contractual arrangements made with suppliers to supply goods and services.

Supply chain The series of activities that moves materials from suppliers, through operations to customers.

Supply chain management Management of the flow of materials through the entire supply chain.

Supply network design The configuration of the organization's relationship with its suppliers and the decision about which activities the organization should undertake internally and which should be subcontracted to other agencies.

Supply-side influences Factors influencing costs that vary according to location and are, therefore, taken into account when making the location decision. See also demand-side influences.

Systems thinking An approach that uses the idea of holism to study the whole organization instead of breaking it down into parts in order to understand it.

Tangibility If goods are tangible they are physical things you can touch. A service is intangible and can be seen as a process that is activated on demand.

Target-oriented quality An approach that strives through the process of continuous improvement to keep as close as possible to the target specification.

Technical analysis Determining whether the technical capability to manufacture the product or deliver the service exists.

Time study The use of statistical techniques to arrive at a standard time for performing one cycle of a repetitive job.

Time-constrained project A project that must be completed within a specific time frame and, therefore, may need to use alternative resources. See also resource-constrained project.

Total preventative maintenance A programme of routine maintenance that will not only help to reduce breakdowns, but also to reduce downtime and lengthen the life of the equipment. See also prevention costs.

Total quality control An approach that emphasizes a commitment of effort on the part of management and employees throughout an organization to improving quality.

Total quality management (TQM) A philosophy that aims to make high quality, as defined by the customer, a primary concern throughout the organization and to ensure that all parts of the organization work towards this goal.

Trade-off A situation where to excel in one objective results in a poor performance in one or more other objectives.

Upstream suppliers   Those who supply the organization with goods or services. See also **downstream customers**.

Utilization   The proportion of time a process is in actual use compared with its design capacity. See also **efficiency**.

Value chain   The set of processes used to create value for a customer.

Value engineering (VE)   The elimination of unnecessary features and functions that do not contribute to the value or performance of the product.

Vertical integration   The amount of ownership of the supply chain by an organization.

Virtual organization   An organization in which e-Business is used to outsource more and more supply-chain activities to third parties so that the boundaries between and within organizations become blurred.

Visual control   The maintenance of an orderly workplace in which tools are easily available and unusual occurrences are easily noticeable.

Warehousing   The use of locations to hold a stock of incoming raw materials used in production or hold finished goods ready for distribution to customers. Warehousing is also used to store work-in-progress inventory or spares for equipment.

Web services   A collection of industry standards which represents the most likely technology connecting services together to form a service-oriented architecture.

Weighted scoring   The process by which a list of factors that are relevant to the location decision is compiled and each factor given a weighting that indicates its relative importance compared with the other factors. Each location is then scored on each factor and this score is multiplied by the factor value. The alternative with the highest score is chosen.

Work measurement   Determining the length of time it will take to undertake a particular task.

Work sampling   A method for determining the proportion of time a worker or machine spends on various activities; work sampling can be very useful in job redesign and estimating levels of worker output.

Work study   Measuring the performance of jobs through two elements: method study and work measurement.

Workforce schedule   This determines the daily workload for each member of staff.

Work-in-progress inventory   Inventory at some point within the operations process.

Yield management   The use of demand management strategies aimed at maximizing customer revenue in service organizations. It is particularly appropriate when the organization is operating with relatively fixed capacity and it is possible to segment the market into different types of customers.

INDEX

Double-Sampling Plan

In a double-sampling plan a smaller sample is taken than in a single-sampling plan. If the quality is very good or very bad the lot is accepted or rejected as before. If the result is inconclusive then a second sample is taken and the lot is rejected or accepted on the combined results of the two samples. The technique should allow an overall saving of inspection costs by the use of a smaller sample, which will usually provide a definite result.

Multiple-Sampling Plan

Here an initial sample (which can be as small as one unit) is taken. If the number of defectives is above or below a specified limit the lot is rejected or accepted as appropriate. If the number of defectives is between these limits, a second sample is taken and the total number of defects is compared to an increased set of upper and lower limits. The process repeats until the lot is accepted or rejected. Multiple-sampling plans are particularly appropriate when inspection costs are relatively high. For example for destructive testing, when the cost of testing the whole sample would be prohibitive.

Variable-Sampling Plan

A variable-sampling plan takes samples from a measure that can take a range of values, as opposed to an attribute plan, which is a discrete value. Variable sampling plans are constructed in a similar way to attribute plans but instead of the binomial and Poisson distribution, a normal distribution is assumed (especially for a sample size greater than 30). This means the trial and error approach to develop the plan is not needed, but standardized variable tables are available to develop plans for various AQL values.

SUMMARY

- The concept of quality can be viewed from different perspectives.

- Measurements of quality can be categorized as operational (for example, scrap rates), financial (for example, quality costs) and customer based (for example, measures from SERVQUAL).

- Techniques for quality improvement can be categorized as operational (for example, SPC), financial (for example, cost of quality) and customer based (for example, quality gaps).

- Total quality management is a philosophy that aims to ensure high quality is a primary concern for the organization.

- Deming proposes a TQM implementation plan that emphasizes continuous improvement to achieve conformance to specification. Crosby proposes a TQM implementation plan that emphasizes changing people's perception of the cost of quality.

- Six Sigma is a company-wide initiative to reduce costs through process efficiency and increase revenues through process effectiveness.

- ISO 9000 provides a quality standard between suppliers and customers.

- Statistical process control is a sampling technique that checks the quality of an item that is engaged in a process.

- Acceptance sampling consists of taking a random sample from a larger batch or lot of material to be inspected.

CASE STUDY 17.2

A Disciple of Japanese Quality Management

Order and efficiency are hallmarks of the TVS motorbike factory near Bangalore in southern India. To direct foot traffic, arrows are painted on the shiny shop floor of India's third-largest motorcycle maker. Large banners with exhortations such as 'Let Us Achieve Zero Defects' and 'Quality is a Way of Life' hang across the bright facility where nearly 2000 vehicles are built each day on neat assembly lines. Tea breaks are 9:15 to 9:22 and 14:15 to 14:22, according to a memo on the wall. Japan's veneration for order has been fully transplanted to this TVS factory in the city of Hosur. Venu Srinivasan, the mild-mannered 55-year-old managing director and chairman

of TVS, has indoctrinated the company with the Japanese management strategy of total quality management (TQM). TVS's turnaround has hinged on principles of attention to process, consistency, transparency and employee involvement.

Total quality management was launched at TVS in 1989 and is credited with reviving the ailing company. Since then, TVS and sister companies in the $2.2 billion TVS Group have won the prestigious Japan Quality Medal and the Deming Prize, a quality award from Japan. TVS rolled out 923 000 motorbikes last fiscal year in India with sales growing 19% to reach about $900 million. It recently opened a